Between Reform, Reaction, and Resistance
Studies in the History of German Conservatism
from 1789 to 1945

D0205427

Between Reform, Reaction, and Resistance

Studies in the History of German Conservatism from 1789 to 1945

Edited by

Larry Eugene Jones *and* **James Retallack**

BERG

Providence • Oxford

Published in 1993 by

Berg Publishers, Inc.

Editorial offices:
221 Waterman Street, Providence, RI 02906, U.S.A.
150 Cowley Road, Oxford OX4 1JJ, UK

©Larry Eugene Jones and James Retallack

**A CIP catalogue record for this book is available from the British
Library.**

Library of Congress Cataloging-in-Publication Data

Between reform, reaction, and resistance : studies in the history of
   German conservatism from 1789 to 1945 / edited by
Larry Eugene Jones and James Retallack.
      p.   cm.
   Includes bibliographical references and index.
   ISBN 0–85496–787–7
   1. Germany—Politics and government—1789–1900. 2. Germany
—Politics and government—20th century. 3. Conservatism—Ger-
many—History—19th century. 4. Conservatism—Germany—Histo-
ry—20th century. I. Jones, Larry Eugene. II. Retallack. James N.
DD204.B48   1992   92–26391
320.943—dc20   CIP

Printed in the United States by Edwards Brothers, Ann Arbor, MI.

To our teachers and our students

Contents

Contents

Preface

This collection of essays represents a cross section of the most recent research in Germany, Great Britain, Canada, and the United States on the history of German conservatism. The volume originated as a complement to the collection of essays on the history of German liberalism that Konrad H. Jarausch and Larry Eugene Jones published in 1990 under the title *In Search of a Liberal Germany*. As in the case of the anthology on German liberalism, this collection addresses three distinct audiences. First, it seeks to provide the specialist in modern German history with a survey of the most recent scholarship on the topic of German conservatism. In this respect, this collection views conservatism not merely in its party political form but also in terms of its relationship to conservative currents in culture, society, and politics. Second, the collection provides the generalist in either German or European history with fresh insight into the historiographical debates that have done so much to shape current thinking about conservatism and its place in modern German history. In doing so, the volume argues for a more differentiated approach to the study of German conservatism than has heretofore been the case and suggests that historians must focus on regional and local developments in order to develop a true appreciation of its role in German political culture. Third, the collection provides comparative historians with a strong empirical foundation upon which new and possibly divergent conclusions about the relative strengths and weaknesses of German conservatism can be based. This, in turn, will shed new light on the perennially vexing problem of the German *Sonderweg* and make it easier to arrive at a more meaningful understanding of the differences between conservatism in Germany and other industrialized countries.

The collection is introduced by a general survey of the historiography of German conservatism from the 1920s to the present. This is followed by fifteen individual contributions that reflect the vitality of current research on the topic of German conservatism. In soliciting contributions to the collection, the editors have employed a catholic definition of conservatism that goes beyond the discussion of conservative ideas or their embodiment in specific institutions to an analysis of the social, religious, and cultural context in which these ideas and institutions have developed. Accordingly, these essays represent a wide range of methodologies and conceptual approaches. Some are more traditional explorations of political conservatism in both its ideological and institutional representations; others are more innovative and enrich our understanding of German conservatism through the analysis of its relationship to factors of gender, regionalism, and culture. By the same token, the editors have taken special care to solicit essays that reflect the full chronological sweep of German conservatism from its earliest manifestations in the era of the French Revolution to its confrontation with Nazism.

The first four contributions offer varying perspectives on the emergence of new religious, social, and political views among Prussian conservatives in the middle of the nineteenth century. Christopher Clark opens the discussion with an examination of the social and ideological functions of Christian fundamentalism before 1848. Concentrating on the aristocratic officials, estate owners, and military men who became the leaders of the Prussian "Awakening" after the wars of liberation, Clark suggests that the conspicuous degree of aristocratic participation in the Awakening constituted a response to a perceived decline in the corporate function and identity of the aristocratic estate. That the Awakening also had a social component is clear from Clark's discussion of pious aristocrats who willingly submitted to personal humiliation at the hands of social inferiors in congregational meetings. The conservative response to the social question is discussed in a different light in the next two essays by Hermann Beck and Wolfgang Schwentker. Beck's essay shows how opposition to the Stein-Hardenberg reforms of 1807–1813 combined with growing conservative dissatisfaction over a Prussian state that seemed incapable of addressing the problem of pauperism to produce an ostensibly new brand of conservatism articulated by critics such as Josef Maria von Radowitz, Victor Aimé Huber, Carl Rodbertus, and Hermann Wagener and characterized by its commitment to a solution of the so-called social question. Schwentker's sketch of Huber's social thought reveals how conservatism underwent a fundamental "change of heart" in more respects than one when it stopped thinking of the social problem as a question of charity and began to view it in political terms. Huber's concept of "association" provided a blueprint for a more progressive form of social conservatism than had inspired conservatives in the *Vormärz*. David Barclay's study of the camarilla of Frederick William IV shifts the focus from the level of social policy to that of courtly intrigue. In his examination of the personalities and pecadilloes that made up the king's *ministère occulte*, Barclay explains that Ludwig von Gerlach and other members of the camarilla were often more interested in finding the right formula for a new conservative party than in preserving the personal prestige of the monarch to whom they gave the nickname *Butt* or "flounder."

The second group of four essays examines the extreme flux that characterized party political relationships on the German Right from the late 1880s to the outbreak of World War I. Dirk Stegmann's essay on efforts to found a new right-wing party between 1887 and 1894 explores how the very conception of "party" was evolving on the German Right. In the opinion of right-wing activists ranging from inexperienced hotheads to staid boardroom executives, the National Liberal and Conservative parties were no longer "adequate" to represent the interests of agriculture or heavy industry. Social policy toward workers, radical nationalism, and the need to redefine the style of conservative politics all fed the acrimonious debate that splintered the old Bismarckian alliance. Geoff Eley offers an alternative reading of the crisis of conservative politics at the beginning of the 1890s with conclusions that diverge from Stegmann's in several important respects. Eley's main goal is to set another historical orthodoxy on its ear, namely, the argument developed most forcefully by Hans-Jürgen Puhle that Prussian Junkers called the agrarian movement of the early 1890s into existence by a conscious and calculated act of will. In exploring the regional content of these developments, Eley turns his attention to the hinterland, where he discovers that the friction between "in groups" and "out groups" produced different kinds of political "heat" for established political elites in virtually every province and state of Germany. More broadly, Eley argues that we should "reconsider the completeness and stability of the Agrarian League's achievement."

George Vascik's essay on Diederich Hahn revolves around many of the issues addressed by Eley. Vascik too considers the "sudden" appearance of agrarian radicalism in the 1890s, the relationship between leaders and led, and the image of the Agrarian League as a unitary, all-powerful, quintessentially modern political machine. But Vascik's approach is diametrically opposed – and thus complementary – to Eley's in that he provides a political biography of a man who gained almost unrivaled notoriety in Wilhelmine politics. In the last essay devoted to Wilhelmine conservatism, James Retallack addresses many of the questions that vexed conservatives both in the 1890s and after 1909. Like Stegmann and Eley, Retallack explores the new pressures that destabilized the relationship between conservatives and the government in late Wilhelmine Germany. Retallack examines the internal development of the German Conservative Party and its impact upon Reich policy under the chancellorship of Theobald von Bethmann Hollweg and suggests that the fate of Bethmann's own reform agenda became inextricably linked to the fate of reformism within the party itself. But in the end, neither the conservatives nor the government espoused a viable form of "reformist conservatism" or found ways to chart a rational political course between the dictates of reason and sentiment. Thus both the Conservative Party and Imperial Germany met their Philippi in 1918.

The next three essays explore the intellectual and cultural dimensions of conservative politics in the Weimar Republic. In his essay on the conservative response to the November Revolution of 1918–19, Peter Fritzsche demonstrates how the social and political upheavals that accompanied the collapse of the Second Empire produced a fundamental caesura in the development of German conservatism. While most conservatives – and particularly those with close ties to the prewar conservative establishment – viewed the November Revolution as a collapse, or *Zusammenbruch*, a group of young conservative activists led by Arthur Moeller van den Bruck, Max Hildebert Boehm, and Eduard Stadtler looked upon the events of November 1918 as a "breakthrough," or *Durchbruch*, to an entirely new political order that had little in common with the established social and political hierarchies of the Wilhelmine era. This brand of conservatism, as Fritzsche points out, was not restorationist but profoundly revolutionary and sought nothing less than the political rebirth of the German nation. In his essay on conservatism, National Socialism, and the cultural crisis of the Weimar Republic, Alan Steinweis examines the way in which influential conservative publications such as the *Deutsche Rundschau*, *Der Ring*, and *Die Tat* tended to equate Weimar with cultural decadence. Even here, however, Steinweis detects a surprising ambivalence on the part of many young conservative intellectuals toward the cultural revolution that had swept Germany since the beginning of the century. Steinweis also explores the extent to which antipathy toward modernist culture constituted a common ground upon which conservatives and Nazis could unite. In his essay on conservative plans for a revision of the Weimar Constitution, Hans Mommsen shifts the focus of attention from cultural policy to the search for conservative alternatives to the Weimar party state. With the increasing paralysis of Germany's republican institutions at the beginning of the 1930s, neoconservative pundits such as Hans Zehrer from *Die Tat* and Heinrich von Gleichen from *Der Ring* began to propagate plans for the creation of a new governmental system in which political parties would no longer play the central role they had assumed after 1919. But, as Mommsen points out, conservative advocates of a "government without parties" fell victim to a fundamental misreading of the Nazi movement that, in turn, did much to immobilize conservative opponents of Nazism in the period surrounding the formation of Hitler's cabinet of national concentration in January 1933.

The last four essays in the collection explore the question of conservative culpability for the collapse of the Weimar Republic and the establishment of the Third Reich. Renate Bridenthal's essay on the role of women in the conservative mobilization of the German countryside in the Weimar Republic represents an extension of Eley's essay on the Agrarian League. The focal point of Bridenthal's essay is the National Federation of Agricultural Housewives' Associations (RHLV), an organization founded in the 1890s as part of the Agrarian League's campaign to mobilize Germany's rural population in support of a conservative and protectionist political agenda. After the collapse of the Second Empire, the RHLV allied itself with the National Rural League and played a central role in organizing rural opposition to Germany's new republican order. But, as Bridenthal argues, the RHLV's dependence upon male-dominated agricultural interest organizations severely compromised its own autonomy as a member of the women's movement and greatly facilitated its "coordination" into Nazi-controlled agricultural front organizations after 1933. Shelley Baranowski continues an examination of agrarian conservatism in the Weimar Republic with an analysis of the relationship between Pomerania's rural elites and National Socialism in the critical years from 1928 to 1933. Baranowski's thesis is that beginning in 1928 there was a convergence "between the elevated radicalism of [Pomeranian] agrarian elites and the Nazis' accelerated efforts to attract aggrieved rural voters." Although this combination generated some of the mass support that Hitler used to secure the chancellorship, the NSDAP's relationship to the agrarian elites in Pomerania remained "a volatile mixture of accommodation and competition."

In an essay on the conservative resistance to Hitler and the fall of the Weimar Republic, Theodore Hamerow undertakes a critical analysis of what future leaders of the anti-Hitler resistance thought about the Weimar Republic and the rise of Nazism in the final and decisive years of the republic's existence. Hamerow's conclusion is that "virtually all of those who later came to form the nucleus of the conservative resistance to Hitler initially greeted the establishment of the Hitler regime – or, more precisely, the end of the republican system – with relief, if not enthusiasm." Men such as Ludwig von Beck, Ulrich von Hassell, and Carl Goerdeler looked upon National Socialism as a useful ally in the struggle against the hated Weimar system and, for the most part, were prepared to collaborate with the Nazi state as long as it served their own political interests. Larry Eugene Jones, on the other hand, suggests that there were limits to conservative collaboration with the new Nazi regime. In an essay on the background to the Röhm purge in the summer of 1934, Jones argues that Germany's conservative elites were so badly fragmented along political as well as structural lines that they were incapable of formulating a coherent response to the rise and challenge of Nazism. Influential conservatives were in fact so disaffected from the new regime that they drafted elaborate plans for a conservative coup that ended in failure with Hitler's celebrated strike of 30 June 1934.

* * *

Financial support from a variety of sources facilitated completion of this book. Larry Eugene Jones received grants from the German Marshall Fund and the Woodrow Wilson International Center for Scholars as well as a sabbatical leave from Canisius College that made it possible for him to devote his time and energy to this and related projects. James Retallack was the beneficiary of support for research and sabbatical leaves in 1990–92 from the Social Sciences and Humanities Research Council of Canada and the University of Toronto. The editors would also like to express their appreciation to Steven Kirchgraber and Lynn Stievater of Canisius College and Marven Krug of the University of Toronto for their invaluable assistance at various stages of the project. And finally, they would like to thank Marion Berghahn of Berg Publishers not only for her commitment to the project but also for her patience with an enterprise that took longer to materialize than the editors had originally anticipated.

Buffalo/Toronto, July 1992
L.E.J./J.N.R.

German Conservatism Reconsidered: Old Problems and New Directions

Larry Eugene Jones and James Retallack

I

The specter of the Third Reich has understandably clouded much of the historical writing on nineteenth- and twentieth-century Germany. The enormity and sheer inhumanity of the crimes committed in the twelve years of Nazi rule have created a special optic through which historians – not just in Germany but throughout the Anglo-American world – have come to view the vicissitudes of Germany's social, political, and cultural development since 1789. The net effect of this has been to produce a body of historical literature that selectively highlights those features of the German past exhibiting a degree of continuity with the Third Reich, yet discounts those suggesting an alternative trajectory to the one Germany followed from 1789 to 1945. This, in turn, has left us with a flat, one-dimensional, and overly deterministic reading of modern German history that regards the establishment of the Third Reich as little more than the inevitable culmination of certain factors present in German political culture since the French Revolution.

Recently, however, the master narrative that has governed the writing of German history since the end of the Second World War has been challenged not only by developments within the historical profession but by the actual course of history itself. If nothing else, the fact that the German Federal Republic has lasted longer than the combined life-span of the Weimar Republic and Third Reich would suggest that a more positive reassessment of Germany's democratic and liberal potential is long overdue.[1] Moreover, the recent unification of

---

1. K.H. Jarausch and L.E. Jones, "German Liberalism Reconsidered: Inevitable Decline, Bourgeois Hegemony, or Partial Achievement?" in *In Search of a Liberal Germany: Studies in the History of German Liberalism from 1789 to the Present*, ed. K.H. Jarausch and L.E. Jones (New York, Oxford, and Munich, 1990), pp. 1–23.

the two Germanys will almost certainly prompt a fresh look at nationalism and its role in Germany's historical development, though ideally without the venom and underlying political agenda that accompanied the much celebrated *Historikerstreit* of the mid-1980s. In fact, the *Historikerstreit* may very well have been the opening volley of a much more protracted struggle within the German historical profession over how the German national tradition is to be reinterpreted in the light of recent historical developments.

In the meantime, one of the most contentious issues associated with the *Historikerstreit* – namely, the primacy of political history and the study of organized political power within the context of the nation state – has been challenged by recent developments within the profession itself. Both the "new social history," with its turn toward social anthropology and its emphasis upon the primacy of experience over structure, and the "new cultural history," with its linguistic turn and emphasis upon the role of language in the constitution of social and political reality, have done much to undermine the privileged position that political history has always held within the German historical profession. At the same time, the rise of multiculturalism as a central component of the postmodernist agenda for a reform and revitalization of the historical sciences has underscored the need for a remapping of the German past, both to explore hitherto neglected aspects of that country's national history and to affirm the inherently international character of all national histories.[2]

All of this underscores the state of extreme flux that characterizes current scholarship on modern German history. If nothing else, the postmodernist challenge has succeeded in drawing attention to the need for a critical reassessment of the existing body of literature on Germany's social, political, and cultural development since 1789. Nowhere is that need more apparent than in the case of German conservatism. For although the literature on this subject is indeed prodigious, much of it is badly outdated and in need of substantial revision. To be sure, several recent studies have made important strides in over-

2. In this respect, see the collection of papers from the conference sponsored by the Deutscher Akademischer Austauschdienst on "German Histories: Challenges in Theory, Practice, and Technique" at the University of Chicago, 4 and 5 October 1989, in a special issue of *Central European History* 22 (1989): 227–457.

coming this deficit and in indicating where the emphasis of future research might lie. Still, research on the topic tends to be dictated by a peculiar Anglo-American bias that has viewed German conservatism as a deviation from the more pragamatic and politically responsible forms of conservatism that developed in the United Kingdom and the United States. The debate over the nature and function of German conservatism has thus found a comfortable niche within the more general debate over the German *Sonderweg*.

The study of German conservatism has also been frustrated by the lack of a scholarly consensus over what the term conservatism actually means. "Conservatism," wrote Clinton Rossiter in 1968, "is a word whose usefulness is matched only by its capacity to confuse, distort, and irritate."[3] Problems of definition stem in large measure from the fact that, unlike liberalism or socialism, conservatism did not originate as an ideology with a fully articulated concept of human nature, the state, and society, but rather as a reaction on the part of specific social strata to the sudden and dramatic changes that began to transform the face of Europe in the second half of the eighteenth century. Insofar as conservatism identified itself with the defense of the status quo, however, it suggested patterns of behavior that clearly antedated the French and industrial revolutions. As a result, the term has come to embrace both a disposition frequently identified as "traditionalist" and the specific ideology within which this disposition has been articulated.[4] Historians and social theorists have thus found it convenient to juxtapose traditionalism as a means of identifying the subjective, instinctive, and natural disposition to keep things the way they are to a formally articulated ideology of conservative principles, values, and ideas. This distinction, however, tends to be more artificial than real and obscures the extent to which traditionalism and conservatism complement each other as the two poles of an analytical tension that defines the parame-

---

3. C. Rossiter, "Conservatism," in *International Encyclopedia of the Social Sciences*, ed. D.L. Sills, vol. 3 (New York, 1968), p. 290. On the evolution of the term since 1789, see R. Vierhaus, "Konservativ, Konservatismus," in *Geschichtliche Grundbegriffe. Historisches Lexikon zur politisch-sozialen Sprache in Deutschland*, ed. O. Brunner, W. Conze, and R. Koselleck, vol. 3 (Stuttgart, 1982), pp. 531–65.

4. For the classic statement of this position, see M. Oakeshott, "On Being Conservative," *Rationalism in Politics* (New York, 1962), pp. 168–96.

ters of recent research on conservatism and its place in modern German history.

II

The historiography of German conservatism since the 1920s has generally reflected changing emphases in the research and writing of German history. Initially historians placed great emphasis on the intellectual roots of German conservatism and its contribution to the German *Sonderweg*. Attempts were made to identify various strands of conservative ideology or stages in conservative development and then to link these with prominent individuals and their writings. Early and conceptually innovative forays into the field of social history were interrupted or ignored, only to be pressed once again at a later stage with new vigor and insight. Gradually methodological tools adopted from the social sciences broadened the scope of the inquiry and introduced much-needed theoretical considerations, though generally 1933 continued to be taken as the terminal point of conservative development. And in the most recent phase, the fracturing of the historical guild has impelled research in promising new directions. Nevertheless, the separate strands of analysis and modes of inquiry into German conservatism have all too often remained isolated from one another: theory and empiricism coexist unhappily like partners in a bad marriage, while studies of the nineteenth century say nothing about the twentieth (or vice versa). Great works are studied without any attempt to identify their readership or political impact, just as the tactics of parliamentary parties are divorced from the ideology that allegedly underpinned them. How have these deficiencies colored past scholarship on German conservatism, and how might they be overcome?

The sociologist Karl Mannheim, writing in the 1920s, was one of the first to explore the intellectual roots of conservatism. To the concept of "traditionalism" he opposed a type of conservatism "oriented to meanings that contain different objective contents in different epochs."[5] The significance of

5. See the editors' "Introduction: The design of *Conservatism*," in K. Mannheim, *Conservatism: A Contribution to the Sociology of Knowledge*, ed. D. Kettler, V. Meja, and N. Stehr (London and New York, 1986), pp. 1–26. For Mannheim's distinction between "traditionalism" and "conservatism," see pp. 72–77.

Mannheim's pioneering contribution remains undiminished, not least because his habilitation thesis from the 1920s was recently discovered and published in full in both German and English. Since Mannheim first raised the question of locating conservatism within its concrete historical context, historians have suggested many categories or "ideal types" for the analysis of German conservatism. Usually these ideal types are discussed in one of two ways: either as components of a comprehensive "system" of conservative thought – less frequently a system of politics or a social order – or as chronological stages through which conservatism allegedly passed on the way to some more or less modern form. Sigmund Neumann's book on the "stages" of Prussian conservatism (1930) set the pattern for both lines of analysis in three important respects. First, Neumann combined the ideal-typical and the chronological models. Second, he linked prominent individuals with each distinct brand of conservatism. And third, he identified two antithetical strands within nineteenth-century conservatism – romantic conservatism and liberal conservatism – that combined to produce a "higher third." This synthesis was identified by Neumann as realistic conservatism, which supposedly dominated the period after 1848. As representative figures of these three stages in the development of German conservatism, Neumann selected the romantic conservatives Justus Möser and Ludwig von der Marwitz, the liberal conservatives Joseph Maria von Radowitz and Moritz August von Bethmann-Hollweg, and the realistic conservative Otto von Bismarck.[6]

Mannheim's and Neumann's concentration on political thought rather than political action, their interest in ideal types, and their emphasis on the period from 1770 to 1848 influenced writing on the subject for many decades.[7] In his study of German constitutional history since 1789, Ernst Huber identified four categories of conservatives: estate-bound (*ständisch*) conservatives, social conservatives, national

6. S. Neumann, *Die Stufen des preußischen Konservatismus. Ein Beitrag zum Staats- und Gesellschaftsbild Deutschlands im 19. Jahrhundert* (Berlin, 1930; reprint Vaduz, 1965).

7. See the bibliography to this volume for the collections of essays published in the early 1970s by H. Grebing, M. Greiffenhagen, and G.-K. Kaltenbrunner. For a review of this literature, see K. Schmitz, "Konservatismus – eine ideengeschichtliche Nostalgie?" *Archiv für Sozialgeschichte* 15 (1975): 536–46.

conservatives, and state conservatives.[8] Fritz Valjavec was somewhat less categorical in his 1951 study of the emergence of political movements in Germany between 1770 and 1815. He pointed instead to the decisive interplay between political forces of the late Enlightenment and early romantic periods, and though his contribution was seldom acknowledged, he provided the first real analysis of key conservative individuals and texts.[9] By far the most important American contribution to this discussion was Klaus Epstein's seminal study of the genesis of German conservative thought from 1770 to 1806. Building on Valjavec's work, Epstein not only stressed the specificity of German conservatism as a defense of the *ancien régime* against the universalist principles of the Enlightenment and French Revolution, but he offered a comprehensive definition of conservatism that embraced three distinct ideal types: status quo conservatives, reform conservatives, and reactionaries.[10] Although this book, like Valjavec's, was theoretically less challenging than Mannheim's, it surpassed any work of its era in the richness of its empirical detail.

By the time of Epstein's early death in 1967 the students of conservative ideas had begun to turn their attention to the period after 1871. In this respect the work of two emigré historians, Fritz Stern and George Mosse, merits special consideration. Stern was most interested in the emergence of a particular brand of conservatism known in the Weimar Republic as "revolutionary conservatism." By studying the writings of three self-styled "conservative revolutionaries" – Paul de Lagarde, Julius Langbehn, and Arthur Moeller van den Bruck – Stern depicted the irrational, antimodernist, and racist currents that helped to create the cultural environment in which the Nazis could come to power.[11] Mosse, on the other hand, directed his attention to the emergence, dissemination, and institutionalization of a *völkisch* and racist ideology from the beginning of the nineteenth century through the Nazi seizure of power in

---

8. E.R. Huber, *Deutsche Verfassungsgeschichte seit 1789*, 4 vols. (Stuttgart, 1957–69), vol. 2, pp. 331ff.

9. F. Valjavec, *Die Entstehung der politischen Strömungen in Deutschland 1770–1815*, 2nd ed. (Kronberg/Ts. and Düsseldorf, 1978).

10. K. Epstein, *The Genesis of German Conservatism* (Princeton, N.J., 1966), esp. pp. 7–11.

11. F. Stern, *The Politics of Cultural Despair: A Study in the Rise of the Germanic Ideology* (Berkeley, Ca., 1961).

1933.[12] By focusing on "cultural despair" and "liturgical impulses," Stern and Mosse explored the more virulent forms of conservative ideology and charted later strains of anti-Semitism, antimodernism, and nihilism back to their roots in the nineteenth century. Their work paralleled that of Peter Pulzer, a prominent English scholar, whose work on political anti-Semitism in Germany and Austria represented the beginnings of a sociopolitical as well as an intellectual analysis of what had certainly become one of the most vexing problems of modern German history.[13] The work of all three – but particularly that of Stern and Mosse – was predicated upon the assumption that there was a fundamental liberal deficit in Germany's political culture that made the collapse of the Weimar Republic and the triumph of Nazism virtually inevitable.[14]

Neumann's argument that German conservatism developed in coherent stages has also led historians to distinguish between two "styles" of conservative politics: *Weltanschauungspolitik* and *Interessenpolitik*. Those who make this distinction have tended to argue that these styles were mutually exclusive and that they appeared sequentially, although in contradiction to this they have also identified many variations and alleged turning points in conservative development – for instance the *Junkerparlament* of 1848, the Agrarian League (Bund der Landwirte) founded in 1893, and the anti-democratic condominium of big business and agrarianism after 1930. For the most part, however, these models have included normative assumptions that were more often implied than explicitly argued. Ignoble, unreflective, and materialist motives were thus ascribed to German conservatives, while high-mindedness, insight, and a continuing attachment to idealism were alleged to have inspired conservatives in other countries,

---

12. G. Mosse, *The Crisis of German Ideology: The Intellectual Origins of the Third Reich* (New York, 1964); and idem, *The Nationalization of the Masses: Political Symbolism and Mass Movements in Germany from the Napoleonic Wars Through the Third Reich* (New York, 1975).

13. P. Pulzer, *The Rise of Political Anti-Semitism in Germany and Austria* (New York, 1964, rev. ed. Cambridge, Mass., 1988).

14. The most explicit statement of this position is to be found in the introduction to F. Stern, *The Failure of Illiberalism: Essays on the Political Culture of Modern Germany* (New York, 1972), pp. xi–xliv. For a critique of this position, see K.H. Jarausch, "Illiberalism and Beyond: German History in Search of a Paradigm," *Journal of Modern History* 55 (1983): 268–84.

particularly in western Europe. In making such a distinction, however, historians have been guilty of a conceptual slippage between social and political categories. By identifying conservatism exclusively with aristocrats, historians have failed to appreciate the extent to which conservatism penetrated into the ranks of the middle and lower classes. Whereas this error of interpretation has been addressed recently by historians of liberalism – who rightly note that bourgeois aspirations have historically been accommodated by regimes that fall far short of liberal goals[15] – little attention has been devoted to the way in which this sort of imprecision has skewed our understanding of German conservatism.

Normative assumptions such as these informed even the most innovative early studies of German conservatism by social historians such as Hans Rosenberg and Alexander Gerschenkron. In these works German conservatives/Junkers were condemned for being incapable of playing the historical role that British conservatives/lords accepted with such good grace. According to this line of analysis, the British aristocracy learned to preserve what Edmund Burke called "the pleasing draperies of life" while waving the white flag of economic decline as a class – in effect, voluntarily submitting and contributing to their own demise. But the German Junkers were anomalous because they could not, or would not, read the writing on the wall. Refusing to do the gentlemanly thing, they ignored the pronouncement of the elite theorist Vilfredo Pareto that history is the graveyard of aristocracies; instead they fought ruthlessly to preserve their many privileges. The political consequences of this were enormous. As Gerschenkron expressed it in applying his model of "backwardness" to Germany, the price of bread and the fate of democracy were not unconnected issues. By preserving the power of the grain-growing Junkers on their large landed estates in the rural east, German history was encumbered with a fateful and essentially negative legacy.[16] Rosenberg, on the other hand, believed that the Junkers' "pseudo-democratization" involved the incorporation of techniques of mass mobilization and pop-

---

15. See especially D. Blackbourn and G. Eley, *The Peculiarities of German History: Bourgeois Society and Politics in Nineteenth-Century Germany* (Oxford and New York, 1984).

16. A. Gerschenkron, *Bread and Democracy in Germany* (New York, 1946).

ulist demagoguery that also contributed to their survival into the twentieth century.[17] This, too, set the German Junkers apart from elites anywhere else in the western world.

By 1970 this view of German conservatism had become a crucial component of *Sonderweg* theory. No book was more influential in defining the essential contours of this theory than Ralf Dahrendorf's *Society and Democracy in Germany* (1967). Writing from the perspective of a committed liberal, Dahrendorf asked: "Why is it that so few in Germany embraced the principle of liberal democracy?"[18] In answering this question, Dahrendorf argued that the extremely rapid pace of German economic modernization after 1871 took place within a social and political system that was still essentially feudal. The net effect of this temporal disjunction was to retard the social and political development of the German bourgeoisie, thus making it possible for a conservative, landowning elite to perpetuate its political dominance by means of an alliance against democracy with Germany's industrial leadership. This line of analysis found immediate echoes in the work of a group of historians at the University of Bielefeld, who in the 1960s and 1970s confirmed the essential elements of Dahrendorf's thesis with a wide range of empirical and theoretical treatises. In 1966 Hans-Jürgen Puhle published a densely empirical study of the Agrarian League, in which he argued that in the 1890s German conservatives abandoned their distaste for mass politics and learned better than their rivals how to mobilize a rural constituency for the defense of elite interests. Having adopted a political style that Puhle called "prefascist," German conservatism bequeathed a tragic inheritance to the Weimar Republic.[19] An equally critical view of German

17. H. Rosenberg, "Die Pseudodemokratisierung der Rittergutsbesitzerklasse," in idem, *Machteliten und Wirtschaftskonjunkturen. Zur neueren deutschen Sozial- und Wirtschaftsgeschichte* (Göttingen, 1978), pp. 83–101; and idem, *Bureaucracy, Aristocracy and Autocracy: The Prussian Experience, 1660–1815* (Boston, Mass., 1958).

18. R. Dahrendorf, *Society and Democracy in Germany* (New York, 1967), p. 14.

19. H.-J. Puhle, *Agrarische Interessenpolitik und preußischer Konservatismus im wilhelminischen Reich 1893–1914. Ein Beitrag zur Analyse des Nationalismus in Deutschland am Beispiel des Bundes der Landwirte und der Deutsch-Konservativen Partei* (Hanover, 1966; 2nd ed. Bonn Bad-Godesberg, 1975). See also idem, *Von der Agrarkrise zum Präfaschismus: Thesen zum Stellenwert der Agrarischen Interessenverbände in der Deutschen Politik am Ende des 19. Jahrhunderts* (Wiesbaden, 1972). For an English summary of Puhle's central thesis, see idem, "Conservatism in Modern German History," *Journal of Contemporary History* 13 (1978): 689–720.

conservatism was to be found in Hans-Ulrich Wehler's enormously influential *The German Empire* (1973). Here Wehler painted a picture of conservatives working with tragic effectiveness to counter the threat of democracy by manipulating interest-group politics, religious and secular education, class justice, constitutionalism, imperialism, and alleged foreign threats. Indeed, in Wehler's analysis it seemed as if the conservatives had succeeded in bringing history to a halt before 1914.[20]

From the perspective of Puhle and Wehler, the political mobilization of the "little man" in Wilhelmine society was nothing more than the penultimate act in a drama of political manipulation that stretched from the failed bourgeois revolution of the mid-nineteenth century to the failed conservative counterrevolution of January 1933. The same argument was espoused, though informed by different conceptual approaches, by Theodore S. Hamerow in the United States,[21] Volker Berghahn in the United Kingdom,[22] and Fritz Fischer and his circle of students from the University of Hamburg,[23] while historians of the former German Democratic Republic equated conservatism with fascism and focused unremittingly on the united opposition of the Junkers and the bourgeoisie to Germany's working classes.[24] By the end of the 1970s, however, a

20. H.-U. Wehler, *The German Empire 1871–1918*, trans. K. Traynor (Leamington Spa, 1985). The historiography can be charted through R.J. Evans, "Introduction: Wilhelm II's Germany and the Historians," in *Society and Politics in Wilhelmine Germany*, ed. R.J. Evans (London, 1978), pp. 11–39; R.G. Moeller, "The *Kaiserreich* Recast? Continuity and Change in Modern German Historiography," *Journal of Social History* 17 (1984): 655–83; and J. Retallack, "Social History with a Vengeance? Some Reactions to H.-U. Wehler's *Das Deutsche Kaiserreich*," *German Studies Review* 7 (1984): 423–50.

21. T.S. Hamerow, *The Social Foundations of German Unification, 1858–1871: Ideas and Institutions* (Princeton, N.J., 1969), esp. pp. 181–221.

22. V.R. Berghahn, *Der Tirpitz-Plan. Genesis und Verfall einer innenpolitischen Krisenstrategie unter Wilhelm II* (Düsseldorf, 1971).

23. It would be impossible to cite all the major works of relevance here. The general outlines of the Fischer thesis are to be found in F. Fischer, *War of Illusions: German Politics from 1911 to 1914* (London, 1975); and idem, *From Kaiserreich to Third Reich: Elements of Continuity in German History 1871–1945*, ed. and trans. R. Fletcher (London, 1986). For a sample of what Fischer's disciples have produced, see *Industrielle Gesellschaft und politisches System: Beiträge zur politischen Sozialgeschichte. Festschrift für Fritz Fischer zum siebzigsten Geburtstag*, ed. D. Stegmann, B.-J. Wendt, and P.-C. Witt (Bonn, 1978); and *Deutscher Konservatismus im 19. und 20. Jahrhundert. Festschrift für Fritz Fischer zum 75. Geburtstag*, ed. D. Stegmann, B.-J. Wendt, and P.-C. Witt (Bonn, 1983).

24. For example, see the special issue on "Konservative Politik und Ideologie" edited by H. Gottwald in the *Jenaer Beiträge zur Parteiengeschichte* 44 (July 1980); K. Gossweiler, "Junkertum und Faschismus," in *Preußen in der deutschen*

reaction against this particular reading of German history – with its obvious implications for an understanding of German conservatism – had begun to materialize. Among those who spearheaded this reaction was Richard Evans, a British historian who argued in the introduction to a collection of essays on the Second Empire that Wehler's *Kaiserreich* was presented as "a puppet theatre, with Junkers and industrialists pulling the strings, and middle and lower classes dancing jerkily across the stage of history towards the final curtain of the Third Reich."[25] At the heart of Evans's challenge lay a profound dissatisfaction with the manipulative model that both Wehler and Puhle used to explain the relationship between Germany's conservative elites and the masses they sought to mobilize in defense of their vested social and economic interests.

Evans's critique marked the beginning of a general broadside against what came to be known as the "new orthodoxy" of the Bielefeld School. In this endeavor, Evans was joined by two British historians, David Blackbourn and Geoff Eley, whose original monographs on different aspects of Wilhelmine political culture challenged the notion that Germany's conservative elites had somehow "duped" or "manipulated" subordinate classes of society into supporting policies inimical to their own interests.[26] In the revisionist assault that followed, politics in the Wilhelmine era was seen less as a matter of political manipulation from above than as combined social-political self-mobilization from below.[27] In Eley's allu-

Geschichte nach 1789, ed. G. Seeber and K.-H. Noack (East Berlin, 1983), pp. 290–302; and *Falsche Propheten. Studien zum konservativ-antidemokratischen Denken im 19. und 20. Jahrhundert*, ed. L. Elm (East Berlin, 1984). See also the various entries on conservative parties and interest organizations in *Lexikon zur Parteiengeschichte. Die bürgerlichen und kleinbürgerlichen Parteien und Verbände in Deutschland (1789–1945)*, ed. D. Fricke et al., 4 vols. (Leipzig, 1983–86).

25. Evans, "Introduction: Wilhelm II's Germany," p. 23. See also D. Blackbourn, "Politics as Theatre: Metaphors of the Stage in German History, 1848–1933," in idem *Populists and Patricians: Essays in Modern German History* (London, 1987), pp. 246–64.

26. See D. Blackbourn, *Class, Religion and Local Politics in Wilhelmine Germany: The Centre Party in Württemberg before 1914* (New Haven, Conn., and London, 1980); and G. Eley, *Reshaping the German Right: Radical Nationalism and Political Change after Bismarck* (New Haven, Conn., and London, 1980).

27. For further discussion of the problem, see R. Chickering's review of Eley's book cited in the previous note in *American Historical Review* 86 (1981): 159–60; as well as Eley's review of M.S. Coetzee's *The German Army League: Popular Nationalism in Wilhelmine Germany* (New York, 1990), in *American Historical Review* 96 (1991): 1569–70.

sive phrase, subordinate groups "registered a profound seismic shift at the base of German society, which sent heavy tremors of social aspiration upwards to the political surface of the new German state."[28] Eley and other contributors to Evans's volume of essays suggested that radical nationalists, Catholics, artists, youth, peasant groups, workers, and women had all challenged the social and political status quo with such vigor that it was no longer possible for historians to maintain that they had been "bought off," "cowed into submission," or "negatively integrated" into the existing system of rule. Moreover, even the Kaiser and his chancellors competed for the right to transform their divergent political ambitions into practice; heavy industrialists who claimed to serve the state sought to protect their own vested interests; and established right-wing politicians adapted to the pressures of subordinate groups in widely differing ways. As the decade of the 1980s dawned, then, historians were beginning to examine not only Wilhelmine history but also the history of conservative elites in new, pluralistic ways.

III

The next decade witnessed a continuation and intensification of the assault against the Bielefeld paradigm. In speaking of a paradigm shift at the beginning of the 1980s, one must be careful not to obscure the diversity that existed within each of the competing camps. For the decade witnessed a remarkable divergence of views and approaches on each side that cannot be ascribed simply to the pursuit of personal scholarly agendas. Conversely, the intensity with which this campaign was conducted often obscured the many areas of interpretation in which the historians of the Bielefeld School and their critics found common ground. Evans, Blackbourn, and Eley have all continued to affirm the importance of the structural as opposed to the narrative mode of analysis, and they have remained committed to the critical reappraisal of German historiography as an ongoing enterprise. Moreover, the revisionist critique of the Bielefeld paradigm did not result in the substitution of a new orthodoxy for the one that was supposed

28. G. Eley, "The Wilhelmine Right: How It Changed," in *Society and Politics*, ed. Evans, p. 124.

to have been dismantled. On the contrary, the net effect of the historiographical debates of the 1980s has been to open up the reassessment of the German past to new methodologies, new conceptual approaches, and new lines of empirical inquiry. What has emerged from this is a much more nuanced and differentiated picture of Germany's historical landscape than seemed imaginable in the 1960s.[29]

This, in turn, has led to a fundamental reassessment of conservatism and its place in modern German history. One of the major weaknesses of the Bielefeld paradigm was its tendency to refer to conservative elites without regard to their actual positions in the hierarchies of wealth, prestige, and power. Depending on the requirements of the argument, these elites included not only Junkers but also members of the Prussian army, court, and bureaucracy, heavy industrialists, imperialists, Protestant clergy, educators, and – in the broadest view – all those who opposed the advance of social democracy and the threat of revolution. As historians began to appreciate the exceedingly diverse social, ideological, and political interests of those who rallied to the conservative cause, they became increasingly skeptical of the argument that conservatives could have devised or implemented the grand strategy necessary to deflect the threat of modernization. For far from taking the initiative to steer economic, social, and political modernization into paths that did not threaten their material interests, conservatives were forced to respond as best they could – ambivalently, unwillingly, and inadequately – to these challenges. Furthermore, historians now recognize that it is no longer necessary to choose exclusively between the notion of "politics from the top down" with its emphasis upon political decision making at the highest echelons of the government, and that of "society from the bottom up" with its emphasis upon the autonomous experience of subordinate social groups and their capacity for self-mobilization in the political realm. Instead, both perspectives can be combined to address the more complex – and more interesting – questions about how the many worlds of German society and politics collided. From this perspective, conservative strategies were neither "fatefully successful" nor "hopelessly inadequate," but rather

29. See further J. Retallack, "Wilhelmine Germany," in *Modern Germany Reconsidered, 1870–1945*, ed. G. Martel (London and New York, 1992), pp. 33–53, esp. pp. 48–50.

part of an ongoing story of partial and incomplete adaptation to the challenges of industrialization, social upheaval, and democratization. Nonetheless, such strategies were, in David Blackbourn's telling phrase, "akin to riding the tiger."[30] An escalating spiral of radicalism and ruthlessness began in the nineteenth century, thus helping to set the stage for the rise of German fascism in the twentieth.

Because the fate of German agriculture and the manipulation of Germany's rural population figured so prominently in the Bielefeld paradigm, some of the most exciting new work involves a fresh look at the social and political relationships of the German countryside. No longer can we agree with an American observer who wrote from Berlin in 1833 that this world was populated by only two classes: "the von's and the not von's."[31] Instead a much richer and more complicated picture has emerged in which patterns of authority and subordination between Junkers and peasants were more differentiated than previously believed. Any picture of the German countryside must now also include non-noble landowners and various categories of peasants stretching from independent proprietors to landless wage laborers. Moreover, the avenues available for expressing grievances and the long-term political consequences of doing so were far more varied than once imagined. This has been illustrated by William Hagen's essays on the "Junkers' faithless servants" in rural Brandenburg in the early modern period,[32] by two volumes of essays on the German peasantry in the nineteenth and twentieth centuries,[33] by

30. D. Blackbourn, "Peasants and Politics in Germany, 1871–1914," *European History Quarterly* 14 (1984): 47–75; and idem, "The Politics of Demagogy in Imperial Germany," *Past and Present* 113 (1986): 152–84, both reprinted in Blackbourn, *Populists and Patricians*, pp. 114–39, 217–45.

31. John Lothrop Motley, letter of 4 November 1833, cited in E. Engelberg, *Bismarck*, 2 vols. (Berlin, 1986–90), vol. 1, p. 126.

32. W. Hagen, "The Junkers' Faithless Servants: Peasant Insubordination and the Breakdown of Serfdom in Brandenburg-Prussia, 1763–1811," in *The German Peasantry: Conflict and Community in Rural Society from the Eighteenth to the Twentieth Centuries*, ed. R.J. Evans and W.R. Lee (New York, 1986), pp. 71–101; idem, "Seventeenth-Century Crisis in Brandenburg: The Thirty-Years' War, the Destabilization of Serfdom, and the Rise of Absolutism," *American Historical Review* 94 (1989): 302–35.

33. For example, see I. Farr, "'Tradition' and the Peasantry: On the Modern Historiography of Rural Germany," and other essays in *German Peasantry*, ed. Evans and Lee, pp. 1–36; and R.G. Moeller, "Introduction: Locating Peasants and Lords in Modern German Historiography," in *Peasants and Lords in Modern Germany: Recent Studies in Agricultural History*, ed. R.G. Moeller (Boston, 1986), pp. 1–23.

Francis Carsten's survey history of the Junkers,[34] and by Robert Berdahl's exploration of conservative ideology and its relationship to the contours of social class before 1848. Of these studies, Berdahl's shows most clearly how early conservative principles emerged from the day-to-day experience of landownership in rural Prussia. Because estate owners exercised both private and public functions, paternalism and domination were central to this ideology. Nonetheless, social differentiation made conservative ideology – like conservative authority and conservative "interests" – problematic from the very beginning.[35] Just as recent studies of the German bourgeoisie have put to rest the notion that the German middle classes were "feudalized" by a pre-industrial Junker elite,[36] studies of peasants and lords have undermined the notion of a single cohesive conservative constituency in the countryside.

A similar breakthrough can be seen in efforts to explore the intellectual and cultural dimensions of German conservatism in the nineteenth century. By reexamining the theoretical works of early conservative theorists such as Ernst Brandes, Friedrich von Gentz, August Wilhelm Rehberg, and Adam Müller, Jörn Garber reminds us that models of conservatism before 1810 varied enormously in both substance and style, and that many of them offered highly sophisticated analyses of the historical impact of revolution in Germany.[37] Wilhelm Füßl provides the same service for the mid-nineteenth century with his exemplary study of Friedrich Julius Stahl. On the one hand, Füßl reconsiders the way in which Stahl stifled the Prussian conservatives' allergic reactions to constitutional monarchy after March 1848 with careful ministrations of con-

---

34. F.L. Carsten, *A History of the Prussian Junkers* (Aldershot, 1989).

35. R.M. Berdahl, *The Politics of the Prussian Nobility: The Development of a Conservative Ideology, 1770–1848* (Princeton, N.J., 1988), chs. 1–2. See also J. Retallack, "'Ideology without Vision'? Recent Literature on Nineteenth-Century German Conservatism," *Bulletin of the German Historical Institute London* 13 (1991): 5–11.

36. See especially D. Blackbourn, "The German bourgeoisie: an introduction," in *The German Bourgeoisie: Essays on the Social History of the German Middle Class from the Late Eighteenth to the Early Twentieth Century*, ed. D. Blackbourn and R.J. Evans (London and New York, 1991), pp. 1–45, as well as the editors' preface, pp. xiv–xviii.

37. J. Garber, "Drei Theoriemodelle frühkonservativer Revolutionsabwehr. Altständischer Funktionalismus, spätabsolutistisches Vernunftrecht, evolutionärer 'Historismus,'" *Jahrbuch des Instituts für Deutsche Geschichte* 8 (1979): 65–101.

stitutional compromise and political calculation. On the other hand, Füßl's book illustrates the fruitfulness of considering conservative theory in its larger social and cultural context. As his account illustrates, political ideology in the nineteenth century was formulated and disseminated through many channels, including teaching, indoctrination, the exercise of authority, parliamentary debate, *Publizistik*, and myriad other forms of political communication.[38] A similar approach informs Roger Chickering's methodologically innovative study of the Pan-German League (Alldeutscher Verband) from 1886 to 1914. Here Chickering employs analytical strategies borrowed from social psychology and cultural anthropology to explain the Pan-German League's appeal and influence in Imperial Germany. By exploding the methodological boundaries that have traditionally encapsulated the study of political history, Chickering's work opens up exciting new lines of inquiry at the intersection of culture and politics.[39]

One of the more important elements of the revisionist critique of the Bielefeld paradigm is its rejection of the Prussocentric bias that had colored historical writing on modern German history ever since the wars of national unification. Two studies of conservative party politics published in 1988 use a regional perspective to explain the forces acting on conservatives from above and below. Although the principal focus of Wolfgang Schwentker's account of conservative *Vereine* in the revolution of 1848/49 is Prussia, he devotes considerable attention to the different ways in which conservatives were activated in Brandenburg, Pomerania, East and West Prussia, and other provinces. In this respect, he approaches the problem not only from the perspective of the camarilla but also from that of the local election committees and patriotic *Vereine*. In documenting the *attempts* of conservative leaders to impose their political line on local *Vereine*, Schwentker also stresses the role that local conservative leaders played in the remarkably successful electoral mobilization of January and February 1849.[40] James Retallack advances similar arguments in his monograph on the German

38. W. Füßl, *Professor in der Politik: Friedrich Julius Stahl (1801–1861). Das monarchische Prinzip und seine Umsetzung in die parlamentarische Praxis* (Göttingen, 1988).
39. R. Chickering, *We Men Who Feel Most German: A Cultural Study of the Pan-German League, 1886–1914* (Boston, Mass., 1984).
40. W. Schwentker, *Konservative Vereine und Revolution in Preußen 1848/49. Die Konstituierung des Konservativismus als Partei* (Düsseldorf, 1988).

Conservative Party (Deutsch-Konservative Partei). Here Retallack argues that German conservatives were caught between the demands of mass politics and *Honoratiorenpolitik* and failed to make an effective choice between the two. After Bismarck's fall in 1890, the consequences of the conservatives' inability to choose between political exclusivity and mass mobilization alienated the Kaiser and his government without winning new recruits among the masses.[41] Rejecting suggestions that the conservatives "hovered" in a "quasi-oppositional" role[42] or that they "oscillated between the extremes of a status-bound old-conservative club of notables and a 'populist' mass movement of the Right,"[43] Retallack argues that the conservatives' assessment of their own role differed so radically from time to time and from place to place that only a close analysis of regional particularities can properly situate them within Imperial Germany's political culture.[44]

As historians have begun to free themselves from the fetters of Prussocentrism, it has become increasingly clear that German conservatism assumed many different forms and possessed many different faces. One of the faces that historians in the 1960s and 1970s so conveniently neglected was that of Catholic conservatism, a movement closely tied not only to the Catholic nobility in Bavaria, the Rhineland, Westphalia, Silesia, and Württemberg,[45] but also to the Christian labor move-

---

41. J. Retallack, *Notables of the Right: The German Conservative Party and Political Mobilization in Germany, 1876–1918* (Boston, Mass., and London, 1988). See also idem, "Conservatives *contra* Chancellor: Official Responses to the Spectre of Conservative Demagoguery from Bismarck to Bülow," *Canadian Journal of History* 20 (1985): 203–36.

42. Puhle, *Agrarische Interessenpolitik*, pp. 204, 212.

43. *Deutscher Konservatismus im 19. und 20. Jahrhundert*, ed. Stegmann, Wendt, and Witt, p. vii.

44. See J. Retallack, "Anti-Semitism, Conservative Propaganda, and Regional Politics in Late Nineteenth-Century Germany," *German Studies Review* 11 (1988): 377–403; idem, "'What is to Be Done?' The Red Specter, Franchise Questions, and the Crisis of Conservative Hegemony in Saxony, 1896–1909," *Central European History* 23 (1990): 271–312; and idem "Anti-Socialism and Electoral Politics in Regional Perspective: The Kingdom of Saxony," in *Elections, Mass Politics and Social Change in Modern Germany: New Perspectives*, ed. L.E. Jones and J. Retallack (New York and Cambridge, 1992), pp. 49–91.

45. For example, see H. Gründer, "Rechtskatholizismus im Kaiserreich und in der Weimarer Republik unter besonderer Berücksichtigung der Rheinlande und Westfalens," *Westfälische Zeitschrift* 134 (1984): 107–55; and F. Keinemann, *Soziale und politische Geschichte des westfälischen Adels* (Hamm, 1976). On the Bavarian nobility, see K.O. Aretin, "Der bayerische Adel. Von der Monarchie zum Dritten Reich," in *Bayern in der NS-Zeit*, ed. M. Broszat, E. Fröhlich, and A. Grossman, 6 vols. (Munich and Vienna, 1977–83), vol. 3, pp. 513–67.

ment that had emerged at the end of the nineteenth century in response to the social encyclicals of Leo XIII.[46] David Blackbourn's monograph on the German Center Party (Deutsche Zentrumspartei) in Württemberg before 1914 demonstrates how local party leaders recast the Center in a populist mode and identified it more closely with the economic interests of conservative social classes in the cities and countryside.[47] Similarly, Jonathan Sperber's study of popular Catholicism in the mid-nineteenth century shows that after 1848 social change, political engagement, and industrialization combined to produce an upsurge of religious piety as well as a "clerical-conservative symbiosis" within Germany's Catholic population.[48] With the collapse of the Second Empire, Catholic conservatives found themselves increasingly estranged from the Center in the wake of its transformation from an opposition to a government party. Gabriele Clemens's detailed study of Martin Spahn, a onetime Centrist who went over to the right-wing German National People's Party (Deutschnationale Volkspartei or DNVP) in 1921,[49] represents the most recent contribution to a still meager, yet growing, body of literature on Catholic conservatism in nineteenth- and twentieth-century Germany.[50]

IV

For the most part, historical writing on the period after 1918 has remained impervious to the implications of the debates that have done so much to stimulate a revival of historical interest in the Bismarckian and Wilhelmine periods. With few exceptions, historians writing on the Weimar Republic have subscribed either consciously or unconsciously to a conceptu-

46. For example, see E.D. Brose, *Christian Labor and the Politics of Frustration in Imperial Germany* (Washington, D.C., 1985).

47. See Blackbourn's monograph cited above, n. 26, as well as D. Blackbourn, "The Problem of Democratization: German Catholics and the Role of the Centre Party," in *Society and Politics in Wilhelmine Germany*, ed. Evans, pp. 160–85.

48. J. Sperber, *Popular Catholicism in Nineteenth–Century Germany* (Princeton, N.J., 1984). See also M.L. Anderson, "Piety and Politics: Recent Work on German Catholicism," *Journal of Modern History* 63 (1991): 681–716.

49. G. Clemens, *Martin Spahn und der Rechtskatholizismus in der Weimarer Republik* (Mainz, 1983).

50. Of the few early works on the topic, the most important is K. Breuning, *Die Vision des Reiches. Deutscher Katholizismus zwischen Demokratie und Diktatur (1929–1934)* (Munich, 1969).

al paradigm that views Germany's experiment in democracy from 1919 to 1933 as little more than a passing stage in the transition from the authoritarianism of the Second Empire to the totalitarianism of the Third Reich. From this perspective, the Weimar Republic seems doomed to failure, if not by what Puhle and Wehler define as the persistence of elite intransigence to democratic reform from the 1890s to the 1930s, then certainly by what their former colleague at the University of Bielefeld, Jürgen Kocka, identifies as the "strength of pre-industrial, pre-capitalist, and pre-bourgeois traditions" within both the German elites and the lower strata of German society.[51] More recently, however, historians such as Geoff Eley and Larry Eugene Jones have argued that by assigning causal primacy to structural deformities in Germany's political development since the middle of the nineteenth century or to the persistence of pre-industrial traditions among specific sectors of the German population, the Bielefeld School produced a skewed understanding of the Weimar Republic and seriously oversimplified the social and political dynamics that led to Hitler's installation as chancellor in 1933. At the very least, such an approach had the unintended effect of absolving the historian of any responsibility for explaining the collapse of Weimar and the rise of National Socialism in terms of the specific crises, both economic and political, that gripped Germany between 1918 and 1933.[52]

Both the leading representatives of the Bielefeld School and their critics were specialists in the history of the Bismarckian and Wilhelmine periods and therefore only indirectly involved in extending the frontiers of historical knowledge for the period after 1918. Insofar as they had anything to say about developments from 1918 to 1945, they did so primarily in the form of critical essays that extended conclusions drawn from research on the period before 1918 to the Weimar Repub-

51. For the most concise statement of this position, see J. Kocka, "Ursachen des Nationalsozialismus," *Aus Politik und Zeitgeschichte*, 21 June 1980, pp. 9–13.

52. For example, see G. Eley, "What Produces Fascism: Preindustrial Traditions or a Crisis of the Capitalist State?" *Politics and Society* 12 (1983): 53–82, reprinted in idem, *From Unification to Nazism: Reinterpreting the German Past* (Boston, 1986), pp. 254–82; and Jones, "Why Hitler Came to Power: In Defense of a New History of Politics," in *Geschichtswissenschaft vor 2000. Perspektiven der Historiographiegeschichte, Geschichtstheorie, Sozial- und Kulturgeschichte. Festschrift für Georg Iggers zum 65. Geburtstag*, ed. K.H. Jarausch, J. Rüsen, and H. Schleier (Hagen, 1991), pp. 259–62.

lic and Third Reich.[53] In the meantime, research and writing on the history of German conservatism in the Weimar Republic demonstrates remarkable vigor both in Germany and the Anglo-American world. For the most part, this body of work explores three general areas of historical inquiry: conservative and right-wing organizations such as the DNVP, the Stahlhelm, and the German National Union of Commercial Employees (Deutschnationaler Handlungsgehilfen-Verband); anti-liberal and anti-democratic ideas with particular emphasis on the much debated notion of the "conservative revolution"; and the role that conservative elites in agriculture, industry, and the military played in the destruction of the Weimar Republic and the establishment of the Third Reich. Much of the early work on Weimar conservatism, however, is already obsolete, not only on account of its theoretical blandness but also because expanding access to new archival sources has dramatically altered both the quality and quantity of the empirical evidence available for an interpretation of conservatism and its place in the history of the Weimar Republic.

No conservative organization in the Weimar Republic has received more attention than the German National People's Party. By last count, no fewer than a dozen books and dissertations have been produced on different aspects of the DNVP's history. In the 1950s and 1960s Lewis Hertzman and Werner Liebe published monographs on the early years of the DNVP's existence; both are now badly outdated and generally inferior to Jan Streisow's dissertation on the relationship between the DNVP and the radical racists from 1918 to 1922.[54] Although John Williamson has produced a useful, though hardly definitive, biography of Karl Helfferich,[55] the DNVP's strategy and tactics during the crisis years of 1923/24 remain something of a mystery. The DNVP's development from 1924 to 1928, on the other hand, has been the subject of a detailed dissertation by Manfred Dörr, who devotes considerable attention to an

---

53. For example, see G. Eley, "Conservatives and Radical Nationalists in Germany," in *Fascists and Conservatives: The Radical Right and the Establishment in Twentieth-Century Europe*, ed. M. Blinkhorn (London, 1990), pp. 50–70.

54. See L. Hertzman, *DNVP: Right-Wing Opposition in the Weimar Republic, 1918–1924* (Lincoln, Nebr., 1963); W. Liebe, *Deutschnationale Volkspartei 1918–1924* (Düsseldorf, 1956); and J. Streisow, *Die Deutschnationale Volkspartei und die Völkisch-Radikalen 1918–1922*, 2 vols. (Frankfurt am Main, 1981).

55. J.G. Williamson, *Karl Helfferich, 1872–1924: Economist, Financier, Politician* (Princeton, N.J., 1971).

analysis of the party's social composition and the split that the DNVP's two attempts at governmental participation in 1925 and 1927 produced at all levels of the party's national organization.[56] No comparable study of the DNVP in the last years of the Weimar Republic exists, although Elizabeth Friedenthal wrote an early, superbly documented dissertation on the internal party crises of 1929/30.[57] In the meantime, Alfred Hugenberg's role in the party is the subject of major studies by John Leopold, David Walker, and Heidrun Holzbach. Of the three, Holzbach's monograph on the "Hugenberg system" is by far the most resourceful in exploring the full scope of Hugenberg's activities. Concentrating on the years preceding Hugenberg's election as DNVP party chairman in October 1928, Holzbach uncovers the instrumental role Hugenberg played behind the scenes in organizing the anti-republican Right before Nazism arrived on the scene. In doing so, Holzbach succeeds in revealing the extent to which Hugenberg was able to bring not only the DNVP party leadership but also the so-called "young conservatives," nationalist workers' organizations, and the paramilitary Right within the compass of his influence.[58]

Other conservative organizations have also been the subject of intensive investigation. The various splinter parties that broke away from the DNVP and other established bourgeois parties between 1924 and 1930 have all been the topics of specialized studies. Conservative economic interest organizations have also received their fair share of attention. Bernd Weisbrod's monograph on the organization and representation of Ruhr heavy industry during the period of Weimar's political and economic stabilization from 1924 to 1929 documents the extent to which conservative economic elites were successful in sabotaging the social and economic fabric of Weimar democracy well before the outbreak of the world economic crisis.[59] Jens Flemming and Dieter Gessner perform a similar ser-

56. M. Dörr, "Die Deutschnationale Volkspartei 1925 bis 1928" (Ph.D. diss., University of Marburg, 1964).

57. E. Friedenthal, "Volksbegehren und Volksentscheid über den Young-Plan und die deutschnationale Sezession" (Ph.D. diss., University of Tübingen, 1957).

58. H. Holzbach, *Das "System Hugenberg". Die Organisation bürgerlicher Sammlungspolitik vor dem Aufstieg der NSDAP* (Stuttgart, 1981), esp. pp. 99–166.

59. B. Weisbrod, *Schwerindustrie in der Weimarer Republik. Interessenpolitik zwischen Stabilisierung und Krise* (Wuppertal, 1978). See also idem, "Economic Power and Political Stability Reconsidered: Heavy Industry in Weimar Germany," *Social History* 4 (1979): 241–63.

vice for the agrarian sector with their respective works on the reestablishment of conservative hegemony in the countryside after the revolution of 1918/19[60] and the crisis of agrarian protectionism in the last years of the Weimar Republic.[61] In a similar vein, William Patch and Hartmut Roder examine the Christian labor movement and its relationship to the various nonsocialist parties, including the DNVP.[62] The increasing integration of conservative industrial, agrarian, and working-class interests into the fabric of Weimar democracy, however, provoked a sharp counterreaction that drew its impetus from the "new nationalism" of paramilitary organizations such as the Stahlhelm and Young German Order (Jungdeutscher Orden). This phenomenon has been the subject of intense investigation and has produced a spate of specialized monographs, the most important of which is Volker Berghahn's study of the Stahlhelm.[63] American scholars have produced two works of note: James Diehl's survey of Germany's paramilitary Right before the advent of National Socialism and, more recently, Peter Fritzsche's monograph on the modes of bourgeois political mobilization in Lower Saxony.[64] Both studies underscore the extent to which the rise of Nazism was predicated upon factors that were already present in Germany's bourgeois political culture prior to the outbreak of the world economic crisis.

The role that conservative industrial, agricultural, and working-class interest organizations played in Weimar's

---

60. J. Flemming, *Landwirtschaftliche Interessen und Demokratie. Ländliche Gesellschaft, Agrarverbände und Staat 1890–1925* (Bonn, 1978), esp. pp. 161–327.

61. D. Gessner, *Agrarverbände in der Weimarer Republik. Wirtschaftliche und soziale Voraussetzungen agrarkonservativer Politik vor 1933* (Düsseldorf, 1976); idem, *Agrardepression und Präsidialregierungen in Deutschland 1930–1933. Probleme des Agrarkonservatismus am Ende der Weimarer Republik* (Düsseldorf, 1977). For an English summary of Gessner's central thesis, see idem, "Agrarian Protectionism in the Weimar Republic," *Journal of Contemporary History* 12 (1977): 759–78.

62. See W. Patch, *Christian Trade Unions in the Weimar Republic, 1918–1933: The Failure of "Corporate Pluralism"* (New Haven, Conn., 1985); and H. Roder, *Der christlich-nationale Deutsche Gewerkschaftsbund (DGB) im politisch-ökonomischen Kräftefeld der Weimarer Republik* (Frankfurt am Main, Bern, and New York, 1986).

63. V.R. Berghahn, *Der Stahlhelm – Bund der Frontsoldaten 1918–1935* (Düsseldorf, 1966).

64. See J.M. Diehl, *Paramilitary Politics in the Weimar Republic* (Bloomington, Ind., 1977); and P. Fritzsche, *Rehearsals for Fascism: Populism and Political Mobilization in Weimar Germany* (New York and Oxford, 1990).

short-lived political stabilization from 1924 to 1929 also met with strong resistance from Germany's young conservative intelligentsia. The efforts of young conservative intellectuals such as Arthur Moeller van den Bruck, Oswald Spengler, Ernst Jünger, and Edgar Jung to mobilize the forces of counter-revolution against the Weimar Republic and all that it suppos-edly stood for have been the subject of specialized monographs that are far too numerous for detailed attention here. Many of these, such as Klemens von Klemperer's study of Germany's "new conservatism" or Kurt Sontheimer's work on anti-democratic thought in the Weimar Republic, were essentially attempts to develop a typology of neoconservative ideas with-out properly situating these ideas in a broader social, econom-ic, and political matrix.[65] More recently, historians have tried to explode the boundaries that have traditionally encapsulat-ed the study of intellectual history in hopes of developing a better understanding of the institutional and cultural context in which these ideas developed and flourished.[66] Particularly noteworthy in this respect is the pioneering study by Joachim Petzold from the former German Democratic Republic, whose analysis of young conservative ideas in the Weimar Republic explores the multifarious relationships that existed between the young conservative movement and conservative economic elites in industry and agriculture.[67] In a somewhat different vein, Gary Stark's monograph on the neoconservative pub-lishing industry from 1890 to 1933 examines the material and institutional infrastructure that allowed right-wing critics of Weimar democracy to disseminate their particular brand of revolutionary conservatism – with all its antimodernist, anti-liberal, and anti-Semitic overtones – throughout German society as a whole.[68] Similarly, Jeffrey Herf shows how young

65. See K. von Klemperer, *Germany's New Conservatism: Its History and Dilemma in the Twentieth Century* (Princeton, N.J., 1957); and K. Sontheimer, *Antidemokratisches Denken in der Weimarer Republik. Die politischen Ideen des deutschen Nationalismus zwischen 1918 und 1933* (Munich, 1962).

66. For example, see L.E. Jones, "Culture and Politics in the Weimar Repub-lic," in *Modern Germany Reconsidered*, ed. Martel, pp. 74–95; as well as M. Eksteins, *Rites of Spring: The Great War and the Birth of the Modern Age* (Boston, Mass., 1989); and D. Peukert, *The Weimar Republic: The Crisis of Classical Moder-nity*, trans. by R. Deveson (New York, 1992).

67. J. Petzold, *Wegbereiter des deutschen Faschismus. Die Jungkonservativen in der Weimarer Republik* (Cologne, 1978).

68. G. Stark, *Entrepreneurs of Ideology: Neoconservative Publishers in Germany, 1890–1933* (Chapel Hill, N.C., 1981).

conservative ideologues such as Spengler and Jünger appropriated the modernist fascination with technology and
placed it at the service of a reactionary political agenda
under the rubric of what Herf appropriately calls "reactionary modernism."[69]

The role that Germany's conservative elites played in the
collapse of the Weimar Republic and during the transition
from Weimar to the Third Reich has remained a topic of considerable controversy. For although these elites felt little loyalty to the Weimar Republic and actively sought its replacement
with a more authoritarian regime, the degree to which they
supported the solution that eventually emerged in January
1933 is far less clear. Karl Dietrich Bracher's *Die Auflösung der
Weimarer Republik* from the late 1950s remains the most comprehensive treatment of this problem. Bracher's central thesis
was that the progressive paralysis of Germany's republican
institutions created a power vacuum that made it possible for
conservatives with access to Reich President Paul von Hindenburg – men such as Franz von Papen and General Kurt von
Schleicher – to use the deepening economic crisis of the early
1930s to dismantle the last vestiges of Weimar democracy and
create a more authoritarian governmental system over which
they and their peers in agriculture, industry, and the military
would exercise effective control. Bracher thus combined a
structural approach to the dissolution of the Weimar Republic
with close attention to the role that individual conservatives
played in this process.[70]

More recently, David Abraham has tried to improve upon
Bracher's analysis of how and why Weimar failed by
approaching the question from a neo-Marxist perspective
informed by the theoretical insights of Antonio Gramsci and
Nicos Poulantzas. Like Bracher, Abraham views the collapse
of the Weimar Republic from a structural perspective but
eschews the notion of a power vacuum that played such an
important part in Bracher's analysis and disputes the emphasis that Bracher placed upon the agency of individual conservatives such as Hugenberg, Papen, and Schleicher. At the same

69. J. Herf, *Reactionary Modernism: Technology, Culture, and Politics in Weimar
and the Third Reich* (Cambridge, 1984).
70. K.D. Bracher, *Die Auflösung der Weimarer Republik. Eine Studie zum Problem des Machtverfalls in der Demokratie*, 3rd ed. (Villingen/Schwarzwald,

time, Abraham sees a causal relationship between the crisis of bourgeois hegemony and the collapse of the Weimar Republic and devotes considerable attention to the conflicts that made it necessary for Germany's conservative elites to turn to National Socialism as an "extra-systemic solution" to the crisis of the capitalist state. This crisis was characterized not only by the inability of Germany's republican institutions to generate a viable domestic consensus for the formulation and conduct of national policy, but also by the republic's loss of legitimacy among increasingly large sectors of the German population. Only by allying themselves with the Nazis would it be possible for Germany's conservative elites to provide themselves with the mass political base they needed to legitimize their claims to social and political hegemony. The minimalist program of the Hitler-Papen-Hugenberg cabinet in January 1933 thus represented the lowest common denominator upon which Germany's economic elites could unite at a time of intense conflict both between and within the industrial and agricultural sectors of the German economy.[71]

For all of its empirical shortcomings,[72] Abraham's work has drawn renewed attention to the role that Germany's conservative elites played not merely in bringing about the collapse of the Weimar Republic but, more importantly, in securing Hitler's appointment as chancellor. In this respect, Abraham's conclusions complement those of another historian, Dirk Stegmann, who published a major article in 1973 on the relationship between German big business and National Socialism. Here Stegmann emphasizes the continuity in the political behavior of Germany's economic elites from the end of the Second Empire through the collapse of the Weimar Republic and the establishment of the Third Reich. Preferring a structural mode of analysis over one that concentrates on questions of individual motivation, Stegmann sees the formation of the Hitler cabinet in January 1933 as an attempt by conservative elites in industry and agriculture – but particularly in the former – to domesticate the Nazi movement by saddling it with the burden of political responsibility so that, in the long run, it

71. D. Abraham, *The Collapse of the Weimar Republic*, 2nd ed. (New York, 1986), esp. pp. 1–41.
72. See G.D. Feldman, "A Collapse in Weimar Scholarship," *Central European History* 12 (1984): 159–77; and P. Hayes, "History in an Off Key: David Abraham's Second *Collapse*," *Business History Review* 61 (1987): 452–72.

could be used to stabilize their own social and political hegemo-ny.[73] This line of analysis, however, encountered sharp criticism from Henry Turner, who argues on the basis of extensive prima-ry research in German firm archives that, with few exceptions, German industrialists neither provided the Nazi Party with financial support prior to 1933 nor played a role in the actual decision to entrust Hitler with the chancellorship. Among other things, Turner denies the existence of a causal relationship between the general crisis of German capitalism in the 1920s and early 1930s and the establishment of the Third Reich.[74]

The controversy over Abraham's use of evidence quickly obscured the larger theoretical questions he raises about the nature of the state and its relationship to civil society. If the episode had any positive benefit, then it lay in the new studies it spawned during the 1980s by historians on both sides of the controversy who were trying to come to terms with its impli-cations. Peter Hayes's detailed study of the German chemical industry in the Third Reich and Reinhard Neebe's monograph on Paul Silverberg and the National Federation of German Industry (Reichsverband der Deutschen Industrie) in the last years of the Weimar Republic both confirm the essential out-lines of the Turner thesis.[75] On the other hand, a more critical perspective that had much in common with Abraham's basic approach could be seen in Jane Caplan's study of civil admin-istration in the Weimar Republic and Third Reich.[76] The same is true of Shelley Baranowski's work on the attitude of conser-vative Protestant elites toward the Nazi regime and, more recently, on the east-Elbian aristocracy during the transition from Weimar to the Third Reich.[77]

73. D. Stegmann, "Zum Verhältnis von Großindustrie und Nationalsozialis-mus 1930–1933," *Archiv für Sozialwissenschaft* 13 (1973): 399–482.

74. For Turner's critique of Stegmann, see H.A. Turner, Jr., "Großun-ternehmertum und Nationalsozialismus 1930–1933. Kritisches und Ergänzen-des zu zwei neuen Forschungsbeiträgen," *Historische Zeitschrift* 221 (1975): 18–68. See also idem, *German Big Business and the Rise of Hitler* (Oxford, 1985).

75. P. Hayes, *Interest and Ideology: I.G. Farben in the Nazi Era* (Cambridge, 1987); and R. Neebe, *Großindustrie, Staat und NSDAP. Paul Silverberg und der Reichsverband der Deutschen Industrie in der Krise der Weimarer Republik* (Düssel-dorf, 1981).

76. J. Caplan, *Government with Administration: State and Civil Service in Weimar and Nazi Germany* (Oxford, 1988).

77. S. Baranowski, *The Confessing Church, Conservative Elites, and the Nazi State* (Lewiston, N.Y., 1986); and idem, "Continuity and Contingency: Agrari-an Elites, Conservative Institutions and East Elbia in Modern German Histo-ry," *Social History* 12 (1987): 285–308.

Interest in the role that Germany's conservative elites played in the establishment of the Nazi state has carried over into the historiography of the Third Reich. In this respect, however, historians have focused less on the conservative role in the stabilization of the Nazi regime between 1933 and 1938 than on conservative involvement in the anti-Nazi resistance after 1938. Hans Rothfels, Gerhard Ritter, Wilhelm Ritter von Schramm, and the first generation of historians writing in the shadow of World War II placed strong emphasis upon the religious and moral motives that lay at the heart of the conservative resistance to Hitler, depicting the abortive coup of 20 July 1944 as an act of national self-redemption on the part of Germany's traditional conservative elites.[78] This particular reading of the resistance and the motives that inspired it has found a sympathetic echo on this side of the Atlantic in the work of Peter Hoffmann and Klemens von Klemperer.[79] A second generation of resistance specialists led by Hans Mommsen and Klaus-Jürgen Müller, however, argues instead that the emergence of the resistance must be understood as a functional response to the collapse of the alliance that Germany's conservative elites had concluded with the Nazis at the founding of the Third Reich. Both Mommsen and Müller stress the extent to which conservative elites in German civilian and military life were prepared to collaborate with the Nazi regime as long as Hitler honored the concessions he had made at the time of his installation as chancellor. It was only when this was no longer the case – as, for example, after the infamous Fritsch-Blomberg affair at the beginning of 1938 – that the seeds of a conservative resistance began to take root and grow.[80]

78. For the classic statements of this position, see H. Rothfels, *The German Opposition to Hitler* (Hinsdale, Ill., 1948); G. Ritter, *Carl Goerdeler und die deutsche Widerstandsbewegung* (Stuttgart, 1954); and W. v. Schramm, *Conspiracy among Generals*, trans. R.T. Clark (London, 1956).

79. For example, see P. Hoffmann, *The History of the German Resistance, 1933–1945*, trans. R. Barry (Cambridge, Ma., 1977); and K. von Klemperer, "Glaube, Religion, Kirche und der deutsche Widerstand gegen den Nationalsozialismus," *Vierteljahrshefte für Zeitgeschichte* 28 (1980): 293–309.

80. On the historiography of the German resistance, see H. Mommsen, "The Political Legacy of the German Resistance: A Historiographical Critique," in *Contending with Hitler: Varieties of German Resistance in the Third Reich*, ed. D. C. Large (Cambridge, 1991), pp. 151–62. For a sample of Müller's work, see K.-J. Müller, "The Structure and Nature of the National Conservative Opposition in Germany up to 1940," in *Aspects of the Third Reich*, ed. H.W. Koch (New York, 1986), pp. 133–78, and idem, *The Army, Politics, and Society in Germany, 1933–45: Studies in the Army's Relation to Nazism* (New York, 1987).

V

In retrospect, it is clear that the study of German conservatism has demonstrated remarkable vitality since the end of World War II. Prompted by the perennially vexing question of responsibility for the series of national catastrophes that befell Germany between 1890 and 1945, historians on both sides of the Atlantic have produced a body of literature that is prodigious and varied. Beginning in the late 1960s and early 1970s, historians abandoned the idealistic theory of the state that had informed so much of the early writing on the history of German conservatism in favor of new analytical strategies that derive much of their legitimacy from the theoretical legacies of Karl Marx and Max Weber. This was accompanied by a shift from the narrative to the structural mode of analysis and by the introduction of new methodologies and analytical techniques appropriated from the social sciences. As the work of both the circle around Fritz Fischer and the Bielefeld School clearly suggests, a reassessment of conservatism and its role in modern German history stood very much at the heart of the paradigm shift that defined German historical writing in the early 1970s. More recently, however, thinking on the history of German conservatism has been affected by a second and ultimately more radical change in conceptual perspective. For not only has the postmodernist challenge effectively shattered the master narrative that has governed the reconstruction of the German past for almost five decades, but it has opened up exciting new lines of historical inquiry that have great potential to enrich our understanding of conservatism and its place in modern German history.

It remains to be seen how far the postmodernist challenge will succeed in actually transforming the landscape of historical scholarship in Germany and the Anglo-American world. At present, however, one can identify several distinct dimensions of the postmodernist agenda for a reform and revitalization of the historical sciences that may be of future relevance to the way in which German conservatism is studied. *Alltagsgeschichte*, or the history of everyday life, invests our understanding of the past with an intimacy and texture that is conspicuously absent from the more structurally oriented modes of historical analysis. This, in turn, complements the attention that historians such as Wolfgang Schwentker, James Retallack, and Peter Fritzsche have focused on the constitution of political conservatism at the local and regional levels of Germany's political culture.[81] At the same time, postmodernism has redefined the nature of power to include societal, familial, and sexual relationships previously excluded from the compass of political history and has linked the study of power to questions of gender, culture, and language in ways that historians are just beginning to appreciate. Renate Bridenthal's work on the organization and mobilization of rural women in the Weimar Republic, for example, shows how historians can – and indeed must – bridge the gender gap in order to write a truly comprehensive history of German conservatism.[82] By the same token, Roger Chickering's study of the Pan-German League offers a particularly telling example of just how essential an understanding of the general cultural milieu is for the analysis of political behavior and the development of political institutions.[83] More recently, Thomas Childers has refined this line of inquiry by using the linguistic analysis of political discourse as the point of departure for an interpretation of voting behavior in the Weimar Republic.[84]

At the very least, it is safe to say that the agenda for future research on the history of German conservatism is far from exhausted. Major areas of investigation still require careful attention. Historians are still waiting for the comprehensive social history of the Junkers that Hans Rosenberg promised, but never wrote. Recent studies of estate life before 1848 have also shown just how much remains to be learned for the later periods as well. Historians know very little about the rhythms and rituals of aristocratic culture and have much to gain from the "history of everyday life" with its emphasis upon the reconstruction of social experience. Perhaps greater accessibility to archives in the former German Democratic Republic and Poland will spur historians to this task. In a more traditional vein, accessibility to these resources might also encourage historians to undertake full-scale studies of the National Liberal, Free Conservative, and Christian Social parties at both the

---

81. See the works cited above, nn. 40, 41, 44, as well as P. Fritzsche, *Rehearsals for Fascism*.

82. For example, see Bridenthal's contribution to this volume.

83. See the work cited above, n. 39.

84. T. Childers, "The Social Language of Politics in Germany: The Sociology of Political Discourse in the Weimar Republic," *American Historical Review* 95 (1990): 331–58.

regional and national levels. Nor, for that matter, is there an adequate history of the German National People's Party that places its development in the context of the social and economic history of the Weimar Republic. Similarly, the role of religion as a factor in conservative culture and conservative politics will continue to attract scholarly interest. In this respect, the history of Catholic conservatism in the Second Empire and the Weimar Republic deserves particular attention. Historians also need to know more about the terms and mechanisms of conservative collaboration with Nazism both before and after the establishment of the Third Reich. Whereas the part that conservatives played in the anti-Hitler resistance from 1938 to 1944 has received its share of scholarly attention, neither the role that Germany's conservative elites played in the stabilization of the Nazi regime from 1933 to 1938 nor the extent to which patterns of conservative collaboration persisted after 1938 have received the attention they deserve. Whether one prefers the more traditional modes of analysis associated with political history or the more innovative analytical techniques that have been developed in connection with the postmodernist agenda, much important work on the history of German conservatism remains to be done.

All of this suggests that it would be premature to relegate political history to Karl Marx's infamous "dustbin of history." On the one hand, the study of power and its constitution within the framework of not only the state but society as a whole will remain an important component of historical scholarship well into the postmodern era. This will be particularly true in the case of Germany, where the events of 1989/90 have revived the specter of an unrepentant and aggressive German nationalism at home and abroad. This, in turn, will almost certainly lend new impetus to a reexamination of Germany's national traditions and their relationship to the political forces that have shaped the general course of modern German history. On the other hand, the study of political history itself is undergoing a revitalization as a result of its interaction with the most fruitful developments in collateral fields of historical inquiry. Just as political history reaped enormous benefit from its exposure to social history in the 1960s and 1970s, so now it stands to benefit from new advances in the fields of cultural history, women's studies, and linguistics.

1

The Politics of Revival

Pietists, Aristocrats, and the State Church in Early Nineteenth-Century Prussia

Christopher M. Clark

I

In December 1827, an Englishman returned from Berlin to London with "pleasing testimonies to the increase in religion amongst influential persons in the Prussian dominions." This Evangelical traveler told a prominent London missionary society of a prayer meeting in Berlin at which he had met "30 persons of the first rank." He reported that the king and his ministers were at one in the pursuance of pious projects, he recalled his numerous meetings with army officers of "truly Christian spirit," and he concluded that "it was a blessing to have such men at the helm."[1] The capital city of the German Enlightenment had become a center of fundamentalist Christian sentiment.

The visitor from England had witnessed the "Berlin Awakening" at the zenith of its social and political influence. The Awakening rejected the "lordship of intellect," as Heinrich von Treitschke put it, in favor of an emphasis on the immediate quality of religious experience. The church service was esteemed as one possible route to edification, but awakened Christians preferred "the private devotional meeting, the sermon in the house, the barn or the field, the conventicle. Here one could find a statement of faith that was more vigorous, more lively, more intimate, more in tune with a sense of broth-

*I would like to thank Timothy Blanning, Jonathan Steinberg, and Charles Turner for their comments on an earlier draft of this paper.
    1. Letter from Mr. R. Smith to the Committee of the London Society for Promoting Christianity among the Jews, 17 December 1827, cited in *The Jewish Expositor and Friend of Israel* 13 (1828): 262–67; here p. 266.

31

erly community."[2] The relative indifference of the awakened to ecclesiastical forms and confessional boundaries was strongly reminiscent of the pietist movement that had grown during the early eighteenth century from a small and embattled reformist sect within Lutheran orthodoxy to the "state religion" of Brandenburg-Prussia. Penitence and rebirth as necessary steps on the way to grace, the conventicle as the locus of a community bound together in shared devotion – these were familiar pietist themes. Strong parallels with the language of the older movement seemed to justify the view that the Awakening was indeed a "revival," a *re*awakening of something that had gone into hibernation during the long "night of rationalism." The Protestant historiography of the nineteenth and early twentieth centuries frequently evoked the continuity implicit in the notion of renewal with metaphors of seasonal change and natural succession. Thus, the Awakening was the spring after the "spiritual winter" of the Enlightenment, an epoch of relief after floods, or the breaking forth of a river that had been reduced to a meager stream by the silt of rationalism.[3]

For all their ideological baggage, such metaphors did not generate an entirely false picture of the Awakening in Prussia. Throughout the Frederician *Aufklärung*, the traditions of the old Pietism had been perpetuated in the dispersed communities of the *Brüdergemeinde* – the Moravian Brethren who maintained an extensive network of religious communities linked by correspondence and traveling missionaries. Pietist traditions also persisted in the households and conventicles of the *Stillen im Lande*, those "quiet ones" who cultivated a religiosity diametrically opposed to the rationalist Christianity that prevailed in the churches and universities. At the height of the Prussian *Aufklärung*, in the 1770s, the Moravian preacher Servus led prayers in the home of a Berlin baker, despite an

2. E.L. v. Gerlach, "Das Königreich Gottes," *Evangelische Kirchenzeitung* 68 (1861), cols. 438–54; here cols. 438–9 (Gerlach's emphasis).

3. See J. Richter, *Geschichte der Berliner Missionsgesellschaft, 1824–1924* (Berlin, 1924), p. 1. For examples of the impact of these metaphors, see L. von Rohden, *Geschichte der Rheinischen Missionsgesellschaft* (Barmen, 1856), p. 1; F. Weber, "Reiseerinnerungen aus Norddeutschland vom Juli 1870," *Saat auf Hoffnung* 7 (1870): 341–51, here p. 348; F. Hauß, *Erweckungspredigt. Eine Untersuchung über die Erweckungspredigt des 19. Jahrhunderts in Baden und Württemberg insbesondere über die Ursachen ihrer Fruchtbarkeit, als Hilfe in der Predigt heute* (Bad Liebenzell, 1924/25), p. 7.

official prohibition of the meetings on the grounds that they constituted a "dangerous conventicle."[4] In Berlin as elsewhere, the Moravians and the *Stillen im Lande* played an important role in the propagation of awakened religion.[5]

Nevertheless, the Berlin Awakening was not and could not be a mere revival of the old pietism – it was too closely linked to the specific problems of the postwar period.[6] The Christian charitable foundations of the 1810s – workhouses, orphanages and poor schools – were largely a response to the social and economic dislocation caused by the French occupation and wars of liberation. The profound psychological impact of defeat and occupation lent force to a spiritual movement capable of endowing the task of reconstruction with a transcendental significance. But the fundamental, if obvious, difference between pietism and its nineteenth-century revival was that the awakened had lived through the French revolution and observed its effects in Germany. For Protestant historians writing near the end of the era, it was clear that the beginnings of the Awakening were to be found in that "barren and stormy time when faith was everywhere extinguished and love grown cold," a time when the "storms of revolution from France filled our German fatherland with their poisonous breath." The Awakening was directed not only toward the salvation of

4. L. Witte, *Das Leben D. Friedrich August Gottreu Tholuck's*, 2 vols. (Bielefeld and Leipzig, 1884–86), vol. 1, p. 99.

5. See, for example, F.W. Kantzenbach, *Die Erweckungsbewegung. Studien zur Geschichte ihrer Entstehung und ersten Ausbreitung in Deutschland* (Neuendettelsau, 1957); idem, *Baron H.E. von Kottwitz und die Erweckungsbewegung in Schlesien, Berlin und Pommern* (Ulm, 1963); idem, "Erweckungsbewegungen am fränkischen Hahnenkamm und im Altmühlgrund," in *Pietismus – Herrnhutertum – Erweckungsbewegung. Festschrift für E. Beyreuther,* ed. P. Meyer (Cologne, 1982), pp. 347–61; R. Schäfer, "Skizzen aus der Oldenburger Erweckungsbewegung," *Oldenburger Jahrbuch* 85 (1985): 77–88; J. Althausen, "Kirchliche Gesellschaften in Berlin, 1810–1830. Ein Beitrag zur Geschichte der Erweckungsbewegung und des Laienapostolats in den evangelischen Kirchen des 19. Jahrhunderts" (Ph.D. diss., University of Halle-Wittenberg, 1965), pp. 8–16. In the Rhineland, almost all the significant preachers of the Awakening came from households of the *Stillen im Lande,* and the conservation of traditions within certain families guaranteed a degree of continuity. See F.W. Krummacher, *Gottfried Daniel Krummacher und die niederrheinische Erweckungsbewegung* (Berlin and Leipzig, 1935), pp. 62–63.

6. On the question of continuity and novelty in movements for religious renewal, see H. Lehmann, "Neupietismus und Säkularisierung. Beobachtungen zum Sozialen Umfeld und politischen Hintergrund von Erweckungsbewegung und Gemeinschaftsbewegung," *Pietismus und Neuzeit* 16 (1990): 40–58.

Christian souls but also against the corrosive rationalism of the revolution in France, where the "blinded populace, intoxicated by the chalice of enlightened frenzy," had rejected church and king.[7] This view proved persuasive, and the celebration of the "victory" of positive Christianity over Enlightenment and revolution became a commonplace of nineteenth-century German historiography.[8]

The early nineteenth-century Awakening in the German states was a regionally varied, socially and politically heterogeneous phenomenon.[9] In this essay I consider one particular variant: the neo-pietist revival that centered on the city of Berlin in the years following the end of the wars of liberation. The most distinctive feature of the Berlin postwar revival was the conspicuous and unusual degree of aristocratic participation. The predominance of von Gerlachs, von Thaddens, von Oertzens, von Thiles, von Stolbergs, and Senfft von Pilsachs in the neo-pietism of the postwar period poses an interesting and important question: why was a popular, low-church religious revival embraced by well-connected and high-born aristocrats? The "natural" constituency of revivalist neo-pietism in Prussia was the unworldly milieu of pious artisans and Herrenhut missionaries. Why was it enlarged after 1815 to include a wealthy, long-established, and influential segment of the Prussian aristocracy? Farm workers, weavers, booksellers, coppersmiths, and pastors were the characteristic protagonists of early nineteenth-century revival in the German states. Even in Berlin, the guardians of anti-rationalist religion at the turn of the century had been bakers, tailors, and shoemakers.[10] This essay proposes some reasons for the "conversion" of certain segments of the aristocracy to awakened religion after 1815. It suggests that the pietist revival offered a threatened aristocracy one means of articulating its resistance to the centralizing

7. L. von Rohden, *Geschichte der Rheinischen Missionsgesellschaft*, p. 1.

8. M. Greschat, "Die Aufklärung. Einleitung," in *Die Aufklärung* (*Gestalten der Kirchengeschichte*), ed. M. Greschat, vol. 8 (Stuttgart, 1983), pp. 7–41; here p. 8.

9. See H. Lehmann, "Pietism and Nationalism: the Relationship between Protestant Revivalism and National Renewal in Nineteenth-Century Germany," *Church History* 51 (1982): 39–53. Lehmann lists six distinct strands of late eighteenth-century neo-pietist revival. For a persuasive rejection of the view that "Awakening" and "Reaction" were equivalent, see Kantzenbach, *Baron H. E. von Kottwitz*, p. 26.

10. W. Wendland, *Das Erwachen religiösen Lebens in Berlin* (Berlin-Steglitz, 1925), p. 5.

state and to reform from above. It then considers the impact of this conflict on voluntarist Christian activism in the 1820s and 1830s.

II

Contacts with the Moravian Brethren played an important role in the spread of the Awakening in Berlin. As early as 1810–12, Prussian officers were attending the services of the elderly Moravian Johann Jänicke and gathering for communal prayer.[11] In 1816, a group of young men founded the political and literary discussion group known as the *Maikäfer* (maybugs or ladybugs). The group included the elder brothers von Gerlach, Carl von Voß, Carl von Rappard, Friedrich Karl von Bülow, Count Caius von Stolberg, and Gustav von Below. Ludwig von Gerlach later described the main interest of the group as "patriotic-romantic-inspirational-Christian poetry" interspersed with anti-revolutionary political discussions based on the works of the conservative Swiss state theorist Carl Ludwig von Haller. Religious issues initially played little or no role in these discussions: the "pietistic-Christian element was not represented."[12] But a number of the *Maikäfer* were closely involved in the city's religious life. The Gerlachs, August Wilhelm Goetze, Moritz August von Bethmann-Hollweg, Adolf Le Coq, and Adolf von Thadden-Trieglaff were among those *Maikäfer* who preferred the unvarnished, inspirational sermons of the preacher Justus Gottfried Hermes to the more worldly and intellectual style of Friedrich Schleiermacher.[13] The years 1814 to 1816 saw the migration of a significant segment of the conservative elite in Berlin from Schleiermacher to Hermes.[14] Some, like Bethmann-Hollweg and Plehwe,

11. F. Wiegand, "Der Verein der Maikäfer in Berlin," *Deutsche Rundschau* 160 (1914): 279–91. Wiegand cites (p. 279) the case of Lieutenants von Knebel, von Schmeling and von Manderode who met with a Captain von Hüfer for devout discussions. Manderode held weekly gatherings for Christian edification.

12. E.L. von Gerlach, *Ernst Ludwig von Gerlach. Aufzeichnungen aus seinem Leben und Wirken 1795–1877*, ed. J. von Gerlach (Schwerin, 1903), p. 95.

13. For a characteristic comparison of Schleiermacher with Hermes, see the remarks by Hans Rudolf von Plehwe recorded in Ludwig von Gerlach's diary (10 March 1817), Gerlach, *Aufzeichnungen*, p. 99.

14. H.-J. Schoeps, *Aus den Jahren preußischer Not und Erneuerung. Tagebücher und Briefe der Gebrüder Gerlach und ihres Kreises 1805–1820* (Berlin, 1963), p. 14.

remained sympathetic with Schleiermacher, but a definitive rejection of his rationalism was more characteristic. Adolf von Thadden-Trieglaff, for example, vehemently repudiated Schleiermacher's "soul-murdering arrogant principle of the congruence of reason and grace."[15] Ludwig von Gerlach, Friedrich Karl von Bülow, and Goetze also attended the evening prayer groups of Johann Jänicke: "I have never heard anyone preach so beautifully about the transformation of the individual through faith," Gerlach wrote in October 1816.[16]

A series of intense and semi-public conversions marked the entry of many of the *Maikäfer* into a self-consciously awakened community that continued to draw them together in later life after they had dispersed to their various estates and public offices. In the second half of 1816, Carl von Lancizolle, Thadden-Trieglaff and Bethmann Hollweg all travelled to Munich to visit Johann Nepomuk Ringseis and Johannes Gossner, the leading figures of the Bavarian Awakening.[17] Lancizolle's conversion occurred soon after his return on 30 November 1816, in the company of various members of his circle at the house of an awakened preacher. Many of the awakened could date their conversions to a specific day and hour. Bethmann-Hollweg's conversion took place close to midnight on New Year's Eve 1816/17 at the house of the awakened pastor Johann Georg Seegemund: "With a deep inward shock and a hot stream of tears I recognized my sin which stood before my eyes like a mountain."[18]

In April 1819, Thadden and Senfft von Pilsach introduced

15. Adolf von Thadden to Ludwig von Gerlach, Good Friday 1818, printed in ibid., pp. 593–95; here p. 594.

16. Gerlach, *Aufzeichnungen*, p. 97 (5 October 1816).

17. H. Kadel, *Johann Nepomuk Ringseis. Erlebnisse aus der bayrischen Erweckungsbewegung* (Marburg, 1981), p. xx. The house of the jurist von Savigny served as the focus for early contacts between the Bavarian Awakening and the *Maikäfer* circle; see Schoeps, *Aus den Jahren*, p. 14. See also K. Aland, "Berlin und die bayrische Erweckungsbewegung," in *Verantwortung und Zuversicht. Eine Festgabe für Otto Dibelius*, ed. K. Aland (Gütersloh, 1950), pp. 117–36; and R. Bigler, *The Politics of German Protestantism. The Rise of the Protestant Church Elite in Prussia 1815–1848* (Berkeley, Los Angeles, and London, 1972), pp. 127–34.

18. Cited in F. Fischer, *Moritz August von Bethmann Hollweg und der Protestantismus* (Berlin, 1937), p. 70. Seegemund was the son of a Stettin barge-driver who had been wounded at Dennewitz and experienced his conversion in the field hospital. He subsequently specialized in ministering to awakened circles within the officer corps. C. Nagel, "Zeit zwischen den Zeiten. Bilder aus dem Berliner Vormärz," *Der Bär von Berlin* 11 (1962): 7–26; here p. 21. For Seegemund's influence on the Gerlachs, see Bigler, *Politics*, pp. 133–34.

the Gerlachs to the members of an aristocratic circle with a strong mystical tendency that had formed, after the death of Hermes in 1818, around the awakened Pomeranian preacher Löffler. Thadden, Senfft, and Ludwig von Gerlach were later to recruit their wives – the sisters Henriette, Ida, and Auguste von Oertzen – from the *Löfflerkreis*. This recruitment is a clear example of the way in which kinship relations strengthened the cohesion of the growing pietist "community." By the end of 1819, the *Maikäfer* had been replaced by "a close-knit brotherly circle" that met every week for songs and prayer.[19] In the increasingly polarized ecclesiastical world of postwar Berlin, Schleiermacher and the rationalists on the one hand, and the awakened preachers with their growing neo-pietist following on the other, occupied diametrically opposed positions. Ludwig von Gerlach recalled hearing a sermon in which Jänicke criticized those who refused to believe that the devil was anything more than an idea: "Oh if only the veil [*Schleier*] would fall from the eyes of the veil-makers [*Schleiermacher*] and veil-weavers!"[20]

Young conservative nobles were attracted to the anti-rationalist preachers not merely because their anti-revolutionary and anti-liberal theology rejected reason as a yardstick for truth, but also because a sense of belonging to a close-knit community characterized their church services and parochial life. This was a recurring motif in contemporary accounts and recollections of the Berlin Awakening. Describing his visit to Hermes' church service on 26 November 1815, Bethmann-Hollweg recalled finding in the "small, homely church" a "densely-packed" crowd, a gathering of people who "[strove] for the truth and [sought] the Good in the middle of the great city full of worldly chaos and commotion." This congregation, Bethmann-Hollweg added, seemed to be "animated by a single spirit."[21] Clemens von Brentano confided to the awakened Bavarian preacher Ringseis in February 1816 that he "often envied these people [Goetze and the Gerlachs] the rousing, intimate sense of community in Hermes' little church." Count Alexander von der Goltz recalled that "the love which pre-

---

19. Gerlach, *Aufzeichnungen*, pp. 117–119.
20. Ibid., p. 103 (16 June 1816). Jänicke publicly withdrew the remark at the request of von Plehwe.
21. Fischer, *Bethmann-Hollweg*, pp. 59–60.

vailed in our circle had something overwhelming that drew others in as soon as they came near it."[22]

This quest for community that motivated so many *Maikäfer* to convert to awakened Christianity is not without significance. Men returning from wars – and officers in particular – are frequently reluctant to relinquish the security of a soldierly community. Most of the *Maikäfer* had recently seen active military service. Le Coq had fought at Ligny and Belle Alliance; Goetze had been lamed by a French bullet at Dennewitz; Leopold von Gerlach and Gustav von Below had served on Blücher's staff and later on the General Staff under Gneisenau; Ludwig had thrice been wounded and received the Iron Cross; Carl von Voß and Wilhelm von Gerlach had served with the Neumark Dragoons; and Senfft von Pilsach and Lancizolle had joined the Voluntary Riflemen in 1813. The desire for security and solidarity was also rooted in the decade of political and economic upheaval that followed the defeat of the Prussian army by the French in 1806. The French occupation of 1806/7, the demand for indemnities, the seizure of Prussian livestock, the conscription of farm hands, the collapse of the grain market, and the steep rise in the cost of agricultural labor placed severe economic burdens upon the landowning aristocracy.[23] During this period of economic distress, moreover, the Prussian government embarked on a series of legislative reforms designed to centralize and streamline the Prussian state. A number of these reforms, such as the abolition of certain noble monopolies, the emancipation of the peasants and the removal of tax exemptions on noble land, were clearly intended to undermine – or at least to redefine – the privileged corporate status of the aristocracy in Prussian society.[24]

22. Cited from a letter to Ringseis in Gerlach, *Aufzeichnungen*, p. 95. The citation from Goltz is in W. Wendland, *Siebenhundert Jahre Kirchengeschichte Berlins* (Berlin and Leipzig, 1930), p. 225.

23. On the long-term economic decline of the aristocracy, see R. Koselleck, *Preußen zwischen Reform und Revolution. Allgemeines Landrecht, Verwaltung und soziale Bewegung von 1791 bis 1848* (Stuttgart, 1967), pp. 81–85. On the impact of the occupation on the nobility, cf. B. von Münchow-Pohl, *Zwischen Reform und Krieg. Untersuchungen zur Bewußtseinslage in Preußen 1806–1812* (Göttingen, 1987), esp. pp. 108–109. On the financial difficulties of the Gerlach family during this period, see Agnes von Gerlach's letter of 17 March 1810 to her son Leopold, cited in Gerlach, *Aufzeichnungen*, p. 41.

24. The political impact of the reforms on the Prussian aristocracy is well documented. Robert Berdahl has shown that the responses of the aristocracy to the reform movement varied – as one would expect – from edict to edict and from province to province. See Berdahl, *Politics*, p. 118. For aristocratic

The resumption of hostilities after 1812 could not make good the political damage inflicted by the defeat of the Prussian army in 1806, at least from the vantage point of many conservative aristocrats. In February 1813, when Leopold von Gerlach went to join the armed forces at Breslau, he observed with some ambivalence how the populace was preparing for the campaign: "What a chaos of views, ideas, and revolutionary attitudes is this suddenly animated crowd of the people! I would fear atrocities of every kind from such a war if I were fifty-two instead of twenty-two and if the steady, loyal sense of the countryman and the burgher were not a sure counterweight to these things."[25] Gerlach observed further that there were three "camps" in Breslau – the "aristocratic," the "democratic," and the "anarchist." The first was "without anything positive and without power. It does not dare to show itself as a party and merely works weakly and secretly against the others, even tries, out of a kind of desperation, to join the democrats so as to weld an aristocratic element onto [them]." The democrats, by contrast, were "the most excellent and robust of our land."[26] The "anarchist" party consisted of students, academics, and book traders who followed the patriot leader Friedrich Ludwig Jahn, and were without great political significance. One thing above all was clear: "The attitude that prevails among the most independent men is extremely Jacobinical and revolutionary. Those who seek to ground the future in history, or who want to graft the new shoots onto the still healthy stems [of the past] are subject to mockery, so that even I begin to waver in my certainty."[27]

For Leopold von Gerlach, these observations had important political implications. As he recognized in 1813, the political future of postwar Prussia would depend upon whether the "half-dead forms of the old regime, which still contain so much of the beautiful life of the past," would be repaired and renewed or "boldly destroyed to make way for the new."[28] As the famous "constitutional promise" of 22 May 1815 indicated,

---

opinion on such attempted reforms as the Gendarmerie Edict of July 1812 (which was not implemented), see ibid., pp. 142–43.

25. Diary of Leopold von Gerlach, Breslau, February 1813, Bundesarchiv, Abteilungen Potsdam (henceforth BA Potsdam), NL von Gerlach 90 Ge 1 (transcription [ms.] by Otto Koser of the former Reichsarchiv), Bl. 60.

26. Ibid., Bl. 43.

27. Ibid., Bl. 60.

28. Ibid., Bl. 45.

the king's position on this fundamental issue was unclear. The announcement of a forthcoming constitution gave an ambiguous impression of the government's intentions. The body of the text reassured estate-conscious aristocrats that the provincial *Landstände*, the traditional organs of aristocratic representation, would continue to operate in the kingdom of Prussia. But the opening paragraph announced that the king intended to create "a representation of the people." This provision was politically anathema to conservative estate owners. As Carl von Lancizolle later complained: "How much fruitless and even harmful scribbling and chatter could have been prevented by the exclusion of that completely meaningless and pointless §1!"[29] While the constitutional promise unnerved those aristocrats who opposed the policies of the crown-sponsored reform bureaucrats, it also awoke expectations among the constitutionalists which the king had no wish to meet. To make an offer that whetted the hopes of the constitutionalists while allaying the worst fears of the *altständisch* aristocrats had been Hardenberg's immediate intention,[30] but the promise had disruptive long-term effects. The king's subsequent refusal to keep his word cast him in a negative light and intensified the feeling in political circles that the constitutional question was still open.[31]

The collaboration between the crown and the bureaucratic reformers nourished the fears of conservative aristocrats that the result would be a bureaucratized, homogenized monarchical state. In such a state, conservatives feared, the representation of provincial and estate-bound interests would have little or no role. The *Maikäfer* who read Carl von Haller's *Restauration der Staatswissenschaft* were passionate opponents of the "Rousseauian state from below";[32] but they were also becoming increasingly aware of the threat from above posed by a centralizing absolutist monarch. In April 1816, Leopold von Gerlach speculated anxiously that if Hardenberg were to

---

29. C. von Lancizolle, *Über Königthum und Landstände in Preußen* (Berlin, 1846), p. 206. Lancizolle was professor of law at the University of Berlin when this work was published.

30. For a discussion of the motives and intentions behind the constitutional promise of 1815, see H. Obenaus, *Anfänge des Parlamentarismus in Preußen bis 1848* (Düsseldorf, 1984), pp. 55–88.

31. Cf. Koselleck, *Preußen zwischen Reform und Revolution*, pp. 286–87.

32. Gerlach, *Aufzeichnungen*, p. 102.

resign or to be unseated by an intrigue, the result might be a return to cabinet government. Only solidarity among the conservative protagonists of provincial and aristocratic freedoms would forestall a return to the old absolutist forms. "He must only be defeated by a *party*," Gerlach concluded.[33] A fortnight later, after discussions with the jurist Friedrich Karl von Savigny, he wrote: "Savigny fears that Hardenberg's departure will bring an end to the respect for public opinion and make way for a despotism that is now already creeping in the shadows." He went on to observe that as a "royal concession," the edict concerning the estates contained a "despotic element." It was not in the interest of the estates to accept such a concession, "for what is granted to them by grace can be taken away as such."[34] In January 1820, the king dissolved the *Landschaft* of the Kurmark. (The *Landschaften* were provincial credit institutes that lent funds for the improvement of noble estates.) For the conservative aristocrats, this high-handed abuse of prerogative illustrated the danger royal absolutism posed to estate institutions. A petition from representatives of the nobility and the cities of the Kurmark, begging the government to reconsider its decision, was rejected out of hand by Hardenberg and Frederick William III, who described the petition as a "presumption" and threatened the aristocratic deputies with "severe legal action" for the "failure to recognize his sovereign legislative authority." Ludwig von Gerlach characterized this episode as a "one-sided absolutist violation of the rights of the estates."[35]

Aristocratic opposition to the excesses of royal absolutism was not new. The argument that the nobility constituted both a bulwark against princely despotism and a safeguard against republicanism was one of the commonplaces of late eighteenth-century conservatism.[36] Like many of his peers, Leopold von Gerlach the elder, father of the Gerlach brothers, had welcomed the beginnings of the French Revolution, "on account of the slovenly-despotic goings-on since the Regency of 1715."[37] But the failure to repel French aggression and the

33. Diary of Leopold von Gerlach, 9 April 1816, BA Potsdam, NL von Gerlach, 90 Ge 2, Bl. 5.

34. Ibid., Bl. 6.

35. Gerlach, *Aufzeichnungen*, p. 120.

36. See K. Epstein, *The Genesis of German Conservatism* (Princeton, N.J., 1966), p. 192.

37. Gerlach, *Aufzeichnungen*, p. 15.

wish to forestall a revolution at home greatly accelerated the process of centralization in Prussia. As Leopold von Gerlach the younger observed, the growth of the central bureaucracy effectively supplemented the power of the monarch with an "administrative despotism that eats away at everything like vermin."[38] For *altständisch* aristocrats, the experience of reform strengthened their conviction that anti-particularist bureaucratic liberalism and royal absolutism were animated by the same inner logic.

III

Most of the *Maikäfer* and their close friends were still too young in the years immediately following the war to be directly engaged in high politics.[39] As students of Haller and of Adam Müller, they were keenly aware of the broader issues involved; yet the rigor of their pietism and their self-conscious absorption in local affairs rendered them insensitive to the tactical dimensions of court life and day-to-day politics.[40] Nonetheless, religion was one area in which the pietists, for all their initial political quietism, were unable to avoid a direct collision with the reforming state.

The Protestant churches of Prussia were among those institutions that felt directly the impact of bureaucratic reform and modernization. The reconstruction of the administration in 1808 completely abolished the church consistories, the last vestiges of an independent ecclesiastical governing body. In April 1815, the provincial consistories were reestablished by a

38. Diary of Leopold von Gerlach, 1 May 1816, BA Potsdam, NL von Gerlach, 90 Ge 2, Bl. 9.
39. Gustav von Below was twenty-four when the war ended, Friedrich Karl von Bülow twenty-six, Adolf le Coq eighteen, August Wilhelm Goetze twenty-three, Karl Wilhelm von Lancizolle nineteen, Carl von Rappard twenty-one, Ernst von Senfft-Pilsach twenty, Count Caius von Stolberg eighteen, and Adolf von Thadden nineteen. Wilhelm, Leopold and Ludwig von Gerlach were twenty-six, twenty-five, and twenty respectively.
40. In this respect, the Pietist aristocrats of early nineteenth-century Prussia exemplify one of the general trends in German party formation throughout the nineteenth century, namely an orientation toward ideological and theoretical positions and an ambivalent relation to the realities of political practice. See T. Nipperdey, "Grundprobleme der deutschen Parteiengeschichte im 19. Jahrhundert," in *Deutsche Parteien vor 1918*, ed. G. Ritter (Cologne, 1973), pp. 32–55, here p. 34; F. Valjavec, *Die Entstehung der politischen Strömungen in Deutschland, 1770–1815* (Munich, 1951), p. 36.

royal Cabinet Order, but their area of competence was severely reduced. The "Protestant consistory" now dealt with the affairs of both Protestant confessions. A distinction was made between "internal" and "external" church affairs, so that the most important business – appointments, ordination, discipline and surveillance – fell to the relevant government departments.[41] The ground was thereby prepared for the legal union, by royal order, of the two Protestant confessions in 1817. The confessions continued to differ in their liturgical and sacramental practice but they were joined within the greater unity of the Prussian state church headed by the king himself as *summus episcopus*. Prussia was not the only German state to introduce such a reform: church unions occurred almost simultaneously in Nassau, the Palatinate, Baden, Waldeck, Rhine-Hessen and elsewhere. But only in Prussia was it implemented from above, without consultation.[42] The Prussian church union was not forced upon the king by the reform bureaucrats.[43] On the contrary, it represented the realization of an old Hohenzollern policy. A union of the two Protestant confessions had been sought by Prussian monarchs since the conversion of Johann Sigismund to the Reformed Church in 1613, and Frederick William himself enthusiastically oversaw the drafting of the necessary legislation.

On 26 October 1817, the forthcoming union was announced in the churches of Prussia. The united rite was to be introduced on 31 October 1817, to coincide with the tricentennial of the Reformation – the 300th anniversary of the day on which Luther had nailed his theses to the church door in Wittenberg. After hearing the announcement from the pulpit, Ludwig von Gerlach wrote in his diary: "At the time, it made a very unpleasant impression upon me, as [something] soulless and

41. O. Hintze, "Epochen des evangelischen Kirchenregiments in Preußen" (orig. 1906), in *Moderne preußische Geschichte 1648–1947. Eine Anthologie*, ed. O. Büsch and W. Neugebauer (Berlin, 1981), pp. 1217–42, here pp. 1231–33; H. von Treitschke, *Deutsche Geschichte im 19. Jahrhundert*, 3 vols. (Leipzig, 1882), vol. 2, p. 240.

42. G. Ruhbach, "Die Religionspolitik Friedrich Wilhelms III von Preußen," in *Bleibendes im Wandel der Kirchengeschichte. Kirchliche Studien*, ed. B. Moeller and G. Ruhbach (Tübingen, 1973), pp. 307–30, here p. 308.

43. The king's wish for a church union accorded with the plans of the reformers. The idea of uniting the competence for the affairs of both confessions in one adminstrative body had earlier been put forward by Freiherr vom Stein in his reform plan of 1808; see M. Lehmann, *Freiherr vom Stein* (Göttingen, 1925), pp. 257–58.

external, as 'a division rather than a union'."[44] With regard to changes introduced in the form of communion, Gerlach observed that "not being able to communicate on Reformation Day as we have in the past – this is already the beginning of compulsion. If this thing does not die away, as is very much to be hoped, then the compulsion will remain."[45] Far from dying away, the Act of Union was supplemented in the following years by legislation increasing its scope. In 1821, the United church received a new liturgy, the hybrid product of a variety of Protestant liturgical traditions, which the king himself had composed.[46] It was henceforth to be binding for both confessions within the state church.

The growing alienation of the aristocratic neo-pietists from the church during the late 1810s and 1820s should be seen against the background of the monarch's attempt to create a unified, centralized state church during these years. As Ludwig von Gerlach recalled, it was fashionable among the awakened to call church buildings "stone houses" and church pastors "men in black gowns."[47] Such outbursts had an inescapably political dimension. To belittle and reject state ecclesiastical institutions in this way meant turning down a crown project with which the king himself was increasingly personally associated. The early 1820s saw a widening of the gap between the Prussian state church and the neo-pietists. Nothing illustrated this divergence more clearly than the involvement of pietist aristocrats with groups that claimed the right to secede or "separate" from the state church. During their periods of office in Naumburg, Ludwig von Gerlach and Goetze came into contact with a community of awakened artisans, saltmakers and wage laborers in and around the town of Sulza. "For the first time," Gerlach later recalled, "I entered into real, often difficult – but for that very reason instructive and edifying – contact with Christians of the humblest station, their conventicles and home prayer groups, their lively opposition to the rationalized

44. Gerlach, *Aufzeichnungen*, p. 104. The quotation is from a contemporary diary entry.

45. Diary entry, 26 October 1817; ibid., p. 105.

46. The new Church Agenda, as it was called, incorporated elements from the liturgies of Hohenzollern predecessors, the Pomeranian church calendar of 1563, the formulae of Martin Luther, the prayers of the French Colony, and historical liturgies from Sweden and England. E. Foerster, *Die Entstehung der preußischen Landeskirche*, 2 vols. (Tübingen, 1905–7), vol. 2, p. 57.

47. Gerlach, *Aufzeichnungen*, pp. 132, 149–50.

and worldly clergy all around them."[48] The awakening in Sulza soon spread to Naumburg and other towns in the area. By 1822 the attempt to establish an independent Christian congregation had brought the awakened worshippers of Sulza into direct conflict with the church authorities. Those prayer meetings that did not take place within the framework of an individual family were prohibited on pain of severe penalties. The awakened aristocrats responded with sympathy for the Sulza community. Count Dohna, Carl von Rappard and Bethmann-Hollweg were in favor of establishing a special congregation on Pinne (Rappard's estate) or in Berlin, and money was collected to permit a collective emigration of the Sulza community.[49] In August 1822, as the conflict grew more serious and the first arrests occurred, the Merseburg government warned Ludwig von Gerlach not to associate himself with the separatists. In November 1824, after further visits to Sulza, Gerlach was summoned by the district governor in Merseburg and asked to give an account of his links with the community there.[50]

While Gerlach was cultivating the friendship of pious craftsmen in Naumburg and Sulza, a more radical form of revivalism was spreading on the estates of other pietist aristocrats. In 1819, Carl von Below and his brother Gustav, a former *Maikäfer* and landlord of the Pomeranian estate Reddenthin, were "awakened" by the ex-*Maikäfer* Goetze. They began to hold prayer meetings and services in the estate house, with seventy to eighty people in attendance. Here, as elsewhere among the awakened, there was a strong missionizing impetus. Converts were made among the "little people." Among these were a housemaid at Reddenthin, whose uncomplicated piety is said to have humbled her noble patrons, and one of the shepherds from the estate, whose sermons moved audiences to tears. A clash with the ecclesiastical authorities was inevitable. Immediately after his conversion, Heinrich von Below, brother of Gustav and Carl, approached the local superintendent Tischmeyer and confessed himself to be the greatest of sinners. Tischmeyer replied that the Herr Baron was, on the contrary, the noblest of men. In Below's eyes, this

48. Ibid., p. 125.
49. Ibid., p. 136.
50. Ibid., pp. 136, 145.

response was clear proof of the superintendent's rationalism. After a service in the village of Mützenow, during which Tischmeyer had preached that God-fearing folk of *all* nations were pleasing to God, Heinrich von Below upbraided him publicly and warned the congregation not to continue attending his services.[51] The provincial consistory at Stettin responded in 1820 by commissioning Tischmeyer and another preacher, Metger, to report on the activities of the Below brothers. When Metger refused, the consistory ordered police surveillance of the prayer meetings. All attendants who were not from the estate itself were to be identified by gendarmes stationed at the entrance to the house and fined by the authorities. News of the events on the Below estates quickly permeated the network of the awakened. A neo-pietist physician by the name of de Valenti, whom Ludwig von Gerlach had met after moving to Naumburg as acting director of the District Supreme Court, reported to Gerlach and Goetze. De Valenti was concerned at the radicalism of the Belows' separatist pietism and pleaded with Gerlach to call for moderation: "The knot must be loosened gently, not chopped apart." But Gerlach was in sympathy with the beleaguered pietists.[52] The separatism on the Below estates in the districts of Stolpe, Rummelsburg, and Schlawe soon spread to the neighboring Thaddens in Trieglaff, the Senfft von Pilsachs in Rottnow, and the Puttkamer family estates in Versin and Reinfeld. The influence of these estate-based pietisms went far beyond the immediate circle of those who lived and worked there. It was at Reinfeld that Bismarck met his later wife, Johanna von Puttkamer. He experienced his conversion to "serious Christianity" while visiting the Thaddens at Trieglaff.[53]

If the growing involvement of landed aristocrats in various forms of ecclesiastical separatism is seen in the context of the

51. For a short but evocative account of the separatism espoused by von Below, see F. Wiegand, "Eine Schwärmerbewegung in Hinterpommern vor hundert Jahren," *Deutsche Rundschau* 189 (1921): 323–36.

52. Gerlach, *Aufzeichnungen*, p. 126.

53. On the connections between Bismarck and the Pomeranian separatism of the von Belows, see H.G. Bloth, *Die Kirche in Pommern. Auftrag und Dienst der evangelischen Bischöfe und Generalsuperintendenten der pommerschen Kirche von 1792 bis 1919* (Vienna, 1979), p. 92. On Bismarck's conversion, see Bigler, *Politics*, p. 142. On the spread of pietist Christianity in this area, see P. Haake, "Ernst Freiherr Senfft von Pilsach 1795–1882," in *Pommersche Lebensbilder*, ed. W. Menn (Cologne and Graz, 1966), vol. 4, pp. 324–60, here pp. 327–28.

Church Union of 1817 and the new liturgy of 1821, the political implications are clear. In urging the faithful not to attend the services of an employee of the state church, they were asserting the traditional clerical patronage rights of the aristocratic landowner. The socially disparate charismatic Christian gatherings of the converted, in which noblemen knelt with bowed heads before shepherds and peasants, were unthinkable outside the estate context. That the noble estate should become the focus of Christian-aristocratic defiance of the central authorities was hardly surprising; the social and political function of the noble landowner constituted one of the fronts on which *ständisch* aristocrats fought their losing struggle against the centralizing state. The Gerlachs are a good example. In accordance with the "good, conservative doctrine for which Haller had made me so enthusiastic," Ludwig negotiated with the officers of the General Commission in the summer of 1818 to preserve the traditional "law and constitution" of the family's Rohrbeck estate. The General Commission was charged with putting into effect the Declaration of 29 May 1816 that granted certain categories of peasants proprietary rights to the land they occupied and permitted others to buy themselves out of their feudal obligations. The Commission rejected Gerlach's proposals, pointing out that the relationship of lord to peasant had been "fundamentally altered." The Gerlachs refused to ratify the documents, but, after taking note of the Gerlach family's "obstinacy and ignorance of the law," the General Commission proceeded to confirm the separation of peasant lands from the Rohrbeck estate.[54] The General Law Regarding the Establishment of Provincial Estates (5 June 1823), which specified that the longstanding ownership of aristocratic property conferred eligibility for participation in the *Ritterstand*, opened the first estate to non-noble landowners.[55] But it also confirmed the paramount importance of the landed estate as the basis for an aristocratic political identity. As Robert Berdahl has pointed out, the ideology of the conservative nobility in the 1820s and 1830s turned on the (mythologized) concept of the *"ganzes Haus"*: the ideal of the noble estate on which a close-knit community of mutual obligation could co-exist harmoniously with social hierarchy.

54. Gerlach, *Aufzeichnungen*, p. 115.
55. Koselleck, *Preußen zwischen Reform und Revolution*, pp. 337–39.

Much has been made of the pseudo-egalitarian quality of the neo-pietist communities.[56] This critique is founded on the assumption that the pietists' belief in the equality of all Christian souls was fundamentally inconsistent with their allegiance to the existing social order. But such a reading plays down the subversive potential of separatist pietism in the period. Among the extraordinary individuals who participated in the Pomeranian conventicles was the peasant Dubbach, who is reported to have leapt into the audience after a sermon and kicked the kneeling faithful – Heinrich von Below included – in the napes of their necks, crying "get deeper down into humility!"[57] Denunciations of the pietists as "Jacobins," and the complaint by Karl von Altenstein, minister for church, health and educational affairs, that they encouraged "complete disrespect for the social relationships that have previously existed"[58] testify to the serious threat that some contemporaries saw in the estate-based separatisms of the 1820s. This suggests that it might be more fruitful to interpret these movements as sporadic plebiscitary experiments by a rural aristocracy whose link to "the people" had been severely attenuated by the administrative reforms of the central government. There was a certain symmetry in this posture. The desire to win the trust and approval of "the people," and to eliminate alternative foci for popular loyalties, had been an important motive for administrative reform. In a recommendation to Hardenberg in 1818, a Coblenz bureaucrat argued that it would be possible, with the help of a constitution, to "separate the people from the *Landstände.*"[59] The king himself became a participant in this contest for the people's allegiance. Thirty years after the estates paid homage to Frederick William III in 1798, Friedrich von der Marwitz recalled with distaste the way in which the "Berlin mob, or as one now prefers to say, the people," had been permitted to witness the ceremony as spectators. He saw in the innovation a sign of the "spirit of the new age" and observed that the French Revolution had made a tra-

56. See, for example, Berdahl, *Politics*, pp. 249–50; M. Scharfe, *Die Religion des Volkes. Kleine Kultur- und Sozialgeschichte des Pietismus* (Gütersloh, 1980), pp. 136–37.
57. Wiegand, *Eine Schwärmerbewegung*, p. 333.
58. Both cited in Berdahl, *Politics*, p. 249.
59. Cited in Koselleck, *Preußen zwischen Reform und Revolution*, p. 298.

ditional homage impossible: "One will have to invent a new kind [of homage] for the next accession to the throne."[60] Marwitz was right. The spectacle offered by Frederick William IV's homage exhibited even more clearly the impact of the "spirit" that Marwitz had found so offensive. The king's speech to the huge crowd gathered before the palace contained an unmistakably plebiscitary element:

> Knights! Burghers! Countrymen! And all you countless ones who have gathered here! . . . I ask you: will you with heart and mind, with word and deed . . . stand by me and help me to maintain Prussia as it is . . . and as it must stay, if it is not to go under? . . . Then answer me with the clearest, most beautiful word of the mother language, answer me with your word of honor Yes![61]

The estate-based pietist separatisms of the 1820s and 1830s should be seen in the context of these competing bids for popular legitimacy: liberal calls for popular "participation" in the life of the state, the mystical union of king and people, and the paternalistic relationship between peasant and landlord. As Karl Holl observed in 1917, looking back through the lens of late nineteenth-century German conservatism, it was on the landed estates of eastern Prussia – where barons and wage laborers prayed together and addressed each other with the familiar *Du* – that the Prussian nobility claimed to have discovered its alliance with the common people.[62]

IV

In addition to "penitence, heartfelt belief, [and] brotherly love," the Awakening in Prussia was characterized, as Ludwig von Gerlach later recalled, by "proselytising aggression and the drive to make conquests."[63] Count Anton von Stolberg-

---

60. F.L.A. von der Marwitz, *Aus dem Nachlasse Friedrich Ludwig August von der Marwitz auf Friedersdorf*, ed. M. Niebuhr, 2 vols. (Berlin 1852), vol. 1, pp. 93–94.

61. For a stimulating discussion of the plebiscitary elements in this speech and in Frederick William's conception of the relationship between people and king, see W. Bußmann, *Zwischen Preußen und Deutschland. Friedrich Wilhelm IV. Eine Biographie* (Berlin, 1990), pp. 116–18.

62. K. Holl, "Die Bedeutung der großen Kriege für das religiöse und kirchliche Leben innerhalb des deutschen Protestantismus (1917)," in K. Holl, *Gesammelte Aufsätze zur Kirchengeschichte*, vol. 3: *Der Westen* (Tübingen, 1928), pp. 302–84; here pp. 357–58.

63. Gerlach, *Aufzeichnungen*, p. 117.

Wernigerode called upon his peers to "become missionaries, not among the wild tribes in India and Africa, but among the heathens of the Fatherland."[64] Voluntary religious societies – missions, bible-societies, book clubs, and charitable associations – proliferated in Berlin during the 1810s and 1820s. They were another aspect of the post-Napoleonic Christian revival that threatened to conflict with the interests of the state church. As with the rural separatist movement, church authorities dominated by rationalists and jealous of their remaining authority confronted groups of highly motivated anti-rationalist laymen. The activities of the voluntary societies, though "religious" in the widest sense, fell outside the immediate authority of the institutional church.

Many of the aristocrats and their associates who passed through the post-Napoleonic awakening in Berlin subsequently became involved in voluntary religious societies. They directed missionary societies, religious book clubs, and Bible societies, founded poor schools, and visited the inmates of prisons.[65] One variety of Christian activism that attracted the interest of a particularly broad cross-section of the awakened community was the mission among the Jews established in Berlin in 1822. Among the members of the Gerlach circle who became involved in this enterprise were Ludwig, Otto, and Leopold von Gerlach, Moritz August von Bethmann-Hollweg, Ernst Senfft von Pilsach, Friedrich Focke, Count Anton Stolberg-Wernigerode, Ernst Hengstenberg (with whom Ludwig collaborated in found-

64. Cited in Althausen, "Kirchliche Gesellschaften in Berlin," p. 20.
65. Carl von Bülow and August Wilhelm Götze, for example, were both vice-presidents of the Berlin Missionary Society, founded in 1829 to carry on the work of the missionary seminar of the Bohemian preacher Jänicke. Von Bülow was also a committee member of the Evangelical Book Club and the Society for Released Prisoners; Leopold and Ludwig von Gerlach were committee members of the Berlin Missionary Society and the Prussian Central Bible Society. In the late 1820s, Ludwig von Gerlach, his childhood friend Friedrich Focke, his brother Otto von Gerlach, Ernst von Senfft-Pilsach, and other members of their circle were involved in the running of free schools for poor children. These men also made regular visits to the prisons for the purpose of edifying and converting the inmates. Bethmann-Hollweg, Lancizolle, Lecoq, and Leopold von Gerlach were also committee members of the Berlin Society for the Promotion of Protestant Missions among the Heathens. See Gerlach, *Aufzeichnungen*, pp. 162, 172, 174. The original statutes and membership list of the Gesellschaft zur Beförderung der evangelischen Missionen unter den Heiden, dated 29 February 1824, are in the Geheimes Staatsarchiv Preußischer Kulturbesitz (GStA) Merseburg, Geheimes Zivilkabinett, 2.2.1. Nr. 23566, Bd. 1, Bl. 64–66.

ing the *Evangelische Kirchenzeitung*), and the anti-rationalist theologian Friedrich August Tholuck, whom Ludwig had befriended in Naumburg.[66] Focke and Otto von Gerlach were also committee members of the Society for the Christian Care of Proselytes from Judaism. This group met at Focke's home in Berlin and concerned itself with securing money, clothes, and gainful employment for impoverished converts.[67]

The social milieu of missionary activity in Prussia during the 1820s and 1830s reflected the broader social composition of the Awakening. Aristocrats, especially military men and senior bureaucrats, set the tone in committee meetings and acted as "lightning rods" to deflect criticism and attract the patronage and support of the powerful.[68] But the rank-and-file membership and the provincial auxiliaries were dominated by artisans, school teachers, and local manufacturers. The committee that met at the Berlin home of General Job von Witzleben in 1822 to found the Berlin Society for the Promotion of Christianity among the Jews, for example, was an august assembly: it boasted a major general and adjutant general of the Prussian army, an army lieutenant, a university professor, a legation councillor, the British envoy in Berlin, the chargé d'affaires of the Grand Duchy of Baden, the court chaplain, and a senior government councillor. Its rural support, however, came from minor local officials, master tradesmen, and school instructors. Typically for the voluntarist groups of the period, the Society's wider membership showed a relatively low level of clerical participation: an aggregate of 14 percent for the years 1822/23.[69]

The early career of the Berlin Society for the Promotion of Christianity among the Jews provides an illustration of the

---

66. For a full list of the founding committee members of the Gesellschaft zur Beförderung des Christenthums unter den Juden zu Berlin (GBCJ), see *Jahresbericht der GBCJ* 1 (1924): 34. On the activities of this society, see C.M. Clark, "Jewish Mission in the Christian State. Protestant Missions to the Jews in Eighteenth- and Nineteenth-Century Prussia" (Ph.D. diss., University of Cambridge, 1991).

67. Conferenz-Protocolle des Vereins für christliche Fürsorge für jüdische Proselyten, 30 October 1829, 13 November 1829, 27 November 1829, 8 January 1830, etc., GStA Merseburg, Rep. 199, Nr. 70.

68. This metaphor was employed by the awakened Berlin merchant Samuel Elsner to describe the function of socially elevated persons who took on directorships in the religious societies. Cited in Witte, *Das Leben*, vol. 1, p. 216.

69. For a list of donors and subscribers to the Berlin Mission to the Jews, see *Jahresbericht der GBCJ* 1 (1824): 35ff.

kinds of resistance that Christian voluntarism encountered from the church authorities in the 1820s and 1830s. Thanks to its distinguished patronage and the accordance of its aims with those of the anti-emancipatory Jewish policy of the Prussian government after 1815, the Berlin Society enjoyed the full support of King Frederick William III.[70] But the consistories of the Prussian provinces viewed with distaste the rapid institutionalization of the new society. They objected to its largely lay membership and the millenarian tone of its prayer meetings and publications. Church officials clearly suspected links between all non-church associations with "religious" interests and the separatism that they feared would undermine the Prussian Union. In 1823, the ministry for church, health, and educational affairs announced that the statutes of all new provincial missionary societies were to be submitted to the provincial governments for official approval.[71] In 1826, the ministry issued a circular warning the superintendents of the Prussian United Church of the harmful effects of pietism, mysticism, and separatism. "These words," Ludwig von Gerlach observed, "were used in the commonplace, hollow sense they had when they were deployed against the stirrings of living Christianity."[72] When Ernst Hengstenberg, then a private tutor in the faculty of theology at the University of Berlin, published a short treatise stressing the positive import of these terms in their original context, he received a sharp warning from the ministry.[73]

The tension between lay religious associations and the state church was exacerbated by the fact that missionary and voluntarist culture in Prussia was largely a product of the Awakening. The public bearing and religiosity of the missionaries of the Berlin Society marked them as neo-pietists who had come to spread the word among Christians as well as Jews. During his stay in the town of Strzellno in the province of Posen in 1825, missionary Friedrich Händes, an employee of the Berlin

70. The king, the crown prince and his wife, and the princes Wilhelm, Carl, and Albrecht all made annual donations to the Society. See for example *Jahresbericht der GBCJ* 14 (1837): 15.

71. Von Schön to Provincial Governments, 20 March 1823, GStA Berlin, XIV, 181/10018, Bl. 9.

72. Gerlach, *Aufzeichnungen*, p. 159.

73. Otto and Ludwig von Gerlach and Adolf le Coq strongly approved of Hengstenberg's outspoken criticism, and his treatise became the "seed of the *Evangelische Kirchenzeitung*." Ibid., pp. 159–60.

Society, was able to "awaken" the Protestant inhabitants of the town.[74] In May 1826, however, the consistory of the province of Prussia in Königsberg complained to the ministry that Händes had "gathered about him the inexperienced female youth of Neidenburg, so that after his departure a regular society for religious purposes had formed in the house of the dyer Oettinger." The consistory argued that the meetings in Oettinger's house constituted a "sect" in the "general sense of any separatist gathering." As a result of these meetings, the young women of Neidenburg had been "filled with fantasy," rendered "mentally confused and physically exhausted," and were "unfit for chores and numb to all appeals."[75] This complaint exemplifies the kind of hostility that organized, non-ecclesiastical religiosity could arouse among the officials of the state church. The emphasis upon a conspiratorial meeting behind closed doors and the claim that the excessive zeal of the "converted" was having a disruptive social effect – these were classic motifs in the campaign against separatism. In order to avoid further clashes with the officials, Major General Job von Witzleben, president of the Berlin Society, sent Minister von Altenstein a revised copy of the mission's instructions to its missionaries. The new instruction booklet stressed the importance of friendly relations between missionaries, local pastors, and superintendents. It also urged the employees of the Berlin Society to avoid any actions that might seem to endanger the "relationship between the congregations and their appointed ministers" or encourage the "founding of sectarian and separatist associations."[76] Perhaps in response to Witzleben's assurances, Frederick William issued a Cabinet Order in September 1826 ordering provincial authorities not to hinder the missionaries in their work.[77]

The mission to the Jews also came into conflict with the consistory of Brandenburg. In an effort to subordinate the society,

74. The Protestant Christians of the town of Strzellno to Committee of the GBCJ, 25 January 1826, GStA Merseburg, Rep. 199, Acta der GBCJ zu Berlin, Nr. 16.

75. Royal Prussian Consistory to the Ministry of Church, Health, and Educational Affairs (hereafter MGUMA), Königsberg, 18 May 1826, GStA Merseburg, Rep. 76 III Sekt. 1, Abt. XIV, Bl. 55–57.

76. See Witzleben for Committee GBCJ to von Altenstein, Berlin, 5 September 1826 and accompanying document. Ibid., Bl. 61–63.

77. The Order is cited in MGUMA to Marienwerder government, Berlin, 13 November 1826, GStA Berlin, Rep. 181/5132.

the consistory waged a guerilla campaign of bureaucratic obstruction. It complained to the ministry for church affairs when the mission committee announced its first annual general meeting, pointing out that no permission had been sought from the consistory as the mission's "immediate clerical superior." It observed missionary meetings and reported any improprieties to the ministry. And it raised objections when the mission applied for a church building in which to hold its services for Jews, advising the secular authorities not to support the work of the mission on the grounds that it was ineffective and wasteful of resources.[78] The Berlin Society was generally able to extricate itself from these difficulties by appealing to Altenstein and, if necessary, to the king himself. Frederick William had informed Witzleben personally in February 1822 that the new foundation expressed his "innermost wishes." As an intimate associate of the king, Witzleben provided the committee with a direct route of appeal to the highest authority in the Prussian state.[79] When, for example, the consistory opposed a move by the Berlin Society to install a permanent missionary to the Jews in Berlin, arguing that such an appointment would encourage the establishment of "special conventicles," it was overridden by a Cabinet Order from the king.[80] Collaboration of this kind between the highest state authorities and the "perfumed pietists" – as Arnold Ruge called the awakened aristocrats in the *Hallesche Jahrbücher* – prompted the observation by the liberal theologian Philipp Conrad Marheineke that "it was terrible how the church [in Berlin] was ruled by the adjutants."[81]

78. See governor of the Province of Brandenburg to MGUMA, 30 August 1827, Royal Prussian Police Presidium to Brandenburg Consistory, 31 August 1827, Brandenburg Consistory to MGUMA, 6 September 1827, MGUMA (clerical department) to Brandenburg Consistory, 13 September 1827, and loose notes signed by Nicolai and Ritzschl – both members of the Consistory – dated 22 and 23 August 1827 respectively. Evangelisches Zentralarchiv Berlin (EZA), 7/2912.

79. R. Bieling, *Die Juden vornehmlich 1822–1901* (with a supplement by K. Schaeffer for the period from 1903 to 1912) (Berlin, 1913), p. 12. On Witzleben's personal influence on the king, see *Allgemeine Deutsche Bibliographie*, vol. 34 (Berlin, 1898; repr. Berlin, 1971): 675–77; here p. 676.

80. Brandenburg Consistory to MGUMA, Berlin, 30 August 1827, EZA 7/2912.

81. Marheineke was actually referring to Leopold von Gerlach and General von der Gröben, Witzleben's successor as president of the Berlin Mission to the Jews. Cited in Gerlach, *Aufzeichnungen*, p. 169. The citation from Ruge is in Witte, *Das Leben*, vol. 1, p. 101. Ruge distinguished between "perfumed" and "ordinary" pietists.

By the late 1820s, the United Church of Prussia was faced with a far more formidable problem than the sporadic separatism of the "perfumed pietists." The re-emergence of an aggressive "Old Lutheran" confessional identity posed an existential threat to the Union that Frederick William III had designed. The Old Lutherans refused to relinquish their traditional liturgy and opposed the new state liturgy as the creation of "pagan Calvinists."[82] The government responded with police action. In Hönigern near Namslau in Silesia, for example, the Lutheran church was opened by force, the Old Lutheran pastor dragged off to prison, and the town billetted with 500 soldiers.[83] By 1830, after violence had erupted in Breslau and the lives of various officials had been threatened, it became clear that "the matter was no longer one of theological differences, but one of open rebellion against the authorities."[84] There were waves of arrests and emigration. Old Lutheranism was a predominantly Silesian phenomenon, but its radicalism and the speed of its growth nourished fears that it would spread throughout the whole kingdom. The atmosphere of state paranoia that characterized the late 1820s and 1830s had a very damaging effect on voluntarist culture in Prussia. Altenstein even argued that "excessive piety" (*Frömmelei*) could easily lead to liberalism, since "every aberration from the normal order and every certainty that one has found something better" was politically problematic.[85] The intensified suspicion of extra-ecclesiastical groups, mysticism, and separatism of any kind placed missionary groups in a vulnerable position.

Despite his earlier affirmation of their (avowed) aims, Frederick William now began to suspect that the missionary societies were aligned with the separatists. In the wake of the Old Lutheran agitation, he formed a special censorship commission under the control of the ministry for church, health, and educational affairs, which was to carry out closer surveillance of the printed literature produced by the numerous societies.[86]

82. *Evangelische Kirchenzeitung* (1830): 352, 404, cited in Bigler, *Politics*, p. 110.
83. Hintze, "Epochen des evangelischen Kirchenregiments in Preußen," pp. 1230–34.
84. *Evangelische Kirchenzeitung* (1830): 377, cited in Bigler, *Politics*, p. 112.
85. Cited in Foerster, *Entstehung der preußischen Landeskirche*, vol. 1, p. 233.
86. W. Wendland, *Die Religiosität und die kirchenpolitischen Grundsätze Friedrich Wilhelms des Dritten in ihrer Bedeutung für die Geschichte der kirchlichen Restauration* (Giessen, 1909), p. 124.

The government viewed with increasing unease the classical social manifestations of the missionary movement: prayer groups, anniversary feasts, missionary meetings. These half-public, half-private associations, secluded from view and difficult to police, now seemed to provide the ideal breeding ground for separatism and political agitation against the state church. Some missionary societies disappeared altogether during the period of the separatist purges. In 1830, the Academic Mission Club was dissolved. Requests for its reinstatement by the relatively well-established Berlin Missionary Society (BMG) were unsuccessful. In 1833, when the committee of the BMG asked for permission to hold regular mission meetings, its request was turned down. In 1833, apparently in reply to a direct complaint from the Berlin Society for the Promotion of Christianity among the Jews, Frederick William confirmed in a Cabinet Order to Altenstein that Jewish missionaries were not to be hindered in their task. But he now added the proviso that "the missionaries must hold themselves strictly within the limits of the business of converting Jews." They should at all costs avoid branding "Christian congregations or members of the same as teachers of false doctrine, as has already occurred, since in this case the licence [to missionize] will not only be withdrawn, but these missionaries will be subject to penalty by law."[87] Early in 1834, the government issued an order forbidding conventicles, religious meetings, or private study groups of any kind. The destructive effect of Old Lutheran separatism and the government's responses to it were soon felt close at hand by the Berlin mission to the Jews. In August 1836, on Frederick William's instruction, Altenstein informed the Berlin committee that it was immediately to dismiss one of its employees who had joined the Old Lutherans. The committee tried hard to retain its missionary, but without success. Further dismissals followed.[88] The government had embarked

87. Cabinet Order, 31 March 1833, EZA 7/2912. See also von Altenstein to von der Groeben (president of the GBCJ), Berlin, 31 March 1834, GStA Merseburg, Rep. 76 III, Sekt. 7, Abt. XVII.

88. See Cabinet Order to von Altenstein, 13 August 1836, and Altenstein to GBCJ Committee, Berlin, 18 August 1836, GStA Berlin, HA XIV, Rep. 181/5132; Wedemann to GBCJ Committee, Zülz, 4 March 1836; GBCJ Committee to Wedemann, Berlin, 23 April 1836; GBCJ to Silesian Consistory, Berlin, 2 June 1836; Silesian Consistory to GBCJ, Breslau, 18 June 1836. For the appeal against Altenstein's order, see GBCJ Committee to Altenstein, Berlin, 3 September 1836. GStA Merseburg, Rep. 199, Nr. 25. For later dismissals, see *Jahresbericht der GBCJ* 14 (1837): 6, and ibid., 15 (1838): 8.

upon "that regrettable decade of small-minded police persecution that ended with the virtual bankruptcy of Prussian church policy."[89]

Even as the campaign against the separatists was reaching its height, however, there were signs that the opposition between "centralists" and "voluntarists" was about to be superseded by a larger political and constitutional conflict. By 1830 it was clear that Old Lutheranism had come to serve as a focus for liberal discontents in Prussia. The Silesian separatist leader, Gottfried Scheibel, a pastor and professor of theology in Breslau and the former librarian of the Breslau Society for the Promotion of Christianity among the Israelites, was accused by Hengstenberg in the *Evangelische Kirchenzeitung* of deliberately allowing political agitators into the movement.[90] Although the association with political liberalism helped to heat up the anti-separatist campaign, it also signalled that the long-established opposition between separatists and statists was becoming obsolete. The political impact of the July revolution in France and the emergence of more radical forms of theological liberalism indicated the growing importance of another ideological fault line in Prussian political society. In the fierce journalistic battle fought by Ludwig von Gerlach and the *Evangelische Kirchenzeitung* against the liberal rationalist theologians Wilhelm Gesenius and Julius August Ludwig Wegscheider at the University of Halle, the awakened elite rallied to the cause of Protestant orthodoxy and the state church. The *Evangelische Kirchenzeitung* now argued that it was the propaganda of the liberal rationalists that had fostered the division between the orthodox Protestant church of Prussia and those whom they derided as "pietists." In reality, one anonymous author declared, it was precisely their joint opposition to the camp of "neologistic unbelief" that had helped to resolve the old dispute between pietist and orthodox tendencies within Prussian Protestantism.[91]

89. Richter, *Geschichte der Berliner Missionsgesellschaft*, p. 65.

90. For a full list of the founding members of the Gesellschaft zur Beförderung des Christenthums unter den Israeliten zu Breslau (an auxiliary of the Berlin Society), see the Society statutes dated 15 May 1822, GStA Merseburg, Rep. 199, Nr. 8. The Breslau auxiliary closed down in 1828. On Hengstenberg's campaign against Scheibel, see Bigler, *Politics*, pp. 111–14.

91. See anon., "Der reelle Unglaube und der vorgebliche Mysticismus," *Evangelische Kirchenzeitung* 7 (1833), cols. 521–28, here cols. 521–22. A number of articles published by this journal in the 1830s stressed the orthodox charac-

Christopher Clark

The accession of Frederick William IV in 1840 brought a change in government policy that did much to defuse the tension between the separatists and the Prussian state. The former crown prince had long been known to sympathize with the romantic religious and spiritual aspirations of the neo-pietists. His mellowing influence had helped to smooth official negotiations with the Pomeranian separatists in the 1820s and his attitude to the government's persecution of the Old Lutherans was ambivalent. Moreover, the new king's friends and advisers included Leopold von Gerlach, Ludwig August von Thile (known for his piety as "Bibel-Thile"), Anton von Stolberg, and Ernst Senfft von Pilsach. These men constituted the "pietist party" that the liberals feared would gain control over royal policy.[92] In 1845, the Old Lutheran dispute effectively came to an end with the publication of a General Concession to the separatists by the government of Prussia.

V

Separatism continued to flourish on some of the Pomeranian estates – there were communities of "Belowian" pietists in Pomerania as late as 1933 – but it no longer had the social and political resonance it had enjoyed during the 1820s. For most of the pietist aristocrats, the celebration of separatism and the fanatical atmosphere of the "brotherly circle" belonged to a particular phase of their youth, in the aftermath of occupation and war. Even Adolf von Thadden later regretted the way in

---

ter of the "serious Christianity" known as pietism. See for example, anon., "Lesefrüchte. Was wird gegenwärtig unter dem Pietismus verstanden?" *Evangelische Kirchenzeitung* 11 (1837): cols. 145–48, where it was argued that when the rationalists attacked the "pietists," they were really attacking the Protestant church and its doctrines. For a detailed account of the campaign against Gesenius and Wegscheider, see J. Bachmann, *Ernst Wilhelm Hengstenberg. Sein Leben und Wirken nach gedruckten und ungedruckten Quellen dargestellt*, 3 vols. (Gütersloh, 1876–92), vol. 2, pp. 177–283.

92. H. Wagener, *Die Politik Friedrich Wilhelms IV.* (Berlin 1883), pp. 12, 17. On the "pietistische Partei," see also K.V. Rochow, "Erinnerungen der Karoline von Rochow, geborene von der Marwitz," in *Vom Leben am Preußischen Hofe 1815–1852*, ed. L. von der Marwitz (Berlin, 1908), pp. 219–20. On the extent of the pietists' influence on Frederick William IV, see Bußmann, *Zwischen Preußen und Deutschland*, esp. pp. 110–11. Cf. H.-C. Kraus, "Das preußische Königtum und Frierich Wilhelm der IV. aus der Sicht Ernst Ludwig von Gerlachs," in *Friedrich Wilhelm IV. in seiner Zeit. Beiträge eines Colloquiums*, ed. O. Büsch (Berlin, 1987), pp. 48–93. Kraus stresses the relative autonomy of the king and the limited political influence of the pietist faction.

which, as an angry young man, he had harassed the local *Landrat*. Ludwig von Gerlach, too, eventually came to share his youngest brother Otto's opinion that it was wrong to view churches as "stone houses" and clergymen as "men in black gowns."[93]

As Walter Bußmann has recently observed, the first half of the nineteenth century was a period in which political and ecclesiastical issues were particularly closely intertwined.[94] By the 1840s, when conservative pietists and liberal "friends of light" (*Lichtfreunde*) skirmished in the German journals, the connection between political and religious issues was obvious. In 1846, a liberal author lamented that German politics was dominated by theological debates: "The supposedly religious movement of our age is not, in fact, religious, but political."[95] In the period before 1830, as this essay has tried to demonstrate, the relationship between religion and politics was more subtle, but no less significant. Aristocratic neo-pietism was a response to the upheavals of war and reform. It articulated the political concerns of one section of the landed nobility in a period of rapid political and social change. This is not to suggest that it was merely a mask for political interests. There can be no doubt as to the authenticity and intensity of the religious experiences that bound the neo-pietists together. But aristocratic revivalists were well aware that their spiritual choices had political implications.

Not merely the theological content of neo-pietist religiosity, but also its characteristic social forms – prayer groups, conventicles, missionary and caritative societies – reflected the predicament of the Prussian aristocracy in the post-Napoleonic period. In his book, *Democracy in America*, Alexis de Tocqueville observed that American society, lacking feudal corporations, had invented voluntary association as the new principle of collective action. Much attention has been given to the role of voluntary associations in the formation of bourgeois political society, but a tendency to link them exclusively with the phenomenon of "bourgeoisification" has led to the almost complete neglect of those strands of early nineteenth-century

93. Gerlach, *Aufzeichnungen*, pp. 132, 149–50.
94. Bußmann, *Zwischen Preußen und Deutschland*, p. 119.
95. Robert Prutz, cited in H.-U. Wehler, *Deutsche Gesellschaftsgeschichte*, vol. 2: *Von der Reformära bis zur industriellen und politischen "Deutschen Doppelrevolution" 1815–1848/49* (Munich, 1987), p. 467.

Christopher Clark

organizational culture that were emphatically non-bourgeois.[96] To "organize" in conventicles and caritative associations was one – though certainly not the only – possible response to the threat that bureaucratic modernization posed to the corporate identity of the Prussian aristocracy.

The era of "perfumed pietism" deserves to be considered an important formative experience in the evolution of nineteenth-century German conservatism. Senfft von Pilsach, Kleist-Retzow, Puttkamer, and the Gerlachs were among those significant figures in Prussian conservatism after 1848 who came from a pietist aristocratic milieu. The social conscience, the provincialism, and the populist, plebiscitary appeal of *altständisch* aristocratic pietism made a vital contribution to the crystallization of a conservative agenda in Prussia. No single figure illustrates this better than Bismarck, the conservative champion of universal suffrage and the architect of social insurance. Himself a convert to awakened Christianity, he once described the pietists on the Reinfeld estate as "models in every respect of what I wished to be."[97]

96. See M. Agulhon, "La sociabilité est-elle objet d'histoire?" in *Sociabilité et Société Bourgeoise en France, en Allemagne et en Suisse 1750–1850* (Mission Historique Française en Allemagne, Paris, 1986), pp. 13–23. Agulhon warns against equating voluntarism with bourgeois culture (p. 22), but the close association that Habermas posited between the two continues to exert a strong influence on historical research. See esp. O. Dann, "Die bürgerliche Vereinsbildung und ihre Erforschung," in ibid., pp. 43–52, and the outline of recent research offered in the revised foreword to J. Habermas, *Strukturwandel der Öffentlichkeit. Untersuchungen zu einer Kategorie der bürgerlichen Gesellschaft* (Frankfurt am Main, 1990), pp. 11–53.

97. O. von Bismarck, *Gedanken und Erinnerungen* (Stuttgart and Berlin, 1928), pp. 53–54. The quotation is from Bloth, *Die Kirche in Pommern*, p. 92.

2

Conservatives and the Social Question in Nineteenth-Century Prussia

Hermann Beck

Nineteenth-century Prussian conservatism has customarily been viewed as inextricably linked to the material interests of Prussian noblemen. The temptation is therefore great to see conservative ideas and organizations as serving the Junkers' interest politics exclusively. Yet between 1830 and 1870, in response to the social problems of their time, Prussian conservatives developed a set of ideas and policies that do not fit this simple model. To be sure, in Prussia as elsewhere in Europe, conservatism was in large measure a reaction against the great revolution in France: "Nous ne voulons pas la contrerévolution, mais le contraire de la révolution." De Maistre's famous slogan became the slogan of Prussia's first effectively organized conservative circle that congregated around the *Berliner Politisches Wochenblatt*.[1] And, as in other European countries, Prussian conservatism was conditioned by the history of the Prussian state that, in turn, shaped its idiosyncrasies and specific features. Those particuliarities of Prussian conservatism later influenced the character of German conservatism during the empire and the Weimar Republic.

Nonetheless, another perhaps more immediate factor conditioning the development of Prussian conservatism can be found in the Prussian reforms of 1807 to 1813 that fundamentally reshaped state and society. More specifically, the begin-

---

1. H.J. Schoeps, "Neue Briefe zur Gründung des Berliner Politischen Wochenblattes," in *Zeitschrift für Religions- und Geistesgeschichte* 11 (1961): 114–127; W. Scheel, *Das Berliner Politische Wochenblatt und die politische und soziale Revolution in Frankreich und England* (Göttingen, 1964). See also *Berliner Politisches Wochenblatt*, 8 October 1831.

nings of Prussian conservatism can be traced back to the refusal of Prussian noblemen to comply with the bureaucratic reform measures, such as the liberation of the peasantry, which they claimed threatened their economic position – indeed, their entire way of life – as well as the internal composition and historical traditions of Prussia.[2] It is of great significance, then, that from its very inception Prussian conservatism reacted to problems of an essentially social nature. The reforms, resulting in the liberation of the peasantry, the cancellation of a multitude of other social and economic restrictions, and the disintegration of traditional bonds,[3] brought in their wake a clearly definable *Soziale Frage*, or "social question," generally identified as the problem of widespread pauperism in *Vormärz* Germany.[4] It is difficult to exaggerate the importance of public debate on this issue. In an age when literacy was generally limited to the educated few and literary output amounted to but a fraction of today's, *Pauperismusliteratur* was prodigious. Between 1816 and 1830, forty-two titles on the subject were published, fifty-five between 1831 and 1840, and 231 during the "hungry forties."[5]

2. Two recent studies shed light on the aristocratic fronde and their convictions: F.L. Carsten, *Geschichte der preußischen Junker* (Frankfurt, 1988), pp. 80–105; and especially R. Berdahl, *The Politics of the Prussian Nobility: The Development of a Conservative Ideology 1770–1848* (Princeton, N.J., 1988), pp. 123–58.

3. W. Conze, "Das Spannungsfeld von Staat und Gesellschaft im Vormärz," in *Staat und Gesellschaft im deutschen Vormärz*, ed. W. Conze (Stuttgart, 1962), pp. 207–69. Conze saw the entire period between 1815 and 1848 conditioned by the breakdown of corporate bonds (*Dekorporierung*) and excessive population growth, which dislocated the traditional social structure (*Disproportionierung*) and, in turn, were accompanied by dissolution and profligacy (*Entsittlichung*).

4. The argument that pauperism in Prussia was largely the result of the all-encompassing bureaucratic reforms is convincingly made in R. Koselleck's *Preußen zwischen Reform und Revolution*, 2nd ed. (Stuttgart, 1975). Otherwise there is little agreement about the origins and nature of pauperism in Germany. The vast literature on the subject is succinctly summarized in F. Marquardt's review essay, "Pauperism in Germany during the Vormärz," *Central European History* 2 (1969): 77–89.

5. L. Dilcher, "Der deutsche Pauperismus und seine Literatur," (Ph.D. diss., University of Frankfurt, 1957), p. 156. Not surprisingly, the revolutionary year 1848 alone saw the publication of 59 titles. All were published within the territory of the later Second Reich, most of them in Prussia and Saxony, with Berlin and Leipzig as main publishing centers. For a thorough analysis of the *Pauperismusliteratur* see the older but very comprehensive review article by P. Mombert, "Aus der Literatur über die soziale Frage und über die Arbeiterbewegung in Deutschland in der ersten Hälfte des 19. Jahrhunderts," *Archiv für die Geschichte des Sozialismus und der Arbeiterbewegung* 9 (1921): 169–237, which examines 277 titles. The excellent recent study by K.-J. Matz, *Pauperismus und Bevölkerung* (Stuttgart, 1980), focuses on southern Germany.

In conjunction with the national and constitutional question, the *Soziale Frage* was the pivotal issue of the *Vormärz*. It was widely discussed among the literate and politically aware sectors of the populace, and became a topic of discussion that could be avoided neither in the literary salons and coffee houses of Berlin nor among an expanding circle of state officials. It was, moreover, a subject in which conservatives displayed extraordinary interest. Between the foundation of the *Berliner Politisches Wochenblatt* in 1831 (as a response to the July Revolution of 1830 in France) and the founding of the Second Reich, social issues remained prominent in the discussions and propaganda of Prussian conservatives. Conservative responses to pauperism displayed tremendous variety, which was due in part to the changing nature of the problem itself. While the *Soziale Frage* of the 1830s and 1840s had a predominantly rural character mainly concerning overpopulation in Prussia's east-Elbian provinces, by the 1850s it had become the "workers' question" or *Arbeiterfrage*, concerning principally the rapid rise of an urban proletariat after the mid-1840s.

The plethora of conservative remedies to social ills prompts the question: Why have historians paid such scant attention to the subject? Several investigations into conservative social thought were written between 1910 and 1940.[6] But after that the topic seems to have become moribund. Perhaps Prussian conservatism became too negatively charged, discouraging historians who might have explored its more positive contributions. In any event, studies completed after 1945 have tended to concentrate more on the conservatives' political ideas than on their responses to the social question.[7] The following

6. The subject was also a popular dissertation topic; see H. Goetting, "Die sozialpolitische Idee in den konservativen Kreisen der vormärzlichen Zeit" (Ph.D. diss., University of Berlin, 1920); K.E. Femerling, "Die Stellung der konservativen Partei zur gewerblichen Arbeiterfrage in der Zeit von 1848 bis 1880" (Ph.D. diss., University of Halle, 1927); K.V. von Herberger, *Die Stellung der preußischen Konservativen zur Sozialen Frage* (Meißen, 1914); Walter Früh, "Radowitz als Sozialpolitiker" (Ph.D. diss., University of Berlin, 1937).

7. See, for example, W. Scheel, *Das Berliner Politische Wochenblatt und die politische und soziale Revolution in Frankreich und England* (Göttingen, 1964), which, despite its title, barely analyzes the social ideas of the *Wochenblatt* group. In postwar Germany, there has been very little interest in social conservatism per se. One exception is Johann Baptist Müller's article, "Der deutsche Sozialkonservatismus," in *Konservatismus. Eine deutsche Bilanz*, ed. H. Grebing et al. (Munich, 1971), pp. 67–97, which, however, pays virtually no attention to the period before 1870, focusing instead on Imperial Germany and the Weimar

essay attempts to fill this gap by concentrating on the social thought of Prussian conservatives.

Social conservatism in Prussia was exceedingly diverse and multifaceted. The activities of theorists and activists, moreover, were mutually reinforcing and divisive at the same time. Although in general the common ground shared by conservative thinkers was vast, there was great variety in conservative approaches to the social question. Four of these are highlighted below. The first section examines the influence of a circle of conservatives loosely affiliated with Prussia's first conservative weekly, the *Berliner Politisches Wochenblatt*. The *Wochenblatt's* committee of editors included Leopold and Ludwig von Gerlach who, between 1848 and 1858, gained notoriety as close advisers of Frderick William IV; Carl von Voß-Buch, a close friend of the crown prince (later Frederick William IV); Ernst Carl Jarcke, a legal scholar from the University of Berlin; the Halle historian Heinrich Leo, known as a member of the right Hegelians; and – most notably – Josef Maria von Radowitz, the future foreign minister of Prussia and close friend of Frederick William IV.[8] This group, advancing a solution to the social question within the framework of the social estates or *Stände*, advocated the restoration of social conditions as they had existed in the late medieval period. They used this argument to criticize the rise of absolutism and the modern bureaucratic state, both of which challenged their social and political preponderance, and to suggest that Germany should

---

Republic. The *Berliner Politisches Wochenblatt* should not be confused with the *Preußisches Wochenblatt zur Besprechung politischer Tagesfragen*, published between 1851 and 1861 by a group of *Reformkonservative* (also referred to as "liberal conservatives") around Moritz August von Bethmann-Hollweg. The *"Wochenblattkreis"* was far less concerned with social issues than the circle around the *Berliner Politisches Wochenblatt*. See M. Behnen, *Das Preußische Wochenblatt* (1851–1861) (Göttingen, 1971).

8. On the origins of the *Berliner Politisches Wochenblatt* and its members, see C. Varrentrap, "Rankes historisch-politische Zeitschrift und das Berliner Politische Wochenblatt," *Historische Zeitschrift* 99 (1907): 35–119; R. Arnold, "Die Aufzeichnungen des Grafen von Voß-Buch über das Berliner Politische Wochenblatt," *Historische Zeitschrift* 106 (1911): 325–340; for Voß-Buch's complete notes see, "Die Aufzeichnungen des Grafen von Voß-Buch über das Berliner Politische Wochenblatt," Geheimes Staatsarchiv Preussischer Kulturbesitz, Abteilung Merseburg (hereafter GStA Merseburg), Nachlaß (hereafter NL) Carl von Voß-Buch, No. 32, Rep. 92; W. Scheel, *Das Berliner Politische Wochenblatt*; P. Hassel, *Radowitz* (Berlin, 1905); and L. Salomon, *Geschichte des deutschen Zeitungswesens*, 3 vols. (Oldenburg and Leipzig, 1900–1906), vol. 3, provide further information.

return to an age when estates and guilds still regulated social life.

The second section focuses on Josef Maria von Radowitz, who rose to become Prussia's most original conservative thinker after the demise of the *Wochenblatt* in 1841. Whereas the *Wochenblatt* group was determined to alleviate pauperism outside the modern state, Radowitz rejected a *"ständisch renewal,"* realizing that "the monarchy based on estates is extinct in the consciousness of the masses."[9] Despite his strong mistrust, even open hostility, toward the omnipotence of the Prussian bureaucracy – a mistrust he shared with his former brothers-in-arms around the *Wochenblatt* – Radowitz became convinced that the alleviation of social misery required active state intervention. He argued that pauperism could and should be eliminated only within the framework of the modern centralized state.

In contrast to Radowitz and the members of the *Wochenblatt* group, all of whom suspiciously eyed the progress of industrial development and the rise of a capitalist economy,[10] the two other important conservatives of the *Vormärz* period, Viktor Aimé Huber and Carl Rodbertus, wholeheartedly embraced the achievements of the machine age. Personally they had little contact with the Gerlachs or with Radowitz. Indeed, resentment and animosity poisoned their relations with other conservatives, undermining whatever strength common political goals might have provided.[11] Despite marked differences in

9. J.M. von Radowitz, *Gesammelte Schriften*, 4 vols. (Berlin, 1851), vol. 4, pp. 247–48.

10. In fact, many of their pronouncements are reminiscent of a *"Kulturkritik"* that, in the case of the *Wochenblatt*, was complemented by sentiments of a wistful longing for the bygone days of guild life and *ständisch* rule. In Radowitz's writings one encounters a critique of modern civilization similar to that of the philosophy of life of turn-of-the-century Germany, with its criticisms of urbanization, modern industry, and the corrupting influence of money.

11. During his stay in Berlin (after 1843), Huber maintained cordial relations with Friedrich Julius Stahl, Heinrich Leo, and the conservative minister of culture Eichhorn (who had made a name for himself by forcibly removing left Hegelians from the University of Berlin). For the "Gerlach clique" Huber had nothing but disdain, and in Radowitz he saw little more than a *"beau parleur,"* sentiments that were largely reciprocated. See I. Paulsen, *Viktor Aimé Huber als Sozialpolitiker*, 2nd ed. (Berlin, 1956), p. 74; as well as the older studies by R. Elvers, *Viktor Aimé Huber*, 2 vols. (Bremen, 1872–74); and M. Lenz, *Geschichte der königlichen Friedrich Wilhelms Universität Berlin*, 4 vols. (Berlin, 1910–18), vol. 2, pp. 60–68.

the theories developed by Huber and Rodbertus, the third section examines this affirmative disposition toward the modern age and assesses its significance as a common denominator between the two.

Fourth and finally, the enigmatic figure of Hermann Wagener is considered. Wagener belonged to a different generation from the other conservatives discussed here: he developed his important social ideas only during and after the 1848 Revolution. A more practical politician than the others (except, perhaps, Radowitz), Wagener gained public renown and notoriety as editor-in-chief of the *Kreuzzeitung*, the foremost organ of Prussian conservatism, from 1848 to 1853. Wagener subsequently became editor of the *Berliner Revue*, publisher of a multi-volume conservative encyclopedia, the *Staats- und Gesellschaftslexikon*, and conservative deputy in the Prussian House of Deputies and the Reichstag. Although his career was unexpectedly cut short by one of the scandals of the *Gründerzeit*,[12] his role as Bismarck's adviser for social issues was of central importance, for Wagener provided Bismarck with a series of important memoranda on the *Arbeiterfrage* that appear to have helped shape Bismarck's own ideas on the question.[13] Wagener's social ideas are especially compelling because they anticipate the ideas of later German conservatives in both the nineteenth and twentieth centuries. But in the context of this essay, more important is his role as someone who summed up forty years of development in the social thought of Prussian conservatism. From utter rejection of the modern state as exemplified by the *Wochenblatt* group in the 1830s, a younger generation of conservatives had come to accept that the state could be used as a means to conservative ends. That acceptance suggests that, contrary to many older

12. Wagener had obtained shares for the Pomeranian railroad while lobbying for the concession of this new railroad line. According to his mentor Bismarck, Wagener had merely engaged in an act that had become standard practice at the time. Even though a parliamentary investigation committee cleared Wagener of all criminal charges, the moral blemish could not be undone. See W. Saile, *Hermann Wagener und sein Verhältnis zu Bismarck* (Tübingen, 1958), p. 114.

13. On this, see W. Saile, *Hermann Wagener*; H.-J. Schoeps, "Hermann Wagener. Ein konservativer Sozialist," in *Zeitschrift für Religions- und Geistesgeschichte* 8 (1956): 193–217; and especially Wagener's long memorandum of 1864 to Bismarck, which is preserved with Bismarck's marginal notes: see "Denkschrift von Hermann Wagener für Bismarck," 1 March 1864, GStA Merseburg, NL Zitelmann, p.91.

views, by the 1870s some Prussian conservatives had realized that preserving their own power meant accommodating themselves to fundamentally new social and political conditions. Wagener was even prepared to collaborate with the working class to perpetuate the power of traditional elites.

I

The foundation of the *Berliner Politisches Wochenblatt* in 1831 was a milestone in the history of German conservatism, for it provided an initial political platform for a diverse group of conservatives. The inner cohesion of the group was based on shared opposition to any form of revolution as well as a common understanding of organic growth, right (*Recht*), and law (*Gesetz*). Institutions of state and society had matured only gradually, they argued, just as rights and privileges had developed organically during the course of centuries.[14] Law existed only in its given, organic form, as did claims, titles, and rights of possession. Only the gradual process of development could bestow legitimacy upon these.[15] The members of this group also shared a strong mistrust toward any kind of closed system, and they were unanimous in rejecting general axioms, alleged to be rooted in natural law, such as "the rights of man" or "sovereignty of the people." Abstract principles (as laid down in a constitution, for example) could never be applied to matters of state and society, they argued, for such principles would undermine the "good and vested rights," the traditionalism on which the Prussian state was based.[16] The enemies of these vested rights, sanctified by tradition, were different forms of "absolutism," such as "modern liberal constitutionalism" and the "dictatorship of the civil service," in which those close to the *Wochenblatt* saw the embodiment of the modern

14. "Die Kraft und Schwäche des Liberalismus," *Berliner Politisches Wochenblatt* (hereafter *BPW*), 29 October 1833; "Versuch einer systematischen Darstellung der politischen Parteien," *BPW*, 26 October 1833.

15. "Vom deutschen Bauernstande," *BPW*, 8 December 1832; "Über den erblichen Adel als notwendigen Bestandteil der erblichen Monarchie," *BPW*, 7 May 1835.

16. In a programmatic article commemorating the first anniversary of the *Wochenblatt's* publication, the editors emphasized that the "good and vested rights" were "divine rights, since it was divine will and commandment to hold sacred property and the right of the other." See "Das Berliner Politische Wochenblatt am Schlusse des ersten Jahres seines Bestehens," *BPW*, 29 October 1832, p. 246.

centralized state.[17] In the same vein, monarchical omnipotence was vigorously denounced: "royal absolutism and revolution are but different aspects of one and the same thing, twin children of the same mother."[18]

The early conservatives who wrote for the *Wochenblatt* spurned absolute royal power as an infringement upon their own freedom. In this sense these conservatives were different from conservatives in Imperial Germany, whose relationship to the monarch was characterized by dutiful obeisance, if not outright servility. It was the 1848 Revolution that marked the turning point in the changing relationship between the Prussian nobility and the crown. In the 1830s and 1840s there were still numerous liberal Junkers in east-Elbian Prussia (especially in East Prussia); but the revolutionary uprisings, including numerous rural revolts and peasant insurgencies, made the Junkers more conscious of the interests of their own class.[19] In the 1830s, moreover, the spirit of the noble fronde – as exemplified by the family of Quitzows who had rebelled against the first Hohenzollern when they came to the Mark Brandenburg in 1415 – still remained alive in the aristocratic members of the group. *Wochenblatt* conservatives thus vehemently rejected centralized state power, regardless whether it were wielded by an omnipotent prince or by a well-organized bureaucracy (as was the case in *Vormärz* Prussia). Instead they favored particularist, regional, and *ständische* powers. "If the state has to be the primary source of all law," wrote a contributer to the *Wochenblatt* in 1834, "private law loses its foundation and the only barrier against arbitrariness and despotism collapses."[20]

17. Ibid., p. 247. These "forms of absolutism," as the *Wochenblatt* referred to them, were manifestations of "an absolute principle or authority" that were "set above the good and vested rights."

18. "Revolution und Absolutismus," *BPW*, 30 March 1833, p. 77.

19. See F.L. Carstens, *Die Preußischen Junker*, pp. 105–20; Thomas Nipperdey, *Deutsche Geschichte 1800–1866* (Munich, 1983), p. 397. Nipperdey emphasized that the passing of a constitution tied the political fate of Junkers more closely to that of the monarchy. See also the recently published memoirs of A. Dohna zu Schlobitten, *Erinnerungen eines alten Ostpreußen* (Berlin, 1989), who observed a continuous shift to the right among the members of his own family. Dohna believed that it was above all "the unrest of 1848 and later the great influence of Bismarck" that turned the Dohnas from liberals into conservatives (ibid., p. 163).

20. "Die Lehre von der wahren Freiheit," *BPW*, 22 February 1834. In anticipation of what would become a real danger in modern German history, the article continued that "in this case, even the most brutal outrage can be justified by public interest and the maintenance of the state."

Such statements were typical of early conservatives insofar as they betrayed fear of a renewal of revolutionary terror as had been practiced in the name of the state in 1793/94.

The members of the *Wochenblatt* were aristocratic decentralists like Montesquieu, championing a restoration of the rule of the estates: state power was to be hemmed in by representatives of the estates (*Ständevertretungen*) and their law courts (*Ständegerichte*), acting as natural checks to princely as well as to bureaucratic power in order to preserve the "good old *Recht*."[21] Conservatives favored a resuscitation of an idealized *Ständestaat*, a state ruled jointly by the estates and the king, that would safeguard their independence within their local district. The estates had developed organically, being "created and conditioned by nature," and they were based "on the naturally determined difference of occupation, ways of life, customs, and interests" of the people. Concomitant with spurning the modern centralized state went disdain for the uniformity of law. The conservatives were too deeply rooted in the historical experience of the Margraviate of Brandenburg and the Holy Roman Empire, with their countless free imperial knights, cities, and principalities (each possessed of its own legal customs), not to feel threatened by the standardization of the modern age and its eradication of "natural" inequalities. Inequality was part of the conservatives' self-understanding and identity, just as the restoration of a pre-revolutionary world was their declared goal. In many of their articles, the *Wochenblatt* group conjured up an idealized image of late medieval and early modern times that, in hindsight, had become a world of prosperity without social ills where the individual was firmly integrated into the family and into "corporations of artists and artisans."[22] The reestablishment of

21. "Revolution und Absolutismus," *BPW*, 30 May 1833 (2nd article), p. 77. (Unless indicated otherwise, the following quotations in the text are taken from this article.) Law codifications were scornfully dismissed: "The equality of law and, as its means, the uniformity of law in the whole country, was and is absolutism's real goal and ambition" ("Revolution und Absolutismus," 3rd article).

22. "Betrachtungen über Gewerbe-, Zunft-, und Innungswesen," *BPW*, 19 May 1832, p. 311 (the following quotations are taken from this article); and "Die Doktrinen des Wochenblatts," *BPW*, 29 December 1832, pp. 331–32. In conjuring up this bygone age, conservatives often got carried away by the romantic spirit of their own epoch: "everyone celebrated merry evening hours in the guild-hall or the public house after a hard day's work, keeping many feasts and banquets throughout the year according to their guild statutes and by-laws."

guilds for tradesmen, which had been abolished during the reform era, thus became a central tenet of *Wochenblatt* conservatism and was deemed imperative for the solution of the problems that plagued society. Guilds were praised not only as protective social networks that absorbed the poor but also as moral and religious institutions that saw to the maintenance of public order. The world of the late medieval city was thus held up as the model for an entirely self-regulating social cosmos in which guilds and corporations helped their impoverished members and in which "guild ordinances and by-laws had the force of police regulations."[23]

This backward-oriented, medieval ideal was reproduced in the *Wochenblatt*'s recommendations to remedy contemporary pauperism by holding up the social conditions of the past when seeking solutions for the future. The social organization conservatives espoused resembled the regimented, neo-feudal order of the estate and the socially arrested world of the medieval town: a closed society, self-contained, regimented and secure, whose members were safe and provided for but, at the same time, highly dependent upon one another, a world where conflicts remained controlled because everyone was firmly ensconced in the existing social fabric. According to the *Wochenblatt*, man had to remain bound by social ties such as family, corporations, estates, and the paternalistic relationship of the estate (*Gutsherrschaft*). Subordination and dependence did have their benefits, the members of the group maintained, because the dependent subjects derived obvious advantages from their masters, just as the peasants gained food and shelter in return for their services. Freedom from service was therefore not true freedom, since "it is not given to man to provide for his living in complete independence from others"; subordination, moreover, was considered "reasonable and just."[24] Conservatives were convinced that "in order to reach higher stages of development, greater or lesser restrictions on personal development are necessary" and that mutual dependence was "the only cohesive factor in society." Small wonder then that the *Wochenblatt* group considered the social legacy of

23. On the nature and function of guilds in town, see M. Walker, *German Home Towns* (Ithaca, NY, 1971), pp. 73–108.

24. "Über den Mißverstand der Freiheit in volkswirtschaftlicher Beziehung," *BPW*, 13 May 1837. The following quotations in the text are taken from this article.

the Prussian reform era as disastrous. As one of its members wrote in 1837: "The fragmentation of civil society into individuals and the disintegration of all bonds that give more security to the individual than the state could provide will have grave results."[25]

With the dissolution of journeymen's associations, traditional craftsmen were destined to become extinct and be replaced by a "multitude of dissolute and uncouth workers."[26] The transformation of the pre-industrial journeyman into the industrial laborer thus presaged decline because the journeyman had been integrated into a complex social network, whereas the industrial worker was uprooted and thereby allegedly deprived of moral restraint. For the *Wochenblatt* these developments encapsulated the essence of the social problem: this "multitude of uncouth and dissolute workers," this vast unfettered mass of unemployed journeymen, apprentices, and land- and propertyless peasants, would one day sweep away the existing order. The solution, as ceaselessly reiterated in conservatives' arguments, was to reinstate the old checks and restraints that acted upon the lower classes, for it lay "in the nature of man" to realize the "necessity of certain restrictions and limitations."[27]

While in Prussia itself an industrial working class hardly existed during the 1830s, the importance of an industrial proletariat and the potential danger it posed to society were recognized at an early date. During the first half of the nineteenth century, those Prussians interested in social, political, and economic issues closely followed developments in England, whose strengths they wanted to emulate and whose problems they wanted to avoid.[28] England therefore served as a model

25. Ibid.
26. "Die Lehren des Pauperismus," *BPW*, 12 January 1839, p. 6; "Betrachtungen über Gewerbe-, Zunft-, und Innungswesen," *BPW*, 9 June 1832, p. 152. In the *Wochenblatt's* portrayal of the arrested commonwealth of the medieval town, conflicts were non-existent, as everyone, from master-craftsman to apprentice, was bound by a rigid social code: the master-craftsman who did not abide by guild regulations would be publicly dishonored; journeymen had to greet each other according to a fixed ritual, the *Gesellengruß*; and the journeymen's association, the *Gesellenverband*, kept its members under such tight supervision that deviation from accepted standards of behavior usually resulted in ostracism and subsequent emigration.
27. "Über den Mißverstand der Freiheit in volkswirtschaftlicher Beziehung," *BPW*, 13 May 1837.
28. Already at the beginning of the nineteenth century, it had become customary for high Prussian officials to undertake a "grand tour" to England; see

for the solution of potential social problems, and countless articles in the *Wochenblatt* reflected the growing preoccupation with the specter of an all-engulfing industrial proletariat. The principal target of the *Wochenblatt*'s criticisms, however, was the rising class of industrial entrepreneurs, whose "unbridled, wild, speculative spirit," and "financial despotism" were blamed for the misery of the industrial working class.[29] It would be disastrous, conservatives asserted, if the landed nobility were to be supplanted by the rising industrial entrepreneur, for the well-being of state and society rested on the interplay between the landed nobility in the countryside and guilds and corporations in towns. Behind the pernicious factory system – the *Wochenblatt* referred to it as "modern feudalism" – the "thunder cloud of a great social revolution" was lurking,[30] and the new "aristocracy of money and industry" now exercised "a far more oppressive rule" over the lower classes, "the bondsmen of the new age."[31] The plight of the industrial worker was subsequently reduced to one of "monstrous moral corruption," and conservatives rightly feared that the "untamed licentiousness, profligacy, and dissoluteness," once unleashed, would also endanger their own privileges.[32] The proliferation of morally demeaning factory work

---

W. Treue, *Wirtschaftszustände und Wirtschaftspolitik in Preußen, 1815–1825* (Stuttgart, 1937). Among conservatives, Radowitz, Ludwig von Gerlach and Viktor Aimé Huber, who wrote a celebrated book on the English university system, all spent a longer period of time in England; among Hegel's better known works is his essay on the English Reform Bill of 1832, and even the novelist Theodor Fontane, then an impecunious pharmacy apprentice, spent a week in London in the early 1840s. See his lively account in the autobiography of his early years, *Von Zwanzig bis Dreißig, Werke und Schriften*, vol. 35 (Frankfurt and Berlin, 1980), pp. 127–39.

29. "Die Lehren des Pauperismus," *BPW* 12 January 1839, p. 6; "Über den Mißverstand der Freiheit in volkswirtschaftlicher Hinsicht," *BPW*, 13 May 1837; "Die Kraft und Schwäche des Liberalismus," *BPW*, 19 October 1833.

30. "Der moderne Feudalismus," *BPW*, 10 June 1837, p. 134. The following quotations in the text are taken from this article.

31. Ibid. The *Wochenblatt* contrasted its rival's sins against its own perceived virtues: "[the old aristocratic rule] has been resurrected without poetry, faith, love, and gallantry – and without humility; it is the old luxury, but without taste and without dignity, the old domination, but without the sacrificing generosity, without the disinterestedness, without the voluntary devotion to a higher ideal; it is the old ambition, but without the inbred moral sense and without the feeling of high pride, conceit without honor, in one word: it is the power of gold that has been replaced by the power of iron."

32. Factory work was considered to be "demoralizing," brutalizing the worker: "trustworthiness, moderation, industry, and domestic virtues seem to be wholly extinct among the lower classes."

and the subsequent erosion of the old social order helped create the modern working class that, conservatives held, "might become the most powerful lever of a social revolution."[33]

According to conservatives, it was the instability of modern times, the breakdown of Christian faith, the disintegration of large family units, and the rootlessness of modern man that had given the proletariat its restless, menacing quality. To avoid a revolution, social change would have to be harnessed and the proletariat reintegrated into society on the basis of old beliefs and the traditional political checks. This, *Wochenblatt* conservatives maintained, could not be achieved by "the state," which "is but a dead idea for them [the proletariat], offering punishment and discipline, not commiseration. Compassion is only to be found in charity and human sympathy."[34] Not surprisingly, conservatives believed that the one group in society possessing both "noble-mindedness and the means to help" was the Prussian aristocracy. It alone could take on the task of assimilating the proletariat into society through the foundation of an aristocratic order, "molded after the old knight orders" that would have the function of serving and protecting the poor. Colonies for the poor could be established in Prussia's eastern provinces where, under the tutelage of the nobles, the poor would be allocated a fixed amount of property. Such colonies would not only increase the productive agrarian capacity of the east, but "the aristocracy would also find itself by helping others."[35] Pauperism was thus used as a device to ensure continued aristocratic predominance in the east: for the Junker class, helping the poor provided a new *raison d'être* – "the renovation [and] the conservation of this estate."

Like most nineteenth-century conservatives, the members of the *Wochenblatt* group were steeped in an anti-Enlightenment tradition. They polemicized against the French Revolution and were influenced by political romanticism. It was not cold reason that governed life for them, but tradition, history,

33. "Die Proletarier," *BPW*, 14 November 1835. Especially during the later years of its existence, the specter of a social revolution is frequently conjured up in the columns of the *Wochenblatt*.
34. "Wo tuth Hülfe Noth," *BPW*, 13 February 1841, p. 35. The following quotations are taken from this article.
35. Ibid. "A brotherhood, becoming a knight's shield for poor people, would be . . . the most glorious task of the time, which can only be realized by the German aristocracy."

Hermann Beck

and the organic development of social customs and institutions. General principles, embodied in the codification of laws or a constitution, as well as the modern *Rechtsstaat*, governed by an abstract, codified law, were therefore anathema to them. So was the bureaucracy in which conservatives recognized the instrument of these pernicious forces, a levelling, modernizing agent, bent on destroying the world they loved. Instead, the *Wochenblatt* declared its preference for regional and particularist powers such as estates and corporations, emphasizing natural inequality, a God-given hierarchy, and a social system based on mutual dependence. The group's anti-capitalism, anti-industrialism, and anti-modernism were outgrowths of its uncompromising opposition toward the rising forces of liberalism that threatened to undermine the traditional social order. Another salient feature of their political world that set these conservatives apart from later Prussian conservatives was their strong opposition to "royal absolutism," considered an infringement upon their freedom. This opposition was conditioned by their narrow fixation on Prussian traditions and by an idealization of the *Ständestaat* of the sixteenth century when the Junkers were still politically powerful in Brandenburg-Prussia and the elector was considered merely a *primus inter pares*.

II

From the very beginning, the group around the *Berliner Politisches Wochenblatt* had been divided into an orthodox Protestant and a Catholic section. The Gerlach brothers, Heinrich Leo, and Carl von Voß-Buch were orthodox Lutherans, while Jarcke and Radowitz were Catholics. After the Cologne church conflict of 1837, which polarized Protestants and Catholics in Prussia, the Catholic members of the group became disenchanted with the newspaper's increasingly orthodox Lutheran course. In fact, between 1837 and 1841, when it ceased publication, state support had become necessary to keep the newspaper afloat financially. After the final disintegration of the *Wochenblatt* circle in 1841, Josef Maria von Radowitz gradually emerged as a social thinker in his own right.[36] Countless apho-

---

36. See W. Windelbrand, "Josef Maria von Radowitz," in W. Andreas and W. von Scholz, *Die Grossen Deutschen*, 5 vols. (Berlin, 1936) vol. 3, pp. 357–59; F. Meinecke, *Josef Maria von Radowitz. Ausgewählte Schriften und Reden* (Munich, 1921), pp. vii–xix; and Radowitz's own autobiography in P. Hassel,

risms, epigrams, and short sketches on the growing importance of the fourth estate testified to his interest in the problem
of pauperism. In particular, a discussion of social issues occupied a prominent position in his widely read *Gespräche aus der
Gegenwart über Kirche und Staat* (Contemporary Conversations
on Church and State).[37] In the *Gespräche*, Radowitz contrasted
the political ideologies of the time in the form of a dialogue,
similar to Plato's dialogues, and in doing so he displayed
extraordinary intuition and a great deal of sympathetic understanding for his political opponents.[38] Even though Radowitz
realized that a revival of the *Ständestaat* so ardently propagated by the *Wochenblatt* had "lost its foundation in public opinion,"[39] like many other conservatives of his time he was firmly
convinced that "the consciousness of the masses" would
remain "monarchical conservative."[40] Nevertheless, the era of
absolute monarchy, vociferously rejected by Radowitz despite
his close personal friendship with Frederick William IV, had
also come to an end, and the hated rule of bureaucracy was
bound to vanish with it.[41] Radowitz agreed with his former

Josef Maria von Radowitz (Berlin, 1905). On Radowitz's conservatism in general,
see also P. Kondylis, *Konservatismus. Geschichtlicher Gehalt und Untergang*
(Stuttgart, 1986); James Sheehan, *German History, 1770–1866* (Oxford, 1989),
pp. 710–715, discusses Radowitz's foreign policy.

37. See especially his "Fragmente (1826–1853)" in J.M. von Radowitz,
Gesammelte Schriften, 5 vols. (Berlin, 1851–1853), vols. 4 and 5; and idem,
Gespräche aus der Gegenwart über Kirche und Staat. The *Gespräche* quickly ran
through several editions: the first appeared in April 1846, with subsequent
editions in October 1846, February 1847, and March 1851. See also idem, *Neue
Gespräche aus der Gegenwart über Kirche und Staat*, 2 vols. (Stuttgart, 1851).
Upon the publication of the first edition of the *Gespräche*, the *Augsburger Allgemeine Zeitung*, generally considered the leading newspaper in pre-March Germany, called the book "the most important literary event during the last
decade" (*AAZ*, 16 August 1846, no. 228). Unless indicated otherwise, references refer to the fourth edition published in W. Corvinius, *Radowitz' ausgewählte Werke*, 3 vols. (Regensburg, 1911), vol. 1.

38. The reader is confronted with characters that resemble ideal-types of the
political life of the 1840s. There is an industrial entrepreneur (Crusius), acting
as spokesman for liberalism and constitutional monarchy; a conservative aristocrat (Arneburg), whose younger brother personifies a left-Hegelian radical
(Detlev); a high-ranking official (*Ministerialrat* Oeder); and finally Radowitz
himself, in the guise of a humane nobleman (von Waldheim).

39. Radowitz, *Gesammelte Schriften*, vol. 4, p. 248.

40. Ibid., p. 249. This conviction of the innately conservative character of the
lower classes was shared by Carl Rodbertus and Hermann Wagener; it constituted a prerequisite for the successful establishment of a "social kingdom,"
and later became the basis of Wagener's demand for universal suffrage.

41. Ibid., vol. 4, pp. 246–49.

comrades-in-arms of the *Wochenblatt* that property automatically entailed commitment and responsibility, a conviction to which Ludwig von Gerlach adhered all his life.[42] For Radowitz, as for Gerlach, it was not the private component of property that was sacrosanct, but the public one, because of the obligations attached to it. Radowitz thus strongly opposed "the heathen unrestrictedness of property." Instead, he insisted, all possessions were "borrowed," and the landowner was only the steward of his property.[43] Radowitz and Gerlach both repudiated the liberal conception of the "free disposability" of property.[44] According to Radowitz, the great danger of modern times lay in the discrepancy between political equality and social inequality. The modern proletarian was legally equal and independent, Radowitz believed, but he was socially "exposed" – deprived of shelter and protection due to the destruction of corporations and the resulting atomization of society.[45] Radowitz deplored the fact that individual property to which neither obligation nor service was attached had outstripped property held by corporations to which social duties had once adhered.[46] In his eyes, this was a fateful development. Yet, in contrast to the *Wochenblatt* circle, Radowitz realized that it was futile to attempt to turn back the clock. Instead he advocated the reorganization of property with the help of the state.[47]

42. As Gerlach put it in an 1849 speech: "If property is not linked to an office, it becomes untenable. If you convince me that property does not entail an official duty vis-à-vis the state, nor the obligation towards voluntary service to consume oneself in sacrifice [*zur Aufopferung*], you will make a communist out of me." See H.-J. Schoeps, *Das andere Preußen*, 5th ed. (Berlin, 1981), p. 38.

43. Radowitz, *Gespräche aus der Gegenwart über Kirche und Staat*, p. 390. The higher the rank, the greater was to be the obligation.

44. Gerlach proved to be even more adamant in his denunciation. During the Revolution, in a speech before the *Junkerparlament* (on 18 August 1848), he proclaimed that "property is but a political concept, an office established by God, in order to keep God's law for the state alive; it is only in connection with the obligations engraved on it that property is sacrosanct; merely as a means to enjoyment, property is not sacred, but squalid. In respect to property without obligation, communism is right." See L. von Gerlach, *Aufzeichnungen aus seinem Leben und Wirken* (Schwerin, 1903), p. 541.

45. Radowitz, *Gesammelte Schriften*, vol 4, p. 225.

46. Radowitz, *Gespräche*, pp. 369–70.

47. Radowitz, *Gesammelte Schriften*, vol. 4, pp. 242–45. In his writings, Radowitz used the terms *Staat*, *Regierung*, and *Fürsten* virtually synonymously. Radowitz's favorable predisposition toward the state seemed a contradiction in terms given his strong rejection of the hated rule of officials, since even in his conception of the state, the bureaucracy still remained powerful.

During the 1840s, pauperism assumed ever more menacing proportions in Germany, and Radowitz, being intimately familiar with social developments and socialist thinkers in France, quickly came to regard the social question as pivotal for the survival of the society he knew. The immense problems of pauperism and the relationship between capital and labor would have to be tackled soon, he wrote at one point, while the government still possessed its full authority. "With the proletariat, a fourth estate has arisen," he warned; "how many comparisons does this invite with the history of the rise of the third estate!"[48] To avoid future social and political conflagrations, Radowitz urged his contemporaries, it would be necessary "to drain and cultivate the morass of the proletariat from which deadly fumes ascend."[49] According to Radowitz, this formidable task was to be shouldered by the state – a belief that marked a radical break with the *Wochenblatt* tradition. Radowitz felt driven to the realization that "the state will have to face up to its social mission or else it will be toppled by it."[50]

It was the social upheavals of the 1840s that lay at the root of this sea change in conservative thought: the Silesian weavers' revolt of 1844 and the "hunger revolts" of 1847/48, which forced contemporaries to realize the necessity of preventive state measures for fear that pauperism might assume politically dangerous proportions.[51] By the late 1840s, the social question had acquired such dimensions that few who seriously analyzed the problem believed it could be mastered without state intervention. Carl Rodbertus and Lorenz von Stein preached state help,[52] and even the Prussian bureaucracy, which throughout the *Vormärz* had been reluctant to commit itself on the issue, acknowledged an obligation toward the poor. August von der Heydt, minister of commerce between 1848 and 1862, conceded in a memorandum of 1849 "that one

48. Ibid., vol. 4, p. 149.
49. Ibid., vol. 4, p. 211.
50. Ibid., vol. 4, p. 265.
51. On the uprisings preceding the 1848 Revolution in Prussia see M. Gailus, *Strasse und Brot* (Göttingen, 1990), pp. 210–350.
52. On Carl Rodbertus see section III; L. von Stein, *Geschichte der sozialen Bewegung in Frankreich von 1789 bis auf unsere Tage*, ed. G. Salomon, 3 vols. (Munich, 1921); L. von Stein, *Schriften zum Sozialismus 1848, 1852, 1854*, ed. E. Pankoke (Darmstadt, 1974); D. Blasius and E. Pankoke, Lorenz von Stein (Darmstadt, 1977); *Lorenz von Stein. Gesellschaft-Staat-Recht*, ed. E. Forsthoff (Frankfurt and Berlin, 1972).

of the foremost responsibilities of each government was to bring relief to the misery of the people."[53] The right-Hegelian Heinrich Bernhard Oppenheim argued similarly that it was the duty of the state to elevate the social and educational level of the pauperized masses, lest they threaten its very existence.[54] It was thus high time, Radowitz urged in the early 1850s, that the state embarked upon "the solution of the social question," for otherwise the issue of pauperism would be forced upon the authorities later when they might be "powerless and haplessly confronted with anarchy."[55]

If the state, in Radowitz's conception, still retained its authoritarian and patriarchal character, how was it to harness the proletariat? Even before Lorenz von Stein had popularized the notion, Radowitz promoted the idea of a "kingdom of social reform" as the ideal and most feasible solution. Based on the concept of a monarch actively supported by the lower classes, this program postulated that the lower orders of society were fundamentally royalist in outlook. In Radowitz's *Gespräche*, the Pietist Junker Arneburg praised the potential usefulness of the lower classes as "an unexpected ally against the usurpation of the middle classes."[56] It was Arneburg's hope that the lower classes could be used as a counterrevolutionary force against a liberal bourgeois uprising. Bismarck was later driven by similar expectations when he introduced universal male suffrage in the hope of mobilizing what he imagined to be the royalist and conservative lower classes that would buttress the monarchy. Radowitz proposed to make use of "hired rabble as militia against the revolution" as early as 1831, recommending that military commanders enlist "the most notorious scoundrels and gallow birds" to quell revolutionary uprisings.[57] By the late 1840s, Radowitz had become

---

53. "Votum des Ministers für Handel, Gewerbe, und öffentliche Arbeiten," 7 July 1849, GStA Merseburg, Rep. 120 BB, VII, 1, pp. 84–94.

54. On the political ideas of the Hegelian right see H. Lübbe, *Politische Philosophie in Deutschland* (Munich, 1974), pp. 27–83.

55. Radowitz, *Gesammelte Schriften*, vol. 4, p. 266.

56. Radowitz, *Gespräche*, p. 330.

57. Früh, *Radowitz als Sozialpolitiker*, pp. 24–6. The principle of using the dispossessed against the liberal bourgeoisie surfaced again during the 1848 Revolution, when the chairman of the *Preußenverein*, von Katte, agreed with the commander of the workers' union to lead workers jointly with the military against the liberal *Bürgerwehr*. See E. Jordan, *Die Entstehung der konservativen Partei und die preußischen Agrarverhältnisse* (Munich and Leipzig, 1914), p. 299.

less radical, now proposing to integrate the proletariat into the state by tying it to the monarch through an active social policy. Princes should help the lower classes to help themselves, for it was not the proletariat but the liberal middle classes that posed the gravest and most imminent danger to the survival of the monarchy. Therefore, the government should adopt "the interests of the unpropertied estates as its main objective."[58]

Radowitz was convinced that "the next revolution will be not a political, but a social one." The war-cry of this revolution, he added, "will not be some hollow political theory, but hunger versus gluttony, simplicity versus luxury, the rights of man versus the rights of the citizen."[59] Throughout Radowitz's writings, and most notably in the *Gespräche*, one is astounded to find a great deal of sympathetic understanding both for the plight of the lower classes and for the views of political opponents. In the *Gespräche*, the left-Hegelian Detlev is depicted as an ally on the social question. Here, *les extrêmes se touchent*: Radowitz makes it clear that his conservatism is much closer to the Hegelians' radical idealism than to either liberalism – a purely materialistic position in his eyes – or the ruthlessly modernizing views of the bureaucracy. The spokesman for liberal officialdom, Ministerialrat (Superior Councilor) Oeder, even accuses Waldheim, Radowitz's alter ego, of adopting a socialist point of view.[60] And indeed, in the *Gespräche* there was substantial common ground between the conservative and socialist positions in respect to state intervention (as the indispensable precondition to alleviate pauperism), anti-liberalism, and the advocacy of a social kingdom. In the *Gespräche*, the left-Hegelian Detlev set himself up as the champion of the prince, who was to become the greatest entrepreneur, while the state itself would make its debut "as manufacturer, as industrialist."[61] When recommending that the people should turn to the absolute rulers for help, Detlev anticipates a Lassallean position. In fact, the understanding between Waldheim and Detlev foreshadowed the attempted but stillborn collabo-

58. Radowitz, *Gespräche*, p. 271. In the *Gespräche*, princes were strongly encouraged to turn to the masses: "There, among the lowliest and most numerous class of the population, are their [the princes'] most natural allies." Ibid., p. 270.

59. Radowitz, *Gespräche*, p. 137. This is put forth by the left Hegelian.

60. Ibid., pp. 391–92.

61. Ibid., p. 139.

ration between Bismarck and Lassalle. In Radowitz's treatise of the 1840s, as in Prussian politics of the 1860s, state socialism and anti-liberalism figured as the strongest common denominators.

The main dividing line "in politics as in all other things" lay for Radowitz in the "principal antagonism between idealists and materialists."[62] It was the "moral value" of left Hegelianism that made him feel more affinity for the philosophy of the radical Left; for there could be no common cause with "materialists" in politics. Thus, the conservative and the left Hegelian both promoted the idea that it was the purpose of the state to realize higher principles, "an eternal idea,"[63] rather than to encourage mere material well-being, as liberals advocated. With Radowitz, this anti-liberalism not only had an ideological foundation but was rooted in fear of the rising economic power of the bourgeoisie and its mounting political demands for a constitution. Anti-liberalism was the common denominator shared by all pre-March conservatives. It was naturally exacerbated by the political demands of liberals during the Revolution of 1848 and the constitutional crisis of the 1860s. Radowitz's anti-liberalism is causally connected with reprehension for the modern economic order. Like the *Wochenblatt* before him, he blamed industrial capitalism for social misery: "The great merchant, the factory owner, the speculating entrepreneur – they engulf hundreds of self-supporting social elements."[64] His anti-liberalism turned into anti-industrialism when he denounced the "idolatry of industry,"[65] and

62. Radowitz, *Gesammelte Schriften*, vol. 4, p. 81, in an aphorism entitled "Idealismus – Materialismus in der Politik." This antagonism between idealists and materialists in politics would later become a recurring theme in German political and intellectual life. It was the idealistic element that was mostly associated with "the German character," while the materialistic one was equated with the "civilization of the West," deemed to be infinitely more shallow. This dichotomy became a leitmotif with Ferdinand Tönnies, Oswald Spengler, and in the World War I writings of Thomas Mann, Ernst Troeltsch, and Friedrich Meinecke.

63. Ibid., p. 82.

64. Radowitz, *Gespräche*, p. 141.

65. Ibid., p. 343. Previously, in 1842, he had written in a similar vein that industry was "idolized" and "treated like the most important affairs of state in industrial exhibitions, while people seeking nothing but their own advantage by every means possible are fawned upon by kings down to their lowliest servants and showered with decorations and honors." Radowitz, *Gesammelte Schriften*, vol. 4, p. 113.

Radowitz also bemoaned the disintegration of the town guilds, lamenting the fact that the proper understanding of "working and serving" had been lost.[66]

Radowitz never outgrew his wistful longing for the past. This he shared with his former friends connected with the *Wochenblatt*, together with a strong suspicion of absolute monarchy and of an omnipotent civil service. Otherwise, the two outlooks diverged sharply. For the members of the *Wochenblatt* circle, the social question was one among many problems, but for Radowitz it was the decisive issue of the age. His detailed knowledge of England and France, where industrial capitalism was more fully developed than in Prussia, made him fear for the very survival of the Prussian monarchy. To buttress the monarchy's waning power in the face of the rising bourgeosie, he advocated a kind of state socialism under royal tutelage, a "social kingdom" that would provide mass support for the throne and benefit all ranks of society.

III

Viktor Aimé Huber was an oddity among Prussian conservatives. Anti-modernism was alien to him. Not sharing most conservatives' hostility toward industry and progress, he never advocated the restoration of guilds or looked back longingly to the Middle Ages. This outlook was undoubtedly rooted in his family origins. Like Radowitz, Huber was a newcomer to the world of Prussian Junkers, being born in Stuttgart in 1800 to parents who had achieved considerable literary notoriety. His father was a friend of Schiller's, while his mother had been married to the famous Jacobin, Georg Forster of Mainz.[67] A convinced liberal in his early years, Huber traveled widely in the 1820s, notably to England, France, and Spain, where he fought against the Carlists. During the 1830s, he gradually

66. Ibid., p. 5.
67. I. Paulsen, *Viktor Aimé Huber als Sozialpolitiker*, 2nd ed. (Berlin, 1956); W. Shanahan, *German Protestants Face the Social Question*, vol. 1 (Notre Dame, Ind., 1954); Goetting, *Die sozialpolitische Idee*, pp. 50–64; R. Elvers, *Viktor Aimé Huber. Sein Werken und Wirken*, 2 vols. (Bremen, 1874); and S. Hindelang, *Konservatismus und soziale Frage: Victor Aimé Hubers Beitrag zum sozialkonservativen Denken im 19. Jahrhundert* (Frankfurt a.M., 1983). On his life in general, see the article by his student R. Elvers in the *Allgemeine Deutsche Biographie* (Leipzig, 1881), vol. 13, pp. 249–58; and the brief sketch by H.-J. Schoeps in the *Neue deutsche Biographie* (Berlin, 1972), vol. 9, pp. 688–89.

abandoned his liberal creed and settled down as Professor of History and Occidental Languages in Marburg. There he attracted the attention of the Prussian court with a tract on the feasibility of a conservative party in Germany, directed against the left Hegelians and their *Hallesche Jahrbücher*.[68] Huber believed that a conservative party should not merely consist of an elite but should constitute a broadly based movement of the people. In his eyes, "the conservative point of view" and "the popular one"[69] were virtually identical. Conservatism was the "opposite of torpor and stagnation,"[70] Huber proclaimed, hailing the Prussian monarchy as "a spiritual center for all sane elements of German folk life."[71]

Huber's writings were studied with great interest in the Prussian capital. After the demise of the *Berliner Politisches Wochenblatt*, the Prussian government was searching for a journalistic counterweight to the Hegelians' *Hallesche Jahrbücher*, and Huber seemed to be the man "to foster the good cause of law and truth in the literary field."[72] In the autumn of 1843, Huber was appointed to a newly established chair at the University of Berlin. His principal task, however, was to edit a new conservative journal, *Janus*, whose title symbolized the unity between past and present.[73] Because few other conservatives contributed articles to *Janus*, Huber had ample opportunity to develop and publicize his social ideas in its pages. Pauperism to him was inherently a moral problem, one of *Bildung* and a style of life.[74] It was vitally important, Huber believed,

---

68. V.A. Huber, *Über die Elemente, die Möglichkeit oder Nothwendigkeit einer konservativen Partei in Deutschland* (Marburg, 1841).

69. Huber, *Elemente*, p. 44.

70. Huber, *Elemente*, p. 12.

71. V.A. Huber, *Die Opposition. Ein Nachtrag zu der Konservativen Partei* (Halle, 1842), p. 11.

72. Früh, *Radowitz*, p. 37. Ranke and Dahlmann had been the first choices to edit a conservative journal, but negotiations between them and the Prussian government proved fruitless. See M. Lenz, *Geschichte der königlichen Friedrich Wilhelms Universität Berlin*, 4 vols. (Berlin, 1910–18), vol. 2, pp. 60–68.

73. The journal was published between January 1845 and March 1848. From its inception, it was a commercial failure: only 62 copies were sold during the first six months of its publication, while in 1846, the year of its greatest success, a mere 174 copies (of a total circulation of 750) reached their intended destination. See Elvers, *Huber*, vol. 2, pp. 188–190; Paulsen, *Huber*, p. 51.

74. See V.A. Huber, "Manchester. Das Proletariat," in *Janus* 1 (1845): 641–78, 705–27.

to preserve "the autonomy of family life"[75] and to safeguard "a Christian family life within the proletariat."[76] At the core of the social problem lay atomization, the absence of a supporting social fabric for the individual, and the failure to achieve the individual's integration into a larger whole – familiar themes sounded by many other conservatives. In contrast to his conservative comrades, however, Huber believed that only within "associations . . . of proletarian individuals and families"[77] could man be rescued from his existence "in atomistic masses."[78]

To contemporaries in the 1840s, this central concept of "association" was reminiscent of Charles Fourier and other early French socialists. After the 1848 Revolution it would be popularized by the liberals around Hermann Schulze-Delitzsch and consequently rejected by conservatives. Yet there is no mistaking Huber for a liberal. His moralizing approach marked the dividing line between the liberals' ideal of "help through self-help" and his own concept of association. For the liberals, association was a means to an end. For Huber it was an end in itself, for it was interlaced with the idea of the Christian state and thus bound to strengthen the moral foundations of society. The federation of workers envisioned by Huber would maintain the conservative status quo and facilitate the integration of proletarians into state and society. "Redeeming" them from mass existence meant blunting the cutting edge of their political movement and reducing the social threat they posed.

Huber's model of an association was based on his experience in England where, in 1844, he spent several months in Manchester, studying the actual living conditions of the proletariat. His observations were published the same year as Friedrich Engels's *The Conditions of the Working Class in England*, but the two studies offered radically different conclusions. Although seemingly shaken by the misery around him, Huber reached the astonishing conclusion that the plight of

---

75. V.A. Huber, "Auch ein Wort über den Schwanenorden und dessen mögliche Bedeutung," in *Evangelische Kirchenzeitung*, 7 February 1844, p. 87.

76. V.A. Huber, "Über innere Colonisation," *Janus* 2 (1846): 204.

77. Ibid., p. 205.

78 Ibid., p. 215.

workers could be eased "with more thrifty habits."[79] In the final analysis, Huber believed, misery was the workers' own fault: they were "too dull-witted or too careless, too thoughtless, too disheartened."[80] Huber noted with relief that, for the present, "these starving millions" had not yet found the means "to endanger the existing status quo and the people favored by it."[81] Material improvements he deemed secondary. What truly counted were "improvements in the domain of moral and religious life."[82] The organization of the rural proletariat in England, whose living conditions Huber depicted as almost idyllic, provided the model for his own associations.[83] In contrast to England, however, the key to their success in Prussia lay above all with the state, which had "the inner vocation" to help, although municipal corporations also had a "natural obligation to become partners."[84] It testifies to the influence of his Prussian environment that Huber believed it would be unwise "to execute great things without the state."[85] In contrast to Radowitz, he conceded that he would prefer to act without the state. But Huber was painfully aware of the impossibility of excluding it, knowing that it would be unrealistic to hope that the regulating hand of the bureaucrat could be circumvented in Prussia. Presumably in order not to be recognized as the outsider he was, Huber accommodated himself to what he perceived as the prevailing conservative mood. He went so far as to consider the establishment of a "Ministry of Poor Relief Affairs," for, in the long run, "no civilized state could exist without . . . a ministry for these things."[86]

Nevertheless, despite all his efforts at assimilation, Huber remained a foreigner in the Prussian capital. His continuing inability to formulate his ideas clearly and succinctly exacer-

79. V.A. Huber, "Manchester. Das Proletariat," in *Janus* 1 (1845): 641–78, 705–27, esp. p. 676.
80. Ibid., p. 676.
81. Ibid., p. 652.
82. Ibid., p. 678.
83. See Huber, "Über innere Kolonisation," in *Janus* 2 (1846): 193–255. To avoid being associated with "Fourier's Phalanstères, Owen's Social Colonies or Cabet's Ikaries" (197), Huber made it clear that he was concerned above all with improvements in moral and religious life, while "the acquisition of so-called political rights and liberties for the proletarians" (199) was no matter of urgency.
84. Ibid., p. 229.
85. Ibid., p. 251.
86. Ibid., pp. 251–52.

bated a predilection for impenetrable prose, rendering him a failure as journalist, academic lecturer, and popularizer of conservative ideas alike. The lukewarm reception his ideas found with other conservatives was a cause for personal dismay.[87] After the revolution, the situation did not improve. On the contrary, the gulf widened between those associated with the *Kreuzzeitung*, who supported corporatist solutions to the social question, and those – with the exception of Huber, mostly liberals – who supported the idea of association. The conservatives of the *Kreuzzeitung* recognized "authority ordained by God"[88] as the central principle of artisan corporations, whose inherently hierarchical structure they also wanted to see transferred to industrial establishments. Because this concept was absent from Huber's thought, other conservatives viewed his associations as "a revolutionary order that artificially masses former guildsmen, now deteriorated into factory workers, into groups for the purpose of political agitation."[89]

While Huber put his trust in the state with considerable reluctance, Carl Rodbertus preached state intervention as the sole panacea. Rodbertus, born in 1805 in the old university town of Greifswald on the Baltic, began his professional life as an official in the judicial branch of the bureaucracy after completing his studies in jurisprudence. He later returned to university to study history and economics at Heidelberg, and finally settled down as a gentleman farmer in 1835 at Jagetzow, a manor he had bought in Pomerania. Except for a brief foray into politics – during the 1848 Revolution he served as minister of culture for two months – he is chiefly remembered for his theoretical contributions to the social question, in particular for his advocacy of state socialism. Rodbertus's writings were mainly concerned with the preservation of culture in an age of mass pauperism and the pivotal role of the state in solving social problems.[90] The essence of Rodbertus's social

87. Elvers, *Huber,* vol. 2, pp. 109–10. He complained publicly that other conservatives had shown "neither understanding nor approval ... nor even serious consideration or critical examination" for his ideas. See *Janus* 1 (1847): 290–91.

88. K.V. von Herberger, *Die Stellung der preußischen Konservativen zur Sozialen Frage* (Berlin, 1914), p. 40.

89. *Staats- und Gesellschaftslexikon,* ed. H. Wagener, 23 vols. (Berlin, 1859–67), vol. 8, p. 323.

90. On Rodbertus see E.-H. Jansen, "Das Proletariat im Vormärz in den Anschauungen deutscher Denker" (Ph.D. diss., University of Kiel, 1929), pp.

ideas is encapsulated in his early essay "Die Forderungen der arbeitenden Klassen."[91] According to Rodbertus's own testimony, this article contained "the entire system that I developed piece by piece in my writings on political economy,"[92] while his disciple Adolph Wagner held that "during his entire future life, Rodbertus went beyond his early achievement only in details."[93]

The essay opened by addressing the ultimate goals of the working classes and asking whether the fulfillment of their demands would bring about "the ruination of modern culture?"[94] Rodbertus argued that their real goal was not "political power" but "more property," which was ultimately a cry "for more participation in the blessings of modern culture."[95] The onslaught of the lower classes against the established order had to be taken seriously, Rodbertus insisted, because it was an illusion to assume that the state could be defended against them "with such purely negative means as bayonets." The cohesion of society had to come from within, for it was held together by "moral institutions."[96] These had failed. The

48–59; M. Wirth, *Bismarck, Wagner, Rodbertus* (Berlin, 1883); as well as Wirth's long article on Rodbertus in the *Allgemeine Deutsche Biographie* (Leipzig, 1889), vol. 28, pp. 740–63; H. Dietzel, *Karl Rodbertus* (Berlin, 1886); Herberger, *Die Stellung der preußischen Konservativen zur sozialen Frage.* Though contemporary conservatives regarded Rodbertus as one of their own, more recently he has mainly been viewed as the precursor of state socialism in Germany. For the *Brockhaus* (Wiesbaden, 1973), vol. 16, p. 30, he is the "founder of scientific socialism in Germany, notably of state-socialism." T. Nipperdey, *Deutsche Geschichte 1800–1866*, p. 520, decribes him as belonging "to the intellectual history of socialism," even though he was an "advocate of state-socialist measures and skeptical toward a proletarian revolution"; while to H.U. Wehler, *Deutsche Gesellschaftsgeschichte 1815–1845–49*, 2 vols. (Munich, 1987), vol. 2, pp. 265–66, Rodbertus clearly belongs to the conservative camp.

91. This article on "The Demands of the Working Classes" was written in 1839 and then sent to the *Augsburger Allgemeine Zeitung*, which, however, refused to publish it. It was not until 1872 that an abbreviated version of the essay was printed in the *Berliner Revue*. The article was reprinted, again in a shortened version, in *Briefe und sozialpolitische Aufsätze von Dr. Rodbertus-Jagetzow*, ed. R. Meyer (Berlin, 1895), pp. 575–86, before it was completely reproduced in *Schriften von Dr. Carl Rodbertus-Jagetzow*, ed. A. Wagner, 4 vols. (Berlin, 1899), vol. 3, pp. 195–223.

92. From the preface by A. Skalweit in *C. Rodbertus, Die Forderungen der arbeitenden Klassen* (Frankfurt a. M., 1946), p. 3.

93. *Schriften von Rodbertus-Jagetzow*, vol. 3, p. 193.

94. Ibid., vol. 3, pp. 195–223, esp. 195. Unless indicated otherwise, the following references refer to this article.

95. Ibid., pp. 196–97.

96. Ibid., pp. 200–01.

laboring classes had emancipated themselves from the old "system of discipline" (*Zucht*) without having yet internalized the new "system of education" (*Bildung*) that characterized modern times. Unable to extricate itself from its "culturally hostile tendencies," liberalism had failed abysmally, Rodbertus argued, since it laid the foundations for "the despotism of profit-yielding property" and thereby confined the worker "to standards of minimum subsistance."[97] The liberal system therefore had to be replaced by a state-directed economy, which alone could guarantee the necessary increase in the workers' affluence by implementing "a legally binding assessment of value for all goods that has to be based on labor."[98] Only through a rigid system of state regulation could the social question, which Rodbertus considered "the vital question of modern civilization," be solved. And it was the state's task to assert guardianship over the laboring classes.[99] As productivity rose, the state would ensure that the workers' share in the national product rose correspondingly.

In contrast to the conservatives around the *Wochenblatt*, Rodbertus welcomed the accomplishments of industrial progress, sharply opposed the restoration of guilds, and disavowed any romantic tendencies. He was convinced that "whoever turns to the past to remedy the social question will never contribute to its solution."[100] Rodbertus praised the achievements of modernity and asserted that nothing "could change the world more beneficially than the discovery of machines."[101] Yet, his endorsement of the machine age did not imply acceptance of the political and economic order that accompanied it. Anti-liberalism was a trait he shared with other conservatives. Like the *Wochenblatt* and Radowitz, Rodbertus blamed the "merely

97. Ibid., p. 213.
98. Ibid., p. 222. For Rodbertus this was tantamount to solving the social question, which essentially consisted of "the question of the proportionate share of the working classes in the entire national productive output." See *Schriften von Rodbertus-Jagetzow*, vol. 3, p. xxiv. In addition, Rodbertus called on the state to create paper money based on this value assessment to pay the workers, and to establish storehouses where they could exchange their money for food.
99. Ibid., pp. 217–19. State action was also imperative "to rescue modern culture from the venomous breath of the materialistic system."
100. Dietzel, *Karl Rodbertus*, vol. 1, pp. 20–21.
101. "Forderungen," p. 215. "In days to come machines might be able to take the place of the slaves of antiquity, and all the rest of society represent the free men."

negative character" of liberalism for the misery of the lower classes. According to Rodbertus, only a strong and authoritarian state that was concerned about the welfare of the lower classes could rescue the workers from their plight.

IV

This concept of an authoritarian welfare state was further elaborated by Hermann Wagener. Wagener was a prolific but not an original writer, acquiring most of his ideas from other conservatives such as Stein, Rodbertus, and, despite personal resentments, also from Radowitz.[102] Born in 1815 into a Protestant parsonage, Wagener pursued the study of jurisprudence in Berlin in the 1830s and then became a junior official (*Referendar*) at the higher regional court in Frankfurt an der Oder. There, Ludwig von Gerlach, who was the court's vice-president, became his friend and mentor.[103] Publicly inconspicuous until the 1848 Revolution, Wagener quickly gained notoriety as editor-in-chief of the newly founded conservative *Kreuzzeitung* and later established his reputation as one of the conservative party's best-informed and acerbic speakers in both the Prussian parliament and North German Diet.

As journalist and politician, Wagener's trenchant pen and slashing tongue alienated political adversaries and comrades alike.[104] His confrontational style introduced a new element into conservative politics in Prussia, foreshadowing the rhetoric of the radical conservative movements in late nineteenth-century Austria and France as described by Carl Schorske and Zeev Sternhell.[105] Another salient feature of

102. On Wagener see H.-J. Schoeps, "Hermann Wagener," pp. 193–217; a revised version of the essay appeared in H.-J. Schoeps, *Das andere Preußen. Konservative Gestalten und Probleme im Zeitalter Friedrich Wilhelm IV.*, 5th ed. (Berlin, 1981), pp. 203–28; H.-J. Schoeps, *Deutsche Geistesgeschichte*, 5 vols. (Frankfurt, 1980), vol. 4, pp. 379–411; Saile, *Hermann Wagener*; A. Hahn, Die Berliner Revue (Berlin, 1934); O. Stillich, *Die politischen Parteien in Deutschland*, 2 vols. (Leipzig, 1908), vol. 1, pp. 105–25; and, for occasional references to Wagener's ideas, Kondylis, *Konservatismus*.

103. L. von Gerlach, *Aufzeichnungen aus seinem Leben und Wirken* (Schwerin, 1903), p. 298.

104. E. Nolte, "Konservatismus und Nationalsozialismus," in *Konservatismus*, ed. H.-G. Schumann (Königstein, 1974), pp. 244–61, esp. 251.

105. Z. Sternhell, *La Droite Révolutionaire* (Paris, 1978); C. Schorske, *Fin-de-Siècle Vienna: Politics and Culture* (New York, 1980). *Cum grano salis* one could see in Wagener a German Maurice Barrès, without the violent nationalism, of course, which would have been quite impossible for a Prussian conservative of the 1850s.

Wagener's conservatism was his openness toward the Left, specifically, his readiness to collaborate with socialism to reach his ends. In editing the multi-volume *Staats- und Gesellschafts-lexikon*, a conservative encyclopedia intended to counterbalance existing liberal competitors in the field, his closest associate was the former head of Berlin's left Hegelians, Bruno Bauer. A close friend of Karl Marx in the early 1840s, Bauer later became notorious through his rabid anti-Semitism, with which he infested the *Berliner Revue*, another literary undertaking in which Wagener collaborated with him. Though a conservative journal, the *Berliner Revue* under Wagener's control adopted several socialist demands such as profit-sharing by workers.[106] According to Wagener, socialism constituted a "very vigorous system, encompassing all facets of the human life and species."[107] To counter socialism effectively, it would have to be properly understood, Wagener argued, because the *Arbeiterfrage* could never be solved by men uniformly hostile toward it.[108] Even though the socialists of his own time still acted as "political partisans and collaborators of liberalism and democracy,"[109] Wagener was convinced that once the democratization of state and society had been achieved, the lower classes would turn against liberalism and could then be used as an instrument to stem its political ascendancy.

In this context, Wagener's relationship with the labor leader Ferdinand Lassalle is revealing. In his memoirs, Wagener lavished high praise on Lassalle: his concern for workers "had been salutary," because "what mattered most to him was to get the workers away from the deceptions of the bourgeoisie."[110] In parliament the conservative deputy Wagener referred to Lassalle as an "ingenious, creative man," who had perpetuated old Prussian virtues.[111] The main point of convergence was their mutual propagation of a "social kingdom," a

106. Nolte, "Konservatismus," pp. 251–52.

107. H. Wagener, *Die Lösung der sozialen Frage* (Bielefeld and Leipzig, 1878), p. 19.

108. Wagener pointed this out in a handwritten memorandum to Bismarck, dated 18 April 1863, in the Bismarckarchiv Friedrichsruh; reprinted in Saile, *Hermann Wagener*, pp. 138–44, esp. 142.

109. Wagener, *Lösung*, p. 33.

110. H. Wagener, *Erlebtes. Meine Memoiren*, 2 vols. (Berlin, 1884), vol. 2, p. 39. Wagener also praised Lassalle's "high regard for the state, the misuse of which as a mere caretaker Lassalle opposed energetically" (ibid.).

111. Schoeps, *Deutsche Geistesgeschichte*, vol. 4, p. 404.

concept Lassalle advanced from the Left and Wagener from the Right. In June 1863, Lassalle wrote to Bismarck that he believed "the working class instinctively gravitates toward dictatorship, provided it can be rightfully convinced that this dictatorship is exerted in its own interest." Lassalle continued: "The working class . . . will be prepared, despite its republican convictions, . . . to accept the crown as the natural champion of a social dictatorship."[112] At around the same time, the socialist Wilhelm Liebknecht expressed concern to Marx that Lassalle had made it clear that to fight the bourgeoisie effectively he would "not even shrink back from an alliance with the kingdom."[113]

Wagener was even more emphatic in his promotion of the social vocation of the monarchy. "The European monarchies have a future only if they turn into social monarchies," he asserted in a memorandum to Bismarck.[114] Wagener emphasized to Bismarck that it should be of major concern to conservatives "to acquire and secure the sympathies of the great mass of the population by actively standing up for their material and moral interests."[115] The foremost political task of the future was to break the opposition of the bourgeoisie. This could be accomplished "by satisfying the legitimate material demands" of the petty bourgeoisie on the one hand [Bismarck's marginal note: "which ones?"] and, on the other, by creating a political counterweight in the "small artisan and working class" [Bismarck's note: "by which means?"] whose "political needs will always gravitate toward monarchical power."[116] To create this

112. *Bismarck und Lassalle. Ihr Briefwechsel und ihre Gespräche*, ed. G. Mayer (Berlin, 1928). In a note to Bismarck of 5 February 1864, Lassalle, referring to liberalism, wrote that he hoped "to smash our common enemy" (ibid., p. 103). This correspondence, drafted in a tone of chummy familiarity, naturally caused considerable misgivings among other socialists. When, months after Lassalle's untimely death in a duel, Marx and Engels learned of the negotiations that their wayward disciple had entertained with the Prussian minister president, Marx charged that Lassalle wanted to model himself into "a Richelieu of the proletariat," while to the more straightforward Engels he was simply "a common scoundrel" (ibid., p. 57).

113. Ibid., p. 53.

114. "Justizrat Wagener: Gedruckte Denkschrift von 1. März 1864," 1 March 1864, GStA Merseburg, NL Zitelmann, Rep. 92, no. 91, pp. 1–10, esp. 1. Wagener quoted this sentence with reference to Lorenz von Stein. The memorandum is preserved with Bismarck's marginal notes.

115. Ibid., pp. 9–10.

116. Ibid., p. 2. When Wagener spoke of the "bourgeoisie," he referred only to the haute bourgeoisie, which had amassed enough wealth and education to put forth political demands. When using the term *"Bürgerthum,"* he refers

counterbalance, Wagener believed one should emulate the politics of the absolute princes who had used the burghers to break the resistance of the old estates. The king, Wagener asserted, had the obligation to be "the protector of the weak, the king of beggars, the savior and patron of the popular masses."[117] This policy lay ultimately in the monarchy's own interest.[118] Wagener vociferously demanded universal suffrage and the abolition of Prussia's three-class voting system as necessary "correlatives to the heavy toll of lives [*Blutzoll*]" of compulsory military service.[119] In his memoirs, he insisted that with the introduction of universal suffrage the state had assumed an obligation to implement social reforms because, once unleashed, the proletariat could no longer "be dominated by police-state methods."[120] Wagener also recommended that the state take over private enterprises. At the root of this suggestion lay his belief that property holders should not freely dispose of their possessions but that, on the contrary, ownership entailed an inherent obligation.[121] In turning the "dispossessed into possessors"[122] or, as he put it in his memoirs, in elevating the working classes "to the standard of life of the middle classes,"[123] Wagener intended "to liberate labor of the wage slavery of capital and eliminate the antagonism between capital and labor."[124]

Statements such as this make it clear that hostility to liberalism provided another potential bond between Wagener and Lassalle. To Lassalle, liberalism was "the sole enemy."[125] Wagener, in turn, was convinced that it was not the masses

---

to the petty bourgeoisie that, in his opinion, was still united in a community of interest with the "kleinen Gewerbe- und dem Arbeiterstande."

117. Wagener, *Lösung*, p. 66.

118. In an 1855 draft for a conservative program, Wagener wrote that "in future all the kingdom will either be an empty shadow or a tyranny or it will degenerate into a republic, if it does not muster the high moral courage to become a kingdom of social reform." See H. Wagener, *Die kleine, aber mächtige Partei* (Berlin, 1885), p. 13.

119. *Neue Preußische Zeitung-Kreuzzeitung*, 2 November 1862; Schoeps, *Das andere Preußen*, p. 212.

120. Wagener, *Erlebtes*, vol. 2, p. 42.

121. Wagener, *Lösung*, p. 127. In this respect, he was very much the disciple of Radowitz and Ludwig von Gerlach.

122. Wagener, *Lösung*, p. 150.

123. Wagener, *Erlebtes*, vol. 2, p. 6.

124. Wagener, *Lösung*, p. 150.

125. Mayer, *Bismarck und Lassalle*, p. 53.

that posed the greatest threat to the monarchy but rather "the oligarchs of finance capital as well as the 'Catilinarian characters' of the intellectuals kept in leading strings by them, together with the affiliated liberal notabilities of bureaucratism."[126] Anti-liberalism also lay at the basis of Wagener's concept of a "social kingdom," wherein the monarch would use the lower classes to fight the liberal bourgeoisie. Wagener's own point of view was thus closer to the socialists than to the liberals, even though it was with the latter that he shared the perquisites of upper-class life. Naturally, Wagener was realistic enough to know that the collaboration of the working class could not be assured without substantial concessions. In a memorandum to Bismarck he therefore recommended "continuous collaboration reflected in co-ownership."[127] It was this realism that forced Wagener to part ways with his old friend and mentor Ludwig von Gerlach, to whom he pointed out that "estates have ceased to exist" and "the hallmark of the age is precisely the disintegration and decomposition of all outdated institutions and organisms."[128] Nevertheless, Wagener – "the socialist of the Prussian royal court" (as August Bebel once derisively referred to him) – remained a conservative at heart. His attempt to help the workers was overshadowed by his deep-seated fear of proletarian uprisings that, after witnessing the Commune uprising in Paris in the spring of 1871, turned into an obsession.

Wagener's lasting importance for German conservatism lies in his role as mediator between *Vormärz* social conservatives, whose thought he had absorbed and popularized, and Bismarck, whose social legislation he influenced decisively. Not being a specialist in social affairs himself, Bismarck often had to rely on his collaborator's advice, even though he was too pragmatic to follow Wagener's instructions precisely. Wagener's numerous memoranda on social issues could not, however, fail to leave a lasting mark: they undoubtedly made Bis-

126. From a memorandum of Wagener to Bismarck of 18 April 1863, in the Bismarckarchiv Friedrichsruh; reprinted in W. Saile, *Hermann Wagener und Bismarck* (Tübingen, 1958), pp. 138–144, 142. This sentence encapsulated several pillars of Wagener's *Weltanschauung*: his anti-liberalism, his anti-intellectualism, i.e., his hatred for the uprooted *Literaten*, in whom he saw his ideological enemies, and his deep distrust toward the civil service, a feature typical of many Prussian conservatives from the *Wochenblatt* circle to Radowitz.

127. Saile, *Hermann Wagener und Bismarck*, p. 137.

128. Schoeps, *Geistesgeschichte*, vol. 4, p. 388.

marck more receptive to the plight of the lower classes and drew his attention to the political advantages a shrewd social policy could offer.

All social conservatives, from the members of the *Wochenblatt* circle to Huber and Rodbertus, preferred to see themselves as politicians rather than merely political theorists. This was because the influences acting upon them were of a practical nature. Gerlach and Radowitz knew the problem of pauperism at first hand, while Huber had gleaned his impressions of working-class life from the slums of Manchester, not from books. Nevertheless, their main contribution to the solution of the social question was to remain a theoretical one. The most important development social conservative thought underwent between 1830 and 1870 was its changing attitudes toward the state and the monarchy. The *frondeur* spirit of the *Wochenblatt* quickly faded under the impact of the growing economic power and the political demands of the *Bürgertum*, culminating first in the 1848 Revolution and then in the constitutional conflict of the 1860s. Fear of growing bourgeois influence soon outweighed any misgivings regarding the absolute power of the crown. The "social kingdom" propagated by Radowitz, Rodbertus, and Wagener had the triple goal of tying the proletariat to the monarchy, keeping the power of the bourgeoisie in check with the help of the lower classes, and fortifying royal authority. The conservatives' concept of a "social kingdom," thus, was not a positive one, as it was designed primarily to stem the growth of liberalism. Anti-liberalism soon became the great common denominator among all conservatives and for some, such as Radowitz and Wagener, the bridge to socialism. All conservatives concurred in their hatred for the "oligarchy of finance" and "profit-yielding capital," which was largely blamed for the misery of the lower classes. Yet, in attacking liberalism, they attacked more than an economic or political concept. To conservatives, liberalism embodied a new, menacing way of life that questioned organic growth and rendered obsolete traditions that had become dear to them. With the exception of Huber and Rodbertus, conservatives feared the unbounded freedoms that came in the wake of industrial development. They feared rapid social change, the concomitant breaking up of community, and the atomization of society. These fears largely explain their anti-modernism.

The social question, moreover, was interpreted principally as a moral problem, even by those, like Huber, who did not share the *Wochenblatt*'s rejection of modernity and progress. Consequently, conservatives' fear that the fabric of society was disintegrating made them search for a new element of *Bindung*, of obligation and commitment. This quest in turn explains the inner gravitation of some conservatives toward socialism, which seemed equally intent on rescuing the individual from solipsistic solitude and was therefore of an inherently higher "moral" value than liberalism. With the socialists, conservatives also shared the notion that a strong state would provide for the poor. Indeed, with their dread of isolation and atomization; their nightmare vision of unstructured, directionless masses; their insistence on community, organic growth, authority, and hierarchy; and their virulent anti-liberalism, social conservatives in Prussia between 1830 and 1870 anticipated many of the themes and anxieties that were to become central to twentieth-century German conservatives – including, not least, the "conservative revolutionaries" of the Weimar Republic.[129]

129. For a brief orientation, see K. Sontheimer, *Antidemokratisches Denken in der Weimarer Republik* (Munich, 1978); A. Mohler, *Die konservative Revolution in Deutschland*, 2nd ed. (Darmstadt, 1972); and K. von Klemperer, *Germany's New Conservatism* (Princeton, N.J., 1957).

3

Victor Aimé Huber and the Emergence of Social Conservatism[*]

Wolfgang Schwentker

I

For social and historical reasons the bonds of sympathy between conservatives and the poor are often very weak. Conservatives are usually uninterested in the problems of the lower stratum of society, and vice versa. But in times of political crisis or massive economic and social change, the relationship between conservatives and the poor can become critically important. In such periods many conservatives begin to view the lower orders or substrata of society (*Unterschichten*) as a threat to the political and social order. Conversely, the poor come to regard conservatives as representatives of the wealthy in society and, thus, as responsible for preventing them from obtaining better living conditions. In Germany, the restoration period and the *Vormärz* (1815–48) were years of such fundamental change. Conservatives were well aware of the magnitude of these changes, but after the experience of revolution in France in 1789 and 1830 they saw them mainly as a threat to their positions of power in politics and society. Most German conservatives reacted to these challenges by developing a conservative or even reactionary ideology. The historians Klaus Epstein and Robert Berdahl have described the development of political conservatism in this pre-revolutionary period,[1]

[*] This essay is based partly on a lecture given at St. Catharine's College, Cambridge, on 5 March 1992. My thanks go to Christopher Clark and the other participants for their stimulating comments.

1. K. Epstein, *The Genesis of German Conservatism*, (Princeton, N.J., 1966); R.M. Berdahl, *The Politics of the Prussian Nobility: The Development of a Conservative Ideology, 1770–1848* (Princeton, N.J., 1988).

rightly focusing on reactionary or paternalist Junkers and on reformist bureaucrats. Certainly only a few conservatives believed that the survival of the political order depended on finding answers to the so-called "social question." Yet of those who embraced the idea of social reform, Victor Aimé Huber emerged as the most important and outstanding thinker.[2]

Although Huber wanted to speak for his fellow conservatives in the Prussian aristocracy, in the end he became the spokesman for the poor and the growing working class. Among the conservatives he remained isolated. Nevertheless, his impact on the development of social thought in mid-nineteenth-century German politics was far-reaching. In his later career Huber became an advisor to the Prussian government, and he established close contact with all the principal social reformers, including those who like Hermann Wagener belonged to the conservative faction, those who like Hermann Schulze-Delitzsch were liberals, and those who like Ferdinand Lassalle espoused socialism. Some of these figures assimilated Huber's social ideas and accepted his counsel, though in the main they did not wish to follow his monarchist aims in politics. Yet what distinguished Victor Aimé Huber from the other conservative social reformers of his time – for example, Johann Hinrich Wichern – was his refusal to conceive the social question in terms of charity. Rather, Huber was a political thinker who put his social ideas and his social reform projects in a political framework in order to defend the traditional social and political order.

This essay begins its analysis of how Huber's social ideas were developed and transmitted by examining the "social question" in its historical context. Huber is then discussed as a conservative thinker who developed his views on the social question under unique circumstances. The third section deals with the conservatives' reaction to the revolution of 1848/49 as a crisis of the social order; here Huber's own perspective

2. For the most recent account of Huber's political and social ideas, see S. Hindelang, *Konservatismus und soziale Frage. Viktor Aimé Hubers Beitrag zum sozialkonservativen Denken im 19. Jahrhundert* (Frankfurt, 1983). Important older studies include I. Paulsen, *Viktor Aimé Huber als Sozialpolitiker*, 2nd ed. (Berlin, 1956), and R. Elvers, *Victor Aimé Huber. Sein Werden und Wirken*, 2 vols. (Bremen, 1872–74). Huber's life and work are summarized in "Huber, Victor Aimé," *Neue Deutsche Biographie*, vol. 9 (Berlin, 1972), pp. 688–89; for an older but even more extensive account, see *Allgemeine Deutsche Biographie*, vol. 13 (Leipzig, 1881), pp. 249–58.

and contributions to the debate are studied. A fourth section provides an overview of Huber's program for workers' cooperatives in the 1850s and 1860s, and a final section compares his views as a representative of social conservatism with the social ideas of his contemporaries and followers.[3]

II

From the 1830s onward, poverty became a mass phenomenon in all German states.[4] This development was especially pronounced in the rapidly growing cities. Before 1800 the proportion of urban dwellers who belonged to the lower orders was typically between 50 and 70 percent; in the following decades, however, that proportion rose to between 60 and 90 percent. For example, in Cologne it stood at 78 percent (1817/49), in Weimar at 68 to 78 percent (1820), in Hamburg at 75 to 80 percent (1817/48), and in the northern German town of Flensburg it even registered 90 percent (1835).[5] In Frankfurt, the proportion of bourgeois city dwellers to poor stood at three to one in 1720; a century later the ratio had been exactly reversed.[6] Despite dramatic economic and social changes, a remarkably strong continuity is evident in the social make-up of the poor, who consisted mainly of handymen, day-laborers, porters, country laborers, domestic servants, craft workers, industrial laborers, cripples, invalids, prostitutes, and tramps. The dominant shared characteristic among these groups was their lack of personal property. Half of those who were homeless, for example, lived below the poverty line. In cases of illness or unemployment, most poor families fell immediately into desperate circumstances. Poor-houses (*Armenanstalten*) were of limited aid because their budgets were always inadequate. Thus hundreds of thousands of people had to live in dirty

3. For a general introduction to the history of German social conservatism, see J.B. Müller, "Der deutsche Sozialkonservatismus," in *Konservatismus*, ed. H.-G. Schumann, 2nd ed. (Königstein, 1984), pp. 199–221.

4. F.D. Marquardt, "Pauperism in Germany During the Vormärz," *Central European History* 2 (1966): 77–88; *Die Eigentumslosen: Der deutsche Pauperismus und die Emanzipationskrise in Darstellungen und Deutungen der zeitgenössischen Literatur*, ed. C. Jantke and D. Hilger (Freiburg i. Br., 1965).

5. H.-U. Wehler, *Deutsche Gesellschaftsgeschichte*, 2 vols. to date (Munich, 1987), vol. 2, *Von der Reformära bis zur industriellen und politischen "Deutschen Doppelrevolution," 1815–1845/49*, p. 279.

6. W. Fischer, "Soziale Unterschichten im Zeitalter der Frühindustrialisierung," *International Review of Social History* 8 (1963): 415–35.

shacks or on the streets, suffering from hunger and threatened by illness, without any hope for a better future. In Cologne nearly 30 percent of the population was registered on the poverty rolls in 1848. Forty percent of Berlin's annual budget was spent on suppporting the poor in 1847, while approximately 75 percent of Berlin's artisans did not have to pay taxes because their income was so low. As early as the 1820s nearly 80 percent of the inhabitants of Hamburg paid no taxes for the same reason.[7]

Contemporaries called these people "paupers" or simply "the poor,"[8] appropriating terms that first appeared in French and English. Through Friedrich Bülau's pamphlet of 1834, "State and Modern Industry: A Contribution to Commercial Policy and Poor Police," as well as through the writings of Robert von Mohl and the philosopher Franz von Baader, the term *"Pauperismus"* was introduced, triggering widespread discussion of social issues.[9] In 1836 a prominent conservative Junker from Prussia, Friedrich Ludwig August von der Marwitz, referred to the poor and paupers in his attempt to identify a new class of society.[10] One year later the liberal Freiburg Professor Buß warned his colleagues in the Baden Landtag about the new social problem, predicting that pauperism would soon become a political and social danger.[11] Then in 1846 the *Brockhaus Conversations-Lexikon* used pauperism as a new term signifying an important and fatal phenomenon that could no longer be described simply as "mass poverty." Pauperism, claimed the *Brockhaus*, did not describe the kind of natural poverty that can befall anyone; rather, it identified a situation when masses of people, although they work hard, cannot afford a basic existence, and when there are no signs of progress or expectations of better living conditions in the future.[12]

7. Wehler, *Deutsche Gesellschaftsgeschichte*, vol. 2, p. 280.

8. See W. Conze, "Proletariat, Pöbel, Pauperismus," in *Geschichtliche Grundbegriffe. Historisches Lexikon zur politisch-sozialen Sprache in Deutschland*, ed. O. Brunner, W. Conze, and R. Koselleck, vol. 5 (Stuttgart, 1984), pp. 27–68.

9. Ibid., p. 39.

10. F.A.L. von der Marwitz, "Von den Ursachen der überhandnehmenden Verbrechen" [1836], in *F.A.L. von der Marwitz, Ein märkischer Edelmann im Zeitalter der Befreiungskriege 1808–1815*, ed. F. Meusel, 3 vols. (Berlin, 1908–13), vol. 2, p. 453.

11. See W. Fischer, *Der Staat und die Anfänge der Industrialisierung in Baden 1800–1850*, vol. 1 (Berlin, 1962), p. 385.

12. "Pauperismus," in *Brockhaus' Conversations-Lexikon der Gegenwart*, vol. 4 (Leipzig, 1840), p. 65.

From the early 1840s onward, the problem of pauperism became a dominant topic in public discussion. Civil servants and parsons, writers and scientists, landowners and journalists all took part in this debate. Most participants believed that pauperism threatened social and political stability and that it could lead, in the worst case, to a revolution by the poor.[13] It was in this atmosphere that a heated controversy arose concerning the principal reasons for this new kind of poverty. Two main positions were taken. Some political observers – such as the young Friedrich Engels in his 1845 study of the condition of the working class in England – regarded pauperism as a necessary consequence of industrialization.[14] Engels and those who followed in the orthodox-Marxist historiographic tradition thought that pauperism meant proletarization: they regarded the development of industrial capitalism as the major reason the masses were kept in inhuman living conditions. But other contemporaries ascribed pauperism mainly to the dissolution of agrarian feudalism from the pre-modern period.[15] Due to rapid increases in population, the feudal agrarian economy seemed no longer able to provide people with enough work or food.

Recent empirical research has found that the problem was much more complex than either of these analyses suggested. Clearly a combination of factors was responsible for the pauperism of the *Vormärz* period. The basic reason for the increasing mass poverty was doubtless the so-called "demographic revolution" that took place in the first half of the nineteenth century.[16] In Prussia, for instance, the population increased by 90 percent between 1815 and 1865, from 10.3 million to 19.5 million. However, the employment market – especially the agrarian economy and the traditional artisan sector – was not able to integrate more people into an obsolete economic system. The traditional cottage industry provided by the putting-out system (*Verlagssystem*) fell into bitter competition with the first industrial factories. In the first decades after 1815, the early success of technological discoveries left thousands

13. Wehler, *Deutsche Gesellschaftsgeschichte*, vol. 2, p. 290.
14. F. Engels, *The Condition of the Working-Class in England in 1844. With a Preface Written in 1892*, trans. F. Kelley (London, 1950).
15. See, for example, S.P. Gans, "Von der Verarmung des Landmanns" [1831], in *Die Eigentumslosen*, ed. Jantke and Hilger, pp. 83–92.
16. Wehler, *Deutsche Gesellschaftsgeschichte*, vol. 2, pp. 10–24.

behind; only a few people chose emigration as an escape from lifelong poverty. Before the revolution things became even worse. The structural crisis produced by an increase of population and by a continuing constriction in the employment market was aggravated by an acute famine in which thousands of people starved to death. The director of Berlin's state statistical office, Friedrich W. Dieterici, estimated that in the dreadful situation in 1847 about 50–60 percent of the Prussian population had fallen into misery.[17] It was only after the revolution, in the mid-1850s, that contemporaries began to realize that industrialization was not the principal threat – indeed, that industrialization could provide people with new jobs and help them escape from a tragic existence.

Germans in the *Vormärz* were of course not only investigating the reasons for pauperism, but also trying to find permanent solutions to the problem. It is difficult to separate the analyses advanced by the different political movements in those years; but we can distinguish between three broad strategies for dealing with the social question.[18] First, a powerful analysis based on the principle of revolution started with Engels' investigation into the English working class; this analysis can be said to have culminated quickly in Marx and Engels' *Communist Manifesto* of 1848, which demanded a fundamental change in the distribution of property. Second, we have the proposals of the bourgeois liberals, who sought a solution to pauperism through improved education, through associational life, and through subsidiary voluntary organizations. They believed in the power of the individual and in free competition in both the economy and society. Liberals such as Friedrich Harkort supported efforts that aimed at strengthening the role of the individual but also promoted the idea of self-help through cooperative associations. The third view – the conservative one – postulated that the dramatic increase in the number of poor in Germany was due to liberalism, the ideology of a free-market economy, and the atomization of society. Embracing a romantic, organic view of historical development, the conservatives sought to solve the social question

17. F.W. von Dieterici, "Erwerbsmangel, Massenverarmung, Massenverderbnis, deren Ursachen und Hilfsmittel," *Zeitschrift des Vereins für deutsche Statistik* 1 (1847): 118–35.
18. T. Nipperdey, *Deutsche Geschichte 1800–1866: Bürgerwelt und starker Staat*, 2nd ed. (Munich, 1984), pp. 244–46.

by urging the Prussian government to give up its course of liberalization and to strengthen the traditional manufacturing and agrarian sectors. Most conservatives – for instance Adam Müller and Heinrich Leo – looked back to the past for their social ideas, and most were also politically reactionary. Only a few looked forward and considered the process of industrialization as something irreversible. Of these, the most prominent was Victor Aimé Huber.

III

Born in the southwestern German town of Stuttgart in 1800, Huber studied medicine and European languages at the universities of Göttingen and Würzburg. Soon he became interested in political issues, abandoned university study, and began his extensive travels within Europe. In the 1820s he joined liberal circles in Paris, where he met Benjamin Constant and Alexander von Humboldt. Then he took up the cause of the liberal opposition in Spain, earning his keep there by writing about his travels. In 1826/27 he became the Paris correspondent for various journals published by Johann Cotta in Stuttgart, and after this relationship ended he travelled again to England and Italy. In 1828 Huber accepted a job as a teacher and settled in the northern town of Bremen, where he converted from Catholicism to Protestantism before he was married. Then in 1833 he was appointed professor for west European languages and modern history at the University of Rostock, and his career as a scholarly writer began, reaching its most productive phase in the 1840s. He published a book on English poetry, and in 1839/40 his major work appeared: a two-volume history of English universities.[19] In 1836 he accepted a position at the University of Marburg, and in 1843 he finally took the chair for the history of European literature in Berlin; this he kept until 1851, when he gave it up for personal and political reasons.

As a young man Huber was at first fascinated by liberal ideas. Soon, however, he came to believe that rationalism, which he regarded as the philosophical foundation of liberalism, would lead to the destruction of both the monarchist state and religious belief. He therefore turned to conservatism,

19. V.A. Huber, *Die englischen Universitäten*, 2 vols. (Kassel, 1839–40).

which became the main source for his social ideas. It was probably the experience of the French Revolution of 1830 and its tremendous impact on German politics that made him more critical of liberalism. In his view, the liberal and democratic movements of the day, gaining strength through the Hambach gathering of 1832 and through the flowering of liberal newspapers and associations (*Vereine*), could lead to social and political instability. Soon he regarded liberalism in the same terms as another conservative thinker of this era, Friedrich Julius Stahl – as "the party of revolution." These concerns brought him finally into the political arena.

Huber's earliest and most important political contribution was a brochure published in 1841 about the "possibility or necessity" of a new conservative party: *Über die Elemente, die Möglichkeit oder Notwendigkeit einer konservativen Partei in Deutschland*.[20] Even though he was still a professor in Marburg, this publication made Huber a prominent figure in Berlin's political circles exactly one year after Friedrich Wilhelm IV became king of Prussia. Huber argued that it was time for conservatives to take a stand against the rising influence of liberalism in public affairs, and he stressed the need to influence public opinion through the establishment of new conservative newspapers and journals. Between the lines Huber already expressed uncertainty whether the king would be able to retain his position of absolute sovereignty and withstand a possible political challenge from the liberal bourgeoisie. Therefore another purpose of his pamphlet was to strengthen conservatives' political resolve and to push them forward to some kind of new political organization. As Huber argued, conservatives should be prepared in times of crisis or even revolution to defend the political order on behalf of a weakened monarch.[21]

In other writings from this time Huber also argued that the Prussian bureaucracy was fascinated by liberal ideas; one example he selected was its support for freedom of trade (*Gewerbefreiheit*) to promote the further development of a free market economy. But most important in Huber's writing – and this remained a longstanding characteristic of his political thought – was his staunch defense of the absolutist position of

20. Marburg, 1841.
21. Ibid., p. 42.

the Prussian monarch. Even though he was sometimes skeptical about the personal qualities of Friedrich Wilhelm IV, he criticized any kind of constitutional sovereignty of the people. "At the highest level of politics," he wrote, "there is room for only one power, and the so-called balance of power is a fiction that cannot be tolerated as anything but a fairy tale for grown children."[22]

Huber rejected all constitutions in which parliament had the right to take part in political decision making. From his point of view this would lead automatically to a republican order and would give way to the rule of the bourgeoisie. To be sure, Huber recognized that times were changing, and he accepted that the people wished to take part in political affairs. For this reason he supported political education of all kinds. However, he believed that such education should be limited, enabling the individual to play a role only at the level of self-government in the cities, towns, and villages. The main political decisions at the top levels of government should be prepared by a chamber of advisors representing the social estates (*Stände*) and should be executed by the monarch himself. Huber believed that the estates were socially and politically responsible for the whole of public affairs: they represented the people in a truly organic way.

Huber's strong defense of the organic order of society, his commitment to historical traditions, and his unquestioned belief in transcendental authority were typical of conservative thought in his day. Most conservatives were still strongly under the influence of ideas advanced earlier in the century by the "political romantic" Adam Müller. Even history, as "the sum of all experiences," was for Huber a conservative principle:[23] conceived in a linear and deterministic way, it culminated in the "kingdom of God." Thus Huber criticized liberalism and rationalism because they weakened religious faith and put the free individual at the center of historical development, without any respect for the values of the organic order or regard for the principles of nature and tradition. In this sense, then, much of Huber's political thought was more oriented toward the past than that of some of his political friends: Stahl,

22. Ibid., p. 37. See also David Barclay's contribution to this volume.
23. V.A. Huber, "Staatsmännische Texte mit Glossen eines Laien," *Janus. Jahrbücher deutscher Gesinnung und Tat* (hereafter cited as *Janus*) 1 (1845): 387.

for example, was a much more modern thinker, particularly in constitutional matters. In contrast to Stahl, Huber must be regarded as the defender of an absolutist system of monarchy that in the 1840s had already become obsolete.

This being said, the reactionary elements of Huber's political thought coexisted with remarkably progressive thinking in social matters. In both regards the year 1844 was a turning point in Huber's career. In February 1844 Huber published a commentary about planning for the Order of Swans (Schwanenorden), an aristocratic Christian charity organization for which Friedrich Wilhem IV provided support and even the romantic name. In his article for one of the leading conservative organs of the day, the *Evangelische Kirchenzeitung*, Huber declared for the first time that the question of pauperism and its elimination might be of greater importance than any other political topic.[24] Already heavily involved in these matters, Huber went to England in May 1844. In Manchester, Bolton, and Turton he visited factories and the houses of working-class families in order to acquire first-hand knowledge of living conditions in an industrial system more advanced than Germany's. Based on these journeys, in 1845 he published a travelogue in his new journal, *Janus*, which must be seen as one of the most impressive contemporary analyses of working-class poverty.[25]

At this time in Germany, pauperism was at the top of the political agenda, and Huber was only one among a number of social reformers, bureaucrats, scholars, and publicists who took the opportunity to go to Britain to gather information on conditions there. He, like others, wished to see whether modern industrial society could solve the social question or whether it was about to become worse. For Huber at this time

24. V.A. Huber, "Auch ein Wort über den Schwanenorden und dessen mögliche Bedeutung," *Evangelische Kirchenzeitung* 34 (1844): 81–88. See also Paulsen, *Viktor Aimé Huber als Sozialpolitiker*, pp. 60–61; and J. Reulecke, "Die Anfänge der organisierten Sozialreform in Deutschland," in *Weder Kommunismus noch Kapitalismus. Bürgerliche Sozialreform in Deutschland vom Vormärz bis zur Ära Adenauer*, ed. R. vom Bruch (Munich, 1985), p. 25.

25. V.A. Huber, "Eindrücke und Betrachtungen eines Reisenden. (Aus Briefen an einen Freund.) Manchester. Das Proletariat," *Janus* 1 (1845): 641–78 and 705–27. For German social studies of England in general, see J. Reulecke, "Englische Sozialpolitik um die Mitte des 19. Jahrhunderts im Urteil deutscher Sozialreformer," in *Die Entstehung des Wohlfahrtsstaats in Großbritannien und Deutschland, 1850–1950*, ed. W.J. Mommsen and W. Mock (Stuttgart, 1982), pp. 40–56.

it was obvious that things were getting worse. Therefore his tone was fatalistic and his description was in some ways quite similar to Engels' more famous study published the same year. Like Engels, Huber found that the poor were in a disastrous position due to exploitation (especially of women and children) by employers, their typical daily workshifts of twelve or fourteen hours, unsafe workplace conditions, their vulnerability to market crises, and the permanent danger of unemployment. For this reason he agreed completely with Engels' description of conditions. In his critique of Engels' book he wrote: "Unfortunately we must acknowledge that the description the author gives ('according to his own observations and authentic sources') of the conditions and relations of the English proletariat are largely in accordance with what we have observed ourself."[26] But the conservative Huber came to very different conclusions than Engels. For Huber the solution of the social question could not be found in a revolutionary change of the social and political order. For him the social question remained essentially a question of morality. In Bolton and Turton, Huber had visited some model factories in which working conditions were much better than elsewhere due to the responsibility of the factory owners. Therefore, in his opinion, social responsibility at the top of the social order and self-help at the bottom seemed enough to solve the problem of poverty in a satisfactory way. Under no circumstances, Huber felt, should the working class become the ruling class of society.

IV

In the final years before the revolutionary outbreak of 1848, pauperism continued to dominate political debate in Germany, especially in Prussia.[27] Because of a bad harvest in 1845/46, famine and rapidly rising food prices focused attention on the problem. As purchasing power was reduced, so was the demand for consumer items. As a result, the textile industry soon faced massive losses, the small businesses of artisans and shopkeepers declined, and interest rates climbed

26. For Engels, see n. 14. See also Huber's critique, "Zur neuesten Literatur," *Janus* 1 (1845): 387–89.
27. J. Bergmann, *Wirtschaftskrise und Revolution: Handwerker und Arbeiter 1848/49* (Stuttgart, 1986).

steeply. Two years of relatively good harvests (1846 and 1847) improved the situation slightly. But the country was still in a crisis: craftsmen, factory workers, peasants, and rural laborers all suffered from this general economic instability.

In those years most politicians were concerned with mass poverty among artisans and the peasants. The government was blamed for its liberal course in promoting freedom of trade and the emancipation of the peasantry, both of which had allegedly led to the collapse of the agrarian economy. Only a few commentators were already concerned about evidence of increasing poverty among the nascent working class in industry. Among conservatives, Count Hermann zu Dohna-Kotzenau, a representative of the east-Elbian nobility, analysed the consequences of the economic crisis in his study, *Der freie Arbeiter im preußischen Staate* (1847). Dohna urged the Prussian government to act immediately to reverse the increasing poverty of the proletariat in order to protect state and society from the "poison of communism."[28] He also developed his own model for the "organization of labor," which came rather close to Huber's proposals and those advanced years later by the "socialists of the chair" (*Kathedersozialisten*) in Wilhelmine Germany. The journeymen (*Gehülfen* and *Gesellen*) of the artisan class as well as the factory worker, Dohna wrote, should be protected by the government through control of the public labor market.[29] From Dohna's point of view the government, after promoting a liberal economic course for decades, was obliged to unite the workers in one estate and to give them the opportunity to organize themselves in associations and clubs. It should not, however, consider giving up its political authority.

In March 1848 all previous proposals, whether sophisticated or not, sank into the whirlpool of revolution. In the subsequent struggle for power the main focus was on "high politics" in parliament, not on the concerns of the poor man in the street. This continued to be the case as the major political movements began to organize themselves into independent associations and clubs. The conservatives, at first shocked into

---

28. H. Graf zu Dohna-Kotzenau, *Der freie Arbeiter im preussischen Staate* (Berlin, 1847). See also B. Moore, *Injustice: The Social Bases of Obedience and Revolt* (London, 1978), pp. 140–42.

29. Dohna-Kotzenau, *Der freie Arbeiter*, p. 68.

immobility by the revolutionary upheaval, entered the political fray quite late, but from June 1848 onward they registered decisive successes.[30] The so-called "national question" and constitutional issues dominated political discussion in the various conservative associations that appeared after June: the Preußenvereine, the Patriotische Vereine, and the Vereine für König und Vaterland. In the programs of these associations the social question was addressed, but it was certainly not central. Although these programs offered little encouragement to the oppressed artisans, in the autumn of 1848 more and more people from the petit bourgeoisie – especially craftsmen who already felt the pressure of economic competition from modern industry – joined conservative Preußenvereine and Patriotische Vereine. In the Potsdam Verein für König und Vaterland, for example, artisans working in traditional crafts (shoemakers, tablemakers, blacksmiths, and tailors) represented more than 50 percent of all members.[31] These groups opposed freedom of trade in the liberal sense and they hoped that conservatism could protect them against economic decline and poverty in the future. For this reason, in the later phases of the revolution the programs of conservative associations concentrated on issues such as the restoration of the guilds and neglected the social concerns of the rising working class. The conservative elite in Berlin was much more concerned with the interests of the petit bourgeoisie and the landowning aristocracy. It was a bad omen that during the founding meeting of the Verein für König und Vaterland in Magdeburg, a lecture on the social question had to be cancelled because the members were too busy organizing themselves into a broader network of conservative *Vereine*.[32]

Paradoxically, it was a representative of the old-conservative "fronde" who tried to shift the attention of conservatives

---

30. W. Schwentker, *Konservative Vereine und Revolution in Preussen 1848/49: Die Konstituierung des Konservativismus als Partei* (Düsseldorf, 1988).

31. Ibid., p. 172. Usually the proportion of artisans in the conservative associations was lower. Socially they were dominated by bureaucrats, business owners, landed aristocrats, army officers, and representatives of the Protestant church. The only conservative association that addressed social issues in its name and its program was the Verein für sozial-politische Reform. This association was guided by leading representatives of the Prussian nobility and bureaucracy. Its program was quite sophisticated, but the elitist Verein could not find much support among poor artisans and workers.

32. Ibid., p. 195.

to the social question in 1848. In the *Neue Preußische Zeitung* (known as the *Kreuzzeitung*) – a newspaper, founded in late June 1848, which immediately became a rallying point for all conservatives – Ludwig von Gerlach warned his party colleagues not to underestimate this problem. In July 1848, he wrote: "The working classes are correct in reminding us that they are human beings, not machines."[33] In August another contributor supported Gerlach's views by arguing that, due to the increase in mass poverty and the failure of the liberals in Berlin and Frankfurt to solve the problem, conservatives themselves should seek answers to the social question. Such concerns were not only a Christian duty, this contributor added, but should also be addressed for tactical reasons, because social policy might weaken the revolutionary movements in the cities.[34] To be sure, it soon appeared that other strategies would yield more fruitful results. In late November 1848 Prussia's national assembly in Berlin was dissolved, and shortly thereafter a new constitution was issued by the king. The heated public debate that ensued was dominated by constitutional issues. Yet as attention shifted to elections scheduled for January 1849, the social question became relevant again. At this time the revolution was at a crossroads, between a monarchist-reactionary coup d'état and a second, social revolution. As a result, all political parties scrambled to rewrite their political programs in order to attract new strata of voters.

And so a new opportunity arose for Huber to draw the attention of conservatives and a broadened political public to social issues. In the *Kreuzzeitung* he published a series of articles on the social question in which he pointed out that "for the future of Prussia the solution of social problems is much more important than any constitutional or political topic."[35] He argued that conservatives should now take charge to prevent the political revolution from becoming a social one. In contrast to Wichern's Inner Mission project, Huber argued that charity alone would not be enough. He saw this as just a first step in the right direction and thought it would fail to alleviate a mass phenomenon such as pauperism. Huber proposed to

33. E.L. von Gerlach, *Zwölf politische Monats–Rundschauen vom Juli 1848 bis dahin 1849* (Berlin, 1849), p. 11.

34. *Neue Preußische Zeitung (Kreuzzeitung)*, 16 August 1848.

35. V.A. Huber, "Die sozialen Fragen," *Neue Preußische Zeitung (Kreuzzeitung)*, 16 and 17 December 1848, 17 January 1849.

supplement Wichern's efforts through the creation of workers' associations that would function as free communities of individuals. He wrote that the creation of free workers' associations would be the only way to fight pauperism under the conditions of capitalism as a new economic world order.

With Huber's essays on social policy, the concept of association received a conservative interpretation for the first time. In the 1830s, influenced by the writings of Claude Henri Saint-Simon, Charles Fourier, and Robert Owen, this idea was discussed in all political groups, despite its socialist origins. Liberals such as David Hansemann or Robert von Mohl regarded associations as an advanced stage of private self-help. For socialists it was only one step toward the establishment of a communist society. In contrast to both liberal and socialist models, Huber claimed for the conservatives that workers' associations would help to guarantee the people's basic existence. For Huber, one way to make associations a successful alternative to pauperism was to create vital and productive communities of working people. This concept sounded modern, but the basic idea was nevertheless conservative. The workers were seen as the fourth estate in society, not as a class. Therefore Huber's aim in offering solutions to the social question was neither democracy nor economic independence but the integration of the growing proletariat into the monarchist state. As a basic political strategy, his ideas had much in common with Lorenz von Stein's concept of the "kingdom of social reform."[36] And in practical terms there were many sectors of economic life where the associations modeled by Huber could bear fruit: savings banks and health welfare schemes, old-age relief and house-building subsidies – even the resolution of conflicts between workers and factory owners.

Promoting these ideas in December 1848, Huber remained isolated among conservatives. In their view, Huber's ideas were designed to mobilize the workers against the political establishment rather than to bring more conservative members into the Prussian Landtag. Even Stahl – like Huber a progressive conservative, but only in constitutional affairs – reacted critically. For Stahl and the moderate wing of the *Kreuz-*

36. L. von Stein, *Geschichte der sozialen Bewegung*, ed. G. Salomon, 3 vols. (Munich, 1921). On Stein, see D. Blasius, "Lorenz von Steins Lehre vom Königtum der sozialen Reform und ihre verfassungspolitischen Grundlagen," *Der Staat* 10 (1971): 33–51.

zeitung group, the concept of association smacked of democracy and the "red republic."[37] Out of touch with the living conditions of workers, they compared the relationship between factory owners and workers with that between Junkers and rural laborers. Most of the conservatives preferred new legal restrictions to keep the industrial worker enmeshed in the old feudal order; accordingly, their models for a solution to the social question went in completely different directions. Stahl, the Gerlach brothers Leopold and Ludwig, and the old frondeurs looked on pauperism only as a problem of the traditional artisans and peasants. Huber, with his vision of the future, remained among his political friends just an eccentric outsider.

The lifeblood of social policy depended not on sophisticated theory but rather on a well-organized social project. Huber was well aware of this. In February 1849 he joined the Cooperative Building Society of Berlin (Berliner Gemeinnützige Baugesellschaft),[38] founded in 1847 by C. W. Hoffmann, a member of Prussia's higher civil service who was involved in housing policy. Most members came from the upper stratum of Prussian society – Junkers, bankers, bureaucrats, factory owners, and army officers – and were bound together by the idea of a social aristocracy. Their Building Society had two main purposes. It was designed, first, to promote collaboration between the owning and the non-owning classes. Second, it sought to protect the petit bourgeoisie from falling into misery or "proletarization." Although Huber's personal aims differed in some respects, he saw the Building Society as an opportunity to acquire practical experience in the field of social policy. His conception of "the transformation of a worker without property into a working proprietor" became the motto of the group,[39] and soon practical steps were taken to realize this idea. To combat Berlin's extreme shortage of good apartments affordable to poor people, the society launched building projects to create new living facilities, and some of these became quite successful among artisans and skilled workers.

---

37. H.-J. Schoeps, *Das andere Preußen. Konservative Gestalten und Probleme im Zeitalter Friedrich Wilhelms IV.*, 2nd ed. (Honnef am Rhein, 1957), p. 60. For Stahl, see the recent study by W. Füßl, *Professor in der Politik: Friedrich Julius Stahl (1802–1861). Das monarchische Prinzip und seine Umsetzung in die parlamentarische Praxis* (Göttingen, 1988).

38. Paulsen, *Viktor Aimé Huber als Sozialpolitiker*, pp. 88–107.

39. Elvers, *Victor Aimé Huber*, vol. 2, p. 273.

The society also published its own organ, *Concordia*, which appeared for the first time in May 1849.[40] Huber became its chief editor and in the following months he wrote extensively for this journal. Although the paper never won a broader readership, Jacques Droz has noted correctly that it developed into the most remarkable organ of German social conservatism in the revolutionary period.[41] Because Huber could now take positions independent of the *Kreuzzeitung* group, his articles became increasingly critical of his own party, which he condemned most of all for its mistaken strategy in social affairs. In an article entitled "The Conservative Party and the Social Question," Huber wrote that conservatives had failed to address either the social question or the problem of pauperism. A party, he wrote, "that wants to be a conservative one must take the conservative solution of the social question honestly into its program."[42] For Huber it was impossible to stop the development of modern industry and go back to simple manufacturing. Therefore the protection of craftsmen in the face of factory production would be artificial and useless in practice. He emphasized that even conservatives must recognize that basic changes in production were of world-historical significance.

In other articles Huber dealt with the political impact of social issues. He tried to convince his readers that an alliance of the nobility and the "fourth estate" could be the only way to help the poor and to keep them tied to the social and political order. Before Karl Marx examined class conflict in France from his London exile in 1851, Huber addressed the same issue, though of course from a completely different perspective. In an article entitled "The President Louis Bonaparte and the Social Question" – an unknown masterpiece – Huber argued that a successful solution to the social problem could lead to a coalition between the highest and lowest strata of society and might offset the growing power of the bourgeoisie.[43] Huber

40. *Concordia. Blätter der Berliner gemeinnützigen Baugesellschaft* (hereafter cited as *Concordia*); this journal, published in Berlin in 1849/50, is found only in the University of Marburg library.

41. J. Droz, "Une revue conservatrice allemande peu connue: *Concordia*," *Historisches Jahrbuch* 74 (1955): 485–89.

42. V.A. Huber, "Die conservative Partei und die soziale Frage," *Concordia* 1 (1849): 140.

43. *Concordia* 1 (1849): 7.

regarded Napoleon Bonaparte's *"Extinction du pauperisme"* as one example of how new directions in social policy could succeed without undermining social stability. Bonaparte had recommended the creation of workers' colonies and producers' cooperatives in areas not owned by the landed aristocracy. He was even ready to expropriate some members of the landowning classes to improve living conditions among the poor – a suggestion, however, that Huber vigorously rejected. In France as in Germany, Bonaparte's proposals for the solution of the social question were regarded as a step toward revolution. But for the Prussian conservatives in particular, they also came very close to socialism: an alliance with the poor and the growing working class was tantamount to playing with political fire.

Huber's views elicited no echo from conservative elites in Berlin and the countryside – the *Kreuzzeitung* group, the court camarilla around Friedrich Wilhelm IV, the Prussian bureaucracy, and the network of grassroots conservative *Vereine* in the provinces. This led Huber after the revolution to think about a formal political separation from all conservative groups. From his point of view, old and new conservatives had made too many concessions in constitutional matters. They were willing to accept that politics had become a public matter to be discussed in parliaments and political organizations, but they had shown no interest in social issues at all. Thus Huber was forced to seek support from liberal institutions such as the Berlin Building Society or the Central Association for the Welfare of the Working Classes (Centralverein für das Wohl der arbeitenden Klassen), to which Huber reported on the English cooperative movement in 1851 and 1852.[44] Finally, Huber decided to leave the conservatives altogether. He quit his professorship at the University of Berlin and moved to the Brandenburg town of Wernigerode near the Harz mountains, where he could develop his social ideas in isolation. In his political "farewell" to his conservative critics – entitled *Bruch mit Revolution und Ritterschaft* – he identified the principal differences that separated him from them. These mainly concerned not political issues but the social question.

---

44. V.A. Huber, *Über Association mit besonderer Beziehung auf England* (Berlin, 1851); and idem, *Über die cooperativen Arbeiterassociationen in England* (Berlin, 1852). See also Reulecke, "Anfänge der organisierten Sozialreform," p. 37.

"Even before 1848," Huber wrote, "but more strongly since 1848 – because the social problem became so important – we had to blame the conservative party for its serious sins of omission in lacking curiosity, being reserved, and showing no strength."[45] From Huber's perspective the conservatives simply did not wish to acknowledge social problems – they had failed to transform themselves into an "aristocracy of social reform":

> The principal struggle of our time pits the conservative reaction against the devilish barbarism of revolution in its causes and effects; the decisive battleground for this struggle, however, is in the realm of social issues. . . . The calling of knighthood [*Ritterschaft*] is not a calling of domination [*Beruf der Herrschaft*] in association with the divinely ordained king, who should be at the same time the first knight of the age and of his people – instead it is a calling of triple service: service to God – service to the king – but above all service to the age's poor, to the weak, to the sick.[46]

V

After the apparent failure of political solutions during the revolutionary era, public discussion turned once again to the social roots of poverty. This change of perspective was mainly a response to changes in social and economic relationships in the 1850s.[47] As Germany's industrial economy matured, a skilled labor force emerged, educated enough to use new techniques of production. Entrepreneurs, merchants, and bankers, largely disappointed by politics, returned to business and began to experiment with new forms of industrial organization, investment, and trade. Together with the creation of a better infrastructure in transport and communication, this gave the German economy a fresh start in the process of industrialization that led to further changes in the social structure. Most contemporaries did not doubt that economic and political developments might change the social order again. In 1855 the Prussian statistician Friedrich Dieterici commented on these trends with the observation that "industry is penetrating human affairs with such power and significance that a com-

---

45. V.A. Huber, *Bruch mit Revolution und Ritterschaft (Berlin 1852)*, p. vii.
46. Ibid., p. 39.
47. J. J. Sheehan, *German History 1770–1866* (Oxford, 1989), pp. 730–47.

parison with earlier conditions is scarcely possible."[48] Daily newspapers, scholarly journals, popular encyclopedias, and public discussions of all sorts devoted greater attention than they had in the *Vormärz* to social and economic affairs. Indeed, Germans' whole conception of society and its structures became a matter of central concern at exactly the time that the social order itself was undergoing its most fundamental change. Moreover, if the social question continued to be hotly debated, it was now more contentious than ever and, thus, elicited more diverse proposals to solve it.

As industrialization accelerated after 1850, the problem of pauperism began to disappear and the contours of a working class began to take shape. As a result, scholarly commentators and journalists began to deal with the social question in ways that put the spotlight on workers, not the unemployed poor. In this intellectual and social climate, the term "proletarian" (*Proletarier*) came to be used in a more pejorative way.[49] Huber had already made it clear in his pamphlet of 1853 bidding farewell to the conservatives that a successful solution of the social question depended on distinguishing between the social problems of the working class on the one hand and those of the poor, or *Proletarier*, on the other. For Huber at this time, the solution of the social question was:

> nothing less than the creation of permanent improvements in the condition of the so-called working classes – whether one likes it or not, the great mass, the fundamental stratum of the people – whereby their material, moral, and intellectual existence is raised to such a level that they are protected from the gradual or sudden floods of moral, material, and intellectual suffering that one may call pauperism, or proletariat.[50]

Four years later, in 1857, Huber contributed an article on the "Working Classes" to the *Deutsche Staats-Wörterbuch* that reached a much broader readership and played a more important part in the discussion on social issues.[51] Huber once again criticized the tendency to amalgamate or equate the terms "worker" (*Arbeiter*) and "proletarian" (*Proletarier*), because he wanted to protect the hardworking laborer from mixing with the "dangerous classes" – the unemployed poor. For Huber

48. Ibid., p. 733.
49. W. Conze, "Proletariat, Pöbel, Pauperismus," pp. 57–60.
50. V.A. Huber, *Bruch mit Revolution und Ritterschaft*, p. 40.

the proletariat was the "garbage of bourgeois society." The concept of *"Proletariat"* did not describe a special part of society, but was used to express an aversion to a heterogeneous mass of social elements. As Werner Conze has pointed out, Huber's article was important in popularizing the pejorative interpretation of *"Proletariat"*: "This tendency of Huber's to defend the orderly, energetic worker who secured his existence through labor – as distinct from the impoverished or revolutionary *Proletarier* – and to find a place for him in 'bourgeois society,' was and remains a socio-political principle that was not exclusive to the conservative Christian social circles to which Huber belonged. This intention to limit the conceptual applicability of *Proletariat* was by and large successful."[52]

Together with his involvement in discussions about the lower stratum of society, Huber in his later years concentrated on elaborating his cooperative program. As he pointed out in one of his last lectures at the University of Berlin, central to any solution of the social question was self-help for the working classes supported by members of the upper estates.[53] This idea became the basis of his cooperative program in the 1850s, when he again traveled to Belgium, France, and England to investigate how social problems had developed in more advanced stages of industrialization. This time Huber found the main reason for degrading living conditions to lie in the isolation of the individual worker, followed by low income and an insecure existence.[54] From Huber's point of view, the mutual association of individuals who shared the same interests was the only escape from poverty. He explained his model once by writing:

> The [principle of] association rests on the principle of experience, and in every regard it adheres to the [following] maxim: through the union of a large number of smaller forces – and indeed this holds true for material life (above all, workers' wages) as well as for moral life – a larger force is created, whose strength is not limited according to the law of simple addition but, rather, according to a law roughly analogous to that arithmetic series whereby the

51. V.A. Huber, "Arbeitende Classen," in *Deutsches Staats-Wörterbuch*, ed. J.C. Bluntschli and K. Brater, vol. 1 (Stuttgart, 1857), p. 281.

52. W. Conze, "Proletariat, Pöbel, Pauperismus," p. 58.

53. The lecture was entitled "The Social Question, the Proletariat, and Pauperism"; see Hindelang, *Konservatismus und soziale Frage*, p. 171.

54. V.A. Huber, *Die Selbsthilfe der arbeitenden Klassen durch Wirtschaftsvereine und innere Ansiedlung* (Berlin, 1848).

magnitude [and] the practical value of each individual component is multiplied in similar ways.[55]

Thus, for Huber, the free association of workers would strengthen them individually in their work and in their private life. In the beginning Huber's interest focused on the rental cooperatives (*Mietgenossenschaften*) that he felt should help to provide the working poor with better living conditions. But soon he developed a program of cooperative projects that in theory would involve all aspects of social life.

Here Huber distinguished between passive and active cooperatives. A passive cooperative was a free association that took advantage of a small amount of money to create savings banks for working-class people. The accounts were to be used in cases of illness or death, with special funds designated for funerals (*Begräbniskassen*). A characteristic of these passive cooperatives was that capital was retained in savings banks and assistive cooperatives – that is, it was not used to support further projects. Therefore their value was limited. For Huber the active cooperatives were much more important.[56] Again a distinction was made between consumers' (or economic) cooperatives on the one hand, and producers' (or industrial) cooperatives on the other. The first type was much easier to organize and proved more successful. Huber regarded differentials between wages and prices as the main cause of pauperism, in contrast to socialist analysis, which blamed pauperism on working conditions and the fundamental antagonism between capital and labor. In many of his writings from the 1850s, Huber claimed he wanted to create consumers' cooperatives enabling workers to live in better conditions, and in his proposals he drew on his observations in England. Thus the English penny societies, developed mainly after 1845, became a model for the German savings societies or *Sparvereine*. These associations concentrated on buying food and firewood and distributing them among their members; some years later the first cooperative stores and mills were founded. In many of his lectures and pamphlets Huber gave decisive support to these

---

55. Huber, *Bruch mit Revolution und Ritterschaft*, p. 42.

56. V.A. Huber, "Die ökonomische Association," in *V.A. Hubers Ausgewählte Schriften über Socialreform und Genossenschaftswesen*, ed. K. Munding (Berlin, n.d. [1894]), pp. 747–69; Hindelang, *Konservatismus und soziale Frage*, 236–43.

examples of consumers' cooperatives. In an article on "Association" he contributed to Johann Caspar Bluntschli's *Deutsches Staats-Wörterbuch*, Huber pointed out that consumers' cooperatives were designed to allow for large-volume purchases; such goods could then be distributed to members at advantageous prices.[57] In this way the worker could use his limited money more effectively, and the differential between low income and high prices would become less marked. In this article Huber also described how consumers' cooperatives might evolve into cooperatives that produced exclusively for their own members. He discussed cooperatives that owned their own mills, bakeries, or butcher shops, and noted that some of these could become relatively independent from their surrounding village economies.

Another aspect of Huber's program, described in his brochures and put into practice in his home town of Wernigerode, was the creation of housing cooperatives (*Siedlungsgenossenschaften*). Back from his travels in 1855, Huber wrote the following account in his *Reisebriefe*: "Poor housing conditions are a major reason for the rise of pauperism [and] the increasing corporal, ethical, and economic disorder [*Zerrüttung*] of the proletariat. Without a reform of housing conditions there can be no solution to the social question! The reform of housing conditions is therefore a principal goal of the association that, moreover, stands in need of considerable numbers of buildings for its economic and productive aims."[58] In the 1850s Huber already had experience with the Berlin Cooperative Building Society, and this he now used to promote new building cooperatives and housing cooperatives. Their main purpose was to gather capital that could be used to buy land and build new houses for workers and their families. Because of his observations in Manchester, Huber sought to avoid housing projects designed as huge "rental barracks" (*Mietskasernen*). Instead his favorite model – harmonious perhaps, but certainly unrealistic for his time – was a housing cooperative where workers lived with their families in small cottages (complete with gardens) and used consumers' coop-

---

57. V.A. Huber, "Assoziation," in *Deutsches Staats-Wörterbuch*, vol. 1, p. 481.
58. V.A. Huber, *Reisebriefe aus Belgien, Frankreich und England im Sommer 1854*, 2 vols. (Hamburg, 1855), vol. 1, p. 38.

eratives to supply themselves with everyday needs and goods. Thus Huber's goal was actually a combination of various types of cooperatives: this, he believed, would provide workers with ideal living conditions.

The second type of cooperative Huber described was the producers' or industrial cooperative.[59] Huber knew that it was nearly impossible to establish this kind of cooperative in the industrial sector: lack of capital and insufficient managerial experience among workers would always conspire against its success. In factories and mining, in spheres of production that fell between modern industrial output and traditional craftsmanship, and in sectors that depended upon raw materials and extensive economic ties, it seemed to him impossible to create producers' cooperatives for workers. Such cooperatives seemed viable only for those who practiced traditional trades: tailors, shoemakers, brewers, and blacksmiths, for example. Therefore Huber conceded that workers would benefit mainly from consumers' cooperatives, and he did not develop his idea of producers' cooperatives further. But he kept his model as an option for the future.

Huber, in short, was convinced that cooperative organizations could lead to a better life for workers at an early stage of industrialization. In the 1850s and 1860s his main purpose was to improve the material living conditions of the developing working class. In addition, the cooperative associations were intended to help the individual working man, isolated and adrift, in moral and intellectual ways. At the end of his life Huber looked back on his many plans and endeavors, and concluded:

> To these external and tangible advantages of cooperatives discussed so far can be added still other advantages – just as significant, indeed, more significant spiritually and ethically – that under prevailing conditions of massive atomization are all too often unavailable to the individual within the generality. The worst aspects of ethical and spiritual life among the lower orders, namely their lamentable lack of cooperative spirit, their lethargy, and their coarseness, are more or less directly related to the lack of any assistive, healthy, invigorating community in daily life.[60]

59. V.A. Huber, "Die industrielle Association," in *V.A. Hubers Ausgewählte Schriften*, pp. 821–35; Hindelang, *Konservatismus und soziale Frage*, pp. 243–51.
60. V.A. Huber, "Das Wesen der Genossenschaft und ihre Bedeutung für die Innere Mission," *Fliegende Blätter aus dem Rauhen Hause zu Horn bei Hamburg* (1862): 363.

VI

Recent historical scholarship has regarded Victor Aimé Huber as one of the social thinkers in the early stage of industrialization who in comparison to other conservatives developed a relatively modern perspective.[61] Though he failed personally to establish cooperatives in his own hometown, he played an important role in the public discussion of social issues. During the period of reaction and the "new era," the Prussian government and the political parties also regarded him as an expert on social affairs. But Huber's political calculations were often imprudent. His timing was bad, not least on those occasions when he sought to put his social ideas at the top of the political agenda. He was doctrinaire, without any sense of tactical flexibility and compromise. And his move from Berlin to Wernigerode – occasioned by his growing personal and political isolation – kept him away from the centers of decision making, technological innovation, and economic development that might have given his social program more immediate relevance.

In his political career Huber was a man who continually fell between two stools. After failing to gain support for his political ideas among his conservative contemporaries, he sought contact with his liberal and socialist counterparts. Thus he participated in meetings of the Central Association for the Welfare of the Working Classes and the Congress of German Political Economists (Kongreß deutscher Volkswirte); he also published essays in various liberal journals. In 1856 he traveled to Delitzsch to meet Hermann Schulze – a leading liberal social reformer and, in Huber's words, the "father of the concept of cooperatives" in Germany.[62] Due to the social environment in Saxony, Schulze-Delitzsch's efforts concentrated on the social problems of artisans. On several occasions he made it clear that in comparison to the working classes, artisans were still numerically more significant and their living conditions much worse. He agreed with Huber's analysis that working-class social ills were caused by insufficient income, extremely long working hours, and a generally insecure mate-

---

61. Nipperdey, *Deutsche Geschichte 1800–1866*, p. 245.
62. See further, R. Aldenhoff, *Schulze-Delitzsch: Ein Beitrag zur Geschichte des Liberalismus zwischen Revolution und Reichsgründung* (Baden-Baden, 1984).

rial existence. Nevertheless, Schulze-Delitzsch's own social projects were designed principally to protect artisans from descending further into poverty. The liberal concept of self-help characterized his answers to the social question. By successfully establishing raw-material cooperatives (*Rohstoffvereine*) and lending associations (*Vorschußvereine*), Schulze-Delitzsch became one of the outstanding protagonists of the cooperative movement in Germany. Huber applauded his ideas and discussed with him his own idea of consumer cooperatives, which Schulze-Delitzsch found extremely interesting. Huber disagreed with his fellow reformer, however, on two important points. First, Huber was ready to accept financial support from the state in establishing cooperatives, while Schulze-Delitzsch was not. Second, he believed that Schulze-Delitzsch's ideas and projects, though extremely helpful, were leading social policy in the wrong direction because they concentrated on improving the living conditions of artisans.

On this point Huber's criticism of Schulze-Delitzsch was similar to that of Ferdinand Lassalle. In his public debate with Schulze-Delitzsch, Lassalle used Huber's argument that, in contrast to any "gambit with the dead skeleton of the old guild system," only a social policy for the working class had relevance for the future.[63] Lassalle was also in favor of producers' cooperatives under governmental guidance as a solution to the social and political conflict of interests between workers and capitalists.[64] But in contrast to Huber, Lassalle demanded not only the economic emancipation of the working class, but also political emancipation, to be achieved initially through a campaign for universal suffrage. Huber regarded this strategy as an ill-considered attempt to eliminate the separation of state and society.

Both Schulze-Delitzsch and Lassalle were impressed and influenced by Huber's social ideas; however, they regarded him politically as a reactionary monarchist who could not understand the signs of the times. Even Hermann Wagener and other conservatives associated with the *Kreuzzeitung* and, later, with the *Berliner Revue*, criticized Huber for his lack of political sense. It took several years before another generation of conservatives set the social question again on the political

63. V.A. Huber, *Die Arbeiter und ihre Rathgeber* (Berlin, 1863), p. 24.
64. See further, S. Na'aman, *Lassalle* (Hanover, 1970).

agenda.[65] During the Bismarckian empire many of Huber's ideas were revived, especially among the *Kathedersozialisten* and Stöcker's Christian Social movement; but with their different political aims these groups proceeded in other directions. Thus, although Huber was the first German conservative to devote his career to solving the social question, it may be true that he had no direct successor. The internal contradictions within his program – political backwardness and socioeconomic modernity – undermined his position and weakened his message. Huber failed personally because he did not wish to accept that in the age of emancipation and democracy it was impossible to help the lower orders overcome their underprivileged status and poverty while excluding them from full participation in politics. Nonetheless, even in later decades this contradiction remained an essential part of conservative ideology and continued to present German conservatives with one of their most basic dilemmas.

65. In this regard one might mention Carl Rodbertus and the Catholic reformer Franz Hitze, as well as Rudolph Todt and Adolph Wagner, who together founded the Zentralverein für Socialreform auf religiöser und konstitutioneller Grundlage in 1877. For this tradition in conservative thought, see Müller, "Der deutsche Sozialkonservatismus," pp. 203–36.

4

The Court Camarilla and the Politics of Monarchical Restoration in Prussia, 1848–58[*]

David E. Barclay

I

Historians have long (and rightly) emphasized the remarkable ability of Prussia's traditional elites to adjust to changing political, social, and economic circumstances. Perhaps at no time in the nineteenth century was that adaptability better illustrated than in their response to the revolutionary upheavals of 1848. Although temporarily confused and even paralyzed by the events of March, they were quickly able to regain the political initiative, neutralize and counteract much of the revolutionary dynamic that had emerged during that year, and survive Prussia's transition to a form of parliamentarism and constitutionalism with much of their power and authority intact. Crucial to the process of conservative elite mobilization after the spring of 1848 was what Edwin von Manteuffel, an officer with a passion for politics, called a "carefully considered, carefully prepared restoration" of monarchical authority.[1] The crown had been the focal point of the Prussian state for generations, and to most Prussian conservatives a powerful and effective monarchy was indispensable to the maintenance of all other kinds of authority. Thus the so-called "Camarilla" or

*The research for this essay was made possible by a fellowship from the Alexander von Humboldt Foundation (Bonn-Bad Godesberg), a Summer Stipend from the National Endowment for the Humanities, and financial assistance from the Kalamazoo College faculty development program.

1. E. von Manteuffel, "Anfang Juli 1848 (Ueber Revolutionen)" (ms.), Geheimes Staatsarchiv Preußischer Kulturbesitz, Abteilung Merseburg (hereafter: GStA Merseburg), Hausarchiv (hereafter: HA) Rep. 192 M, Edwin von Manteuffel, D, Nr. 5², Bl. 7.

David E. Barclay

"court party" of King Frederick William IV, which helped to pave the way for the counterrevolution of November 1848 and the policies of the decade of reaction thereafter, has figured prominently in analyses of the revolution and its aftermath.[2]

Descriptions of the Camarilla have often conjured up images of a *ministère occulte*, a "kitchen cabinet," an unofficial and even semi-secret collection of *éminences grises*, court officials, and longtime associates of the mercurial Frederick William IV. This group of people was determined to "insulate the king from his liberal official ministry" and to subvert Prussia's nascent constitutional order.[3] In fact, according to many historians, after April 1848 the Camarilla constituted a "counter-government" (*Gegenregierung*) or an alternative government-in-waiting (*Nebenregierung*), biding its time until the Prussian National Assembly could be dispersed and replaced with a new, truly "monarchical" regime.[4]

No one has ever denied the existence of the Camarilla at the court of Frederick William IV after 1848. Contemporaries were keenly aware of its existence, while its members actually used the term "Camarilla" to refer to themselves. It even provided literary inspiration to the democratic writer Karl Gutzkow, whose multivolume novel, *Die Ritter vom Geiste* (1850–51), described a conspiratorial clique of reactionaries at what was obviously supposed to be the Prussian court.[5] It is a bit surprising, therefore, that until the 1960s little was known about the exact composition and internal workings of the Camarilla. Recently, however, the critical evaluation of a number of important sources has made it possible to reassess the nature of the Camarilla and to reconsider the larger processes by

2. For a recent assessment of the Camarilla's long-term significance, see R.M. Berdahl, *The Politics of the Prussian Nobility: The Development of a Conservative Ideology 1770–1848* (Princeton, N.J., 1988), p. 376.

3. Ibid.

4. M. Kliem, "Genesis der Führungskräfte der feudal-militaristischen Konterrevolution 1848 in Preußen" (Phil. Diss., Humboldt-Universität zu Berlin, 1966), pp. 393–94, differentiates between the *ministère occulte* as a *Gegenregierung* and the Camarilla as a *Nebenregierung*; this distinction, however, is problematic.

5. K. Gutzkow, *Werke*, ed. R. Gensel, vols. 13–15, *Die Ritter vom Geiste* (Berlin, 1910), esp. the chapter entitled "Die 'Gesellschaft' und die kleinen Zirkel," vol. 13, pp. 386–97; see also the analysis of the novel in E.K. Bramsted, *Aristocracy and the Middle-Classes in Germany: Social Types in German Literature 1830–1900*, rev. ed. (Chicago, 1964), pp. 80–91.

which conservative elites helped to shape the institutional environment of postrevolutionary Prussia.[6]

This essay is intended as a contribution to that process of reassessment. It advances four major propositions. First, it suggests that the influence and size of the Camarilla have been greatly exaggerated. Always a loose and exceedingly informal arrangement, its membership was smaller than has usually been supposed. After the spring of 1848 it had to contend with several other groups and individuals for influence over a monarch who managed to be at once highly impressionable, and yet unbending in his adherence to certain idiosyncratic and strongly held views. Second, it argues that the Camarilla's influence was greatest in the autumn of 1848, reaching its zenith with the establishment of a government headed by Count Friedrich Wilhelm von Brandenburg. Third, after December 1848 it is arguably very difficult to speak of a "Camarilla" at all. One might better think of a shifting and amorphous collection of conservative court officials, of whom the most notable was Leopold von Gerlach, one of the king's confidants since the late 1820s and adjutant general after 1850. Gerlach remained the vestigial Camarilla's pivotal figure, and on various occasions after 1848 he used his access to the king and queen to advance his own views and those of his fellow

6. Among the more important titles, see K. Canis, "Der preußische Militarismus in der Revolution 1848" (Inaug.-Diss., Universität Rostock, 1965), pp. 53–60; idem, "Ideologie und politische Taktik der junkerlich-militaristischen Reaktion bei der Vorbereitung und Durchführung des Staatsstreiches in Preußen im Herbst 1848," *Jahrbuch für Geschichte* 7 (1972), pp. 459–503; Kliem, "Genesis," pp. 390–400; H. Diwald, introduction to *Von der Revolution zum Norddeutschen Bund. Politik und Ideengut der preußischen Hochkonservativen 1848–1866. Aus dem Nachlaß von Ernst Ludwig von Gerlach*, ed. H. Diwald, 2 vols. (Göttingen, 1970), vol. 1, pp. 55–57; W.J. Orr, Jr., "The Foundation of the *Kreuzzeitung* Party in Prussia, 1848–1850" (Ph.D. diss., University of Wisconsin-Madison, 1971), pp. 131–36; R. Schult, "Partei wider Willen. Kalküle und Potentiale konservativer Parteigründer in Preußen zwischen Erstem Vereinigten Landtag und Nationalversammlung (1847/48)," in *Deutscher Konservatismus im 19. und 20. Jahrhundert. Festschrift für Fritz Fischer zum 75. Geburtstag und zum 50. Doktorjubiläum*, ed. D. Stegmann, B.-J. Wendt, and P.-C. Witt (Bonn, 1983), pp. 53–54; G. Grünthal, "Bemerkungen zur Kamarilla Friedrich Wilhelms IV. im nachmärzlichen Preußen," in *Friedrich Wilhelm IV. in seiner Zeit. Beiträge eines Colloquiums*, ed. O. Büsch (Berlin, 1987), pp. 39–47. Among older works, two are still very helpful: E. Jordan, *Die Entstehung der konservativen Partei und die preußischen Agrarverhältnisse von 1848* (Munich and Leipzig, 1914), pp. 297–368; and F. Hartung, "Verantwortliche Regierung, Kabinett und Nebenregierungen im konstitutionellen Preußen 1848–1918," *Forschungen zur Brandenburgischen und Preußischen Geschichte* 44 (1932), pp. 3–17.

conservatives aligned with the famous conservative newspaper founded in 1848, the *Kreuzzeitung*. Fourth, the significance of the Camarilla – or, more precisely, of "high conservative" court elites – between 1848 and 1858 needs to be evaluated in terms of a continuing set of compromises and political arrangements with other conservative interests, including the king himself; for Frederick William IV was by no means merely a creature of either the Camarilla or the *Kreuzzeitung* party.[7]

II

On 28 March 1848, only ten days after the events that had so dramatically and fundamentally transformed the bases of Prussian politics, the country's first constitutional chief minister stepped down. Count Adolf Heinrich von Arnim-Boitzenburg had hardly been a popular choice, and now, he argued, it was essential that he be replaced by a more truly representative ministry. The liberal Rhenish businessman Ludolf Camphausen succeeded him, leading a cabinet that included the Aachen financier David Hansemann as finance minister and the liberal diplomat Heinrich Alexander von Arnim-Suckow as foreign minister.[8]

When word of these political developments reached him,

7. Much of the research for this essay draws upon the hitherto untapped "Abschriften des Nachlasses Leopolds von Gerlach" (hereafter: "Abschriften"), which consist of multivolume, typescript copies of Gerlach's diaries and correspondence. The original copy of Gerlach's *Nachlaß* was lost during the Second World War, and presumably destroyed. During the 1920s, however, the former Reichsarchiv in Potsdam prepared two copies of the *Nachlaß*; the project was initiated by Otto Koser, director of the Reichsarchiv branch in Frankfurt am Main (now an *Außenstelle* of the Bundesarchiv). For various reasons, the project was not completed, and the volumes were never published; but two copies still exist, one in the Gerlach-Archiv at the Institut der politischen Wissenschaft of the University of Erlangen (hereafter: GA), the other in the Bundesarchiv, Abteilungen Potsdam (hereafter: BA Potsdam). These typescripts have only become available to scholars in recent years, and supersede the heavily edited, two-volume version of Gerlach's diaries, *Denkwürdigkeiten aus dem Leben Leopold von Gerlachs. Generals der Infanterie und General-Adjutanten König Friedrich Wilhelms IV.*, ed. A. von Gerlach (Berlin, 1891–92). References in the text below will be to the thirty-five-volume set in Erlangen; where I cite Gerlach's diary, I shall also provide appropriate cross-references to the printed *Denkwürdigkeiten*.

8. Arnim-Boitzenburg to Frederick William IV, 29 March 1848, in *Revolutionsbriefe 1848. Ungedrucktes aus dem Nachlaß König Friedrich Wilhelms IV. von Preußen*, ed. K. Haenchen (Leipzig, 1930), pp. 59–60; J. Hofmann, *Das Ministerium Camphausen-Hansemann. Zur Politik der preußischen Bourgeoisie in der Revolution 1848/49* (Berlin [East], 1981), pp. 48–56, esp. p. 55.

Leopold von Gerlach was spending the evening with the king and queen in Potsdam. Frederick William tried to defend his behavior during the famous ride through the streets of Berlin (*Umritt*) on 21 March, during which, in the eyes of virtually all Prussian conservatives, the monarchy had been more griev-ously humiliated than on any occasion since the catastrophes of 1806/7. Gerlach noted in his diary that the king's "discours-es about the March events – a mixture of resignation, weak-ness, apathy, and desperation – made a frightful impression on me. Everything was confused, listless, and fantastic."[9] Ger-lach went home "heavy with despair," and, after a night of troubled sleep, resolved early the next morning to seek out the king once again and urge him to stiffen his resolve. Accompa-nied by a veteran court official, Ludwig von Massow, Gerlach made three critically important recommendations to the dis-traught monarch: (1) not to go to Berlin, but to require the new parliamentary ministers to come out to him in Potsdam; (2) under no circumstances to appoint the mildly liberal General Wilhelm von Willisen as war minister, for to do so might undermine the political reliability of the armed forces; and (3) to dismiss Foreign Minister Arnim-Suckow. In his diary Ger-lach explained his motives: "I was thinking of the possibility of restoring monarchical authority by proceeding from the army and from foreign policy. The king agreed to everything, but how unreliable he is!" That same day, Frederick William wrote to Camphausen that he intended to stay in Potsdam. This decision ensured that at least one member of the embry-onic Camarilla would always be close to the king's side.[10]

"Camarillas" were themselves nothing new in nineteenth-century Europe. Indeed, the word had first been used in its modern sense to refer to the corrupt system of private favoritism and patronage practiced at the court of Ferdinand VII, king of Spain from 1814 to 1833.[11] Some scholars have also written of a "Camarilla" at the court of Ferdinand's contempo-rary, Frederick William III of Prussia, who always tended to rely on favorites and cronies responsible to no one other than

9. Leopold von Gerlach, diary (29 March 1848), GA, "Abschriften," 6: 37 (not in *Denkwürdigkeiten*).

10. Ibid., 6: 37–38 (partly in *Denkwürdigkeiten*, vol. 1, pp. 149–50); Orr, "Foundation," 139–40; Canis, "Militarismus," 54; Kliem, "Genesis," 395.

11. H.O. Meisner, *Archivalienkunde vom 16. Jahrhundert bis 1918* (Göttingen, 1969), p. 307.

himself.[12] However, his son and heir, Frederick William IV, turned out to be even more susceptible to the ideas and blandishments of unofficial advisers. Notable for his far-reaching intellectual interests, his genuinely creative aesthetic imagination, and his voluble personality, Frederick William loved to surround himself with lively friends and stimulating conversationalists. Several of these interlocutors became indispensable to him, and they represented a wide variety of views, tastes, backgrounds, and interests. Some were architects and art connoisseurs, reflecting the king's lifelong passion for these pursuits, while others, such as the ubiquitous Alexander von Humboldt, could hardly be described as moss-backed Junker reactionaries. Still, the majority of the king's advisers consisted of people who for many years before 1840 had belonged to an informal group of friends, the so-called "Crown Prince's Circle," and had often chafed against what they regarded as the rigid bureaucratic "despotism," unimaginativeness, and sterility of Frederick William III's last years. In many cases, the members of the Crown Prince's Circle were bound by ties of marriage, blood, and shared generational experience. Above all, the liberation wars of 1813–15 and the postwar religious "Awakening" (*Erweckungsbewegung*) had encouraged in many of them a veneration for *ständisch*-corporative institutions in a "Christian-German" monarchical state.

After his accession to the throne in 1840, Frederick William continued to draw upon the advice and expertise of these old friends. As he put it on one occasion, "I am not like so many rulers, big and petty, who act as though no one can influence them. I choose my ministers and my entourage so that they can exercise influence over me, but that has its definite limits; and on this point there is nothing more to be said."[13] His last observation, however, raises a key issue, for Frederick William rarely allowed himself to be dominated permanently by any group or individual. To be sure, he was often swayed by the informal advice of certain special favorites, most notably Joseph Maria von Radowitz, Christian Carl Josias Bunsen

---

12. For example, see Thomas Stamm-Kuhlmann, *König in Preußens großer Zeit. Friedrich Wilhelm III. der Melancholiker auf dem Thron* (Berlin, 1992), pp. 416–24, 458–64.

13. Leopold von Gerlach, diary (5 January 1852), GA, "Abschriften," 9: 4–5 (also in *Denkwürdigkeiten*, vol. 1, p. 719).

(Prussia's emissary to London from 1841 to 1854), and, after 1848, Carl Wilhelm Saegert, a Berlin school director with whom the king regularly conferred on the highest matters of state policy. This led Leopold von Gerlach to complain that, in comparison with Bunsen and Radowitz, the king regarded the narrower Gerlach circle as "cattle."[14] But such preferment did not deter the monarch from accepting Radowitz's resignation during the autumn crisis of 1850, or from agreeing to Bunsen's departure at the time of the Oriental crisis four years later; for even his closest friends were, in his view, only executors of his own will and his own wishes.

In an odd and often contradictory way, Frederick William combined an adherence to ideas of "historical" group rights and *ständisch* freedom with an exalted, Romantic, and even mystical vision of his own office, believing that kings were privy to certain truths inaccessible to ordinary mortals. Leopold von Gerlach once remarked ironically that the king often acted "as if royal persons were descended from another Adam."[15] Indeed, Frederick William often treated his advisers, officials, and the members of his entourage badly, loading them with unnecessary work, interfering with their daily routines, and publicly scolding them for their alleged failings. There was an extraordinarily high turnover among his ministers, especially before 1848, and throughout his entire reign the king's confidants bitterly complained about his "indifference" and "ingratitude" toward his servants. Moreover, Frederick William consistently tried to manipulate his advisers to his own advantage. In the words of the British minister to the Prussian court, the "king thinks that by not avowing his partiality for any particular Party, by playing fast and loose with all, that he maintains his own independence and freedom of action, and though he pleases none he also quarrels with none."[16] The minister was right; Frederick William IV was not likely to remain for long under the thumb of any group or individual, and no "Camarilla" would ever hold permanent

14. Leopold von Gerlach, diary (19 November 1848), GA, "Abschriften," 6: 238 (passage somewhat different in Gerlach, *Denkwürdigkeiten*, vol. 1, p. 244); cf. Orr, "Foundation," p. 238.

15. Leopold von Gerlach to Theodor Heinrich Rochus von Rochow, 25 July 1850 (draft), GStA Merseburg, Rep. 92, Leopold von Gerlach, Nr. 10, Bl. 139–139^v.

16. Lord Bloomfield to Earl of Clarendon, 10 February 1854, Public Record Office, Kew, FO 64/368.

sway over him. To this extent, Heinrich von Sybel was not far off the mark when he contended that Frederick William was in fact directly and personally responsible for the major decisions taken during his reign.[17]

Many contemporaries noted that, shortly after mounting the throne, the new king continued to solicit advice from a number of quarters, including "unofficial" friends such as Leopold von Gerlach and Radowitz. As early as 1842 some people were already beginning to hint darkly that the monarch was surrounded by a "Camarilla" of "pietists" and reactionaries.[18] One recent historian actually describes Frederick William's supposed *Vormärz* Camarilla as "the apex of a political party, which, though not organized, was nevertheless full of confidence in itself. The Camarilla had . . . become a center of power in *Vormärz* Prussia."[19] This argument is difficult to sustain. When one looks carefully at the apex of the Prussian state between 1840 and 1848, one encounters an amorphous, fluid structure of temporary coalitions and overlapping factions that only partially stabilized after 1845, when Ernst von Bodelschwingh emerged as the country's *de facto* prime minister. On the whole, there was little unity and much confusion among the king's advisers, many of whom came to disagree vehemently with each other during those years, despite shared bonds of friendship and experience before 1840. Moreover, in this preconstitutional, semiabsolutist era, distinctions between the "formal" and "informal" functions of government, or between the government and the court, remained blurred. Many of the people to whom the king listened most attentively in fact occupied formal positions in government or in the royal entourage. The insightful and well-connected Russian emissary in Berlin, Peter von Meyendorff, once

17. H. von Sybel, *Die Begründung des Deutschen Reiches durch Wilhelm I. Vornehmlich nach den preußischen Staatsakten*, 4 vols., 4th ed. (Munich and Leipzig, 1902), vol. 1, p. 104.

18. Peter von Meyendorff to Foreign Minister Nesselrode, 21 April 1842, in P. von Meyendorff, *Ein russischer Diplomat an den Höfen von Berlin und Wien. Politischer und privater Briefwechsel 1826–1863*, ed. O. Hoetzsch, 3 vols. (Berlin and Leipzig, 1923), vol. 1, p. 232; K.A. Varnhagen von Ense, *Tagebücher*, ed. L. Assing, 15 vols. (Leipzig and Berlin, 1862–1905), vol. 2, p. 354 ("Einiges aus Humboldt's Mittheilungen," 31 August 1844); Count Maximilian von und zu Lerchenfeld to King Ludwig I, 2 November 1845, Bayerisches Hauptstaatsarchiv, Munich, MA III, Nr. 2623.

19. E.R. Huber, *Deutsche Verfassungsgeschichte seit 1789*, vol. 2, *Der Kampf um Einheit und Freiheit 1830 bis 1850*, 3d ed. (Stuttgart, 1988), p. 483.

remarked that Frederick William's regime before 1848 was "personal government personified"; but no one was in a position to cajole or push the king where he did not want to go.[20]

In fact, Leopold von Gerlach and his closest friends attributed many of the difficulties and setbacks of the *Vormärz* years to the *absence* of a Camarilla (or its equivalent). The king could never be expected to hold the reins of power firmly in his own hands, they believed. As a result of his unsteadiness, Leopold's younger brother Ludwig wrote in January 1848, "demoralization" had spread throughout the entire land. A constant theme of Leopold von Gerlach's pre-1848 correspondence with Ludwig and like-minded associates was the need for a firm and fixed *"conseil"* that would enjoy the king's full confidence and that could develop a clear, steady, and consistent plan of governance for the monarchy. Such a *conseil*, Leopold argued, could also constitute a conservative alternative to what he regarded as the twin evils of constitutionalism and bureaucratic absolutism.[21] But would such a goal ever be attainable? Leopold had his doubts, at least until the traumas of March 1848 necessitated a fundamental rethinking of the available political options.

III

The new *"ministère occulte"* that began to take shape after 29 March 1848 felt obliged to proceed with great caution, and at first its aims were relatively modest: to save what could be saved of effective crown authority. But Leopold von Gerlach found a sympathetic ear in one of Frederick William's several adjutants, General Friedrich Wilhelm von Rauch, and the two men quickly became the Camarilla's moving spirits. Before long, as Gerlach later wrote, he and Rauch were in perfect accord on every political issue.[22] Personally, however, the two men could hardly have been more different. Most historians

20. Meyendorff to Nesselrode, 19 December 1841, in Meyendorff, *Briefwechsel*, vol. 1, p. 199; Orr, "Foundation," p. 130.
21. Leopold von Gerlach to Ludwig von Gerlach, 12 January and 31 July 1842, GA, Fasz. CS; Leopold von Gerlach to Baron Karl von Canitz und Dallwitz, draft of letter not sent, 13 January 1842, ibid., "Abschriften," 17: 32–35; Leopold von Gerlach to Count Albrecht von Alvensleben-Erxleben, 6 January 1842, ibid., 17: 36–38.
22. Leopold von Gerlach to Ludwig von Gerlach, 10 June 1850, in *Von der Revolution*, ed. Diwald, vol. 2, p. 678.

now agree that, if anything, Rauch was the Camarilla's real leader before November 1848, although in contrast to Gerlach he was never personally close to the monarch. Born into a Potsdam officer's family in 1790, he had served with distinction in the wars of 1813–15. In 1829 he was named aide-de-camp to Frederick William III, and four years later he became the Prussian military plenipotentiary to the Russian court at St. Petersburg. Personally seconded to the tsar, he quickly became an admired confidant of Nicholas I, Frederick William IV's brother-in-law. Laconic, earnest, and conscientious, Rauch was not drawn into Frederick William's shimmering intellectual orbit. But he was unreservedly devoted to the monarchical cause, which for him was inseparable from the person of the monarch himself; thus he vigorously rejected calls for the king's abdication in the spring and summer of 1848. Conversely, the psychologically and intellectually complex Prussian king always responded favorably to Rauch's blunt, direct ways. As Frederick William wrote in early 1849: "Don't expect to find any extraordinary political wisdom, cleverness, artfulness, etc., in him; don't look for a Russophile or a born aristocrat. Rather, look alone for the Potsdam officer, that is, the *genuinely* unselfish nobleman motivated by feelings of honor, the *Prussian* from head to toe."[23]

Though still officially posted to the tsar's court, Rauch found himself in Berlin in March 1848, and he was nauseated by what he encountered there. He had spent several critical hours with the king and queen on 18 and 19 March. He had stood by them as the royal couple were forced to pay their respects to those who had been killed in the street fighting, and he had joined the king on his *Umritt* of 21 March. "It was almost more than an old soldier's heart could bear," he later remarked. "It was as if I had come from the madhouse."[24] As

23. Marginal comment on letter from C.W. Saegert, 7 January 1849, Geheimes Staatsarchiv Preußischer Kulturbesitz, Berlin, Brandenburg-Preußisches Hausarchiv, Rep. 192, Carl Wilhelm Saegert, Nr. 17, Bl. 4. Emphasis in original. The best description of Rauch is in Orr, "Foundation," pp. 134–36. See also *Soldatisches Führertum*, ed. K. von Priesdorff, 10 vols. (Hamburg, 1937–42), vol. 5, pp. 30–33; H.-J. Schoeps, "Berichte aus St. Petersburg," in idem, *Neue Quellen zur Geschichte Preußens im 19. Jahrhundert* (Berlin, 1968), pp. 441–42; O. von Bismarck, *Die gesammelten Werke*, vol. 15, *Erinnerung und Gedanke*, ed. G. Ritter and R. Stadelmann (Berlin, 1932), p. 38; H. Wagener, *Die Politik Friedrich Wilhelm IV.* (Berlin, 1883), pp. 59–60.

24. Excerpts from Rauch's reports in K.L. von Prittwitz, *Berlin 1848. Das*

an "old soldier," though, he believed that his duty required him, even in an age gone mad, to do everything possible to protect the monarch and thus the kingdom itself.

We have already met Leopold von Gerlach (1790–1861), the other main player in the 1848 Camarilla. He was a far more complex personality than Rauch. Like his younger colleague, Edwin von Manteuffel, Gerlach was the very prototype of the political general. One of several talented sons of Berlin's first mayor, Gerlach had entered military service in 1806 and participated in the campaigns of that year and in the wars of liberation thereafter. It was during the latter conflict that he first met the crown prince, who was five years his junior.[25] Only after the late 1820s did he begin corresponding with the crown prince on a regular basis; by 1830, however, he was regularly appearing in Frederick William's company, along with several other friends connected to the "Crown Prince's Circle." Before 1849 Gerlach held no official position in the court entourage or in the *maison militaire*, but in 1842 he secured a military sinecure that guaranteed him frequent access to the monarch.

Two experiences – the struggle against the "revolutionary" Bonaparte in 1813–14 and the intense moral earnestness of the Awakening after 1815 – had left an indelible impression upon the young Gerlach. Until the end of his life he remained an advocate of the Holy Alliance, of a *ständisch*-corporative monarchy, and of a renewed Christianity as a counterweight to the Satanic snares of revolution. Crucial to his *ständisch* views was a distaste for "absolutism" in all its forms, whether monarchical, bureaucratic, or revolutionary. In fact, he argued, bureaucratic centralization antedated the French Revolution in many parts of Europe, and was just as destructive of "historical" right and of historically sanctioned liberties and privileges. With these views, it is not surprising that Gerlach gravitated into Frederick William IV's orbit, where he firmly remained until their deaths, eight days apart, in January

---

Erinnerungswerk des Generalleutnants Karl Ludwig von Prittwitz und andere Quellen zur Berliner Märzrevolution und zur Geschichte Preußens um die Mitte des 19. Jahrhunderts, ed. G. Heinrich (Berlin, 1985), pp. 331, 392.

25. Leopold von Gerlach to Frederick William IV, 21 September 1856, GStA Merseburg, HA, Rep. 50, J, Nr. 455, Bl. 148ᵛ; Leopold von Gerlach, "Familiengeschichte," in *Aus den Jahren preußischer Not und Erneuerung. Tagebücher und Briefe der Gebrüder Gerlach und ihres Kreises 1805–1820*, ed. H.-J. Schoeps (Berlin, 1963), p. 103.

David E. Barclay

1861.[26]

Leopold von Gerlach's relationship with his royal master, both before and after 1848, was full of contradiction and ambivalence. On the one hand, Gerlach constantly professed his love and affection for Frederick William IV. In 1855 he wrote, "I do not believe that there is anyone among the king's servants who so completely agrees with him politically, which His Majesty himself knows very well. From 1827 until 1840, indeed until 1848, I regarded him – precisely him – as the head of my party."[27] On the other hand, although he was under no illusions about the king's weaknesses and foibles, his highly developed sense of duty and religious responsibility always obliged him to speak bluntly and directly to that agitated, hypersensitive monarch. Loud altercations and vehement arguments frequently resulted, and Gerlach often gave vent to his frustration with the king's "arrogance, this inability to recognize the beam in his own eye, this criticism of the mote in the eyes of others, this insincerity, this ill-humor, this irritability. . . ."[28] Ingratitude was the inevitable lot of kings' servants, Gerlach sighed on numerous occasions. He often tried to resign, most frequently after 1850; but Frederick William, for whom the usually affable Gerlach was absolutely indispensable, invariably rejected his aggrieved adjutant's requests.

Despite a gossipy streak and a love of backroom intrigue, Gerlach never managed to become a Richelieu, an Olivares, or a Metternich, much less a Bismarck. For one thing, Frederick

26. No full-scale biography of Gerlach has ever been written. For biographical information, see, above all, *Aus den Jahren*, ed. Schoeps; L. von Keyserling, *Studien zu den Entwicklungsjahren der Brüder Gerlach. Mit Briefen Leopolds von Gerlach und seiner Brüder an Karl Sieveking* (Heidelberg, 1913); A. Clausen, *Die Stellung Leopold von Gerlachs zum Abschluß des preußischen Verfassungswerkes unter Friedrich Wilhelm IV.* (Inaug.–Diss., Universität Leipzig [printed]; Weida i. Thür., 1914); S. Nobbe, "Der Einfluß religiöser Überzeugung auf die politische Ideenwelt Leopold von Gerlachs" (Phil. Diss., Friedrich-Alexander-Universität Erlangen-Nürnberg, 1970); K. Canis, "Leopold von Gerlach," in *Preußen in der deutschen Geschichte nach 1789*, ed. G. Seeber and K.-H. Noack (Berlin [East], 1983), pp. 153–72. Crucial for an understanding of his political views is his famous correspondence with Bismarck in the 1850s: *Briefe des Generals Leopold von Gerlach an Otto von Bismarck*, ed. H. Kohl (Stuttgart and Berlin, 1912). Bismarck's letters to Gerlach can be found in O. von Bismarck, *Die gesammelten Werke*, vol. 14, *Briefe, Erster Band: 1822–1861*, ed. W. Windelband and W. Frauendienst (Berlin, 1933).

27. Leopold von Gerlach, diary (13 October 1855), GA, "Abschriften," 12: 127 (also in *Denkwürdigkeiten*, vol. 2, p. 345).

28. Leopold von Gerlach, diary (28 November 1850), GA, "Abschriften," 7: 233 (not in *Denkwürdigkeiten*).

William was too determined to be his own man and rule for himself; for another, the phlegmatic Gerlach was always a fatalist, even a pessimist, with a melancholic and wistful strain. As his famous correspondence with Bismarck during the 1850s demonstrated, he abhorred an amoral politics of state interest. He was not really a man of action, but first and foremost a *Prinzipienreiter*, a man of principle who believed that he could best serve the monarchical cause by acting as the king's conscience. Accordingly, many observers have argued that in 1848 the "pragmatic" Rauch's concrete influence may have exceeded that of Gerlach. Certainly Rauch's connections in the officer corps, many of whose members distrusted and disliked Gerlach, were crucial to the Camarilla.[29] Peter von Meyendorff, a Russian diplomat whose ties to the Camarilla were close but discreet, once remarked: "Without Rauch it is difficult to act on the king. Gerlach does not have Rauch's energy, nor, as a consequence, his influence." Although Gerlach's "political principles are as excellent as Rauch's," Meyendorff continued, he did not have "the same nerve, the same dexterity of judgment."[30] In fact, one historian from the former German Democratic Republic has gone so far as to argue that in 1848/49 *"Adjutant General von Rauch unquestionably became the head of the principal feudal-militaristic forces in Prussia."*[31] This contention is, however, greatly overdrawn.

During the critical months between the spring and autumn of 1848, Gerlach and Rauch could count on the active support of only a relatively small number of allies. "Rauch, Massow, Ludwig, and I were the only ones from April 1848 to November 1848," Leopold wrote several years later. Most of the king's old ministers had retired from public life and, in the new spirit of responsible constitutional government, had urged the king not to seek their counsel but to rely on his new cabinet instead. Other friends, such as Count Carl von der Groeben or Count Anton zu Stolberg-Wernigerode, were not present in

29. Varnhagen, *Tagebücher*, vol. 6, p. 376 (29 September 1849).

30. Meyendorff to Nesselrode, 4 May 1850, in Meyendorff, *Briefwechsel*, vol. 2, p. 293; Meyendorff to Empress Alexandra Feodorovna, 20 September 1849, in ibid., vol. 3, p. 382.

31. Kliem, "Genesis," p. 397; emphasis in original. See also idem, "Die Rolle der feudaljunkerlichen Reaktion in der Revolution von 1848/49," *Zeitschrift für Geschichtswissenschaft* 17 (1969), p. 320; and the more balanced analysis in Orr, "Foundation," p. 136.

Berlin or Potsdam during those months. The king's chief reporting adjutant general, August Wilhelm von Neumann-Cosel, was "utterly weak and useless," according to Gerlach. And Radowitz, who was elected that spring to the Frankfurt National Assembly, had become, Gerlach declared, "our opponent in the Paulskirche."[32]

As Gerlach noted, Ludwig von Massow (1794–1859) has to be regarded as a "member" of the Camarilla in 1848. In that year he was serving as intendant of the Royal Gardens, but that innocuous-sounding title masked his real importance. A long-serving court official with an impeccable aristocratic pedigree, Massow had served as marshal of the court under Frederick William III, and was intimately acquainted with the details of the court's finances. He was in a position to see Frederick William IV virtually every day as long as the monarch was staying in Potsdam or at his nearby summer residence in Sanssouci, and in 1848 he played a much more significant role than has sometimes been realized.[33]

If Massow could be counted on wholeheartedly to support the efforts of Rauch and Gerlach at court, the same could not be said of Leopold's brother Ludwig. Five years younger than Leopold (and thus the same age as the king), Ernst Ludwig von Gerlach (1795–1877) was far more energetic, emphatic, and uncompromising in his views. He too had been decisively stamped by the wars of liberation and the Awakening; but whereas Leopold had entered the military, Ludwig had pursued a judicial career. In 1848 he held a senior position at the appellate court in Magdeburg. Over the years he had become a devotee of Haller's patrimonialism and Evangelical orthodoxy. In the words of one scholar, his engagement with the intensely individualistic Awakening after 1815 had "led him and some of his friends into politics, where, however, they moved from the individual to the *basileia*, from pietism to

32. Leopold von Gerlach, diary (12 July 1851), GA, "Abschriften," 8: 217 (not in *Denkwürdigkeiten*).

33. The documents in GStA Merseburg, Rep. 92, Familienarchiv von Massow, Nr. 13, demonstrate clearly that Massow was consistently able to reinforce the views of Rauch and Gerlach in 1848. For a characterization of his personality, see C. von Rochow and M. de la Motte-Fouqué, *Vom Leben am preußischen Hofe 1815–1852*, ed. L. von der Marwitz (Berlin, 1908), pp. 154–55. The entry on Massow in the *Neue Deutsche Biographie* (Berlin, 1990), vol. 16, pp. 362–63, argues – incorrectly, in my opinion – that he cannot be regarded as a member of the Camarilla.

'churchliness'; in the end they supported an entirely hierarchical and orthodox conception of the church."[34] He had also discovered in himself a journalistic talent and a zest for fierce political and ideological controversy, to which he gave free rein in the pages of Ernst Wilhelm Hengstenberg's *Evangelische Kirchen-Zeitung* after 1827 and in the *Berliner Politisches Wochenblatt* after 1830.

Ludwig was never an intimate of Frederick William IV, and he never shared Leopold's feelings of personal attachment and devotion to that monarch. For all his loyalty to the monarchist cause and his conviction of the divinely ordained quality of monarchical authority, Ludwig deplored Frederick William's erratic style. As early as 1841 he had concluded that the king was probably doomed to be a "complete nullity."[35] Moreover, as he constantly liked to remind Leopold, Frederick William's exalted and even mystical views of his own office were arrogant and inflated. *All* men are kings, Ludwig liked to insist, a notion that he derived from Haller's ideas about the divine quality of all authority.[36]

When the revolution that he had long anticipated finally arrived in March 1848, Ludwig von Gerlach remained fiercely critical of the king's performance and skeptical about his future. Frederick William had not shown sufficient "penance" (*Buße*) for the sins of his past, Gerlach felt; thus it would be false pity to "go easy" on the monarch now. As early as 17 March, Ludwig wrote: "*Self-reliant* men, who nevertheless stand with the king, are what he needs. . . . The delicacy that Leopold recommends reminds me of a man who sees his neighbor fall into a fire but thinks it too indelicate to grasp him firmly."[37] In the weeks immediately after the revolution, Ludwig began to work feverishly on concrete strategies to defeat or at least slow down the progress of the revolution. Convinced that conservatives could learn from their enemies and take advantage of the new freedom of the press, in the spring

34. *Aus den Jahren*, ed. Schoeps, p. 24.
35. H.-C. Kraus, "Das preußische Königtum und Friedrich Wilhelm IV. aus der Sicht Ernst Ludwig von Gerlachs," in *Friedrich Wilhelm IV.*, ed. Büsch, p. 62.
36. Ibid., pp. 87–88.
37. Ludwig von Gerlach to Ernst Wilhelm Hengstenberg, 17 March 1848, Staatsbibliothek Preußischer Kulturbesitz Berlin, Handschriftenabteilung, Nachlaß Ernst Wilhelm Hengstenberg, Briefe Ernst Ludwig von Gerlachs 1829–1867, Bl. 158.

and summer of 1848 he devoted most of his prodigious energy to the creation of a conservative newspaper and to the closely related task of encouraging new forms of conservative political organization. The outcome of the newspaper idea was, of course, the decision to launch the *Neue Preußische Zeitung*, which because of the iron cross on its masthead quickly became known as the *Kreuzzeitung*. Celebrated for its flamboyant and often scabrous style, the *Kreuzzeitung* was certainly not a creation of the court Camarilla, but the two were closely intertwined thanks to the Gerlach brothers. As is well known, after 1848 the newspaper itself became a focus for adherents of what came to be called the "*Kreuzzeitung* party."[38]

Ludwig was less immediately concerned with the personal fate of the king than with the establishment of an effective conservative political organization, and in the spring and early summer of 1848 the work of the nascent court Camarilla was of secondary importance to him. As has been suggested above, Ludwig consistently drew a sharp distinction between the office of king, which was sanctioned by God, and the sinful nature of its occupant. The king had lost sight of his responsibility before God, Ludwig argued; his arrogance and willfulness had led him astray, and now he would have to be led back to the paths of righteousness and humility. Though the king was God's deputy on earth, Ludwig contended, he always

38. Orr, "Foundation," pp. 55–87, is still the best description of the paper's establishment, though it needs to be brought up to date by reference to sources that were unavailable to the author when he wrote his study; among them are the letters of Ludwig von Gerlach in GA, "Abschriften," 18 (or, alternatively, in BA Potsdam, 90 Ge 6, Nachlaß Leopold von Gerlach, Bd. 16), and the papers of Hermann Wagener in BA Potsdam, 90 Wa 3. See also H. Wagener, *Erlebtes. Meine Memoiren aus der Zeit von 1848 bis 1866 und von 1873 bis jetzt*, 2 vols. (Berlin, 1884), vol. 1, pp. 4–19; and the recent analyses by W. Füßl, *Professor in der Politik. Friedrich Julius Stahl (1802–1861). Das monarchische Prinzip und seine Umsetzung in die politische Praxis* (Göttingen, 1988), pp. 127–37; and W. Schwentker, *Konservative Vereine und Revolution in Preußen 1848/49. Die Konstituierung des Konservativismus als Partei* (Düsseldorf, 1988), pp. 60–62, 175–76. Schwentker describes the emergence after the summer of 1848 of "grass roots" conservative associations (*Vereine*), which, he argues, were astonishingly "autonomous" and certainly not instruments of the military or of the "reactionary court clique": ibid., p. 142. For an insightful review of the Füßl and Schwentker volumes, as well as of R.M. Berdahl's book cited above, see J. Retallack, "'Ideology without Vision'? Recent Literature on Nineteenth-Century German Conservatism," *German Historical Institute London. Bulletin* 13, no. 2 (May 1991): 3–22. The forthcoming studies of Ludwig von Gerlach by H.-C. Kraus, of the conservative press by J. Retallack, and of Hermann Wagener by H. Dieckwisch should also be important contributions.

remained a fragile and fallible vessel, a sinner like all other human beings – and, Ludwig frequently noted, Frederick William IV had sinned mightily. If that ruler failed to correct his ways, he hinted, supporters of the monarchical cause "should in *no* case be permitted to fall *with* the king."[39] Accordingly, Ludwig warned Leopold in mid-April not to associate himself too closely or personally with the king and to avoid "infection whenever you enter Butte's house." (*"Butt"* or *"Butte"* was an old nickname for Frederick William.)[40] On at least two occasions Ludwig compared Frederick William to the hapless Emperor Ferdinand of Austria, and he indicated that he was not at all averse to the idea of abdication. Conservative efforts should focus on rescuing the institution of monarchy, he contended, and not on bailing out a "nullity" such as Frederick William IV.[41] Only later in the summer did he drop the idea of abdication, principally because there was no clear alternative to the present monarch. But even in the autumn of 1848 Ludwig was still making barbed comparisons between Frederick William and the unfortunate English monarchs Richard II and Henry VI.[42] Such views were, of course, anathema to Leopold, for whom monarchical values were most obviously embodied in "a human being of flesh and blood," *"mon naturel maître,"* the *real* king whom God had granted to the Prussians. "If authority comes from above," Leopold wrote to Ludwig in June 1848, "so too does Frederick William IV, and he can only be dismissed from above."[43]

Rauch shared Leopold's views unreservedly, and so did Edwin von Manteuffel (1809–1885), who, though not a "member" of the Camarilla's inner circle, may still be regarded as one of its close associates. A thirty-nine-year-old *Rittmeister* at the beginning of a long, colorful, and controversial career, Manteuffel was inspired by feelings of personal loyalty and obligation to the monarch that were even stronger than

39. Quoted in Grünthal, "Bemerkungen," p. 42.

40. Ludwig von Gerlach to Leopold von Gerlach, 16 April 1848, GA, "Abschriften," 18: 10. A *Butt* is a flounder; Frederick William was amused by this nickname, and often drew caricatures of himself as a fish.

41. Ludwig von Gerlach to Leopold von Gerlach, 22 and 29 June 1848, ibid., 18: 45, 49; Kraus, "Königtum," p. 68.

42. Ludwig von Gerlach to Leopold von Gerlach, 29 June and 26 October 1848, GA, "Abschriften," 18: 47–50, 95.

43. Leopold von Gerlach to Ludwig von Gerlach, 20 June 1848, in *Von der Revolution*, ed. Diwald, vol. 2, p. 529; cf. Orr, "Foundation," p. 138.

Leopold's. During the most harrowing days of March 1848 he had stayed close to the king's side, even while his wife was giving birth to a baby son. Shortly thereafter he was named a royal aide-de-camp. In that capacity Manteuffel often served as a kind of courier between Berlin and Potsdam during the summer and autumn. The marshal of the court, Count Alexander von Keller (1801–1879), was also increasingly taken into the Camarilla's confidence during the summer months of 1848. Other "associates" of the Camarilla were the Halle historian Heinrich Leo, a conservative writer and theorist who was consulted by the Gerlachs from time to time in 1848; and Ludwig's brother-in-law, the Pomeranian aristocrat Baron Ernst Senfft von Pilsach, who had long specialized in earnest sermons to the king regarding his various moral and political shortcomings.

But what kind of practical service could the Camarilla provide to the beleaguered monarch? Would the dispirited and depressed Frederick William have the will or the energy to listen to his friends? Would an opportunity present itself for Manteuffel's "well-considered, well-prepared restoration"? And what form would such a restoration take? Confronted with these difficult questions, the Camarilla proceeded cautiously, even timorously, as the summer of 1848 unfolded.

IV

If the restoration of effective monarchical authority was the Camarilla's main concern in the summer of 1848, Frederick William's behavior constantly gave its members ample grounds for pessimism. By turns lachrymose, self-pitying, apathetic, resigned, and angry, the king spent weeks on end in Sanssouci deluging his ministers with angry letters and diverting himself with far-fetched projects to resurrect the defunct Holy Roman Empire. Throughout those months Frederick William consistently denied any responsibility for events in Berlin. The calamities that were transpiring in the capital, he said, were entirely the fault of the politicians there. In August, for example, he wrote to one longtime confidant: "If you find a lack of consequence in the policies of the government, just remember that we have been blessed with the *monstrum horrendum ingens* of a responsible cabinet, which takes pride in ruling without and against the king. *I do not rule.* For God's sake, don't forget that for a single moment."[44]

Frederick William's tactics of "self-effacement" (*Effacieren*) in the summer of 1848 reflected both the advice of Joseph Maria von Radowitz and his own inclinations. Radowitz urged the monarch to avoid a premature confrontation with the Prussian National Assembly or with the revolutionary masses in Berlin, and to bide his time and wait for an opportune moment.[45] Leopold von Gerlach constantly derided Radowitz's ideas and darkly hinted that they simply encouraged the king's "apathy and indifference"; but in fact the Camarilla had nothing better to offer in their place.[46] It would be necessary to come up with a "firm" and "reliable" ministry, Leopold warned, before Frederick William could seriously contemplate a restorationist strategy. In the summer of 1848, however, no such ministry was in sight, in part because many powerful conservative leaders had lost faith in the monarch and were unwilling to serve him. Many members of Prussia's traditional elites seemed to share Georg Wilhelm von Raumer's bleak diagnosis that the Hohenzollern were "a fallen race," and, as the famous *Junkerparlament* of August 1848 demonstrated to an irritated Ludwig von Gerlach, many more seemed to be interested primarily in salvaging as much as possible of their older economic and social privileges.[47] In this situation the Camarilla too urged a temporizing policy. As Leopold von Gerlach put it in a revealing memorandum of 1 June 1848:

> For now it seems essential that the king deal, as much as currently possible, with reliable, loyal, and insightful persons (Rauch, Massow, Keller), and that he give them his full confidence. He must do everything through them and nothing without them. He must inform them of his arrangements with other people; and through them he must establish contact with other persons whose advice, discernment, and power might be important. Then the king will

44. Frederick William IV to Count Carl von der Groeben, 30 August 1848, GStA Merseburg, Rep. 92, Graf Carl von der Groeben, B Nr. 4ᵉ 1848, Bl. 13ᵛ.

45. Radowitz to Frederick William IV, 24 May and 22 June 1848, in J.M. von Radowitz, *Nachgelassene Briefe und Aufzeichnungen zur Geschichte der Jahre 1848–1853*, ed. W. Möring (Stuttgart and Berlin, 1922), pp. 48–49, 58–59.

46. Leopold von Gerlach, diary (23 August 1848), GA, "Abschriften," 6: 124 (not in *Denkwürdigkeiten*).

47. Ludwig von Gerlach to Leopold von Gerlach, 29 June 1848, GA, "Abschriften," 18: 49. On the *Junkerparlament* and Ludwig von Gerlach's response to it, see especially Schwentker, *Vereine*, pp. 100–110, and Berdahl, *Politics*, p. 380.

have to try to gain ground in the cabinet, especially by arranging for the foreign ministry to get a new occupant and by maintaining close contacts with the minister of war.

Eventually, Gerlach suggested, the king would be in a position to dissolve the existing National Assembly and call for elections to a new one. Only in an extreme case – such as the proclamation of a republic – could drastic action be undertaken immediately.[48]

Two months later, at the end of July, Gerlach was still warning Frederick William to avoid any confrontation with the Assembly in Berlin. The king could only think seriously about its dissolution once he had the firm backing of a united cabinet, wrote Gerlach, and such a ministry was not yet in sight. "Whether such a step, which could almost be called a coup d'état, would currently be advisable, is very doubtful. I at least would not advise Your Majesty to do it right now, but would prefer to proceed step by step, though with resolute determination."[49] Ludwig, preoccupied during these weeks with political organizing and the establishment of the *Kreuzzeitung*, echoed his older brother's sentiments, agreeing that it would be necessary to wait "until ripe fruit falls into the king's lap, and, in the meantime, let us prepare a ministry. . . ." As early as 17 July, Ludwig suggested that Count Friedrich Wilhelm von Brandenburg, commander of the VI Army Corps in Breslau, might play a role in such a government. And by late August, Ludwig was suggesting that a suitable cabinet might include Brandenburg, Otto von Bismarck, and Karl Ludwig von Prittwitz, who had commanded army units in Berlin during the street fighting of 18 and 19 March.[50]

Still, there were few signs in the late summer that the "fruit" to which Ludwig had alluded was about to ripen. In June the Camphausen government had resigned in the wake of street

48. Leopold von Gerlach, "Promemoria," 1 June 1848, GA, "Abschriften," 18: 172–75.

49. Leopold von Gerlach to Frederick William IV, 28 July 1848 (draft), ibid., 18: 182–83; the final version, sent to the king the next day, excluded any reference to a coup d'état: Leopold von Gerlach to Frederick William IV, 29 July 1848, in Leopold von Gerlach, diary (29 July 1848), ibid., 6: 107–8. On the Camarilla's lack of initiative, see also Orr, "Foundation," pp. 146–47.

50. Ludwig von Gerlach to Leopold von Gerlach, 17 July and 27 August 1848, GA, "Abschriften," 18: 54, 71; see also Ludwig von Gerlach to Leopold von Gerlach, 9 July 1848, in H. von Petersdorff, "Briefe Ludwigs von Gerlach an seinen Bruder Leopold," *Konservative Monatsschrift für Politik, Literatur und Kunst* 63, no. 1 (October 1905), p. 71; Orr, "Foundation," p. 152.

violence in Berlin, which had culminated in the storming of the government arsenal (*Zeughaus*) on 14 June. Although the new cabinet was headed by one of the king's childhood playmates, the East Prussian aristocrat Rudolf von Auerswald, its driving force remained Finance Minister David Hansemann, who was determined to end the special privileges enjoyed by Prussia's traditional elites. Meanwhile, a special committee of the National Assembly, chaired by the respected democrat Benedict Waldeck, was preparing a revised constitutional draft that provided the king with a suspensive rather than an absolute veto. That draft also called for the creation of a popular militia and the abolition of patrimonial privilege in the countryside.[51] Conservative responses to the so-called *Charte Waldeck* were, of course, predictably and vehemently negative.

Then, suddenly, a crisis emerged that neither king nor Camarilla had anticipated. On 31 July regular army units in the Silesian town of Schweidnitz had fired on a crowd of civilians and killed fourteen people. On 9 August outraged deputies in the Berlin National Assembly considered a motion by the Breslau democrat Julius Stein demanding that Prussian officers "distance themselves from all reactionary tendencies" and present concrete evidence of their commitment to constitutional values. The Auerswald-Hansemann cabinet, aware of the extreme sensitivity of civil-military relations in Prussia, tried to dampen the controversy for several weeks, but by early September the issue could no longer be avoided. On 7 September the National Assembly called upon the government, by a 219 to 143 vote, to carry out the stipulations of the Stein Resolution.[52]

Frederick William IV was convinced that the hour of decision had arrived, and that the use of force against his "disloyal and good-for-nothing" capital was inevitable.[53] Unable to find a suitable candidate to head a new government, Frederick William proceeded to draft a series of statements on 11 and 19 September in which he indicated that he would annul the Stein Resolution, move the National Assembly from Berlin to the city of Brandenburg, and eliminate the *Charte Waldeck* and

51. Huber, *Verfassungsgeschichte*, vol. 2, pp. 730–32; M. Botzenhart, *Deutscher Parlamentarismus in der Revolutionszeit 1848–1850* (Düsseldorf, 1977), pp. 538–41.

52. Botzenhart, *Parlamentarismus*, pp. 527–32.

53. Frederick William IV, "Die Lage der Dinge heute 4. September 1848 ist folgende," GStA Merseburg, Rep. 92, Familienarchiv von Massow, Nr. 13, Bl. 62.

Hansemann's anti-Junker "confiscatory" laws. The Assembly would be dissolved if it objected to these measures.[54] This so-called *Kampfprogramm* of September 1848 has long been regarded as evidence of a carefully planned coup, worked out by the king with the Camarilla's connivance, in anticipation of the actual course that events took in November and December 1848. The historian Günther Grünthal has convincingly shown, however, that throughout the autumn of 1848 Frederick William failed to adhere to the details of his September program, to which the Camarilla itself responded cautiously and skeptically. It is, in fact, impossible to regard the counter-revolution of November–December 1848 as a coup concocted in advance by the king and his conservative advisers in the court Camarilla. That counterrevolution was a much more complex affair, and its results were, from the Gerlachs' stand-point, exceedingly ambiguous.[55]

Always an informal and even disorganized group, the Camarilla was at first unprepared for the crisis that attended the collapse of the Auerswald-Hansemann cabinet.[56] Indeed, on 6 September, the day before the National Assembly's cru-cial vote on the Stein Resolution, Rauch and Leopold von Ger-lach had talked with each other for the first time in almost a month; a week earlier, at the end of August, Ludwig had had his first serious conversation with the king since the March revolution.[57] Though initially caught off guard, Rauch, the Gerlachs, and Massow quickly barraged Frederick William with advice. While recognizing the gravity of the situation, the

54. Frederick William IV, "Kampfprogramm" of 11 September 1848, in F. Frahm, "Entstehungs- und Entwicklungsgeschichte der preußischen Verfas-sung (vom März 1848 bis zum Januar 1850)," *Forschungen zur Brandenburgi-schen und Preußischen Geschichte* 41 (1928): 266–67; and in *Dokumente zur deutschen Verfassungsgeschichte*, ed. E.R. Huber, vol. 1, *Deutsche Verfassungs-dokumente 1803–1850* (Stuttgart, 1961), p. 374; "Denkschrift König Friedrich Wilhelms IV.," 15 September 1848, in *Revolutionsbriefe 1848*, ed. Haenchen, pp. 175–78.

55. G. Grünthal, "Zwischen König, Kabinett und Kamarilla. Der Verfas-sungsoktroi in Preußen vom 5.12.1848," *Jahrbuch für die Geschichte Mittel- und Ostdeutschlands* 32 (1983): 135–37; idem, "Bemerkungen," pp. 42–43.

56. For details leading up to the cabinet's resignation, see W.J. Orr, Jr., "König Friedrich Wilhelm IV. und der Sturz des Ministeriums Auerswald-Hansemann," *Jahrbuch für die Geschichte Mittel- und Ostdeutschlands* 25 (1976), pp. 124–44.

57. Ludwig von Gerlach, diary (30 August 1848), in *Von der Revolution*, ed. Diwald, vol. 1, p. 109; Leopold von Gerlach, diary (6 September 1848), GA, "Abschriften," 6: 131–32 (not in *Denkwürdigkeiten*); cf. Orr, "Sturz," p. 140.

Camarilla continued to caution the king against a rash or premature collision with the Assembly in Berlin. Rather, they said, he should remain "moderate, clear-headed, almost passive," but also "conscientious, fully consistent, and true to his principles."[58] In a conversation with Frederick William on 9 September, Leopold von Gerlach raised the vague possibility of a "military ministry," but decided not to pursue the matter further, because to do so would be premature. Count Brandenburg had not been sounded about his willingness to accept a ministerial post, and otherwise the Camarilla was not at all confident that the king was prepared to act decisively.[59] As Ludwig noted to Leopold after returning to Magdeburg in mid-September, "No one is yet able to discern the king's banner, depend on it, and rally around it. . . . You will have to do everything in your power to *organize* the king and the Camarilla – or else all is lost." To his diary, however, Ludwig confided his skepticism that this could be done: "Everything is still as it was. We need heroic deeds, everything is ready, only the hero is missing."[60]

As it happened, the Camarilla had no influence whatsoever over the king's choice for a stopgap minister president. On 21 September 1848, General Ernst von Pfuel, a highly regarded liberal and former friend of Heinrich von Kleist, became head of a new cabinet that from the very outset was intended to be short-lived. Its main function was to mediate between the National Assembly and an increasingly angry and estranged

58. "Vereinbarung der beiden Gerlachs vom 9.9.1848," GA, "Abschriften," 18: 194–96. See also Ernst Ludwig von Gerlach, "Regierungsplan für den König, Herbst 1848," in idem, *Aufzeichnungen aus seinem Leben und Wirken 1795–1877*, ed. J. von Gerlach, 2 vols. (Schwerin i. Meckl., 1903), vol. 2, pp. 511–18, and GA, "Abschriften," 18: 184–91 (with marginal comments by Leopold); Leopold von Gerlach to Ludwig von Gerlach, 7 September 1848, in *Von der Revolution*, ed. Diwald, vol. 2, pp. 567–69.

59. Leopold von Gerlach, diary (9 September 1848), GA, "Abschriften," 6: 141 (also in *Denkwürdigkeiten*, vol. 1, p. 193, with slight textual variations); Ludwig von Gerlach, diary (9 September 1848), in *Von der Revolution*, ed. Diwald, vol. 1, pp. 111–12. In a report dated 14 September and presented to the king in the presence of Rauch and Leopold von Gerlach, Massow developed similar arguments: GStA Merseburg, Rep. 92, Familienarchiv von Massow, Nr. 13, Bl. 112. See also Canis, "Militarismus," pp. 135–36; idem, "Ideologie und Taktik," p. 478.

60. Ludwig von Gerlach to Leopold von Gerlach, 12 September 1848, GA, "Abschriften," 18: 77; Ludwig von Gerlach, diary (10 September 1848), in *Von der Revolution*, ed. Diwald, vol. 1, p. 112. See also Grünthal, "Zwischen König, Kabinett und Kamarilla," p. 137; idem, "Bemerkungen," pp. 42–43.

monarch. Despite claiming to be a closet republican, Pfuel had
served the king well for many years. Thus Frederick William
was shocked and horrified when he learned, at the end of September, that the new minister president had issued his own
"Anti-Reaction Decree" which echoed the major provisions of
the hated Stein Resolution! At the same time, the National
Assembly continued to press for a series of important social
and political reforms, including the abolition of the death
penalty, the introduction of habeas corpus, and an end to
landowners' special hunting rights. Finally, in mid-October,
the Assembly voted to eliminate Frederick William's designation as king "by the Grace of God" (*durch Gottes Gnaden*).[61] For
a monarch who was literally convinced of his *Gottesgnadentum*
and its mystical qualities, this was the last straw. The Assembly had twice seriously intruded upon his monarchical role –
first, attempting to undercut his direct control over the army,
and, second, publicly casting doubt upon the divinely
ordained nature of his own station – and this even the "self-
effacing" Frederick William IV could never tolerate. Pfuel's
situation immediately became untenable, and on 16 October
he and his cabinet resigned.[62] This time the Camarilla was
ready with an alternative government to present to the king.
Its hour had finally struck.

V

Count Brandenburg's name had first come up in discussions
about a new cabinet in mid-July, and at the end of September,
recognizing the importance of Pfuel's Anti-Reaction Decree,
Ludwig von Gerlach insisted that the time had come to put
together an antirevolutionary ministry including Brandenburg, Bismarck, and the young ultra-reactionaries Hans Hugo
von Kleist-Retzow and Marcus Niebuhr. The prince of Prussia
– Frederick William's younger brother and heir to the throne –
could serve as "Generalissimo."[63] Having broken with the

---

61. V. Valentin, *Geschichte der deutschen Revolution von 1848–1849*, 2 vols.
(Cologne, 1977; originally published 1931–32), vol. 2, pp. 246–51; Huber, *Verfassungsgeschichte*, vol. 2, pp. 741–45; Canis, "Ideologie und Taktik," pp.
479–87; Botzenhart, *Parlamentarismus*, pp. 543–44.

62. See the documents in *Revolutionsbriefe*, ed. Haenchen, pp. 199–200, 206–7.

63. Ludwig von Gerlach to Leopold von Gerlach, 29 September 1848, GA,
"Abschriften," 18: 85.

Pfuel cabinet, and alarmed that the authority of his office was fast slipping away, the ever-hesitant Frederick William had run out of options; he really had no choice at this point but to go along with the Camarilla's prescriptions. As Leopold put it in a letter to Brandenburg on 21 October: "Our lord the king is stuck in a swamp, he feels that he is sinking, he is calling out for help, but no one is willing to extend a hand to pull him out." Then, outlining the Camarilla's restorationist strategy, Gerlach continued: "The task is simple and clear. It is a matter of declaring that the king is master of the land, and not the Assembly in the comedians' house; it is also a matter of accepting the consequences of this declaration, based on the army, which is still loyal, and the subjects of the crown, who are still loyal. This decision deserves our enthusiasm."[64]

In October and early November, Rauch, Massow, and the two Gerlachs were in virtually daily contact with the king, constantly reminding him of his "duty" and urging upon him a policy of firmness and steadiness.[65] The Camarilla was also more numerous in the autumn of 1848 than at any other time. Heinrich Leo and Senfft-Pilsach participated in its discussions, while the young journalist and financial expert Marcus Niebuhr (1817–1860) became its newest "member." Son of the famous historian Barthold Georg Niebuhr and a protégé of Ludwig von Gerlach in Magdeburg, the zealous, even fanatical young man quickly became one of Leopold's confidants as well.[66]

On 6 October, as the crisis within the Pfuel cabinet was unfolding, Rauch and the Gerlachs met with the king and convinced him that Leopold should travel to Breslau, where Count Brandenburg was still serving as a corps commander, to discuss with him the possibility of heading a new government. The illegitimate result of one of Frederick William II's frequent dalliances, Brandenburg was thus the king's uncle

---

64. Leopold von Gerlach to Brandenburg, 21 October 1848, in Leopold von Gerlach, diary (21 October 1848), GA, "Abschriften," 6: 198 (also in *Denkwürdigkeiten*, vol. 1, pp. 224–25); cf. Grünthal, "Bemerkungen," p. 44.

65. During those weeks (11–19 October and 1–13 November) Ludwig von Gerlach maintained a daily "Journal der Camarilla," in *Von der Revolution*, ed. Diwald, vol. 1, pp. 120–29, 131–40.

66. Ludwig von Gerlach to Leopold von Gerlach, 22 and 28 October 1848, GA, "Abschriften," 18: 94–95, 98; Leopold von Gerlach, diary (1 November 1848), ibid., 6: 210 (not in *Denkwürdigkeiten*). For biographical details on Niebuhr, see *Allgemeine Deutsche Biographie* (Berlin, reprint, 1967–71), vol. 23, pp. 662–64, and Orr, "Foundation," pp. 163–64.

and had spent his entire life in the country's highest aristocratic circles. A thoroughly military man, he was under no illusions about the tasks that would confront him in Berlin and
Potsdam, but after much arm-twisting and soul-searching he
agreed. On 1 November, the Assembly learned to its great dismay that Pfuel had stepped down and that Brandenburg was
the new minister president. The significance of this announcement was obvious. The time had come, Leopold von Gerlach
insisted, to put an end to the idea of parliamentary sovereignty, "to show in every possible way that the king still rules in
this country, and not the Assembly."[67] Three days later, on the
evening of 4 November, the Camarilla – the Gerlachs, Rauch,
Massow, Keller, and Leo – met in Count Brandenburg's rooms
at the *Neue Kammern* near Sanssouci to hear the new cabinet's
plans to move the Assembly from Berlin to the city of Brandenburg, to urge the king to contain his rhetorical excesses,
and to shield the monarch from "destructive" outside influences. Despite a steady downpour, the participants left the
conclave in an "elated mood." Moreover, with the designation
of a "firm" government committed to the monarchical cause,
the Camarilla itself had, according to Ludwig, fulfilled its
major purpose: "The Camarilla (the king says, 'my friends')
faded away in the presence of the presiding minister."[68]

On 9 November General Friedrich von Wrangel's troops
occupied Berlin, encountering virtually no resistance; the
National Assembly was adjourned and removed to Brandenburg, and a "state of siege" was proclaimed in the capital
itself. The Assembly tried to resume its activity on 27 November, but by then it was too late. On 5 December it was dissolved, and on that same day Brandenburg's government
announced the promulgation of a new constitution. This document was, in many respects, surprisingly moderate, providing
for a two-house parliament to be elected on the basis of a

67. Leopold von Gerlach to Brandenburg, 2 November 1848, GA,
"Abschriften," 6: 211 (also in *Denkwürdigkeiten*, vol. 1, pp. 232). See also
Leopold's diary for the period from 17 October to 3 November 1848, in GA,
"Abschriften," 6: 190–214 (much more complete than *Denkwürdigkeiten*, vol. 1,
pp. 218–35); also Ludwig von Gerlach's "Journal der Camarilla, Fortsetzung," in
Von der Revolution, ed. Diwald, vol. 1, pp. 131–40, for the days after 1 November.
Cf. the extremely detailed description in Jordan, *Entstehung*, pp. 354–67; and the
analysis in Grünthal, "Zwischen König, Kabinett und Kamarilla," p. 146.

68. Ludwig von Gerlach, diary (4 November 1848), in *Von der Revolution*, ed.
Diwald, vol. 1, p. 134.

rather broadly defined franchise. The king remained, of course, monarch "by the Grace of God" and the ultimate source of political authority. But at some future date he would have to take an oath to the constitution and accept the permanence of parliamentary institutions and ministerial responsibility.[69] In short, Frederick William's "November ministry" had brought him and the Prussian state irreversibly into the constitutional age.

Frederick William was at first aghast when he learned of the Brandenburg government's decision to impose a constitution, for he had dreamed of returning to the older projects of *ständisch* reform that he had pursued so enthusiastically before 1848. On 23 November he proclaimed, in one of his innumerable outbursts, "If I were not a Christian I would take my own life." A few days later he appeared to Rauch, Massow, and Leopold von Gerlach to be in a state of "complete despair": "They could declare him mad, he said, they could call him a dog, but he could never agree to sign this thing."[70] Still, the king had no choice. And, in any case, he had won, despite the concession of a constitution. He had survived the revolution with much of his authority intact, for in the new constitutional age, the power of the Prussian crown would remain formidable indeed. Despite his initially hysterical reactions, Frederick William gradually began to accommodate himself to the new situation after 5 December. It began to dawn on the king that the constitution could be revised to reflect "monarchical principles" – as, indeed, it was with the imposition of three-class suffrage in 1849 and the reorganization of the upper chamber into a "House of Lords" (*Herrenhaus*) in 1854.[71]

As Günther Grünthal has put it, the constitutional document of 5 December 1848 was the result of a three-way compromise among the king, the Camarilla, and the Brandenburg cabinet.[72] The new minister president himself had gone out of

69. Botzenhart, *Parlamentarismus*, 545–50; *Dokumente*, ed. Huber, vol. 1, pp. 382–94; Frahm, "Verfassung," 288–91. As it happened, the oath was finally administered on 6 February 1850, after long months of political wrangling and constitutional revision.

70. Leopold von Gerlach, diary (23 November and 5 December 1848), GA, "Abschriften," 6: 247, 267 (only portions in *Denkwürdigkeiten*).

71. Grünthal, "Zwischen König, Kabinett und Kamarilla," pp. 169–70.

72. Ibid., p. 164. See also W.J. Orr, Jr., "The Prussian Ultra Right and the Advent of Constitutionalism in Prussia," *Canadian Journal of History/Annales canadiennes d'histoire* 11, no. 3 (December 1976): 299–303; Füßl, *Professor*, pp. 153–62; Schwentker, *Vereine*, pp. 232–47.

his way to show that he was "not a creature or a tool of the Potsdam Camarilla."[73] The very embodiment of the bureau-cratic-military strand in Prussian conservatism, Brandenburg was virtually impervious to *ständisch*, "pietist," or "Christian-German" sentiments. The leaders of the Camarilla were at best marginally involved in the discussions leading up to the con-stitution's promulgation. On 26 November Leopold observed that "the power of the Camarilla has largely been absorbed by the cabinet," and on 3 December – two days before promulga-tion – the general admitted that he had not discussed any political issues with the king for more than a week. Both Ger-lachs had, of course, been worried about the rumors of a pos-sible constitution. Ludwig himself only found out about the constitutional draft while riding the train on 6 December. He immediately began thinking about "reconstructing the Camar-illa and coming up with ministers in reserve," and he fired off an angry article for the *Kreuzzeitung*.

But just as the king had had no alternative to the Branden-burg government in October, so too had the vestigial Camaril-la run out of options in December.[74] Leopold shared Ludwig's disappointment, but he was always more cautious than his belligerent younger brother. For the time being, he believed, the Camarilla's members, while distancing themselves from the government's actions, would have to accept the constitu-tion. Besides, Leopold consoled himself, Prussia's dose of con-stitutionalism was "not too strong."[75] Quite a few, perhaps even most, conservatives seemed to agree with him. Many of the popular conservative associations (*Vereine*) that had sprung up in large numbers, especially in Brandenburg and Pomerania, since the summer of 1848 were quite willing to accept the promulgation of a constitution; in fact, since mid-November many of them had been urging the king to take this

73. Leopold von Gerlach to Ludwig von Gerlach, 19 November 1848, in *Von der Revolution*, ed. Diwald, vol. 2, p. 599.
74. Ludwig von Gerlach, diary (8 and 12 December 1848), in ibid., vol. 1, pp. 145–46.
75. "Bruchstück eines politischen Résumés von Leopold von Gerlach, Pots-dam," 7 December 1848, GA, "Abschriften," 18: 252–53; Leopold von Gerlach to Ludwig von Gerlach, 14 December 1848, in *Von der Revolution*, ed. Diwald, vol. 2, p. 615. See also Leopold von Gerlach, diary (3 and 4 December 1848), ibid., vol. 6, pp. 264, 266 (also in *Denkwürdigkeiten*, vol. 1, pp. 257–58, 259, though incorrectly dated); Leopold von Gerlach to Brandenburg, 23 December 1848, GA, "Abschriften," 6: 275–78 (also in *Denkwürdigkeiten*, vol. 1, pp. 263–65).

step.[76] At the same time, prominent conservative scholars and publicists such as Friedrich Julius Stahl contended that the new constitution was compatible with the maintenance of monarchical institutions in Prussia.[77]

VI

It is difficult to speak of an identifiable or coherent court Camarilla after December 1848, and thereafter the Gerlachs only rarely used that term to refer to themselves and their friends. Friedrich Wilhelm von Rauch, who had never much cared for politics anyway, was happy to return to his beloved St. Petersburg in 1849; his health declined rapidly, however, and he died in June 1850. Massow and Keller resumed their administrative duties at court, and there is no evidence that they ever again concerned themselves with explicitly political matters. Leopold von Gerlach was frequently absent from court during the first months of 1849, while Ludwig increasingly focused his energies on the newly constituted upper house or First Chamber, to which he was elected in early 1849 – the beginning of a long, active, and often controversial parliamentary career. Indeed, just as the Camarilla largely acceded to constitutionalism after December 1848, so too were its members essentially absorbed into the "*Kreuzzeitung* party," which emerged during the decade of reaction after 1848 as the major political voice of "high" conservative interests. For years before 1848 Ludwig von Gerlach had argued that conservatives should learn from their enemies how to organize politically. Now, like his fellow conservative Stahl, Ludwig was quick to appreciate the utility of constitutionalism for the conservative cause. Throughout the 1850s, as recent studies have made abundantly clear, neither Ludwig nor any other member of the Camarilla ever seriously considered departing from the constitutional path or undertaking a counterrevolutionary coup d'état.[78] Moreover, after 1849 Leopold von Gerlach became convinced that the war against "the revolution" had to be directed simultaneously against "Bonapartism" and

---

76. Schwentker, *Vereine*, pp. 242–47; Hans Wegge, *Die Stellung der Öffentlichkeit zur oktroyierten Verfassung und die preußische Parteibildung 1848/49* (Berlin, 1932), pp. 44, 54–59.

77. Füßl, *Professor*, p. 154.

78. These arguments are summarized in Grünthal, "Bemerkungen," p. 46.

David E. Barclay

"bureaucratic despotism," and during the 1850s he was often concerned that a Hardenberg-style bureaucratic system was reemerging in Prussia. Thus, like his brother and Stahl, Leopold decided that the present constitution, though less desirable than a *ständisch* arrangement, offered the best protection against both Bonapartists and bureaucrats.[79] Frederick William IV understood just how much things had changed when he began to complain that people like Stahl and the Gerlachs, indeed the entire *Kreuzzeitung* party, had, "may God have mercy!, suddenly become constitutional!!!"[80] But in fact the king himself had become "constitutional." Although he swore, until the onset of his debilitating illness in 1857, that he wanted to replace the "French-modern" constitution with "real German, *ständisch* institutions," he also realized that he had taken a sacred oath to the constitution in February 1850, "and my word is sacred, and I will not break it." In the meantime, "as long as we are afflicted by the French constitution, and especially as we free ourselves from it, we still need majorities!!"[81]

Frederick William remained, of course, an unhappy and unwilling constitutional monarch, and until the end of his active reign in 1857/58 he continued to seek advice from both his old cronies and new, extraconstitutional advisers. After 1849 Leopold von Gerlach's own position at court became official for the first time; in that year he was promoted to general *à la suite* in the royal entourage, and in 1850 he succeeded Rauch as one of the king's reporting adjutants general. This position guaranteed him virtually unlimited access to the monarch. He also forged a close political alliance with Queen Elizabeth after 1848, and thus was able to use his famous "coffee ministry" – his daily briefing of the king and queen over breakfast – to good effect during the years of reaction. Marcus Niebuhr became Leopold's closest political ally during this decade,

79. Leopold von Gerlach to Frederick William IV, 20 February 1853, GStA Merseburg, HA Rep. 50, J, Nr. 455, Bl. 84–85; Leopold von Gerlach to Graf Münster, 27–30 May 1853, in Nobbe, "Einfluß," *Quellen*, pp. 162–63; Leopold von Gerlach to Edwin von Manteuffel, 29 October 1858, in ibid., pp. 180–82; Clausen, *Stellung*, pp. 76–78; Nobbe, "Einfluß," pp. 109–14.

80. Frederick William IV to Baron Ernst Senfft von Pilsach, 9 July 1854, GStA Merseburg, Rep. 92, Ernst Freiherr Senfft von Pilsach, B, Nr. 8, Bl. 12^v.

81. Frederick William IV to Emperor Francis Joseph I, 28–29 September 1853, GStA Merseburg, HA Rep. 50, J, Nr. 939, Bl. 59^v–60.

and, as the king's secretary and, later, privy councillor, he was always a reliable watchdog of the Gerlachs' interests.[82]

Nevertheless, Gerlach and his friends at court and in the *Kreuzzeitung* party by no means enjoyed an uncontested position of primacy in Prussia during the reaction era. Nor could Leopold ever count on the king's unqualified confidence, despite his personal indispensability to that mercurial monarch. Four main factors combined to circumscribe the influence of these men. First, there was the long struggle against Radowitz's Union project, which ended with the autumn crisis of 1850 (during which Brandenburg suddenly died and was succeeded by Otto von Manteuffel) and the Olmütz accords at the end of November. The *Kreuzzeitung* and its court allies emerged victorious from this conflict, after which they were able to place a number of their supporters – including Bismarck, Kleist-Retzow, Senfft-Pilsach, Ferdinand von Westphalen, and Karl von Raumer – in key state positions. In contrast to 1848, however, this time the *Kreuzzeitung* group opposed the king, who thereafter remained deeply embittered by that newspaper's ferocious assaults against his "divine" friend, Radowitz.[83]

Second, between 1850 and 1854 many conservatives became embroiled in another long struggle with Frederick William, this time over the reorganization of the upper house. Third, Leopold von Gerlach became involved in endless squabbles with Minister President Otto von Manteuffel, especially after the onset of the Oriental crisis in 1853. Fourth and finally, after 1848 Frederick William became increasingly concerned with security issues; accordingly, he sought out new confidants, such as Berlin's Police President Carl Ludwig von Hinckeldey or the bizarre school director Carl Wilhelm Saegert, who could satisfy his growing obsession with police and surveillance matters. So distressed was Leopold von Gerlach with these developments that after 1852 he began to complain of a "second Camarilla" that had intruded itself between the king and his older friends.[84] Thus the center of the Prussian state

82. Leopold von Gerlach to Ludwig von Gerlach, 26 October 1851, 10 August 1852, 7 October 1857, in *Von der Revolution*, ed. Diwald, vol. 2, pp. 766–67, 807, 930.

83. Frederick William IV to Christian Carl Josias Bunsen, 9–10 January 1854, GStA Merseburg, HA Rep. 50, J, Nr. 244a, Bl. 188.

84. Leopold von Gerlach, diary (29 January 1852 and 18 April 1856), GA, "Abschriften," 9: 25 and 13: 77 (neither in *Denkwürdigkeiten*).

remained a swirling and chaotic arena of competing interests and influences throughout the decade of reaction, with no single group or individual in a position to dominate the others or impose its will upon the king. In the caustic words of the British envoy to Berlin in 1854: "There is perhaps no Court in Europe at the present moment where such a maze of intrigue is being carried on as in Berlin."[85] To Ludwig von Gerlach, though, things could be a lot worse, as he sighed on one occasion: "All we can do is accept this anarchy, as the French say; we must accommodate ourselves to the fact that it exists and that we cannot get rid of it. Anarchy is not totally intolerable for us. We have more or less gotten used to it."[86] It is therefore beyond any doubt that the political constellation of the autumn of 1848 – when Frederick William found himself in perfect accord with his "high" conservative allies – was unique. The vestigial Camarilla of the reaction era never became anything remotely resembling a *ministère occulte*, a *Nebenregierung*, or a *Gegenregierung*.

The Gerlachs themselves had never overestimated the Camarilla's significance, nor did they ever express exaggerated hopes for its durability. In October 1848 Ludwig von Gerlach had argued that a Camarilla was "inevitable" whenever "the king has fallen out with his ministry or is simply alienated from it, . . . but it is incompatible with a solid, powerful government, especially in times of serious struggle."[87] Writing eight years later, Leopold noted: "Our position is based on resolute unity with the king, in some respects as an extension of the constitutional ministers."[88] Of course, after December 1848, as has been noted above, it was often difficult for Gerlach to maintain "resolute unity" with Frederick William. However, like his monarch, Gerlach remained convinced that, even in a constitutional state based on a responsible government, the king was entirely within his rights to heed his informal advisers. Gerlach always insisted that it was "nonsense"

85. Lord Bloomfield to Earl of Clarendon, 10 February 1854, Public Record Office, Kew, FO 64/368.

86. Ludwig von Gerlach to Leopold von Gerlach, 16 July 1852, GA, "Abschriften," 22: 210.

87. Ludwig von Gerlach, "Promemoria über das Verhältnis des Grafen Brandenburg zu den übrigen Ministern," 19 October 1848, in *Von der Revolution*, ed. Diwald, vol. 2, pp. 593–94; cf. Grünthal, "Bemerkungen," pp. 44–45.

88. Leopold von Gerlach, diary (18 April 1856), GA, "Abschriften," 13: 77 (not in *Denkwürdigkeiten*).

to believe that a *"Camarilla-Regiment"* could not be reconciled with a constitutional system. He also admitted, however, that in such a system responsible ministers were entirely within *their* rights to demand that the king remove his unofficial advisers.[89]

It was this sort of reasoning that helped the king adjust himself, however reluctantly, to the new constitutional arrangements and the changed political realities of the post-1848 period. Therein lies the Camarilla's real historical significance. It represented a relatively short-lived, transitional stage in the process by which conservative elites were able to undertake a kind of counterrevolution while simultaneously adapting themselves to permanently changed circumstances. In the process those elites were able to bring the unhappy king along with them, and this was in itself a remarkable achievement.[90] It is thus no coincidence that the court Camarilla of 1848 essentially dissolved into the *Kreuzzeitung* party, which itself contributed so significantly to the modernization of conservative political practice in the second half of the nineteenth century. Of course, like the conservative acceptance of constitutionalism after December 1848, that practice remained ambivalent and full of contradictions. As this essay has emphasized, the *Kreuzzeitung* party and its court allies decided that constitutional structures could help maintain an authoritarian social and political system rooted in a powerful monarchy; but this decision was largely based on tactical and strategic considerations. Accordingly, the "modern" styles of conservative political practice should be understood within the framework of what Günther Grünthal describes as the "pseudoconstitutionalization" of the Prussian Right after 1848.[91] Many conservatives continued to sympathize with their king's distaste for "French-modern" constitutions, parliaments, elections, and mass politics.[92] They also shared his dark forebodings about the future of the monarchical and conservative cause. In the summer of 1857, after almost a decade of political reaction, Frederick William IV remained convinced that, in the end, he

89. Leopold von Gerlach, diary (1 January 1849), GA, "Abschriften," 6: 280–81 (also in *Denkwürdigkeiten*, vol. 1, p. 266, though not dated). See the discussion of the same passage in Grünthal, "Bemerkungen," pp. 45–46.

90. Berdahl, *Politics*, p. 376.

91. Grünthal, "Bemerkungen," p. 46.

92. Retallack, "Literature," pp. 14, 18–19.

was still going to lose. "The revolution is stalking the world once more," he wrote to one close friend. "May God have mercy!"[93]

93. Frederick William IV to Groeben, 29 June 1857, GStA Merseburg, Rep. 92, Graf Carl von der Groeben, B Nr. 4ᵍ 1855–1857, Bl. 45–46.

5

Between Economic Interests and Radical Nationalism

*Attempts to Found a New Right-Wing Party in Imperial Germany, 1887–94**

Dirk Stegmann

In September 1889 Johannes von Miquel, one of the leading politicians of the National Liberal Party, diagnosed a far-reaching crisis in German party politics. This was during a period of social discontent brought on by the agricultural crisis and the depression in industry. He stated that "all our political parties were out of date long ago, that they are products of the past but not of the living present and future, and that these very questions of the future, which have no place in the present party programs, will lead to the disintegration of these parties."[1] Miquel did not follow up this observation with any concrete suggestions for a solution to the problem. Yet he was not the only person to offer such criticism. Some years before, in 1885, Arnold Steinmann-Bucher, the general secretary of the Cologne branch of the Association of Industrialists (Verein der Industriellen or VdI), had compared the parliamentary system, with its political parties, to groups organized according to the corporate interests of agriculture, industry, trades, and artisanry or skilled crafts. Steinmann-Bucher concluded: "Today, the individual citizen is much more closely connected with his corporate group [*Verein*] than with parliament, and the latter is already beginning to become unpopular."[2]

---

* This essay was translated by Dirk Stegmann and Gary Walsh.

1. Speech by Miquel, 22 September 1889, in *Johannes von Miquels Reden*, eds. W. Schultze and F. Thimme, 4 vols. (Halle, 1911–14), vol. 3, p. 259.

2. A. Steinmann-Bucher, *Die Nährstände und ihre zukünftige Bedeutung im Staate* (Cologne, 1885), p. 87.

Dirk Stegmann

Because the government had also made itself the advocate and supporter of corporate (*berufsständisch*) organizations – this was particularly true in the field of social policy after 1884, with the establishment of professional cooperative associations (*Berufsgenossenschaften*) for accident insurance "as a counterbalance to parliament" – Steinmann-Bucher believed that in the long run a rivalry would emerge between the two.[3]

This view was symptomatic of the anti-party feeling prevalent in conservative industrial circles at this time. It was based on the assumption that political parties could not address real social needs because they did not proceed from the "economic basis of human existence." Whereas the rapidly expanding "economic" system inevitably had more in common with associations (*Vereine*) representing corporate interests – that is, "genuine" interests – the "party" system was considered simply an artificial product of society. Cooperation had become nearly impossible between party and association, for the latter was held to be an "organic" part of society, a microcosm of society itself. Steinmann-Bucher felt the gap could only be bridged by the founding of a so-called Senate for Economic Affairs (*Volkswirtschaftlicher Senat*) that would safeguard corporate interests when dealing with the Reichstag. In his opinion, the best solution was to introduce an intrinsically corporate voting system (*berufsständisches Wahlrecht*) that would be supplemented with appointments by the monarch. Ultimately this program had an authoritarian corporate state as its aim; no provisions were made for the masses to have any political input. Bismarck, of course, was also in favor of constraining parliament by strengthening the political influence of economic associations. Such considerations had been behind his social policy initiatives – aimed broadly at a general reorientation of society since 1884.[4]

The impact of such ideas, particularly on the propertied classes, had accelerated since the mid-1870s. The deliberate cultivation of corporate associations during these years should be seen primarily as a reaction to political and social crisis, namely, as a means to establish an alternative power base to the existing party structure. The initiative was supported more

3. Ibid., p. 88.
4. In particular see K. Born, *Staat und Sozialpolitik nach Bismarcks Sturz* (Wiesbaden, 1957), pp. 25ff.

strongly by industrialists than by artisans and tradesmen. A dominant role was played here by associations with a strong regional influence, such as the so-called Langnamverein (Verein zur Wahrung der gemeinsamen wirtschaftlichen Interessen in Rheinland und Westfalen), founded in 1871, or one of the regional branches – the northwestern group – of the Association of German Iron and Steel Industrialists (Verein Deutscher Eisen- und Stahlindustrieller or VDEStI), founded in 1874. Both associations were diligently managed by Henry Axel Bueck. From the 1880s to the mid-1890s they were the dominant voice in the formulation of corporate association policy, eclipsing quite clearly the influence exerted by the national associations in Berlin, such as the Central Association of German Industrialists (Centralverband Deutscher Industrieller or CVDI), founded in 1876, or the VDEStI.[5]

The alignment of firms and business branches along economic and socio-political lines was supported at an early stage by a subsidized press, which had an impact not only on their clientele but also on society: "Sound, practical economic principles should be passed on to the masses."[6] The CVDI in Berlin founded its own "press committee" in 1885 that coordinated the allocation of funds for the subsidized press reports known as *Korrespondenzen*.[7] These reports were used in the "large" papers to influence the educated classes, and were also distributed free of charge to those "smaller local papers" that were usually "available in pubs" and calculated to reach "the people" easily.[8]

In the agricultural sector, the Association of Tax- and Economic Reformers (Vereinigung der Steuer- und Wirtschafts-Reformer or VdSWR), founded in 1876, attempted under the leadership of Baron Julius von Mirbach-Sorquitten to speak for agricultural interests. However, this association represent-

---

5. Richter (Hauptverein des VDEStI) to Servaes (Nordwestliche Gruppe), 12 October 1891, Duisburg, Haniel-Archiv, 3001070/7.

6. Circular of the CVDI, June 1885, Haniel-Archiv, 3001873/1.

7. *Deutsche Volkswirtschaftliche Korrespondenz* (hereafter cited as *DVK*), 1876ff. See also H.A. Bueck, *Der Centralverband Deutscher Industrieller 1876–1901*, 3 vols. (Berlin, 1902–05), vol. 1, p. 163; especially *Berliner Politische Nachrichten* (hereafter cited as *BPN*), 1882ff, and *Neue Reichskorrespondenz* (hereafter cited as *NRC*), 1884ff. See also Bueck's circular of 13 November 1882, Haniel-Archiv, 3001075/5, and note 6. The *NRC* provided material free of charge to 465 newspapers in 1893 and 925 newspapers in 1900. For further details, see the CDVI circular from June 1900, Haniel-Archiv, 3001073/2.

8. CDVI circular, 31 May 1893, Haniel-Archiv, 3001073/2.

ed mainly the interests of large landowners in Prussia. Even though the VdSWR remained an organization of notables and never had more than about 700 members, in its role as a *comité directeur* it provided the ideological weapons for the alignment of agricultural interests in Protestant areas. The VdSWR, which was also linked to the CVDI through the membership of a few conservative industrialists, also aimed at the complete reformation of society into a corporate system. Since the beginning of the 1880s, board members such as Baron Karl von Thüngen-Roßbach had tried to convey this plan to farming circles through regional farmers' associations in order to give the movement more political force.[9]

The deteriorating agricultural situation from the mid-1880s onward[10] gave rise to a supraregional political farmers' movement more strongly oriented toward the property interests of farmers. Beginning in the Prussian province of Saxony and founded in 1885, the German Peasants' League (Deutscher Bauernbund)[11] spread rapidly to Brandenburg, Pomerania, Lower Silesia, parts of West Prussia, the states of Thuringia and, in 1891, throughout the Kingdom of Saxony. Its approximately 40,000 members came to form the backbone of a new agricultural association, the Agrarian League (Bund der Landwirte or BdL), founded in February 1893. The artisans' associations, on the other hand, remained for the most part without any supraregional representation, even beyond the turn of the century. The interests of artisans diverged so widely that local and regional alignments either failed to come into being or lasted only fleetingly. Corporate social ideologies and a reserved attitude toward the established parties were widespread, particularly in the conservative wing of German artisans organized in the General German Union of Artisans (Allgemeiner Deutscher Handwerkerbund or ADH), founded in 1882, which established ties to the VdSWR. In the course of this formation of organized interest groups, the split between the corporate groups and the parties became more and more

9. See the open letter from Thüngen-Roßbach, quoted in Steinmann-Bucher, *Nährstände und ihre Bedeutung*, pp. 228ff.

10. See in particular J. Flemming, *Landwirtschaftliche Interessen und Demokratie: Ländliche Gesellschaft, Agrarverbände und Staat 1890–1925* (Bonn, 1978), pp. 20ff.

11. See *Konservatives Handbuch* (Berlin, 1892), pp. 58–59. Before 1890 there were 10,000 members; in 1890, 18,000; in 1891, 35,000. See *Agrarisches Handbuch*, ed. Bund der Landwirte, 3rd ed. (Berlin, 1911), pp. 155–56.

evident. In this respect, the parties that came under the strongest pressure were those confronted by well-organized corporate groups.

Since the 1860s the National Liberal Party had been a stronghold of industrial interests. But in the late 1880s it became involved in a fundamental conflict with the large industrialists in the area of Rhineland-Westphalia. This crisis of confidence was brought about by the socio-political initiatives of a National Liberal deputy named Wilhelm Oechelhäuser, who sat in the Reichstag from 1878 to 1893. In 1852 Oechelhäuser had served as mayor of Mülheim an der Ruhr; from 1856 to 1890 he was the general director of the German Continental Gas Company in Dessau; and from then until his death in 1902 he was the chairman of its board of directors. He was also on the board of directors of private and joint stock banks as well as enterprises in the machine-building industry, and, as the owner of a plantation in the Cameroons, he was actively involved in the colonial movement of the 1880s. In 1886 Oechelhäuser published a brochure entitled *Die Arbeiterfrage. Ein soziales Programm*, and in 1887 he published another entitled *Die sozialen Aufgaben der Arbeitgeber*. Both publications encountered strong opposition from the Langnamverein and the CVDI, because Oechelhäuser, unlike such authoritarian patriarchs as Friedrich Alfred Krupp or Baron Karl Ferdinand von Stumm-Halberg, advocated the recognition of liberal workers' organizations (*Gewerkvereine*) and the establishment of workers' chambers (*Arbeiterkammern*) presided over by state factory inspectors. In a new book published in 1888, *Über die Durchführung der sozialen Aufgaben im Verein der Anhaltischen Arbeitgeber*, Oechelhäuser called for his ideas to be put into practice through freely elected workers' committees, through relief funds, and through industrial and consumer cooperatives in particular. He was able to implement these ideas in the Anhalt Employers' Association, which he had founded himself that same year.[12] In doing this, he rather openly attacked his industrial colleagues in the Ruhr district and their idea of "imposed welfare, which seeks to have everything done for the workers but nothing done by the workers." In his *Deutsche*

---

12. For Oechelhäuser's career, see W. von Geldern, *Wilhelm Oechelhäuser als Unternehmer, Wirtschaftspolitiker und Sozialpolitiker*, Beiheft der Zeitschrift für Firmengeschichte und Unternehmerbiographie "Tradition," no. 7 (Munich, 1971).

Arbeiterzeitung, founded in September 1888, he further tried to popularize his ideas within the employers' camp.

All of these activities were an alarm signal to Bueck, the managing director of the Langnamverein. He had already pointed out in 1887 that Oechelhäuser could not be dismissed as an outsider, since his strong position in the National Liberal Party was due to the fact that Miquel especially shared his views. In addition, he was regarded as an expert on the state bureaucracy.[13] There was more reason for concern when not only Miquel but also the National Liberal leader Rudolf von Bennigsen openly supported the program of the *Arbeiterzeitung*. It became clear that influential National Liberal industrialists who represented large chemical industries in the Reichstag – men such as Gustav Siegle (BASF) or Carl Clemm (BASF) – did not disapprove of Oechelhäuser's initiatives. These initiatives were also viewed favorably by left-liberal members of the Reichstag such as Richard Roesicke, the Berlin brewery industrialist, who had published his own social program, entitled *Arbeiterschutz,* in 1887.

The big Westphalian industrialists became all the more concerned about this development as signs increasingly indicated that this reorientation was met with approval within the Prussian state bureaucracy. Proof of this could be found, for example, in the initiatives of Baron Hans Hermann von Berlepsch, district governor (*Regierungspräsident*) of Düsseldorf at that time,[14] who was promoted in 1890 from the *Oberpräsidium* of the Rhine province to Prussian minister for trade and industry. The reactions to the Ruhr workers strike of 1889 also showed that these fears were not unfounded. As this conflict developed into Wilhelmine Germany's first mass strike, the Ruhr industrialists found themselves with no support from the general public or from the political parties close to them, including the Conservatives; nor did they receive backing from either the government or Kaiser Wilhelm II.[15] These industrialists severely criticized Wilhelm's "idea of being able

13. Bueck to Servaes, 13 April 1887, and Bueck to the members of the board of the Langnamverein, 25 April 1887, both in Haniel-Archiv, 3001071/2.

14. Berlepsch supported the founding of the Linksrheinischer Verein für Gemeinwohl in 1886, a fact that Oechelhäuser clearly emphasized in his book.

15. That is the tone of the long letter from Emil Kirdorf (GBAG) to Adolph von Hansemann (Disconto-Gesellschaft), 1889, quoted in F.A. Freundt, *Kapital und Arbeit* (Berlin, 1927), pp. 57ff.

to find in a 'social monarchy' a new basis of legitimacy for the whole system,"[16] because, as they argued,[17] in practice this meant increasing the state's control over workers – eventually seen in the amendments to the Trade Law of 1891 and the Prussian Mining Law of 1892. As Wilhelm Beumer, the new general secretary of the Langnamverein, declared categorically on 12 April 1890, "the workshop and the army are very much alike in that strict discipline must prevail for all classes."[18]

Bismarck's fall from power in March 1890, together with the rout suffered in the Reichstag elections a few weeks earlier by the three right-wing parties that had rallied together in Bismarck's so-called *Kartell* of 1887, considerably reduced the influence of the big western industrialists in Berlin.[19] The new ministers in Berlin, especially Miquel and Berlepsch, were viewed with distrust and open antagonism. On the whole, the result was shattering. With the clear swing to the left in the Reichstag and weaker contacts with the government, "most serious dangers threatened"[20] these Rhenish and Westphalian industrialists. Their response was two-fold: first, to develop an industrial press policy to influence public opinion more strongly; and second, to pave the way for closer contacts with organized agricultural groups, with whom the industrialists believed the political-economic alliance dating from 1879 could be defended. This analysis was directed at the National Liberal Party with the warning that the big industrialists would not accept a swing to the left without taking counter-measures: "[representatives of] industry in Rhineland-Westphalia will answer any move toward left-wing liberalism [*Deutschfreisinn*] with a secession from National Liberalism."[21]

16. K. Saul, "Zwischen Repression und Integration: Staat, Gewerkschaften und Arbeitskampf im kaiserlichen Deutschland 1884–1914," in *Streik: Zur Geschichte des Arbeitskampfes in Deutschland*, ed. K. Tenfelde and H. Volkmann (Munich, 1981), p. 219.

17. "Die Gewerbeordnungsnovelle," *DVK* 15, no. 36 (9 May 1890); "Zur Annahme der Gewerbeordnungsnovelle ohne den §153," ibid., no. 37 (8 May 1891); and "Die Gewerbeordnungsnovelle," ibid., no. 39 (15 May 1891). See also Freundt, *Kapital und Arbeit*, p. 62.

18. *Mitteilungen des Langnamvereins*, nos. 4–6 (April–June 1890), p. 89.

19. See the tone in the articles entitled "Die Reichstagswahlen und die Industriellen," *DVK* 15, no. 9 (31 January 1890); "An die deutschen Industriellen" and "Das Wahlresultat," ibid., no. 18 (4 March 1890).

20. "An die deutschen Industriellen," *DVK* 15, no. 18 (4 March 1890).

21. "Zuschrift aus nationalliberalen industriellen Kreisen am Rhein," *DVK* 15, no. 20 (11 March 1890).

The political dissension came to a head in the winter of 1890/91. In a Reichstag by-election in Bochum-Witten, a glass manufacturer named Hermann Müllensiefen was the National Liberal candidate. With tacit permission from the general secretary in party headquarters in Berlin, plus considerable support from Wilhelm Kulemann, a former member of the Reichstag who also was Miquel's protégé, all the miners' demands from the strike year 1889 were endorsed by Müllensiefen during his campaigning for the second ballot.[22] A strong protest against these electoral tactics was made by the chairman of the election committee, the wealthy Bochum industrialist Louis Baare, who until that point had supported Müllensiefen with ample backing from heavy industry in the Ruhr.[23]

In this incident the traditional politics of notables, or *Honoratiorenpolitik*, practiced by the decentralized election committee under the control of local employers, suddenly clashed with the overriding interests of the party bureaucracy in Berlin. At the general meeting of the Langnamverein on 31 January 1891, the National Liberal Party was strongly condemned for its "vote-catching" tactics. Emil Kirdorf, general director of the Gelsenkirchen Mining Company (Gelsenkirchener Bergbau Aktien-Gesellschaft or GBAG), demanded a reappraisal of the relations between heavy industry and the National Liberal Party.[24] Kirdorf's speech expressed more than mild disapproval and showed that ill-feeling ran deep, as illustrated by an article – published the day before the meeting of the Langnamverein – in a newspaper that sided with big industry interests. The article called for the founding of a new political party, a German "Economic Party" (Deutsche Wirtschaftspartei).[25] The tenor of this initiative was similar to the spirit of Kirdorf's subsequent speech, so it is highly probable that the impulse came from the circle of people around Kirdorf. In any case the CVDI denied having anything to do with it.[26]

Economic objectives were at the heart of the program.

22. See W. Kulemann, *Politische Erinnerungen: Ein Beitrag zur neueren Zeitgeschichte* (Berlin, 1911), pp. 155ff.

23. Ibid., p. 155. See also "Rheinisch-Westfälisches," *DVK* 16, no. 17 (27 February 1891).

24. See Freundt, *Kapital und Arbeit*, p. 61.

25. "'Wirtschaftliche' oder 'politische' Fraktionen," *DVK* 16, no. 9 (30 January 1891).

26. For the dementi of the *BPN*, the mouthpiece of the CDVI, see *DVK* 16, no. 12 (10 February 1891).

Explicitly "political" questions took second place, and a voting system favoring the old *Kartell* parties was recommended. The primacy of economics and the solidarity among the "big corporate groups" (industry and agriculture) came together in the suggestion that both groups form an "independent parliamentary group" in economic matters. Basically, the program oscillated between the founding of a new party and the revival of the political *Kartell* idea in the form of a reincarnation of the Economic Union (Wirtschaftliche Vereinigung) that had been formed among Reichstag deputies back in 1878. A demand for the creation of a German Economic Council (Deutscher Volkswirtschaftsrat) further indicated these men's distrust of a political parliament.

The assault on the National Liberal Party was obvious. The party was reproached for flirting with left-wing liberalism and for tolerating "Herr Oechelhäuser's socio-political fantasies."[27] The dissidents also emphasized their argument that political parties had outlived their usefulness and should be replaced by economic parties by citing similar statements from Miquel and, for further proof, from Bismarck, whose mouthpiece, the *Hamburger Nachrichten*, openly supported this program. On several occasions early in 1891, Bismarck himself said things to the same effect.[28] It was surely more than a coincidence that Kirdorf and other big industrialists went on a pilgrimage to Friedrichsruh during these months.[29]

The discussion about the "Economic Party" continued in political circles into early 1891 but then died down.[30] On the whole, this discussion about the founding of a new party must be understood as a warning shot fired at the National Liberals and as a means of urging the Conservatives to continue to make common cause with the Ruhr industries in the field of economic policy – to oppose, in other words, Chancellor Leo von Caprivi's foreign trade policy. At the National Liberal Party congress in Berlin on 31 May 1891, the party leaders showed they acknowledged the Kirdorf faction's dissatisfac-

27. *DVK* 16, no. 11 (6 February 1891).

28. "Die 'Deutsche Wirtschaftspartei' und die 'Hamburger Nachrichten'," *DVK* 16, no. 23 (20 March 1891). See also H. Hofmann, *Fürst Bismarck, 1890–1898*, 3 vols. (Stuttgart, 1913–14), vol. 3, p. 131.

29. Freundt, *Kapital und Arbeit*, p. 63.

30. "Die Deutsche Wirtschaftspartei," *DVK* 16, no. 32 (21 April 1891). Unfortunately, the volumes of the *DVK* for 1892 and 1893 are missing.

tion. They now sought to prevent the big industrialists in the Rhineland and Westphalia, or at least the influential groups among them, from swinging to the right to the Free Conservatives or even to the Conservative Party. They argued that it was "time to pause"[31] in socio-political matters, justifying this to other groups by making reference to the industrial crisis. Yet at the same time the party leadership clearly stressed the primacy of politics, by rejecting all proposals aimed at making economic matters the basis of a political party.

This response can be interpreted either as a rejection of the "Economic Party" or as a new compromise within the party. The compromise sought to mediate between the advocates of protective tariffs and those of free trade, for the dispute between them had become more serious in the course of the combined agricultural and industrial crisis. Agricultural interests in North Germany and in the Palatinate now confronted the commercial interests of industry, trade, banking, and small business. In 1892 Oechelhäuser, for example, attempted to ease the continual crisis within the party by advising Bennigsen to establish a firm economic program advocating moderate free trade. Oechelhäuser had not forgotten recent National Liberal election losses in North Germany. Therefore, in order to find new voters and to win back others, he directed his efforts at the urban propertied classes and small farm owners – both being groups that benefited little from high protective tariffs on agricultural products.[32] Bennigsen, however, rejected these suggestions in a memorandum of December 1892[33] because he feared for the survival of the party in the Reichstag. The party, he believed, could be torn apart in the ensuing dispute between the majority, who favored protective tariffs, and the minority, who favored free trade. This would also further lessen the party's chances of influencing government policy. Moreover, Bennigsen had to consider that the party caucus in the Prussian House of Deputies was traditionally right-wing and would not have gone along with even a cautious swing to the left as proposed by Oechelhäuser.

The extent to which the party's course would satisfy the

31. For the text of the resolution, see *DVK* 16, no. 43 (2 June 1891).
32. See Oechelhäuser to Bennigsen, 2 January 1892, quoted in H. Oncken, *Rudolf von Bennigsen, ein liberaler Politiker: Nach seinen Briefen und hinterlassenen Papieren*, 2 vols. (Stuttgart, 1910), vol. 2, pp. 569–70.
33. Ibid., pp. 575–76.

industrialists around Kirdorf remained to be seen. Kulemann, for example, saw this group already marching toward the Free Conservative Party.[34] On the other hand, ever since the Free Conservatives had been badly weakened in the Reichstag elections of 1890 and, more clearly, from 1891 onward, the industrial wing around Wilhelm von Kardorff (one of the founders of the CVDI) was increasingly forced onto the defensive by the agricultural wing. In addition, relations were very strained between the Ruhr industrialists and Stumm, who represented the views of Saarland industrialists within the party. In 1891, the party political scene became even more explosive with the advent of an autonomous imperialist movement – a kind of second front – that directed its main attacks against the government and particularly against the National Liberal Party. On 9 April 1891, the General German League, later renamed the Pan-German League (Allgemeiner Deutscher Verband, later Alldeutscher Verband, or ADV),[35] was founded in Berlin. The Pan-Germans claimed to form "the central rallying point for all national endeavors," independent of parties and of government, an "organization of ardent national elements."[36] This was at the same time a guarded challenge directed at the National Liberal Party – the very party that had been so involved with Friedrich Hammacher, Miquel, and Oechelhäuser in implementing and propagating colonial policy in the 1880s, and the party that until that time had claimed to be the most determined representative of the national idea.

This new nationalist, imperialist, agitational association, which in the historian Eckart Kehr's words considered itself to be a "holding company" of the national idea in Germany, attracted primarily Conservative and Free Conservative deputies[37] in Prussia and the Reich, but no National Liberal

34. Kulemann, *Erinnerungen*, p. 157.

35. See the founding manifesto attached as a supplement to the *Deutsches Wochenblatt* (hereafter cited as *DWbl*) 4, no. 18 (30 April 1891). On the founding of the General German League, see E. Hartwig, "Zur Politik und Entwicklung des Alldeutschen Verbandes 1891–1914" (Ph.D. diss., University of Jena, 1966).

36. Otto Arendt (editor of the *DWbl*, a Free Conservative member of the Prussian House of Deputies, and a close friend of Wilhelm von Kardorff), in "Der Allgemeine Deutsche Verband," *DWbl* 4, no. 19 (7 May 1891): 219.

37. On the six-member board sat Kardorff (Free Conservative member of the Prussian House of Deputies [MdPAH] and of the Reichstag [MdR]) and Mirbach-Sorquitten (Conservative MdR and president of the VdSWR). On the fourteen-member executive committee sat for the Free Conservatives: Arendt

167

deputies from the Reichstag. Only a few prominent members of the Prussian House of Deputies and some former members of the Reichstag represented the National Liberal element.[38] The rationale for this new association had produced such little response in 1886 that it had been abandoned after a short time. But in 1891 it resurfaced and was embraced by early colonial enthusiasts,[39] professors (historians, geographers, biologists and zoologists),[40] and prominent industrialists. Among the industrialists a leading role was taken by representatives of the mining and engineering industries in Rhineland-Westphalia[41] and by individual representatives of the iron industry in northern Germany, upper Silesia, and the Saarland.[42] There were only a few representatives of merchants[43] and none for artisans or small traders. On the other hand, the large landowners[44] provided several prominent signatories, all of whom – like Mirbach-Sorquitten – either belonged to the pro-*Kartell* wing of the Conservative Party or were closely connected to the Association of Tax- and Economic Reformers.

(MdPAH), Count von Arnim-Muskau (MdR); von Pilgrim (MdPAH); and for the Conservatives: von Below-Saleske (MdR); Mehnert (MdR); Olzem (MdPAH). On the seventy-three-member committee sat for the Free Conservatives: von Baumbach (MdR), Count von Behr-Behrenhoff (MdR); von Hellmann (MdR); Leuschner (MdR); von Tiedemann-Labischen (MdPAH); Ritter (MdPAH); and Schultz-Lupitz (MdPAH); for the Conservatives: Count von Douglas (MdR); von Helldorff-Bedra (MdR); Baron von Plettenberg-Mehrum (MdR); von Jagow (MdPAH); Schier (MdPAH); and Hansen (MdPAH).

38. On the board sat von Fischer (Oberbürgermeister of Augsburg, MdR); on the executive committee sat Tramm (MdPAH); on the committee sat von Eynern (NLP caucus leader in the PAH); and Enneccerus (MdPAH).

39. Fabri; Bley; Peters (honorary member); Hübbe-Schleiden; and Schweinfurth.

40. Hasse, Haeckel, Preyer (all members of the executive committee); Credner, v. Duhn, Eimer, Ermann, Fick, Fischer, Joest, von Koch, Liszt, and Ratzel (all members of the committee).

41. Theodor Reismann-Grone, managing director of the Bergbaulicher Verein, was a member of the executive committee. Other members were: C. Lueg, president of the Verein Deutscher Eisenhüttenleute and general director of the Gutehoffnungshütte; Bernhardi, managing director of Dortmund's chamber of commerce and a close friend of Bueck of the CVDI; Kirdorf, general director of the GBAG and, since 1893, head of the board of the Rhenisch-Westphalian Coal Mine Syndicate; Kleine, member of the board of the Bergbaulicher Verein; and von Schwarze, manager of a coal mine.

42. G.L. Meyer, head of the board of the Ilseder Hütte and president (1893–96) of the VDEStI; Seebohm, general director of the Stumm'sche Hüttenwerke; and Ritter, the Generalbevollmächtiger of the Pless'sche Gruben in Upper Silesia.

43. Besides others: Lange, president of Lübeck's chamber of commerce.

44. For example, Mirbach-Sorquitten and Thüngen-Roßbach. Most of the Conservative and Free Conservative deputies were large landowners as well.

That the new association's founding appeal was signed by industrial managers such as Emil Kirdorf, colonial ideologues such as Carl Peters, or new men such as the 25-year-old *Regierungsassessor* Alfred Hugenberg, showed that *Honoratiorenpolitik* would not be pursued. Another indication of the fundamental reorientation of these men's aims was the fact that the same big Rhenish-Westphalian industrialists who had openly supported Caprivi's policy toward England in their press organs the year before and who had not taken seriously the founding of an oppositional National Association (Nationalverein) by Peters and Hugenberg,[45] now supported the General German League through the Langnamverein.[46]

Its organizational structure and its emphasis on the building of local groups – stressed by founding members such as Hugenberg – also illustrated that the ADV represented a new element in German politics: there was an obvious contrast between it and such older agitational associations as the German Colonial Association (Deutscher Kolonialverein), founded in 1882, and the German Colonial Society (Deutsche Kolonialgesellschaft), founded in 1887. The majority of people on the board or on the executive committee of the ADV were in the 34 to 40 age group. Apart from people such as the chairman of the board, Carl von der Heydt, Jr. – a partner in the Elberfeld bank of v. d. Heydt, Kersten & Sons and since 1881 a friend of Carl Peters – most of them had not previously been prominent in politics. They now wanted to have their say at a time marked by industrial and agricultural crises, by a relative power vacuum in post-Bismarckian Berlin, and by the emergence of social conflicts. Moreover, these groups wanted to appeal to the "masses"[47] because they were aware that success could only be achieved if the masses were mobilized. A Pan-German manifesto from 1895 made this clear: "Today the individual is powerless. Great achievements can only be accomplished with the help of the masses."[48] Though not stated explicitly, it was clear that control over the association and its policy was to be determined solely by the representatives of the educated and propertied classes.

45. *DVK* 15, no. 47 (20 June 1890); no. 50 (1 July 1890); and no. 57 (25 July 1890).

46. *Mitteilungen des Langnamvereins*, nos. 4–6 (April–June 1891), pp. 177–78.

47. "Manifesto," *DWbl* 4, no. 18 (30 April 1891). See above, n. 35.

48. *Alldeutsche Blätter*, 1 April 1895, no. 13 (supplement).

Dirk Stegmann

The gap between the ADV's leaders and the "masses" was to be bridged with the heavy-handed ideology of a national *Machtstaat*, with the stress on cultural hegemony. Fulfillment of the "popular" demand for *Weltpolitik* was to be included, as was "the solution of our most important national problems such as emigration and, last but not least, socialism."[49] This was formulated at the end of 1891 in an article probably written by von der Heydt himself. It quite distinctly revealed the manipulatory level on which nationalism was to be introduced. The socio-imperialist element was obvious in the sense that the "masses" were not only to be diverted away from socialist demands but were also to provide added momentum to the national idea.

Pan-German references to "the people" must not be misunderstood as "populism."[50] On the contrary: the appeal to the masses did not mean that they were to be given political responsibility; they were merely to serve as a political backdrop. That appeal, moreover, remained a rhetorical figure of speech, used continually by agitators in nationalist associations – including the *Kartell* parties – in order to give them increased legitimacy. As late as 1918, shortly before the collapse of the monarchy, the leader of the ADV, Heinrich Claß, had to concede that the League had never succeeded in offering something "to the masses"; that is why, Claß concluded, it is "always better to have a leader and a general staff than nothing at all."[51] Nevertheless, in many respects the war-aims debate in Germany from 1914 to 1918 was anticipated by the imperialist aims of the Pan-German League, for the ADV linked together expansion on the continent and overseas, and incorporated an anti-English bias – for example, by supporting the building of a battle fleet – that accepted the possible outcome of a world war.[52]

49. "Auf der Schwelle des Weltkrieges II," *DWbl* 4, no. 42 (15 October 1891): 497, also printed in *Mitteilungen des Alldeutschen Verbandes*, 1892, no. 2, p. 4.

50. This is the general idea suggested in G. Eley, *Reshaping the German Right: Radical Nationalism and Political Change after Bismarck* (New Haven, Conn., 1980).

51. Meeting of the ADV managing committee, 13 September 1918, BA Potsdam, Alldeutscher Verband, 120. For the Conservatives, see von Thielmann-Jacobsdorf, *Deutsche Volkswirtschaft oder Weltwirtschaft?* (Breslau, 1895), pp. 31, 57–58.

52. See above, n. 49. See also von der Heydt, "1891," *Mitteilungen des Alldeutschen Verbandes*, 19 January 1892; Schroeder-Poggelow, "Die Annäherung zwischen Deutschland und Frankreich," *DWbl* 7, no. 3 (18 January 1894): 26–27, and "Vom Kap zum Nil," ibid., no. 24 (14 June 1894).

Initially the ADV met with considerable success. The establishment of a local group in Berlin was followed in early 1892 by a group in Hamburg.[53] That group quickly gained 300 members, most of whom were representatives of respected Hamburg merchant families.[54] By its own account, the League's total membership rose to between 16,000 and 17,000 in early 1892 and to 21,000 by the end of the year.[55] Politicians such as Kardorff or Mirbach-Sorquitten saw the ADV primarily as a binding agent that, through the use of the national idea on a long-term basis, might make it possible for the former *Kartell* parties to stop drifting apart and reach some kind of reconciliation. On the other hand, a group was soon formed that wanted to expand the association into an independent party. The three leading protagonists of this group were the ADV's chairman, Carl von der Heydt; a member of the executive committee, Wilhelm Schroeder-Poggelow; and the managing director of the ADV, Hans van Eycken. With the rapid growth of the League, these men saw an opportunity to expand their extra-parliamentary agitation association into a "National Party."[56] Von der Heydt had been actively involved in the founding of the colonial movement in the 1880s and was a member of the Free Conservative Party.[57] Schroeder-Poggelow was a committee member of the German Colonial Society and a member of the German East Africa Society. Politically he was close to the National Liberal Party,[58] but because he maintained the lifestyle of a Junker on the Poggelow estate near Teterow in the Grand Duchy of Mecklenburg-Schwerin and served as a committee member of the VdSWR, he had established close links with agrarian interest groups. It is impossi-

53. Staatsarchiv Hamburg, Politische Polizei, V 452, vol. 1.
54. In this case, the president of the local committee in Hamburg, Mönckeberg, on 15 March 1892. See *Hamburgischer Correspondent*, 16 March 1892, no. 192.
55. See above, n. 53.
56. For information on the Nationalpartei, see Hartwig, "Politik und Entwicklung des Alldeutschen Verbandes," pp. 38ff.; D. Stegmann, *Die Erben Bismarcks: Parteien und Verbände in der Spätphase des Wilhelminischen Deutschland: Sammlungspolitik 1897–1918* (Cologne, 1970), pp. 106ff.; see also Eley, *Reshaping the German Right*, pp. 49ff.
57. H. Pogge von Strandmann, "The *Kolonialrat*, its Significance and Influence on German Politics, 1890–1906" (D.Phil. diss., Oxford University, 1970), p. 83.
58. Ibid. See also *Bericht über die Verhandlungen der 18. Generalversammlung der Vereinigung der Steuer- und Wirtschafts-Reformer in Berlin, 21. Februar 1893* (Berlin, 1893), p. 111.

ble to determine to which party van Eycken belonged, but he was probably also a member of the Free Conservative Party since he enjoyed von der Heydt's confidence.

A number of influential figures behind the scenes had been informed of these men's plans:[59] These included the Free Conservative Silesian magnate, Count Guido Henckel von Donnersmarck; Hugo Prince zu Hohenlohe-Oehringen, Duke of Ujest, a member of the Prussian *Herrenhaus*; and Prince Karl Egon von Fürstenberg, head of the family line at Donaueschingen and owner of one of the largest entailments in the Reich. Fürstenberg represented the higher nobility of southern Germany and the large landowners. Politically speaking these men were close to the Conservative Party. The arch-conservative Count Alfred von Waldersee, the former chief of staff of the Prussian army and commanding general of the Ninth Army Corps in Altona at the time, was also informed. As a candidate of this fronde, he was in contact with both the wing of the Conservative Party close to Adolf Stöcker and with Free Conservative circles around Otto Arendt of the *Deutsches Wochenblatt*. Adolph von Hansemann, the proprietor (*Geschäftsinhaber*) of the Disconto-Gesellschaft – the financial bank of the big Rhenish-Westphalian industrialists – provided contacts with large capitalist industrial groups, and thus Krupp was also informed. In party circles, people sympathetic to this plan included such Free Conservative politicians as Kardorff, Arendt, and the Silesian magnate who sat in the Reichstag, Count Hermann von Arnim-Muskau.

These men were united, first, by their determined stand against Chancellor Caprivi's "New Course" and, second, by their unreserved acceptance of Bismarck's political ideas about authoritarian government and about a monarchy that would not threaten the political status quo.[60] The "older" generation of politicians such as Hansemann, Kardorff, and Henckel von Donnersmarck were in agreement with the goals of the "younger" generation around von der Heydt; they differed only on the means to achieve those ends. Both groups were of the opinion that a national public would first have to

59. Diary entries, 2 October 1892 and 10 February 1893, in A. von Waldersee, *Denkwürdigkeiten des Generalfeldmarschalls Alfred Grafen von Waldersee*, ed. H.O. Meisner, 3 vols. (Stuttgart and Berlin, 1922–23), vol. 2, pp. 265, 285.

60. See von der Heydt, "Gibt's in Preußen ein Ministerium?" *DWbl* 5, no. 12 (24 March 1892): 134ff.; and Arendt, ibid., no. 32 (11 August 1892): 377ff.

be created systematically. The older generation of politicians saw the rapid expansion of the mass press as a means to achieve this. The younger generation agreed, but also considered it necessary to ensure popular support by founding associations and by influencing public opinion in a permanent way through political parties in parliament. Thus it was the group around von der Heydt that promoted the idea of "new thoughts and new men" and stressed that a "strong popular government would have to be achieved through a strong popular party."[61] They considered themselves to be Bismarck's legitimate heirs, and as the "young generation" it was their duty to propagate the "new spirit" that had already been created.[62]

These calls for political realignment seemed to be particularly promising because they came at a time in mid–1892 when Caprivi's government faced its most serious political crisis in the wake of the failed School Bill. At this time Caprivi had to relinquish the post of minister-president in Prussia to his reactionary rival, Count Botho zu Eulenburg. Von der Heydt firmly believed that a National Party could provide the political basis for new policies in Prussia and in the Reich, and he and his friends hoped that Caprivi would be replaced by a man who shared their views – perhaps Count Waldersee. The timing also seemed auspicious with regard to the status of the former *Kartell* parties. In 1892 the Conservative Party was in the throes of its most serious internal crisis since its founding in 1876. This crisis had become apparent as the party came into conflict with Caprivi's economic policies, but the situation was exacerbated when the Conservative leadership came under attack on two fronts: from its agricultural constituency in rural areas, and from the oppositional wing of the party around Stöcker and the editor of the *Kreuzzeitung*, Baron Wilhelm von Hammerstein-Schwartow. This so-called *Kreuzzeitung* group forced the Conservative Party leader, Otto von Helldorff-Bedra, to relinquish his post in the early summer of 1892. Helldorff had pleaded for a policy of supporting the government and had called repeatedly for a revival of the *Kartell* of 1887. Despite the fact that the Stöcker wing had already refused to back any "middle-party action"[63] in July 1892, von der Heydt

61. "Politisches Denunziantentum," *DWbl* 5, no. 51 (22 December 1892): 606.
62. "Die Gründung einer neuen politischen Partei," in ibid., p. 606.
63. Stöcker in July 1892, quoted in W. Frank, *Hofprediger Adolf Stoecker und die christlichsoziale Bewegung*, 2nd ed. (Hamburg, 1935), p. 231.

still hoped for cooperation from the pro-government Conservatives.

In December 1892 the Conservative Party appeared to move in a new political direction with its Tivoli Program, which opened the door to a form of demagogic anti-Semitism that had gone from strength to strength in Reichstag by-elections in the autumn of 1892 and contributed decisively to the defeat of Conservative candidates. The agrarian protest movement forming in the countryside at the same time was to be ideologically bound to the Conservatives in a similar way: "If we do not take the matter into our hands," wrote one agrarian leader, "socialists and anti-Semites of the worst kind will do it."[64] However, the party crisis could not be so easily resolved because the Agrarian League, founded in February 1893, was an autonomous agrarian "pressure group" that from the very outset brought strong pressure to bear on the Conservative Party.

Within the National Liberal Party, too, internal conflicts remained obvious between the agrarian and industrial wings on the one hand and the groups wanting to give the party a stronger socio-political profile on the other. In December 1892 Oechelhäuser sought to draw Bennigsen's attention to a "fermentation process."[65] He was afraid that the party could "collapse" or vanish "in the sand of the next elections." He unambivalently considered the "National Party" a direct threat, although he remained optimistic because he could not imagine such a new foundation succeeding without an explicit economic program. Finally, the Free Conservative Party had also been suffering since 1891 from an internal conflict between its agricultural and industrial wings. This conflict was intensified by intraparty disagreements between the supporters of bimetallism (Kardorff, Arendt, Leuschner) and the advocates of a "gold only" currency standard (Stumm, Krupp, Zedlitz-Neukirch).[66]

---

64. Conrad von Wangenheim to his brother, 24 December 1893, quoted in *Conrad Freiherr von Wangenheim-Klein-Spiegel*, ed. H. von Wangenheim (Berlin, 1934), p. 21.

65. Oechelhäuser to Bennigsen, 18 December 1892, quoted in Oncken, *Bennigsen*, vol. 2, p. 575.

66. For the controversy with Stumm, see Arendt, "In eigener Sache," *DWbl* 5, no. 32 (11 August 1892): 377ff. For further information, see von Kardorff, "Audiatur et altera pars," ibid., no. 8 (18 February 1891): 86ff., and no. 9 (26 February 1891): 99ff; "Die deutsche Landwirtschaft und ihre Zukunft," ibid., no. 38 (17 September 1891): 445ff., and no. 39 (24 September 1891): 458ff., as well as F. Hellwig, *Carl Ferdinand Freiherr von Stumm-Halberg* (Heidelberg, 1936), pp. 454, 469, 479.

Because their party had suffered unparalleled electoral defeats in the Reichstag elections of 1890, Arendt and Kardorff (among others) hoped to guarantee their survival as a political group through incorporation into the new "National Party."

The *spiritus rector*, von der Heydt, believed in the ideologically integrating power of the national-imperialistic idea; as he put it, the new party would have to avoid the mistake of "putting economic questions of the day or fashionable trends in the forefront" of any party program. To him, the greatest mistake of the Bismarck era had been the "directing of public attention to purely materialistic matters." Instead he advocated an appeal to "great political ideas" and to "idealistic movements": their strength alone would determine "whether we will become a world power in the coming century or sink as a fragmented people into the population migrations of the future."[67]

As previously noted, von der Heydt had urged the adoption of these ideas as early as 1886, but at that time they had achieved no political resonance.[68] Now, in 1892, at a time of general crisis in domestic and foreign policy, Pan-German imperialism in combination with decisive opposition to Caprivi seemed to constitute a more viable ideological focus for the new political party. One thing was particularly clear to von der Heydt: the old *Kartell* parties had doomed themselves by becoming fixated on economic goals. As a result, plans for the "National Party" could not be reconciled with the idea of an "Economic Party" as it had been spelled out by representatives of the mining, iron, and steel industries, despite their marked programmatic emphasis on the goals of imperialism. Nonetheless, individual industrialists such as Kirdorf were quite prepared to think in terms of a double strategy; this underlines the significance of their willingness actively to support both the ADV and the "Economic Party."

Press support for the "National Party" came especially from Otto Arendt's *Deutsches Wochenblatt*, which had increasingly supported Pan-German imperialism.[69] From the National Lib-

---

67. von der Heydt, "Gibt's in Preußen ein Ministerium?" *DWbl* 5, no. 12 (24 March 1892): 135.

68. See von der Heydt to Hammacher, 30 June 1886, quoted in H.-U. Wehler, *Bismarck und der Imperialismus* (Cologne, 1969), p. 485.

69. See above, n. 52.

eral side came the demand for a "German Middle Party,"[70] to be based on the idea of the *Kartell* or, more concretely, on a fusion of the former *Kartell* parties of 1887. A National Party would come into being "from the grass-roots level upward, directly from the voters themselves, if the leaders should fail to recognize the signs of the time." The zoologist Ernst Haeckel of Jena, a founding member of the ADV and evidently the source of the term "National Party," argued along the same lines. So did many anti-Semites sympathetic to Pan-German goals – for instance, Friedrich Lange, who prior to the establishment of his German League (Deutschbund) in 1894 had supported the idea of a National Party in the *Tägliche Rundschau*. Lange demanded that the fight against Judaism be an essential point of the party's program,[71] and although this thought stood in complete opposition to the intentions of the founders,[72] it is illustrative of the hopes cherished by radical nationalists on the right wing of German society.

Of all the program drafts and circulars that sought to launch the "National Party," one copy is preserved in the private papers of Maximilian Harden, the publisher of *Die Zukunft* and an enthusiastic Bismarckian at that time.[73] The cover letter to a select circle mentioned the "discontent" of the "best elements of the population," once again identified the Caprivi government's "weakness and lack of clarity" in all areas of domestic and foreign policy, and claimed that the existing parties and parliament as a whole were lacking initiative or were incompetent. The program defended the constitutional status quo, but showed a willingness to attach greater value to the

70. "Die Bildung einer deutschen Mittelpartei," *DWbl* 5, no. 42 (20 October 1892): 498ff.

71. Lange, "Vom deutschen Reich zum deutschen Vaterlande," 11 October 1892, in F. Lange, *Reines Deutschtum: Grundzüge einer nationalen Weltanschauung*, 4th ed. (Berlin, 1904), pp. 194ff. On the anti-Semitic tendencies within bourgeois circles sympathetic to the League – including lawyers, publicists, and members of the German League. See the ADV's *Mitteilungen*, 8 July 1892, no. 6, pp. 58–59, as well as sources cited in n. 55.

72. See von Kardorff, "Die antisemitische Bewegung," *DWbl* 5, no. 51 (22 December 1892): 609ff. The founding manifesto ofthe "National Party" (see the following note) contained the following statement: "We acknowledge that the anti-Semitic movement finds its nourishment in the prevailing bad social and economic conditions, and we are striving to improve this, but we strongly disapprove of the demagogic form in which anti-Semitism has appeared on the political scene."

73. Bundesarchiv Koblenz, Nachlaß Maximilian Harden, Nr. 140, H. 1.

role of parliament. It met the demands of industry by opposing reform on the workers' question (*Sozialpolitik*), but
remained very general and imprecise with regard to economic
policy. While "demagogic" anti-Semitism was rejected, the
group interests often targeted by anti-Semites were mentioned
under the rubric of a "healthy farming and middle class" that
would have to be organized in guild and agricultural chambers in order to represent their interests in the same manner as
industry and trade. The military posture of the government
was criticized as weakening German power, and in the arena
of foreign policy the program stressed Germany's "future as
an economic and political world power."

As might be expected, the government opposed the founding of such a party, despite the fact that some of Wilhelm's
advisors now supported the political view that challenged
Caprivi's tactic of mustering alternating majorities in parliament, and advocated instead a revival of *Kartell* policies.[74] The
Foreign Office in particular, whose Department for Colonial
Policy under Paul Kayser had often been the focus of massive
attacks by the imperialist enthusiasts around von der Heydt,[75]
sought to thwart the founding of the new party by using a
semi-official government newspaper, the *Kölnische Zeitung*, to
leak plans for the enterprise.[76] At the same time it described
the barely-concealed criticism of Wilhelm's "personal regime"
in the program drafts as an affront to the emperor (*Majestäts-
beleidigung*). This move was intended to push the Kaiser into
coming out against the establishment of the party. Friedrich
Alfred Krupp, who had to report to Wilhelm personally (probably as a result of this article), was not able to dispel these
doubts. As Waldersee remarked, Wilhelm was "furious with
the people involved."[77] Krupp himself withdrew from the circle of founders and was no longer willing to make a financial
contribution toward the transfer of the *Münchener Allgemeine
Zeitung* from Munich to Berlin on 1 December 1892 – a move
intended to provide press support for the "National Party."

74. See especially J.C.G. Röhl, *Deutschland ohne Bismarck* (Tübingen, 1968),
pp. 79ff.
75. "Die heutige deutsche Kolonialpolitik," *DWbl* 5, no. 38 (22 September
1892). See also Schroeder-Poggelow, "Der heutige Stand der deutschen Kolonialpolitik," ibid., no. 44 (3 November 1892): 322–23.
76. "Politisches Denunziantentum," *DWbl* 5, no. 51 (22 December 1892): 606.
77. Diary entry, 10 February 1893, in Waldersee, *Denkwürdigkeiten*, vol. 2, p.
285.

Thus the plan to found the party officially on 15 January 1893 in Berlin failed.[78]

Within the General German League itself, strong opposition arose against the founding of the new party. Leading figures in the ADV who regarded these plans as a direct threat to their own organization, who disapproved of von der Heydt's sharp anti-governmental course, and to whom Alfred Hugenberg had access, were: Ernst Hasse, a Leipzig statistician and university professor who was a member of the ADV's executive committee (*geschäftsführender Ausschuß*); Hasse's Leipzig colleague, Hermann Credner, a member of the ADV's committee (*Vorstand*); and the historian Karl Lamprecht.[79] These men believed that the ADV should continue to act as an agitation group over and above the other parties. It proved convenient for them that the managing director (*Geschäftsführer*) of the ADV, Eycken, had maneuvered the ADV into relatively large financial losses as a result of the publication of a *Kalender aller Deutschen*; these losses threatened the existence of the League. On 5 July 1893, in a meeting in Frankfurt that was not attended by the Berlin leaders von der Heydt and Eycken, von der Heydt was replaced as ADV leader by Hasse, who had been elected a National Liberal Reichstag deputy in May.[80]

On 10 December 1893 most of the League's debts were paid off, but Eycken had to turn over management of the League's finances to Adolf Lehr from Leipzig, who was also a good friend of Hasse.[81] Hasse's plan to strengthen the ADV as an organization independent of the parties – for instance, by transferring the business office from Berlin to Leipzig – was strongly supported by Hugenberg, by the representative of the Ruhr coal mining industry in the executive committee, Theodor Reismann-Grone, and by the manufacturer Simons from Elberfeld.[82] This support provided another clear indication that this group rejected the plan for a "National Party," at least at this particular time. The reorganized ADV, which called itself the Pan-German League from 1894 onward, never-

---

78. Diary entries, 2 October 1892 and 10 February 1893, in ibid., pp. 265, 285.
79. Hartwig, "Politik und Entwicklung des Alldeutschen Verbandes," pp. 38ff.
80. Hasse to Lehr, 10 November 1893, BA Potsdam, Alldeutscher Verband, 180.
81. Hasse to Lehr, 12 December 1893, ibid.
82. Ibid.

theless could not keep such leading Conservatives as Mirbach-Sorquitten, Paul Mehnert, Nicolaus von Below-Saleske, Fritz Olzem, and Adolf von Pilgrim, or Free Conservatives such as Arendt, from resigning from the executive committee and from the board (*Präsidium*).[83] In some cases these men went so far as to turn their backs completely on the organization.[84] The ADV's membership fell in 1894 to 5,000 people, organized into thirty-three local groups.[85]

Ultimately it was the founding of the Agrarian League in February 1893 that altered the domestic situation and spelled doom for the "National Party." As a direct response to this action by the agricultural community, and as a further step toward the development of an economic program that would help in the struggle against other political parties, the advocates of the "Economic Party" of 1891 became active once again. On 18 February 1893, the day the BdL was founded in Berlin, the Association of Industrialists in the government district of Cologne declared that the new agricultural organization must be expanded into a "general German Economic League unifying industry and agriculture."[86] Then somewhat later, in April 1893, the supporters of the "Economic Party" once again addressed the public with a new appeal, this time directed to agriculture, the guilds, and industry.[87] They described Bismarck as the chief witness to their own goals: through newspapers friendly to his views, he had repeatedly called for representation according to economic interests through an "alliance of all productive forces." Similar efforts on the part of the agrarians were mentioned as well, with reference to Alfred Ruprecht-Ransern's famous appeal for "lobby politics" on 21 December 1892 and to Baron Conrad von Wangenheim's proclamation on 28 January 1893. This proclama-

83. O. Bonhard, *Geschichte des Alldeutschen Verbandes* (Leipzig, 1920), pp. 271ff.

84. Lehr deplored the fact that "people from the upper strata of society" were leaving the ADV. See Lehr to Hasse, 5 June 1894, BA Potsdam, Alldeutscher Verband, 180.

85. K. Schilling, "Beiträge zu einer Geschichte des radikalen Nationalismus in der Wilhelminischen Ära" (Ph.D. diss., University of Cologne, 1958), p. 32, n. 81.

86. See the *Bericht über die Verhandlungen der 18. Generalversammlung der Vereinigung der Steuer- und Wirtschafts-Reformer, 2.February 1893*, p. 31.

87. "Aufruf der Deutschen Wirtschaftspartei an die Landwirtschaft, das Handwerk und die Industrie," n.d., Haniel-Archiv, 3001075/5.

tion had been signed by forty prominent landowners and also supported a "large economic party in the parliaments," specifically including industry and trade. The new "German Economic Party" should demonstrate "independence" in "political questions," should incorporate agriculture "as the most important field of German professional activity [*Gewerbe*]"; handicrafts and small businesses as the "second largest class"; then "national industry"; and finally "national" trade. An economic program with an accent on tariffs and neo-mercantilism was to be pushed through parliament, and there was to be mutual support of agriculture and industry in the elections.

Comparing the major points of this program with those of 1891, the stronger orientation toward agriculture is particularly noteworthy, as is the inclusion of handicrafts and small business, both of which had previously been lacking. The agrarian middle-class components of this originally industry-oriented program were calculated to incorporate the large agrarian protest movement that had appeared. Apart from that, it was also an indication that the necessity of a mass movement was more clearly recognized in 1893 than in 1891 and, as such, had to be incorporated into the new political strategy.

A preparatory committee presented itself by name this time. It was a collection of fifteen people, of whom the majority – nine – belonged to agriculture.[88] One signatory was a judge on Nürnberg's court of appeals, and most of the remaining five signatories had connections to the iron and coal industry along the Rhine and in the Ruhr.[89] Prominent industrialists, with the exception of C.F. von Tenge and Anton Unckell, were absent from the list, as were prominent names on the agrarian side except for Edmund Klapper, the chief editor of *Fühling's Landwirtschaftliche Zeitung*. No representatives of guilds or small businesses had signed.

Even though the appeal emphasized the solidarity of inter-

88. Four untitled Junkers from Saxony, East Prussia, and West Prussia; the others were Guts- or Bauerngutsbesitzer, normally leaders of agrarian societies.

89. A Bergrat from Upper Silesia; a factory owner from Barmen; the editor of the *DVK* himself (who was a member of the executive committee of the Langnamverein); the president of the Verein Deutscher Eisengiessereien, von Tenge-Rietberg; and A. Unckell, general director of the Kohlenverkaufsverein at Dortmund and a close friend of Kirdorf.

ests between industry and agriculture, certain undertones directed against the Agrarian League showed how improbable such an alliance appeared to be. In fact, despite all claims to the contrary, the leaders of the Agrarian League wanted their new organization to be just an "agricultural party" and not a comprehensive "economic party." Unity existed only in the shared goal of overcoming parties by means of economic lobby groups. Baron von Wangenheim, who in 1898 would become one of the chairmen of the League, believed that the "population was tired of parties" and considered success possible only "on the basis of the current economic movement."[90] Chances for realizing an "Economic Party," in short, were no longer viable for the big industrialists in the Ruhr. The executive committee of the Association of Iron and Steel Industrialists referred to the program in its meeting of 25 April 1893 as merely "information to be filed."[91]

Meanwhile, despite a deep-seated conflict of interest, the supporters of the "National Party" once again tried to put together an appeal based on national "idealism." Early in the summer of 1893 they launched a new campaign, this time consciously directed at the Agrarian League. This campaign tried to reconcile the program of the "Economic Party" with that of the "National Party." The *Deutsches Wochenblatt* emphasized that the "core of a large economic party" was to be established through agriculture, and added that the BdL could be considered the "foundation for the great national party of order [*Ordnungspartei*] of the future."[92] At the same time, Schroeder-Poggelow spoke out in favor of a brochure by Moritz Naumann – entitled *Hie Bismarck! Eine Wahlparole für alle national Gesinnten* – that in his opinion represented "a kind of programmatic statement" of the "National Party."[93] Naumann emphasized that the party was "moderate" and preferred "quiet development along its own lines over titanic chauvin-

90. Von Wangenheim to his brother, 24 December 1893, quoted in *Wangenheim*, ed. Wangenheim, pp. 20–21.
91. "Die Interessensolidarität," *DVK* 18, no. 28 (11 April 1893), in Haniel-Archiv, 3001070/10. See also the minutes of the meeting of the VDEStI, ibid., 3001075/5.
92. "Die nationale Bedeutung der agrarischen Bewegung," *DWbl* 6, no. 23 (8 June 1893): 265–66.
93. Ibid., p. 276, with the abbreviation "W. S." Naumann held a D.Phil. and was a retired *Regierungsassessor*; his brochure, published in Berlin in 1893, appeared with the same publishing company that published the *DWbl*.

ism." This meant a departure from the extreme positions of von der Heydt. In point of fact, Naumann repeated familiar criticisms of Caprivi by comparing his "New Course" unfavorably with the principles of Bismarckian policy and by arguing that Caprivi's policy on school matters and the Polish question, as well as the government's entire social, economic, colonial, and foreign policy, should be rejected. Naumann's criticism of the old *Kartell* parties was just as emphatic; they were accused of lacking independence and constantly making compromises. Considering himself closer to the Conservatives than to the National Liberals, Naumann deliberately argued from the "royalistic"[94] perspective of "youth" – the generation after Bismarck – who demanded more than servility and accommodation. This was an undisguised swipe at the Kaiser's absolutism and at Byzantinism, both of which were deemed unworthy of "free men" and held responsible for the growing general displeasure with the Kaiserreich. With reference to Bismarck's speech in Jena in 1893, Naumann called for "a parliament with the ability to provide leadership [*führendes Parlament*],"[95] but not a copy of English parliamentarianism. This body should be strong enough to force the crown to grant existing constitutional rights, and not be a parliament "without a will of its own." To achieve this aim, the "old forms" of the *Kartell* parties – which had "become rotten" – would have to be "destroyed."[96]

Naumann continued to hold onto the integrating motto of nationalism without establishing a firm program. Bismarck was stylized as a national hero and as a symbolic figure for the new party. The implicit social base was the educated middle class with its Bismarckian enthusiasm: "those occupied with handicrafts and agriculture" who were dissatisfied with the economic and social politics of the New Course were explicitly mentioned, and the Agrarian League was specifically praised.[97] Its organizational structure was held up to the "other productive classes" as an example to be imitated. In addition to the residents of the eastern frontier districts (*Ostmark*) and the "ordinary common people," "German youth"

94. Naumann, *Hie Bismarck!*, p. 25.
95. Ibid., p. 20.
96. Ibid., p. 22.
97. Ibid., p. 26.

was explicitly championed as constituting the party's base.[98] These programmatic statements were aimed at integrating the agrarian protest movement of the Agrarian League, but they missed the mark. Germany's party landscape did not experience any movement until 1893, and then only on the left wing of the party spectrum, when the German Radical Party (Deutsch-Freisinnige Partei) underwent a schism in the controversy over the government's military program. The right-wing parties, on the other hand, came under the influence of the new radical economic pressure group represented by the BdL, which subsequently proved successful in winning over an impressive number of representatives to its "agrarian" mandate, not only from the Conservatives but also from the Free Conservatives and the National Liberals.[99]

Alfred Hugenberg was a member of the ADV's executive committee from early 1894 onward. In the summer of 1894 he complained to the ADV's director, Lehr, that in these circumstances "our goals" were receiving "little attention."[100] "We need a great success in some matter or another," Hugenberg stated. It would therefore be necessary to find new strategies, namely "*mass* (not A.d.V.) meetings," where the ADV would remain in the background but in reality would be responsible for providing the speakers. With this suggestion the tactic of concealed influence (*verdeckte Einflußnahme*) in nationalist publicity was born, a tactic the ADV was to practice with great success following Wilhelm's official inauguration of *Weltpolitik* in January 1896. In 1894 Hugenberg had still thought of making the Polish and emigration questions topics of agitation; in the spring of 1896, however, he turned to such issues as the construction of a naval fleet and imperialism.[101]

The increased emphasis on economics in party politics can be conceived of as, among other things, a direct reflection of the combined agrarian and industrial crisis in the years 1891–94. An economic boom did not develop until 1896, after

98. Ibid.

99. See H.-J. Puhle, *Agrarische Interessenpolitik und preußischer Konservatismus im wilhelminischen Reich, 1893–1914: Ein Beitrag zur Analyse des Nationalismus in Deutschland am Beispiel des Bundes der Landwirte und der Deutsch-Konservativen Partei*, 2nd ed. (Bonn-Bad Godesberg, 1975), pp. 167–68.

100. Lehr to Hasse, 5 June 1894, BA Potsdam, Alldeutscher Verband, 180.

101. See Hugenberg's speech in Celle at the end of February 1896, cited in *Weser-Zeitung*, 21 February 1896.

which the agrarian sector, too, attained relative prosperity, particularly after the establishment of new protective tariffs in 1902. The call for a "purely" lobbyist party developed out of this long-lasting economic crisis. The "Economic Party" planned by industrial circles in 1891, like the "Agricultural Party" of the BdL of 1893 or the call for an autonomous "middle-class party [*Mittelstandspartei*]"[102] in 1895, provide impressive evidence of this relationship. As a result of the economic boom beginning in 1896, these ideas lost their mobilizing power. Yet in the long run they signaled the arrival of a kind of political activity that was not confined to occupational lobbying. The result was a partial political activation of the broad mass of voters in the agricultural sector and among the middle classes of artisans and small businessmen. Caprivi's economic policy had provided the initial impulse, but a further burst of political activity began in 1891 when the debate on German foreign policy became a central issue in politics. Foreign policy ceased to be a domain of the rich and the educated, and this development manifested itself in the successful founding of such nationalist agitation groups as the ADV.

This political mobilization continued, although improved economic conditions no longer provided the compulsion to focus exclusively on the defense of special interests. The political activity of the nationalist groups increased in strength in the late 1890s and the number of such organizations grew. The right-wing spectrum of German parties was so totally fractured that a political market for the allegiance of the masses gradually developed. A contributing factor to this development that should not be underestimated was the relative power vacuum in Berlin under Caprivi that had begun with Bismarck's surprising fall from power but that continued to evolve in dramatic fashion in 1892 and 1893.

The general political context for these changes continued to be the economic interests within the so-called productive classes and the deliberate use of nationalism as an integrating ideology, combined with attacks on socialism. In times of systemic political crisis – as in 1912/13, when parliamentary elec-

---

102. For example, see the manifesto of a Deutsche Mittelstandspartei from the master goldsmith Fischer in Berlin, printed in *Vorwärts*, 18 April 1895, no. 90. There were similar tendencies in Halle in Prussian Saxony. See *Deutsches Blatt*, 10 June 1895, no. 133.

tions produced a leftward swing, or in 1917/18, when the Kaiserreich underwent its final agonies – these strategies came to life in more radical and extensive forms. The so-called "Cartel of Productive Estates" (Kartell der schaffenden Stände) of 1913, like the German Fatherland Party (Deutsche Vaterlandspartei) of 1917, reveal a strong continuity in right-wing political culture, where the appeal to the "masses" never had more than a declamatory character and a largely instrumentalist function.

6

Anti-Semitism, Agrarian Mobilization, and the Conservative Party

Radicalism and Containment in the Founding of the Agrarian League, 1890–93[*]

Geoff Eley

> Anti-Semites today are as revolutionary as the Social Democrats and should be rejected by the Conservative Party as completely contrary to the principles of conservatism.
>
> *Norddeutsche Allgemeine Zeitung*, April 1892

> For where does Anti-Semitism lead, what does it want? . . . All who generate dissatisfaction today work to the good of the Social Democrats.
>
> Speech of Reich Chancellor Leo von Caprivi to the Reichstag, 30 November 1893

I

Discussion of agrarian politics in Imperial Germany is understandably dominated by Hans-Jürgen Puhle's study of the Agrarian League (Bund der Landwirte or BdL) and its impact on the politics of the German Conservative Party (Deutsch-Konservative Partei). First published in 1966, Puhle's work demonstrated convincingly how Prussian conservatism was

---

[*]This essay was originally written for a collection of essays that was to have been edited by John C. Fout but failed to materialize. It elaborates upon themes I first addressed in the second chapter on "Honoratiorenpolitik and the Crisis of National Liberalism" in my book *Reshaping the German Right: Radical Nationalism and Political Change after Bismarck* (New Haven, Conn., and London, 1980), and complements an essay I recently published with the title "Notable Politics, the Crisis of German Liberalism, and the Electoral Transition of the 1890s" in *In Search of a Liberal Germany: Studies in the History of German Liberalism from 1789 to the Present*, ed. K.H. Jarausch and L.E. Jones (New York, Oxford, and Munich, 1990), pp. 187–216.

captured by a radical agrarianism militantly at odds with the accommodating governmentalism of the past.[1] In the campaign for higher tariffs between 1893 and 1902, the BdL recast the Conservative Party in its own image, transforming its organization, broadening its popular base, and delivering an apparatus for winning elections. Above all, it overwhelmed the stiff and royalist state-mindedness of the Prussian nobility with a new kind of "biologically oriented *völkisch* nationalism," which incorporated social-Darwinist and anti-Semitic currents into an existing authoritarianism and perfected a demagogic and plebiscitary style of politics. Building on the socioeconomic discontent of the peasantry and *Mittelstand*, the BdL linked popular grievances to the specific class interests of the east-Elbian aristocracy and created a new type of agrarian coalition. Centered on the issue of protective tariffs, this coalition was moved by a generalized hostility to the emerging urban-industrial civilization, bitterly resisted the logic of progress, and amounted to a major impediment to liberal and democratic conceptions of change.

For our purposes, three points in Puhle's interpretation are worth noting. First, its underlying conception seems to be essentially a manipulative one, in which powerful vested interests – in this case, the Junkers – defended the "status quo" against a left-wing challenge by manufacturing new sources of

---

1. The following exposition is condensed from several of H.-J. Puhle's works, especially *Agrarische Interessenpolitik und preußischer Konservatismus im wilhelminischen Reich (1893–1914). Ein Beitrag zur Analyse des Nationalismus in Deutschland am Beispiel des Bundes der Landwirte und der Deutsch-Konservativen Partei,* 2nd ed. (Bonn-Bad Godesberg, 1975), pp. 274–89; and idem, "Conservatism in Modern German History," *Journal of Contemporary History* 13 (1978): 701–07, from which the quotations have been taken. Puhle's other publications are essentially straightforward restatements of the arguments originally presented in his book. For example, see idem, *Politische Agrarbewegungen in kapitalistischen Industriegesellschaften. Deutschland, USA und Frankreich im 20. Jahrhundert* (Göttingen, 1975), pp. 28–112; idem, "Der Bund der Landwirte im wilhelminischen Reich. Struktur, Ideologie und politische Wirksamkeit eines Interessenverbandes in der konstitutionellen Monarchie (1893–1914)," in *Zur soziologischen Theorie and Analyse des 19. Jahrhunderts,* ed. W. Rüegg and O. Neuloh (Göttingen, 1971), pp. 145–62; idem, "Parlament, Parteien und 1890–1914," in *Das kaiserliche Deutschland. Politik und Gesellschaft 1871–1918,* ed. M. Stürmer (Düsseldorf, 1970), pp. 143–67; idem, *Von der Agrarkrise zum Präfaschismus. Thesen zum Stellenwert der agrarischen Interessenverbände in der Politik am Ende des 19. Jahrhunderts* (Wiesbaden, 1972). For Puhle's more general ideas about Wilhelmine history, see his essay "Zur Legende von der Kehrschen Schule," *Geschichte und Gesellschaft* 4 (1978): 108–19.

popular support. Puhle's research seemed to establish that the Agrarian League was easily dominated by the Junkers – i.e., the large estate-owners from the regions of Prussia east of the Elbe River – despite the numerical preponderance of smaller farmers in the membership and despite the national range of its operations. Moreover, as well as accepting their own political subordination in an organization dominated by an arrogant and undemocratic aristocratic elite, smaller farmers are thought to have had no objective interest in supporting grain tariffs, which were allegedly tailored to the specific circumstances of the grain-producing large estates in East Elbia. In other words, the BdL was called into existence as a nationally based agrarian movement by intelligent Junker politicians, both to secure their economic demands and to legitimize their social and political privileges through a general agrarian ideology. In effect, the smaller farmers were duped. The BdL claimed to speak for rural society as a whole, but in reality it was concerned with preserving the social and political power of aristocratic estate owners in a special region of the country.

Second, Puhle suggested that the Agrarian League made a vital contribution to the overall radicalization of the German Right before 1914. The BdL established a paradigm of "modern" agitational organization that "other right-wing leagues and federations" tried to follow – "organizations such as the German National Union of Commercial Employees [Deutschnationaler Handlungsgehilfen-Verband], the Society for the Eastern Marches [Ostmarkenverein], the Pan-German League [Alldeutscher Verband], the Navy League [Flottenverein], and numerous other agitational, imperialist organizations representing the so-called 'old middle class' [*alter Mittelstand*] of shopkeepers, tradesmen and artisans." Around this variegated extra-parliamentary activity there developed "a protectionist and social-imperialist consensus as the exclusive ideological consensus of the propertied classes." The BdL was a central feature of this radical Right, and its militant agrarianism became subsumed in the larger ideological enterprise: "Conservatism lost its separate identity and became merged with a newer and wider *völkisch* nationalist, social-imperialist, militant and militaristic ideology that was distinctly '*mittelständisch*,' markedly anti-Semitic and inclined to organic, integrationist theories of social harmony." Though it used the forms of popular democratic mobilization, "the new ideology sought to undermine parliament and the political parties, and in its radically dichotomized view of society – a direct response to liberal and socialist theories – played a decisive part in the polarization of political debate during the Second Empire."

Third, there is an extremely strong argument about continuity. Puhle describes the above process as a transition "from traditional conservatism to prefascist *völkisch* nationalism," and the reference to "prefascism" raises the now familiar claims regarding the question of "continuity between *Kaiserreich* and Weimar Republic." This is perhaps the least specified element in the argument. Quite apart from its teleological implication that the Wilhelmine era was a staging post for an already predetermined destination, the concept of "prefascism" has never been properly explained in Puhle's work. In one of his more explicit statements, he associates it with the combination of "revolutionary" and "reactionary" components – the adoption of a "modern" agitational practice for the pursuit of extremely "backward" goals, including undermining the parliamentary system and safeguarding agrarian interests "by enforcing a return to preconstitutional politics and to the institutional conditions existing before the Bismarckian Empire." As he says: "it is this dual potential, the fusion of reactionary aims and modern, seemingly 'progressive,' and often revolutionary methods and ideologies, which actually makes the new Right prefascist and establishes a clear line of descent from it to the National Socialist takeover and Nazi rule."

Superficially, there may be little to quarrel with in these three positions: the Junkers' dominance within agrarian politics, the centrality of the Agrarian League in the ideological formation of a Wilhelmine "new Right," and the continuity between the latter and National Socialism. But each of them has recently been the subject of considerable discussion. The difficulties with the concept of continuity in the wake of the Fritz Fischer controversy have been extensively aired, though as yet without any definitive resolution.[2] Similarly, while Puhle's estimate of the BdL's general importance cannot be

2. For an introduction to these discussions, see J.A. Moses, *The Politics of Illusion: The Fischer Controversy in German Historiography* (London, 1975); and R.J. Evans, "Introduction: Wilhelm II's Germany and the Historians," in *Society and Politics in Wilhelmine Germany*, ed. R.J. Evans (London, 1978), pp. 11–39. My own thoughts on this question can be found in G. Eley, "The Wilhelmine

seriously disputed, it seems clear that he overgeneralizes the impact of its ideological innovation and conflates some very different phenomena into his synthetic concept of the "new Right." To discuss the agrarian movement and the nationalist pressure groups such as the Pan-German League, the Society for the Eastern Marches, and the Navy League in the same breath, for example, is a serious oversimplification and obscures the serious contradictions between the "rural" and "urban" sectors of the radical Right. On the one hand, these groups' recruitment of social classes was quite distinct. Though the old *Mittelstand* was certainly present, the nationalist associations were preeminently organizations of the educated bourgeoisie (*Bildungsbürgertum*) and prosperous middle class. On the other hand, they pursued conflicting ideological goals. Pan-Germans and Navy League activists had fewer qualms about Germany's transition to an *Industriestaat* and were quite happy to envisage the taxation of landed interests, while agrarians could view *Weltpolitik* and the construction of a big navy only with suspicion. More prosaically, anti-Polish agitation threatened the seasonal labor market of the east-Elbian estates. These differences were accommodated only after 1912 – and then only partially, unevenly, and under the force of pragmatic, defensive necessity.[3]

It is with the first of these three points abstracted from Puhle's work – the question of manipulation – that this essay will be concerned. Enough has been published over the last few years to suggest that Puhle's picture of farsighted and manipulative Junkers is heavily overdrawn. The idea that peasant farmers were duped into supporting agricultural protection against their own best interests is certainly wrong; James Hunt, Robert Moeller, and, in a different way, David Blackbourn and Ian Farr have made a convincing case for the peasants' economic rationality and market adaptation.[4] Moreover, smaller farmers had their own organizations in most

Right: How it Changed," in *Society and Politics*, ed. Evans, pp. 112–35; and Eley, *Reshaping the German Right*, pp. 1ff., 335–61. See also J. Caplan, "'The Imaginary Universality of Particular Interests': The 'Tradition' of the Civil Service in German History," *Social History*, 4 (1979): 299–318.

3. On right-wing unity, see Eley, *Reshaping the German Right*, pp. 293ff., 316ff.

4. J.C. Hunt, "Peasants, Grain Tariffs, and Meat Quotas: Imperial Protectionism Re-Examined," *Central European History* 7 (1973): 311–31; R.G. Moeller, "Peasants and Tariffs in the Kaiserreich: How Backward were the

parts of western Germany, whereas in east Elbia self-sufficient family farms were far less significant to the rural economy. The Agrarian League never penetrated into the Catholic countryside of the south and extreme west, while in the central Protestant regions of the country – Schleswig-Holstein, Oldenburg, Hanover, Hesse, Saxony, Thuringia, and the northern parts of Bavaria, Baden, and Württemberg – it spread very unevenly. Furthermore, even when the BdL absorbed local and regional farmers' organizations – as it largely did after the turn of the century – this did not automatically translate into votes for the Conservative Party at the polls. Different kinds of rural radicalism maintained an independent political existence right up to the outbreak of the First World War.[5]

If this is so, we should reconsider the completeness and stability of the Agrarian League's achievement. At issue here, really, is the nature of the relationship between the BdL's inner leadership and the popular constituency it sought to mobilize – the texture of political relations that brought landowners and peasants together in the same agrarian movement. Unfortunately, it is precisely this question that Puhle's work, for all its pioneering virtues, fails to discuss. Its focus is the BdL's national apparatus and leadership, and the detailed analysis concentrates on the movement's ideology, especially its anti-Semitic dimension, its journalistic and electoral activity, its relationship to the different parties and pressure groups, and its parliamentary record. The movement's success as a popu-

---

Bauern?" *Agricultural History* 55 (1981): 370–84; D. Blackbourn, *Class, Religion and Local Politics in Wilhelmine Germany: The Center Party in Württemberg before 1914* (New Haven, Conn., and London, 1980), pp. 44ff, 196–230; I. Farr, "Populism in the Countryside: The Peasant League in Bavaria in the 1890s," in *Society and Politics*, ed. Evans, pp. 136–59. See also the excellent synthesis in A. Hussain and K. Tribe, *Marxism and the Agrarian Question*, vol. 1: *German Social Democracy and the Peasantry, 1890–1907* (London, 1981), pp. 20–71; and the authoritative economic analysis by S.B. Webb, "Agricultural Protectionism in Wilhelminian Germany: Forging an Empire with Pork and Rye," *Journal of Economic History* 62 (1982): 309–26.

5. Here I am thinking especially of anti-Semitism in Hesse, Thuringia, and Saxony, and particularism in Hanover, Hesse, and Bavaria – not to speak of the national minorities (Poles, Alsace-Lorraine) or the Catholic peasant leagues (*Bauernvereine*), which in terms of total national membership always maintained their numerical superiority over the BdL. For reasons that are hard to understand, it is commonly held that the anti-Semitic parties disappeared from the scene after 1900. This thesis, which also seems to be shared by Puhle, is to be found in the otherwise useful book by R. Levy, *The Downfall of the Anti-Semitic Parties in Imperial Germany* (New Haven, Conn., 1975).

lar movement is attributed to "the extraordinary integrative power of the militant new conservative-agrarian, *völkisch-national* ideology of economic harmony, with its social-Darwinist, *mittelständisch* and anti-Semitic strains."[6] Yet there is no discussion of how the ideology was mediated, no analysis of the interactions between leaders and led, and no understanding of the movement's relationship to rural society. In fact, rural society as such is completely absent from Puhle's book, except for three perfunctory pages on "the social context" at the very beginning.[7] The author displays no interest in the actual process through which the smaller farmers west of the Elbe were incorporated into the new agrarian movement. Similarly, the analysis is completely Prussocentric, and the non-Prussian regions of Germany – or, for that matter, the western provinces of Prussia as well – are deliberately excluded from consideration.[8]

The aim of this essay is to recover some of the agrarian movement's larger context by examining the specific circumstances that surrounded the founding of the Agrarian League in 1893 and the process by which it emerged during the course of the 1890s as Germany's leading farmers' organization. It will argue that the current body of secondary literature on the BdL has both exaggerated the Junker leadership's constructive achievement and underestimated the strength of independent agrarian agitation. It will place the founding of the BdL within a larger field of political developments that also includes the growth of autonomous small farmer activity in most parts of Germany, the related emergence of political anti-Semitism, the convergence of the anti-Semites with a Christian Social current inside the Conservative Party, and the general attempts to form new right-wing parties after the fall of Bismarck. As I have argued elsewhere, these developments amounted to a gradual break up of the Bismarckian system of politics.[9] On this basis, it should be possible to explore the complexity of agrarian agitation in the 1890s, to reexamine the relationship

6. Puhle, *Von der Agrarkrise zum Präfaschismus*, p. 41.

7. Puhle, *Agrarische Interessenpolitik*, pp. 18–20.

8. Ibid., pp. 64–68. It should be clearly understood that these remarks are not meant to disparage the value of Puhle's overall achievement or to suggest that his pioneering research on the BdL should be discarded. They are meant instead to define the limits of his analysis.

9. Eley, *Reshaping the German Right*, pp. 19–40.

between the Conservative Party and the BdL, and to discuss the dynamics of right-wing radicalization before the First World War. In other words, this analysis represents a further contribution to an understanding of the general process in the 1890s that David Blackbourn and I have characterized as a "reconstitution of the political nation."[10]

II

The bare facts of the BdL's foundation may be easily stated. On 21 December 1892 an unknown Silesian tenant farmer named Alfred Ruprecht-Ransern published a militant agrarian manifesto in the *Landwirtschaftliche Tierzucht*, a local agricultural newspaper published in Bunzlau. This manifesto produced a dramatic political response – more dramatic perhaps than the obscurity of the author and place of publication might have warranted. At a time of growing agrarian resentment against the Caprivi government's trade policies, this manifesto proved the catalyst for a major organizational departure. A month later, on 28 January 1893, the same newspaper published a second manifesto by Baron Conrad von Wangenheim-Klein-Spiegel calling for the creation of a "great economic party" to lobby for agricultural interests. Following this, approximately 120 agrarian politicians convened in Berlin on 4 February to create the Agrarian League. They established an organizing committee of twenty-five members and scheduled a founding convention for 18 February. The convention duly ratified the new organization, in two back-to-back rallies of about 4,000 to 5,000 participants each. Regional meetings ensued in many parts of Germany. The new organization abjured specific party affiliations and opened its ranks to "any farmer and friend of agriculture" who could claim German nationality and the Christian religion. It envisaged a vigorous campaign of public agitation for the interests of agriculture by holding regular membership meetings, influencing elections, and making use of the press. By May 1893, the organization claimed 162,000 members, and after the Reichstag elections of June 1893, it had the affiliation of some 140 parliamentary deputies in the so-called Economic Union (Wirtschaftliche

10. This is one of the principal arguments in both Eley, *Reshaping the German Right*, and Blackbourn, *Class, Religion, and Local Politics*.

Vereinigung).[11]

How are we to interpret these events? Puhle describes the BdL as an organization "continuously dominated by the interests of the large estates east of the Elbe, whose share of the membership was less than 1 percent and declined from year to year."[12] In an obvious sense this was true. The first national committee, comprising the forty-three regional chairmen and their deputies, contained nineteen owners of a large estate (*Rittergut*) and seven owners of a small estate (*Gut*), two counts, three barons, a general, and five state officials. Altogether there were twenty-eight aristocrats. By 1909 the picture was much the same. The larger landowners, invariably aristocratic, predominated at each level of the leadership. In 1913 over 50 percent of the 250 constituency chairmen were *Rittergut* owners, as were 45 percent of the 120 committee members and over 70 percent of the council. This contrasted with the overall structure of the membership, which by 1913 had risen to 328,000. Members paying dues of over 20 marks, i.e., those who owned more than 200 hectares of land, represented 2 percent of the total membership in the early years before declining to about 0.5 percent after 1900 (1,500 in 1902, 1,733 in 1913). So-called "middle landowners" represented the vast majority, making up 85 to 89 percent of the BdL membership. To use a related yardstick, by 1906 only 44 percent of those on the membership list came from east of the Elbe, as against 53 percent in 1896. What this meant was that a growing proportion of the BdL's membership was drawn from areas where large estates were not dominant.[13]

Most historians have taken these figures at face value. There

11. For the proceedings of the constituent meeting, see *Stenographischer Bericht über die Konstituirende Versammlung des Bundes der Landwirte am 18. Februar 1893 im Saale der Tivoli-Brauerei zu Berlin* (Berlin, 1893). There is a good account of the founding of the BdL in S.R. Tirrell, *German Agrarian Politics after Bismarck's Fall* (New York, 1951), pp. 159ff.; to which Puhle's account, *Agrarische Interessenpolitik*, pp. 32ff., adds nothing new. The key texts, including Ruprecht-Ransern's manifesto, are published in O. von Kiesenwetter, *Zehn Jahre wirtschaftspolitischen Kampfes* (Berlin, 1903).

12. Puhle, "Bund der Landwirte," p. 148.

13. Details from Tirrell, *German Agrarian Politics*, p. 182; Puhle, *Agrarische Interessenpolitik*, pp. 37ff., 68ff.; and Puhle, "Bund der Landwirte," p. 149; as well as D. Fricke, "Bund der Landwirte (BdL) 1893–1920," in *Die bürgerlichen Parteien in Deutschland. Handbuch der Geschichte der bürgerlichen Parteien und anderer bürgerlicher Intessenorganisationen vom Vormärz bis zum Jahre 1945*, ed. Dieter Fricke et al., 2 vols. (Leipzig, 1968 and 1970), vol. 1, p. 133.

is a great temptation to view the process of agrarian mobilization through the eyes of the large landowners who provided the BdL's national leadership. It is indeed very easy to construct a manipulative model of political mobilization in which the Agrarian League's mass membership served essentially to prop up the Junkers' political position, and in most existing accounts of the Wilhelmine polity this view has tended to prevail.[14] But the formal preponderance of the large estate owners in the organizational structure of the BdL should not obscure the political constraints on the landowners' power once they had established the practice of popular political mobilization. The existence of any mass movement on the scale of the BdL implies some degree of reciprocity between leaders and led. An exclusive stress on the demagoguery or "manipulative" achievement of the former obscures the true dynamics of the relationship.

This becomes clearer when we consider the context of the BdL's formation. Puhle stresses very strongly the reaction of the Conservative Party leadership to Chancellor Caprivi's trade treaty legislation as the decisive factor, at the same time somewhat discounting the significance of the radical manifesto issued by Ruprecht-Ransern, which is otherwise taken to be the crucial initiative. He argues that the primary impetus came from "the recognition by the key group in the Conservative leadership that the party had lost influence and the conviction that the dilemma of serving a state whose government had to be fought against could not be resolved by means of the received conservative wisdom." Consequently, the radical and unprecedented step of a formal declaration of opposition was taken. Puhle draws special attention to an article published in the *Kreuzzeitung* on 14 December 1891 by Count Friedrich von Limburg-Stirum, the chairman of the Conservative caucus in the Prussian House of Deputies, in which he attacked the Austrian trade treaty that was then being pushed through the Reichstag.[15]

14. A good test is the incidental descriptions of the BdL in the literature at large, where it appears very much as a simple instrument of Junker power. For example, see H.P. Ullmann, *Der Bund der Industriellen* (Göttingen, 1976), p. 24; S. Mielke, *Der Hansa-Bund für Gewerbe, Handel und Industrie* (Göttingen, 1976), p. 19; and M. Kitchen, *The Political Economy of Germany, 1815–1914* (London, 1978), p. 210.

15. Puhle, *Agrarische Interessenpolitik*, pp. 32f.

It is not so much that Puhle's assertions are in themselves wrong as that they present an extremely truncated account of the process by which the BdL came into existence and, as a result, blur the larger determinations at work. In effect, Puhle draws a simple correlation between the well-known weaknesses of east-Elbian agriculture, the formal preponderance of large estate owners in the BdL's leading organs, and the uneven development of the opposition to Caprivi's trade policies within the Conservative Party. Puhle then makes this correlation serve as a causal statement. But it is by no means clear that this adds up to a sufficient explanation for the BdL's founding. For one thing, Limburg-Stirum's *Kreuzzeitung* article was published a full year before Ruprecht-Ransern's later initiative, and from this point of view Puhle's emphasis is disproportionate. Moreover, at the time of Limburg-Stirum's outburst, the Conservative opposition was by no means unequivocal. While thirty-five Conservative deputies voted against the Italian trade treaty and thirty-six voted against the Austrian treaty in the ratification debate on 18 December 1891, fourteen and eighteen deputies respectively still voted in favor of these two bills. In addition, the opposition to these early treaties revealed some interesting features. Less than half the deputies who voted against the Italian treaty (twenty-five out of sixty-six) – and slightly more than half of those who voted against the Austrian treaty (twenty-seven out of forty-eight) – came from east of the Elbe. The rest came from regions where the smaller farmer was much more important. One such region was Baden, where deputations of winegrowers managed to detach five Center deputies for a vote against the Italian treaty. The treaty's lowered grape and wine duties were a special grievance to those who lived in the south and along the Rhine, and the same atmosphere of resentment characterized resistance to the Austrian treaty as well. Thus Georg Orterer felt obliged to give voice to the general disquiet of Bavarian farmers, even though he and other Bavarian Centrists decided not to join the opposition.[16]

16. For an account of these events, see Tirrell, *German Agrarian Politics*, pp. 121ff. For a useful discussion of the atmosphere surrounding the Austrian and Italian treaties, see J.A. Nichols, *Germany after Bismarck: The Caprivi Era, 1890–1894* (New York, 1986), pp. 138–53. For the general context there are several more recent works. In particular, see P. Leibenguth, "Modernisierungskrisis des Kaiserreichs an der Schwelle zum wilhelminischen Imperialis-

Of course, it might be argued that this scarcely affected the Conservatives as such, inasmuch as the party was overwhelmingly an east-Elbian one. Yet in the 1893 Reichstag elections, seventeen of the Conservatives' seventy-two seats came from west of the Elbe: five from Saxony, three from central Germany, four from the south, and five from the northwest. The loss of this supra-regional base could never have been a matter of indifference to the party. Moreover, considering the agrarian movement as a whole over the following years – i.e., as a national movement – the south, center, and northwest of the country were to prove at least as important as the Junker heartlands east of the Elbe. To put it another way, the vote on the Italian treaty was compelling evidence that when the farming constituency called the tune, most rural deputies – whatever their party – felt obliged to dance. Thus, twelve National Liberals and three deputies representing the south-German People's Party (Deutsche Volkspartei) from Württemberg and the Central Franconian province of Bavaria voted against the Italian treaty under pressure from the winegrowers. In the absence of such pressure, National Liberals were much freer to support the Austrian treaty, yet five National Liberals still entered the opposition lobby – four from the Bavarian Palatinate and one from Hesse. By the time of the vote on the Russian trade treaty in March 1894, the opposition's geographical spread was much clearer. Now only 40 percent of the votes opposed to the treaty – 59 of 146 – came from the six east-Elbian provinces of Prussia and the two Mecklenburgs, whereas thirteen came from four western provinces, thirty-five from central Germany (the provinces of Saxony and Hesse-Nassau, and the states of Hesse, Saxony, and the smaller principalities), and thirty-seven from the south (Bavaria, Baden, Württemberg, and the Hohenzollern lands). The Conservatives were the largest single contingent in the opposition, providing fifty-

---

mus. Politische Probleme der Ära Caprivi (1890–1984)" (Ph.D. diss., University of Cologne, 1975); R. Weitowitz, *Deutsche Politik und Handelspolitik unter Reichskanzler Leo von Caprivi 1890–1894* (Düsseldorf, 1977); W. Stribrny, *Bismarck und die deutsche Politik nach seiner Entlassung 1890–1898* (Munich, 1977); J.C.G. Röhl, *Germany without Bismarck: The Crisis of Government in the Second Reich 1890–1900* (London, 1967); D. Stegmann, "Wirtschaft und Politik nach Bismarcks Sturz. Zur Miquelschen Sammlungspolitik 1890–1897," in *Deutschland in der Weltpolitik des 19. und 20. Jahrhunderts. Festschrift für Fritz Fischer*, ed. I. Geiss and B.-J. Wendt (Düsseldorf, 1973), pp. 161–84.

four votes against the treaty and only six in favor. The Free Conservative vote, by contrast, was sixteen against and nine in favor. But these opponents of the bill were joined by thirty-nine members of the Center, sixteen National Liberals, four deputies from the Bavarian Peasants' League (Bayerischer Bauernbund), and seventeen assorted Anti-Semites and independents.[17]

For the Catholic Center Party (Deutsche Zentrumspartei) at least, this opposition resulted from a powerful rural backlash against the previous policies of its Reichstag caucus; that rural constituency, in addition, was vigorously hostile to the party's traditional aristocratic leadership. In the 1893 Reichstag elections the Center returned no nobles in Silesia and only two in the south, while only twelve of the thirty-one aristocrats who had represented the party in the previous Reichstag were re-elected, most of them from western constituencies. Most ominously, the Bavarian Peasants' League won four seats, and for a time the launching of a separate Bavarian Center Party seemed possible. Much of this was anger at the support given by the Center's governmental wing for the big army bill of 1892/93, which had been the formal occasion of the Reichstag's dissolution. But opposition to increased military expenditure was heavily overdetermined by peasant radicalism and sharpened by the pressure of a recent agricultural crisis. The signs of discontent were already visible in October 1892, when Johann Baptist Sigl, who edited the anti-Prussian *Bayerisches Vaterland*, fought the Center candidate in a Reichstag by-election in the constituency of Kelheim-Rottenburg-Mallersdorf and was narrowly defeated. The League of Lower Bavarian Peasants (Niederbayerischer Bauernbund) fought the 1893 elections with the slogan "no nobles, no clergy, no officials."[18]

In other words, the political activation of the smaller farm-

17. For a breakdown, see Tirrell, *German Agrarian Politics*, p. 294.

18. There is no adequate study of the Bavarian Peasants' League. The best account presently available is Farr, "Populism in the Countryside." For the context of Bavarian politics, see K. Möckl, *Die Prinzregentenzeit. Gesellschaft und Politik während der Ära des Prinzregenten Luitpold in Bayern* (Munich, 1972), pp. 431–77. See also H. Gottwald and W. Fritsch, "Bayerischer Bauernbund (BB) 1895–1933," in *Die bürgerlichen Parteien*, ed. Fricke, vol. 1, pp. 66–78; and H. Gollwitzer, "Der Bayerische Bauernbund (1893–1933)," in *Europäische Bauernparteien im 20. Jahrhundert*, ed. H. Gollwitzer (Stuttgart, 1977), pp. 562–86; as well as the contemporary study by A. Hundhammer, *Geschichte des bayerischen Bauernbundes* (Munich, 1924).

ers, easily dismissed as the dupes of the BdL's noble leadership, has to be accorded a weight of its own. By the time the
BdL was launched, a series of factors had conjoined to produce a mood of extreme volatility among the central and
south-German peasantry. These included not only falling
prices and the threat of higher taxation from increased arms
spending, but also long-term trends such as rural depopula-
tion, indebtedness, the erosion of ancillary enterprises such as
brewing and rural crafts, and the apparent cultural bias of
government in favor of urban areas.[19] In 1892 smaller farmers
had special problems of their own, independent of the effects
imputed to the new trade treaties. They bore the brunt of a
severe foot-and-mouth epidemic. In 1887 12,723 head of cattle
had been affected by this epidemic, but by 1891 the number
had risen to 394,640 and in 1892 to a disastrous 1,504,308.
Although this abated in 1893, a bad drought produced a continuity of crisis for livestock farmers. Moreover, smaller farmers
were turning increasingly to mutual self-help. Between 1890
and 1900 the number of peasant cooperatives increased from
3,006 to almost 20,000, while in the same period the number of
Bavarian peasants who participated in such organizations rose
by 130 percent.[20]

From the small farmer's point of view, recourse to self-help
was already an oblique commentary on the inadequacy of the
existing agricultural corporations, and the emergence of distinctive peasant organizations reflected a widening gap
between large and small landowners. The semi-official agricultural councils (*Landwirtschaftsräte*) and agricultural associations (*landwirtschaftliche Vereine*), for instance, had been gradually transmuted from agencies of technical and scientific information into the primary units of formal consultation between
the bigger farmers and the respective state governments, a
process ratified as early as 1872 in Saxony and Hesse, in 1894
in Prussia, and between 1900 and 1906 elsewhere.[21] When this

19. For the syndrome of rural backwardness and its political consequences
among the peasantry and rural Mittelstand, see in particular Blackbourn,
Class, Religion and Local Politics, pp. 61–99.

20. See Tirrell, *German Agrarian Politics*, pp. 197–98; and Nichols, *Germany
after Bismarck*, p. 217; as well as K.D. Barkin, *The Controversy over German
Industrialization*, 1890–1902 (Chicago, 1970), pp. 125–26.

21. Puhle, *Von der Agrarkrise zum Präfaschismus*, pp. 21–28. See also D. White,
The Splintered Party: National Liberalism in Hessen and the Reich, 1867–1918
(Cambridge, Mass., 1976), pp. 40, 141–42.

happened, the "landed interest" inevitably received a socially restrictive definition, and this more visible exclusiveness was a standing invitation to an independent peasant initiative. The more perceptive agrarian commentators realized this. But it proved difficult to translate public concern for what Gustav Schmoller called "the preservation of a strong agricultural middle stratum" during the 1880s into adequate political practice.[22] In an academic discussion of moneylending abuses in 1887 that anticipated the political rhetoric of the Hessian Anti-Semites, one leading National Liberal from the north of Hesse made an urgent plea for greater adaptability. He attacked the Grand Duchy's combined agricultural associations as "an organization that more often makes allowances for refined bureaucratic form than it promotes practical achievement," and called for a thorough-going reorientation toward local communities in order to close the gap between large and small farmers.[23]

III

The political consequences of this gap may be illustrated by two regional examples: Schleswig-Holstein and the Grand Duchy of Hesse. The former shows the agricultural systems of independent peasants and large estates existing as separate economies in virtually contiguous proximity. In many ways the province was a microcosm of German agriculture's main features at the turn of the century: a highly productive rich and middle peasantry in the fertile marshlands of the west enjoying vigorous traditions of political freedom and conducting a commercial, mechanized agriculture that had quickly converted to livestock farming; large noble estates in the hilly east, more persistent in grain cultivation and slower to respond to the changed conditions of the world market; and sandwiched between them, the poor freeholding peasants of the sandy Geest, generating only small surpluses that had to

22. G. Schmoller, "Die neuesten Publicationen über die Lage des preußischen und deutschen Bauernstandes," *Jahrbuch für Gesetzgebung, Verwaltung und Volkswirtschaft im Deutschen Reich* 7 (1883): 629, cited in White, *Splintered Party*, p. 104.
23. F. Schade, Die Wucher auf dem Lande im Großherzogtum Hessen, Schriften des Vereins für Sozialpolitik, vol. 27 (Berlin, 1887), pp. 82–83, cited in White, *Splintered Party*, pp. 141–42.

be supplemented by wage labor for other farmers and in industry. Here the agricultural associations had long been dominated by the eastern estate-owners, and their influence was further enhanced by the legal incorporation of the new Chamber of Agriculture (Landwirtschaftskammer) in 1895 on a restricted franchise. But in the meantime some agronomists had launched a Cooperative Federation in 1883 for smaller farmers not catered to by the agricultural associations, and by 1900 this numbered some two hundred affiliates. The economic division corresponded to a political one, for the Conservatives could maintain a serious presence only in the eastern districts. The two conservative parties had never won more than two of the province's ten Reichstag seats before 1893, and by 1903 they had been eliminated altogether. By contrast, the liberals maintained and even extended their hold on the peasantry between the 1890s and 1914, taking seven out of the ten seats in 1912. In this setting there was little scope – or even need – for an organization like the BdL. Its field of activity was circumscribed by the peasantry's historic liberal radicalism, and its 8,000 members compared poorly with the 21,000 members of the now defunct agricultural associations, or the 80,000 members who joined the farmers' cooperatives later in the 1920s.[24]

In other words, the contradiction between peasant and estate agriculture in Schleswig-Holstein was articulated within an existing division of political allegiances in which the confident liberalism of prosperous independent farmers drew fresh strength from a direct comparison with the big estates. Here the juxtaposition between peasant and estate agriculture validated liberalism as an ideology of rural radicalism, enabling the old populist coalition against the Prussian aristocracy to persist much longer than elsewhere.[25] But in the sec-

24. G. von Schrötter, "Agrarorganisation und sozialer Wandel (dargestellt am Beispiel Schleswig-Holstein)," in *Zur soziologischen Theorie*, ed. Rüegg and Neuloh, pp. 123–44; Rudolf Heberle, *From Democracy to Nazism: A Regional Case Study on Political Parties in Germany* (New York, 1970), pp. 23ff; and Tirrell, *German Agrarian Politics*, p. 142.

25. Although we remain extraordinarily ignorant about the social basis of German liberalism at the regional and local levels, the state of Oldenburg, large parts of Hanover, and parts of the Rhineland may prove to be comparable to Schleswig-Holstein in the sense suggested here. The term "populist" is used in this essay only as a general term denoting a broadly based appeal to the "people in general" against unrepresentative dominant interests – in this case the landowning aristocracy. In this respect, see E. Laclau, *Politics and Ideology in Marxist Theory* (London, 1977), pp. 143–99.

ond example, that of Hesse, liberalism was itself the political vehicle for the land-owning oligarchy and adapted itself to peasant dissatisfactions with far greater difficulty. Of the three Hessian provinces, something akin to the buoyant farming society of western Schleswig-Holstein was reproduced in only one. This was Rhenish Hesse, "where the influence of the relatively weak territorial aristocracy had been crushed under the French occupation of 1793–1815," and where the "better-off peasants and townsmen" had been the main beneficiaries.[26] Significantly, perhaps, the National Liberals fared better politically in the two Rhenish-Hessian constituencies of Bingen-Alzey and Worms-Heppenheim than elsewhere in the Grand Duchy.

In the two other provinces of Starkenberg and Upper Hesse, the social contrasts were much stronger. Starkenberg encompassed an industrial belt in its north running from Darmstadt to Offenbach, a fertile farming zone in the southwest along the Rhine and the Bergstraße, and the much poorer Odenwald in the southeast. Upper Hesse was more uniformly agricultural, but it was divided by the Vogelsberg into a more prosperous west and a backward east. It was in Upper Hesse, the most northerly of the Hessian provinces where the disparities were greatest and the larger farmers controlled the best land and facilities, that the existing political alignments were most vulnerable. Here the poor smallholding peasantry had to confront the combined liberal predominance of local nobility and improving farmers without the benefit of an existing peasant radicalism to provide a strong counter-hegemonic alternative. Of course, the Hessian National Liberals had originally built their political success on a broad popular coalition against the traditional aristocratic order. As late as 1881, liberals in the adjacent Prussian constituency of Hanau-Geinhausen-Bockelheim had issued the slogan "Junkers and priests together/Put townsmen and peasants in tether."[27] But by the end of the 1880s that popular leadership had ossified into a fresh set of paternalistic relations that could only be fractured by new and independent peasant politics. In fact, Upper Hesse formed the southern rim of a region stretching westwards to Siegen,

---

26. White, *Splintered Party*, pp. 20–21.
27. "Junker und Pfaffen im Bund/Richten Bürger und Bauer zu Grund!" cited in ibid., p. 100.

northwards to Göttingen, and eastwards into Thuringia – a region that was to return a fairly stable bloc of anti-Semitic and radical agrarian deputies from 1893 to the First World War, and thus a similar penetration of radical elements could be achieved in the Hessian context only by a frontal collision with the landed, liberal establishment.[28]

The failure of the Hessian National Liberals to accommodate the needs of smaller farmers, either by adapting the existing agricultural associations or by some organized innovation of the party itself, had far-reaching implications. Basically, they had vacated a political space whose occupation by others eventually brought their survival as a major political force in the countryside into serious question. The challenge to their moral authority had modest beginnings. In 1887 Otto Boeckel, a librarian at the University of Marburg, captured that town's safe Conservative seat, which had been virtually uncontested since 1871. He fought the campaign on the slogan "Against Junkers and Jews," and harkened back to the days of 1848 by adopting the black-red-gold banner as his standard. Known as the "peasant king" and the "second Luther," Boeckel demanded among other things a progressive income tax, cheaper litigation, freedom of speech and the press, abolition of the Prussian three-class franchise, and more accessible credit. Boeckel thus built himself a position as the self-appointed spokesman of a rejuvenated peasant radicalism. By 1890 he was strong enough to extend his agitation from Prussian Hesse into the Grand Duchy, where he found an important ally in the ex-liberal farmer Philipp Koehler. In 1891 his peasant constituency was organized into the Central German Peasants' Association (Mitteldeutscher Bauernverein), which by mid-1882 had 15,000 members in some 400 branches.[29] Its aim was to combine the peasant farmers into a great cooperative with the closest possible connection to the party, to work for the party in parliamentary elections on all levels, and to create thereby a

28. While the specific inflection is my own, this account is condensed from the following sources: White, *Splintered Party*, pp. 123ff; Levy, *Anti-Semitic Parties*, passim; R. Mack, "Otto Boeckel und die antisemitische Bauernbewegung in Hessen 1887–1894," *Wetterauer Geschichtsblätter* 16 (1967): 113–47; and K.E. Demandt, "Leopold von Sacher–Masoch und sein Oberhessischer Volksbildungsverein zwischen Schwarzen, Roten und Antisemiten," *Hessisches Jahrbuch für Landesgeschichte* 18 (1968): 180–84.

29. For further details, see Levy, *Anti-Semitic Parties*, pp. 55–60, and White, *Splintered Party*, pp. 136ff.

free peasant class.[30] Significantly, Boeckel won most of his support in poorer agricultural areas in the north of the Grand Duchy of Hesse, where chronic indebtedness, bad soil, inadequate transportation, and backward technology combined to depress the smallholding peasants. On the other hand, in areas to the west of the Rhine, as in the marshlands of Schleswig-Holstein, a prosperous class of rich peasants with strong traditions of political independence predominated. Here Boeckel's anti-Semitic radicalism made few inroads into support for the established liberal parties.[31]

What do these regional examples signify? First, they illustrate that the agrarian movement of the 1890s cannot be linked solely or even mainly to the politics of the Junkers. On the contrary, the latter were rather slower off the mark than other agrarian spokesmen when it came to organizing a popular movement against the government, the main centers of which were in any case outside the immediate purview of the east-Elbian aristocracy. When the latter acted decisively early in 1893, they did so largely in response to the prior activity of others. Before that time, the salient feature of agrarian mobilization, apart from its sheer novelty, was its character as a movement of smaller and less prosperous farmers. Second, at this stage the movement was not primarily motivated by hostility to Chancellor Caprivi's trade treaties or the threat of lower tariffs, even though specific categories of smaller producers, such as the winegrowers, had certainly opposed the earlier treaties.

Third, the animus and sense of grievance behind the peasantry's political activation were strengthened by the institutional effects of Germany's capitalist transformation on the social relations of the countryside. Smaller farmers confronted their problems not only at a time of accelerating social and economic change, but also when the institutional consolidation of the rural class structure was creating greater distance from the landowning notability through the growth of state agricultural bureaucracies, the cooptation of agricultural associations, and the incorporation of chambers of agriculture. The peasants seemed to suffer most of the costs of economic transformation without any of the gains. Small producers had little

30. Levy, *Anti-Semitic Parties*, p. 59.
31. White, *Splintered Party*, pp. 20–21, 137–40.

hope of participating in the potential benefits of a growing economy – including the expanding urban demand for foodstuffs, new opportunities for consumption, and the greater availability of machinery, implements, and fertilizers – without the benevolent intervention of the state through such means as tax relief, cheaper credit, or a more extensive local railway network. The new consultative arrangements between government and private interests, let alone the larger power structures of which they were a part, normally excluded such people.

Fourth, for this reason peasant grievances tended to be expressed through a kind of antiplutocratic populism. The aristocrat, the priest, the civil servant, the moneylender, the merchant, the educated gentleman, also the professional expert (the agronomist, the lawyer, the veterinary surgeon, the surveyor, or the public health inspector) – these could all be denounced as outsiders in one form or another, as parasites preying on the vitality of rural society. Whenever the aristocrat could be stigmatized as a "Junker," the priest as a "papist," the civil servant as a "Prussian," or the moneylender as a "Jew," so much the better. This, in turn, was invariably linked to local particularism or patriotic sentiments, most notably in Bavaria or in those parts of Prussia like Hanover and Hesse that had been annexed during the wars of unification. Anti-Semitism was also a dominant motif in the rhetoric of peasant radicalism in both the Protestant and Catholic parts of Germany.

Fifth and finally, the same broad scenario of rural unrest was common to most regions of the country, though most pronounced in the center and south. Its political forms varied, including political anti-Semitism in Prussian and Grand Duchal Hesse, independent peasant radicalism in large parts of Bavaria, and a re-deployed social Catholicism in Baden, Württemberg, and again Bavaria. In some regions – Schleswig-Holstein, Württemberg, or parts of Hanover – it was expressed, for a time at least, through the existing liberal parties. But in most cases National Liberalism was the main object of hostility from small producers, although in the early 1890s the Center also received its fair share of abuse in Bavaria.[32]

32. Apart from the works by Levy, White, Farr, Möckl, Blackbourn, and Tirrell cited above, see the following: H. Busch, *Die Stoeckerbewegung im Siegerland. Ein Beitrag zur siegerländischer Geschichte in der zweiten Hälfte des 19. Jahrhunderts* (Siegen, 1968); J.C. Hunt, "The 'Egalitarianism' of the Right: The Agrarian League in South-West Germany, 1893–1914," *Journal of Contemporary*

IV

The geography of the agrarian movement in the early 1890s gave it a pronounced anti-Prussian bias, largely because Prussia signified the social power of the Junkers. As an organ of the Bavarian Peasants' League exclaimed: "It is time to warn our Bavarian peasants not to be cheated by north-German Junkers and big estate owners. The interests of the latter are not always the same as those of the Bavarian peasantry, who are middle and small peasants."[33] Such hostility already spelled trouble for the Conservatives, because they always seriously contested a number of parliamentary seats outside Prussia. But the hostile particularist equation of Prussia with the Junkers began to hit closer to home in those areas that had been annexed only in 1866. The Guelphs in Hanover remained a thorn in the flesh of the Conservatives.[34] But Otto Boeckel's noisy eruption into the cozy Conservative backwater of Marburg, where the incumbent had scarcely needed to put in a public appearance in previous campaigns, was infinitely more threatening. Not only was Boeckel's agitation replete with anti-Junker tirades, but his election to the Reichstag in 1887 began the process of what the Nazi historian Walter Frank called "the secession of radical anti-Semitism from the Conservative Party," a process that reached a stormy conclusion in the spring of 1893.[35]

The political dangers of a disaffected peasantry were forcefully driven home for the Prussian Conservatives by the extraordinary career of Hermann Ahlwardt, who burst onto the scene in the summer of 1891. A middle-aged headmaster who had been suspended from his school in 1889 for embezzlement, Ahlwardt built an alternative career by peddling sensational anti-Semitic stories swathed in lurid personal revelations. After seizing dramatic national publicity by slandering Gerson Ble-

---

History 10 (1975): 513–30; D. Blackbourn, "Roman Catholics, the Center Party and Anti-Semitism in Imperial Germany," in *Nationalist and Racialist Movements in Britain and Germany before 1914*, ed. P. Kennedy and A.J. Nicholls (London, 1981), pp. 106–29.

33. Gottwald and Fritsch, "Bayerischer Bauernbund," p. 68.

34. See S. Stehlin, *Bismarck and the Guelph Problem, 1866–1890: A Study in Particularist Opposition to National Unity* (The Hague, 1973). For the far less important Hessian particularism, see E. Knobel, *Die Hessische Reichspartei. Konservative Opposition gegen das Bismarckreich* (Marburg, 1975).

35. W. Frank, *Hofprediger Adolf Stoecker und die christlichsoziale Bewegung* (Berlin, 1928), p. 257.

ichröder, Bismarck's banker, and serving a four-month prison sentence for his pains, he embarked on a new political career in the spring of 1892. At this point, his progress converged with the ambitions of Stöcker and Baron Wilhelm von Hammerstein-Schwartow, whose so-called *Kreuzzeitung* group was rapidly driving the Conservative Party toward an internal leadership crisis. In effect, Ahlwardt was quickly appropriated as the stalking horse for a far-reaching reorientation of the Conservative Party toward a much more populist kind of political practice.[36]

In the spring of 1892 the Conservative leadership came under increasingly heavy fire. The upper echelons of the party leadership had become progressively isolated within the party as a consequence of their support for the *Kartell* with the Free Conservatives and National Liberals against the Center Party; for their equivocal response to the government's withdrawal of Culture Minister Robert von Zedlitz-Trütschler's heavily clerical school bill; and for the effacing governmental orientation and patrician style of party chairman Otto von Helldorff-Bedra.[37] In these circumstances, the reluctance of those closer to Helldorff to oppose the government's trade treaties was but one confirmation among many of their general ineffectiveness. The principal spokesmen for the opposition – Stöcker, whose relationship to the official Conservative Party was already an ambiguous one, and more erratically Hammerstein, who occupied the strategically crucial editorship of the *Kreuzzeitung* – had already clashed fiercely with Helldorff in 1889/90; the formation of a "Committee of Eleven" as a new executive organ of the party was partly a means of contesting Helldorff's control over policy.[38] It is a serious mistake to conflate this internal opposition to the movement against Caprivi's trade treaties. The latter may have postdated, overdetermined, and eventually superseded the factional conflict within the Conservative

36. For Ahlwardt's career, see Levy, *Anti-Semitic Parties*, pp. 77ff.

37. For details of the political maneuvering in 1892/93, see Nichols, *Germany after Bismarck*, pp. 157–264; and Röhl, *Germany without Bismarck*, pp. 85ff. The difficulties in the Conservative Party may also be traced through the Helldorff-Eulenburg correspondence in *Philipp Eulenburgs politische Korrespondenz*, ed. J.C.G. Röhl, 3 vols. (Boppard am Rhein, 1976–83), vol. 2: *Im Brennpunkt der Regierungskrise 1892–1895*, pp. 788ff., 824ff., 858ff., 876ff., 964ff., 988ff., 1233ff.

38. T. Nipperdey, *Die Organisation der deutschen Parteien vor 1918* (Düsseldorf, 1961), pp. 252–53.

Party, but it was initially discrete from it. The Stöcker-Hammerstein axis had a separate basis and originated mainly in the new populist milieu of the Berlin movement in the early 1880s.[39]

Ideologically the *Kreuzzeitung* faction was a curious transitional amalgam. Hammerstein himself managed to combine the desire to convert the Conservative Party from a club of the Prussian high nobility into a genuine popular formation with an unreconstructed traditional conservatism of "throne and altar," and he was never far from embracing a rather unstable opportunism. Stöcker, on the other hand, represented an entirely different breed of politician. His politics were far more innovative, and, though formally concerned with reconciling the alienated "fourth estate" to the monarchical order, he was actually much more preoccupied with channeling the new anti-Semitic radicalism into a modernized Conservative Party. In both cases, however, the powerful antigovernment animus, the two-fronted hostility against both liberals and orthodox Conservatives, and the belief in some kind of "social" conservatism facilitated a political convergence with the emerging Anti-Semitic parties. Moreover, there were obvious sociological similarities between Stöcker's rural constituency of Siegen, the nearby outposts of Westphalian Conservatism in Minden-Ravensberg, Herford, Bielefeld, and Rinteln, and the anti-Semitic heartlands of Hesse. Similarly, in Berlin, where Hammerstein's supporters had tried to coordinate their efforts through the so-called "Citizens' Clubs" or *Bürgervereine*, the line between the Conservative opposition and the Anti-Semites was blurred.[40]

By the spring of 1892, the political authority of the Helldorff group was at low ebb. By skillful domination of the Conservative press, by exploiting the resentment over the withdrawal of the school bill, and by drawing rhetorically upon the popu-

39. The conflation is implicit in Puhle's work. See also Levy, *Anti-Semitic Parties*, p. 71.
40. The best account of the Stöcker movement in the provinces is Busch, *Stoeckerbewegung*. See also Nipperdey, *Organisation der deutschen Parteien*, pp. 241ff.; and Frank, *Stoecker*, pp. 290ff. In addition to Frank, *Stoecker*, the best source of information on the Berlin movement is W. Kampmann, "Stoecker und die Berliner Bewegung," *Geschichte in Wissenschaft und Unterricht* 13 (1962): 558–79. S. Volkov, *The Rise of Popular Antimodernism in Germany: The Urban Master Artisans, 1873–1896* (Princeton, N.J., 1978), pp. 251ff., is disappointing in this respect and adds nothing new.

lar conservatism of Westphalia and the Anti-Semitic currents in the capital, Hammerstein and his associates were able to win over a significant number of Reichstag and Landtag deputies to their view. For adherents of the *Kartell*, who continued to believe that a coalition with the so-called "middle parties" – i.e., the Free Conservatives and National Liberals – constituted the natural basis of government, this was a particularly depressing time. On the one hand, Hammerstein seemed to be angling for some sort of clerical condominium with the Center Party. On the other hand, the association with the Anti-Semites and the growing tendency to cultivate the masses seemed to be taking the Conservative Party dangerously close to "democratic" waters. In either case, the *Kartell* strategy stood to lose. Moreover, in the background lurked the recently deposed Bismarck, who was widely suspected of encouraging the *Kartell*'s fragmentation in order to make himself again indispensable.[41] In this situation Helldorff pleaded urgently for a "rallying of the reasonable Conservative elements" and for their separation from Hammerstein's "witless demagogy, which served partly papist and partly Social Democratic goals."[42]

Under the impact of the school bill crisis, Stöcker initiated an open power struggle with the current party leadership in a speech to the Berlin Conservatives in March 1892. Simultaneously and in close liaison with Stöcker and other Prussian Conservatives, Ahlwardt began a fresh set of sensational revelations concerning Jewish corruption. By this time, Helldorff's allies had dwindled to a few individuals, including Baron Otto von Manteuffel-Crossen, Baron Hermann von Erffa-Wernburg, and Wilhelm von Rauchhaupt, who represented the solid governmental tradition of the Prussian Conservatives. As the future chancellor Bernhard von Bülow wrote in April 1892, this "little group . . . warm themselves in the sun of the Kaiser's grace," but "have little backing in the country" and could be dismissed as "*Postenjäger* with no ability." By contrast, "the majority of the party is speaking a downright anti-royalist language."[43] The

41. Speculation about Bismarck's intentions was a major factor in the high politics of the early 1890s. See Stribrny, *Bismarck*, pp. 63ff.; and Hank, *Kanzler ohne Amt*, pp. 271–429.

42. Helldorff to Eulenburg, 23 May 1892, *Eulenburgs politische Korrespondenz*, ed. Röhl, vol. 2, p. 877.

43. Bülow to Eulenburg, 6 April 1892, ibid., vol. 2, p. 844.

other "moderate elements" in the Conservative Party – namely, those whom Helldorff called "the group of dependent people, civil servants et cetera, who tack with the wind" – temporized in the absence of a strong lead from the Kaiser or his ministers.[44] On 4 April 1892 Helldorff demanded a clean break with Stöcker, only to be repudiated two days later by the Conservative caucuses in both the Reichstag and Prussian *Herrenhaus* and then by the Prussian House of Deputies shortly thereafter. In a crescendo of anti-Semitic hysteria at the end of April, Ahlwardt published his famous pamphlet on *Die Judenflinten*, whereupon the Conservatives in the Prussian House of Deputies voted by a ninety-five to one margin to adopt a new anti-Semitic program.[45]

In point of fact, this radical triumph proved short-lived. Two days after Helldorff's resignation from the leadership of the Conservative Party on 27 May 1892, the Prussian ministry of war issued a flat denial of Ahlwardt's allegations of corruption in arms contracts, thus setting the stage for Ahlwardt's arrest once again.[46] This rather took the wind from the sails of the *Kreuzzeitung* faction and prompted second thoughts on the part of some prominent Conservatives. In the lull that followed, the Prussian Landtag caucus reconvened and overturned the previous decision by a slim twenty-one to twenty margin at a poorly attended meeting. This suggested a state of some confusion in Conservative ranks, and pressure continued to mount for a clarification of both program and leadership. During the summer Stöcker mobilized resolutions from Westphalia and Saxony, with the result that a national party congress seemed increasingly likely. In the meantime, Ahlwardt maintained a constant barrage of demagogic extravagance, touring the country to accolades of popular acclaim, bristling with wild accusations, and accumulating libel suits as he went. The anti-Semitic fever was further heightened by the Xanten "ritual murder" case, in which an innocent Jewish butcher was made the object of prolonged anti-Semitic speculation and much popular violence.[47]

44. Helldorff to Eulenburg, 23 May 1892, ibid., vol. 2, p. 877.
45. For further details, see Tirrell, *German Agrarian Politics*, pp. 147ff.; Levy, *Anti-Semitic Parties*, pp. 72–79; Nipperdey, *Organisation der deutschen Parteien*, pp. 244ff.; and Nichols, *Germany after Bismarck*, pp. 218ff.
46. Levy, *Anti-Semitic Parties*, pp. 79–80.
47. Nichols, *Germany after Bismarck*, p. 218.

This long summer of fermenting extremism was brought to a fitting climax when Ahlwardt, glorying in the repeated martyrdom of still another prison sentence, was adopted as an official Anti-Semitic candidate for an impending by-election in the Brandenburg district of Arnswalde-Friedeberg. The political choices were conveniently dramatized by the fact that Ahlwardt was opposed by an aristocratic Conservative and a left liberal. After the constituency had been saturated by an unprecedented wave of anti-Semitic agitation, Ahlwardt triumphantly carried the seat on 5 December 1892, just a few days before being sentenced in the largest of his libel indictments. Three days later, on 8 December, the Conservative Party held its first national congress since 1876 in the Tivoli Beer Hall in Berlin, and amidst scenes of anarchic but inescapable pressure from the floor an unequivocal anti-Semitic commitment was incorporated into the party program. Twenty-two Reichstag deputies, all supporters of Helldorff's position, tried rather unconvincingly to interpret this new program as a mere elaboration of the old. But this could not disguise the momentary triumph of Stöcker and Hammerstein. The populist character of the opposition came through strongly in the demand for a reconstruction of the party's executive committee and for the nomination of more non-aristocratic candidates for election.[48]

V

The Tivoli congress was disturbing for Prussian Conservatives in a number of ways. The form of the meeting was itself disquieting. Conservatives were unused to public accountability and rarely needed even to campaign publicly in an election. To submit their deliberations to the proceedings of a mass meeting was thus a new experience. Moreover, the absence of a party constitution made it difficult to control the composition of the audience. There was no procedure for choosing delegations and no scrutiny of credentials at the congress itself. Attendance was open to ordinary members of the party, and in light of the distinctions mentioned above it was inevitable that this should prove the thin end of an Anti-Semitic wedge. It is

48. Nipperdey, *Organisation der deutschen Parteien*, pp. 245, 256; Levy, *Anti-Semitic Parties*, pp. 80ff.

clear that, of the 1,200 delegates who attended the congress, perhaps as many as several hundred belonged to the different Anti-Semitic parties. The Tivoli affair consequently drama-tized the problem of regularizing Conservative relations with these newer political formations, not just organizationally but programmatically as well. Due to the debilitating indetermi-nacy of its official politics, the Conservative Party had been momentarily overwhelmed by the populist drive of its radical minority. As Stöcker observed some weeks later: "This was no congress of black dress suits and white kid gloves, but one of ordinary jackets." Or, as the lawyer August Klasing from Bielefeld expressed it from the perspective of the Westphalian Conservatives: "We thought that for many of our parliamen-tarians too much time in Berlin is likely to impair the energy of resolution, the hardness and strength of the backbone, and the tension of the muscles. . . . We are fed up with the opportunism that has crippled the Conservative Party's real strength for years." The non-aristocratic petty bourgeois militancy of the anti-Semitic turn was unmistakable. Another of Stöcker's sup-porters, an anti-Semite from Chemnitz named Eduard Ulrich, called on the party to be "demagogic in the good sense," for "the banner of anti-Semitism is not to be hauled down until the Jews are as small as they are now great."[49]

Coming as the grand climax to a year of anti-Semitic agita-tion and in the immediate, emotional aftermath of Ahlwardt's remarkable by-election victory, the peculiar radical ambience of the Tivoli proceedings placed the Conservative leadership under enormous pressure. The new party chair, Otto von Manteuffel, held much the same orthodox Conservative views as the supplanted Helldorff and had originally proposed a simple renewal of the 1876 program. But sensing the mood of the moment, he acquiesced to more radical departures. As he later said, "The Jewish question was not to be avoided unless we wanted to leave the full wind of the movement to the dem-agogic Anti-Semites; with it they would have sailed right past us."[50] As it was, Stöcker – along with Hellmut von Gerlach, editor of Stöcker's organ *Das Volk* and at that time a self-described "Tory Democrat," after the fashion of Lord Ran-dolph Churchill, and Hans Leuß, another prominent Anti-

49. All three quotations are from Frank, *Stoecker*, pp. 302–04.
50. Ibid., p. 302.

Semitic leader – had successfully nipped in the bud the leadership's proposals for fresh anti-Socialist laws, and it was still unclear where the boundaries of "popular" conservatism actually lay.[51] Helldorff for one had no doubts. Hammerstein – "the adroit and unscrupulous tactician" – and Stöcker – "the popular agitator" – had "exploited the Anti-Semitic movement with a true genius," but the "end effect" of the Tivoli congress had been "capitulation of the Conservative Party before the mob."[52] Hammerstein was definitely no democrat, but many of his supporters were much more ambivalent. At all events, Conservatives were fast being trapped into uncongenial positions, whose implications were temporarily fudged by the unaccustomed pleasures of popular success. Both the logic of the situation and the recklessness of many Junker Conservatives had been revealed in one declamatory intervention at the Tivoli congress, when Ahlwardt's defeated Conservative opponent shouted from the floor: "better ten Ahlwardts, ten Anti-Semites, than one left liberal."[53]

The wider implications of these events were not lost on the Conservative leadership. When the confused radicalism of the congress and the frenetic events of early December 1892 were added to the variant forms of agrarian radicalization described earlier in this essay, they rounded off into an extremely threatening conjuncture. The sharpening structural contradictions between small and large farmers had already had clear political implications, but these had been more of a problem for the other parties, the National Liberals and the Center, than for the Conservatives themselves. Boeckel's success in Marburg on an anti-Junker platform had been ominous, and Stöcker's support in Westphalia was equally disconcerting. But so far there had been little evidence of agrarian radicalism's penetration into the Conservative heartlands east of the Elbe. This made Ahlwardt's triumphal progress through the Brandenburg countryside all the more threatening, coming as it did so soon after the Anti-Semites' victories in Hesse and Sigl's narrow defeat in the Kelheim by-election in October. When even the dependent peasantry of the east could be galvanized from political torpor by Ahlwardt's volatile millenarian invocations

51. H. von Gerlach, *Von Rechts nach Links* (Hildesheim, 1978), pp. 131ff.
52. Helldorff to Eulenburg, 11 December 1892, *Eulenburgs politische Korrespondenz*, ed. Röhl, vol. 2, p. 989f.
53. Levy, *Anti-Semitic Parties*, p. 83.

of Luther, Hus, and Christ, the survival of the Conservative Party in its existing form was being brought into question.

It is true that the radical victory at Tivoli could have only occurred because the national leadership was divided and its politics in transition.[54] But the transitory nature of the populist success – in two years the Hammerstein-Stöcker wing would be in disarray – should not obscure its decisive contribution to the conjuncture of 1892/93 that led to the further development of the Conservative Party. Anti-Semitism continued to feed on the deteriorating conditions of agricultural life, and the potential for agrarian mobilization had so far only been glimpsed. In these circumstances, orthodox Conservatives were rightly concerned about their political credibility. At the time of Ruprecht-Ransern's agrarian manifesto toward the end of December 1892, Wilhelm von Kardorff wrote that he had never before witnessed the bitterness currently seething around him in Silesia, adding that the Conservatives would "experience the consequences in the next election."[55] If the Conservatives were not to lose their political leadership in the countryside, it was imperative for them to devise a means of rallying agricultural interests or rural society *as a whole*, and of reemphasizing the lines of solidarity between large and small farmers.

In evaluating the circumstances that surrounded the founding of the Agrarian League in February 1893, therefore, it is important to observe the full complexity of this immediate conjuncture. The BdL was formed not from some spontaneous realization in the Conservative Reichstag delegation that new methods were needed if the trade treaties were to be defeated. Such a reading of these events exaggerates the overall coherence of Conservative interventions in this period. It also ignores the main dilemma of official Conservatives who were forced to face two ways: to reconcile opposition to the trade treaties with received pro-governmental assumptions certainly, but at the same time to cope with the equal novelty of an independent agrarian mobilization beyond their political control. Ruprecht-Ransern's public call for a new agrarian party

54. Nipperdey, *Organisation der politischen Parteien*, p. 244.
55. S. von Kardorff, *Wilhelm von Kardorff. Ein nationaler Parlamentarier im Zeitalter Bismarcks und Wilhelms II. 1828–1907* (Berlin, 1936), pp. 275–76. See also F. Hellwig, *Carl Ferdinand Freiherr von Stumm-Halberg 1836–1901* (Heidelberg, 1936), p. 464.

came just as the Conservative establishment was struggling to reestablish its control over events. In this sense, his initiative was eagerly grasped by the more perspicacious Conservative politicians. It was a chance to deflect all the causes of rural unrest onto the single issue of the treaties while simultaneously containing the new Anti-Semitic unruliness. A decisive response to Ruprecht-Ransern's manifesto could both terminate the recriminations about the party program by imposing a fresh priority and obscure the contradictions between landowners and peasants. But the Junkers, it cannot be stressed too strongly, had not created this situation for themselves. The BdL was not, as Puhle suggests, the product of some manipulative strategy "called into life by east-Elbian estate-owners and Conservatives, who for economic reasons moved into active and radical opposition and set themselves against state and government."[56] On the contrary, the possibility of a new organization such as the BdL was first determined by the agrarian radicalism that preceded it. The latter was immensely disquieting for most orthodox Conservatives. Although they were responsible for launching the Agrarian League, they did not do so under circumstances chosen by themselves.

VI

The BdL appeared at a time of agricultural crisis but also in the wake of prior agrarian mobilization. This *double* condition of existence was clearly responsible for the immediate circumstances surrounding its founding. A few days after the Anti-Semites' apparent victory at Tivoli, Otto Boeckel poured scorn on the Conservatives' sincerity and simultaneously reemphasized the social contradiction at the center of the agrarian movement. "A party of the nobility and great landowners is still a long way from being a people's party, even though its program is patched up with a piece of the Jewish question."[57] Then, on 21 December 1892, Ruprecht-Ransern issued his call for a "single, great agrarian party." Three days after that, Baron Conrad von Wangenheim, the future chairman of the BdL and the owner of a *Rittergut* in Pomerania, laid bare the

56. Puhle, "Bund der Landwirte," p. 148.
57. Cited in Levy, *Anti-Semitic Parties*, p. 84.

Conservative dilemma in a letter to his brother. Repudiating any suggestion of "demagogy," he admitted that "initially an extremely vigorous agitation" would be necessary to hold "the indolent masses" to the standard. His remarks revealed both contempt for popular intelligence and fear that others might exploit it. He argued that "the government can only be grateful to us if we seek to guide the uneducated masses. The discontent there is quite enormous and the language hellishly sharp. If we don't take the matter in hand, then Socialists and Anti-Semites of the worst sort will."[58]

Concrete action followed. After consulting colleagues, Wangenheim issued a second manifesto on 28 January 1893 that was followed on 4 February by a self-constituted meeting of approximately 120 farmers in Berlin. The latter elected an organizing committee of twenty-five that included Ruprecht-Ransern but conspicuously omitted leading associates of Stöcker – let alone the Anti-Semites – and was heavily aristocratic. The constituent meeting of the Agrarian League duly convened on 18 February 1893. In contrast to the Tivoli congress of two months before, the meeting was orderly, formal, and tightly controlled in advance, with no unexpected incidents despite the attendance of some 10,000 farmers. The leading speakers repudiated demagogic intentions and proclaimed their royalism. The eleven-point program consisted of straightforward economic demands for the defense of agriculture as an interest, and the twin themes of the keynote speeches were the essential unity of all farmers, whether large or small, and the need to oppose the trade treaties. Significantly, there was no commitment to anti-Semitism and no trace of the crude egalitarianism that characterized the rural mobilization in central and western Germany. Equally significantly, a resolution affirming support for the army bill was passed at a time when peasant spokesmen were girding themselves to reject it.[59]

The new organization's authentic political function was revealed by its impact in the regions. The founders of the BdL were conscious of their east-Elbian origins but made efforts to

58. *Conrad Freiherr von Wangenheim-Klein-Spiegel*, ed. H. von Wangenheim, 2 vols. (Berlin, 1934), vol. 2, pp. 20–21.

59. Apart from the *Stenographischer Bericht* cited in n. 11, see Tirrell, *German Agrarian Politics*, pp. 159ff.; Puhle, *Agrarische Interessenpolitik*, pp. 33ff.; Fricke, "Bund der Landwirte," p. 132; and Levy, *Anti-Semitic Parties*, pp. 87ff.

Geoff Eley

establish roots in southern Germany as well. A special meeting was scheduled in Mainz for 25 March 1893, to which farmers from Baden, Württemberg, Alsace-Lorraine, Bavaria,
Prussian Hesse, and the Grand Duchy of Hesse were invited.
In Baden and Württemberg the returns were moderate, in
Alsace-Lorraine there were none at all. In Bavaria, moreover,
matters were complicated by the indigenous radicalism of the
peasants' leagues.[60] The efforts were most rewarding in the
Grand Duchy of Hesse, where the beleaguered National Liberals were already facing the mass defection of rural voters that
the Conservatives only anticipated in eastern Prussia. In one
month the BdL had acquired an organization in Hesse with a
six-man executive committee. Almost without exception, the
leading lights at the provincial and district levels were National Liberal notables, and the local structure meshed neatly with
that of the agricultural associations. Significantly, in terms of
the state's socioeconomic topography, it was most successful
in the prosperous areas of Rhenish Hesse, the Main flatland,
and the Wetterau region in the west of Upper Hesse, whereas
it made little headway in the poorer parts of the Odenwald
and Vogelsberg.[61]

As suggested above, the BdL's implantation in the countryside was a response not merely to the agricultural crisis, but
also to the greater politicization of the peasantry that this crisis
was starting to produce. In the Hessian context it was a clear
attempt to erect defensive walls against Boeckel's Central German Peasants' Association. In 1892 the latter was maintaining
an impressive level of mobilization – an average of twenty-
five to thirty "major political gatherings" a month, accompanied by "lectures, discussions, and entertainments"[62] – and
this was bound to disturb established politicians whose activity moved at a far more leisurely and informal pace. In the
spring of 1891, a government survey had already reported the
existence of Anti-Semitic majorities in twenty-three villages
around Büdingen and the germs of similar situations in most
other areas of Upper Hesse.[63] Unless National Liberals were to

60. For further details, see Blackbourn, *Class, Religion, and Local Politics*, pp.
196–230; Hunt, "'Egalitarianism' of the Right," p. 515; Tirrell, *German Agrarian
Politics*, p. 169; White, *Splintered Party*, p. 149; Puhle, *Agrarische Interessenpolitik*, p. 68; and Farr, "Populism in the Countryside," pp. 144ff.
61. White, *Splintered Party*, p. 143.
62. Levy, *Anti-Semitic Parties*, p. 62.

218

abdicate their rural hegemony completely, therefore, some means of counterattack had to be found, and in 1893 the newly established BdL was tailor-made for the purpose. In the June 1893 Reichstag elections, seven of the National Liberals' nine parliamentary candidates were endorsed by the BdL, and the other two were broadly sympathetic with its purpose. The results were mixed. Although the Anti-Semites held two of their three seats in Upper Hesse and gained another in Bensheim-Erbach, the National Liberals recovered Friedberg-Büdingen with a heavily agrarian candidate, Waldemar von Oriola, the BdL's provincial chairman in Upper Hesse. The Anti-Semitic advance was checked, but only at the expense of far-reaching concessions to the new Conservative-led agrarian movement.[64]

Arguably, the Agrarian League's most important achievement was to equip the Conservative Party with stable allies west of the Elbe, where rural politics had previously been dominated by forces less sympathetic and often directly hostile to the Junkers. The largest of these allies was the Center, but its cooperation was also the least problematic, for on most questions its politics converged independently with those of the Conservatives.[65] The Anti-Semites also adopted positions that were often consonant in the sphere of agricultural policy, but their social radicalism prevented cooperation elsewhere. Here the collaboration was far more difficult for reasons already discussed above, with the result that the BdL found itself contesting the Anti-Semites' popular support and partly adjusting to it. But it was the support of the National Liberals, who dominated large areas of northern, central, and southwest Germany, that proved the most rewarding in the long run. The BdL's ability to interpose itself between the National Liberal Party and its historic rural support was one of the most significant developments of the 1890s. As they entered the decade, liberal parties faced important challenges not only from the Social Democrats in the towns in Baden, Hesse, Thuringia, and Saxony but also from variegated rural agitations in Baden, Württemberg, the Palatinate, the Grand Duchy

---

63. Eugen Schmal, *Entwicklung der völkischen Bewegung. Die antisemitische Bauernbewegung in Hessen von der Boeckelzeit bis zum Nationalsozialismus* (Giessen, 1933), pp. 80–83.

64. White, *Splintered Party*, pp. 143–44.

65. See Puhle, *Agrarische Interessenpolitik*, pp. 172–73.

of Hesse, Prussian Hesse, and Hanover. Rather than developing their own agrarian organization, the National Liberals in effect contracted a political alliance with the newly created BdL. While this may have been an effective short-term expedient for stemming the defection of rural voters to independent agrarian parties, it did so at the doubtful expense of surrendering a certain amount of the National Liberals' own political autonomy.[66]

The insertion of the BdL into traditional liberal territory undermined the National Liberals' claim to be a party of disinterested principle that embodied the general interest of society as a whole. As the BdL was an independent national organization with its own apparatus and policies, the National Liberals increasingly relinquished control over agrarian politics by maintaining such an alliance. And as the BdL began absorbing some of the Anti-Semites' rural constituency after 1900, its practical autonomy further increased. This was apparent by the next Reichstag elections in 1898. In Hesse, for example, the National Liberals' electoral fortunes had become far more dependent upon the BdL's own national machinery, in spite of the fact that they continued to staff the BdL's local committees. Thus Wilhelm Haas, a liberal civil servant who was both the architect of the Hessian cooperative movement and a leading figure in the agricultural associations, was nominated in two Hessian districts and won Bensheim-Erbach away from the Anti-Semites by deliberately disguising his liberal affiliations as an "indepedent" agrarian commitment. Fritz Schade, another leading liberal, was sponsored by the BdL in Alsfeld-Lauterbach-Schotten, where he lost to the incumbent Anti-Semite even though he presented himself as a "non-party" man. The clearest case of all was Oriola, who retained his seat in Friedberg-Büdingen by paying meticulous attention to the parish-pump contacts on which the Anti-Semites had previously fed. But the brightest ideological and organizational auspices clearly belonged to the BdL and not to a revitalized rural liberalism.[67]

Similar trends could be seen elsewhere. In Baden and

66. The 1887 Reichstag elections were the last in which the National Liberals regained something approximating their previous strength from the 1870s. For further information, see Eley, *Reshaping the German Right*, pp. 19–40, 293–315.

67. White, *Splintered Party*, pp. 44–45, 131, 144–45.

Schleswig-Holstein, for example, the National Liberals were not so organizationally dependent upon the BdL, with the result that the latter caused the liberals far less trouble than in Hesse. But in Hanover, where the Hessian syndrome had been broadly reproduced after 1893, serious tensions developed in the fall of 1897 as the National Liberals and the Agrarian League entered the elections with daggers drawn. Here the party had already expelled Diederich Hahn, the BdL's extravagant director, and now it did the same to Johann Friedrich Schoof, the BdL's provincial chairman and a National Liberal Landtag deputy.[68] In the Bavarian Palatinate, where the National Liberals held all six Reichstag seats in 1893, the adjustment to the BdL's new organizational presence proved stormiest of all. Massive pressure was exerted by the BdL on National Liberal district organizations to ensure the nomination of sympathetic candidates. Where this proved impossible, as in Kaiserslautern, an independent BdL candidate was nominated. This produced a traumatic upheaval in the region's National Liberal Party; the atmosphere was in fact "so embittered and disordered by the invasion of unscrupulous agrarian rabble-rousers" that all six incumbent deputies declined renomination.[69] Here the National Liberals held on to four of their six seats, but at the cost of becoming thoroughly "agrarianized."

All of this suggests that the impact of the Agrarian League was ultimately far greater in regions west of the Elbe River. Its contribution to *national* politics, therefore, cannot be assessed merely by the Junkers' parochial concerns east of the Elbe, where, despite the alarmism after Ahlwardt's success in 1892, their control was never brought into serious question. In a sense, the east was the *least* important area of the BdL's operations. In the five Reichstag elections between 1893 and 1912, the Conservative Party retained a solid bloc of deputies in the Protestant agricultural areas of East Prussia, West Prussia, Pomerania, Brandenburg, Posen, and Silesia. Here the BdL's contribution was administrative rather than properly agitational; it oiled an existing machinery of domination that rested ultimately upon the social relations of large-scale estate agriculture and transmuted seigneurial jurisdiction. Arguably, the BdL's importance to the Conservatives was greatest where

68. Puhle, *Agrarische Interessenpolitik*, pp. 195–97.
69. See the detailed report in the *Heidelberger Zeitung*, 14 May 1898.

election battles with other parties were most hotly contested. With the exception of the Polish areas of Posen and West Prussia, this was not the case in east Elbia before 1900. Moreover, while official Conservative candidates always drew a significant number of votes in Hanover, parts of Westphalia, Thuringia, Saxony, Baden, Württemberg, and the Protestant parts of Franconia, Conservative intervention in these areas usually took the form of pressuring the existing rural parties. A Prussocentric obsession with the Junkers' special circumstances east of the Elbe River can obscure this related aspect of Conservative survival – namely, the need to construct political alliances both in the Reichstag and at the polls.[70]

The importance of regionalism cannot be assessed simply by searching for regional *caucuses* in the Agrarian League or the Conservative Party, which is how Puhle tends to treat the problem.[71] Nor can the two organizations be conflated, at least not for the period from 1893 to 1903. As I have already suggested, it is dangerous to evaluate the BdL's "significance for German conservatism in general" by reference to the "Prussian provinces east of the Elbe" alone.[72] As early as 1896, the majority of the BdL's members came from west of the Elbe. From 1895 to 1899 the BdL's eastern membership actually declined and thereafter grew much more slowly than in the west. More to the point, the BdL had little impact on the *texture* of Conservative domination in the east, or even on its extent. Between 1903 and 1912 the Conservative vote in the eastern provinces of East and West Prussia, Silesia, and Brandenburg continued to fall, whereas the areas of expansion included Württemberg (7 percent), Baden (3.4 percent), Bavaria (3.1 percent), Hanover (1.4 percent), and the Rhineland (1.1 percent).[73] Furthermore, as suggested above, we need to consider the BdL's impact on other parties such as the National Liberals in Hanover, Hesse, and the Palatinate or the Anti-Semites in Prussian Hesse, Thuringia and Saxony either directly or by forcing them into alliances with the Conservatives. It was no accident that Diederich Hahn, the League's most demagogic agitator, occupied a

70. For the dangers of "Prussocentrism" and the "centrality" of the regions for an understanding of national policies in the 1890s, see Blackbourn, *Class, Religion and Local Politics*, pp. 13ff.; and Evans, "Wilhelm II's Germany and the Historians," pp. 24ff.

71. Puhle, *Agrarische Interessenpolitik*, p. 276.

72. Ibid., pp. 10, 64.

73. Ibid., p. 219. Membership figures are taken from ibid., p. 309.

Hanoverian seat in what had previously been National Liberal territory. Indeed, west of the Elbe River the BdL required a more vigorous and sophisticated agitation, not just because it was interfering with the established primacy of other parties, but also because it was dealing not with a dependent agricultural proletariat but with a free peasantry enjoying its own recently discovered capacity for independent political action.

There was a clear difference between the agrarian movements in the eastern and western halves of Germany. In the east the BdL serviced an apparatus of Conservative domination structurally rooted in the productive organization and social relations of large-scale estate agriculture. At the local level the Agrarian League did not so much *represent* the Junkers' interests as *administer* them. In the west, by contrast, the BdL not only had to establish its political credibility with an independent farming class that was often deeply hostile to the Prussian aristocracy, it also had to compete with existing agrarian agencies. Given this distinct *modus operandi*, the BdL's contribution to the long-term evolution of the German Right was much greater in the west than in the east. The arrival of the BdL in the west had the effect of unlocking the party fronts, a process that the Anti-Semites had already begun at the local levels. It fundamentally "agrarianized" the National Liberal Party, partly by offering valuable assistance in the retention of rural votes, but partly also by making itself the arbiter of that retention. By a protracted and uneven process, the BdL also assimilated the radicalism and popular constituency of previous radical agrarian movements in most parts of Protestant Germany. In the longer term, mainly after 1900, the BdL built a political bridge between the agrarian populism of the 1890s and the national structures of the Conservative Party. But to return to the vexing question of manipulation, these contributions were more a response to a variegated, fragmented, and locally conditioned popular challenge than an act of spontaneous innovation by farsighted east-Elbian Junkers.

VII

It remains to pull the various threads of this argument together. The first major point should require no further elaboration. It emphasizes the national, as opposed to the east-Elbian, range of the agrarian movement; its beginnings in the specific problems of small farmers west of the Elbe; and its disruption of existing political alignments, particularly those dominated by the National Liberals in Protestant central Germany. The second point concerns the precise significance of this mobilization and its role in the founding of the Agrarian League in February 1893. Here it is important not to consider the BdL's founding in isolation from the events that surrounded it. In particular, it should be directly related to the political turbulence in the Conservative Party two months before. Differing kinds of rural radicalism – the startling progress of Hessian Anti-Semitism, the agitation of the Bavarian peasants' leagues, the stirrings of Catholic agrarianism in the southwest, and even the SPD's "turn to the countryside" after 1890 – were sources of great uneasiness for Conservative notables. By the end of 1892, the Hammerstein-Stöcker machinations combined with Ahlwardt's demagogic adventures to bring the populist ferment right to the center of the east-Elbian Conservative Party itself.

The sinister implications of the Anti-Semitic agitation – with its plebeian backbone, antiplutocratic rhetoric, and egalitarian intimations – should not be underestimated. One "eastern agrarian," as Count Julius von Mirbach-Sorquitten called himself, saw "the danger that the accession of many propertyless people would turn the movement against property as such, so that it would degenerate into a variant of Social Democracy."[74] Helldorff echoed these sentiments: "If our good country folk, the small official [and] the clergyman are fed a diet" of slanderous allegations about "the rotten conditions in all high places, then when the time comes we should not expect the masses to halt before the *Rittergut* – or, in the final instance, before the throne." In this sense, the Anti-Semitic movement was "in the end the certain harbinger of Social Democracy."[75] These observations cast a powerful light on the launching of the Agrarian League. By objective function certainly – and in the minds of Wangenheim and the other founding fathers probably – the creation of the BdL was an attempt to defuse the crisis in the Conservative Party, an agrarian counterrevolution against the populist offensive of Stöcker, Hammerstein,

74. Cited in Frank, *Stoecker*, p. 304.
75. Helldorff to Eulenburg, 11 December 1892, in *Eulenburgs politische Korrespondenz*, ed. Röhl, vol. 2, p. 990.

and the Anti-Semites. It was a bid to coopt the agrarian mobilization, to divert in onto the less threatening terrain of opposition to the trade treaties, and to bring it under the tutelage of the Junkers. But the BdL was not the instigator of the agrarian movement; it was an effect of the latter, not its cause. It was not some farsighted intervention of the established Conservative leadership, conceived twelve months in advance with Limburg-Stirum's public stand against the Austrian trade treaty, but an improvised response to a double problem: the crisis of Conservative Party unity and a crisis of social relations in the countryside.

Ultimately, it can be argued, this double problem was resolved on terms favorable to the Junkers. By the time high tariffs were reinstituted in 1902, most of the central German Anti-Semites had made their peace with the BdL, while the latter had brought the National Liberals into line in rural Hesse, the Palatinate, and Hanover. Moreover, as Puhle forcefully argues, the Conservative Party had become comprehensively agrarianized, so that by 1914 it was for all intents and purposes identical with the BdL's east-Elbian organization. Between 1893 and 1902 the BdL essentially made the demand for tariff protection the all-dominating priority of conservative politics in a ploy that proved extremely effective in displacing the more broadly based popular conservatism associated with Stöcker and Hammerstein. In Bielefeld and Minden-Ravensburg, for instance, the vitality of the party's popular Protestantism was gradually sapped by the remorseless encroachments of the agrarians; while in 1895/96 Stöcker and his supporters abandoned the Conservative Party altogether and went off in different political directions.[76] Finally, if Puhle is right – and there is strong evidence to suggest that he is – the BdL also took on board so much of the Anti-Semites' radical ideology, including their "biologically oriented *völkisch* nationalism" and their appeal to the *Mittelstand*, that there was increasingly little reason for the Anti-Semites to oppose it.

Nevertheless, the founding of the BdL did not miraculously conjure the problems and resentments of the small farmers out of existence. In attempting to sublimate deep social contradic-

---

76. For further details, see Frank, *Stoecker*, pp. 312ff. For the local response, see Busch, *Stoeckerbewegung*, pp. 83ff.

tions into a unitary ideology representing agrarian interests, the BdL was committing itself to hard political labor. That labor was likely to remain permanently unfinished, for the conflicts between large and small farmers were a structural feature of an unreformed agricultural economy and were therefore not likely to go away. The integration of small farmers could only be achieved by adapting the forms of Conservative politics to the local predilections of a diverse rural radicalism. However, since there was no comparable effort to adapt the Conservative Party's national profile to this sort of radicalism, the foundations of the agrarian synthesis that began to emerge from the 1890s was bound to be insecure. The Agrarian League had been launched by a conservative establishment in the hopes of preempting a threatening radical rebellion in the party's own midst. Its introduction into the west-German countryside then proved the lever of a far-reaching realignment of rural politics. But although this completed the disintegration of one political configuration, it did not definitively produce a new one in its place.

This is the third major point of this essay. One of the beguiling features of Puhle's account is the completeness of the BdL's victory. According to Puhle, the BdL dominated the agrarian movement after having virtually called it into life, going on to conquer the Conservative Party – all, it seems, within a few years of its founding. From this perspective, it is of marginal interest but of little real historical significance what may or may not have been happening in the Hessian or south-German countryside. In the end, agricultural policy and the direction of government were determined by the power elites at the top. Nowhere was this supposedly more true than in the case of the Agrarian League, the instrument of the Junkers' class interests. The views from the BdL's Berlin headquarters and the east-Elbian *Rittergut*, after all, were the ones that ultimately counted. Yet enough should have been said to suggest an alternative view. In 1893 the Conservatives were in total disarray. The party system was in a state of general flux, and there was widespread speculation, invariably associated with the name of Bismarck, about the possibility of a new right-wing party.[77] The National Liberals were losing ground as the hegemonic force in the central German countryside. The

77. In this respect, see D. Stegmann's contribution in this volume.

Center Party faced a major agrarian revolt of its own, encompassing both southern Germany and Rhineland-Westphalia. Anti-Semites were agitating among the peasantry and the *Mittelstand*. The Social Democrats were also turning to the countryside. In other words, the BdL entered a national situation of exceptional volatility. In the long term, it proved the agency of a far-reaching rural realignment that provided Conservatives west of the Elbe with badly needed allies. It also eventually brought the independent Anti-Semitic agitation broadly within the Conservative fold, though on a far less stable basis than Puhle assumes. But it is less the conclusion than the *process* itself that is interesting. For it is only by carefully examining the friction – the interactions, tensions, and incompletely resolved contradictions – between the Agrarian League and the larger agrarian movement in the country it sought to discipline that we are able to grasp the dynamics of German conservatism's unstable radicalization.

7

Agrarian Conservatism in Wilhelmine Germany

Diederich Hahn and the Agrarian League

George Vascik

The Agrarian League (Bund der Landwirte or BdL) is often identified in historical literature as a radical, unitary, all-powerful interest group that manipulated German farmers and peasants into supporting conservative, Junker-oriented political and economic aims. Given the continued resonance of the model first postulated by Alexander Gerschenkron and Hans Rosenberg – a model that explains Germany's tragic path by the persistence of pre-modern feudal elites – the Agrarian League remains a focus of historians' interest, even though an expanding body of research suggests that our understanding of the BdL needs to be reevaluated.[1] The need for such a reassessment becomes even more compelling when one considers the career of Diederich Hahn. Hahn, scion of Lower Saxon building contractors, gave up a promising career in banking to become organizer of the Hanoverian BdL; he later served as League director and as a member of its leadership troika. In the course of this unorthodox career path, Hahn used his considerable organizational skills (augmented by radical, anti-Semitic, and populist rhetoric) to build a personal following among peasant voters in Protestant areas west of the

---

1. See Charles Maier's introduction to the third edition of A. Gerschenkron, *Bread and Democracy in Germany* (Ithaca, N.Y.,1989). H.-J. Puhle, *Agrarische Interessenpolitik und preußischer Konservatismus im wilhelminischen Reich 1893–1914* (Hanover, 1967); and S. Tirrell, *German Agrarian Politics after Bismarck's Fall* (New York, 1951) are the standard works on the Agrarian League. J. Retallack, *Notables of the Right: The Conservative Party and Political Mobilization in Germany, 1876–1918* (Boston, 1988), is the best recent study.

George Vascik

Elbe. In doing so, he gained notoriety and attracted animosity unrivaled in Wilhelmine politics.[2]

No reliable study exists of Hahn's life and works. Although he was a meticulous diarist and correspondent who worked diligently to put the BdL's archives in order, the majority of Hahn's letters and papers have not survived.[3] However, new archival material has become available in the past two years that will enable historians to begin reassessing Hahn's impact on the Agrarian League and Wilhelmine rural politics. This material reveals that our previous understanding of the Agrarian League as a unitary interest group dominated by the interests, ideals, and figures of Junkerdom is far from adequate. Diederich Hahn's career, more than any other, reveals the tensions present within the BdL. The League, far from being monolithic, was riven with cleavages: east and west, peasant and Junker, dairy producers and cereal growers, Conservatives and members of other parties who saw the League as nonpartisan, as well as accommodaters and maximalists. Overlaying all these conflicts were a series of bitter personal quarrels and vendettas within the leadership.

Hahn was at the center of these conflicts. As a non-agrarian, bourgeois historian from the west-Elbian peasant heartland who possessed neither horse nor plough (to paraphrase a famous speech by Chancellor Leo von Caprivi), Hahn depend-

2. Hahn is thought by some scholars to have been the model for Diederich Hessling in Heinrich Mann's satirical novel, *Der Untertan*. In the early drafts of *Der Untertan*, Diederich Hessling was Diederich Hänfling. See H. Eggerrt, "Das persönliche Regiment. Zur Quellen- und Entstehungsgeschichte von Heinrich Manns 'Untertan'," *Neophilologus* 55 (1971): 298–316; and E. Kirsch and H. Schmidt, "Zur Entstehung des Romans 'Der Untertan'," *Weimarer Beiträge* 6 (1960): 118.

3. The majority of these, housed in the BdL archives, underwent a series of disasters, including flood and fire damage. All traces of Hahn's papers within the still existing League archives have disappeared. Hahn's wife held a *Splitternachlaß*, which devolved into the possession of Hahn's oldest son, Christian Diederich. For years, Hahn denied historians access to his father's papers, until in 1990 he delivered substantial portions of the *Nachlaß* into the care of the Niedersächsisches Staatsarchiv Stade (hereafter NStA Stade). He has, however, not brought himself to donate his parent's correspondence, so even this splinter at this writing remains incomplete. The press archive of the Agrarian League held at the Bundesarchiv Potsdam contains only press clippings on Diederich Hahn's speeches and career. The Kreisarchiv Otterndorf in Hahn's home county of Hadeln possesses a small collection of printed works by and about the Hahn family. This biographical study would not have been possible without the help of Archivrat Dr. Schultze of the NStA Stade who prepared the Hahn *Nachlaß* for my use.

ed upon the income from his position with the League to support his lifestyle and his political prominence. He tried to maintain this position by doggedly representing both his well-to-do peasant constituents and the radical wing of the BdL. With his fiery temperament and fierce oratory, Hahn became the prototype of the kind of patriotic activist that so bedeviled the German governments of that era.[4] Reclaiming Diederich Hahn for history could significantly broaden our appreciation of the diversity – and destructiveness – of radical political behavior in the *Kaiserreich*.

I

Diederich Hahn was born in 1859 to a well-to-do family in the village of Osten, in the flat, fertile marshlands where the Elbe empties into the North Sea. For over 200 years, his forefathers had operated a dike-building and lock-repairing business. In a land oppressed by frequent, life-threatening floods, this made the Hahn family very important – and, one might add, very rich. Business was so good that two years before Diederich's birth, his father had left the established family firm and begun his own dike-building enterprise.[5] Thus it was into a world of prominence and privilege that the future self-styled peasant leader was born.

Diederich developed comfortably in this environment. As a youth, he often accompanied his father as he checked on weather damage, settled accounts, and solicited new business.[6] Undoubtedly the deference accorded the father (and his pampered son) as they made their rounds was a factor in the creation of Hahn's remarkable self-confidence. These were

4. Described by Max Weber, "Parlament und Regierung im neugeordneten Deutschland" and "Politik als Beruf," in *Gesammelte Politische Schriften* (Tübingen, 1971), pp. 306–443, 505–560. The growth of this cadre of professional associational activists is forcefully described in G. Eley, *Reshaping the German Right: Radical Nationalism and Political Change after Bismarck* (New Haven, Conn., 1980).

5. H. Lefevre and J. Bohmbach, *Von Johann Hane 1664 bis J.D. Hahn 1984: Ein Bau-Chronik aus dem Elbe-Weser-Dreieck* (Hechthausen, 1985), p. 1. The German-American historian Alfred Vagts remembers *Vater* Hahn more distinctly than the son, since the firm's rooster logo was prominently displayed on A.D. Hahn's ubiquitous projects. A. Vagts, "Diederich Hahn – ein Politikerleben," *Jahrbuch der Männer vom Morgenstern* 46 (1965): 155–92, esp. 156.

6. C.D. Hahn, "Erinnerungen an Diederich Hahn," *Stader Jahrbuch* 75 (1985): 82–98, esp. 83; Lefevre and Bohmback, *Von Johann Hane*, p. 13.

George Vascik

especially prosperous years for the Hahn family, as it acquired numerous contracts given out by the triumphant Prussians after the Danish war, and no doubt provided a further material basis for the pro-Prussian sentiments present in the Hahn home. The outbreak of war in 1870, followed swiftly by the triumph of the German army over the French and the proclamation of the Empire in the Hall of Mirrors at Versailles, were pivotal events in the emergence of young Hahn's world view. Unlike most of his Hanoverian countrymen, Hahn saw Prussia (and particularly the Prussian army) as a positive force, and he soon worshipped Bismarck, the architect of unification, as a demigod.[7]

For his secondary education, Hahn was sent to the Royal Gymnasium in the district capital of Stade, where he lodged at the home of his uncle, Carl Bertram Hahn. This uncle, a teacher and philologist of some note, imparted to the future agrarian leader a love of languages – particularly in the local peasant dialects of northwest Germany.[8] Because the Royal Gymnasium was an elite school, favored by numerous prominent Hanover and Berlin families, Hahn acquired many well-connected friends.[9]

It was surely one of these friendships that provided Hahn with the first step in his career. Upon graduation Hahn enrolled as a junior officer in the 3rd Foot Guards Regiment. How did Hahn – a commoner and a non-Prussian – come into such illustrious company? Throughout a life in which he was very loud in celebrating his successes, Hahn remained strangely silent about those pivotal moments when the influence of highly placed friends or acquaintances opened doors for him. Quite possibly he was helped by the father of a school chum, Under-State Secretary Justus von Grüner, who was a friend and advi-

7. Hahn, "Biographische Anmerkungen und Literaturverzeichnis zu Diederich Hahn (1859–1918)," *Deutsches Geschlechterbuch* 180: 244. A devoted Bismarckian, Hahn was organizer of the "Bismarck Kommer," a Berlin banquet held every year on the chancellor's birthday (April 1). He presided at the head table and often gave the after-dinner speech, on one occasion directly after returning from Schönhausen. "Berliner Gedanken an Diederich Hahn," *Deutsche Tageszeitung*, 27 February 1918, p. 1. Heinrich Mann skillfully transmuted Hahn's ebullient adoration of Bismarck into Heßling's fawning Kaiser worship.
8. R. Wiebalck, "Diederich Hahn," *Niedersächsische Lebensbilder* 2 (1954): 98.
9. Vagts, "Diederich Hahn," p. 155; and Hahn, "Biographische Anmerkungen," p. 243.

sor to Crown Princess Victoria.[10] In any case, Hahn leapt whole-heartedly into Prussian military life, where he acquired further contacts and a reputation as "the big Fresian *Kerl.*"

Having climbed so high, Hahn was not about to return to Osten to build dikes at the completion of his military service in 1878. Supported by his family's wealth and an inheritance from a rich uncle, Diederich moved smoothly from the spit-and-polish of the barracks to the lecture halls and fraternity houses of the universities of Berlin and Leipzig. He took up residence in the fashionable Grüner home, and was introduced into the dazzling world of Berlin high society and politics.[11] In Berlin, Hahn began the study of history, economy, and law, attending the lectures of such eminent scholars as Gustav Schmoller and Adolph Wagner. If his attendance was less than perfect, it was because Hahn had found a more satisfying outlet for his irrepressible ambition – student politics.

In 1880, following the contemporary pattern of studying at several universities, Hahn moved to Leipzig, where he immediately became caught up in the anti-Semitic, conservative social reform movement led by Adolf Stöcker. He gave his first political speech to a large assembly of fellow Stöckerites in November 1880, and, along with Friedrich Naumann, helped organize the Leipzig student movement. By summer semester 1881 the movement had begun to reach critical mass. Hahn and Naumann initiated a series of evening lectures, and invited Stöcker himself as their initial lecturer. In a valedictory speech at semester's end, Hahn summed up the movement's guiding ideals as "Germandom and Christianity . . . the roots of our strength." A telegram the students sent to Bismarck at the conclusion of the evening received the following reply: "The spirit that speaks through your words allows me an insight into the future of our Fatherland. In it I foresee relief from the problems that the present has inherited from the past."[12]

10. Hahn, "Erinnerungen," p. 87; *Amtliches Reichstags-Handbuch* (Berlin, 1889), p. 1290; Diederich Hahn was First Lieutenant in the Reserves. It is interesting that the young Hahn, already a convinced Bismarckian, kept his political opinions to himself in this liberal milieu.

11. G. Klauder, "Diederich Hahn zum 100. Geburtstag," *Akademische Blätter* 61 (1959): 182, claims that Hahn's diary entries condemned the anti-Bismarckian Grüners and their circle. On Berlin society, see G. Masur, *Imperial Berlin* (New York, 1970).

12. Klauder, "Diederich Hahn," p. 183.

Bismarck's rather generic reply was enough to set the young Hahn on fire. Together with Naumann, he began to lay plans to "nationalize" the Leipzig movement. The result was the creation of the Association of German Students (Verein Deutscher Studenten or VDSt), which Konrad Jarausch has characterized as "a confusing blend of radical nationalism, political anti-Semitism, and positive Christianity."[13] Hahn's genius as a political organizer became apparent when he organized the association's first *Kyffhäuserfest* in August 1881. This was a swashbuckling, hypernationalistic, naively mystical affair. Hahn staged the founding meeting of the VDSt on the slopes of the Kyffhäuser, the mythical resting place of the medieval hero-emperor Friedrich Barbarosa, and delivered the opening address in the florid hyperbolic style that would latter typify his political oratory. Throughout his speech he dramatically clutched the imperial flag in one hand and raised his saber with the other.[14] After salubrious rhetorical contributions from other student spokesmen, as evening drew near Hahn brought the meeting to a close with a *Hoch* to the Kaiser.

Curiously, after making this initial splash Hahn retired from VDSt activities. Possibly he had begun to wear on people's nerves. But the Leipzig episode foreshadowed four aspects of Hahn's later political life: he was a determined and successful political organizer, he loved the limelight of the podium, he knew how to throw his audience into raptures, and he was too "idealistic" to work well with others – even within organizations that he himself had created.

At the conclusion of winter semester 1882, Hahn moved back to Berlin to continue his historical and legal studies. At this time one of the strangest incidents in Hahn's career transpired. Hahn and a group of classmates decided to cheer Bismarck as he left by train for his country estate at Schönhausen. The crowds were so thick that the group of young devotees arrived on the platform just as the chancellor's train was pulling out. Impetuously, Hahn threw himself at the car in which Bismarck was riding, grabbed an overhead bar, and

---

13. K. Jarausch, *Students, Society and Politics in Imperial Germany: The Rise of Academic Illiberalism* (Princeton, 1982), p. 270. Also see H. v. Petersdorf, *Die Vereine deutscher Studenten: Zwölf Jahre akademische Kämpfe* (Leipzig, 1890). For a first-person account of this environment, see H. von Gerlach, *Erinnerungen eines Junkers* (Berlin, 1926), pp. 107–09.

14. Vagts, "Diederich Hahn," pp. 158–59.

swung back and forth before the window at which Bismarck was sitting. All the time that he was swinging back and forth like a chimpanzee, he was shouting out his fealty. Probably relieved when he ascertained that Hahn was not an assassin, the unflappable Bismarck opened the window and, after a short conversation, said: "Why don't you come to see me at Schönhausen some time?" What to Bismarck was no doubt only a quickly forgotten pleasantry was to the self-absorbed Hahn much more than an invitation to tea. He took the chancellor seriously, believing he heard in Bismarck's words vindication of his life and political activities.[15]

Returning to academic life after such spirited involvements must have been difficult, particularly for a student with eclectic interests who was inclined to coast on his native perspicacity and volubility. Hahn was at something of a loss as far as his future was concerned. He loved politics and he loved the dashing figure he cut in Berlin society as an earnest student and junior officer in the reserves. He clearly contemplated both an academic and a political career, but both required money. His social expenses were high, even with the free room at the Grüner's, and the immediate monetary rewards of the long academic career path were minimal. Out of respect for his family's financial situation, Hahn in November 1884 passed the state exam for probationary teaching in history. Now Hahn could make some money by teaching in a gymnasium, though this was hardly the level to which he aspired. His further advancement required one of nineteenth-century Germany's most respected titles: Doktor.

Hahn convinced his dissertation director, Adolph Wagner, to allow him to write a "legal" and historical dissertation that was essentially philological in nature.[16] From the archaic low

15. Hahn, "Erinnerungen," p. 86–87; Hahn, *Dein Vater*, 79–80. Exactly when Hahn took up Bismarck's invitation is hard to ascertain. Some sources suggest it was while he was still a student, others that it was not until many years later. Klauder, "Diederich Hahn," p. 182; Hahn, "Erinnerungen," p. 87. Most of Hahn's dealings with Bismarck that can be traced in the Schönhausen guest books were in the form of formal homages and telegrams. See Bundesarchiv (BA) Koblenz, NL Bismarck, Bestand A, Nr. 35, "Friedrichsrüher Gästebücher 1887–1895" On a visit in April 1895, Hahn took up a whole page writing out a birthday greeting. Only Wilhelm II used up so much space.

16. On Wagner, see H. von Gerlach, *Von Rechts nach Links* (Zurich, 1937), pp. 68–69; and K. Barkin, *The Controversy over German Industrialization, 1890–1902* (Chicago, 1970), pp. 139–47. Hahn completed his doctoral studies sometime between 1884 and 1886.

German he translated a dike register that had come into his possession while he had roved the dikes as a youth with his father. To this translation, Hahn added thirty-six pages of legal, economic and philological analysis, topped off with a four-color, fold-out map.[17] As Hahn's son and biographer, Christian Diederich Hahn, has charitably remarked, it was a tribute to his father's determination that he was able to convince Wagner of the worthiness of this project.[18] Although Hahn would later pose as a great scholar of East Fresian manuscripts and historian of his *Heimat*, this dissertation only demonstrated his unsuitability for an academic career.[19] In any case, once Hahn had earned his doctorate he needed a job.

Salvation came once again from the Grüner family.[20] Justus von Grüner secured Hahn a position at the Queen Augusta Gymnasium, a prestigious Charlottenburg institution catering to the capital's wealthy. In his semester at the Queen Augusta, Hahn was by all accounts an enthusiastic teacher whose lectures earned the rapt devotion of his students. Ever the climber, Hahn was careful to cultivate the parents of his pupils as well, for he considered the gymnasium and his career as a history teacher to be only a step toward more lucrative, prestigious employment.[21] The father of one student proved to be particularly helpful. Henry Villard, a high-ranking employee of the Deutsche Bank, was greatly impressed with his son's passionate, articulate teacher[22] and put Hahn in contact with Georg von Siemens, head of the bank and one of the most important men in Germany.[23] Siemens was impressed with Hahn as well, and took him on in the bank's research section. Thus a new chapter of Hahn's life began, and he became

---

17. *Dat diekrecht der Oldendorper schowinge. Nach der Handschrift herausgegeben, übersetzt und mit einer Einleitung* (Stade, 1896). Copy found in the *Nachlaß* Hahn at the Kreisarchiv Otterndorf.

18. Hahn, "Erinnerungen," p. 83.

19. M. Hahn, *Kämpfer* (Leipzig, 1920). A rough draft, newspaper serialization and correspondence regarding Margarethe Hahn's thinly veiled biography of her husband are contained in NL Hahn, Ha VII/B/M/52–53.

20. Wiebalck, "Diederich Hahn," pp. 98–99.

21. Haushofer, "Diederich Hahn," p. 503.

22. O.G. Villard, *Fighting Years* (New York, 1939), p. 74. Henry Villard, an emigré 1848-er, had many prominent friends in Berlin liberal circles.

23. G. Sossinka, "Diederich Hahn, Direktor des Bundes der Landwirte. Sein Beitrag zur Diskussion um die Agrarpolitik des wilhelminischen Reiches" (Ph.D. diss., Göttingen University, 1974), pp. 57–58; C. Hahn, "Biographie von Diederich Hahn," in *Dein Vater*, p. 242.

known throughout Berlin society as "Georg Siemens' young man."[24]

Technically speaking, Hahn was engaged as an archivist. The functions he actually performed for Siemens are hard to pin down, for his employment file was destroyed and Hahn later offered differing accounts of his time with the bank to different audiences. Sometimes he claimed to have worked on the Berlin-Baghdad railroad project, sometimes to have set up the bank's "Bureau of Political Economy," and sometimes to have created its newspaper archives.[25] Given Hahn's managerial success in the Agrarian League, the latter two functions seem quite likely. Alfred Vagts has suggested yet a fourth function – that of publicity agent – for Hahn not only plied the bank's causes on the social circuit but also made speeches around the country extolling freer trade policies.[26]

Hahn in this period (1886 to 1890) was distinctly *salonfähig* – handsome, eager to please, polite, and subservient. At home in the company of the Grüners, in the regimental mess, or out on the town, Hahn experienced the best Berlin society had to offer. It was at this juncture that Hahn began to visit Bismarck frequently. At first they talked about dikes, Bismarck having begun his political career as a dike superintendent. Bismarck counseled Hahn to continue his studies. Hahn even brought some rustic dike watchers of his acquaintance to breakfast with the great man. It was allegedly noted in Berlin society that "Siemens' young man" was making frequent visits to Schönhausen.[27]

But then, in 1890, a series of shocks buffeted the young archivist and changed his life. His fiancée tragically drowned, his closest friend from the regiment committed suicide, and his younger brother, tapped to take over the family firm, died.[28] These personal tragedies left Hahn in a very vulnerable, shaken state. Then came a great political shock: the impetuous young Kaiser Wilhelm II, for whom Hahn felt nothing but contempt, dismissed Bismarck. Much as the Armistice in November 1918 was to transform and gal-

---

24. Hahn, "Biographische Anmerkungen," p. 87.
25. Haushofer, "Diederich Hahn," p. 503.
26. Vagts, "Diederich Hahn," p. 161.
27. Hahn, "Erinnerungen," p. 87.
28. Ibid., p. 87. These events are alluded to in M. Hahn, *Kämpfer*. See *Unterhaltungsbeilage der Täglichen Rundschau*, 30 January 1914, p. 1.

vanize a troubled Austrian corporal, Bismarck's dismissal became the focus for all Hahn's turbulent emotions. It marked a turning point in Hahn's life. He found it difficult to abide those who criticized Bismarck, and this immediately strained relations with his liberal social circle. He refused to attend regimental banquets when the Kaiser was to appear,[29] and while he continued his public speaking tours for the Deutsche Bank, his talks increasingly became tributes to Bismarck and denunciations of his successor, Chancellor Caprivi.[30] Hahn had not yet discovered agrarianism (where his hatred of Caprivi would ultimately lead), but the bright young *arriviste* from the provinces had begun to alienate himself from liberal Berlin.

Hahn's chance to strike back came in the winter of 1891. There was a sympathetic notion amid National Liberal circles to give Bismarck a seat in the Reichstag, and the former chancellor had already turned down several such offers.[31] But then Hermann Gebhard, city manager of Bremerhaven and Reichstag delegate from Hahn's home district – the Hanoverian constituency of Neuhaus-Hadeln – resigned from the Reichstag due to poor health. Having retained ties to his old friends back home, a number of whom had become prominent in local politics, Hahn moved quickly to bring them together with Bismarck.[32] With the district's Landtag deputy Johannes Schoof and Wilhelm Klussmann, the mayor of Geestemünde, in tow, Hahn turned up at Schönhausen.[33] There, the three convinced Bismarck that the Fresian mandate was his for the taking. Bismarck was drafted, and Hahn was exultant.

There were problems, though. National Liberal leader Rudolph von Bennigsen and provincial party chief Johannes Flathmann had coveted the seat for Bennigsen's young pro-

---

29. Hahn, "Biographische Anmerkungen," p. 238; Hahn, "Erinnerungen," p. 94. After Bismarck's interment, Hahn lingered over the grave with Count Lehndorf, muttering under his breath that "the Hohenzollerns have dug their own grave. . . ."

30. Hahn, "Erinnerungen," p. 87.

31. Sossinka, "Diederich Hahn," p. 57, suggests that the whole Bismarckian candidacy was Diederich Hahn's idea. Vagts, "Diederich Hahn," pp. 167–168.

32. Haushofer, "Diederich Hahn," p. 503; Hahn, "Biographische Anmerkungen," p. 243; B. Ehrenfeuchter, "Politische Willensbildung in Niedersachsen zur Zeit des Kaiserreiches" (Ph.D. diss., Göttingen University, 1951), p. 166.

33. O. von Bismarck, *Die gesammelten Werke* (Berlin, 1924), vol. 4, p. 165.

tégé, Carl Sattler.[34] Sattler, like Hahn, was an archivist and the two had been on friendly terms. Hahn's quick action, however, had presented Bennigsen and Flathmann with a nettlesome choice: to continue to push Sattler or to ratify Bismarck's nomination in the local party associations. Deciding that they had no real choice, they reluctantly advised Sattler to await another opportunity.

If Hahn was well on his way toward creating life-long political enemies, he seemed oblivious to the fact. Instead he jumped into his great love: politicking. He managed Bismarck's campaign – not an easy matter, as the Old Man refused to campaign. Hahn had to draft "statements" to local groups, push them under Bismarck's nose for his signature, and then pass these off as Bismarck's own sentiments[35] – and because the former chancellor would not speak on his own behalf, Hahn had to do so for him. At the same time, Hahn was also busy arranging rallies, directing campaign workers, and recruiting volunteers to pass out ballot papers around the constituency. That Bismarck failed to achieve a first ballot majority (he won only 43 percent of the vote) and was forced into a runoff with a Social Democrat was an embarrassment, but in the end Bismarck did manage to win.[36]

For the next two years, Hahn's work at the Deutsche Bank became secondary to his main occupation: serving as Bismarck's agent to the constituency of Neuhaus-Hadeln. In modern terms, we would call Hahn a district staffer. He brought district concerns to Bismarck's attention, and curried favor with constituents back home.[37] Neither task was easy, for Bismarck was a woefully slothful deputy. He quite obviously cared not a wit for his constituents, and had only accepted the mandate as a means of tweaking the Kaiser's nose. Once Wilhelm had seen the necessity of making an outward reconcilia

34. An undated address book, NStA Stade, NL Hahn, Ha VII/13/b/35, contains Sattler's name, suggesting that Hahn and Sattler were more than casual acquaintances. On the election, see Ehrenfeuchter, "Politische Willensbildung," pp. 166–67; J. Flathmann, *Die Reichstagswahlen in der Provinz Hannover 1867–1896* (Hanover, 1897), p. 75; NStA Hannover, Hann. 122a, Oberpräsidium, I/106, "Vierteljahresbericht 1893," IV, p. 36.

35. Vagts, "Diederich Hahn," p. 17.

36. L. Gall, *Bismarck. Der weisse Revolutionär* (Frankfurt, 1980), p. 711.

37. Vagts, "Diederich Hahn," pp. 169, 172–73; and Klauder, "Diederich Hahn," p. 182.

tion, any need for Bismarck to address the Reichstag (whether to denounce Caprivi or to bemoan the silting up of Geestemünde harbor) became superfluous.[38]

When it became apparent that Bismarck would not stand for reelection in 1893, Hahn made plans to step in as his anointed successor.[39] From his local friends, Hahn knew the depth of local anger over falling grain prices and American meat imports – the two products upon which the well-being of the district's peasant electorate depended. He also realized how Caprivi's proposed trade treaties with Austria-Hungary and Russia represented a threat (mostly symbolic) that agriculture was being abandoned by the urban, industrial Germany of the future.[40] It was at this point that the already virulently anti-Caprivi Diederich Hahn became an agrarian. Thus a professionally and socially successful young Berlin Doktor, from a prominent provincial bourgeois family, employed by the very symbol of finance capitalism, began his remarkable self-transformation into the tribune of Lower Saxony's peasants.[41]

II

Hahn was able to transform himself into an agrarian by virtue of his commitment to the goals of the Agrarian League. Founded in February 1893, shortly before new Reichstag elections were called, the Agrarian League became the focus of Hahn's energies and the vehicle for his rise to the upper reaches of the Wilhelmine political world. Hahn was already well acquainted with a number of the men who founded the League, particularly Georg Oertel, Felix Telge, Ernst Reventlow, and Paul von Heydebrand und der Lasa.[42] He was also instrumental in setting up a newspaper sympathetic to the

38. Bismarck, *Werke*, vol. 9, p. 394; and E. Eyck, *Bismarck: Leben und Werk* (Zurich, 1941–44), vol. 3, pp. 613–15.

39. Hahn, *Dein Vater*, pp. 79, 243; Haushofer, "Diederich Hahn," p. 503; Hahn, "Erinnerungen," p. 88.

40. Barkin, *German Industrialization*, pp. 210–12. On the local political climate see Vierteljahresbericht 1893/III, NStA Hannover, Ha 122a I 106.

41. C.F. Bötticher, "Diederich Hahn," *Deutsches Biographisches Jahrbuch*, p. 251; Wiebalck, "Diederich Hahn," p. 103; Hahn, "Erinnerungen," p. 89, claims that Hahn joined the Agrarian League at Bismarck's suggestion, "in order to win over the north German peasants and create a counterweight to the east-Elbian Junkers."

42. O. von Kiesewetter, *Zum fünfundzwanzigjährigen Jubiläum des Bundes der Landwirte* (Berlin, 1918), p. 59.

League, the *Deutsche Tageszeitung*.[43] After the League was founded he became its director for the province of Hanover; this position gave him the opportunity to create a province-wide political machine loyal to himself. Hahn would later use this base to reinforce his own position within the League and attempt (unsuccessfully) to set himself up as *Bauernführer* of the entire west-Elbian peasantry.

Hahn had a number of natural advantages. First, he had no problem turning on its head everything he had been saying for the previous six years while in the employ of Georg Siemens. Once a "free trader," Hahn now armed himself with empirical data gathered from his own research to argue for agricultural protection. His statistical expertise and doctor's title combined to lend his statements an air of credibility, particularly among those already disposed to believe him. As a former employee of the Deutsche Bank, for instance, he was especially effective in arguing for a new stock exchange law.

Hahn's power as an orator, already manifest in his *Kyffhäuserfest* speech and in his duties for Siemens, was his greatest weapon. Eugen Richter (himself no shy orator) called Hahn "a man of demonic eloquence."[44] Always an avid student of philology and local dialects, Hahn addressed his audiences in their own voice. When speaking in a local hall or tavern, Hahn was sure to slip into *plattdeutsch* and tell a few local jokes. Throughout his life, he kept extensive notebooks of folk stories and local dialectic peculiarities in order to be able to create a warm and immediate aural bond with his audience.[45] When he spoke, his crudity and his recklessness could be compared with that of Adolf Hitler. Like Hitler, he knew no bounds of taste or propriety. Like Hitler, he summoned the very worst demons and fears of his audience and gave them names. And like Hitler, he forged an emotional bond with his audience that summoned it to political action.

---

43. On Hahn's relationship with the *Deutsche Tageszeitung*, see NStA Stade, NL Hahn, Ha VII/13/M/9. On the *Deutsche Tageszeitung* itself, see H. Pacyna, "Die Entstehung der 'Deutschen Tageszeitung', ihr Wirken und Charakter vom 1894 bis 1914, dargestellt am Beispiel einiger wirtschaftspolitischer Entscheidungen dieser Zeit" (Dr. agr., University of Bonn, 1957).

44. Hahn, "Biographische Anmerkungen," p. 244. See Margarethe Hahn's story about how the Reichstag used to fill up to hear Hahn speak in *Dein Vater*, pp. 43–45.

45. Hahn's notebooks were destroyed in 1934; Hahn, "Erinnerungen," p. 94.

In the Reichstag, Hahn quickly developed a distinctive speaking style. He was always combative. His maiden speech pointed the way: concluding a long speech on the proposed stock exchange law, Hahn ended with the phrase "leave me my peasant, I'll leave you your Jew."[46] His style rarely became more elevated. He fancied himself a fine rhetorical duelist, skilled at stilletto-like thrusts, but in fact his speeches were heavy with ponderous nationalist catch-phrases and personal invective.[47]

But what ideas did he express? From his maiden speech on, he was quick to employ anti-Semitic phrases in his speeches and writings, but whether he actually believed these things or was only using them as populist window-dressing is hard to ascertain. He had friendly relations with various Jewish people, but then he always took a perverse pride in being "friendly" with his political enemies. One thing is certain: with his rhetoric Hahn helped make anti-Semitism – often an explicitly racist anti-Semitism – a normal part of rural political discourse.

The major focus of his activity was the protection of agriculture, and here several major points emerge. Hahn espoused the essential unity of peasant and large estate owner interests in agricultural protection, and his maxim was simple: the profitability of agriculture must be maintained to keep as many people as possible on the land, for the countryside was the bastion of the monarchy. This necessitated the highest amount of protection for the greatest number of agricultural commodities, with the lowest possible tax burden on the peasantry.[48] Between 1893 and 1914, Hahn consciously developed the notion of Germany being a land of agricultural autarchy. Only with a healthy peasantry could the established institutions of monarchy, army, and faith be maintained, and only a nutritionally self-sufficient Germany could insure the country's physical security.

This concern for the profitability of agriculture forced Hahn to support some contradictory policies after the turn of the

46. *Stenographische Berichte über die Verhandlungen des Reichstags,* 7 December 1893.
47. "Der Reichstag aus der Vogelschau," *Berliner Tageblatt,* 3 August 1903, p. 1; Hahn, *Dein Vater,* pp. 43–44.
48. Sossinka, "Diederich Hahn," pp. 66–76, on the evolution of Hahn's agricultural policies.

century. As a militarist, he was always eager to support a strong army, though he absolutely abhorred the expansion of the Imperial navy. Hahn realized, as some of his fellow conservatives and agrarians failed to realize, that the fleet cost money – so much money that agriculture would have to be tapped for additional revenue. Hahn argued that agriculture was already "drowning" under over-taxation; it could bear no further burdens. Of course, as a monarchist, it was not possible for Hahn to work publicly against the navy. When a Center delegate publicly jeered at Hahn for the duplicity of his position, Hahn challenged the offending member to a duel.[49]

Opposition to the navy did not, however, make Hahn a pacifist.[50] He periodically called for war against Russia and Great Britain, advocated a preventive war against France, and mistrusted Austria-Hungary and the Balkan states. The economic policies he advocated were a source of friction with other states, and they contributed much to the international ill will generated by Germany in the decade before 1914. Hahn's domestic posture was similarly aggressive. He supported a reintroduction of the socialist laws and the hard-labor bill for the imprisonment of Social Democratic activists, and he backed the army's handling of the Zabern affair in 1913. Given his head, Hahn would have filled the country's jails and silenced its dissidents.

A distinguishing feature of Diederich Hahn's radicalism was his conflict with the National Liberal Party (Nationalliberale Partei or NLP).[51] Initiated in 1891, deepened in 1893, this conflict exploded when Hahn was demonstratively banned from the NLP's Reichstag caucus in 1894. Others in the Agrarian League recognized the importance of working with the NLP: twenty-two National Liberals had campaigned with League endorsement in 1893, and some constituency-level Agrarian League leaders were themselves National Liberals.[52] If the League was to be a nationwide organization, it had to co-opt such rural liberals. In any event, enactment of measures to

49. H. Delbrück, "Politische Korrespondenz," *Preußische Jahrbücher* 99 (1900): 564; Vagts, "Diederich Hahn," p. 180.

50. Vagts, "Diederich Hahn,"pp. 185–190.

51. See George Vascik, "Rural Politics and Sugar: A Comparative Study of National Liberal Politics in Hannover and Prussian Saxony, 1871–1914" (Ph.D. diss., University of Michigan, 1988).

52. Puhle, *Agrarische Interessenpolitik*, p. 146.

aid agriculture would require a broad coalition of National Liberals, Free Conservatives, Conservatives, and occasional Center party participation, and thus it was clear to more pragmatic League leaders that the National Liberals could not be simply stricken from all political equations; a formally "nonpartisan" policy was considered more advantageous.

Hahn would have none of this. His race against Carl Sattler in 1893 had been brutally contentious. Hahn secured the support of the local National Liberal associations in the counties of Neuhaus, Hadeln, and Kehdingen, but the provincial party refused to accept these endorsements, naming Sattler instead as its man in the race. Thus Hahn's victory was secured by the destruction of what the provincial party chair called the best constituency organization in Hanover.[53]

After the election, Hahn took his seat as a "guest" (*Hospitant*) of the National Liberals, but he was an unwelcome guest. In July 1894, the party formally expelled him from its caucus. Making the best of it, Hahn dramatically picked up his papers and crossed the aisle from the liberal backbenches to those of the Conservatives, causing Eugen Richter to joke, "now that the National Liberals have lost their rooster [Hahn], they will lay only crooked eggs."[54] Hahn was enthusiastically supported in this move by his constituency organization, for the locals had already come to view him as their champion against an unresponsive provincial leadership.[55]

When the date was set for the 1898 election, Hahn was once again nominated by the local liberal associations, but the provincial leadership refused to accept this nomination as well, taking the unprecedented step of dissolving the Hadeln constituency party. Yet the election for a new committee produced a group even more beholden to Hahn, which declared its independence from Berlin and Hanover. After that move, the provincial leadership once again dissolved the Hadeln organization and expelled its members formally from the party.[56]

Hahn's response was to challenge the National Liberal Party

---

53. Flathmann, *Die Reichstagswahlen*, p. 75.

54. Puhle, *Agrarische Interessenpolitik*, p. 194; Klauder, "Diederich Hahn," p. 183.

55. Ehrenfeuchter, "Politische Willensbildung," p. 167.

56. On the dissolution of the Otterndorf Verein, see *Hannoversche Courier*, 25 May 1898, "Aus der Partei," p. 1.

electorally on all fronts. He had already written to his confederate Johannes Schoof the previous year:

> If it would not endanger my health, I would fight all the current National Liberal Reichstag deputies from the province [of Hanover] if they were to be renominated. They have all without exception endangered us with the Russian trade treaty, as well as the Kanitz proposal, and I have no future trust in these people in political matters.[57]

Some National Liberal constituency organizations responded to Hahn's blackmail by nominating candidates more sympathetic to the Agrarian League.[58] Those that did not, the League warned, would bear the onus for a defeat of the patriotic forces.[59] When proper candidates were not forthcoming in six other constituencies, Hahn put up independent BdL nominees.

Hahn's tactics succeeded in displacing three liberal deputies.[60] His willingness to countenance the elections of anti-Prussian Guelphs further indicates the depth of his animosity. Indeed, Hahn's unwillingness to support his National Liberal enemies even against Social Democrats was notorious[61] and he was repeatedly accused of this in the National Liberal press, although he always claimed his words were misconstrued.

The disruptive effects of Hahn's activities in the northern counties of Hanover can be gauged from the political reports of the local county administrators. The Landrat of Kehdingen reported in 1900 that the National Liberals in his district who once predominated now lacked a solid organizational base.[62] In the county of Jork, the BdL was "the largest organization, with party agents in every community under the direction of the constituency committees and the central [League] leadership." Earlier, the Landrat reported, the National Liberals had possessed an electoral committee, but that "has been entirely taken over by the Agrarian League . . . the peasants who were its strongest supporters are now all devoted to Dr. Hahn."[63]

57. Vascik, "Rural Politics," p. 314.
58. Ibid., pp. 197–235, 249–65.
59. "Parteifragen," *Korrespondenz der Bund der Landwirte,* 28 October 1897, p. 1.
60. Ibid., p. 2.
61. Puhle, *Agrarische Interessenpolitik,* p. 197.
62. Report of Landrat Kreis Kehdingen to the Regierungspräsident Stade, 2 August 1902, NStA Stade, Rep. 80 P/VII/795.
63. Report of Landrat of Kreis Jork to the Regierungspräsident Stade, 3 August 1902, NStA Stade, Rep. 80 P/VII/795. For a comprehensive analysis of

Hahn's intentions toward the Hanoverian National Liberals were clear when he declared in 1902 that the League planned to replace the liberals as the province's "nationalist" representative in the Reichstag.[64] Provincial National Liberal chair Johannes Flathmann responded by asking the party's 250 agents (*Vertrauensmänner*) in rural counties to complete a survey on their local agricultural economies. They were asked a series of specific questions about the structure of the local farming population and economy, as well as about local peasant actions to the new tariffs.[65] In this way, the party was able to run candidates targeted to each constituency's narrow economic interests: it could challenge Hahn head-to-head, accommodate local agrarian radicals, or ignore agrarian issues altogether. Hahn complained that "if the National Liberal party had enough urban voters behind it, it would make no secret of its direct unfriendliness to agriculture."[66]

Flathmann's strategy of wooing Hanoverian peasants away from Hahn's agrarians paid off for the National Liberals in the Reichstag elections of 1903, when the two groups faced each other in ten of the province's nineteen constituencies. After a bitter campaign the National Liberals prevailed in seven of the ten contests.[67] Only Count (later Prince) Edzard zu Inn- und Knyphausen retained his Fresian mandate, the other two seats being won by the particularlist German-Hanoverian party. Hahn himself was defeated by Hugo Böttger, an anti-League editor and publicist. Appealing to narrow sectional interests in the Bülow tariff negotiations, obstructing the *Mittellandkanal*, and excoriating Free Conservatives had backfired on Hahn, as Hanoverian liberals found they could be simultaneously more "patriotic" and more economically particularist than Hahn himself could be in his position as League director.

---

political alignments in the marsh district, see the report of the Regierungspräsident Stade to the Oberpräsident Hannover, 25 August 1902, NStA Stade Rep. 80 P/VII/795. Much the same conditions prevailed in East Fresia. See the report of Landrat Kreis Nordern to Regierungspräsident Aurich, 10 August 1900, NStA Aurich, Rep. 21a.

64. A. O'Donnell, "National Liberalism and the Mass Politics of the German Right, 1890–1907" (Ph.D. diss., Princeton University, 1974), p. 301.

65. J. Flathmann, *Die Landbevölkerung der Provinz Hannover und die Agrarzölle* (Hanover, 1902); "Die Nationalliberale Partei und die Landwirtschaft," *Hannoverscher Courier*, 20 March 1902, p. 5.

66. "Sand in die Augen," *Bund der Landwirte*, 18 April 1903, p. 121.

67. Vascik, "Rural Politics," 285–294.

The five years after the election of 1903 witnessed a remarkable attempt on the part of the Hanoverian National Liberals to buttress their position vis-à-vis Hahn and his agrarian radicals. More farmers were brought into the party's associational life and local electoral committees made a greater attempt to recruit candidates with agricultural backgrounds.[68] Butter producers were reassured that the party would support a law prohibiting margarine (or insisting that it be dyed blue), meat producers were promised that the party would represent the interests of fodder users against those of the cereal-producing Junkers who "controlled" the Agrarian League, and sugar beet growers were courted with a law prohibiting artificial sweeteners.[69]

The profoundly anti-Hahn content of Hanoverian National Liberalism was sharpened via the party's predominant position in the provincial press – party chief Flathmann edited the *Hannoversche Courier*, the province's leading newspaper. Three of the province's five mass circulation dailies were aligned with the party, as was the leading provincial weekly, the *Niedersächsische Wochenzeitung*. Of the 151 newspapers published in the province in 1912, almost half of those that professed a party affiliation were National Liberal. The League and its Conservative allies could count on only thirteen newspapers, eight with circulations under 5,000.[70]

That Hahn was able to claw his way back into the Reichstag in 1907 against these odds was remarkable indeed, although doing so had meant allocating the lion's share of the resources made available by the League to the province to his own campaign. This had allowed only two other candidates to run against National Liberals.[71] In the afterglow of his return to the Reichstag, Hahn sensed the tide once again turning his way. Speaking before the League's annual assembly in February 1908, Hahn claimed that the influence of agrarians within the

68. The party was so successful in this that urban liberals complained that agriculture was overrepresented. See "Die NLP und Landwirtschaft," *Hannoversche Courier*, 20 March 1902, p. 5.

69. G. Vascik, "Sweet Affinity: National Liberals and the German Sugar Industry, 1867–1914," unpublished essay.

70. H. Schüter, *Die politische Tagespresse der Provinz Hannover* (Bad Essen, 1919), pp. 37–38.

71. Vascik, "Rural Politics," pp. 305–08. On the race in constituency 5 (Melle-Diepholz) see NStA Osnabrück, Rep. 450, Landratsamt Wittlage, Nr.

NLP had grown.[72] He even had the audacity to claim – inaccurately – that four Hanoverian liberals elected would not have been elected without League backing.

Buoyed by what was a patently unique election outcome, Hahn once again went on the offensive, this time by joining the Conservative Reichstag caucus and announcing that the BdL would challenge National Liberal control of the province's delegation to the Prussian House of Deputies.[73] Hahn managed to wrest seven seats from the liberals, but at the cost of his political future. Building upon the organizational initiatives that had followed in the wake of the Flathmann survey, the province's rural liberals established their own Peasant League.[74] This nascent liberal agrarian interest group failed to stop Hahn in 1908, but the effort provided the foundation for a new peasant league created the succeeding year when the Bülow Bloc collapsed over the projected imperial finance reform. Ultimately, it was to destroy Hahn's power within his constituent base in the northwestern peasantry and leave him exposed to his enemies within the Agrarian League.

III

It was in his work for the BdL that Diederich Hahn first emerged as a fully professional politician in the sense of being both an organizational apparatchnik and a tactical politician. Hahn succeeded in building the Hanoverian branch of the BdL in an extremely hostile environment by combining organizational genius with demagogic skill. He appointed chairmen to each constituency and recruited local chairs for every village chapter, all of this organized along a strict chain of command, with League agents (*Vertrauensmänner*) carrying orders to the villages and overseeing local activities. Moreover, the provincial apparatus published its own weekly

72. Bundesarchiv, Abteilungen Potsdam (hereafter cited as BA Potsdam), *Reichskanzlei*, Nr. 1128, "Bund der Landwirte," 16–17.

73. "BdL und Landtagswahl", *Hannoversche Courier*, 8 May 1908, p. 1; *Niedersächsisches Wochenblatt*, 12 May 1908.

74. G. Vascik, "The German Peasant League and the Limits of Rural Liberalism in Wilhelmian Germany," *Central European History*; 24 (1991): 147–75, G. Mundle "The German National Liberal Party, 1900–1914" (Ph.D. diss., University of Illinois, 1975); and T. Eschenburg, *Das Kaiserreich am Scheideweg: Bassermann, Bülow und der Block* (Berlin, 1929), pp. 119–20.

newspaper and distributed the flood of literature and agitational material produced by the Berlin central office. Hahn used his time away from Berlin to visit the branches, recruit new members, and urge his troops forward. From the tribune of the Reichstag and before audiences large and small, he denounced Caprivi's trade treaties and proposed laws and amendments that stood no chance of enactment – all for the benefit of his Hanoverian followers.

It was a ticklish business to first establish a provincial organization and to then control the League at its grassroots, for Hanover was National Liberal territory. The Hanoverian National Liberal party, following Bennigsen's lead, was unsure about the BdL. Confronting the NLP's entrenched power province-wide would have been impossible, so the Hanoverian BdL adopted a nonpartisan stance, hoping to ensnare all in its net. The Guelphs of course declined to work with the League, as did its Center party ally, because the BdL was staunchly "national" and the Guelphs would have none of it. Still, the League's nonpartisan stance enabled it to recruit members from across the "national" spectrum.[75] Inn- und Knyphausen was the province's most prominent Conservative, Free Conservatives and National Liberals served as local and county chairs, and Hahn himself, of course having defeated Carl Sattler, initially took his seat in the Reichstag as a *Hospitant* of the National Liberal party.

While the apparatus Hahn created was loyal to himself personally, the broader allegiance of the provincial membership was another question. To gain their loyalty, Hahn had to first gain their trust and he sought to do this, in a process described below, both in the Reichstag and on the stump. The result was that by 1898, Hahn had spread his influence in ever-expanding circles, winning followers first among his constituents in Neuhaus-Hadeln, then throughout Hanover, and finally throughout the whole of northwest Germany. It was this large personal following that gave Hahn his most enduring power base within the League. And all the while, Hahn successfully maintained a dynamic reciprocity between organization and agitation, aiming to make the Agrarian League more influen-

---

75. J. Hunt, "The 'Egalitarianism' of the Right: The Agrarian League in Southwest Germany, 1894–1914," *Journal of Contemporary History* 10 (1975): 513–30.

tial and himself more prominent and indispensable within it.

Drawing upon his experiences as a student leader and as a Hanoverian agitator, Hahn recognized that one key to power within the Agrarian League was through control of its organization. In the spring of 1896 the League's original director, Heinrich Suchsland, suffered a stroke,[76] and Hermann Plaskuda, Suchsland's deputy, was nominally delegated to run the League office. Here, Hahn saw his opening. He moved into an apartment at Hafenplatz 4, around the corner and less than fifty feet from the League's offices on Dessauerstraße.[77] From this point on, Hahn lived and breathed League business. With his nonstop activity and willingness to take on any task, he had soon displaced Plaskuda as the central office's essential actor. When Suchsland died the following summer, Hahn was seen as his logical successor, even though Gustav Roesicke, deputy to League chair Bernhardt von Ploetz, worried that Hahn was determined to found an exclusively agrarian party.[78]

Hahn's climb to the directorship of the BdL reflects the pattern he had already established: hard work, innovation, and cultivation of his social and organizational superiors. All contemporary sources speak of Hahn's incredible energy and drive. With his sharp gray eyes and commanding character, he bulldozed through projects. He put this drive to use in building up a personal empire within the central office. Where, in 1894, the League was serviced by 65 officials and functionaries, by 1914 their number had increased to 352 (67 classified as "upper" officials) and the League's publishing operations, which fell under Hahn's purview, were staffed by a further 400 workers.[79]

Hahn was also entrusted with direction of the electoral division (*Wahlabteilung*), and this he expanded beyond anything known in the other non-socialist parties or interest groups. The League's budget for 1907 was around one million marks, surpassing that of the Social Democrats, and this necessitated collecting dues from League members (for the support of gen-

76. Kiesewetter, *Zum fünfundzwanzigjährigen Jubiläum*, p. 59.
77. Ibid., pp. 59–60. Personal observations of Dessauerstraße and Hafenplatz.
78. D. Fricke and E. Hartwig, "Bund der Landwirte," in *Lexikon zur Parteiengeschichte*, ed. D. Fricke et al., 4 vols. (Berlin, 1983–86), vol. 1, p. 249.
79. Retallack, *Notables of the Right*, p. 109.

eral League activities), demanding special extraordinary dues to build up a war chest for election campaigns, and soliciting or subtly extorting funds from wealthy backers. The League received lists of candidates supported by its constituency organizations, and Hahn in turn distributed the amassed funds to worthy candidates.[80]

To support the League's electoral activities, Hahn created a speaker's school and a speaker's bureau. In this school, Hahn trained professional traveling agitators. These agitators would make stump speeches during election campaigns and give informative or inspirational talks to local chapters between elections. By 1909, Hahn's corps of traveling agitators had grown to over 100, with all expenses covered by Hahn's budget. The school also provided instructions to local volunteers, who took Hahn's course at their own expense. In this way, Hahn imparted his own hyperbolic, emotional speaking style to a whole cadre of rural activists and left a mark on rural political discourse that lasted far beyond his own lifetime.[81]

These speakers, functionaries, and unpaid local activists could not operate in an informational vacuum: policy positions had to be made known, talking points delineated, and convincing evidence assembled. For these purposes, Hahn established a weekly *Korrespondenz* to which every BdL functionary and official subscribed. This kept the cadre abreast of current issues and enabled the League throughout the Reich to speak, for the most part, with one voice. As the man in charge, Hahn's imprint lay heavy upon the *Korrespondenz*, and allowed him to impart his own "spin" on issues facing the League. The *Korrespondenz* was supplemented by a series of publications destined for the broader membership: the League published its own weekly newspaper, the *Bund der Landwirte* (with a circulation of nearly 250,000), which was sent to individual member's homes, as well as provincial newspapers (with circulations totalling 120,000). Hahn's projects included special topical monographs, guides for elections, a yearly League calender, and eleven mobile libraries.[82]

As League director, Hahn was *de jure* co-chair of the corporation that published one of the German Right's preeminent

80. On Roesicke's unhappiness with Hahn's use of the funds in 1910, see Roesicke to Wangenheim, 6 April 1910, BA Potsdam, NL Roesicke, Nr. 2/i.
81. Sossinka, "Diederich Hahn," p. 63.
82. See Fricke and Hartwig, "Bund der Landwirte," pp. 241–70.

newspapers, the *Deutsche Tageszeitung*. Hahn had been one of the co-founders and original shareholders of the *Deutsche Tageszeitung* in 1894, and had made numerous contributions to its columns prior to 1897. For the next two decades, he would use the paper as a sounding board for his own ideas and as a vehicle for attempting to outmaneuver his fellow leaders in the BdL. His personal friendship with editors Georg Oertel and Felix Telge ensured sympathetic treatment from the paper and became a source of chagrin to his opponents.[83]

Recognizing the importance of at least the appearance of factual integrity from his days with the Deutsche Bank, Hahn expanded the League's press archive that had been founded by Gustav Roesicke in 1893. Under Hahn's direction the archive increased its subscriptions from 60 to 310 newspapers by 1914, all clipped and filed by category.[84] A further innovation under Hahn was the creation of a pension plan for League functionaries, the first of its kind: a certain amount was deducted from each functionary's salary, then invested by the League's business manager. Some of these funds were invested in the League's own buying cooperative (which always paid a hefty dividend) as well as the *Deutsche Tageszeitung* (which also paid a yearly dividend of ten percent).[85] Finally, Hahn was responsible for overseeing relations between the Berlin leadership and the regional branches in northwestern Germany.

Within the League's directorate, Hahn was always a difficult colleague. On the one hand, he was too "idealistic," by which his contemporaries meant he was unwilling to compromise. Hahn never settled for a half loaf, and as a result, was often left with nothing. This "idealism" naturally grated on his more pragmatic colleagues in the League. On the other hand, he was extremely defensive about his personal empire, demanding that his colleagues both recognize the boundaries of his authority and respectfully seek his opinion in general

83. Roesicke to Hahn, 17 December 1897; and Roesicke to Ploetz, 20 December 1897, BA Potsdam, NL Ploetz.

84. G. Meyer, "Das Pressearchiv des Bundes der Landwirte (1893–1945)," *Zeitschrift für Geschichtswissenschaft* 5 (1959): 1121–23.

85. Hahn was a founder and frequent contributor to the *Deutsche Tageszeitung* according to Haushofer, "Diederich Hahn," p. 503. Conscious of Hahn's financial difficulties, Roesicke wanted to provide him with a nest egg (5,000–6,000 M. annually). See Roesicke to Wangenheim, 31 May 1907, BA Potsdam, NL Roesicke, Nr. 2/i.

League matters. When individuals ran afoul of Hahn on either point, he took the matter personally.

This irritability was not obvious before 1897, largely because Hahn was still making his way within the League. As he had demonstrated while working for Siemens, he could be very engaging when it suited his purposes. Even after joining the BdL directorate, Hahn did not immediately experience major difficulties with his colleagues. The period from 1897 to 1903 witnessed a gradual (though profound) radicalization of the League's rhetoric and activities, a radicalization that mirrored Hahn's own development.[86] In the Reichstag elections of 1903, however, Hahn's attempt to profit from the League's hostile relationship to the other parties failed. Indeed, the League lost many supporters in the Reichstag, and after 1903 a more moderate face had to be shown to the outside world.

That this was difficult for the pugnacious Hahn was demonstrated in the Bloc elections of 1907. While the conservative, liberal, and progressive parties had agreed to mount a common campaign against their socialist and Catholic foes, Hahn played by his own rules. His fellows in the Hanoverian BdL challenged incumbent National Liberals in several districts, and most spectacularly, Hahn led a crusade against the Free Conservative leader Wilhelm von Kardorff.[87] Kardorff had proposed the compromise that broke the log-jam over the Bülow tariffs in 1902. Although this compromise gave the agrarians almost all that they wanted, it was unacceptable to Hahn and his radicals. Seeking revenge, Hahn had sponsored a BdL counter-candidate, whom he generously supported with funds from the electoral division treasury. Kardorff's subsequent defeat demonstrated to the outside world and to Hahn's BdL colleagues that Bloc solidarity would stand in the way of neither Hahn's personal vendettas nor his own agrarian agenda.

These tensions reached a critical level in 1908, and reflected Hahn's difficulties with Gustav Roesicke, now chair of the BdL. The setback of 1903 had already convinced Roesicke that compromise was necessary, and that Chancellor Bülow was the man to make those compromises. In the negotiations over

---

86. Recounted in Retallack, *Notables of the Right*, pp. 131–47.
87. S. von Kardorff, *Wilhelm von Kardorff. Ein Nationaler Parlamentarier im Zeitalter Bismarcks und Wilhelms II.* (Berlin, 1936), pp. 342–60, 367.

the Imperial finance reform of 1908/09, Roesicke and Wangenheim pushed Bülow for the best possible deal, but they were unwilling to break the Bloc if all their demands were not met.[88] The radicals, in Roesicke's opinion, failed to understand the political situation. The League needed to work with the Center, although this was difficult because of that party's strong democratic elements. The trick was to attract the Center with a common position on the inheritance tax, which would make the Center's position unacceptable to the Left, and leave the BdL and the Conservative Party in a pivotal position. In all instances, one had to be careful about seeming to come into direct conflict with the Kaiser, for this course would alienate the Conservatives from the League. As for Bülow, Roesicke wrote to Wangenheim that, "we know what he is like, and where we stand with him. His eventual successor is an unwritten page."[89]

The necessity for compromise was lost on Hahn. He had promoted the overthrow of Chancellors Caprivi and Hohenlohe, and had spent the preceding five years publicly deriding Bülow (even while seeking his favors). Why should he stop now? Moreover, his stature within the BdL was founded upon his unalloyed radicalism. Roesicke and Wangenheim might represent the pragmatists within the League, but Hahn was the spokesman for the red-hots. By agreeing to compromise, Hahn would be betraying not only his "ideals" but also the very group of supporters who insured his place within the League's leadership.

Hahn's relationship with Roesicke deteriorated precipitously through 1908. In January, they began to quarrel about a proposed stock exchange bill. Roesicke sought a compromise, but Hahn would not agree. Hahn tried to use the pages of the *Deutsche Tageszeitung* to put forward his own position as that of the League's, but Roesicke was able to convince the paper's editor, Georg Oertel, to fall into line.[90] By summer, Hahn felt so frustrated that he contemplated jumping ship. He journeyed to the resort island of Norderney to visit the vacationing

88. Roesicke to Wangenheim, 14 August 1908, BA Potsdam, NL Roesicke, Nr. 3.
89. Roesicke to Wangenheim, 2 November 1908, BA Potsdam, NL Roesicke, Nr. 3.
90. Roesicke to Wangenheim, 9 January 1908, BA Potsdam, NL Roesicke, Nr. 3.

Chancellor Bülow, to whom Hahn explained that he felt so physically exhausted by League in-fighting that he wanted to resign his directorship. But if he did so, he would lose both the income from that position and the considerable sum he earned as co-editor of the *Tageszeitung*. And if he resigned from the League leadership, would Bülow support his appointment as provincial governor of Hanover? Hahn believed he had extracted a positive response from the man he had harried so long, but that was not the case. Bülow leaked word of their conversation to the press, which scuttled the appointment and caused Hahn a serious loss of face within the League.[91]

For his part, Roesicke used the incident as an occasion to try to push Hahn aside.[92] Realizing his future was on the line, Hahn went to Roesicke and explained that his difficult behavior had been the result of a severe tooth infection. Now he was going to have to undergo root canal work! Roesicke accepted the whole story and was relieved that their recent difficulties had a physiological cause.[93]

As a result of his dental problems, Hahn was forced to sit out the finance negotiations between August and November 1908. These negotiations began to falter at the same time that Hahn was able to reenter the arena. With his usual "idealism," Hahn was sure that Roesicke's policy of pursuing negotiations with the Conservatives and the Center was inappropriate – Hahn wanted no new taxes on agriculture of any kind. Sensing he might have a majority of BdL members on his side, Hahn decided to confront Roesicke, something he hoped would establish his complete ascendency in the League. In a stormy meeting on 5 November, Hahn confronted Roesicke with the charge that Roesicke had failed to carry out the League's mandate in the tax negotiations and accused Roesicke of speaking out against him in the Reichstag. The meeting went so poorly that Roesicke fled Berlin by train to his country home where, in a letter written in the middle of the

91. Diederich Hahn to Margarethe Hahn, n.d., in private possession of Christian Hahn, cited in Hahn, "Erinnerungen," p. 97. B. v. Bülow, *Denkwürdigkeiten*, 4 vols. (Berlin, 1930) vol. 1, p. 302, grouped Hahn with Roesicke and Oldenburg as agrarian radicals who could not be satisfied. He remembered Hahn as a bare-knuckled fighter (*Klopfechter*) who transformed himself from a free trader into an agrarian extremist.

92. Wangenheim to Roesicke, 27 July 1908, BA Potsdam, NL Roesicke, Nr. 3.

93. Roesicke to Wangenheim, 6 August 1908, BA Potsdam, NL Roesicke, Nr. 3.

night, he described the situation to Wangenheim. "[Hahn's] irritated frame of mind against me is very deeply felt and has developed into hate," Roesicke complained, adding that it had become impossible for them to work together. If Hahn stayed with the League, the rivalry and irritability would only continue; if Hahn left, he would no doubt continue his vendetta and paralyze the work of the League: in short, Roesicke concluded that he himself would have to resign.[94] Wangenheim immediately counseled Roesicke to do no such thing. If Hahn persisted in oppressing Roesicke in such an insane manner, Wangenheim would call a meeting of the League executive committee, which would put Hahn in his place. And that is exactly what transpired. In the end, it was Hahn, not Roesicke, who backed down, and from this point onward Hahn's influence within the League began to wane.[95]

Hahn tried to maintain his position by recourse to his popularity with the peasantry west of the Elbe, but even that was not secure. The foundation of the German Peasant League in July 1909, shortly after the disintegration of the Bülow Bloc, ultimately sealed Hahn's fate.[96] Hahn's claim to power within the Agrarian League – that he was uniquely qualified to articulate the grievances of the western peasantry – was challenged in the most public way possible.

The Reichstag elections of 1912 were a disaster for the Agrarian League: a full sixty of the 138 seats that had been won in 1907 were lost. Only 32 percent of League-sponsored candidates survived the second round of balloting, the worst record the League ever recorded. Hahn, Roesicke, and Oldenburg all lost their seats in parliament. As director of the BdL's electoral operations Hahn naturally had to bear a certain share of the blame for these setbacks.[97]

In the campaign leading to the Reichstag elections of January 1912, Hahn mounted the most intense campaign many dis-

---

94. Roesicke to Wangenheim, 5/6 November 1908, BA Potsdam, NL Roesicke, Nr. 3.

95. Wangenheim to Roesicke, 7 November 1908, BA Potsdam, NL Roesicke, Nr. 3. As late as 1917, Hahn was still concerned about what he suspected were moves on Roesicke's part to limit his role in the League. See Hahn to Roesicke, 21 April 1917, BA Potsdam, NL Roesicke, Nr. 2a.

96. Vascik, "The German Peasant League," pp. 167–68.

97. Puhle, *Agrarische Interessenpolitik*, pp. 168–69; and A. Peck, *Radicals and Reactionaries: The Crisis of Conservatism in Wilhelmine Germany* (Washington, 1978), p. 84.

tricts had ever seen, staging 9,478 rallies and deploying 151 paid speakers.[98] Still, Hahn's electoral machine could not swim against the political tide that League radicals had done so much to create. National Liberals and Progressives, working together with the new Peasant League, were able to capture rural seats formerly held by BdL sympathizers. This compensated those two parties for urban seats that were lost to the Social Democrats. Indeed, SPD successes were due in no small part to food policies the League had forced upon the government.[99]

Hahn's loss in the first round of the general election was a traumatic blow to him. Desperately ill from a sore throat that had hampered his campaigning, Hahn took the loss very badly. Graceless in defeat, he refused to support The National Liberal Victor against his Social Democratic opponent in the run-off ballot – an incredible act of defiance against accepted bourgeois political norms. Next time, Hahn told a local meeting, he would "take out an insurance policy" by accepting a mandate in the east.[100]

Although Hahn still retained his Landtag seat and his directorship, he seems to have put some distance between himself and his Berlin duties. In October 1913, he took over the provincial chair of the Hanoverian BdL, finally enjoying the honorific title that Inn- und Knyphausen had held for twenty years.[101] Perhaps responding to some deeper need to prove he was in fact an agrarian, Hahn purchased a large chunk of land on the moor near Basbeck, which he claimed had belonged to the Hahn family before it was laid to waste in the Thirty Years' War.[102] There he built a large brick home in the style of a Lower Saxon *Landhaus*, and moved in with his family. Now he would live like Roesicke!

Building up Haneworth (Hahn's modest name for the

98. J. Bertram, *Die Wahlen zum deutschen Reichstag vom Jahre 1912* (Düsseldorf, 1964), pp. 187–88.

99. William Carl Mathews, "The Food Crisis of 1910–1911: Meat, Potatoes and the Politics of Food," unpublished paper presented at the German Studies Association conference, October 1989.

100. "Wahlen zum Reichstag 12.1.1912," Kreisarchiv Otterndorf, A I d, Nr. 2, Nr. 109.

101. Roesicke supported Hahn for the post in the hope that it would "make his entire temperament more peaceful." Roesicke to Wangenheim, 15 October 1913, BA Potsdam, NL Wangenheim.

102. Haushofer, "Diederich Hahn," p. 503.

estate) became a full-time occupation. Hahn was convinced that by applying the latest techniques of moor cultivation he could make a go of it, but in the two years between his purchase of Haneworth and the outbreak of war, the estate failed to show a profit. August 1914 must have come as something of a relief. Hahn put on his uniform and immediately reported to his unit, where he was assigned to the *Etappenkommando*, first of the Tenth Army Corps and then Second Army Corps. Here Hahn's organizational genius could once again shine. He established cordial relations with French and Belgian businessmen, procuring local supplies for the corps. In recognition of his outstanding work, Hahn was awarded the Iron Cross Second Class.[103]

The war also held political lessons for him, seeming to confirm his long-standing anti-socialism and to promise the basis for a new "national" political fusion. Hahn was impressed by the patriotism of his former political enemies, and took great joy in sharing moments of Teutonic comradeship with Social Democrats and Progressives.[104] This "confirmed" his old belief that if "so-called" Social Democrats were removed from party discipline they would show themselves to be dedicated monarchists.[105] Expanding upon these beliefs, Hahn became an ardent supporter of the German Fatherland Party in 1917, for he believed that the war had made possible a "new orientation" in German politics.[106] Sickness and the worries of managing his estate precluded an all-out effort on his part for the new party, though Hahn did speak on its behalf during short trips around Lower Saxony.

After two years at the front, Hahn returned home and he convinced the war department to establish a prisoner-of-war camp at Basbeck. He then used the POWs as laborers on his estate. Alfred Vagts remembered Hahn riding around supervising his workers "like a Roman landlord on a vast latifundium."[107] Even with convict labor, Hahn was not able to succeed with his fledgling empire. He had taken advantage of his

103. NStA Stade, NL Hahn, VII/13/B, Nr. 32.
104. See articles by A. Rosenthal in the *Kölner Volkszeitung*, 14 September 1914; and A. Bernstein in the *Berliner Morgenpost*, 15 October 1914.
105. BA Potsdam, Pressearchiv der Bundes der Landwirte, 61 Re 1, 3398/89.
106. Ibid., p. 89. Hahn's speech to a Berlin conservative assembly in 1917 calling for a "new orientation" of Conservative politics was so successful that the Berlin party published it as a leaflet.
107. Vagts, "Diederich Hahn," p. 156.

neighbors by buying or leasing land from widows and absentee farmers, greatly increasing his debt burden. Moreover, he had secured a contract to provide hogs to the navy. Contrary to his expectations, however, these contracts were rarely profitable and forced numerous farmers to go out of business.[108] By the late summer of 1916, Hahn was forced to go hat in hand to Wangenheim to ask for help from the Agrarian League's purchasing office. Wangenheim wrote to Roesicke, no doubt with a certain *Schadenfreude*, that "economically, Hahn has himself caught in the nettles."[109]

All these problems left Hahn in a weakened condition, and shortly after Christmas, he collapsed and was transported to a military hospital in Hamburg. In the middle of February 1918 his strength seemed to return, and he wrote to friends that he would be well enough to leave the hospital at the end of the month to address the League's annual assembly in Berlin. On 20 February, however, his condition worsened, and he died four days later.[110]

IV

Diederich Hahn's career is historically significant for three reasons. It demonstrates that for all Wilhelmine society's supposed rigidity a young man from the provinces – if talented and moderately well-to-do – could make it to the highest reaches of society and politics. Educated and energetic, Hahn gained power and prominence through his skills as a bureaucratic organizer and populist agitator. His activities while director of the BdL are the very model of the new type of professional politician foreseen by Max Weber – men who derived their livelihood from their political activities.[111]

Second, Hahn's career provides an important insight into the Agrarian League, Wilhelmine Germany's most determined and vocal interest group. The BdL's opponents were quick to tar it with the brush of Junkerism, pointing to the class origins of its titular leaders and the thrust of its protec-

---

108. Roesicke to Hahn, 27 August 1916, BA Potsdam, NL Roesicke, Nr. 2a.
109. Wangenheim to Roesicke, 8 August 1916, BA Potsdam, NL Roesicke, Nr. 2a.
110. *Berliner Zeitung*, 25 February 1918; and *Bund der Landwirte*, 2 March 1918.
111. Weber, "Parlament und Regierung," p. 389.

tionist policies, but his canard was inaccurate on both counts. The real work in the League was carried out by a whole cadre of middle-class functionaries, of whom Diederich Hahn was only the most prominent. Moreover, small and medium-sized peasant landholders also had a vested interest in agricultural protection.[112] If they belonged to the League, perhaps it was because they genuinely believed their interests were best served by the BdL's policies and – not least – because they felt they had their own political tribune in Diederich Hahn.

The third reason Hahn's career is significant is that hate-mongering, anti-modern, anti-democratic, hypernationalistic Wilhelmine politicians, of whom Diederich Hahn was one of the most prominent, sowed the harvest that was to be reaped in the 1930s. As a speaker at local rallies and as head of the League's propaganda apparatus, Hahn made anti-Semitism the common currency of rural political discourse in the Wilhelmine era. Diederich Hahn in many ways was for the feudal elite of Wilhelmine Germany what Franz von Papen and his friends thought they had found in Adolf Hitler: a drummer for the disaffected. That Hahn did not achieve supreme power may say more about the persistent influence of those elites before 1918 than it does about the relative abilities and fanaticism of the two drummers.

112. R. Moeller, "Peasants and Tariffs in the *Kaiserreich*: How backward were the *Bauern*?" *Agricultural History* 55 (1981): 370–84.

8

The Road to Philippi

The Conservative Party and Bethmann Hollweg's "Politics of the Diagonal," 1909–14*

James Retallack

We will see each other at Philippi.

– Chancellor Bernhard von Bülow, to the Conservatives,
upon resigning from office in July 1909[1]

At Philippi, indeed! . . . It is now a matter for all positive, constructive forces to *close ranks*. . . . In this effort may we finally be granted a government that forcefully and decisively takes the lead in the struggle against all destructive elements.

– Wilhelm Albers
(general secretary of the Conservative Party in Westphalia)
1912[2]

To reform Prussia is impossible; it will remain the *Junkerstaat* it is at present, or go to pieces altogether. . . . Everything works for a great crisis in Germany.

– August Bebel
(leader of the Social Democratic Party of Germany), 1910[3]

* This essay was to have been included in a collection of papers on politics, parties, and the authoritarian state in Imperial Germany. Due to a disastrous series of delays with that volume, the essay was withdrawn in early 1992 and revised to address the themes of the present volume more directly. The author wishes to thank Hartmut Pogge von Strandmann, James Sheehan, and Ulrich Trumpener for their comments on early drafts, and the Social Sciences and Humanities Research Council of Canada for generous financial support.

1. B. von Bülow, *Denkwürdigkeiten*, 4 vols. (Berlin, 1930), vol. 2, pp. 520–1.
2. W. Albers, *Die Besiegten von Philippi! Ein Wort zu den Reichstagswahlen von 1912* (Bielefeld, 1912), pp. 1, 18–19.
3. Cited in V. Berghahn, *Germany and the Approach of War in 1914* (London, 1973), title page.

James Retallack

> Heydebrand is leading the Conservatives down demagogic
> paths. If, in our non-parliamentary system, the government no
> longer finds support . . . even from the Conservatives and the
> moderates, then in the end there will be no one left to carry on.
>
> – Chancellor Theobald von Bethmann Hollweg to Carl von
> Eisendecher (Prussian envoy in Baden), November 1911[4]

> Now the Conservative Party has sunk to complete insignifi-
> cance, and the Center and the Social Democrats are trump.
> Philippi is here.
>
> – Ernst Bassermann (leader of the National Liberal Party),
> to Bülow, April 1912[5]

I

Historians of Wilhelmine Germany have argued since the
1970s that sometime shortly before the outbreak of World War
I there was a major change in the structure and style of politics
in Germany, especially on the political Right. Most of these
historians have tried to define political culture and right-wing
mobilization by concentrating their attention on the leading
nationalist and economic pressure groups.[6] Along the way,
however, they have neglected the three right-wing parties in
Imperial Germany: the German Conservative Party (Deutsch-
konservative Partei or DKP), the Imperial or Free Conserva-

4. Letter of 26 November 1911, in the Political Archive of the German For-
eign Office, Bonn (hereafter PA AA Bonn), Nachlaß (hereafter NL) Carl von
Eisendecher, Nr. 1/2, Bl. 24–25.
5. Letter of 3 April 1912, Bundesarchiv Koblenz (hereafter BA Koblenz), NL
Bernhard von Bülow, Nr. 107, Bl. 153.
6. G. Eley, *Reshaping the German Right. Radical Nationalism and Political
Change after Bismarck* (London and New Haven, 1980); R. Chickering, *We Men
Who Feel Most German. A Cultural Study of the Pan-German League 1886–1914*
(Boston, 1984); D. Stegmann, *Die Erben Bismarcks. Parteien und Verbände in der
Spätphase des Wilhelminischen Deutschlands* (Cologne, 1970); idem, "Zwischen
Repression und Manipulation: Konservative Machteliten und Arbeiter- und
Angestelltenbewegung 1910–1918. Ein Beitrag zur Vorgeschichte der
DAP/NSDAP," *Archiv für Sozialgeschichte* 12 (1972): 351–432; idem, "Vom
Neokonservatismus zum Proto-Faschismus: Konservative Partei, Vereine und
Verbände 1893–1920," in *Deutscher Konservatismus im 19. und 20. Jahrhundert*,
ed. D. Stegmann, B.-J. Wendt, and P.–C. Witt (Bonn, 1983), pp. 199–230; and
idem, "Literaturbericht. Konservatismus und nationale Verbände im Kaiser-
reich," *Geschichte und Gesellschaft* 10 (1984): 409–20; cf. A.J. Peck, *Radicals and
Reactionaries: The Crisis of Conservatism in Wilhelmine Germany* (Washington
D.C., 1978). The most recent contribution is M. Shevin Coetzee, *The German
Army League. Popular Nationalism in Wilhelmine Germany* (New York and
Oxford, 1990). See also the contributions to this volume by G. Eley and D.
Stegmann.

tive Party (Reichs- und Freikonservative Partei or FKP), and the National Liberal Party (Nationalliberale Partei or NLP).[7] These parties have never been integrated into our picture of interest groups struggling to safeguard their own interests and working in opposition to the government of Chancellor Theobald von Bethmann Hollweg. The central importance of the German Conservative Party, the most right-wing of these three parties, has been most conspicuously ignored. Geoff Eley and others have pointed out the insufficiency of Hans-Jürgen Puhle's early study[8] of the Conservatives' auxiliary interest group, the Agrarian League (Bund der Landwirte or BdL), in defining the Conservative Party's position within the Wilhelmine Right. Yet only a few participants in the debate have directly addressed one central question: whether or not traditional Conservative notables maintained their influence with the government of Bethmann Hollweg after 1909.[9]

This essay will suggest what further research could help fill this gap, but it has other aims too: to present new evidence about the relationship between the Conservatives and the government; to consider which personalities dominated that relationship; and to reconsider past interpretations of it in a new light. It will argue that historians can draw upon a substantial body of previously unpublished archival material to provide new insights into the relationship between party and state in late Imperial Germany. Special attention will be paid to the framework of party alignments within which the Conservatives and Bethmann tried to work out their differences before 1914, in order to consider whether contemporaries – with Bethmann and his predecessor, Bernhard von Bülow, in the forefront – viewed the Conservative Party as the legitimate representative of conservative principles in these years. Certainly Bethmann had some conservative supporters who had been alienated by the DKP or who found the other right-wing

7. That the National Liberal Party was "right-wing," and, indeed, that the Catholic Center Party was not, is acknowledged as anything but self-evident.
8. H.-J. Puhle, *Agrarische Interessenpolitik und preußischer Konservatismus im wilhelminischen Reich 1893–1914*, 2nd ed. (Bonn-Bad Godesberg, 1975); cf. J. Retallack, *Notables of the Right. The Conservative Party and Political Mobilization in Germany, 1876–1918* (London and Boston, 1988), esp. chs. 8 and 10.
9. This question is discussed broadly in D. Blackbourn and G. Eley, *The Peculiarities of German History: Bourgeois Society and Politics in Nineteenth-Century Germany* (New York and Oxford, 1984); on p. 119 Eley notes our continuing uncertainty about Bethmann's political philosophy.

parties more to their taste. But when we ask why Bethmann could not abandon the Conservative Party altogether, is the answer simply that he had no alternative source of support for his government? Can we conclude that there was no other constellation of parties capable of supporting Bethmann's policies? Or, could Bethmann simply not *conceive* of an alternative arrangement?

Bethmann had definite political reasons for not breaking with the Conservatives. When he discussed these reasons with colleagues, his tone was often one of frustration and resignation, as we shall see. But at other times, his attitude was confident, even arrogant. To understand these changes in attitude, we must understand the ties that bound Bethmann to the Conservatives and, just as important, the ways the chancellor believed he could improve, loosen, or otherwise redefine these ties. It appears that there was indeed an intangible authority, a right to claim a pivotal position, that Bethmann ceded to the Conservatives, consciously or not. For many reasons he could not turn to the Kaiser, the administration, the interest groups, the other right-wing parties, or even the forces on the left as alternative sources of authority. Does this mean Bethmann was incapable of seeing the "antediluvial" Conservative Party (as one critic described it) for what it was, and is he thus to be condemned for misjudging the DKP? Or were his options in fact as limited as they appeared? If Bethmann was paying lip service to one political group, was it to the Left or the Right?

The problem of defining late Wilhelmine conservatism is bound up with questions about Bethmann's so-called "politics of the diagonal": the method whereby the chancellor relied on shifting parliamentary majorities to permit the collaboration of all non-socialist (*bürgerlich*) parties. In 1917, Bethmann looked back on the success of this policy and commented: "The present party alignment and our constitutional structure force [me] to rely basically on a policy of diagonals. But even the diagonal is a straight line, and I believe I have followed it."[10] Perhaps Bethmann meant to imply here that his policy was less problematic than supposed. Yet it is difficult to say whether the elements of Bethmann's strategy toward the Con-

---

10. Bethmann to Clemens von Delbrück, 8 September 1917, cited in K. Jarausch, *The Enigmatic Chancellor. Bethmann Hollweg and the Hubris of Imperial Germany* (London and New Haven, Conn., 1973), p. 349.

servatives were mutually reinforcing or contradictory. To some, Bethmann's apparent love-hate relationship with the DKP was a carefully considered program to reconcile progressive and reactionary forces in the Reich. Perhaps it could have been as successful as Bismarck's manipulative strategies in the 1870s and 1880s, when ad hoc majorities, sometimes excluding the Conservatives, had yielded a steadfastly "national" policy. To others, Bethmann's efforts were doomed to failure because he could not decide whether to treat the Conservative Party as an essential prop of the status quo or to regard it as a threat to reasonable, farsighted policy. Elements of both these points of view will be examined in the following argument.

This essay has a second theme. Bethmann and his political philosophy have been defined in many ways: as "enigmatic," "without character," and caught between "power and morality."[11] The term "reformist conservatism," however, which appears frequently in Konrad Jarausch's 1973 biography of Bethmann,[12] is a particularly useful shorthand description of Bethmann's political outlook. With this concept of reformist conservatism, the historian can juxtapose two apparently contradictory terms to explore different dimensions of party-state relations in Imperial Germany. By examining how the chancellor and the Conservative Party leaders worked – without ultimate success – to reconcile the forces of change and stability in both party and state, this essay will suggest how the debilitating effects of dichotomous thought conspired against any resolution of the estrangement between the Conservatives and the government after 1909. Bethmann honestly believed, as he told the Reichstag in February 1912, that the Reich "could not be governed through either reactionary or radical means."[13] In this thought the chancellor was certainly not without his supporters among the moderate Conservatives. Yet neither side successfully balanced desires for reform and retrenchment. Neither side successfully reconciled new ideas and old prejudices. Neither side successfully found ways to chart a rational

11. K. Hildebrand, *Bethmann Hollweg – der Kanzler ohne Eigenschaften?* (Düsseldorf, 1970); E. von Vietsch, *Bethmann Hollweg. Staatsmann zwischen Macht und Ethos* (Boppard am Rhein, 1969); W. Gutsche, *Aufstieg und Fall eines kaiserlichen Reichskanzlers* (Berlin, 1973).

12. See n. 10 above.

13. *Stenographische Berichte über die Verhandlungen des Reichstags* (hereafter *RT Sten. Ber.*), vol. 283, pp. 64–65, 16 Feb. 1912.

political course between the dictates of reason and sentiment.

This concept of reformist conservatism will also be used to study the close interconnection between efforts to resurrect the Conservative Party's popularity after the debacle of the finance reform crisis of 1909 and efforts to reestablish the party as a permanent element within the phalanx of "state-supporting" parties in Germany. It was the party's estrangement from the government in 1909 that brought to the fore demands from the DKP's rank-and-file members for a redefinition of the party's whole political strategy. At the center of this redefinition lay many vexing questions about how the party should or could be reformed. Conversely, Bethmann hoped that the Conservatives could be "enlightened" about the realities of political life in a more democratic age. This prevented him from abandoning these old – though no longer trusted – allies of the monarchical state. Thus, Bethmann's overall plan to retain Conservative participation in the governing of Germany while compelling them to accept moderate reform was influenced by the fate of the Conservatives' campaign to popularize their party and to win elections. Whether trying to enlighten the Conservative leadership, to engineer a reconciliation between Conservatives and National Liberals, to create a workable majority in the Reichstag, or to dampen radical nationalist opposition to his foreign policy, Bethmann found that the success or failure of his own reform agenda was inextricably linked to the fate of reformism within the Conservative Party.

This essay can address only certain aspects of relations between the Conservatives and the government between 1909 and 1914. In selecting which events could illuminate this relationship, considerable weight was given to Bethmann's own account, written in July 1914, indicating where he felt the decisive turns on the Conservatives' road to Philippi had been taken: "Whoever, as in 1909, Morocco, and 1913, not only fails to spare the cabinet, but directly attacks it in an hour of need, and whoever, alleging that the regime does not sufficiently defend public authority, undermines it as the Conservatives ceaselessly do, has lost his right to a special position."[14] Thus the legacy of Chancellor Bülow's finance reform legislation of

---

14. Bethmann's marginalia to an article in the *Vossische Zeitung* entitled "Der Reichskanzler als Handlanger," 18 July 1914, in BA Koblenz, R43F, Reichskanzlei-Akten (hereafter Rkz.) Nr. 1392, Bl. 37.

1909 will be examined first, to emphasize the overwhelming importance of this caesura in the history of Wilhelmine Germany. Bülow's own ambivalent attitude toward the DKP will be highlighted, for Bethmann was not alone in failing to understand the larger implications of the Conservatives' drift toward opposition. Attention will be paid to Bethmann's ambivalent view of the Conservative Party during his first years of office, followed by a brief survey of the Conservatives' own attempts to reform and popularize their party. There will be a discussion of Bethmann's efforts to undermine the authority of Ernst von Heydebrand und der Lasa, the de facto leader of the Conservative Party who, the chancellor believed, had to be removed before DKP-government relations could be improved; and the acute conflict between Bethmann and Heydebrand over the Moroccan issue in 1911 will be considered from a number of points of view. Bethmann's military and tax legislation in 1912–13 will be discussed, and some concluding remarks will analyze the apparent political deadlock in Germany after 1912 by considering the personal and structural dimensions of the party-state relationship.

II

How did contemporaries view the political legacy Chancellor Bülow handed to his successor in July 1909? When the Conservatives provided the crucial votes to defeat Bülow's finance reform bill,[15] most observers knew that the end of this legislative battle did not resolve the deepest domestic crisis of Wilhelm II's reign. Even the finance reform question itself was too large to disappear immediately from political debate. The bitterness of the dispute in 1909 made it clear that the parties would continue to defend or attack the final legislation in the years ahead. The Conservatives claimed that the taxes they passed against Bülow's wishes were fair and provided the necessary added revenue. The liberals claimed with more justification that the Conservatives had refused any significant self-sacrifice for the national good because they had defeated an inheritance tax on estates; instead, the Junkers had placed

15. For details and further references, see P.-C. Witt, *Die Finanzpolitik des deutschen Reiches von 1903 bis 1913* (Lübeck and Hamburg, 1970); Katharine Anne Lerman, *The Chancellor as Courtier: Bernhard von Bülow and the Governance of Germany, 1900–1909* (Cambridge, 1990), pp. 235–47.

the increased fiscal burden of indirect taxation on the shoulders of less prosperous consumers. Thus the finance reform of 1909 came to symbolize the refusal of Germany's aristocracy to recognize and accept the consequences of economic decline.

At the height of the battle over the finance reform in April 1909, even Bülow painted a stark picture of conservatism digging its own grave. In marginalia to notes prepared by his chancellory chief, Friedrich Wilhelm von Loebell, Bülow predicted that the Conservative Party's opposition to the inheritance tax would leave a legacy of "confusion, bitterness, [and] depression among wide circles of Conservatives, especially in middle Germany, in the cities, among officials, lower-middle classes, etc." Bülow also foresaw "real (not imaginary) compensations to the liberal-democratic idea in Prussia," meaning that the Conservatives would be forced to accept a Prussian franchise reform.[16] In his last major Reichstag speech of 16 June 1909, Bülow told the Conservatives it would be a long time before they had another chancellor who represented "true conservative interests" and who defended the legitimate long-term needs of agriculture.[17] Overturning the government's proposed finance reform, Bülow continued, would be a grave political error, for "victory in the present is often the road to defeat in the future." The Conservatives, however, refused to heed Bülow's warning. Therefore, on 13 July 1909, the day before his resignation, Bülow declared in an interview[18] that future socialist gains at the polls would prove that the Conservatives had played a "frivolous gambit" with the interests of the monarchy and the nation. Although Bülow later wrote that, like Cassandra, he hoped his prophesies would not come true, he predicted in this interview that the Conservatives' action could be "the starting point of a trend that creates embittered party conflicts, brings forth unnatural party groupings, and is detrimental to the welfare of the nation." To the Conservatives he declared: "We will see each other at Philippi."

In the summer of 1909, then, Bülow was utterly alienated from the Conservative Party; he sincerely believed that the DKP

16. Marginalia (8 April) to notes of 6 April 1909, cited in Witt, *Finanzpolitik*, p. 275.

17. *RT Sten. Ber.*, vol. 237, pp. 8585–8589.

18. For the following, Bülow, *Denkwürdigkeiten*, vol. 2, pp. 520–22; K. von Westarp, "Die Konservative Partei und das Ende des Bülowblocks," in *Süddeutsche Monatshefte* 28, no. 6 (Sonderheft: *Fürst Bülow*): 416ff.

was rushing to its ruin.[19] In drafting his resignation speech in July, he included more far-reaching criticism than finally appeared in his Reichstag address. In taking quite different attitudes toward the DKP in his private thoughts than in his public statements, Bülow adopted contradictory positions characteristic of Bethmann. Asking Loebell – whom he regarded as his "political conscience" – for comments on his draft speech, Bülow wrote: "I might also say: the Conservative Party is using a great national question to initiate a trial of strength [*Machtprobe*] against the government and the chancellor. . . . It thereby damages the authority of the government . . . [and] the foundations upon which the Conservative Party rests."[20]

Nevertheless, in his Reichstag speech of 16 June and in his correspondence in years to come, Bülow continued to assert that he was "politically conservative."[21] In his first sustained retrospective look at the events of 1909,[22] he distinguished between "State Conservatism" and "Party Conservatism." The government's espousal of the latter "partisan" form of conservatism, he felt, would prove fatal. Although Bülow was "absolutely convinced that the Conservative faction went astray in the year 1909," he wrote that "we must never fail to appreciate what the conservative element has achieved for the political life of Prussia and Germany." It would be a "sad loss" if the party ceased to occupy a position in parliamentary and political life that was worthy of its past. In fact, the only indication of Bülow's stormy break with the Conservatives was his insistence on applying adjectives such as "sound" conservatism or conservatism's "best ideals." With these qualifying words and thoughts, Bülow groped to identify the necessity of a moderate or reform-oriented brand of conservatism in Wilhelmine Germany.

19. See Bülow to Loebell, 23 January 1910, for reflections on the political irresponsibility of contemporary parties and parliament; in BA Koblenz, NL Friedrich Wilhelm von Loebell, Nr. 6, Bl. 91. I am grateful to Wolfgang von Loebell for allowing me to use this collection.

20. Undated notes [July 1909] and Bülow to Loebell, 9 Aug. 1909, in ibid, Nr. 6, Bl. 48, 58.

21. Bülow to Rudolf von Valentini, 31 August 1909, in Geheimes Staatsarchiv Preußischer Kulturbesitz, Abteilung Merseburg (hereafter cited as GStA Merseburg), NL R. von Valentini, Nr. 3, Bl. 6–7; Bülow to Axel von Kaphengst, 31 March 1911, in BA Koblenz, NL Loebell, Nr. 7, Bl. 23; Bülow, *Denkwürdigkeiten*, vol. 2, p. 522.

22. B. von Bülow, *Imperial Germany* (New York, 1914), pp. 163ff.

If the Conservative leadership faced a Herculean task in defending its actions before the public and in making good the damage wrought by Bülow's Parthian shot, Bethmann Hollweg's task of reestablishing Conservative-government relations could better be described as Sisyphean. A common thread running through contemporary assessments was that Bülow had left Bethmann an "unfortunate legacy."[23] What was Bethmann's political grand strategy to "liquidate" this legacy? The complexities of Bethmann's personal and political motives must be emphasized at the outset, as must the Conservatives' suspicions of him even before he assumed office.

Neither Bethmann's personality nor his politics much impressed Conservative leaders. Ernst von Heydebrand, the Conservative leader in the Prussian House of Deputies, had told Bülow in March 1905: "As minister of the interior we need a man with a strong hand and backbone. . . . Instead you give us a philosopher."[24] But Heydebrand was neither fair nor accurate in describing Bethmann as a mere philosopher. For the chancellor indicated with his first major legislative initiatives that he would take practical steps to mollify public opinion regarding the Conservative Party. In the first Prussian state ministry meeting over which he presided as chancellor,[25] Bethmann told his colleagues that his aim was "to help the Conservatives make good the errors they had committed," or, as he later put it, to help them "regain touch with the mood of the people." With this goal in mind, Bethmann attempted in early 1910 to achieve a compromise between the Conservatives and the National Liberals over a bill to reform the Prussian three-class franchise.

The chancellor certainly had reason to expect success. As Bülow had predicted, both the Conservatives and the government were under extreme pressure to avoid being tarred with the reactionary brush. A great coup could be scored if, con-

23. *Das Tagebuch der Baronin Spitzemberg*, ed. R. Vierhaus (Göttingen, 1960), p. 520; see also Crown Prince Wilhelm to Bülow [n.d.] in Bülow, *Denkwürdigkeiten*, vol. 2, p. 520, and Kaiser Wilhelm to Bethmann, 31 December 1911, cited in H.-G. Zmarzlik, *Bethmann Hollweg als Reichskanzler 1909–1914* (Düsseldorf, 1957), p. 43.

24. Bülow, *Denkwürdigkeiten*, vol. 2, p. 181; cf. *Walther Rathenau. Tagebuch 1907–1922*, ed. H. Pogge von Strandmann (Düsseldorf, 1967), p. 141.

25. Prussian state ministry meeting protocol in GStA Merseburg, Rep. 90a B III 2 b Nr. 6, Bd. 158, 14 July 1909, Bl. 200–201 (hereafter cited as GStA Merseburg, St. Min., Bd., date, Bl.).

trary to expectations, the Conservatives proved generous in sharing a small part of their considerable power in Prussia. Bethmann's modest reform bill, however, pleased no one. When the government finally withdrew its legislation, it was obvious to most contemporaries that the Conservatives were still reactionaries. The Baroness von Spitzemberg, a shrewd observer of Wilhelmine politics and personalities, wrote in her diary in March 1910 that "the Conservatives are advocating barren, obtuse reaction," although she added that "the liberals are turning more and more into radicals."[26] Bethmann's choice between the two policy positions, however, was no choice at all, at least when he considered the political realities of the situation, not his personal inclinations. For as the baroness noted, during the franchise reform crisis Bethmann became all the more "firm and 'conservative'" as he saw "how little reliance can be placed on the liberals, with whom he would really gladly govern."

Because the chancellor's first major initiative to modernize the Conservative Party had failed, the government suffered a double defeat. Bethmann recognized in May 1910 that the franchise reform debate had widened "the chasm between Conservatives and National Liberals" and driven the latter further to the left.[27] More pointedly, he observed that the Conservatives, "with their personal, social, religious, and political hubris and intolerance, . . . have succeeded in focusing everyone's disgust and dissatisfaction on the three-class suffrage, which is generally seen as an expression of Junker predominance." Nonetheless, when Bethmann told his Prussian state ministry colleagues, as they were considering another franchise reform bill in December 1913, that any future reform had to be agreeable to the Conservatives, he illustrated the impossibility of proceeding decisively against the self-proclaimed protectors of Prussian interests.[28]

III

The Conservatives had their own solutions to the problem of overcoming the debacle of June 1909. Two parallel efforts can

26. *Tagebuch Spitzemberg*, ed. Vierhaus, p. 519.

27. For this and the following, see Jarausch, *Enigmatic Chancellor*, pp. 78–79, 445.

28. GStA Merseburg, St. Min., Bd. 162, 31 Dec. 1913, Bl. 192ff.

be identified. First, the Conservatives sought to assert their independence from the government and the other right-wing parties. They emphasized that their party was a "people's party" capable of standing alone; they worked to regain the allegiance of groups they had alienated in 1909; and they attempted to expand their constituency to new social groups and geographical regions. Thus they aimed simultaneously to explain their actions in 1909 and to breathe new life into the party apparatus. Second, some Conservatives, especially at the provincial level, sought to reestablish contact with whomever in government or National Liberal circles was willing to consider an alliance on terms that did not require an abandonment of fundamental Conservative policies. These two strategies were contradictory in some ways but mutually enhancing in others. The second strategy more directly affected the party's relationship with Bethmann. However, as noted previously, Bethmann could not afford to ignore any signs from within the DKP that a new orientation might be considered.

For Heydebrand, for the Conservative Reichstag caucus chairman, Oskar von Normann, and for Normann's eventual successor, Count Kuno von Westarp, the first priority in the second half of 1909 was to dampen dissent among the party rank and file.[29] Between the defeat of the government's finance reform in June and the staging of a general party congress in November, the German political press was filled with reports of defections from the party. The National Liberals printed a twenty-eight page brochure chronicling this disaffection with the party leadership in virtually all regions of Germany.[30] Pastors, government officials, retired army officers, members of the *Mittelstand,* and Conservatives in urban and semi-urban areas figured prominently in this rebellion. Bülow's prophecy about the internal agonies the DKP would experience seemed to be coming true with a vengeance.

29. Fuller references for the following section are found in J. Retallack, "Reformist Conservatism and Political Mobilization: A Study of Factionalism and Movements for Reform within the German Conservative Party, 1876 to 1914" (D.Phil. diss., University of Oxford, 1983).

30. *Konservative unter sich* (Berlin, 1909); provincial reverberations are found in *Die Reichsfinanzreform 1909 im Lichte der Öffentlichkeit*, ed. W. Schmidt [general secretary of the Conservative Party in Baden], 2nd ed. (Karlsruhe, 1909); and *Zur Steuer der Wahrheit*, von einem ostpreußischen Konservativen (Königsberg, 1909).

Members of Conservative associations in the Berlin suburbs led the grass-roots rebellion in that summer of discontent. The Pankow Movement or Conservative Union argued for new policies and new organizational initiatives to help the Conservative Party "regain its force of attraction."[31] Although the Conservative Union attacked the party leadership's handling of the finance reform issue directly, it did not abandon traditional conservatism. It claimed it wished to work within the party, to help men from academic, industrial, trade, small-business, and working-class backgrounds gain more influence in policy formation. The participation of these elements, the union claimed, would free the DKP from the overwhelming influence of the Agrarian League and set it on the path to becoming a true people's party.

When Conservatives met for their long postponed general party congress in November 1909, the party leadership regarded the congress, not incorrectly, as a useful outlet for these reform proposals and general frustrations. It called on local and regional Conservative associations to establish new and "independent" organizations throughout the Reich. A deeper and more critical self-evaluation, however, was impossible. The need to present an image of party unity and steadfastness overwhelmed all other considerations. Hence, despite these efforts on the part of the DKP leadership to suppress the issue, the debate about Conservatism's "renewal" and "modernization" persisted. In response, Heydebrand abandoned his disinclination to speak at provincial rallies[32] and did his utmost to emphasize the party's confidence, unity, and progressive character. As he declared at a congress of Pomeranian Conservatives in late 1910: "We are destined to be a party of the future, . . . a true people's party, . . . a liberally oriented party."[33]

The Conservative Party's *Sturm und Drang* of 1909 prompted a number of other novel campaigns to increase its following. One of these was the so-called "drive to the west." In December 1909 the leading Conservative newspaper, the *Kreuzzeitung,* published a letter from Cologne in which the correspondent noted that most western Germans believed in liber-

31. "Konservative Männer in Stadt und Land!" Founding proclamation of the Konservative Vereinigung.

32. K. Graf von Westarp, *Konservative Politik im letzten Jahrzehnt des Kaiserreiches,* 2 vols. (Berlin, 1935), vol. 1, pp. 397–98.

33. *Parteitag des Konservativen Provinzialvereins für Pommern* (n.p., n.d. [1910]), pp. 31, 87, 94.

al demonologies of reactionary, boorish east-Elbian Junkers. To counter this notion, Conservative test-candidacies were to be launched in the west. The west's rising demographic importance, the potential reservoir of Protestant conservatives there, and the dissatisfaction with the leftward trend of the National Liberal Party under its leader, Ernst Bassermann, also argued for a long-term commitment from the Conservatives. Such a commitment, the *Kreuzzeitung* wrote, could help undermine the arguments of the Conservative Unionists about Conservative one-sidedness and unpopularity; it could show that the DKP was "a people's party in the best sense of the word."[34]

By prompting discussion about conservatism's role in an industrializing society and the DKP's function as a party of all interests and classes, the "drive to the west" prompted another controversy about "urban conservatism." In 1910 Heydebrand announced that party secretariats would be set up in Westphalia and the Rhine Province, two of the most urbanized provinces in Prussia. Then in May 1911 the Conservatives staged their first large party congress in a west-German metropolis, attracting 2,000 supporters in Cologne. In the next two years urban associations were founded or expanded in many localities, including the Hansa cities. These initiatives, like that of the Conservative Union earlier, were greeted enthusiastically by less traditional editors of Conservative newspapers. A contributor to the influential *Reichsbote*,[35] for example, wrote that "in the time of the universal franchise, a party must *go out among the people*: it must show the masses where their true friends lie." What was needed was "a Conservative people's party," this writer added, true to old Christian-Conservative principles but incorporating "the challenge of Conservative progress!" The Conservatives' opponents, however, heaped scorn on the party's achievements in this westward drive. After the Reichstag elections of 1912, tangible evidence was available to chronicle DKP failure: the Conservatives' share of the vote in cities of over 100,000 inhabitants was only 2.2 percent. Yet Conservative efforts in the cities did not end in 1912, and the hope persisted that the DKP could, by representing itself as a party of progress, expand beyond its traditional domains in rural eastern Prussia.

34. *Kreuzzeitung*, 10 February 1910.
35. *Reichsbote*, 13 August 1912, original emphasis.

The crisis of 1909 also compelled the party to seek new social groups for support. Press reports as early as 1909 alleged that Conservative women were organizing themselves. In 1912, the *Kreuzzeitung* printed a letter from an unnamed Conservative countess who claimed that previous Reichstag elections would have turned out very differently if Conservative women had been more active in politics.[36] Educated women from the upper classes were discovering too late that they had a duty to protect "everything that is holy to mankind." (As this countess observed, many of the 110 Social Democratic deputies in the 1912 Reichstag had had "bad mothers.") A positive but careful tone was adopted by the Conservative press when a Conservative Women's Union was finally established in April 1913. The *Reichsbote* saw the union as another defence against "disbelief" and "cosmopolitan anti-nationalism," while the *Kreuzzeitung* observed that although "politics is without doubt a hateful business," the new age demanded "new comrades in arms." Yet doubts quickly arose in Conservative circles about the organization's reliability as a bulwark against women's emancipation. By the beginning of the war, the majority of Conservatives appeared to believe that the organization of Conservative women in 1913 had merely opened another Pandora's box full of modern, progressive, democratic spirits.

The same conclusion emerged from the shorter prewar history of the Young Conservative movement. In early July 1914, an Imperial Young Conservative Association was founded by a collection of academic youths in Bonn, presenting Heydebrand and Westarp with a fait accompli that was made all the more painful by the left-wing press's emphasis on the association's idealism. The liberal press linked the group's manifesto to earlier calls from within the Conservative Party for a broader commitment to urban, academic, and non-agrarian elements within the conservative milieu.[37] Worried by the implications of this new departure, Westarp spoke of needing to put a "good face on a bad affair."[38]

36. See *Kreuzzeitung*, 4, 8, and 11 March 1912; *Deutsche Tageszeitung*, 15 November 1912.

37. *Freisinnige Zeitung*, 12 July 1914; *Berliner Tageblatt*, 22 July 1914.

38. Westarp to Heydebrand, 8 and 15 July 1914, from the archive of Dr. Friedrich Freiherr Hiller von Gaertringen, Gaertringen: Heydebrand-Westarp Korrespondenz (transcription). I am grateful to Freiherr Hiller von Gaertringen for providing me with a copy of this correspondence.

It is significant that the party congress of November 1909 and the provincial rallies at which Heydebrand spoke in 1910 were Conservative, not merely right-wing, assemblies. There was no serious talk of forming unified associations with either women or youth groups within the National Liberal and Free Conservative parties. Even urban conservatism and the "drive to the west" were hailed in the Conservative press as means to make the Conservative Party independent. But running parallel to these efforts was another campaign to revive the party's influence. This campaign was pursued by various groups and individuals inside and outside the party who wanted to moderate Conservative policies, engineer a Conservative-National Liberal rapprochement, and resurrect a workable parliamentary majority against the Left.

A good deal is known about certain features of this effort, and relatively little is known about others. The work of Dirk Stegmann and others has confirmed the important ties between Conservative agrarians and large industrialists in 1909 and after.[39] We also know many details about the cooperation between the Agrarian League, the Central Association of German Industrialists, and certain *Mittelstand* groups. This cooperation, influenced by a deepening gulf between radical nationalists and Bethmann, eventually led in the autumn of 1913 to the formation of the so-called Cartel of Productive Estates (Kartell der schaffenden Stände).[40]

Essentially, these efforts were carried out in boardrooms, in the halls of parliament, in government offices, and in correspondence between the leaders of the party caucuses and executive committees. However, they were all complicated by the need to find a workable antisocialist consensus at the middle and lower party levels. The rallying together (*Sammlung*) of agricultural, industrial, and *mittelständisch* interest groups failed to overcome the gulf between the National Liberal and Conservative parties, reflected in the continuing polemics between Bassermann and Heydebrand. This was true even after the 1912 elections, which are too easily assumed to have compelled parties facing a common threat to "bury the hatch-

---

39. See Stegmann, *Die Erben Bismarcks*, passim.

40. I doubt whether this Cartel had the practical political effect that is commonly ascribed to it. Stegmann, *Die Erben Bismarcks*; Eley, *Reshaping the German Right*; and Peck, *Radicals and Reactionaries*, all discuss it in some detail.

et" (as the contemporary press frequently, but incorrectly, announced).

In many regions of Germany, it was the antagonism between the NLP and DKP, not their cooperation, that led to marked increases in organizational and agitational activity. Far from subsiding after the "red" elections of 1912, this activity accelerated substantially.[41] On 14 January 1912, at the height of the Reichstag election campaign, Bassermann wrote to the left-wing National Liberal leader in Saxony, Gustav Stresemann, lamenting the NLP's failure to win Pomerania or East Prussia from the Conservatives.[42] But in 1913, the debate whether the National Liberals' efforts in the eastern provinces of Prussia would pay off still raged in the party's executive committee meetings. Local NLP chairmen in these provinces continued to express confidence that Conservative ascendence could be broken down, and their correspondence concentrated more than ever on problems associated with the disruptive NLP-DKP relationship.[43] Though the Conservatives claimed that the socialists were their main enemies, the National Liberals saw themselves in a two-front war against radicals on both the left and right.

As both parties attempted to invade the traditional political territory of the other, spectacular clashes resulted. Old Conservative domains in the east suddenly came within the view of National Liberal eyes still smarting from the finance reform defeat. The German Peasants League (Deutscher Bauernbund), formed in 1909 to attract farmers who did not condone the Agrarian League's extreme interest politics, spearheaded

41. Space does not permit elaboration here. This accelerating organizational effort was evident in the agenda for a delegates' meeting of the East Prussian Conservative Association in October 1913: every point on the meeting's agenda dealt with some aspect of organization: finances, a "winter work plan," speakers' courses, a party secretariat, by-elections, support of the local press, and so on. GStA Merseburg, NL Wolfgang Kapp, CVIII Nr. 3, Bl. 255. A major function of the *Mitteilungen aus der konservativen Partei*, a party newssheet launched in 1908, was to disseminate organizational information to local DKP groups.

42. BA Koblenz, NL Eugen Schiffer, Nr. 9, H. 1, Bl. 23.

43. See "Sitzungen des geschäftsführenden Ausschusses" [1913], meeting of 12 November 1913, in BA Koblenz, R45I, Nationalliberale Partei, Nr. 4, Bl. 65ff.; the NLP's "Organisations-Statistik 1907–1912" (ibid., Bl. 19); and the "Jahresberichte landschaftlicher Organisationen und Wahlkreise" (ibid., Bl. 21ff. and 31ff.), to compare reports for 1911 and 1912. On East Prussia and West Prussia, see the report of A. Wynecken to the NLP's executive committee, 18 October 1913, in BA Potsdam, NL Ernst Bassermann, Nr. 9, Bl. 87.

this "drive to the east." Conversely, the Conservatives' "drive to the west" signalled an unwillingness to concede constituencies west of the Elbe River to the National Liberals. Even the Free Conservative Party, despite its claim to be the ideal "middle party,"[44] had to shape its policies within the constraints of this antagonism. This led it to reorganize and expand for the first time into regions where it had previously been willing to support candidates from the other two parties.[45] Thus the period after 1909 saw many conservative "refoundings" on the local level, as the two conservative parties strove to build up their separate provincial organizations.

It is impossible to document this process in detail here. But these signs of the continuing estrangement between the right-wing parties are a salutary reminder that any claims for the hegemony of the *Sammlung* must be limited. Nor should one forget that the intentions of the leaders of the economic and nationalist interest groups were restated, compromised, and often condemned to failure by the political necessity of working through the established parties. As long as these pressure groups wanted to exert their influence in parliament, they had to work in part through the traditional party machines, themselves undergoing disruptive and unpredictable changes. The parties, as David Blackbourn has put it, were an essential link between the functionaries in the various interest groups and the wirepullers in government.[46] Therefore, before an accurate picture of right-wing dynamism can emerge, greater attention will have to be paid to party leaders at all levels – including personalities such as Bassermann and Heydebrand whose commitments, first and foremost, were to their individual parties.

IV

By 1910/11 it had become apparent that Heydebrand's personal authority within the Conservative Party, together with

44. The *Frankfurter Zeitung*, 19 October 1912, referred to it as the "little club with room for all."

45. See, for example, E. Deetjen, *Freikonservativ! Die nationale Mittelpartei* (Breslau, 1913); *Die Partei der Zukunft*, von einem Deutschen (Leipzig, 1914); *Die Bayerische Reichspartei 1911–1913* (Munich, 1914); and the FKP's *Rundschreiben*, n.d. [early 1912], to regional party leaders, in BA Koblenz, NL Alfred Hugenberg, Nr. 31, Bl. 22ff.

46. D. Blackbourn, *Class, Religion and Local Politics in Germany: The Centre Party in Württemberg before 1914* (New Haven, Conn., and London, 1980), p. 11.

Bassermann's refusal to seek an alliance on the right, was undermining all efforts to end the NLP-DKP impasse. In December 1910 and then again almost a year later, Bethmann Hollweg wrote to the Prussian envoy in Baden, Carl von Eisendecher, that Heydebrand was leading the Conservatives on "disastrous" and "demagogic" paths.[47] By February 1912 he had concluded that "as long as Bassermann and Heydebrand remain as leaders, I see a very black future."[48] By May 1912, the Baroness von Spitzemberg reported that Bethmann was "disconsolate" due to "the lack of political maturity and reliability among the leaders of the bourgeois parties."[49]

During these years, Bethmann sought to overcome the personal antagonism between Bassermann and Heydebrand, and between them and himself, through personal diplomacy. He repeatedly attempted, usually indirectly, to engineer personal meetings between these party leaders; but invariably he failed, and not only because of Heydebrand's obstinacy. In August 1910, for example, Bethmann tried to act as a middleman, allegedly having received conciliatory gestures from both men. However, the attempt misfired, "due to the stupidest blindness of the National Liberals."[50] Bethmann then turned his attention to recruiting pro-government figures within the Conservative Party to report on internal party relations and to undermine Heydebrand's authority.[51]

A confidential letter that Bethmann wrote in mid-1911 to a leading Conservative and the president of the Reichstag, Count Hans von Schwerin-Löwitz, illustrates the tense and ambiguous relationship between the Conservatives and the government.[52] Because Schwerin was highly respected within

47. For this and the following, see Bethmann Hollweg to Eisendecher, letters of 27 December 1910, 16 November 1911, and 22 February 1912, in PA AA Bonn, NL Eisendecher, Nr. 1/2, Bl. 20–21, 24, 29–30.

48. The double meaning here derived from the "black" Catholic Center Party, which was aligned with the Conservatives after 1909 in the "Black-Blue Bloc."

49. Diary entry for 27 May 1912; *Baronin Spitzemberg*, ed. Vierhaus, p. 545.

50. Comments taken from Bethmann to Loebell, 16 August 1911, in BA Koblenz, Rkz. Nr. 1391/5, Bl. 192; see also below.

51. This was certainly not a novel practice. On similar tactics pursued by earlier chancellors, see J. Retallack, "Conservatives *contra* Chancellor: Official Responses to the Spectre of Conservative Demagoguery from Bismarck to Bülow," *Canadian Journal of History* 20, no. 2 (1985): 203–36.

52. Bethmann Hollweg to Schwerin-Löwitz, 1 July 1911 [draft 29 June 1911], in BA Koblenz, Rkz. Nr. 1391, Bl. 110.

the party and had just received national press attention by disavowing Heydebrand's campaign tactics,[53] this letter is especially noteworthy. Bethmann appealed to Schwerin's more traditional antiparliamentary and antipopular instincts by linking criticism of Heydebrand to a broader attack on recent developments in party politics. Bethmann said he could understand how the flagrant fraternization of left liberals with the Social Democrats, the unreliable policies of Bassermann, and the radicalism of the liberal Hansa League (Hansabund) might provoke the Conservatives and make them stubborn. However, it would be "to deny the traditions of the Conservative Party" and to "parliamentarize" it if the DKP were to compete with the other parties for partisan profit: "Political principles are thereby thrown overboard."[54] Then Bethmann pointed out the dangers of a Conservative policy explicitly calculated to appear "popular." The Conservatives seemed to fear that if their party did not fish for votes like other parties, it would not remain competitive at the polls. This might be true, the chancellor wrote, "if we were steering toward the parliamentary system of government." But such a system was "constitutionally impossible" for both Prussia and the Reich.

> Therefore, all this newly inaugurated policy achieves is that the Conservatives, by giving up the traditions that provide their strongest support in the countryside, are degraded to the level of the other parties who live from party egoism, and that the long-standing reciprocal relationship between it and the government is destroyed. The end result will be the weakening of the conservative principle and thereby the acceleration of democratization. I am watching this unhealthy process with growing concern.

Finally, Bethmann lauded Schwerin for speaking out against "party egoism" in his recent speech, because he wanted to encourage such independent thinking in the party. Although he did not express himself so explicitly in the final version, the deleted phrases in Bethmann's draft clearly suggest this strat-

53. In a speech of 27 June, Schwerin had criticized Heydebrand's declaration that Conservatives could never give their support to a left liberal, even when he was running against a socialist.

54. This argument, in fact, had been made by Bethmann on many other occasions. See Bethmann to Eisendecher, 27 December 1910, in PA AA Bonn, NL Eisendecher, Nr. 1/2, Bl. 20–21; Bethmann Hollweg to Bülow, 14 July 1911, in BA Koblenz, NL Bülow, Nr. 64, Bl. 26–36.

egy. He wrote that "improvement can emerge only from the midst of the Conservative Party itself."

Schwerin's correspondence with Bethmann reinforces other evidence that leading Conservatives outside Heydebrand's small circle were deeply worried by antagonisms among Conservatives, National Liberals, and the government. This evidence comes most notably from Conservative leaders in the provinces. The reasons these men were willing to speak out against Heydebrand's policies are not difficult to discern, for they faced the troubling task of reconciling local and national interests by adapting official Conservative doctrine to circumstances and attitudes in their smaller homelands. In middle and western Germany, they tried to deemphasize the Prussian roots of Conservatism, highlighting instead the party's alleged progressive, enlightened, and up-to-date character. Yet they also had to respect Heydebrand's immense personal authority within the DKP and work within the limitations of the National Liberal-Conservative conflicts that his attitude perpetuated. Moreover, the Conservative Party's national leaders and their war-cry of "no surrender" after 1909 made it much more difficult, if not impossible, for these regional leaders to form ad hoc Landtag alliances. This was true especially in regions where members of both parties recognized that only right-wing unity could hold back the socialist tide.[55]

There is little doubt that a study of party relations in the states and provinces of the Reich could tell us a great deal about the viability of the German political system in the years before 1914. Yet considerable evidence already exists to suggest that provincial observers recognized the difficulty the DKP faced in reconciling regional and national priorities.[56]

55. The Kingdom of Saxony was perhaps exemplary in this regard; see further, J. Retallack, "Antisocialism and Electoral Politics in Regional Perspective: The Kingdom of Saxony," in *Elections, Mass Politics, and Social Change in Modern Germany: New Perspectives*, ed. L. E. Jones and J. Retallack (New York and Cambridge, 1992), pp. 49–91; idem, "'What Is to Be Done?' The Red Specter, Franchise Questions, and the Crisis of Conservative Hegemony in Saxony, 1896–1909," *Central European History* 23, no. 4 (1990): 271–312.

56. See, for example, the brochures by W. Albers (cited in note 2) and by W. Schmidt, general secretary of the Conservative Party in Baden: *"Großblock" oder "bürgerlicher Block"? Ein politischer Wegweiser für alle rechtsstehenden Wähler in Baden* (Heidelberg, n.d. [1911]). For a perspective on how Conservatives confronted this problem in the 1870s and 1880s, see J. Retallack, "Anti-Semitism, Conservative Propaganda, and Regional Politics in Late Nineteenth-Century Germany," *German Studies Review* 11, no. 3 (1988): 377–403.

One such account is the unpublished memoir of a leading Conservative Landtag deputy from Silesia, Alfred von Goßler.[57] Like so many others, Goßler's retrospective commentary on caucus life under Heydebrand's leadership was filled with contradiction and inconsistency. For example, he combined an enthusiasm for traditional Conservative ideals with a regret that the party "defended its position in such an obstinate manner" by pursuing "partisan and interest politics." At one point Goßler reported his outrage at Heydebrand's boast that "the Prussian ministers dance to my tune." Yet later he praised Heydebrand's "eminent talents." In a similar tone, a Baden party leader, Baron Udo von La Roche-Starkenfels, wrote to Arnold Wahnschaffe, chief of the Reich chancellory, in October 1910, asking for government funds to support his "energetic" and "loyal" Conservative organization struggling in Baden, that "little land of liberalism."[58] La Roche described Conservatism in Baden as "not feudal-conservative in the narrow Prussian sense, but rather more Christian-conservative, with inclusion of the Christian-national workers and also with the wish to see the right-wing elements of the National Liberals à la Heyl[59] join us."

The urgency with which Conservatives in the Kingdom of Saxony confronted this dilemma was particularly acute because of the socialist threat there. As leader of the Saxon Conservative *Landesverein*, Dr. Paul Mehnert[60] wrote to Loebell in the late summer of 1911 that it was a "duty to the Fatherland" for the right-wing elements to "stress what unites them and push into the background what divides them." Mehnert

57. BA-Militärarchiv, Freiburg i. Br., NL Alfred von Goßler, Nr. 1, Bl. 40ff., "Erinnerungen." I am grateful to Frau Toni von Goßler for allowing me access to this collection.

58. La Roche to Wahnschaffe, 7 October 1910, BA Koblenz, Rkz. Nr. 1391, Bl. 86. The Baden case is illuminated in an unpublished manuscript by H.-J. Kremer, "Die Konservative Partei im Großherzogtum Baden 1876–1914: Geschichte und Politik der Konservativen Partei Badens in der Korrespondenz der Parteiführung. Eine Dokumentation."

59. He is referring to the National Liberal agrarian, Baron Cornelius von Heyl zu Herrnsheim, who had resigned from the NLP's Reichstag caucus in protest against its vote on the finance reform bill of 1909.

60. For more information on Mehnert, his dealings with the Reich and Saxon governments, and his broader assessment of relations between the NLP and DKP, see my essays cited in nn. 51 and 55. The correspondence between Mehnert, Loebell, and Bethmann in August 1911 is in BA Koblenz, Rkz. Nr. 1391/5, Bl. 192–98.

hoped that the "expected" ouster of left-wing National Liberals such as Stresemann would remove an "extremely unfortunate influence" on Bassermann. As he wrote: "If one allows the National Liberals to march further and further to the left, without making the attempt to hold to our side the better and – at least in national affairs – relatively sympathetic elements," then one could not later complain that the Reich was drifting into "liberal-democratic channels." Mehnert's letter is particularly interesting because he had not turned to Heydebrand or the official party leadership with this report: "I fear that at the moment they are not to be won for such considerations." Thus, although Mehnert described himself as a "strict party man," he wrote to Loebell that his allegiance to the DKP also compelled him "to keep in mind the general political situation." When Loebell sent a copy of Mehnert's letter to Bethmann, he acknowledged that Mehnert's opinion was shared by all "reasonable men on the right and on the right wing of the National Liberals." Loebell also emphasized that Mehnert was correct "when he thinks skeptically about the Conservative Party leadership – that is, Heydebrand," and he added: "The errors have not yet ceased, and there is no understanding for farsighted politics."

At this point wholly preoccupied with the Morocco crisis, Bethmann replied that if the government were "not to come wholly and irrevocably under the domination of the Center, a bridge between the National Liberals and the Conservatives must be established." This, he wrote to Loebell, was exactly what had been attempted a year ago, but at that point the plan had been torpedoed by the National Liberals: "They demanded as conditions for a reconciliation with the Conservatives Prussian franchise [reform] and [an] inheritance tax!" Displaying his characteristic ambivalence, Bethmann wrote that "in the intervening time the chances [for this reconciliation] have become worse and become better." Most of what followed, however, was pessimistic. That pessimism was predicated not only on Bassermann's "unreliability" and "radicalism," but also on Heydebrand's "intractable dictatorial strain" and his clear indications that he wanted nothing to do with the National Liberals. As if struggling to identify his own allegiance, Bethmann finally conceded that he blamed conflicts between National Liberals and Conservatives more on Bassermann and Stresemann than on Heydebrand. The NLP's criticism of the government's position in the Morocco question was evidence of the party's "lack of political understanding," its "parliamentary swagger," and its "unscrupulousness" in exploiting national crises for partisan purposes. It was "no wonder," Bethmann observed, "that Conservative men feel their gorge rise" in the face of such conduct.[61] On the positive side, Bethmann saw a possibility for improvement because members of both parties were "beginning more and more to recognize the errors of leadership."

Were Bethmann and Loebell realistic in hoping that Heydebrand's opposition to reform or his authority within the Conservative Party could be shaken? The evidence suggests they were not. In fact, both men seriously underestimated Heydebrand's personal and political influence. A common thread running through contemporary descriptions of Heydebrand is the single-minded commitment with which he worked to preserve the power of the Conservative Party and of his native Prussia. Franz Sontag, the Pan-German enthusiast who once served on the staffs of the Conservatives' *Kreuzzeitung* and the Free Conservatives' *Post*, remarked in his unpublished memoirs that for Heydebrand, the logic of the Reich ended at the Prussian border: "On these frontier posts stood Herr v. Heydebrand . . . always ready to fight for Prussia, even against his king."[62] Eugen Schiffer, a leading right-wing National Liberal who periodically met secretly with Heydebrand, was also impressed by the directness of his manner and the sureness with which he pursued his goals.[63] Theodor Wolff, chief editor of the left-liberal *Berliner Tageblatt*, referred to the Conservative leader as a "huge talent,"[64] and Goßler, despite his differences with Heydebrand, described him as the "most important" and "most interesting" personality in parliament – "not only with-

61. Apparently, Bethmann's general impression of the NLP had not changed greatly since late 1910, when he had written that the Conservative defeat he foresaw in the next elections would lead to a more stable situation only if that defeat signified the victory of "moderate" [i.e., not left-wing] liberalism.

62. BA Koblenz, NL "J. Alter" [pseud. for Franz Sontag], Nr. 6, "Kampfjahre der Vorkriegszeit," pp. 27–28, for this and the following remarks.

63. BA Koblenz, NL Eugen Schiffer, Nr. 1, "Memorien," Heft 1, Bl. 34–47; unfortunately these entries cannot be dated precisely.

64. *Theodor Wolff. Tagebücher 1914–1919*, ed. B. Sösemann (Boppard, 1984), pt. 1, pp. 160, 350.

in the Conservative Party but in the whole political world of the day." Heydebrand possessed an "exceptional power-consciousness" that in combination with "a steel-like, unbending will" made him "a born leader."[65] The state secretary of the Reich treasury, Reinhold von Sydow, recalled in his own memoirs that one question was repeatedly asked in the Prussian state ministry when a crucial issue of domestic policy was discussed: "What does von Heydebrand say about this?"[66] When Heydebrand and Bethmann clashed in early 1911, Bethmann's secretary and confidant, Kurt Riezler, spoke of Heydebrand's ambition to topple the chancellor in almost titanic terms: he referred to the conflict as "German chancellor versus Prussia."[67] The same images were conjured up by Sontag, who described Heydebrand as a "knight without fear or reproach,"[68] and by Schiffer, who provided what remains the most compelling portrait of Heydebrand:

> He is actually called, not without reason, the uncrowned king of Prussia. In parliament and in the government he is known as "the little one," also not without justification. For he is remarkably small of stature, and therefore never stands behind, but rather beside, the speakers' podium. Naturally on the righthand side, in order to remain close to his gardes du corps and as far as possible from the Left. There he stands, shaking his little head back and forth, while, in a not very strong voice, he formulates his phrases, which are often more like a throne speech than a parliamentary one. Time and again he addresses the government benches and upbraids the men sitting there, sometimes with condescension, sometimes in a challenging or even threatening way; or he hurls lightning-bolts upon the Left, which are accompanied by the thunder of applause from his myrmidons.[69]

Heydebrand, then, was a superstar among Wilhelmine politicians. But was Bethmann justified in describing his attitude within the party as "dictatorial"? Could the governmental Conservatives within the DKP have moderated or disavowed Heydebrand's policies? If this second question were answered in the affirmative, Bethmann's strategy of under-

65. BA-Militärarchiv, Freiburg i. Br., NL Goßler, Nr. 1, Bl. 43.
66. Cited in D. Schoenbaum, *Zabern 1913* (London and Boston, 1982), p. 34.
67. *Kurt Riezler. Tagebücher, Aufsätze, Dokumente*, ed. K. D. Erdmann (Göttingen, 1972), pp. 168, 172.
68. BA Koblenz, NL "Alter," "Kampfjahre der Vorkriegszeit," pp. 27–28.
69. BA Koblenz, NL Schiffer, Nr. 1, "Memorien," Heft 1, Bl. 46.

mining Heydebrand's position would appear less baffling. However, contemporary reports suggest that Bethmann was simply deluding himself. Franz Sontag noted that Heydebrand headed an "absolutist regime" in the party executive, and other memoirs confirm this view. For although the Conservative Party had its "magnates' wing" and its governmentalists who often caused Heydebrand consternation, he always carried the day because the party was aware that it had no "Führer personality of comparable rank." The bankruptcy of Heydebrand's personal war on democracy became open to world view when the Conservative Party collapsed along with the monarchy in 1918. But to party insiders, the consequences of Heydebrand's intransigence were evident even before 1914. This is why so many anti-Semites, Pan-Germans, and other radical nationalists turned away from the party in the years after 1909.[70]

V

The story of Bethmann's unsuccessful policy in the second Moroccan crisis of 1911 is well-known.[71] On 9 November 1911 Bethmann defended his French settlement in the Reichstag.[72] It was on this occasion that Heydebrand, scheduled to speak after the chancellor, chose to prove that the DKP was indeed a "nationally-minded" party. He called the Morocco settlement a "worthless" agreement and charged that "these yieldings . . . will not secure us peace, . . . only our good German sword can do that." The import of Heydebrand's speech was not lost on anyone. For the first time, Heydebrand's bitter, pugilistic attitude – toward England and toward Bethmann himself – rivalled what Pan-Germans had been saying for years. Indeed, the crown prince highlighted the occasion by applauding conspicuously from the royal box when Bethmann's policy was called "a *defeat*, whether we say so or not."

Contemporaries and historians since have argued correctly that Heydebrand's dramatic attack on the government was a clear indication that the Conservatives were willing to join the

70. See further, Retallack, *Notables of the Right*, ch. 15.

71. See inter alia F. Fischer, *War of Illusions. German Policies from 1911 to 1914* (London, 1975), pp. 71–94; and Chickering's briefer account in *We Men Who Feel Most German*, pp. 262–67.

72. *RT Sten. Ber.*, vol. 268, pp. 7721ff. (9 November), and pp. 7756ff. (10 November 1911).

nationalist opposition to Bethmann. But Heydebrand was also attempting to redefine the Conservative Party's popular image and to reinvigorate a moribund antisocialist campaign for the Reichstag elections in January 1912. Whereas the SPD charged in its propaganda that the DKP was a chauvinistic agrarian interest group responsible for the new taxes of 1909 that had created such economic hardship in 1911, now Heydebrand was determined to show that his party was a dynamic, committed, independent, and "national" party, worthy of the allegiance of all the little men of Germany who shared his shame over the defeat of Bethmann's Moroccan policy.

The confrontation between Heydebrand and Bethmann in November 1911 undoubtedly opened more questions about the viability of Bethmann Hollweg's government than most Conservatives wished to address at this critical juncture. Liberals immediately anticipated a new direction for government policy and a new alignment of pro-government parties.[73] Some even dared to hope for a "grand bloc" of left-wing parties from the National Liberals to the socialists.[74] But just as interesting is the response from members of what might be called the moderate conservative establishment.[75] Rudolf von Valentini, chief of the Kaiser's civil cabinet, wrote to the shipping magnate Albert Ballin in mid–November that Bethmann's political standing had been "considerably improved" with the help of two people: "Heydebrand and the crown prince!"[76] The Baroness von Spitzemberg concurred, concluding that the Kaiser must be firmly behind Bethmann if the latter was able to reply to Heydebrand's attack with equally harsh words. Bethmann's speech, she noted, had "thrown the house into blank astonishment and brought about the 'retreat

73. See, for example, Albert Ballin to Bethmann, 17 November 1911, in GStA Merseburg, 2.2.1, Nr. 667, Bl. 86–87; and Arthur von Huhn (of the NLP's *Kölnische Zeitung*) to Bülow, 20 November 1911, in BA Koblenz, NL Bülow, Nr. 108, Bl. 55.

74. See Beverly Heckart, *From Bassermann to Bebel. The Grand Bloc's Quest for Reform in the Kaiserreich, 1900–1914* (New Haven, Conn., and London, 1974).

75. See BA Koblenz, Rkz. Nr. 1391/5, Bl. 204, discussing the election campaign; and reports from Prussian envoys in Stuttgart, Munich, and Dresden, in PA AA Bonn, Deutschland Nr. 125, Nr. 3 (Reichstagswahlen), Bd. 25, and Sachsen (Königreich), Nr. 48, Bd. 20. Still indispensible is J. Bertram, *Die Wahlen zum Deutschen Reichtag vom Jahre 1912* (Düsseldorf, 1964).

76. [Valentini] to Ballin, 15 November 1911, in GStA Merseburg, 2.2.1., Nr. 667, Bl. 80–81.

to a standstill.'"[77] That standstill – or standoff – was to many Conservatives preferable to acute conflict in the Reichstag. A contributor to the *Konservative Monatsschrift* in December 1911 spoke for these Conservatives in suggesting that the current political situation – "so infected with the spirit of negativism" – called for the DKP to preserve its "political independence" not through opposition but rather through a kind of "moderate governmentalism."[78]

The upcoming elections, however, precluded a normalization of relations. Thus, when the crown prince, after his "childish, student-like" display, remarked that "Heydebrand's speech was certainly splendid!" the Bavarian envoy in Berlin said to him: "Y[our] H[ighness], that was an election speech!" Heydebrand's motives were recognized by another conservative who was pleased that Bethmann had shown his teeth on 10 November. Count Karl von Wedel, the senior official (Statthalter) in Alsace-Lorraine who had once been considered as Bülow's successor, regretted that the Conservatives under Heydebrand had used the "most hateful, demagogic means to further their party goals." They had done this under Bismarck too, Wedel noted – but now the Conservatives were "seeking to excite the chauvinistic instincts of the people in order to secure their votes."[79]

One of the most enlightening perspectives on the Moroccan crisis is provided by a moderate Conservative who had already proven himself able to bridge the gap between party and state. Before he accepted the position as Bülow's chancellory chief in 1904, and in the midst of a distinguished civil service career that culminated in his appointment as minister of the interior in 1914, Friedrich Wilhelm von Loebell served on the Conservative Party's Committee of Five, where he must have worked closely with Heydebrand. Yet like the two chancellors he served, Loebell was incapable of reconciling a critical stance toward the DKP with an underlying commitment to conservatism. In his unpublished memoirs he wrote that "even though I was naturally aware of the constraints and

77. *Baronin Spitzemberg*, ed.Vierhaus, pp. 537–38, and for the following comments on the crown prince.

78. "Die Regierung und die konservative Partei. Ein Exkurs in die deutsche Verfassung," *Konservative Monatsschrift* 69, no. 3 (December 1911): 233.

79. Wedel to Eisendecher, 12 November 1911, PA AA Bonn, NL Eisendecher, Nr. 2/3, Bl. 95–96.

weaknesses of any party institution, I still always believed that one could work productively within the bounds of the German Conservative Party, if one always kept its great goals in sight."[80] To be sure, this creative enterprise required more clever tactics as the party's program became "sharper" and "more rigid," Loebell wrote. Experience in later years further tempered his original optimism about how easily one could pursue these larger goals, and replaced it with a "certain skepticism." Nevertheless, concluded Loebell, "in my innermost heart I always remained loyal to the fundamental beliefs of my party."

In November 1911, just two days after Heydebrand's outburst in the Reichstag, Loebell wrote to Bethmann. He was as critical of Heydebrand as were countless others on the moderate Right; but he appealed to the chancellor not to abandon the right-thinking elements among the Conservatives. With reference to Heydebrand's speech, Loebell asked: "Is it loyal, conservative policy to speak of washing away sins, to excite popular passions, . . . and to bellow for the applause of the rabble?" Loebell acknowledged that Heydebrand had delivered "a fine speech, a spirited and clever speech" – but it had been "the speech of an advocatus diaboli." Heydebrand's words had been neither respectful nor fair, and they had done more harm than good to the Fatherland by "tearing down the authority that, according to tradition and the party program, one should protect." Heydebrand erred, Loebell continued, if he believed that such a speech represented the mood of the party. Therefore, Bethmann was advised to take no action against the Conservatives, since "we must first survive [the elections of] 12 January without new complications." Loebell saw the possibility that the Reichstag elections might represent "the beginning of an improvement in our situation." Yet it was clear that he conceived of this new beginning, as Bethmann did, as a direct repudiation of Heydebrand's tactics: "It will indeed be a terrible Philippi for my poor party, which is led so falsely." Posterity would be hard on Heydebrand, Loebell concluded: "One will later say of him that he was a courageous man but a calamitous party leader."[81]

---

80. BA Koblenz, NL Loebell, Nrn. 26–27, "Erinnerungen."

81. Loebell to Bethmann Hollweg, 12 November 1911, in BA Koblenz, Rkz. Nr. 1391/5, Bl. 201; cf. P.-C. Witt, "Konservatismus als 'Überparteilichkeit'. Die Beamten der Reichskanzlei zwischen Kaiserreich und Weimarer Republik 1900–1933," in *Deutscher Konservatismus*, ed. Stegmann et al., pp. 231–80.

A similarly revealing retrospective on the crisis of November 1911 was provided by the National Liberal Eugen Schiffer. Schiffer felt that Bethmann's indecisive character had caused a great opportunity to be missed. At a parliamentary dinner, Bethmann once asked Schiffer why the National Liberals seemed to regard him as a "political ox." "Do I not do what I can?" inquired the chancellor:

> In plenary session I am attacked by Heydebrand. I answer him and earn generous applause. I do not believe I exaggerate when I say that I almost always emerge the victor from speaking duels with him. But after three days everyone has forgotten my triumph, and I am dealt with, attacked, and mobbed precisely as if I had not beaten him.

Schiffer's (alleged) reply to Bethmann was startling in its insight and forthrightness. The chancellor did not exploit his victories over the Conservatives, Schiffer explained, because he believed that he had to excuse himself for striking out at them too harshly. Schiffer told him: "You lay Heydebrand out in the sand; but then you help him up, shake the dust off his coat, and ask him if he has been hurt." Perhaps Bethmann felt himself "inwardly too closely bound to this party and its members." Or maybe it was his nature to avoid "brutal decisiveness." Perhaps Bethmann found it tactically important that things not come to a climax, to a full break. But what was at stake was not a matter of personal or party enmity but of great objective issues. One could not evade such issues. "Evasion can prepare the battle, but not replace it," Schiffer warned Bethmann. The battle had to be "taken up and fought out."[82]

Can we say that Schiffer's admonition had any effect on Bethmann's attitude toward the Conservatives? There is no clear answer. In his correspondence with Loebell, Riezler, Bülow, Valentini, and the Kaiser during November 1911, Bethmann explained why he replied so sharply to Heydebrand's attack and how he viewed the Conservatives' new strategy for popularity.[83] To Loebell he wrote that "you know me and

82. BA Koblenz, NL Schiffer, Nr. 1, "Memorien," Heft 2, Bl. 85–86.

83. Bethmann to Loebell, 20 November 1911 (reply to letter from Loebell of 12 November 1911), in BA Koblenz, Rkz. Nr. 1391/5, Bl. 201ff.; cf. Bethmann to Eisendecher, 16 November and 26 December 1911, in PA AA Bonn, NL Eisendecher, Nr. 1/2, Bl. 24ff.; Bethmann to Bülow, 21 November 1911, in BA Koblenz, NL Bülow, Nr. 64, Bl. 26ff.; Bethmann to Valentini, 17 November 1911, and Bethmann's telegram to Wilhelm, 11 November 1911, in GStA Merseburg, 2.2.1, Nr. 667, Bd. 1, Bl. 86–87, 74–75.

understand that I do not like to speak in this tone, and all the less toward a Conservative." But, he added, the Conservatives "could have kept the national wind in their sails without making such irresponsible noises and distancing themselves so openly from the government." Thus, instead of leading them back into the government fold, the Conservatives' effort to achieve popular appeal had set them further at odds with the chancellor. "I follow no policy of revenge," Bethmann wrote to Loebell, "but I fear that the Reich government – whether it is led by me or by another chancellor – will find it more and more difficult to preserve a fundamentally conservative orientation in its policies if there is no change in the leadership of the Conservative Party."

VI

After November 1911 the chancellor drifted toward more explicit criticism of the Conservative Party, and they more directly opposed his policies. Bethmann still claimed he could steer a diagonal course, enlighten the Conservative Party, and avoid his own Philippi. Just as vehemently, the Conservatives claimed that their uncompromising policy toward liberalism (and National Liberalism) had been the correct one, in 1909 and afterward. The government's military and fiscal legislation in 1912/13 illustrated that Bethmann and his ministers were objectively aware that there existed an alternate majority – one excluding the Conservatives – for these bills. Yet the government continued to regard a decisive anti-Conservative policy as too fearsome a leap in the dark.

In a Prussian state ministry meeting of March 1912, Bethmann indicated that he still thought he could help the Conservatives overcome their errors of political judgment.[84] He told his colleagues that the same Reichstag majority should pass the army bill and the new taxes necessary to cover its expense. The Conservatives had declared that they would support the army increases but would never vote for an inheritance tax. In refusing to compromise, Bethmann felt, the Conservatives were merely reopening the political wounds they had first

84. GStA Merseburg, St. Min., Bd. 161, 4 March 1912, Bl. 25ff., and for the following. See further, K. von Westarp, *Die Wehr- und Deckungsvorlagen des Jahres 1913 und die konservative Partei* (Berlin, 1913); Witt, *Finanzpolitik*, pp. 337–376; and Shevin Coetzee, *German Army League*, pp. 30–43.

inflicted – on themselves and the nation – in 1909. On the other hand, if they were to sacrifice for the needs of the military, the Conservatives would thereby remove forever the hatred and demagoguery that had been directed against the party in the winter of 1911/12.[85] Despite these determined words, however, Bethmann proposed entering into negotiations with the parties with no firm program. He conceded that this tactic would leave the government open to the charge of "indecisiveness" and that negotiations were made more difficult by the National Liberals' "wavering attitude." But the issue was too serious to approach any other way, and the Conservatives could not be challenged directly. Bethmann concluded: "If the defense bill were to be defeated because no agreement as to funding could be achieved, should one then dissolve the Reichstag? From which parties would one want to draw support?" In any case, Bethmann observed, a new Reichstag "would be no better than the present one."

By May 1912, "a kind of truce" had been reached in "the wretched war over the inheritance tax."[86] The army increases had been approved. But the left liberals and the National Liberals were outraged that the government always paid more heed to Conservative wishes than to those of the Left. In the Reichstag, Bassermann pointedly asked the chancellor why the National Liberals were always called upon to abandon their principles.[87] And in private he complained to Bülow that his prophecy had been fulfilled: "Philippi has arrived. In the Wilhelmstraße complete helplessness. . . . Everything has fallen through!"[88] Because of this frustration and anger at the government's apparent rebuff, the National Liberals and the Center pushed through a resolution calling for the government to reintroduce a comprehensive inheritance tax within a year. This was the *Lex* Bassermann-Erzberger, which signified a sharp reduction in National Liberal-Center antagonism and left the Conservatives standing on the sidelines.

85. See the SPD's campaign brochure, *Worte und Taten der Konservativen. Material zur Bekämpfung der konservativen Parteien* (Berlin, 1911), pp. 21, 38–39.
86. Wahnschaffe to Valentini, 19 May 1912, cited in Zmarzlik, *Bethmann Hollweg*, p. 59.
87. *RT Sten. Ber.*, vol. 284, p. 1301, 22 April 1912.
88. Cited in Bülow, *Denkwürdigkeiten*, vol. 3, p. 89. The letter to which Bülow is apparently referring – Bassermann to Bülow, 3 April 1912 – contains the passage cited in note 5.

By late 1912 the Reich treasury, now under Hermann Kühn, again had to draft a tax bill acceptable to the Conservatives.[89] In notes Bethmann prepared after reading Kühn's proposal, the chancellor indicated his expectation that the Conservatives and the Center would oppose the tax.[90] But if the government were to carry it through with the help of the Left, the Black-Blue Bloc's defeat would be "so devastating that the conservative principle would suffer a blow from which it could hardly recover." This defeat, in turn, would "put off the possibility of renewed cooperation among the bourgeois parties far into the future." Bethmann observed that "the government could not retreat from such a conflict, even against the conservative elements in the country, if it were a matter of national necessity and if the liberal elements found themselves in a mood that would make it appear possible that we could govern with them for some length of time." However, the chancellor concluded that "both prerequisites are not at hand."[91]

As usual Bethmann was frustrated and angered by the DKP's continued opposition when a compromise tax bill was finally passed in June 1913. He countered Westarp's and Heydebrand's polemics – they denounced the government's "feeble performance" against the "democratic" Reichstag – with an attack of his own in the *Norddeutsche Allgemeine Zeitung*.[92] Privately, Bethmann evidently derived some satisfaction from the Conservatives' isolation. He complained that they demanded that "the government march through thick and thin for them," but that they did not "want to support it in return." Bethmann was even happy to see "this democratic Reichstag" accept "such a gigantic military bill." Yet he was

89. For this and the following, see [Reichsschatzamt], "Denkschrift über die Einführung einer allgemeinen Besitzsteuer im Reiche," n.d. [October 1912]; and Bethmann's "Aufzeichnungen," n.d.; both in GStA Merseburg, 2.2.1, Nr. 27426, Bl. 8; copies also in PA AA Bonn, NL Eisendecher, Nr. 1/8, Bl. 52ff.

90. See Witt, *Finanzpolitik*, pp. 357ff.

91. In a state ministry meeting of 24 February 1913, Bethmann declared that if the government dissolved the Reichstag and launched an election campaign against the parties – meaning primarily the Conservatives – who approved the army bill, it would find itself in a "fatal situation." GStA Merseburg, St. Min., Bd. 162, Bl. 36ff. In the same meeting Bethmann declared that an inheritance tax, if unacceptable to the Conservatives, would represent a "capitulation" to the Left and, as such, could not be considered on either "objective" or "moral" grounds; such a bill would be "incompatible with the essential requirements of the state and the Reich."

92. For this and the following citations, except where noted, see Jarausch, *Enigmatic Chancellor*, pp. 98–99, 104–107, and Witt, *Finanzpolitik*, pp. 372–73.

fully aware that further difficulties loomed on the horizon, for the consequences of his failure to win over the Conservatives were going to be large. First, the liberals' "revenge" for 1909 did not satisfy their eagerness to break down the bastions of conservatism and expand the powers of the Reichtag (as the Zabern affair subsequently illustrated). Second, Bethmann had aroused the indignation of the Kaiser by appearing to concede too much to the Left on an issue that touched on Wilhelm's unchallenged authority in military matters.[93] Third and most important for our discussion, the Conservatives' defeat did not induce them to be more reasonable in the future.

The Conservatives were not yet willing to campaign openly for Bethmann's dismissal. As in 1908–09, they had no wish to convey the impression that a parliamentary crisis had caused the resignation of a German chancellor. Nonetheless, as they began to spin their "secret intrigues" against Bethmann – intrigues that were not dissimilar to those of leading Pan-Germans – Westarp, Heydebrand, and the leaders of the Agrarian League saw little chance of a reconciliation with the chancellor.[94] Bethmann's hope that the two sides could commit themselves to an "objective program" for the future was regarded by Westarp as too dangerous a "blank check" to give the government. Heydebrand agreed. When he replied to Westarp's letter in early July 1913,[95] he observed that Bethmann had "the correct impression that we . . . cannot govern [!] with him, that is, with the policy he represents." The chancellor was "finally beginning to see that even he, properly speaking, cannot do so." The preceding four years provided ample evidence of that, Heydebrand believed: Bethmann's "scoffing remarks," "connivance," and "declarations of loyalty" could neither change the Conservatives' attitude nor induce "votes or

93. By the end of the year, the combination of the Kaiser's displeasure and the Conservatives' intrigues had already prompted Bethmann to consider resignation. He wrote to Eisendecher on 1 Oct. 1913: "Precisely the factors that should ease my burden professionally, H[is] M[ajesty] and the Conservatives, make things more difficult for me, according to their whims and powers. I should have drawn the consequences of this fiction at the beginning of July, since in any case it is unavoidable in the long run." PA AA Bonn, NL Eisendecher, Nr. 1/2, Bl. 44ff.

94. See Westarp to Heydebrand, 3 July 1913, cited in Westarp, *Konservative Politik*, vol. 1, p. 388; Wangenheim to Roesicke, 20 June 1913, in BA Potsdam, NL Conrad von Wangenheim, Nr. 7, Bl. 50.

95. Heydebrand to Westarp, 5 July 1913, in BA Potsdam, NL Westarp, Nr. 1, Bl. 162.

promises of support, to which he cannot lay claim." As Heydebrand wrote in his final words for Westarp, it was Bethmann himself who would be kept in check[96] by "the pentacle in Prussia" – the five bastions of Conservative power in the Prussian House of Deputies, *Herrenhaus*, administration, ministry of state, and royal court. Thus Germany's last major battle over domestic legislation before the war, originally planned to bring together the government and the right-wing parties, had ended in another standoff. Further crises in party-government relations in the winter of 1913/14 – over Zabern, tariffs, and rumors of another Prussian franchise reform bill – added no new ingredients to the volatile mixture of optimism and pessimism on both sides.[97]

VII

The time has come to offer some conclusions about the relative importance of structural and personal factors shaping the relationship between the Conservatives and the government. The earlier discussion of Bethmann's relations with Heydebrand demonstrated that Bethmann's hopes, insights, and expectations for the direction of Conservative Party leadership were a mass of contradictions. The chancellor at the same time hoped for a change of Conservative chairmen, recognized that it had to come from within the party, and (in his more fatalistic moments) expected that Heydebrand would prevail. Yet one can say that these perceptions, however idiosyncratic, were all reactions to the larger, general problem of conservative leadership in the Reich. This too was recognized by all the principal figures involved.[98] Westarp condemned Bethmann primarily for his willingness to consider parliamentary cooperation with the Social Democrats. Heydebrand claimed the mistrust between himself and the chancellor was rooted in the latter's "inner sympathy for liberalism and democracy [and] insuffi-

96. Literally, "made small": "das Pentagram in Preußen macht ihn klein!"
97. See further, Westarp to Heydebrand, 18 and 25 December 1913, and Heydebrand's replies, 20 and 27 December 1913, in BA Potsdam, NL Westarp, Nr. 1, Bl. 190ff.
98. For the following, see Westarp, *Konservative Politik*, vol. 1, pp. 338ff. and 378ff.; E. von Heydebrand und der Lasa, "Beiträge zu einer Geschichte der konservativen Partei in den letzten 30 Jahren (1888 bis 1919)," *Konservative Monatsschrift* 77 (1920): 605–6; and Bethmann to Gustav Schmoller, 9 April 1910, cited in Zmarzlik, *Bethmann Hollweg*, p. 44.

cient consideration of Prussia and Prussian circumstances."
Bethmann, of course, had often considered the larger question
of conservatism's role in Prussia and the Reich. As he wrote in
1910: "Our Prussian landed aristocracy is certainly not free of
faults. However, it provides us, in the army, state administration, and local government, with forces that we can as little do
without in the present as in the past."[99] Believing that the DKP
could be shown the way toward a reformist conservative policy, Bethmann observed that one could never think of shutting
the aristocratic Conservatives out of political life; instead, one
had to "modernize" them.

Unable to turn to the forces of the Left after 1909 because he
considered them politically radical or intellectually mediocre,
Bethmann proved unable to overcome political deadlock on
the domestic front. Because so many conservatives in the German establishment shared Bethmann's view of liberalism, the
prospect of a reformist conservative course remained an ideal
that was inspiring but, in the long run, disastrous. It prevented
a break from unyielding men such as Heydebrand, and it
blinded Bethmann and others to the possibilities for fundamental reform. In fact, the Conservatives saw more clearly
than Bethmann the options that lay open for a liberal,
reformist policy in Germany, a policy that might have arisen
directly from a head-on clash between the Conservative Party
and the government.[100] That these hard-nosed politicians
should have seen these options, and that the philosophical

99. Cf. Bülow's assessment of conservative traditions in Prussia, discussed
in section 2 of this essay; and Philipp Eulenburg's less delicate formulation, in
a letter to Bülow, 1 March 1901: "The thick-headedness of our Junkers has
something bullish about it. For breeding and in battle – that is, in war –
tremendous. In the stalls of culture,. . . unsteerable, unruly. They do not recognize the dangers." BA Koblenz, NL Philipp Eulenburg, Nr. 57, Bl. 23.

100. Circa 1910 Heydebrand allegedly declared to a left-liberal parliamentary deputy: "The future does indeed belong to you, the mass will assert itself
and deprive the aristocrats of their influence. A strong statesman may stem
this tide, but only for a while. We will not, however, abandon our position of
our own free will. Nevertheless, if you force us to, then you will have what
you want." Cited in H. Pachnicke, *Führende Männer im alten und im neuen Reich*
(Berlin, [1930]), p. 63. In May 1912 the agrarian leader Gustav Roesicke replied
to a proposal from a BdL member that the League should leave the government "high and dry" if it failed to defend agriculture: "From the Conservative
side we cannot render the government too afraid that we will abandon it,
because 1) it no longer draws support from us, and does not even want to, and
2) it will find, as soon as it is liberal, a cooperative, jubilant reception on the
left." Roesicke to Joachim von Levetzow-Sielbeck, 2 May 1912, in BA Potsdam,
NL Wangenheim, Nr. 7, Bl. 37ff.

Bethmann did not, may be regarded as either wholly obvious or highly ironic. In any case, due to the person who occupied the highest political office in the land, it was the *perception* of deadlock that prevailed up to 1914.

Despite the importance of these structural dimensions to the problem of modernizing the Reich, neither contemporary assessments nor more scholarly ones since have managed to divert our attention from the personalities involved. Heydebrand may have criticized Bethmann's sympathy for liberalism and democracy, but he concluded that it was the "weakness of his character that precluded an energetic, firm, purposeful, and determined policy, either domestically or in foreign affairs." Westarp was unsure whether Bethmann's apparent willingness to compromise with democracy was the result of a "personal liberalizing policy" or due simply to "indecisiveness" and "lack of fighting spirit." He remembered "occasional conversations in which we [Westarp and Heydebrand] could not decide which of the two faults appeared to us to be the more fateful."[101] Because Bethmann's personal relationship with the Conservative Party reflected and perpetuated these tensions, there is no reason to apologize for concentrating on the decisions of men, not merely the pressures of circumstance, to explain the disasters that befell Germany in the summer of 1914.

In the July crisis Bethmann seemed as determined to oppose the plans of the Conservative Party as Bülow had been in 1909. He insisted as vehemently as his predecessor had that a "reasonable" conservative policy for the state required a position independent from the DKP. Clearly, Bethmann had no wish to fight a war to preserve the Conservatives' ascendence domestically: "If the Conservatives demand special consideration from the government, they themselves must show it first," he wrote at one point.[102] Kurt Riezler, in close contact with Bethmann, described the chancellor's attitude even more starkly: "The chancellor expects from a war, whatever its outcome, a revolution of all existing order." Bethmann felt that "'everything has grown so old,'" Riezler reported. Germany's spiritual and intellectual decline weighed heavily on Bethmann, but in this crisis he dwelt on the practical problems he faced in an

101. See the works by Heydebrand and Westarp cited in note 98.
102. See note 14.

age of mass politics. Some of the blame lay, in Bethmann's eyes, with the liberals – the "intelligentsia" and the "professors." But in the end he turned against much of what Heydebrand, not the liberals, stood for. As Riezler reported: "Heydebrand has said that a war would strengthen the patriarchal spirit and order." Bethmann, however, was "outraged at such nonsense."[103]

Was it insight about the effects of modern war that caused Bethmann to react to Heydebrand's "nonsense" in this manner? Was it a feeling of helplessness? Or was it a sign that he finally began to see the necessity of breaking with the old order in Prussia? We will never know. For as Riezler astutely observed during the final days before Imperial Germany's own Philippi, Bethmann did not understand the implications of his struggle with conservatism. "[Bethmann] is not at all one-dimensional. His shrewdness is probably as great as his ineptitude. The two are mixed and variable."

---

103. Entry of 7 July 1914, BA Koblenz, Kleine Erwerbungen 584–1, Bl. 2ff. (also printed in *Riezler Tagebücher*, ed. Erdmann, pp. 181ff.), and for the concluding observation. It is remarkable how few insights can be won from Bethmann's own account: *Betrachtungen zum Weltkriege*, 2 vols. (Berlin, 1919); see esp. vol. 1, pp. 14–25.

9

Breakdown or Breakthrough? Conservatives and the November Revolution

Peter Fritzsche

Is there any question as to the bewilderment German conservatives felt after the outbreak of the November Revolution? Memories coincide with well-worn portraits: sabers broken in patriotic homes, epaulettes cut off at crowded train stations. Partisan divisions appeared exceedingly sharp as Germans divided neatly along class lines. In towns and cities across the Reich in November 1918, socialist workers dismantled the political power that had been assembled over decades by Wilhelmine notables and Germany's commercial and agrarian elites. Proletarian councilors, anarchist intellectuals, mutinous sailors – these constitute the dominant images of the revolution. Middle-class Germans, and the mostly liberal and conservative politicians who had staffed the wartime ministries in Berlin, by contrast, stood by as onlookers to the revolutionary drama. Indeed, contemporary accounts of the November Revolution generally ignore the reaction of burghers altogether. Except for a small band of convinced democrats around Theodor Wolff, Friedrich Naumann, and other prewar Progressives, middle-class opposition to events in 1918 is taken for granted. Historians since have not added much nuance to this picture and regard Catholic and especially Protestant burghers as mostly passive observers to upheaval and conservatives, in particular, as little more than potential counterrevolutionaries.[1]

---

1. Contemporary accounts of the November Revolution include F. Stampfer, *Die vierzehn Jahre der ersten deutschen Republik* (Karlsbad, 1936); and H. Müller, *Die November Revolution* (Berlin, 1928). On German conservatives in

Peter Fritzsche

Weimar commentators throughout the 1920s reiterated how cataclysmic were the events that overtook burghers in 1918. The November Revolution was nothing less than a vast natural disaster in which most Germans were caught up as victims. On this point, bourgeois Germany seemed to agree. Reflected in the images of nationalist memory, the revolution's perpetrators were small in number and vaguely foreign, its effects were nefarious, and its place in German history dubious.[2] Democrats and even Social Democrats came to look upon the chaos of upheaval with horror and preferred to commemorate Weimar democracy on Constitution Day – 11 August 1919 – rather than on the anniversary of the revolution – 11 November 1918 – precisely in order to distinguish republican order from revolutionary anarchy.[3]

Historians have rejected conspiratorial and excessively circumstantial interpretations of the revolution, but retain the mostly passive bourgeois characters on which those interpretations have rested. The assumption that November 1918 cleaved Germans into opposing camps is a fixed feature in the twentieth century's story of Germany's trial with democracy. Even if the tale is a tragic one, it maintains clear political demarcations between republicans, the proponents of a new Germany, and reactionaries, who, overwhelmed by revolution, struggled to restore a semblance of Wilhelmine order throughout the 1920s and ended up destroying a law-abiding

---

1918, see W. Liebe, *Die Deutschnationale Volkspartei 1918–1924* (Düsseldorf, 1956); A. Thimme, *Flucht in den Mythos. Die Deutschnationale Volkspartei und die Niederlage von 1918* (Göttingen, 1969); M. Greiffenhagen, *Das Dilemma des Konservatismus in Deutschland* (Munich, 1971); M. Weißbecker, "Konservative Politik und Ideologie in der Konterrevolution 1918/19," *Zeitschrift für Geschichtswissenschaft* 27 (1979): 707–20; and J. Petzold, *Wegbereiter des deutschen Faschismus. Die Jungkonservativen in der Weimarer Republik* (Cologne, 1978), pp. 43–110. See also U. Kluge, *Die deutsche Revolution* (Frankfurt am Main, 1985); A.J. Ryder, *The German Revolution of 1918* (Cambridge, 1967); H. Schulze, *Weimar. Deutschland 1917–1933* (Berlin, 1982), pp. 155–88; and W. Bußmann, "Politische Ideologien zwischen Monarchie und Weimarer Republik," *Historische Zeitschrift* 190 (1960): 55–77.

2. For example, see the commemorative volumes published by the nationalist parties ten years after the November Revolution, *Der nationale Wille. Werden und Wirken der Deutschnationalen Volkspartei 1918–1928*, ed. M. Weiß (Leipzig, 1928); and *Deutscher Aufbau. Nationalliberale Arbeit der Deutschen Volkspartei*, ed. A. Kempkes (Berlin, 1927); as well as Thimme, *Flucht in den Mythos*, passim.

3. R. Rürup, "Problems of the German Revolution, 1918–1919," *Journal of Contemporary History* 3 (1968): 109–35.

state altogether. This emplotment of the November Revolution is crucial to the *Sonderweg* interpretation, which highlights the debilitatingly nostalgic and "premodern" aspects of Germany's political tradition and considers Nazism to be the balance of the catastrophe burghers endured in 1918.[4]

If there is good cause to recall the contemporary perception of catastrophe, however, there is also reason to explore the sense of opportunity that middle-class Germans shared in 1918 and 1919. The imagery of crisis used by conservatives portrayed the revolution as a dismal end of tradition, history, and achievement; yet, at the same time, this imagery suggested unforeseen possibilities. The memoirs and histories of the later 1920s are misleading for their black-on-black depictions of the November upheaval. An analysis of immediate responses between October 1918 and March 1920 reveals that many conservatives, especially representatives of the younger generation born in the two decades after the founding of the Reich and pulled into Expressionist currents around Ferdinand Avenarius' journal *Kunstwart* or attracted to the romantic prewar crusades of the Youth Movement, did not dismiss the revolution as a shadowy "stab in the back" or a dangerous anarchic episode. They condemned Marxism and "Western" parliamentary government sharply. Even so, influential critics such as Arthur Moeller van den Bruck, Wilhelm Stapel, Eduard Stadtler, and Max Hildebert Boehm anxiously sought to retrieve from the upheaval the opportunity for national renovation. More than simply a horrifying breakdown or *Zusammenbruch*, November 1918 was also a welcome breakthrough, a *Durchbruch*.

It is this tension between chaos and opportunity that distinguished the political perspective of Weimar's "revolutionary conservatives" and anticipated much of the malleability of bourgeois politics in the 1920s. To understand 1933, it is not nostalgia for kaiser and *Kaiserreich* but the unfulfilled expectations for national renewal that surfaced in 1914 and again in

4. On the *Sonderweg* debate, J. Kocka, "German History before Hitler: The Debate about the German *Sonderweg*," *Journal of Contemporary History* 23 (1988): 3–16; R.G. Moeller, "The *Kaiserreich* Recast? Continuity and Change in Modern German Historiography," *Journal of Social History* 17 (1984): 442–50; H. Grebing, *Der `deutsche Sonderweg' in Europa 1806–1945* (Stuttgart, 1986); and G. Eley, "What Produces Fascism: Preindustrial Traditions or a Crisis of a Capitalist State," reprinted in Eley, *From Unification to Nazism: Reinterpreting the German Past* (Boston, 1986), pp. 254–82.

1918 that historians need to review. The revolutionary conservatives were young adults when the war broke out – Moeller, the oldest, was thirty-eight in August 1914; Boehm, the youngest, twenty-three. They were the restless middle-class sons of the *"Gründerzeit"* generation, the sons who spearheaded the turn-of-the-century revolt against the convention and complacency of Wilhelmine Germany, traded in all sorts of heady literary and artistic projects for cultural renewal before 1914, and thus found the empire's demise in 1918 less troublesome and the postwar future more promising than did older conservatives. Boehm and Stadtler served in the war, but thanks to their cultural rebelliousness before 1914, even established critics such as Moeller van den Bruck and Stapel felt an affinity to the "front generation" and regarded Germany's future as safe in their hands. These literary fraternizations point to a fundamental continuity. Revolutionary conservatism in the Weimar period was, in large part, the elaboration of indictments already prepared against Wilhelmine Germany.[5]

In his classic 1957 study, *Germany's New Conservatism*, Klemens von Klemperer explored the political ground that the theologian Ernst Troeltsch had called the "dreamland of the armistice," the period between the end of hostilities in November 1918 and May 1919, when the terms of the Treaty of Versailles became known. Klemperer argued that a wide range of conservative thinkers, from Thomas Mann to Moeller van den Bruck, had untied themselves from the monarchy, sought

5. R. Wohl, *The Generation of 1914* (Cambridge, Ma., 1979). On the distinctive generations that played political parts in the Weimar Republic, see D. Peukert, *Die Weimarer Republik. Krisenjahre der Klassischen Moderne* (Frankfurt am Main, 1987), pp. 26–31. On "revolutionary conservatism," see K. von Klemperer, *Germany's New Conservatism: Its History and Dilemma in the Twentieth Century* (Princeton, N.J., 1957); H. Gerstenberger, *Der revolutionäre Konservatismus. Ein Beitrag zur Analyse des Liberalismus* (Berlin, 1969); A. Mohler, *Die konservative Revolution in Deutschland 1918–1933*, 2nd rev. ed. (Darmstadt, 1972); K. Sontheimer, *Antidemokratisches Denken in der Weimarer Republik* (Munich, 1968); H. Rudolph, *Kulturkritik und konservative Revolution. Zum kulturell-politischen Denken Hofmannsthals und seinem problemgeschichtlichen Kontext* (Tübingen, 1971); and, more generally, J.P. Faye, *Totalitäre Sprachen. Kritik der narrativen Vernunft, Kritik der narrativen Oekonomie*, trans. I. Arnsperger (Frankfurt am Main, 1977). The anti-Wilhelmine moment in revolutionary conservatism is discussed in J. Müller, *Die Jugendbewegung als deutsche Hauptrichtung neukonservativer Reform* (Zurich, 1971); and R. Pascal, "Revolutionary Conservatism: Moeller van den Bruck," in *The Third Reich*, ed. International Council for Philosophy and Humanistic Studies (London, 1955), pp. 318–19, 344.

new political allegiances, and might have accepted democracy. The almost visceral opposition of conservatives to the new order was not inevitable. This view leads Klemperer to conclude that Germany's postwar tragedy was not Weimar's insufficient liberalism or socialism, but rather its insufficient conservatism and thus the incomplete answers the republic gave to questions of rootlessness and solitude in modern industrial society.[6]

Klemperer's contribution has been to remind historians of the feelings of excitement and opportunity that animated many on the Right immediately after the war. The young journalist Max Hildebert Boehm described the rupture of the November Revolution. Although he could not endorse socialism and remained emotional attached to the monarchy, he recognized "something of that sense of power that grips the entire body when one leaves the narrow byways of the city and steps into the bright expanse of meadows and fields." At the moment of the *Kaiserreich*'s demise, Boehm felt "room – the latitude and perspective of political aspiration."[7] Boehm was not alone in tramping across the political expanse. In Jena that same eventful autumn, Eugen Diederichs, a respected neoconservative publisher, felt compelled to "shout a joyful `Yea' to the revolution, for we feel that true German *Geist* was stifled by the narrow, bureaucratic perspectives of the old regime."[8] There is "a place in the sun for everyone," enthused one writer in the April 1919 inaugural issue of *Gewissen* (or *Conscience*), the most iconoclastic conservative magazine of the postwar years.[9]

What is striking about these confessions is the repeated use of spatial metaphors that serve to delimit the divided terrain of the past, cut up by partisan hostilities, class barriers, and bureaucratic narrows, from the open ground that lay ahead. Assembled around Heinrich von Gleichen's Association for National and Social Solidarity (Vereinigung für nationale und soziale Solidarität) beginning in October 1918, later meeting at

6. von Klemperer, *Germany's New Conservatism*, pp. 12–13.

7. Boehm, "Nationalversammlung und Parteien." *Grenzboten* 77, no. 4 (1918): 197.

8. Diederichs in *Die Tat* 10 (1918/19), cited in G. Stark, *Entrepreneurs of Ideology: Neoconservative Publishers in Germany, 1890–1933* (Chapel Hill, N.C., 1981), p. 155.

9. W., "Bekenntnis," *Gewissen*, 9 April 1919, no. 1. See also Stadtler, "Zum Geleit," ibid., 7 January 1920, no. 2.

the June Club (Juniklub) in Berlin's Motzstrasse, conservative intellectuals contributed dozens of essays to influential journals such as *Grenzboten, Kunstwart, Deutsche Rundschau,* and *Gewissen.* They argued that the challenge of November 1918 was to realize the national community glimpsed in August 1914. Moeller van den Bruck, Boehm, and Stadtler, especially, cited each other repeatedly, and their commentary in 1918 and 1919 adds up to a coherent critique of Germany at the end of the war. The time had come to delete the unnatural divisions, special interests, and particularist claims that had fragmented the Second Reich and repeatedly kept Germans from constructing a unified *"Volksstaat"* or people's state. Political forms had to be made more representative, antique notions of patronage and privilege overturned, and, most importantly, Germany's labor movement, with its virtues of discipline and service, enrolled in the national destiny. Once this work of national reform had been accomplished, conservative thinkers looked forward to a Germany that would reemerge as a powerful subject in twentieth-century affairs. This reformist, future-oriented message was echoed by more mainstream conservative organs such as Oskar Müller's semi-official newspaper, *Deutsche Allgemeine Zeitung,* Scherl's high-brow *Der Tag,* and much of the provincial press.[10]

The resolve to draw on what Moeller van den Bruck called the "bounty of revolution" (*Revolutionsgewinn*) set Weimar's revolutionary conservatives apart from Wilhelmine reactionaries, giving their opposition to the republic an intransigent and restless quality but also marking it with considerable political originality. To be sure, young conservatives were

10. General background is provided by von Klemperer, *Germany's New Conservatism,* and Pascal, "Revolutionary Conservatism," pp. 331–32. See also P. Fritzsche, *Rehearsals for Fascism: Populism and Political Mobilization in Weimar Germany* (New York, 1990), pp. 23–28; G. Hollenberg, "Bürgerliche Sammlung oder Sozialliberale Koalition? Sozialstruktur, Interessenlage und politisches Verhalten der bürgerlichen Schichten 1918/19 am Beispiel der Stadt Frankfurt am Main," *Vierteljahrshefte für Zeitgeschichte* 27 (1979): 393–430; idem, "Bürgertum und Revolution in Frankfurt a.M. 1918/19," *Blätter für deutsche Landesgeschichte* 115 (1979): 69–120; and U. Popplow, "Göttingen in der Novemberrevolution 1918/1919," *Göttinger Jahrbuch* 25 (1976): 205–42. On the conservative press, see K. Brammer, *Das Gesicht der Reaktion 1918–1919* (Berlin, 1919); O. Müller, "Bilanz der Revolution," *Deutsche Allgemeine Zeitung,* 1 December 1918, no. 611; Hirschfeld, "Münchener Brief," *Der Tag,* 23 November 1918, no. 273; and von Hassell, "Wir jungen Konservativen. Ein Aufruf," *Der Tag,* 24 November 1918, no. 274.

never entirely at ease with their equivocal stance toward the November events, and early professions supporting revolution in Germany steadily gave way to harsh condemnations of the spiritual shallowness and crass materialism of the Social Democrats. The frightful chaos of general strikes and civil strife shredded residual sympathy for the fragile republic by autumn 1919. Nonetheless, disappointment with the revolution did not burnish the Wilhelmine past. The new Reich that Moeller van den Bruck or Boehm envisioned required dramatic political rearrangement and demarcated a substantial distance from the guiding social and economic assumptions of the Second Empire. It would be a mistake to regard the endeavors of young conservatives simply as an attempt to save what could be saved in 1918.

The national projects of conservative intellectuals during the revolution have important implications. The political volatility of the 1920s, namely the dissolution of the traditional liberal and conservative parties and the rise of National Socialism, cannot be comprehended without understanding the basic appeal of social reform, particularly in the bourgeois camp. Scholars have generally neglected this task. Nebulous concepts such as the "people's state" (*Volksstaat*) and the "people's community" (*Volksgemeinschaft*) or heavily mortgaged terms such as "*Volk*," "nation," and "public interest" (*Gemeinsinn*) had a popular resonance then that cannot be dismissed. It is the responsibility of historians to try to recover this meaningfulness. Otherwise the road traveled by the German Right in the twentieth century will remain obscure. The point is not to include postwar conservatives in the ranks of potential democrats or tolerant social reformers. Yet, by concentrating on the anti-republican or anti-democratic sweep of their thought, and underscoring their basic opposition to the Weimar Republic, historians have run the risk of flattening out the political body of German conservatism, which put forward social and political reforms and proposed new forms of collective association. These propositions enjoyed widespread public support in 1918 – as they had in 1914 – and, even when abandoned by right-wing politicians over the course of the 1920s, continued to set the standards by which much of the German middle-class electorate measured the Weimar parties until 1933. Although Klemperer takes pains to distinguish

Germany's "new conservatism" from National Socialism, the notions of national solidarity to which the revolution gave voice were common to both.[11]

* * *

Twentieth-century revolution taught German conservatives to approach the future adventurously. The year 1918 was a dramatic moment not simply because the conjuncture of military defeat and the Kaiser's abdication offered opportunities for political renewal that had been postponed for so long, but also because the rapid-fire creation of a new order overturned accepted assumptions about the course of history. In November 1918, the very legitimacy and usefulness of the remembered past was widely questioned by observers in all political camps. As in August 1914, essays, poems, and editorials revealed a sense of "new time" and a flight from history.[12] The sharp breaks with the past came to be endowed with creative potential by anarchists such as Erich Mühsam and Gustav Landauer; by journalists writing for *Die Woche* or *Allgemeiner Wegweiser* who were trying to make sense of the upheaval to their middle-class readers; and by conservative critics anxious to construct a radically different Reich. Moeller van den Bruck, Max Hildebert Boehm, and other young conservatives celebrated the commotion of revolution, even as they had little patience with its specific configuration. The momentum and force, rather than the direction, of revolution caught their imagination.

For the literary critic Arthur Moeller van den Bruck, born into a family of Prussian officials in 1876 and consumed by the austere ideal of Frederican Prussia, there was real treasure to be extracted from upheaval in 1918. His conviction that revolution offered Germany a unique opportunity to throw aside the cheap brilliance of the Wilhelmine era and to fashion itself anew comes across much more forcefully in essays written in 1919 than in their reformulation and republication in *The Third*

11. Valuable reassessments of alternative political visions in the Weimar era include J. Muller, *The Other God That Failed: Hans Freyer and the Deradicalization of German Conservatism* (Princeton, N.J., 1987); and J. Hermand, *Der alte Traum vom neuen Reich. Völkische Utopien und Nationalsozialismus* (Frankfurt am Main, 1988), pp. 9–15.

12. See the important studies by E.J. Leed, *No Man's Land: Combat and Identity in World War I* (Cambridge, 1979), pp. 39–72; and K. Vondung, *Die Apokalypse in Deutschland* (Munich, 1988).

Reich – the book for which Moeller van den Bruck is best known – in 1923. By that time the November Revolution was seen almost exclusively in partisan terms as a horrible Social Democratic catastrophe. Immediately after the war, however, military defeat, the Kaiser's abdication, and the formation of a democratic government seemed to open rather than cut off roads to the future. To Moeller, the revolution confirmed just how implausible actually was the idea of measured progress. The course of history, as it had been crafted in the nineteenth century, was as prosaic and artless as the masses who filled its stage. Only grand, singular moments – August 1914, November 1918 – could inspire political creation and provide nations with meaning and purpose.[13] Revolutions were the great personalities of history, and it was their stature and force that impressed Moeller van den Bruck. He repeatedly stressed the consequence of revolution: It "is always a turning point. What was necessary in the revolution will endure and change the thinking of a people for all times." Revolutions were their own justification and had to be embraced, Moeller explained: "A revolution occurs only once. . . . It is the most private, intimate concern of a people" and "determines a people's fate."[14]

That the German Revolution only came now, in 1918, as the twentieth century opened, was to Germany's advantage, Moeller asserted. England and France had had their revolutions. Whatever opportunities history had extended to these maritime nations had long since passed; they "are older than we. Their people are experienced, tired, matured." Germany, by contrast, was a young nation, poised to wreck the inheritance of the nineteenth century and meet the challenges of the twentieth. About the Second Reich, then, Moeller had little positive to say. It offered only a scant record of timorous materialism and political failure, and had confined Germany's destiny to conventional approaches. After the war, Germany remained impoverished, spiritually as well as economically, but Moeller believed that the November Revolution offered a welcome sense of roominess and possibility – what Boehm had described as the "latitude of political aspiration." Revolution restored national history and

13. Moeller van den Bruck, "Revolution, Persönlichkeit, Drittes Reich," *Gewissen*, 30 May 1920, reprinted in *Der politische Mensch*, ed. H. Schwarz (Breslau, 1933), p. 82.
14. Moeller van den Bruck, "Der Revolutionsgewinn," *Gewissen*, 11 November 1919, no. 31.

Peter Fritzsche

national ambition to Germany by destroying the absolutism of nineteenth-century progress.[15]

It was not long before Moeller lost his enthusiasm for the November Revolution and came to assign to it a much more casual role in German history. It is this more typically conservative Moeller van den Bruck on whom historians focus.[16] In his 1923 book, *The Third Reich*, Moeller reprinted his earlier arguments about revolution and youthfulness, but concluded with an observation that deprived them of their force. In the re-edition, revolutions had been diminished into "only interludes in history:"

> Marx called them steam engines of history. We might rather call them collisions of history: immense railway accidents . . . that may be pregnant with consequences, but that have something of the banality of accidental catastrophes. . . . At best, catastrophes have the virtue of calling attention with a terrible emphasis to existing faults, to which custom and stupidity and self-sufficiency have blinded us. The necessary salvage work after a revolution must, however, be handed over to some experienced person conversant with the whole administration who can set the wrecked, overturned engine in motion again. Life of its own weight resumes its equilibrium and the conservative principle on which all life is based is vindicated.[17]

Four years after the November Revolution, Moeller had come to esteem continuity over catastrophe, and inheritance and endurance over creation. Images of equilibrium, salvaging, and accident suggest a much more mainstream understanding of the course of history. They clash with earlier notions about the singularity and creative endowment of revolution. But it is just these formulations that report the initial enthusiasm of radical conservatives in November 1918.

For Wilhelm Stapel, born the son of a Prussian clockmaker

15. Moeller van den Bruck, "Wir wollen die Revolution gewinnen," *Gewissen*, 31 March 1920, no. 12. See also Boehm, "Die Selbsterneuerung des lebendigen Rechts," *Deutsche Rundschau* 186 (1921): 138–49.
16. See, for example, F. Stern, *The Politics of Cultural Despair: A Study of the Rise of Germanic Ideology* (Berkeley, Ca., 1961), pp. 245–66; Pascal, "Revolutionary Conservatism," p. 331; Sontheimer, *Antidemokratisches Denken*, pp. 237–41; Mohler, *Konservative Revolution*, p. 115; and D. Goeldel, *Moeller van den Bruck: un nationaliste contre la révolution* (Frankfurt am Main, 1984). See also P. Fechter, *Arthur Moeller van den Bruck – Einpolitisches Schicksal* (Berlin, 1934); and H.-J. Schwierskott, *Arthur Moeller van den Bruck und der revolutionäre Nationalismus in der Weimarer Republik* (Göttingen, 1962).
17. Moeller van den Bruck, *Germany's Third Empire* (London, 1934), p. 186.

in 1882, first trained as a book clerk, later an art student and contributing editor to *Kunstwart* during the war and, after 1918, associated with the anti-Semitic German National Union of Commercial Employees (Deutschnationaler Handlungsge-hilfen-Verband), November 1918 offered a welcome chance to make a clean sweep as well. Stapel's rhetoric reveals the lee-way and geography of the moment: "My heart breaks out in jubilation; once again the path is free to reach the destination announced long ago by our prophets."[18] Stapel, like Moeller van den Bruck, linked crisis in the present to renewal in the future. In this regard, he anticipated the quotable slogan of nationalists later in the 1920s: "We had to lose the war in order to win the nation."[19] Predicating the new Reich on dislocation, revolutionary conservatives subscribed to an "ideology of cri-sis" that repudiated the temporal conventions of the liberal age and looked beyond the ruins that so disoriented adherents of the old regime.

In the shadow of Germany's military defeat, the confidence and even exuberance of young conservatives is striking. This rhetorical poise was not the bliss of ignorance, as Troeltsch's term "dreamland of the armistice" might suggest, although the precise terms of the Treaty of Versailles were not yet known and the true extent of demilitarization and territorial revision remained uncertain. Nationalists were hardly san-guine. They had little reason to expect moderation from the Allies, whom they had already accused of "entente imperial-ism" in late 1918. By way of example, Ulrich von Hassell, a Foreign Office official and occasional visitor to the Motz-strasse, foresaw Germany's decline to the lesser-power status of Holland.[20] Certainly no one expected a rapid economic or

18. H. Kessler, *Wilhelm Stapel als politischer Publizist* (Nuremberg, 1967), p. 37; H. Gerstenberger, *Revolutionäre Konservatismus*, pp. 82–84.

19. F. Schauwecker, *Aufbruch der Nation* (Berlin, 1930); Mohler, *Konservative Revolution*, p. 37. For similar sentiments, see V. Mauersberger, *Rudolf Pechel und die 'Deutsche Rundschau'. Eine Studie zur konservativ-revolutionären Publizis-tik in der Weimarer Republik (1918–1933)* (Bremen, 1971), p. 119; and E. Diederichs, *Leben und Werk. Ausgewählte Briefe und Aufzeichnungen*, ed. L. von Strauss and Torney-Diederichs (Jena, 1936).

20. v. Hassell, "Wir jungen Konservativen: Ein Aufruf." *Der Tag*, 24 Novem-ber 1918, no. 274. Born in 1881, the diplomat Hassell was a contemporary of the conservative critics discussed here, but he saw the revolution much more in terms of catastrophe than opportunity. See also G. Schöllgen, "Wurzeln konservativer Opposition. Ulrich von Hassell und der Übergang vom Kaiser-reich zur Weimarer Republik," *Geschichte in Wissenschaft und Unterricht* 38 (1987): 478–89.

military recovery for postwar Germany. But a gloomy sense of pessimism did not prevail among Gleichen and his associates largely because the revolution had reinvigorated what singular, dramatic events could mean. November 1918 confirmed the lessons learned at the outbreak of the world war in August 1914 and of the Russian Revolution in October 1917. Sudden and sharp breaks properly belonged to the rhythm of history. The steady progress of the liberal age had given way to new, intrusive realities at once promising and frightening. Once this discontinuous punctuation was acknowledged, the future of Germany took on shape and possibility in the mind's eye of young conservatives.

The idea of eternal recurrence or restoration that many historians identify in conservative rhetoric was apt only in the most formal sense;[21] it implied discontinuity and infinite malleability and thus ripped from the Weimar Republic the veil of continuity and legitimacy. As Moeller van den Bruck himself recognized, the nostalgic look backward to an allegedly more authentic past was a genre of contemporary criticism, not an itinerary of genuine hope and aspiration.[22] The tactics of asynchronicity, the sharp-edged oppositions that postwar conservatives made between past and present, sketched out what I want to term the delinquency of history. They reported how chance events had disassembled great structures. Seasons of war and revolution had disrupted the autobiographical story line for countless individuals and made it more and more difficult for contemporaries to maintain a coherent or orderly description of reality.[23] Yet it was just this tragic vision of the present that gave radical conservatives the impulse and grammar to conceive of a vastly refashioned German Reich. Their confidence in the possibility of the future and in the transiency

21. Mohler, *Konservative Revolution*; and Sontheimer, *Antidemokratisches Denken*, pp. 119–21. D. Frisby, *Fragments of Modernity: Theories of Modernity in the Work of Simmel, Kracauer and Benjamin* (Cambridge, 1985), pp. 28–37, discusses the intertwined ideas of "eternal return" and transiency.

22. Moeller van den Bruck, "Die Rückkehr zu Friedrich" (ca. 1922), reprinted in *Der politische Mensch*, ed. Schwarz, pp. 110–11. On nostalgia as a modernist genre, see R. Bermann, *The Rise of the Modern German Novel: Crisis and Charisma* (Cambridge, Ma. 1986), p. 11.

23. Vondung, *Apokalypse*, pp. 310–11; and D.M. Lowe, *History of Bourgeois Perception* (Chicago, 1982), p. 39. See also the provocative conclusion of M. Eksteins, "History and Degeneration: Of Birds and Cages," in *Degeneration: The Dark Side of Progress*, ed. J.E. Chamberlin and S.L. Gilman (New York, 1985), pp. 1–23.

of the present profoundly shaped attitudes toward the Weimar Republic in the 1920s. In stark contrast to the order and authority that nineteenth-century conservatives sought to impose, this "Machbarkeitswahn" or intoxication with the possible infused the nationalist opposition to Weimar with a sense of political adventure and recklessness.[24] Indeed, Moeller van den Bruck regarded postwar Germany as a "dangerous land" (*Gefahrland*), a territory surrounded by unfriendly powers yet also rife with its own insurrection and rebellion. Recent history had cast Germans as the "dangerous people" (*Gefahrvolk*) of the twentieth century.[25] As German conservatives looked out at the open, uncertain terrain of the future, they recollected the glories of the Prussian past in order to conjure up the unity of national purpose and the grand mobilization of national energies for which they struggled.

* * *

The rhetoric of the first weeks of Germany's revolutionary season echoed that of the great nineteenth-century revolutions. What Maurice Agulhon has referred to as the "divinization of the people" in the spring of 1848, when revolutionaries appealed to and spoke in the name of "the people", is evident in the autumn of 1918 as well.[26] On the Right and the Left, terms such as the "people's community" (*Volksgemeinschaft*), "people's state" (*Volksstaat*), and "people's party" (*Volkspartei*) saturated the political vocabulary. By their own testimony, young conservatives passionately embraced the *Volk* as well. Germany had changed profoundly since August 1914, noted Wilhelm Stapel. "The entire people had been cast in a new radiance," he wrote at the end of the war. Everywhere there had been "empathy . . . helpfulness, generosity, a quiet celebration."[27] The *Volk* had come to life and finally recognized

24. On "Machbarkeitswahn," see D. Peukert, *Max Webers Diagnose der Moderne* (Göttingen, 1989), pp. 69, 110–11. Nineteenth-century conservative views of revolution are discussed by S. Neumann, *Die Stufen des preußischen Konservatismus. Ein Beitrag zum Staats- und Gesellschaftsbild Deutschlands im 19. Jahrhundert* (Berlin, 1930).

25. Moeller van den Bruck, "Die Ideen der Jungen in der Politik," *Der Tag*, 26 July 1919, no. 159. See also Ernst Jünger, *Der Arbeiter* (Berlin, 1932), p. 55.

26. M. Agulhon, *The Republican Experiment, 1848–1852* (Cambridge, 1983), pp. 9–14.

27. St. [Stapel], "Wohin geht die Fahrt?" *Deutsches Volkstum* 12, no. 1 (January 1919): 1–3. See also Moeller van den Bruck, "Der Revolutionsgewinn," *Gewissen*, 11 November 1919, no. 31.

itself as the proper subject of German history. Unhappily, after four hard winters of war, little survived of the intimate "wonder" of the August days. Yet it remained a remembered treasure of experience that might be retrieved in the postwar era.

Revolution offered the opportunity to rekindle the intimate fraternity and national unity of 1914. According to Karl Bröger, a proletarian poet favored by patriots for his earthy nationalism, both August 1914 and November 1918 composed revolutionary seasons in which Germans hoped to forge a "new Reich" that would dissolve social privileges and vested political interests. If the popular revolution failed, Bröger warned, the violence of either the mob or the money bag would triumph.[28] By invoking the patriotic days of August 1914, conservatives explicitly rejected the class solidarity upheld by soldiers' and workers' councils. But this counter-revolutionary position did not exclude utopian propositions. Conservative visions of national unity lacked a developed notion of political pluralism or an acknowledgement of the economic conflicts spawned by industrial society, but, at the same time, they registered populist frustrations with notables and patricians and thus resisted Wilhelmine authoritarianism. The vocabulary of *Volk* that was so prevalent in 1914 and again in 1918 expressed popular expectations of fraternity, sovereignty, and entitlement.

Harsh condemnations of imperial Germany indicated the scope of political expectations in November 1918. Young conservatives were particularly eager to dismantle the barriers dividing the German people from Germany's political leaders. These were maintained by an undemocratic suffrage and what was taken to be a corrupt and unresponsive party system. But what really muzzled the people, conservatives argued, was not so much unattained parliamentary rights as an undeveloped sense of nation. The German state that Bismarck had constructed left the German *Volk* badly deformed. The Second Reich had turned its back on Germans outside its borders, conceiving the *Volk* only in terms of the existing Bismarckian *kleindeutsch* state and thus forsaking Germans in Austria, Bohemia, and overseas.[29] Even more debilitating to the nation was the

---

28. K. Bröger, "Die Brücke. Eine Geschichte vom neuen Reich," *Illustrirte Zeitung*, 17 July 1919, no. 3968.

29. Boehm, "Die Selbsterneuerung des lebendigen Rechts" (see n. 15).

failure of Germans to generate a common purpose within their borders. According to Moeller van den Bruck, Bismarck's state had merely trained subjects, and had not given them authentic political expression or larger historical roles. The busy patriotic calendar of royal birthdays, Sedan victory days, and silver jubilees had not securely tied the German people to the empire. Without a more popular lay patriotism, in which aristocratic privilege and court choreography no longer occupied pride of place, the Wilhelmine state had simply crumbled in hard times, Moeller explained.[30] To repair the relationship between state and nation was the challenge of the revolution.

Moeller's criticism was echoed by Max Hildebert Boehm, for whom the Reich had proven an incompetent custodian of the national idea. Boehm was not yet thirty when the Second Reich collapsed, but born to a German family in Birkenruh, Lithuania, he was sensitive to the incompleteness of Bismarck's empire. Even as he accepted the editorship of the venerable magazine *Grenzboten* in 1920, Boehm devoted time and energy to protect Germandom abroad and to animate the "deep forces" within the *Volk* until his death in 1964.[31] The lack of popular patriotism that Boehm identified disturbed Wilhelmine observers, who accordingly applauded the activity of the dozen patriotic movements that had sprouted around the turn of the century. But Boehm was not impressed with the Pan-German League, the Navy League, or the Fatherland Party, all of which, in his eyes, were overheated by ambition and arrogance and remained too closely associated with heavy industry and, during the war, with annexationist fantasies to be considered genuine people's movements.[32] Boehm's angry contempt drew on the conviction that strengthening German nationalism required rejecting Wilhelmine patriotism.

Wilhelm Stapel drew the sharpest distinction between the Second Reich and the German *Volk*. Overturning the most basic foundation of German conservatism, Stapel denounced

---

30. Moeller van den Bruck, *Germany's Third Empire*, p. 248. See also the contribution by "a Württemberger" in "Zur Neugestaltung des Deutschen Volksstaates," *Grenzboten* 78, no. 1 (1919): 65–68; and H. König, "Das neue Deutschland und der borussische Sozialismus (Lensch, Plenge, Spengler)" (Ph.D diss., Universität Münster, 1924), pp. 13–15.

31. M.H. Boehm, *Körperschaft und Gemeinwesen* (Leipzig, 1920), p. 61.

32. M.H. Boehm, *Ruf der Jungen*, unrev. ed. (1933 [1919]), pp. 39–40. See also Boehm, "Die Revolution, die wir brauchten," *Grenzboten* 78 (1919): 4–5.

the virtual cult surrounding the state. On the Left and Right, from Lassalle to Ludendorff, Germans had come to regard the state as the only possible and indeed the highest form of social association; "the state has become the god of modern times." Stapel conceded that the state had the right to require citizens to fulfill obligations and obey laws. But duty was "a proud, cold virtue," he wrote, not comparable to what the *Volk* "can demand . . . from us," namely "love" based on common bonds of blood and spirit.[33] A political community founded on the people was necessarily more intimate, more solidary, and more powerful. Like Boehm and Moeller van den Bruck, Stapel sought to replace the state with the *Volk* as the governing principle of the German polity. In the selfless rhythms of going to war, Germans had already glimpsed the features of a popular patriotism far more fulfilling than the beer-swilling imperial birthdays of the Wilhelmine era. The German people did not exist to celebrate *"Fürsten* and *Führer,"* Stapel declared angrily.[34] Populist and anti-monarchist indictments such as these echoed an already extensive debate on German festivity before the war and charted the breadth of public dissatisfaction with authoritarian political conventions in 1918 and 1919.[35]

As revolutionary conservatives commended more popular forms of social fellowship, they also explored questions of political sovereignty. It is difficult not to read the fashionable notion of the *Volksstaat* simply as another code word for reactionary opposition to parliamentary democracy, but the idea was not completely without substance. Although Motzstrasse's conservatives continued to regard the party system with skepticism and remained as suspicious of what they took to be the rule of merely circumstantial majorities as prewar

---

33. W. Stapel, *Volksbürgerliche Erziehung*, rev. ed. (Hamburg, 1920), pp. 37–38. The "spirit of community" was also celebrated by the anarchist Left. See Vondung, *Apokalypse*, pp. 226–57.

34. Kessler, *Stapel*, p. 20.

35. Goldschmidt, "Der Sedantag als Nationalfeiertag 1871–1914," *Deutsche Rundschau* 53 (1926): 181–193; T. Schieder, *Das deutsche Kaiserreich von 1871 als Nationalstaat* (Cologne, 1961), pp. 125–153; G.L. Mosse, *The Nationalization of the Masses* (New York, 1975), pp. 73–99; F. Schellack, "Sedan- und Kaisergeburtstagsfeste," in *Öffentliche Festkultur: Politische Feste in Deutschland von der Aufklärung bis zum Ersten Weltkrieg*, ed. D. Düding et al (Reinbek, 1988), pp. 286, 294; and W. Hardtwig, "Bürgertum, Staatssymbolik und Staatsbewußtsein im Deutschen Kaiserreich 1871–1914," *Geschichte und Gesellschaft* 16 (1990): 280–83.

monarchists, they did so in the name of a more popular representation that the German people still lacked. Since the 1890s, middle-class populists had used the vocabulary of *Volk* to blast the traditional parties for being patrician and elitist and attentive only to the interests of big business and other vocal lobbyists. Anti-parliamentary prejudices were not necessarily signs of political immaturity or political reaction because parliamentary strife seemed so clearly linked to the rude commotion of interest politics.[36] Objections to the horsetrading and political compromise in the Reichstag registered mounting public impatience with existing combinations of privilege and patronage.

When the November Revolution raised the heady promise of the *Volksstaat*, a great many German burghers happily expected what they took to be the cacophony of special-interest parties to be replaced by a single patriotic *Volkspartei* that would be socially responsible but strongly anti-Bolshevik. Liberal and conservative journalists, along with middle-class activists in all the bourgeois parties, repeatedly addressed the issue of party reform. The vigorous debate that took place in 1918 and 1919 has been neglected by historians, yet it reveals widespread impatience with autocratic politics. Among the most vociferous critics of the existing party system was Eduard Stadtler, a Catholic publicist and war veteran who had witnessed the Bolshevik Revolution in Russian captivity. After escaping from prison in early 1918 and making his way back to Germany, Stadtler joined Boehm and Moeller van den Bruck in Gleichen's Association for National and Social Solidarity. Stadtler was best known in revolutionary Berlin for his activity in the Anti-Bolshevik League (Antibolschewistische Liga), but his frantic anti-Communism also contained sharp condemnations of the established parties.[37] Germany could only resist bolshevism, Stadtler argued, by enforcing an ethic

36. D. Blackbourn and G. Eley, *The Peculiarities of German History: Bourgeois Society and Politics in Nineteenth-Century Germany* (Oxford, Eng., 1984), p. 25.

37. On Stadtler's activities during the Revolution, see his own memoirs, *Als politischer Soldat 1914–1918* (Düsseldorf, 1936), pp. 142–56, and idem, *Als Antibolschewist 1918–1919* (Düsseldorf, 1936); as well as R. Stutz, "Stetigkeit und Wandlungen in der politischen Karriere eines Rechtsextremisten: Zur Entwicklung Eduard Stadtlers von der Novemberrevolution bis 1933," *Zeitschrift für Geschichtswissenschaft* 34 (1986): 796–806. On the June Club, see Pascal, "Revolutionary Conservatism," p. 332; and Schwierskott, *Moeller van den Bruck*, pp. 54–61.

of social responsibility and subordinating the claims of special interests. This presupposed not only more patriotism and economic common sense – that is, an end of the strike activity by Germany's socialist workers – but also a more social reformist agenda from the bourgeois camp. Immediately after the revolution, Stadtler's commitment to a brand of state socialism appeared genuine and, as editor of *Gewissen*, he steered the magazine away from "bureaucratic" and "capitalist" forces, although later in the 1920s he came to be regarded as little more than a typical reactionary who spoke out against trade unions on behalf of the veterans' group, Stahlhelm, and thereby "chased" nationalist workers to the left, as one observer put it.[38]

As it was, reform in the bourgeois parties remained a dead letter; the familiar old politicians reassembled in the National Assembly and party factions changed in name only.[39] Stadtler had nothing but contempt for Germany's complacent bourgeois party leaders: it is as if "they do not even recognize that the revolution . . . has thrown into question the relation between the parties and the people."[40] Indeed, the system of proportional representation by which the National Assembly was elected on 19 January 1919 insured that party organizations would control the list of candidates presented to voters. What was the result? According to Stadtler:

> The majority of deputies owed their nomination not to an original intellectual position on the world war or the revolution, but rather to the fact that this shoemaker association or that industrial group demanded that their class-conscious representative be awarded first or second place on party lists.
>
> . . . It was not the free thinkers and leaders of the economic and cultural associations that were elected, but those who had been properly drilled.

38. On the change in editorial policy, see Stadtler, "Zum Geleit!" *Gewissen*, 7 January 1920, no. 1. See also Fritzsche, *Rehearsals for Fascism*, p. 123, and Stutz, "Stetigkeit und Wandlungen," pp. 799–802.

39. See S. Neumann, *Die Parteien der Weimarer Republik*, 3rd ed. (Stuttgart, 1973); and L. Albertin, *Liberalismus und Demokratie am Anfang der Weimarer Republik. Eine vergleichende Analyse der Deutschen Demokratischen Partei und der Deutschen Volkspartei* (Düsseldorf, 1972).

40. Stadtler, "Die Revolution und das alte Parteiwesen," a public lecture held in Berlin on 12 March 1919, republished in E. Stadtler, *Bolschewismus als Weltgefahr* (Düsseldorf, 1936), p. 148.

This combination of bureaucracy and capitalism was fatal to popular representation.[41]

Stadtler's indictment echoed prevailing attitudes among German burghers. Editorials in bourgeois papers across Germany furiously condemned political continuity in the face of upheaval, the prominence of big business representatives in the bourgeois parties, and the inability of party politicians to unify the liberal center. It is difficult to overemphasize how appealing the notion of the *Volkspartei* was to burghers during the first months of the revolution; to be sure, it was an urgent expedient to resist the socialists and thus pulled together unlikely political combinations, but it also expressed widely held standards of public sovereignty.[42]

The judgment against the bourgeois parties was motivated in large part by the conviction that they simply did not give Germans of all social stations a political voice. Along with workers, middle-class constituents throughout the Reich had been disenfranchised in local elections by undemocratic suffrage laws. The three-class voting system in Prussia worked against peasants and plumbers as well as proletarians. The voice of artisans, small businessowners, and employees in the prewar bourgeois parties was feeble indeed. Neither the largely working-class Social Democratic Party nor the existing liberal and conservative parties addressed the populist resentments of middle-class Germans, or actively sought local franchise reform.[43]

From middle-class homes themselves, the *Juniklub* critics agreed that the postwar political structure had to become more "social," that is more accessible to ordinary constituents, but they were divided as to how to achieve equitable representation. Stadtler, for example, held up the revolutionary working-class councils as exemplary vehicles for sidestepping the authority of entrenched party machines. In his view, councils would more nearly reflect the actual organization of the Ger-

41. Ibid., pp. 150–51.

42. L.E. Jones, *German Liberalism and the Dissolution of the Weimar Party System, 1918–1933* (Chapel Hill, N.C., 1988), pp. 16–29; Fritzsche, *Rehearsals for Fascism*, pp. 25–28.

43. That neither the liberal parties nor the Social Democrats championed a reform of the antique and blatantly anti-democratic franchise laws on the local level is noted by R.J. Evans, *Death in Hamburg: Society and Politics in the Cholera Years, 1830–1910* (Oxford, 1987), pp. 80–83; and J.J. Sheehan, "Liberalism and the City in Nineteenth-Century Germany," *Past and Present* 51 (1971): 116–37.

man people who gathered in a market-place variety of occupational interest groups, civic associations, and social clubs. The multitude of local organizations would elect representatives to regional bodies, which in turn would construct the half-dozen national councils needed to oversee the business of economic production, public health, agriculture, national defense, and the arts. According to Stadtler, authentic sovereignty required the state to be built on these "organic" structures; parliamentary parties distorted the will of the German people by conceiving of the electorate only in terms of the material preoccupations of individual voters. Given its overlapping jurisdictions and the formal political recognition it offered all sorts of corporate bodies and civic associations, council government resembled a kind of Holy Roman Empire of German interests. This baroque structure was unworkable if only because sovereignty would be continually contested and thus political legitimacy would remain incomplete. Nonetheless, Stadtler's vision of a "party-free politics," which appeared to delete the claims of privilege, received widespread support from fellow conservatives.[44]

Conservatives welcomed the bourgeois councils that mushroomed throughout Germany in November and December 1918.[45] But the fact is that Germany's *Bürgerräte* never assembled real power and quickly languished.[46] After National Assembly elections on 19 January 1919 secured parliamentary democracy, there was little hope that councils of any sort would assume more than a minor role in the political machinery of the new republic. In many respects, they were unworkable to begin with and hardly provided burghers with reliable political instruments. Workers' and soldiers' councils typically barred bourgeois members and refused to collaborate with the bourgeois councils that emerged on their own. Moreover,

44. Stadtler, *Bolschewismus als Weltgefahr*, p. 159; and Stadtler, "Der Weg zur Tat," *Gewissen*, 17 June 1919, no. 10. See also von Hassell, "Alte und neue Mehrheiten," *Der Tag*, 29 March 1919, no. 66; and Moeller van den Bruck, who refers to Stadtler's concept of "party-free politics" in "Die Ideen der Jungen in der Politik," *Der Tag*, 26 July 1919, no. 159.

45. In this respect, see G. Cleinow, "Wozu brauchen wir die deutschen Volksräte?" *Grenzboten* 78, no. 1 (1919): 185–195; M. Goldstein, "Der Rätegedanke," ibid., pp. 197–202; K. Buchheim, "Die neue deutsche Glaubensspaltung," ibid., p. 224; and Boehm, "Der Irrweg des Bürgerratsgedankens," ibid., 78, no. 2 (1919): 76.

46. On the bourgeois councils, see Fritzsche, *Rehearsals for Fascism*, pp. 28–32.

socialists had nothing to gain by sharing power in the manner that Stadtler and others had imagined. Conservative proponents of the councils conceived of the German population in terms of productive estates, each as viable and essential as the others. It therefore followed that individual constituencies such as industrialists, artisans, or white-collar employees would get as much political representation as industrial workers. This distribution of power insured middle-class groups overproportional representation, relegated the mass of workers to a minority role, and was thus entirely unrealistic in 1918 and 1919.

For all their limitations, however, the bourgeois councils garnered enormous enthusiasm and attracted tens of thousands of supporters to public meetings, giving expression to middle-class expectations for political entitlement. In November 1918, the councils offered a more robust civic voice to artisans, shopkeepers, and employees, constituencies whom the conservative and liberal parties of the Second Empire had largely ignored. Representation by estate appeared to be a congenial political design to middle-class voters because it promised to break up concentrations of power, regardless of whether these were assembled by socialist workers or Ruhr industrialists. Middle-class corporatism, unlikely a political solution as it was for a highly mobile industrial society, thus accounted for the failure of the bourgeois parties to broaden their social base. As long as Weimar politicians continued to confuse parliamentary might with popular representation, Moeller van den Bruck warned, Germans would view the republic skeptically and carefully distinguish it from the "real" democracy he claimed they continued to hope for.[47]

The question of entitlement agitated Max Hildebert Boehm as well. In contrast to Stadtler, however, Boehm called for a reformulation of the German Conservative Party. He chided party leaders for missing critical opportunities. Their blindness had substantially contributed to the collapse of the monarchy. Whatever contributions their statecraft, their nobility of spirit, and their self-assured nationalism had offered Germany, Boehm explained, had been undercut by their exclusive caste mentality.[48] Hardened into awkward reactionary

47. Moeller van den Bruck, *Germany's Third Empire*, p. 118.
48. Boehm, *Ruf der Jungen*, pp. 50–51. For a more cautious restatement, see v. Hassell, "Wir jungen Konservativen. Ein Aufruf." *Der Tag*, 24 November 1918, no. 274.

postures, conservative politicians had reflexively dismissed the principle of political equality, opposed electoral reform, and thus repeatedly denied the mass of Germans a genuine political role. Even after the beginning of the war, Prussian conservatives continued to act like "toothless old men," obstructing democratic suffrage and disregarding the healthy spirit of war socialism.[49] Indeed, as late as 1919, prominent conservatives in the reconstituted German National People's Party (Deutschnationale Volkspartei) had objected to the insertion of the word "*Volk*" in the party name; it was nothing more than "dishonest courting of the masses," according to the Prussian leader Count Kuno von Westarp.[50] Despite these mistakes, Boehm maintained that the German Right had the opportunity to revive itself as an appealing "people's party" if it could bring itself to reject the exclusively Prussian and Protestant character of prewar conservatism, represent Germany's economic and social estates more completely, and cast away traditional class prejudices.[51]

The German National People's Party, a fusion of the two prewar conservative parties along with a number of other *völkisch* and Christian-Social groupings, never realized Boehm's hopes. It was too beholden to the special interests of "rye and iron," too aloof from the concerns of middle-class constituents, too mired in nostalgia for the bygone empire. Nonetheless, the party reform that Boehm and Stadtler sought remained a central political issue. After 1924, the bourgeois parties found their electoral support crumbling. Although party leaders such as Oskar Hergt, Alfred Hugenberg, and Gustav Stresemann repeatedly affirmed their commitment to the ideal of a patriotic "people's party," the old parties remained unrepresentative and elitist in the eyes of most burghers. Throughout the 1920s the search for more congenial political alternatives continued. By the end of the decade, when many observers saw only the hands of big business in the legislative activity of democrats, liberals, and conservatives alike, the Nazi party's emphatic espousal of the "people's

49. Boehm, "Letzte Stunde," *Grenzboten* 77, no. 4 (1918).
50. Liebe, *Deutschnationale Volkspartei*, p. 11.
51. Boehm, "Nationalversammlung und Parteien," *Grenzboten* 77, no. 4 (1918): 200–01; idem, "Konservatismus, Deutschnationale Partei, und Weltrevolution," ibid. 78, no. 2 (1919): 99–100. See also Schöllgen, "Wurzeln konservativer Opposition," pp. 478–89.

community" must have been attractive to Christian workers, small farmers, and artisans who for years had judged their own political bearings according to the post-1918 promise of a "people's party."

* * *

The conservative embrace of the *Volk* was not limited to middle-class constituents. The Germany cherished by the "ideas of 1914" included workers as well. In the afterglow of August 1914, young conservatives breathlessly reported the abiding patriotism and "Germanness" of even Social Democratic workers. In the first year of the war, for example, the neoconservative publisher Eugen Diederichs added a host of proletarian poets to his list and established the national reputations of Heinrich Lersch, Karl Bröger, and Hans Blunck.[52] By contrast, Eduard Stadtler's moment of discovery was more private. It occurred on the western front in 1916, after Stadtler had been promoted to the rank of lieutenant. The sixteen men under his command regarded their new officer warily and loudly cursed the government for prolonging the war. Just as Stadtler was about to denounce this defeatist talk, another officer stepped forward and asked for volunteers to go on a scouting mission. To Stadtler's great surprise, the soldiers who had been most vociferous in their criticisms were the first to volunteer: "I was struck by the contrast between the superficial sloganeering and the basically honest impulse of the simple people."[53]

Similar "revelations" studded the memoirs of nationalists, who after 1914 were sure that Germany's workers had a nationalist core to them. The task was to reach it, to excavate it from beneath the materialism and Marxism they had been taught. The sites of "völkischness" shifted to include working-class districts. Workers were thoroughly German, declared Franz Röhr, a prominent Christian trade unionist:

> Whoever has seen the masses of workers and their wives and children at parades, festivals, and assemblies and has explored their neighborhoods, whoever has compared German workers with

52. Stark, *Entrepreneurs of Ideology*, p. 126.
53. Stadtler, *Als politischer Soldat*, p. 23. See also Gerstenberger, *Der revolutionäre Konservatismus*, pp. 17–18; and M. Kele, *Nazis and Workers: National Socialist Appeals to German Labor, 1919–1933* (Chapel Hill, N.C., 1972).

English, French, and Slav workers, and whoever considers that German Jews are not workers, cannot doubt it. Indeed, in some German cities it is to proletarian quarters that one has to go to see German men, German women, and German children.[54]

Röhr's frankly anti-Semitic celebration of working-class Germans gains significance because it appeared in the definitive statement of young conservative thought, *Die Neue Front*, edited in 1922 by Heinrich von Gleichen, Moeller van den Bruck, and Boehm.

Revolutionary conservatives distinguished themselves by their conviction that the integration of workers was essential to the recovery of German fortunes. Class divisions had gravely weakened the Reich in the past, had persisted to hamper the war effort even after 1914, but must not be allowed to further flaw the nation's future. Germany had to become more proletarian. The role the *Mittelstand* played in conservative thought during the Wilhelmine period was now assumed by workers. Political prosperity no longer depended on the civic spirit and economic independence of the middle classes,[55] but on the allegedly working-class virtues of discipline, militancy, and organization.

Labor acquired a previously unrecognized honor in the eyes of conservatives. Long before the Nazis, it was young conservatives who tinkered with notions of *Deutsche Qualitätsarbeit* or the quality craftsmanship of the Germans in order to recast postwar nationalism in a more popular mold. Boehm, for example, credited trade unions with instilling pride and a commitment to workmanship. He hoped that a labor aristocracy of self-confident German workers would emerge out of the ranks of the industrial proletariat. The crime of Marxism, Boehm maintained, had been to stoke social resentments and incite class warfare rather than to promote the spiritual value of labor. After the war, however, Germany had the opportunity to break out of the materialistic circle "buy – consume – buy" by revalidating labor. Labor could serve either sensual desires (*erwerben . . . um zu geniessen*) as in the decadent West or the idea of production (*leben . . . um zu schaffen*), which was

54. Röhr, "Die deutsche Arbeiterschaft," in *Die Neue Front*, ed. H. von Gleichen (Berlin, 1922), pp. 211–13. See also "Ein Vorgang wie viele," *Gewissen*, 3 December 1919, no. 34.

55. See D. Blackbourn, "The *Mittelstand* in German Society and Politics, 1871–1914," *Social History* 4 (1977): 412.

Germany's mission.[56] Boehm celebrated laborers because they recalled Germans to their true destiny; both were engaged in a vast project of construction.

Boehm's discovery of the German proletariat did not imply a sudden commitment to the pressing questions of wages scales and the eight-hour day that workers faced. Neither Boehm nor other conservatives became advocates of working-class causes in the Weimar period. The discipline of the work force that they envisioned prohibited any unhappy rash of "unjustifiable" strikes, as production was a citizen's first duty.[57] But talk of production meant more than simply breaking strikes and aiding economic reconstruction. It anticipated new conceptions of citizenship based on civic mobilization. The revolution was a good thing, argued Wolfgang Schumann in *Kunstwart*, because it would enlist all Germans in the army of labor. Denied the comfortable life of the rentier, Germans would gain a sense of responsibility. Codes of deference and privilege would crumble as a result, and labor would find the esteem it had been denied in the past.[58] Moeller van den Bruck came to similar conclusions. Only those "young nations" that still honored work and production had a future. The old and sated nations, France in particular, preferred the lazy "ideal of the rentier."[59]

Conservatives despised the materialism and exclusive class loyalties of the socialist movement, yet they admired its sense of organization and service. Social Democracy provided conservatives with important lessons about national mobilization. Out of a formless mass of proletarians, solitary and frightened, trade unions had created an "army" of self-confident members and in doing so had overcome the liberal, laissez-faire principles of the nineteenth century.[60] It was this vast formation,

56. Boehm, "Körperschaftliche Bindung," in *Die Neue Front*, ed. v. Gleichen, p. 42. See also A. Bonus, "Konservatismus und Sozialismus," *Kunstwart* 33 (August 1920): 357–65.

57. See *Gewissen*, 9 April 1919, no. 1; and Bittmann, "Arbeit!" *Grenzboten* 78, no. 1 (1919): 23–26.

58. W. Schumann, "Was ist geschehen? Was muß geschehen?" *Kunstwart* 32, no. 5 (December 1918): 142. See also E.D., "Vom geistigen Sozialismus," *Gewissen*, 26 April 1919, no. 3.

59. A. Moeller van den Bruck, *Das Recht der jungen Völker* (Munich, 1919), p. 24. See also idem, "Das Rechtsgefühl von 1914," *Der Tag*, 16 October 1918, no. 243; and Stadtler, "Die Nationalisierung der deutschen Revolution," in *Die Neue Front*, ed. v. Gleichen, p. 419.

60. P. Bröcker, quoted in W. Lambach, *Ursachen des Zusammenbruchs* (Hamburg, 1919), pp. 5–6; and Röhr, "Die deutsche Arbeiterschaft" (see n. 54), p.

built against prevailing forces of disintegration and abandonment, that revolutionary conservatives hoped to re-enact for the nation as a whole. Long before Ernst Jünger's 1932 historical epic, *Der Arbeiter*, Moeller van den Bruck, Boehm, and others had described the worker not as a distinct social type but as the expression of a new appraisal of the world that was sharper, more relentless. As such, workers provided the means for reviving Germany, which required mass production, national discipline, and, above all, a stern, all-encompassing organization.

Wilhelm Stapel, Eduard Stadtler, and Moeller van den Bruck all promoted the idea of a planned economy and the "science of organization." They repeatedly invoked Karl Renner, an Austrian socialist and economist; Wichard von Möllendorff, undersecretary in Germany's postwar Ministry of Economic Affairs; and especially Johann Plenge, a professor of national economy at the University of Münster, who believed that "organization" would be the guiding principle of the future. The rigors of the world war had already demonstrated the value of cooperation between labor and capital, and the utility of state intervention. "The basic idea of 1914," Plenge wrote, was to put individuals "at the service of the whole," to "step into the ranks." Organization was nothing less than socialism, he asserted; it constituted the very spirit of the twentieth century.[61]

211. See also M.H. Boehm, "Konservatismus," in *Kleines politisches Handwörterbuch* (Leipzig, 1919); A. Bonus, "Konservatismus und Sozialismus," *Kunstwart* 33 (August 1920): 357–65, and (September 1920): 398–402; J. Plenge in *Deutsche Allgemeine Zeitung*, 19 October 1918, no. 535; v. Hassell, "Alte und neue Mehrheiten," *Der Tag*, 29 March 1919, no. 66; and H.S. Weber, "Konservative Ideenwelt und Politik," *Der Tag*, 24 May 1919, no. 111.

61. J. Plenge, *1789 und 1914. Die symbolischen Jahre in der Geschichte des politischen Geistes* (Berlin, 1916), pp. 16, 18, 119. See also idem, "Wirtschaftsstufen und Wirtschaftsentwicklung," *Annalen für soziale Politik und Gesetzgebung* 4 (1916): 495–529; and W. von Moellendorff, "Gemeinwirthschaft," *Die Zukunft* 37, no. 107 (1919): 342. A general survey is provided by R.H. Bowen, *German Theories of the Corporative State* (New York, 1947), pp. 160–209. See also H. König, "Das neue Deutschland und der borussische Sozialismus" (see n. 30); as well as E. Schrader, "Theorie und Praxis. Johann Planges Programm eines organisatorischen Sozialismus," in *Soziologie und Sozialismus – Organisation und Propaganda. Abhandlungen zum Werk von Johann Plenge*, ed. B. Schäfers (Stuttgart, 1967), pp. 17–44; Gerstenberger, *Revolutionäre Konservatismus*, pp. 40–41, 50–57; and D.E. Barclay, "A Prussian Socialism? Wichard von Moellendorff and the Dilemmas of Economic Planning in Germany, 1918–19," *Central European History* 11 (1978): 50–82.

That Germany lost the war did not invalidate the lesson of organization. On the contrary, argued Eduard Stadtler, revolutionary events across Europe confirmed that the outline of the future would be "social-organizational." Stadtler envisioned a postwar Reich in which all citizens would be mobilized to work for the common good: "Organization seizes everyone. Organization is purposeful combination, arrangement, integration. . . . Organizations are ruled by discipline." If Germany followed these basic precepts, "the war of all against all" that had so debilitated Imperial Germany would finally be contained.[62] With its emphasis on regulating labor conflicts and the competition among interest groups, as well as on inculcating the virtues of service, Stadtler's vision of civic organization promised to enforce social peace and, in broad strokes, anticipated the Fordism that Germans hailed six years later. Both Stadtler and Henry Ford subscribed to the political gospel of the preeminence of the engineer and planner, and believed that technical solutions would ameliorate the virulence of social and economic conflicts.[63]

Ideas of social organization and social amelioration caught the imagination of conservatives because of the ambitious mobilization they implied. The mobilization of labor since 1890 and the general regimentation of society by the state during the years of total war provided Weimar's revolutionary conservatives with building blocks for the revival of Germany's nationalist ambitions. Organizational aptitude confirmed national commitment to colonize, to create, to produce. Indeed, for Moeller van den Bruck, twentieth-century practices of organization and management recalled nothing so much as the stern military project of Frederican Prussia, which once had been a pioneering power and ought to inspire Germany's revival in the postwar era.[64]

A year after the revolution, Oswald Spengler, the Munich philosopher, popularized the idea that national mobilization

---

62. E. Stadtler, *Die Diktatur der sozialen Revolution* (Leipzig, 1920), pp. 106–7.

63. On Ford, see H. Weiß, *Abbe und Ford. Kapitalistische Utopien* (Berlin, 1927); and H. Lethen, *Neue Sachlichkeit 1924–1932. Studien zur Literatur des 'Weißen Sozialismus'* (Stuttgart, 1970); and C.S. Maier, "Between Taylorism and Technocracy: European Ideologies and the Vision of Industrial Productivity in the 1920s," *Journal of Contemporary History* 5 (1970): 7–61.

64. A. Moeller van den Bruck, *Der Preußischer Stil* (Munich, 1916), p. 16. See also Moeller van den Bruck, "Der Außenseiter," *Der Tag*, 15 January 1919, no. 6.

expressed German socialism in *Preußentum und Sozialismus*, which he dedicated to Germany's youth. Spengler's opus, *The Decline of the West*, had not appealed to Motzstrasse critics such as Moeller van den Bruck, for whom Spengler was entirely too pessimistic and deterministic. Spengler, who had already drafted his ideas of degeneration before 1914, had little in common with Moeller's heady sense of possibility during the revolution.[65] But Spengler's subsequent analysis of Germany's socialist future, which – however much he linked it to the Prussian past – is unthinkable without the experience of war and revolution, concluded in a far more open-ended fashion. Like many younger conservatives, Spengler lauded the virtues of work, authority, and community, all of which he bundled together and opposed to the liberal values of individual wealth and personal success that allegedly prevailed in France, Great Britain, and the United States. The German laborer provided a striking contrast to the rentier of the West. In Spengler's fantastical vision, the disciplined and energetic German labor movement had steadily revived Prussian statism. Unless Marxist outsiders intervened, German socialism would successfully transform the Reich into a vast Faustian workshop animated by a sense of common national purpose, able to summon the service and self-sacrifice of all its citizens.[66] Imagined this way, socialism suggested itself as a distinctively German path to modernity, a revival of the national compact of total war that would impose a settlement on the social and economic conflicts wrought by industrialization, while at the same time steering Germany toward a grand imperial future.

* * *

The German socialism that Spengler and Moeller van den Bruck envisioned was an unlikely alternative to the powerful Social Democratic movement. Germany's young conservatives had made a cult of workers, yet expended little effort in trying to understand their Marxism. Happy ideals of a people's community could not hide the harsh anti-union aspects of conservative thought. Stadtler, Boehm, and Moeller van den Bruck came to hold most Weimar politicians in contempt, and they found the leadership of German Social Democrats unac-

65. Moeller van den Bruck, "Der Untergang des Abendlandes. Für und wider Spengler," *Deutsche Rundschau* 184 (July 1920): 41–70.
66. O. Spengler, *Preußentum und Sozialismus* (Munich, 1919).

ceptable, because philistine, thus exposing their own social pretensions.[67] Even a republic with a more conservative or nationalist cast would probably not have elicited their support. Yet Germany's new conservatives remained deeply impressed by the revolution. Like their counterparts on the Left, they put forward a variety of utopian projects for a new Germany. Encouraged by the dramatic break the November Revolution had made with the Second Reich, they re-read and re-described the German future in ways that owed surprisingly little to the past.

Influential critics such as Moeller van den Bruck and Stadtler were convinced that Germany would survive and prosper in the postwar era only if state and economy were organized in a more collective fashion. Organization and mobilization were recognized as the new practices that the harsh competition of the twentieth century had made obligatory. The exact form of this restructuring was never precisely delineated, but it was clear that World War I provided a glimpse of the shape of things to come. The war economy had promoted a sense of common purpose and social responsibility among Germans, and Ludendorff's warrior state had played a valuable role facilitating "frictionless" economic cooperation between labor and management. The wartime efforts of German labor provided conservatives with guiding images for a newly mobilized postwar Reich. Workers would not only complete the national community; they would stamp it with what many observers took to be distinctively proletarian virtues: discipline, collective spirit, and a combative bearing. Young conservatives predicated Germany's postwar future on the assumption of this (imagined) proletarian identity. The figure of the "warrior-worker" persisted as a remarkably popular political icon for the new Germany, serving to distinguish nationalist front generation literati such as Ernst Jünger – and eventually the Nazis – from the political practices of the *Kaiserreich*.[68] Neither in temperament nor in substance

67. Pascal, "Revolutionary Conservatism," pp. 342, 347. See also Moeller van den Bruck, "Preußentum und Sozialismus," *Gewissen*, 7 January 1920, no. 1, and Hutten, "Sozialismus und ihr Herr. Neuer Mammonismus," ibid., 10 December 1919, no. 35.

68. For example, see J. Goebbels, *Michael: A Novel*, trans. J. Neugroschel (New York, 1987); as well as M. Kater, "The Work Student: A Socio-Economic Phenomenon of Early Weimar Germany," *Journal of Contemporary History* 10 (1975): 71–94; and more generally, Kele, *Nazis and Workers*.

do the dreamy political sketches of Moeller van den Bruck or Max Hildebert Boehm resemble the much more socially confining and elitist endeavors of prewar nationalists such as Heinrich Claß, whose turgid 1912 book, *Wenn ich der Kaiser wär'*, is perhaps the best known contemporary criticism of Wilhelmine Germany.[69]

If the national community that conservatives prescribed had a distinct military quality, it also called for basic political reform. The new Germany could not simply be a barracks yard or factory floor, mobilized and disenfranchised. Wilhelm Stapel, especially – but also Boehm, Moeller van den Bruck, and Stadtler – cherished the festivity and fraternity of German neighborhoods. They were convinced that the creation of an authentic and powerful national community required a more egalitarian social code and a more accessible political structure. Peasants, shopkeepers, and clerks, as well as workers, deserved social recognition and a political voice. The German *Volk* would not find its historical role until the parliamentary parties had evolved into genuine "people's parties", in which constituents from all backgrounds played political parts. The failure to accomplish these populist reforms had constituted the tragedy of Wilhelmine Germany. For a generation of conservative critics, born in the two decades after unification, the collapse of the Second Reich offered the welcome opportunity to build a more emotionally satisfying and public-spirited *Volksstaat* that would serve as a firm foundation for the revival of Germany as a great power. November 1918 provided Weimar's radical conservatives with a root metaphor for political change: a German revolution was possible and desirable. The dramatic turmoil of revolution untied conservative loyalties to the past, persuading them of the transiency and fragility of the Weimar Republic while marrying their political ambitions to crisis and upheaval.

---

69. H. Claß, *Wenn ich der Kaiser wär'* (Leipzig, 1912). See also L. von Vietinghoff-Scheel, "Die Vorstellungswelt der Alldeutschen," *Der Tag*, 3 June 1919, no. 118.

10
Conservatism, National Socialism, and the Cultural Crisis of the Weimar Republic

Alan E. Steinweis

In seeking to lend coherence to a period of German history that is often treated as a mere interregnum between the Hohenzollern Empire and the Third Reich, Detlev J.K. Peukert has described the Weimar Republic as the "crisis years of classical modernity."[1] The years from 1918 to 1933 saw dramatic breakthroughs in social policy, technology, science, the humanities, and the arts, that, when taken together, constitute what we have come to know as "modernity" throughout much of the twentieth century. "In a mere fourteen years," wrote Peukert, "nearly all the possibilities of modern existence were played out." As it unfolded, however, Weimar modernity generated an intense and widespread backlash. The fierce political and ideological struggles of the Weimar era can, therefore, be understood as the convulsions of a society attempting to come to terms with modernity in all its manifestations.

It was in the area of the cultural arts that the conflict over modernity was the most immediately recognizable to contemporaries. Aesthetic principles and artistic substance served both as causes and as tools of ideological and political struggle. Accordingly, the subject of "Weimar Culture" has received a good deal of attention from historians.[2] Yet our understand-

1. D.J.K. Peukert, *Die Weimarer Republik: Krisenjahre der Klassischen Moderne* (Frankfurt am Main, 1987).
2. Useful studies include *Culture and Society in the Weimar Republic*, ed. K. Bullivant (Totowa, N.J., 1977); P. Gay, *Weimar Culture: The Outsider as Insider* (New York, 1968); J. Hermand and F. Trommler, *Die Kultur der Weimarer Republik* (Munich, 1978); W. Laqueur, *Weimar: A Cultural History* (New York, 1974); H. Pachter, *Weimar Etudes* (New York, 1982); B. Schraeder and J. Schebera, *The "Golden" Twenties: Art and Literature in the Weimar Republic*, trans. K. Vanovich (New Haven, Conn., 1988).

ing of the connections between politics and culture in the Weimar era remains far from complete. Whereas the relationship between art and the political Left in the Weimar Republic has been subjected to detailed examination,[3] analogous connections on the right side of the political spectrum have been explored less fully. Important works on political and social conservatism have devoted little attention to the arts.[4] The major studies of the cultural and intellectual origins of the Third Reich have concerned themselves more with the direct antecedents of National Socialism than with conservatism *sui generis*.[5] This has perhaps been the result of a tendency to view cultural conservatism in the Weimar era from a teleological perspective, according to which National Socialism was the inevitable successor to the Weimar Republic and thus the logical culmination of German history. The tendency to conflate the conservative and National Socialist critiques of culture may very well be, at least in part, a consequence of the very real Nazi-conservative collaboration on the cultural and political front during the latter phase of the Weimar Republic. To the extent that scholars have avoided this conflation and have recognized the conservative critique of artistic modernism as distinct from that of National Socialism, they have depicted the conservative position as monolithic and static, rather than as a diverse set of ideas that evolved in the context of the highly dynamic political, economic, and social circumstances of the years 1918 to 1933.

The purpose of this essay, therefore, is to provide a framework for analyzing conservative reactions to the modernist movements that have collectively come to be called "Weimar Culture." It will show that conservative opinions varied significantly in tone, substance, and militancy. Whereas some

3. Most recently W.L. Guttsman, *Worker's Culture in Weimar Germany: Between Tradition and Commitment* (New York, 1990).

4. K. von Klemperer, *Germany's New Conservatism: Its History and Dilemma in the Twentieth Century*, 2nd ed., (Princeton, N.J., 1968); H. Lebovics, *Social Conservatism and the Middle Classes in Germany* (Princeton, N.J., 1969); W. Struve, *Elites against Democracy: Leadership Ideals and in Bourgeois Political Thought in Germany, 1890–1933* (Princeton, N.J., 1973).

5. G.L. Mosse, *The Crisis of German Ideology: Intellectual Origins of the Third Reich* (New York, 1964); F. Stern, *The Crisis of Cultural Despair: A Study in the Rise of the Germanic Ideology* (Berkeley, Calif., 1961); J. Hermand, *Der alte Traum vom neuen Reich. Völkische Utopien und Nationalsozialismus* (Frankfurt am Main, 1988).

conservatives engaged in little more than reflexive opposition to aesthetically dissonant or politically subversive art, others posited elaborate theories of cultural decline, diagnosing modernism as a symptom of a diseased society. This essay will also depart from the traditional static depiction of cultural conservatism by describing how conservative attitudes toward modernism evolved over time in response to shifts in the political and economic landscape of the Weimar Republic. Finally, this essay will explore the ambiguous relationship between the cultural critique of German conservatism and that of National Socialism. Although opposition to cultural modernism did at times provide a common cause for right-wing enemies of the Weimar Republic, many conservatives could not share in the vulgarity, virulence, and racist essence of the National Socialist position.

* * *

Important elements of the cultural modernism identified with the Weimar era had already been present in the German Empire. As Peter Gay has observed, "The Weimar Style was born before the Weimar Republic."[6] Despite the cultural conservatism of the Kaiser and much of the artistic establishment, the cultural ferment of the empire had produced the experimental theater of Max Reinhardt, the musical atonality of Arnold Schönberg, several schools of expressionism in painting, including *Die Brücke* and *Der Blaue Reiter*, and the beginnings of Bauhaus architecture.[7] Although all these movements were in part the German manifestations of international movements with their own aesthetic dynamics, they were also the products of a German social environment in which the rapid pace of industrialization and urbanization had led artists and intellectuals to question the validity of prevailing bourgeois cultural values. The emergence of a large industrial proletariat challenged the position and confidence of the Ger-

---

6. Gay, *Weimar Culture*, p. 5.
7. Recent important studies of modernism before 1914 include P. Jelavich, *Munich and Theatrical Modernism: Politics, Playwriting, and Performance, 1890–1914* (Cambridge, Mass., 1985); M. Makela, *The Munich Secession: Art and Artists in Turn-of-the-Century Munich* (Princeton, N.J., 1990); P. Paret, *The Berlin Secession: Modernism and its Enemies in Imperial Germany* (Cambridge, Mass., 1980); and J. Weinstein, *The End of Expressionism: Art and the November Revolution in Germany, 1918–1919* (Chicago, 1990).

man *Bildungsbürgertum,* whose outlook had traditionally dominated institutionalized cultural life.[8]

The experience of the Great War, the collapse of the empire, and its replacement by a republic with stated democratic and egalitarian aspirations placed the defenders of traditionalism clearly on the defensive. While in the sociopolitical sphere the working class attained a new level of empowerment and women achieved political emancipation, in the realm of the arts modernism reached its full efflorescence, breaking through the psychological and institutional barriers that had contained it before 1914. Although the actual practitioners of modernism remained a minority among German artists, the public debate over artistic principles focused largely on their work; whether they intended it or not, they became symbols of the new era. Inasmuch as modernism amounted to an assault on bourgeois cultural norms, the attention devoted to it by German critics underscored what was widely perceived as the accelerating erosion of bourgeois cultural hegemony.[9]

Opinion magazines provided an important vehicle for the propagation of the conservative critique of artistic modernism and serve as a main source of information for this essay. The venerable *Deutsche Rundschau,* "one of the oldest and most recognized magazines in Germany," played a leading role in shaping and disseminating elite conservative opinion in the Republic, and, toward the end, in warning conservatives to resist the totalitarian temptation of National Socialism.[10] The *Preußische Jahrbücher,* like the *Deutsche Rundschau,* could also trace its roots well back into the nineteenth century, and counted among its past editors Heinrich von Treitschke and Hans Delbrück. Although both of these publications adjusted to the shifting ideological currents of the Weimar era, their approach to artistic questions remained moderate in comparison to those taken by two newer publications, *Die Tat* and *Der Ring.* Strident in style and substance, *Die Tat* and *Der Ring* served as important forums for the articulation of views connected with

8. For an insightful synthesis, see K.H. Jarausch, "Die Krise des deutschen Bildungsbürgertums im ersten Drittel des 20. Jahrhunderts," in *Bildungsbürgertum im 19. Jahrhundert,* ed. W. Conze and J. Kocka, 4 vols. (Göttingen, 1985–89), vol. 4, pp. 180–205.

9. G. Stark, *Entrepreneurs of Ideology: Neoconservative Publishers in Weimar Germany* (Chapel Hill, N.C., 1981), pp. 172–211.

10. Klemperer, *Germany's New Conservatism*, pp. 110, 124.

the so-called "Conservative Revolution" of the interwar period.

Historians have expended tremendous energy in attempting to make sense of this movement.[11] The phenomenon nevertheless remains elusive. Perhaps its most salient feature was not its actual substance, which was disparate, ambiguous, even contradictory, but rather its utopian, irrational impulse. Several core ideas lent some coherence to the movement. One of these was the juxtaposition of an organic German *Kultur* with the mechanistic societies grounded in liberal capitalism on the one hand, and Marxist socialism on the other. Whereas Germanic *Kultur* was seen as firmly rooted in the people, the other two systems were regarded as artificial constructs. In condemning cultural modernism as an essentially materialistic manifestation of mass society, conservative revolutionaries linked the decline of a supposedly organic Germanic culture with the rise of the working class. In promoting an irrational romanticism, they held up the western rationalist tradition as inherently antithetical to Germandom. And in decrying the culturally corrupting influence of "mammonism," they were as critical of large-scale capitalism as they were of Marxism. The multifaceted crisis confronting Germany could therefore be explained as the result of a decoupling of nation and culture. Thus, the notion of redemption through culture was close to the hearts of the conservative revolutionaries. As early as 1920, Eugen Diederichs, publisher of *Die Tat* and operator of his own press, issued an anthology of *Schriften zur Kulturpolitik*, underscoring the publisher's own declaration that artists, rather than politicians, would lead the way to the "new order in Germany."[12]

Conservative revolutionaries were not nostalgic for the artistic life of the Second Reich. That culture, like the society of which it was a reflection, had grown old, tired, and constipated. Redemption could come only through a restoration of the primacy of irrationalism in German culture. They not only tolerated, but even championed artistic experimentation as being authentically Germanic. The expressionist painter Emil Nolde, an early adherent to National Socialism, exemplified how the

11. A. Mohler, *Die konservative Revolution in Deutschland 1918–1932* (Stuttgart, 1950); J. Herf, *Reactionary Modernism: Technology, Culture, and Politics in Weimar and the Third Reich* (Cambridge, 1984).

12. Stark, *Entrepreneurs of Ideology*, p. 182.

impulse to break through existing artistic barriers could combine with a sympathy for the extreme Right.[13] This affinity, however, was not reciprocal. By and large, the conservative revolution, like National Socialism, was hostile to the artistic modernism of the 1920s, which was generally identified with the Marxist Left. Thus, during the Weimar Republic, cultural antimodernism provided a common denominator between oldline conservatives, conservative revolutionaries, and the *völkisch* Right.

Hardly had the Great War passed into history before artistic issues became a main topic of discussion in conservative journals. The terms of the debate were defined early in the life of the Republic. Writing on the Berlin music scene in the *Deutsche Rundschau* in late 1918, Gustav Ernest, the author of books on Wagner and Beethoven,[14] articulated a complaint that would become common currency among Weimar conservatives: the increasing prevalence of "hypermodernism" had opened up a wide gulf between the "aspirations of the younger of our creative artists" and the "sensibility of the great mass of music-loving and music-understanding audiences." Modern compositions performed with increasing frequency in Berlin, wrote Ernest, suffered from an "inner emptiness," an "affected suprahumanity," and a "nerve-racking uniformity." Yet in a qualifying observation that typified the more sophisticated among the antimodern critics, Ernest pointed out that "modernism as such" did not disturb him so much as did "modernism as an end in itself." After all, Beethoven and Wagner had broken with tradition in their own times. But these two composers had done so because existing musical conventions had constrained their genius; in contrast, most of the new modernists were merely following a fashion. Unlike the critics of the *völkisch* Right, Ernest did not see a conspiracy behind the modernist movement, but only a misdirected youthful enthusiasm.[15]

Albert Dresdner, an expert on art criticism and the history of Scandinavian art,[16] also saw trendiness as the main culprit in

13. B. Taylor, "Post-Modernism in the Third Reich," in *The Nazification of Art: Art, Design, Music, Architecture and Film in the Third Reich*, ed. B. Taylor and W. von der Will, (Winchester, 1990), pp. 128–43.

14. G. Ernest, *Beethoven* (Berlin, 1920); and *Richard Wagner: Sein Leben und Schaffen* (Berlin 1915).

15. G. Ernest, "Berliner Musikleben," *Deutsche Rundschau* 176 (1918): 246–54.

16. A. Dresdner, *Schwedische und Norwegische Kunst seit der Renaissance* (Breslau, 1924).

the assault on tradition in the visual arts. Already before the war, Dresdner maintained in a 1919 *Deutsche Rundschau* article, too many artists had bought into a set of abstract artistic "principles that do not correspond to reality." As a consequence, their works suffered from a "chaotic opaqueness" that was impenetrable even to Germans who were knowledgeable about art. Aside from the obvious aesthetic implications, Dresdner warned of possible economic ramifications. Despite its sacred role in German society, art remained a form of economic activity. By alienating the society around them, German artists ran the risk of financial catastrophe. What was needed, Dresdner argued, was a new concept of artistic utilitarianism that appealed to popular tastes and that restored traditional links between art and the handicrafts. Ironically, in the latter respect, Dresdner shared the impulse toward social relevancy that drove Walter Gropius to found the Bauhaus at around the same time. Their visions differed inasmuch as Dresdner, like other conservatives, sought the restoration of tradition, whereas Gropius and other socially conscious modernists such as Brecht, saw artists as paving the way to a new social reality.[17]

Critics of modernism, such as Ernest and Dresdner, undoubtedly overestimated the popularity and influence of modernism at this still early juncture. Their concerns testify to the power with which artistic movements can evoke, rather than cause, social or political transformations. What was new and worrisome to the likes of Ernest and Dresdner in 1919 was not artistic modernism itself, but rather a nascent political and social order that shared modernism's disavowal of tradition. As Dresdner himself wrote in 1920, "the victory of the November revolution means the victory of expressionism in art."[18] What disturbed Dresdner most was expressionism's new status as a "revolutionary-official" art, before which the state "art bureaucracy had capitulated."

Conservative commentaries on modernism were not universally condemnatory during the earliest phase of the Republic. Some critics understood that artistic life required constant renewal, even if that meant tolerating the "doctrinaire intellectualism" supposedly characteristic of modernism. Thus, it was

17. A. Dresdner, "Die Zukunft der Künstler," *Deutsche Rundschau* 178 (1919): 133–49.
18. A. Dresdner, "Aus dem Berliner Kunstleben," *Deutsche Rundschau* 182 (1920): 301.

not seen as an entirely negative development when the state collections in Berlin were updated to include expressionist paintings in 1919. As one critic opined in the *Deutsche Rundschau*, only time could judge whether the works of Oskar Kokoschka, Max Pechstein, Emil Nolde, and Lyonel Feininger would deserve a permanent place alongside the old masters.[19]

The early National Socialist position left little room for such tolerance. Early in the Weimar Republic, National Socialism represented an extremist version of cultural antimodernism. In its "Twenty-Five Point Program" of February 1920, the Nazi party called for the "legal prosecution of all those tendencies in art and literature that corrupt our national life, and the suppression of cultural events that violate this demand." Like other groups of the *völkisch* Right, the NSDAP saw the threat to traditional German culture as the product of a network of racially, spiritually, and financially interconnected artistic and cultural forces, led by Jews and Marxists, promoted by feminists, and most conspicuously symbolized by the increasing visibility of "Negroes" on the cultural scene. Expressionism, atonality, and other forms of modernism were not artistic trends grounded in a political world view; rather they were manifestations of race. Already in 1920 the Nazi newspaper *Völkischer Beobachter* had ascribed the breakthrough of expressionism to the influence of "Jewry," which had "laid claim to be the cultural ruling class in Germany" by virtue of its control of art galleries, museums, orchestras, theaters, and the press.[20] The celebration of modernism had nothing to do with talent; it was the result solely of the "press dictatorship" of Jews.[21] The Nazi perspective possessed the politically utilitarian virtues of simplicity, consistency, and predictability. Elsewhere on the ideological Right, however, the critique of cultural modernism was more differentiated and ambiguous; as a consequence, it lacked the political punch and popular appeal of the Nazi approach.

Throughout much of the 1920s, the National Socialist critique remained distinguishable from that of most conserva-

---

19. M. von Bunsen, "Die Verjüngung der Nationalgalerie," *Deutsche Rundshau* 180 (1919): 463.

20. B. Funck, "Die Kunstausstellung im Münchener Glaspalast," *Völkischer Beobachter*, 26 August 1920.

21. O. von Kursell, "Max Liebermann," *Völkischer Beobachter*, 27 September 1923.

tives. Simplistic canards such as "art Bolshevism," which the Nazis flexibly invoked to disparage any cultural trend they did not like, appeared far less commonly in conservative journals, which took the trouble at least to differentiate among the modernist trends of which they disapproved. Moreover, for reasons both of conviction and civility, conservative writers on culture refrained from the vulgar, unabashed anti-Semitism of the *völkisch* Right. Even Eugen Diederichs, who believed in the immutability of differences between the German and Jewish *Völker*, in 1922 publicly condemned the crude anti-Semitism of the extreme Right.[22] If race was at the core of the *völkisch* cultural critique, then class served as the primary causal factor for a great number of conservative writers. Their main preoccupation was not with Jews or "foreigners," but rather with the decline of the middle class, which, they believed, had been the wellspring and chief patron of German *Kultur* since at least the nineteenth century.

The severe hyperinflation of 1922/23 exacerbated anxiety over the fate of the middle class and its supposedly attendant culture. The inflation, which was generally interpreted as especially catastrophic for the German *Bürgertum*, seemed to intensify a general cultural and intellectual crisis, one referred to by contemporaries as the "crisis of the intellectual workers."[23] Although applied mainly to describe the increasingly desperate financial situation of academic professionals and artists, this concept, which was widely embraced along the right side of the German political spectrum, contained broader implications for all of German society. In his book on the "crisis" published in 1923, Georg Schreiber, a professor at the University of Münster and a Reichstag deputy for the Catholic Center Party, explored the cultural ramifications of middle-class decline. Its position having deteriorated since the days of the empire, the middle class could no longer patronize the arts at pre-1918 levels. Moreover, the Reich, the federal states, and the municipalities were now too hard pressed in other areas to maintain a sufficiently high level of support for the arts. The new social welfare legislation of the Republic, pushed through primarily by Social Democrats on behalf of their working-class

22. Stark, *Entrepreneurs of Ideology*, pp. 208–09.
23. K.H. Jarausch, "Die Not der geistigen Arbeiter: Akademiker in der Berufskrise," in *Die Weimarer Republik als Wohlfahrtsstaat*, ed. W. Abelshauser (Wiesbaden, 1987), pp. 280–99.

supporters, was particularly damaging, for it forced communities to cut back drastically on subsidies for theaters, orchestras, and museums. Schreiber also pointed to more indirect effects. Higher property taxes, for example, discouraged new construction, leading to reduced opportunities for architects. Monetary instability resulted in a general decrease in publishing activity in the early 1920s, hurting both publishers and authors. Similarly, increased freight expenses rendered art exhibitions costlier and therefore less frequent, depriving artists and sculptors of the possibility of exhibiting and selling their work.[24]

Although Schreiber was undeniably far more moderate a figure than Diederichs and other conservative publicists, he shared their notion that the decline in German cultural values was rooted in the emergence of mass society, one whose economic priorities and cultural values did not correspond to those of the "culture-carrying" middle classes. In their elitism, both had more in common with each other than they did with the National Socialists, who, like the Communists and Social Democrats, preached from the very beginning about the need to make high culture accessible to the masses.

The politico-economic stabilization of the Republic after 1923 did little to dampen the cultural conflict between modernists and their opponents. Throughout the middle part of the decade, modernist influence in the arts continued to grow in Germany. Modernist compositions by Alban Berg and Paul Hindemith premiered in major concert halls. Films by Fritz Lang provoked much discussion, as did stage plays by Bertolt Brecht. Modernists accepted positions in prestigious and powerful institutions. In 1926, for example, Arnold Schönberg was elected to the Prussian Academy of Arts, while in the following year, Otto Dix accepted a faculty post at the Dresden Art Academy. Increasingly, modernist works created public controversy. The 1927 premiere of Ernst Krenek's jazz opera "Jonny spielt auf" was a major *cause celebre* that divided the German public. In the same year, Erwin Piscator launched a new proletarian theater project in Berlin. In 1928, caricaturist George Grosz was tried and convicted on the charge of blas-

---

24. G. Schreiber, *Die Not der deutschen Wissenschaft und der geistigen Arbeiter. Geschehnisse und Gedanken zur Kulturpolitik des deutschen Reiches* (Leipzig, 1923), pp. 108–15.

phemy for an antiwar drawing depicting a crucified Christ wearing a gas mask. To its enemies, then, the new art appeared to be an irreversible juggernaut.

This increasing momentum of the modernist revolt during the Republic's so-called "Golden Years" helps explain why antimodernists intensified their own countermobilization during this period of relative political stability. If one were to seek a symbol for the radicalization of cultural conservatism at this juncture, an ideal candidate would be the architect Paul Schultze-Naumburg. A prominent progressive architect during the empire, Schultze-Naumburg had emerged as a leading detractor of the new architectural style of the 1920s. In his 1928 book *Kunst und Rasse*, he made the leap from a cultural to a racial mode of argumentation, claiming that a direct link existed between modern art and the degenerate condition of its creators. In a subsequent work, *Das Gesicht des deutschen Hauses*, published in 1929, Schultze-Naumburg took issue with the Spenglerian concept of inevitable cultural decline that had achieved fashion among some German conservatives. Changes in architectural style, Schultze-Naumburg asserted, were only partially the result of an evolution in culture; at their root, they were a "biological phenomenon." Schultze-Naumburg's theories thus lent a new legitimacy to the racial determinism that had long defined the *völkisch* point of view.[25]

If the backlash against cultural modernism at times obscured the delineation between conservative and *völkisch* positions in the late 1920s, it was not an entirely coincidental development. Rather, it was the intended result of a National Socialist strategy, implemented in 1928, to broaden Nazism's appeal to the German educated middle class. Although the late 1920s were a period of relative stagnation for the Nazi movement, as measured in electoral and membership terms, the party did initiate new organizational and mobilization strategies that would contribute to its post-1929 successes. The founding in 1928 of the Kampfbund für deutsche Kultur must be understood in this context.[26] Although Hitler and other

25. P. Schultze-Naumburg, *Kunst und Rasse* (Munich, 1928); *Das Gesicht des Deutschen Hauses* (Munich, 1929). For further details see B.M. Lane, *Architecture and Politics in Germany, 1918–1945* (Cambridge, Mass., 1968), pp. 137–39.

26. For a more thorough discussion, see A.E. Steinweis, "Weimar Culture and the Rise of National Socialism: The Kampfbund für deutsche Kultur," *Central European History* 24 (1991): 402–23.

Nazi leaders had been openly contemptuous of artistic modernism since the very beginning of the movement, they had hitherto made no serious attempt to attack artistic issues politically. The mission of the Kampfbund, therefore, was first and foremost to organize grass-roots cultural discontent among educated Germans, and then to harness it to the Nazi movement. In the hope of appealing to "apolitical" Germans, for whom art and culture were far more important than mere politics, the Kampfbund concentrated its efforts on exhibitions, lieder evenings, and lectures. Its publications, most notably the *Deutsche Kultur-Wacht*, presented readers with a combination of serious cultural feature stories and *völkisch* treatises, although the latter tended to be considerably milder in tone than similar pieces found in the *Völkischer Beobachter*. To preserve this nonpartisan facade, until 1932 the Kampfbund took pains to avoid a formal connection with the party, despite the fact that Alfred Rosenberg, a most prominent Nazi, served as national leader of the Kampfbund.

Although the Kampfbund added nothing new of substance to the debate over art, it performed an important function as an institutional bridge between National Socialism and conservatism. Its membership, which had risen to slightly over 2,000 by January 1932, consisted primarily of university instructors, professionals, artists, and intellectuals. Prominent members included Paul Schultze-Naumburg, Winifried Wagner of the Bayreuth Circle, Alfred Heuss, the editor of the prestigious journal *Zeitschrift für Musik*, and Walter von Bogen und Schöstedt, the executive director of the German Nobles Association (Deutsche Adelsgenossenschaft). The Berlin branch counted among its activists Gustav Havemann, a Professor of Violin at the Academy of Music, and the composer Paul Graener, a revered figure among German musical traditionalists.

The readiness of some German cultural conservatives to cast in their lot with a Nazi front organization presaged a further radicalization that ensued with the onset of the Great Depression. Beginning in 1930, the conservative critique of culture underwent a transformation, to some degree in substance, but, even more importantly, in tone. It shifted, to borrow Carl Schorske's formulation, into a new, sharper key.[27] In their con-

27. C.E. Schorske, *Fin-de-Siècle Vienna: Politics and Culture* (New York, 1980), chapter 3. Schorske employed the metaphor to describe the increasingly acrimonious quality of the ideological debate in turn-of-the-century Vienna.

demnation of modernist culture, many conservatives abandoned self-restraint, adopting a harsher, more caustic tone.
Anti-Semitism became far more open and unabashed, and
uses of the "Art Bolshevism" canard grew more frequent.

Conservative opinion continued to flow in several parallel
currents. One current was fundamentally pessimistic. Writing
in *Die Tat* in 1931, Richard Massek pondered the causes and
consequences of the "Auflösung des bürgerlichen Theaters."[28]
"The relentless advance of the masses," Massek argued, had
led to the rise of the "modern" media of cinema and radio,
both of which were well suited to the simplistic outlook of the
masses. Theater, on the other hand, had been a medium rooted
primarily in the *Bürgertum*. As the class composition of German society changed, so, inevitably, would the dominant
forms of artistic expression. Consequently, Massek argued,
attempts to reverse the decline of bourgeois theater through
"great financial sacrifices" contravened the very laws of history. The champions of tradition were fighting a lost cause, for
the "German theater is the expression of an estate [*Stand*] that
no longer exists." Massek even praised Bertolt Brecht's experiment at salvaging theater as an artistic medium by adapting
its form and substance to the working-class milieu, but predicted its ultimate failure.

While Massek and others spread the gloom of cultural
despair, others underscored the urgency of cultural *repair*.
Rather than concede defeat like Massek and other cultural
pessimists or appropriate what were widely regarded as the
aesthetic proclivities of the Left – as Nolde, in the opinion of
many on the right, had done – many conservatives simply
declared total war on modernism.[29] In a front-page article entitled "Kulturbolschewismus" that appeared in *Der Ring* in September 1930, Walther Schotte, a leading conservative and former editor of the *Preußische Jahrbücher*, urged readers to "take
bitterly earnest" the danger confronting German culture.[30] Far
more than a matter of artistic style, cultural bolshevism
embodied a comprehensive world view antithetical not only

28. R. Massek, "Die Auflösung des bürgerlichen Theaters," *Die Tat* 22, no. 12
(March 1931): 993–97.
29. R. Merker, *Die bildenden Künste im Nationalsozialismus* (Cologne, 1980), p.
80.
30. W. Schotte, "Kulturbolschewismus," *Der Ring* 3, no. 36 (7 September
1930): 617–18.

to German culture, but to that of the entire Occident. Having implanted itself in Germany, cultural bolshevism was now helping to pave the way for its political analog. Combatting cultural bolshevism required more than revealing its sinister nature; it required also a reaffirmation of the value of "family, heritage, and property." As if to underscore Schotte's pleas to take art as a politically serious matter, in the very next article Franz von Papen assailed the "poison of class decomposition" dispensed by Erwin Piscator.[31]

Several weeks later, Fritz Nemitz, an art historian who would enjoy a prolific career in the Nazi regime and then in the Federal Republic,[32] provided a quite different analysis of the "life and death struggle" in German art.[33] In an article in *Der Ring* focusing on the visual arts, Nemitz employed socio-logical jargon to describe a multi-dimensional crisis, the main cause of which he attributed to late capitalism. A system pre-occupied with "production" and "utility" must be fundamen-tally hostile to art. "Capitalist man" cannot be fulfilled by art, but only appreciate its decorative function and its function as a vessel of financial value. On a more concrete level, Nemitz pointed out that capitalism "in its present form" had brought about the "disintegration and destruction of the old culture-supporting middle class." Art had thereby become "fully iso-lated and uprooted from its social function." Liberalism, the political concomitant of capitalism, had exacerbated the social alienation of art by imbuing artists with an unhealthy belief in the doctrine of "art for art's sake." Deprived of their historical orientation, German artists were forced to grope for alterna-tives; some turned to American "Negerkunst," while others looked to the "self-styled proletarian art of Russia." What was Nemitz's solution? "Art and *Volk*, Art and Time, Art and Econ-omy – it all fits together in the miracle of a mysterious order that we perhaps may divine [*ahnen*], but that we can never expect to measure in exact proportions." Typifying the abstruse romantic yearnings of many conservative revolution-

31. F. von Papen, "Entschluß!," *Der Ring* 3, no. 36 (7 September 1930): 618–19.

32. Nemitz's publications during the Nazi era included *Gottfried Schadow, Der Zeichner* (Berlin, 1937); *Caspar David Friedrich* (Berlin, 1938), *Junge Bildhauer* (Berlin, 1939); *Unersterbliches Spanien* (Berlin, 1939); *Die Kunst Rußlands* (Berlin, 1940); *Goya* (Berlin, 1940).

33. F. Nemitz, "Was wird aus der Kunst," *Die Tat* 22, no. 9 (December 1930): 679–92.

aries, this particular formulation also reflected an assumption that had become widespread in cultural circles by the end of the Weimar Republic: whatever was wrong, conflicts over art reflected a broader systemic crisis. Paul Ernst, the well-known nationalist writer, observed that this point required continual reiteration, for the general public still did not grasp the sociological importance of art, "what art means to a people."[34]

Increasingly between 1930 and 1933, conservative critics echoed the anti-Semitic sentiments of National Socialism. In his September 1930 article on "Kulturbolschewismus" in *Der Ring*, Schotte smugly noted the special affinity between Jews and modernism. In another contribution to *Der Ring*, one dealing with "Kultur im politischen Kampf," Friedrich Vorwerk listed "Judentum" among the "enemies of the German cultural inheritance," along with Russia, America, "European internationalism," and the "political organization" of the German proletariat.[35] In 1932, Ferdinand Eckhardt used the pages of *Die Tat* to lash out against the "regimentation of the entire artistic life of Germany" by a cabal of dealers and public officials "of one and the same heritage."[36]

At the end of the Weimar Republic there were still conservative critics who resisted the temptation to indulge in open anti-Semitism, references to creeping "Negroidism," and militant denunciation of "cultural bolshevism." The cultural analyses published in the *Deutsche Rundschau* remained largely devoid of such canards. In his call for an emphasis on German *Volkstum* in literature, for example, the nationalist writer Hans Friedrich Blunck stated his case in positive terms, making no reference to "internal enemies," or "degeneracy."[37] Similarly, Hans Joachim Moser, a prolific conservative musicologist, in surveying the state of German music in 1932 acknowledged the contributions of Kurt Weill and Ernst Krenek. Moser

34. P. Ernst, "Die Kunst und das Volk," *Der Ring* 5, no. 7 (12 February 1932): 111–12.

35. F. Vorwerk, "Kultur im politischen Kampf," *Der Ring* 3, no. 47 (28 November 1930): 825–26. Vorwerk emphatically distinguished between the "political organization" of the proletariat, i.e., the Socialist and Communist parties, and the proletariat itself, thus suggesting that artistic modernism had been foisted upon the German working masses by treacherous Marxists.

36. F. Eckhardt, "Schluß mit dem Kunstbetrieb," *Die Tat* 24, no. 6 (September 1932): 498–507.

37. H.F. Blunck, "Volkstum und Dichtung," *Deutsche Rundschau* 233 (1932): 162–76.

reserved his derision for the "pious constructivism" of Arnold Schönberg and his disciples, although even here Moser restricted his critique entirely to an artistic plane. He considered Schönberg a bad composer, not an enemy of the people.[38]

Another voice of restraint was Hans Knudsen, the theater critic for the *Preußische Jahrbücher*. Although hardly a fan of the proletarian theater of Brecht or Piscator, Knudsen usually steered clear of political epithets and reported on the artistic merits and demerits of what he witnessed. In 1931 Knudsen was full of praise for Max Reinhardt, who had recently been forced to close his Deutsches Theater for economic reasons.[39] Adulation for Reinhardt contravened fashion on the political right: to some conservative critics Reinhardt had been guilty of apostasy because of his innovative productions of classical works – Shakespeare and Ibsen were among his favorites – while the *völkisch* Right had latched onto Reinhardt's Jewish heritage from early on.

Even the more strident conservative publications could contain opinion of surprising moderation. In October 1932, for example, Hans Pflug published a fascinating analysis of the "Fall Bauhaus" in *Die Tat*.[40] In August 1932, the Dessau city council had voted 20 to 5 to close the famous school for design. National Socialists and "bourgeois representatives" had voted in favor of the closing, while the Social Democrats on the council abstained for mysterious "party technical" reasons. Only Communists voted against the measure. Pflug noted that the conservative press had warmly approved of Dessau's decision, citing the school's "Marxist and communist orientation" and its "antinational cosmopolitan style." The *Berliner Lokal-Anzeiger* sarcastically recommended a relocation of the school to Moscow. Pflug, however, did not share in the gloating. Invoking the authority of the nationalist-conservative *Deutsche Allgemeine Zeitung*, which had described the Bauhaus as one of Germany's "most serious and most interesting" art academies, Pflug regretted that "philistines and reactionaries" had won the day in Dessau. Pflug ascribed the vote of the bourgeois councilmen to political necessity: so cleverly had the National

38. H.J. Moser, "Die Musik im Gefüge dieser Zeit," *Deutsche Rundschau* 233 (1932): 181–87.
39. H. Knudsen, review of Reinhardt's book *25 Jahre Deutsches Theater*, in *Preußische Jahrbücher* 225 (July–September 1931): 322–23.
40. H. Pflug, "Der Fall Bauhaus," *Die Tat* 24, no. 7 (October 1932): 572–83.

Socialists exploited grassroots resentment of the Bauhaus, the bourgeois councilmen had come to see a vote against the Bauhaus as a way of depriving the Nazis of support. Pflug lamented that an important, and incorrect, decision had been made not on its cultural merits, but out of political expediency.[41]

Pflug had put his finger on what not nearly enough conservatives recognized late in the life of the Weimar Republic, namely, that the impending revolution would not be so much a conservative one as a Nazi one. In the arena of mass politics, conservative critiques of culture, with all of their ambiguities, sociological insights, and impenetrable romantic rhetoric, could not compete with the clear, simplistic message of National Socialism. The very diversity of views that existed along the spectrum of conservatism diluted the potential for political instrumentalization. At the same time, some conservatives, through their bitter attacks on modernism, their submission to the temptation of anti-Semitism, their flirtation with racialism, and their organizational collaboration with Nazism in the form of the Kampfbund, had helped National Socialism win respect as a movement with a legitimate artistic and cultural program.

The complex interplay between National Socialism and cultural conservatism continued beyond Hitler's appointment to the chancellorship. The leading conservative opinion journals were allowed to remain in operation, at least initially. In 1933 the Nazi regime invited established figures such as Richard Strauss and Hans Friedrich Blunck to assume important posts in Germany's revamped cultural institutions.[42] Although the direct, often brutal methods of the regime appalled some conservatives, few mourned the banishment of artistic modernists and the proscription of their works. Conservatives celebrated the generosity with which the new regime subsidized the arts, while artists themselves competed for the flattery and favor of Nazi bigwigs.

Ultimately, however, the Nazis silenced or shoved to the

41. Judging from his later publication record, it seems that Pflug accommodated himself well to the Nazi regime. For example, see Pflug, *Lob der Deutschen Landschaft* (Leipzig, 1938); *Deutschlands Raumschicksal, mit einer farbigen Karte von Mitteleuropa* (Heidelberg, 1941); and *Donau und Donauraum* (Heidelberg, 1941).

42. In late 1933, Strauss became President of the new Reich Chamber of Music, while Blunck was appointed to lead the new Reich Chamber of Literature.

margins anyone who was perceived as a threat to their primacy. By 1939 the conservative journals had been closed down or transformed beyond recognition. Strauss, Blunck, and other conservative collaborators were replaced by Nazis or more malleable personalities. Art historians[43] and musicologists, including Moser,[44] succumbed to pressure to toe the Nazi line in order to maintain their positions and avoid harassment. The paintings of Emil Nolde were removed from museums and placed in an exhibition of "Degenerate Art."[45] The writer Gottfried Benn, who, like Nolde, was an early expressionist who had displayed sympathy for Nazism, also suffered for his aesthetic deviations.[46] In the long run, then, the cultural life that took form in Nazi Germany could not have been satisfying to any conservative of the Weimar era. On the one hand, it was devoid of the profound, redemptive spiritualism yearned for by the conservative revolutionaries. On the other hand, it was not tempered by the aesthetic *noblesse oblige* of traditional conservatism. Its defining logic was race, not culture, and its overriding propagandistic function condemned German artistic life to a decade of kitsch, hate-mongering, and mediocrity.

43. H. Wilmsmeyer, "'Volk, Blut, Boden, Künstler, Gott': Zur Kunstpädagogik im Dritten Reich," in *Wissenschaft im Dritten Reich*, ed. Peter Lundgreen (Frankfurt am Main, 1985), pp. 82–112.

44. P.M. Potter, "Trends in German Musicology, 1918–1945: The Effects of Methodological, Ideological, and Institutional Change on the Writing of Music History," (Ph.D. diss., Yale University, 1991).

45. On the notorious exhibition, see *Nationalsozialismus und "Entartete Kunst": Die "Kunststadt" München 1937*, ed. P.K. Schuster (Munich, 1987); and *"Degenerate Art": The Fate of the Avant-Garde in Nazi Germany*, ed. S. Barron (New York, 1991).

46. G.R. Cuomo, "Purging an 'Art Bolshevist': The Persecution of Gottfried Benn in the Years 1933–38," *German Studies Review* 9 (1986): 85–105.

11

Government Without Parties

*Conservative Plans for Constitutional Revision
at the End of the Weimar Republic**

Hans Mommsen

It is difficult, if not misleading, to trace the destruction of the
Weimar Republic during the phase of the presidential cabinets
from 1930 to 1932 to the actions or failures of specific individuals. By the beginning of the 1930s, the structural weaknesses
of the various parliamentary systems that had been created at
the Paris Peace Conference had become apparent throughout
Europe, with the exception of Czechoslovakia and France.
That the parliamentary system of government in Germany
continued to function until the formation of Heinrich Brüning's cabinet in the spring of 1930 stemmed in no small measure from the diplomatic and fiscal dependence of the Reich,
particularly in the matter of reparations. On the domestic
scene, however, the parliamentary principle was already in
retreat at the time of the June 1920 Reichstag elections.[1] The
transitional regime of Heinrich Brüning, which remained loyal
to the form of constitutional government, was brought down
by the "national" parties at the precise moment that the end of
reparations seemed imminent and factors related to the outbreak of the world economic crisis made it impossible for the
Allied governments to continue the policy of sanctions that
had been employed with such effectiveness throughout the

*This essay was originally published as "Regierung ohne Parteien. Konser-
vative Pläne zum Verfassungsumbau am Ende der Weimarer Republik," in
Die deutsche Staatskrise 1930-1933. Handlungsspielräume und Alternativen, ed.
H.A. Winkler, Schriftenreihe des Historischen Kollegs, Kolloquien 26
(Munich, 1992), pp. 1–18. This translation was prepared by Larry Eugene
Jones with assistance from Steven Kirchgraber.
1. See A. Brecht, "Die Auflösung der Weimarer Republik und die politische
Wissenschaft," *Zeitschrift für Politik* 2 (1955): 291–308.

1920s.[2] It was only then that the political Right overcame its reservations about getting rid of the parliamentary system and assuming power itself.[3]

The ideological justification for the establishment of an authoritarian regime had been formulated some time earlier in the neoconservative writings of Oswald Spengler and Arthur Moeller van den Bruck, as well as in the programmatic statements from the right wing of the German National People's Party (Deutschnationale Volkspartei or DNVP). It was, however, only when influential industrial and agrarian interest organizations began to recoil from the principles of parliamentary government after the formation of the Great Coalition in the summer of 1928 that the German Right's ideological offensive against the principles of parliamentary government found wider political resonance. This offensive united widely different forms of anti-liberalism and merged them irrevocably with an emotionally charged anti-Marxism. The common denominator of right-wing attacks against the republican system of government in the last years of the Weimar Republic lay in a polemic against the supposed "domination of the parties" and the demand that they should either be eliminated altogether or suppressed as instruments for the expression and mobilization of political power. It was precisely this that prompted Ernst Niekisch to comment with characteristic insight that the party system "served as a scapegoat upon which the guilt for all the misery after 1918 had been heaped" so as to distract attention from the responsibility of capitalist economic interests for the situation in which Germany currently found itself.[4]

From the moment of the Weimar Republic's founding, neoconservative political pundits and Catholic corporatist theorists had preached the imperative of overcoming political parties, though without providing any clear idea as to what was supposed to take their place. The anti-parliamentarism propagated first by Spengler, Moeller van den Bruck, and Max Hildebert Boehm and then later by Edgar Julius Jung, Ernst

---

2. For further details, see my analysis in H. Mommsen, *Die verspielte Freiheit. Der Weg der Republik von Weimar in den Untergang* (Berlin, 1989), pp. 363ff., 403.

3. See H. Holzbach, *Das "System Hugenberg". Die Organisation bürgerlichen Sammlungspolitik vor dem Aufstieg der NSDAP* (Stuttgart, 1981), p. 251.

4. Spectator [E. Niekisch], "Der 'autoritäre Staat'," *Das dritte Reich. Blätter für Freiheit und Gemeinschaft* 9, no. 11 (November 1932).

Jünger and the exponents of "soldierly nationalism [*soldatisch-er Nationalismus*]" exhausted itself in the hate-filled rhetoric of civil war. Aside from the fact that the corporatist ideology espoused by Othmar Spann did not so much imply corporate autonomy as a strong, authoritarian state,[5] this rhetoric was characteristically devoid of viable political concepts beyond the vague idea of a corporatist reorganization of state and society. Bourgeois resentment against the existing political parties became increasingly widespread as it became clear toward the end of the 1920s that individual electoral groups could no longer pursue their vested interests by working through the parties of their preference. At the same time, it required a considerable degree of political naiveté to want to abandon the cooperation of the parties altogether. There was, however, a short phase in which ideas of this sort took on an air of practical reality. The idea of government without parties found its most tangible expression in the authoritarian politi-cal course set by the presidential cabinets of Franz von Papen and Kurt von Schleicher in the period after Brüning's fall from power.

Historians have been quick to emphasize the various causes for the functional weaknesses of the Weimar parliamentary system. It would be a mistake, however, to attribute these weaknesses either solely or primarily to a lack of willingness on the part of the middle parties and Social Democrats to enter into coalition arrangements that would have made the forma-tion of majority cabinets possible.[6] The chronic crisis of Weimar parliamentarism[7] stemmed in no small measure from the intransigence and reluctance of the DNVP, the Bavarian People's Party (Bayerische Volkspartei or BVP), the right wing of the German People's Party (Deutsche Volkspartei), and the

5. See M. Schneller, *Zwischen Romantik und Faschismus. Der Beitrag Othmar Spanns zum Konservatismus der Weimarer Republik* (Stuttgart, 1970), pp. 45ff.

6. See K.D. Bracher, "Demokratie und Machtvakuum: Zum Problem des Parteienstaates in der Auflösung der Weimarer Republik," in *Weimar – Selbst-preisgabe einer Demokratie: Ein Bilanz heute*, ed. K.D. Erdmann and H. Schulze (Düsseldorf, 1980), pp. 119–20, 132. The concept of "Selbstpreisgabe" seems to me inadequately defined and does not sufficiently reflect the degree to which the stability of the Weimar parliamentary system was undermined by right-wing organizations and interests.

7. Such was the observation made by Gustav Stresemann at the time of his dismissal as chancellor in the fall of 1923. See G. Stresemann, *Vermächtnis: Der Nachlaß in drei Bänden*, ed. H. Bernhard, 3 vols. (Berlin, 1932–33), vol. 1, pp. 245–46.

organizations that stood behind them to assume governmental responsibility on the basis of Germany's republican constitution. A second, though by no means less significant, factor was the inability of the liberal middle parties to achieve effective integration of the diverse social and economic interests that constituted their material base.[8] It is therefore doubtful whether the desired political stability could ever have been achieved – as a large portion of German public opinion and a majority of Germany's bourgeois parliamentarians demanded – by making the cabinet independent of the Reichstag or by strengthening the powers of the Reich President through a nullification of Article 54 of the Weimar Constitution.

The call for a revision of the Weimar Constitution came not only from the ranks of the republic's enemies but also from liberals such as Walter Jellenik, Willy Hellpach, and Erich Koch-Weser[9] and Social Democrats such as Hermann Heller, Ernst Fraenkel, Hans Simons, and Carlo Mierendorff,[10] all of whom insisted that the powers of the executive should be strengthened at the expense of the Reichstag. It was, however, the conservative constitutional theorist Carl Schmitt who emerged as a particularly eloquent advocate of a fundamental revision of the Weimar Constitution. In a long essay entitled *Legalität und Legitimität* published in the spring of 1932, Schmitt demanded that the first part of the Weimar Constitution – and with it the provisions on the constitutional organs – be subordinated to the second part, which he regarded as the core of the original constitutional decision.[11] The illusions that led the Papen cabinet to promise "the establishment of a truly nonpartisan national state leadership that stood above the entire party system as an unimpeachable bulwark of justice [*unantastbarer*

8. See L.E. Jones, *German Liberalism and the Dissolution of the Weimar Party System, 1918–1933* (Chapel Hill, N.C. and London, 1988), pp. 478–79.

9. In this respect, see W. Jellinek, "Verfassungsreform im Rahmen des Möglichen," *Reich und Länder* 6 (1932): 268ff. On Hellpach, see C. Jansen, "Professoren und Politik. Politisches Denken und Handeln an einer liberalen Universität – Heidelberg 1914 bis 1935" (Ph.D. diss., Heidelberg, 1989), pp. 288ff. For Koch-Weser, see E. Portner, "Koch-Wesers Verfassungsentwurf," *Vierteljahrshefte für Zeitgeschichte* 14 (1966): 280–96.

10. H.-A. Winkler, *Der Weg in die Katastrophe. Arbeiter und Arbeiterbewegung in der Weimarer Republik 1930 bis 1933* (Berlin, 1987), pp. 803ff.

11. For further details, see D. Grimm, "Verfassungserfüllung – Verfassungsbewahrung – Verfassungsauflösung. Positionen der Staatsrechtslehre in der Staatskrise der Weimarer Republik," in *Die deutsche Staatskrise*, ed. Winkler, pp. 183–99.

Hort der Gerechtigkeit]"[12] must therefore be placed against the background of a general willingness within the bourgeois camp to abandon central elements of the parliamentary system. Contemporary observers were quick to stress the illusory character of this political concept, which sought to make everything dependent upon the authority of a popularly elected Reich President at the same time that it pushed aside representative institutions whose legitimacy rested upon precisely the same foundation.[13] As Brüning himself came to realize, the task of carrying through such a reform clearly exceeded the capacities of the Reich President, and no one was willing to run the risk of a renewed debate over the question of Hindenburg's successor to the presidency.

The collapse of the Harzburg Front should have taught Papen that the integration of the NSDAP into the "national opposition" ran counter to Hitler's desire to avoid an association with the so-called "cabinet of barons" that few, if any, of his followers would have understood. That the chancellor continued to believe that it might be possible to secure Hitler's toleration of his cabinet by lifting the ban on the Storm Troopers (Sturmabteilung or SA) and by keeping alive the possibility of the NSDAP's own entry into the national government stemmed from his self-delusion that the NSDAP would lose its own basis for existence with the fulfillment of its anti-parliamentary and "anti-Marxist" demands. The outcome of the July elections, however, had precisely the opposite effect; they only encouraged the equally illusory hope within the National Socialist movement that the takeover of power by Hitler was imminent.[14] The rebuff that ended Hitler's audience with Hindenburg on 13 August 1932 precipitated a severe crisis within the NSDAP that caught the chancellor by complete surprise.

The collapse of the negotiations with Hitler forced the cabinet into an open breach of the constitution. While the minister of the interior, Baron Wilhelm von Gayl, was fully prepared to use the NSDAP's loss of prestige and the tensions this had

12. Radio address by Papen, 12 September 1932, in *Schultheß' Europäischer Geschichtskalender* 73 (1932): 161.

13. See G. Stolper, "Konservatismus?," *Der deutsche Volkswirt* 6, no. 51 (16 September 1932): 1663–65.

14. See the entries for 1, 7, and 9 August 1932, in *Die Tagebücher von Joseph Goebbels: Sämtliche Fragmente*, ed. E. Fröhlich, 4 vols. (Munich and New York, 1987), vol. 1, pp. 211, 217–18.

caused within the party to press for an authoritarian revision of the constitution in spite of increasingly vocal opposition from the state governments, Papen averted an open breach of legality in the hope that the Reichstag scheduled to meet at the beginning of September would go home after several days of debate without challenging the government. After all, the various bourgeois parties, including the NSDAP, were hardly prepared to run the risk of new national elections should their tactics result in the dissolution of the Reichstag. The spectacular no-confidence vote against Papen on 12 September 1932 resulted from two totally unexpected events. First, the DNVP failed to oppose Communist demands in the Reichstag's Council of Elders (Ältestenrat) for a no-confidence vote on the Papen government before proceeding to the order of the day in plenary session. Second, Hitler specifically enjoined the Nazi delegation to the Reichstag from voting against the Communist motion.[15] Throughout all of this, Papen rejected the counsel of his minister of interior both for a *fait accompli* in the matter of constitutional reform and for firm action with respect to the NSDAP. Instead, he continued to hope right up until the last possible moment before the November 1932 Reichstag elections that he would be able to create a fresh political climate and force the NSDAP to accept a humiliating defeat at the polls that would, in turn, make it unnecessary for him and his cabinet to act.

Among the more politically interested segments of the general public as well as in contemporary neoconservative publications, the widespread discontent over parliamentary practice gave way to the expectation that the long-awaited revision of the Weimar Constitution was imminent. The systematic curtailment of the powers of the Reichstag by the first and second Brüning cabinets had given rise to the general impression that the political parties were either about to withdraw from the political stage or had lost their central place in the political process. Ideas of this sort were further encouraged by the progressive dissolution of the liberal middle parties and by the electoral losses of the right-wing DNVP. For example, Hans Zehrer predicted in the influential neoconservative journal *Die Tat* that the "modern political party" had outlived its useful-

---

15. See T. Vogelsang, *Reichswehr, Staat und NSDAP. Beiträge zur deutschen Geschichte 1930–1932* (Stuttgart, 1962), pp. 277ff.

ness as a specific organizational form of the all but defunct liberal order. Drawing upon Spengler's theory of political parties, Zehrer proclaimed the imminent "end of the parties." Virtually all of Germany's non-socialist parties, Zehrer argued, stood on the brink of dissolution. Only the Center, which had a chance to reorganize itself along corporatist lines in accordance with the initiative of the Catholic Action (Katholische Aktion) and the general intent of Pope Pius XI's *Quadragesimo Anno*,[16] was immune from this pronouncement. At the same time, Zehrer dismissed the SPD as a "purely liberalist" party that would also have to withdraw from the political stage, while the socialist labor unions would survive solely as corporatist representatives of the German working class.[17] By no means, insisted Zehrer, should the state try to slow down or prevent the collapse of the various parties. On the contrary, it should strive to bring important fields of activity that had previously fallen within the purview of political parties, among them the education of youth, under its own competence and thereby further restrict the parties' sphere of activity. It should, therefore, come as no surprise that Zehrer supported the government's efforts to establish and build up the National Curatorium for Youth Fitness (Reichskuratorium für Jugendertüchtigung).

The one question with which Zehrer constantly concerned himself was how the NSDAP and KPD were to be integrated into the profound structural transformation he predicted would take place. Zehrer was certain that the rise of National Socialism was part of a secular process of radical change that would ultimately lead to a new synthesis of nationalism and socialism. For him there was no doubt that the NSDAP would eventually attract the KPD's voter potential through a deliberate turn to the left and thus complete the long-awaited merger of the two great anti-capitalist movements. "As a party," Zehrer insisted, National Socialism constituted "the most representative platform of anti-liberal conservatism today"; as a

16. See J. Köhler, "Katholische Kirche und politischer Katholizismus in der Endphase der Weimarer Republik," *Rottenburger Jahrbücher zur Kirchengeschichte* 2 (1983): 141–53, and C. Haffert, "Zwischen Konfession und Klasse. Katholische Arbeitervereine, Katholische Kirche und Zentrumspartei in der Weimarer Republik" (Ph.D. diss., University of Bochum, 1991), pp. 170ff.

17. Zehrer, "Das Ende der Parteien," *Die Tat. Unabhängige Monatsschrift zur Gestaltung neuer Wirklichkeit* 24, no. 1 (April 1932): 68–77.

"movement" it embraced "all the forces that came from the Right and now found themselves on the march in the twentieth century."[18] In another context, Zehrer characterized the two parties as "end-products of liberalism that sucked up and united the masses fleeing from the world of liberal intellect [*liberale Geisteswelt*] for the purpose of using them to destroy the liberal system once and for all."[19] It was precisely to the KPD and NSDAP that the epochal task of sweeping away the remnants of liberalism and clearing the way for a fundamentally new structure had fallen.

Zehrer, whose unusually fragmentary knowledge of communist politics is somewhat surprising, did not doubt for a moment that the KPD was little more than a purely transitional phenomenon. To be sure, there was some truth in the contention that the KPD had profited from the world economic crisis and from the loss of faith by certain sectors of the German working class in the SPD. Still, the Social Democrats did not find themselves in the same state of internal dissolution that afflicted the bourgeois middle parties.[20] Moreover, the extremely high fluctuation in the membership of the KPD suggested that internal stability had eluded the party. The probability that Zehrer's prognosis might come true would have been much greater were it not for the fact that the NSDAP's structure as a movement had been periodically weakened through systematic interventions by the party leadership, interventions designed first and foremost to eliminate the pro-socialist groupings represented by the National Socialist Factory Cell Organizations (Nationalsozialistische Betriebszellenorganisationen or NSBO). Throughout his analysis, the editor of *Die Tat*, like so many other representatives of the bourgeois Right as well as the leadership of the Reichswehr, subscribed to the thesis that National Socialism embodied the comprehensive "national movement" for which they had all been waiting, though in a somewhat primitive and immature form. The distinction between the party as it actually was and the true "national" core of National Socialism can be found in Zehrer's writings in all its conceivable variants. At the outset,

18. Zehrer, "Rechts oder Links?" *Die Tat* 23, no. 7 (October 1931): 547.
19. Zehrer, "Das Ende der Parteien," pp. 74–75. See Zehrer, "Die dritte Front: Revolution des Stimmzettels," *Die Tat* 24, no. 2 (May 1932): 117.
20. See C. Fischer, *The German Communists and the Rise of Nazism* (London, 1991), pp. 190–91.

Zehrer sketched a vision according to which National Social-ism, hitherto trapped in the "slag of the party-movement [*Schlacken der Parteibewegung*]," emerged as the bearer of an epochal social and political transformation. As a logical corol-lary to this point of view, Zehrer warned the NSDAP against entering into coalition alliances that might compromise its integrity and developmental potential.[21] Such an argument was perfectly consistent with the strategy that Zehrer had pro-claimed in 1929 with the motto "*Achtung, junge Front! Draußen bleiben!*" Here Zehrer had hoped to prevent the younger gen-eration from being devoured by an alliance with the "liberal-ist" parties in hopes that they might be held in readiness for the national upheaval that he expected to take place in the next two to three years.[22] The fact that the NSDAP continued to wage a ruthless and uncompromising attack against the exist-ing political system was something Zehrer dismissed as a passing phenomenon that could only be understood as an expression of the revolutionary impulse at work within the party. In this respect, Zehrer was a victim of National Socialist propaganda, which, under the influence of neoconservative ideas, fostered the fiction that the NSDAP represented a fun-damental alternative to the existing system of government.[23] On the other hand, Zehrer argued that the "extremist posi-tion" taken by both the KPD and NSDAP in their agitation against the Weimar Republic was provisional. Precisely because they lacked a clear picture of Germany's future devel-opment, the two parties, he insisted, would "become entan-gled in the system time and time again."[24]

Like the conservative camarilla around Reich President von Hindenburg, Zehrer too believed that the existing parties would collapse in the face of the necessities that confronted the German state. Even the NSDAP would "shatter on this reef in so far as it had become a liberalist party with millions of voters." The only thing that would remain from the NSDAP would be its *bündisch* core, which would form the backbone of

21. Zehrer, "Die eigentliche Aufgabe," *Die Tat* 23, no. 10 (January 1932): 789.
22. Zehrer, "Junge Front! Draußen bleiben," *Die Tat* 21, no. 1 (April 1929): 25–40.
23. For example, see Hitler's speech in Eberswalde, 27 July 1932, in H. Mommsen, *Adolf Hitler als Führer der Nation*, Deutsches Institut für Fernstudi-en (Tübingen, 1984), pp. 159ff.
24. Zehrer, "Wohin treiben wir," *Die Tat* 23, no. 5 (August 1931): 341.

the "New Front" that Zehrer hoped would ultimately rescue German public life from the avarice and pettiness of German party politics. The NSDAP, Zehrer contended, was doomed to failure so long as it failed to dissociate itself from the "dwindling [*abflutenden*] masses" and the "driftwood [*Treibholz*]" of its diverse following, so long as it failed to achieve a greater subordination and stratification of the masses in an elitist "community of leaders committed to combat [*Führer- und Kampfgemeinschaft*]." Paradoxically, it was in the SA and SS that Zehrer perceived the *bündisch*-elitist moment, while the political organization of the NSDAP, on the other hand, seemed intent upon transforming itself into a parliamentary party.[25] As a party, National Socialism had "marched into a vacuum to the beat of a drum [*sich in einen luftleeren Raum hineingetrommelt*]."[26] Opting for the socialist course of Gregor Strasser and his associates on the party's left wing, Zehrer criticized Hitler, whom as late as November 1929 *Die Tat* had ranked among the "greatest numskulls [*Gipsgrößen*] of politics,"[27] for failing to present a "clear intellectual platform."[28]

Step by step Zehrer had to abandon his vision that out of the National Socialist movement the long awaited "Third Front" would spontaneously emerge. Much to his dismay, he was forced to concede that bureaucratic tendencies had gained the upper hand in the NSDAP, that the party was infected by the decomposition of the old system, and that it had fallen victim to the decay of "liberalization."[29] Zehrer's original hope that Gregor Strasser's appeal to the "anti-capitalist longing of the masses" would translate itself into a comprehensive mobiliza-

25. In this respect, see Zehrer, "Das Ende der Parteien," p. 74, and Zehrer, "Die dritte Front," p. 101.

26. Zehrer, "Die dritte Front," 117.

27. See K. Fritzsche, *Politische Romantik und Gegenrevolution. Fluchtwege in der Krise der bürgerlichen Gesellschaft: Das Beispiel des "Tat"-Kreises* (Frankfurt am Main, 1976), pp. 249–50.

28. See note 26, p. 117. In an anonymous article in the *Deutsche Führerbriefe*, 3 June 1932, no. 42, the author argues that the strongest hope that the current transformation of German political life would continue lay in the person of Hitler, who, in contrast to the power hunger and revenge motives of the NSDAP's parliamentary deputies and district party leaders, embodied "a visionary perspective that stands above the things of everyday life." The ideological aims of the movement, the article concluded, were larger than those of the political-parliamentary party.

29. Zehrer, "Rechts oder links?," pp. 551ff. See also Zehrer, "Die eigentliche Aufgabe," p. 793.

tion for the July 1932 Reichstag elections failed to materialize. *Die Tat* was accurate both in its assertion that the NSDAP stood no chance of winning more than 40 percent of the mandates in the July 1932 Reichstag elections and in its prediction that the party would suffer heavy losses at the polls the following November.[30] The cause of this last development lay in the fact that the party had largely exhausted the electoral reservoir of the bourgeois parties by the summer of 1932. It was no doubt in recognition of this that in the late fall of 1932 Joseph Goebbels took the first steps down the suicidal path of trying to compensate for the return of middle-class voters to the ranks of the DNVP by winning the support of sectors of the industrial working class – though without any appreciable success.[31]

Zehrer was not alone in his belief that the collapse of the parliamentary process – something he had confirmed even before the July Reichstag elections – would hasten the internal transformation of the NSDAP. In a similar vein, the *Deutsche Führerbriefe* argued that the outcome of the July elections marked "the end of the revolution from below and the beginning of the revolution from above."[32] According to the same source, the NSDAP had not taken to heart the warning "to confine itself to being a mere movement" but after the election had finally become "a parliamentary party."[33] Hitler's refusal to take his place in the front of "national forces" under Papen and his demand to be entrusted with the chancellorship seemed to confirm the relapse into the cursed "coalition haggling [*Koalitionschacherei*]" of the past. That the NSDAP derived its strength from its numerical success at the polls and

30. In this respect, see Zehrer, "Wohin treiben wir?," *Die Tat* 23, no. 5 (August 1931): 345, and Zehrer, "Deutschland ohne Hindenburg," ibid., 24, no. 9 (December 1932): 713.

31. See T. Childers, "The Limits of National Socialist Mobilisation: The Elections of 6 November 1932 and the Fragmentation of the Nazi Constituency," in *The Formation of the Nazi Constituency, 1919–1933*, ed. T. Childers (London, 1986), pp. 235ff.

32. *Deutsche Führerbriefe*, 12 August 1932, no. 62.

33. Well before the July 1932 elections, the *Deutsche Führerbriefe* had expressed the "nagging fear" that a unilateral takeover of power by the NSDAP would produce little in the way of substantive change and that there existed a real danger of "succumbing to the intoxication of the masses" and "bringing about a renaissance of Weimar" if "the transformation of the parliamentary party into an order" based upon the S.A. and accompanied by the suppression of the civil party did not take place. Ibid., 3 June 1932, no. 42.

not from actual accomplishment was immediately denounced by the leaders of the Ring Movement (Ring-Bewegung) as a "sin against the spirit."[34] Not only had the NSDAP returned to the Reichstag under Papen, but to insiders it was no secret that at least Strasser and a majority of the party's Reichstag deputies had already begun to dissociate themselves from the obstructionist tactics the NSDAP had traditionally employed. Even Göring's election as president of the Reichstag in September 1932 must be seen as an indication that the party was prepared to play a more constructive role in the formation of the parliamentary will.

On the political Right the NSDAP was universally denounced for having suffered a relapse into the parliamentary methods of the past. This argument proved to be a particularly effective line of attack in the campaign for the November 1932 Reichstag elections. By no means, however, did this allegation cause its supporters to write off the NSDAP completely. Even within the NSDAP those who regarded the parliamentary gambit as a tactical failure and who thus wanted to intensify the struggle for power on an extra-parliamentary basis continued to grow in number and volume. Zehrer seized upon statements to this effect as proof that the NSDAP had "reached its turning point," that the "revolution of the ballot box" had come to an end.[35] Zehrer challenged the NSDAP to transform itself into a *Bund*, or order, so that it might take its proper place in the emerging "Third Front," that is, in the "diagonal axis [*Querachse*]" as envisaged by newly appointed Chancellor Kurt von Schleicher. In this respect, Zehrer readily conceded that there had been a marked decline in the mass mobilization he had previously described with such emphasis. The last months of 1932 had in fact witnessed a relaxation of domestic political tensions; the violent conflicts on the streets had visibly declined; and the NSDAP was beginning to show clear signs of exhaustion. All of this prompted Zehrer to conclude that the initiative had temporarily gone over to the "neutral state authority." While much of this may have been wishful thinking, it was nevertheless true that the NSDAP's frontal attacks against the Weimar system had temporarily run out of steam.

34. Cited in Y. Ishida, *Jungkonservative in der Weimarer Republik. Der Ring-Kreis 1928–1933* (Frankfurt am Main, 1988), p. 248.
35. Zehrer, "An der Wende!" *Die Tat* 24, no. 6 (September 1932): 433.

Zehrer's basic position proceeded from the premise that new *bündisch* organizations would take the place of the political parties. "The *Bund*," he wrote in agreement with Spengler's critique of democracy, "belonged to the future, the party to the past."[36] His close ties to Schleicher and his unequivocal partisanship for Gregor Strasser – whose position within the party Zehrer greatly overestimated as a result of his own prognosis that the organizational principle in politics was finally in retreat – caused him to become an unconditional defender of the presidential system and to propagate a thorough-going revolution "from above." Zehrer called upon Schleicher to take up the struggle against party pluralism and called for the creation of a "special people's front of the state."[37] In this connection, Zehrer sketched the outlines of a new national constitution that in many respects anticipated the reform proposals of the national-conservative resistance to Hitler. Zehrer's concept of a new order sought above all else the "de-liberalization" of the existing constitutional structure and the elimination of "today's centralistic [*zentralistische*] parties."[38]

The unusually high analytical level of Zehrer's writing cannot obscure the fact that his views represented the different stages in the development of the presidential system. Zehrer even endorsed the widespread misconception that National Socialism had assumed the guise of a mass movement only in order to emancipate the working class from the influence of the "Marxist parties." Zehrer believed that behind all of this a new state-bearing elite was beginning to take shape, although his immediate concern was that this new elite could be used up and suffocated by the "ruins of the old bourgeois age [*altbürgerliche Trümmern*]."[39] The illusion that the NSDAP could

36. Zehrer, "Das Ende der Parteien," pp. 68ff. For Spengler's critique of democracy, see D. Felken, *Oswald Spengler. Konservativer Denker zwischen Kaiserreich und Diktatur* (Munich, 1988), pp. 131ff.

37. Zehrer, "An der Wende der Innenpolitik," *Die Tat* 24, no. 10 (January 1933): 822–28.

38. Zehrer, "An der Wende!," pp. 447–51.

39. Zehrer spoke of "the growth of an independent stratum" that was active within its own sphere of influence but on the outside only seemed to be waiting. See Zehrer, "Der Sinn der Krise," *Die Tat* 23, no. 12 (Mar. 1932): 952ff. This idea is surprisingly similar in many important respects to the basic conception of the Kreisau Circle (Kreisauer Kreis). See H. Mommsen, "Der lange Schatten der untergehenden Republik. Zur Kontinuität politischer Denkhaltungen," in *Die Weimarer Republik 1918–1933. Politik – Wirtschaft – Gesellschaft*, ed. K.D. Bracher, M. Funke, and H.-A. Jacobsen (Düsseldorf, 1987), pp. 557ff.

somehow be persuaded to follow "the example of the *bündisch* movement in the selection, teamwork, and training" of its leadership, to strive for programmatic substance and qualified cadres, and to cast off its plebiscitarian mass following contributed in no small measure to the tendency of the German public to trivialize, if not ignore, the more terrorist aspects of the Nazi movement. At the same time, Zehrer must accept at least a share of responsibility for the fact that the existing interest organizations and political parties were unable to sustain themselves in the face of the difficult and unavoidable necessities confronting the German state. Zehrer even went so far as to predict that within the NSDAP only those who were bound to each other by the terms of comradeship – including those within Gregor Strasser's political orbit who had embraced neoconservative ideas and who remained in loose contact with the editorship of *Die Tat* – would remain.[40]

With its incantation of a comprehensive crisis that would lead to "total revolution" and a radical new beginning, the Tat-Circle (Tatkreis) distinguished itself from the Ring Movement – which also drew upon Spengler's ideas – by virtue of its concern for the social question and its anti-capitalist rhetoric, which manifested itself in outspoken sympathy for the labor unions and in an explicit commitment to "national socialism."[41] The social exclusivity of the Ring Movement, especially in the membership of the German Lords' Club (Deutscher Herrenklub),[42] precluded close ties to an allegedly collectivist movement such as National Socialism. In the final analysis, however, there were remarkable parallels between Zehrer's analysis and the rhetoric of the Ring Movement. Even more so than Zehrer himself, the Ring Movement advocated the abolition of all political parties and thus became a steadfast defender of the Papen regime and its constitutional experiments. At the same time, the Ring Movement criticized the NSDAP for being a party inextricably tied to parliamentarism, a party that, insofar as it did not "merge" with Alfred Hugenberg's DNVP or ally itself with the KPD, would necessarily complete its own "march into the system." Nevertheless, Heinrich von Gleichen did not hesitate to express hope in his "open letter"

40. See above, n. 23, as well as U. Kissenkötter, *Gregor Straßer und die NSDAP* (Stuttgart, 1978), pp. 128ff.

41. See Fritzsche, *Politische Romantik*, pp. 173ff.

42. See Ishida, *Jungkonservative*, pp. 76–77, 240–41.

to Hitler on 6 November 1931 that there would crystallize within the NSDAP a group of "independent personalities" who would offer a guarantee against the party's descent into chaos.[43] Similarly, Edgar Julius Jung demanded that alongside "the leaders' will to power" and "the longing of the masses" there must be a place for the "creative energy [*Gestaltungskraft*] of those individuals [who] carry in their hearts a picture of the coming century."[44] Such overtures, however, were little more than futile labors of love.

The outspoken antipathy of the Ring Circle toward the very purpose of political parties produced an increasing estrangement from Alfred Hugenberg and – as its strong support for Hindenburg's reelection as Reich president clearly revealed – an initial bias in favor of the presidential regime.[45] With the formation of the Papen cabinet in early June 1932, the Ring Movement emerged as a particularly unabashed defender of the presidential system. With its polemics against "the domination of parties [*Parteiherrschaft*]" and "the self-destruction of the nation by a dying party state," the Ring Movement quickly established itself as a champion of an absolute presidential state that was not even indirectly dependent upon the support of the parties.[46] The close personal ties between the German Lord's Club and members of the Papen cabinet led the government to identify itself more and more closely with the ideas of the Ring Movement. Walter Schotte's program of the "New State" did little to conceal the extent of this relationship. Schotte's program reflected the fact that the cabinet's efforts to insulate governmental responsibility from the influence of political parties – if, in fact, it is possible to characterize the plans that Gayl drafted in the late summer of 1932 for a political coup, or *Staatsstreich*, in such terms – drew much of its intellectual sustenance from the ideas of the Ring Movement.[47]

Schotte's program of the "New State" stressed the unconditional nonpartisanship, or *Überparteilichkeit*, of the government but fell short of renouncing parties altogether for the simple reason that the fragile unity of the German people was closely

43. Cited in ibid., p. 247.
44. Jung, "Aufstand der Rechten," *Deutsche Rundschau* 58, no. 2 (November 1931): 88.
45. Ishida, *Jungkonservative*, pp. 178ff.
46. Ibid., pp. 202–3.
47. *Schultheß' Europäischer Geschichtskalender* 48 (1932): 189ff.

tied to the persistence of the diverse ideological positions they represented. On the other hand, Schotte attacked the ascendancy of special interest parties to which the cabinet had attributed the increasing materialism of German public life. Schotte ascribed the deterioration of Germany's political parties into mere representatives of parochial interests to the disastrous effects of proportional representation, which had made it necessary for the parties to compete for the favor of the masses by means of appeals to their material concerns. This was also the prevailing point of view within the Papen cabinet. The remedies the ideologues of the "New State" had to offer consisted essentially of proposals for increasing the voting age, the introduction of single-member constituencies, and indirect elections at all levels of government above the local level. In this way, Schotte and his associates hoped to stimulate a "re-politicization" of the parties so that they might resume their historical role as representatives of great ideological positions instead of exhausting themselves in parliamentary haggling over special interests. Oblivious to the real consequences of a pluralistic electoral system, Schotte and his supporters entertained great hopes that in Germany's representative bodies highly respected "political personalities" would take the place of political hacks, or *Mandatsträger*, appointed by centralized party bureaucracies.[48] The political concept that lay at the heart of these deliberations dismissed the pursuit of material or social interests as "unpolitical" and defined politics exclusively as the affairs of state. Even then, it was unclear as to whether or not the immediate implementation of these remedies, with the obvious exception of the proposal to increase the voting age, would favor the NSDAP and thereby inhibit the consolidation of state power.

Schotte was realistic enough to assume, at least for the time being, the continued existence of the previous party system, consisting of the KPD, SPD, Center and a right-wing bourgeois party, whereby he expected that the NSDAP would eventually be absorbed into the nationalist Right. At the same time, however, Schotte agreed with Hans Zehrer that in the interim the existing party system would continue to disintegrate before the parties began to reconstitute themselves along

---

48. See U. Hörster-Philipps, *Konservative Politik in der Endphase der Weimarer Republik. Die Regierung Franz von Papen* (Cologne, 1982), pp. 328ff.

oligarchic lines as the purveyors of ideas. In the constitution of the future, Schotte insisted, centralized party organizations with mass memberships would become completely superfluous.[49] In their place one would find elitist combinations such as gentlemen's social clubs, or *Herrengesellschaften*, where expertise and not the strength of numbers would count. Such ideas were also widely held in the young conservative camp, whose leading spokesmen had turned away from the liberal principle of the general public and sought to replace the individual's right to form political associations with a system of corporatist affiliations based upon a procedure of co-option rather than voluntary access. Artur Mahraun had already stressed in his *Jungdeutsches Manifest* that "the *bündisch* organizations of today's front generation [will overrun] the old forms of associational life from the nineteenth century."[50]

Schotte was convinced that, unlike the other great Weimar parties, the NSDAP would not last for long. He defended this conclusion with the argument that National Socialism – and herein he discerned the NSDAP's essential instrument of mobilization – was not suited as a principle for the formation of a political party and would be unable to prevent working-class voters from supporting the workers' parties.[51] The outspoken ambivalence with which the ideologues of the "New State" viewed the NSDAP stemmed in large part from their contention that "the unnatural pressure of our electoral law within the framework of a multiparty parliamentary democracy" could only cause National Socialism to "degenerate into a party."[52] This observation was fully consistent with the strategy the Papen cabinet pursued of trying to separate the "healthy" kernel of the Nazi movement from the fetters of the party organization so that in this form it might be of use to the national government. Only by constituting the authority of the state on an exclusively nonpartisan basis would it be possible to reverse the degeneration of the political system, a degeneration that had found its most visible expression in the deformation of National Socialism as a "people's movement."[53]

In a brochure entitled *Am Grabe der Parteiherrschaft* pub-

49. See W. Schotte, *Der neue Staat* (Berlin, 1932), pp. 33, 146–47.
50. A. Mahraun, *Das jungdeutsche Manifest* (Berlin, 1927), p. 87.
51. Schotte, *Der neue Staat*, p. 27.
52. Ibid.
53. Ibid., p. 164.

lished shortly before the November 1932 Reichstag elections, Count Kuno von Westarp, the leader of the People's Conservatives (Volkskonservativen), protested against such a sweeping rejection of political parties by providing a patently unrealistic assessment of the existing political situation. Agreeing that all of the political parties had "lost their basis in the people," Westarp argued that the suppression of the existing party regiment was the "order of the day" and that the "party absolutism" that had triumphed with the founding of the Weimar Republic was now at an end. But as an experienced parliamentarian who had served in the Reichstag even before the war, Westarp warned against the temptation to do away with "party politics and the influence of political parties" altogether. In this respect, Westarp was well aware of the fact that he was "swimming against the tide" with his contention that political parties would still be necessary for the representation of material and ideal interests, even within the framework of a political system constituted along corporatist lines.

By stressing the role that political parties played as representatives of material interests, Westarp found himself in direct opposition to the program of the "New State," which sought to restrict parties exclusively to the promotion of ideological concerns.[54] What Westarp envisaged was a reform of the existing constitution more or less along the lines of the Bismarckian constitution of 1871. In this respect, Westarp sought to eliminate the overwhelming influence that parties had come to play in German political life by suspending Article 54 of the Weimar Constitution and by introducing a series of supplemental constitutional amendments. Even then, Westarp continued to warn against the dangers of doing away with the parties altogether, though they would certainly have to be reminded of their role as "servants of the state."[55] Such an appeal stood in marked contrast to Westarp's otherwise generally realistic analysis of Weimar's parliamentary development.

Westarp attributed the phenomenal success the NSDAP had experienced – particularly with the younger generation – since the September 1930 Reichstag elections to its categorical rejec-

54. K. von Westarp, *Am Grabe der Parteiherrschaft. Bilanz des deutschen Parlamentarismus von 1918–1932* (Berlin, n.d. [1932]), pp. 127ff.

55. Ibid., pp. 129–30.

tion of Weimar party politics and the parliamentary system of which it was such an integral part. Westarp, however, did not hesitate to criticize the NSDAP for having degenerated from a "movement" into a party. In this respect, Westarp characterized the NSDAP's negotiations with the Center in Prussia after the July 1932 Reichstag election as the "pinnacle of parliamentarism." From here Westarp proceeded to the questionable conclusion that the NSDAP had adapted itself "from top to bottom" to the exigencies of the parliamentary system.[56] By no means, however, was Westarp alone in subscribing to such a point of view. Hitler's constant refusal to place himself at the service of the "national" cabinet under Papen, the threat of a coalition with the Center in Prussia, and his party's uncompromising attacks against the Papen cabinet for having violated the Prussian constitution by deposing state government on 20 July 1932 were all seen by the bourgeois Right as symptoms of a general backslide into the morass of party haggling from which, it was thought, Germany had just emerged.

The bourgeois inability to comprehend the true nature of the Nazi movement reflected not only the success with which National Socialist propaganda was able to prevent the NSDAP from being equated with the other Weimar parties, but also the tenacity with which the NSDAP held on to the fiction that it was not a party restricted to representing the interests of a specific segment of the Weimar electorate, but a "national" movement that transcended existing party barriers and represented the entire German nation. The NSDAP's success at the polls through the summer of 1932 thus stemmed from its strict adherence to the maxim that it represented the antidote to the parties of the preceding thirteen years and from its promise to eliminate these parties "ruthlessly" and without compromise.[57] After the presidential elections in the spring of 1932, the leaders of Reichswehr and DNVP were still naive enough to applaud Hitler's all-or-nothing tactic as a self-conscious disavowal of the existing political system. The same was also true of young conservative pundits such as Jung and Gleichen. It was only after Hitler's break with Hindenburg on 13 August 1932 and the NSDAP's subsequent broadside against the Papen government in the campaign for the November 1932

56. Ibid., pp. 104–5.
57. See above, n. 23.

Reichstag elections that the parties of the "Harzburg Front" began to adopt a more sober assessment of what Hitler and his associates had in mind. Even this, however, did little to dispel the illusory hope on the part of Papen and his associates that in spite of everything it still might be possible "to entice the great and meritorious movement of National Socialism into responsible cooperation in the Reich"[58] and thus separate it from those of its leaders who remained trapped in the party mentality of the existing political system.

The notion that an end to the domination of parties was imminent constituted a response to the all too obvious dissolution of the bourgeois middle parties and the progressive weakening of the DNVP. There was, however, an element of self-delusion in such an idea. At the instigation of DNVP party chairman Hugenberg – and under considerable pressure from the party's neoconservative wing – the DNVP had already taken great pains to portray itself as an analog to the NSDAP and thus disavow its de facto role as a "parliamentary party." The DNVP organ *Unsere Partei* consequently described the Stettin party congress in September 1931 more as a "deployment for battle [*kämpferischer Aufmarsch*] than a deliberative congress," adding that the DNVP had definitively transformed itself from a party organization into "a modern activist movement of the community as a whole [*Gemeinschaftsbewegung*]."[59] Written by Eduard Stadler, this report reflected the programmatic dilemma in which the DNVP found itself as a party demanding an end to the much maligned "rule of the parties." The DNVP thus became entrapped in the rhetoric of its own struggle against the Weimar "party state." What was originally little more than an adjustment to National Socialist propaganda became more and more an end in itself. In his party's election appeal of September 1932, Hugenberg proclaimed that the DNVP would conduct the forthcoming campaign "not as a party but as the political army of the new state," a state that represented "the secret longing of those mil-

58. See the text of Papen's speech before the Bavarian Industrial Association (Bayerischer Industriellenverband), 12 October 1932, reprinted in *Akten der Reichskanzlei: Das Kabinett von Papen. 1 Juni bis 3. Dezember 1932*, ed. K.-H. Minuth, 2 vols. (Boppard am Rhein, 1989), vol. 2, p. 762.

59. See F. Hiller von Gaertringen, "Die Deutschnationale Volkspartei," in *Das Ende der Parteien 1933*, ed. E. Matthias and R. Morsey (Düsseldorf, 1960), p. 625.

lions who to this day still find themselves entrapped in the slavery of the parties."[60]

Friedrich Hiller von Gaertringen has correctly pointed out that there were no concrete proposals behind the DNVP's advocacy of the "New State" or its demands for a revision of the constitution.[61] Hugenberg's widely proclaimed struggle against the "system of the ballot box" could therefore only lead to hara-kiri for himself and his party. Following the March 1933 Reichstag elections, even Hugenberg had to concede that the DNVP had almost certainly outlived its usefulness as a party entity. Hugenberg's foreboding realized itself in May 1933, when the DNVP gave into National Socialist pressure and reconstituted itself as the German National Front (Deutschnationale Front). In an official statement, the party leadership defended this step by explaining that "with the disappearance of the parliamentary system" the party had now taken "the struggle for its *Weltanschauung* to the people."[62] The inherent self-deception in such an explanation was exposed three weeks later when the German National Front had to rationalize its own self-dissolution in terms of "overcoming the party state."[63]

If the quest for a government without parties was important only as a symptom of the self-delusion of the bourgeois Right, then this syndrome would deserve little in the way of special attention. As it was, the idea of an epochal transformation that would replace the pluralistic parliamentary system of the Weimar Republic with a new unity of nation and state – an idea fathered by neoconservative intellectuals, embraced by the Ring Movement and conservative Right, and popularized by the circle around *Die Tat* – contributed in no small measure to a fatal misreading of the NSDAP as a national movement in the temporary guise of a political party from which a new "state-supporting elite [*staatstragende Schicht*]" would eventually emerge. Hatred for the republic, however, prevented the leaders of the German Right from arriving at a more objective assessment of their National Socialist rivals. As a result, Germany's conservative establishment was all the more disap-

60. Ibid., p. 562.
61. Ibid., p. 564. See also R.G. Quaatz and P. Bang, *Das Freiheitsprogramm der Deutschnationalen Volkspartei*, with a foreword by A. Hugenberg (Berlin, 1932).
62. Hiller von Gaertringen, "Deutschnationale Volkspartei," p. 650.
63. Ibid., p. 652.

pointed over what Edgar Jung termed the "falsification of the great movement of regeneration in party egoistic channels" after the formation of the "cabinet of national concentration" in January 1933.[64]

In retrospect, it is difficult to understand why such a discriminating observer as Hans Zehrer would claim that the NSDAP had concluded its revolutionary phase and that it was no longer possible to avoid the "smooth incorporation of the party into the state and the recruitment of its best and most qualified elements for cooperation" with the state. "In light of the fact that the neutral state authority [*neutrale Staatsgewalt*] had already implemented a large portion of their demands and had thus deprived them of more and more of their campaign slogans," the National Socialists could no longer justify their refusal to participate in the government with the argument that "National Socialist demands could only be implemented by members of the party or after Hitler had assumed total power."[65] Such criticism was in fact even more valid now that the party could no longer avail itself of parliamentary means to advance its cause. Zehrer's plans for a revision of the constitution – plans that anticipated the program of the "New State" and that followed constitutional drafts prepared in connection with the discussion of a reform of Germany's federal structure – thus made little, if any, provision for the existence of the National Socialist movement.

The publicly debated details of the expected constitutional revision – particularly those pertaining to the establishment and character of the proposed second chamber – were of secondary importance to the question of precisely how the transition to the new constitution was to be accomplished. For it was clear to the advocates of such a revision that not only was the Reichstag incapable of producing a majority that could amend the constitution, but that the Reich President was reluctant to use the powers of his office to revise the constitution by executive decree. Zehrer himself envisaged the formation of a special presidential committee modeled after the Provisional Economic Council (Vorläufiger Reichswirtschaftsrat), which would take the place of a defunct Reichstag and work out the

64. See B. Jenschke, *Zur Kritik der konservativrevolutionären Ideologie in der Weimarer Republik. Weltanschauung und Politik bei Edgar Julius Jung* (Munich, 1971), p. 167.
65. Zehrer, "An der Wende!," p. 447.

details of constitutional reform to be accorded plebiscitary legitimation through a special bill of indemnification.[66] In the final analysis, however, there were few significant differences between this plan and the political phantasms of the Papen cabinet. After the November 1932 Reichstag elections, Zehrer quickly recognized that the days of the Papen chancellorship were numbered because it stood in unequivocal opposition to the will of the masses. At this point, *Die Tat* began to champion Schleicher's strategy of trying to entice the Strasser wing of the NSDAP into taking part in the creation of a diagonal axis that rested not upon the support of political parties but upon that of the various labor unions, from the socialist General German Trade-Union Association (Allgemeiner Deutscher Gewerkschaftsbund) to the right-wing German National Union of Commercial Employees (Deutschnationaler Hand-lungsgehilfen-Verband). Whereas Schleicher thought essen-tially in terms of the controlled economy from the First World War and behaved somewhat coolly toward the Tat-Circle and its plans for a revision of the constitution, Zehrer and his sup-porters discovered analogies between the new chancellor's idealization of the labor unions and his corporatist schemes for the reorganization of state and society. This, in turn, sup-plied much of the ideological justification for the largely illu-sory notion that economic interest groups and communities of conviction (*Gesinnungsgemeinschaften*) would take the place of political parties.[67]

One of the essential prerequisites for such a development was that the NSDAP, like the various bourgeois parties, was itself in a process of internal dissolution. It soon became clear, however, that the opposite was true and that the NSDAP, in alliance with Hugenberg, had returned to the supposedly obsolete methods of coalition government.[68] Nevertheless, Zehrer found it difficult to abandon his illusion that the NSDAP, now that the parties to its left had been driven out of existence, would cast off its character as a party and become a political order once again. Like most politically unaffiliated conservatives such as Jung and his circle of followers, Zehrer

66. Ibid., p. 449.
67. See A. Schildt, *Militärdiktatur mit Massenbasis. Die Querfrontkonzeption der Reichswehrführung unter General von Schleicher am Ende der Weimarer Republik* (Frankfurt am Main, 1981), p. 98.
68. See Fritzsche, *Politische Romantik*, p. 262.

regarded the formation of the Hitler cabinet as a break with the previous course of development. Given Hindenburg's inclination to withdraw from politics altogether, Zehrer saw this as a "temporary liquidation of the authoritarian form of government" and as a "victory of parliamentarism" that, he feared, would eventually carry the day.[69] Even then, however, Zehrer refused to abandon his dreams. After the March 1933 Reichstag elections, Zehrer called for the dissolution of the Weimar party system in a single step as a prelude to restoring the unified foundation of the state.[70] No doubt Zehrer's remarks were colored by his desire to reach some sort of *modus vivendi* with the new regime.[71] But he was not alone in arguing that the NSDAP had itself become superfluous with the dissolution of the other political parties. It is therefore surprising to discover that in May 1933 Zehrer, in order to remain ideologically consistent, had suddenly become an advocate of the "nationalization [*Verstaatlichung*] of the NSDAP." In what was certainly a peculiar reading of the so-called "March converts," Zehrer suggested that "the nationalization of the NSDAP" was all the more necessary in light of the fact that the party had succeeded in winning over increasingly large sectors of the German people in the five months since Hitler's appointment as chancellor.[72] At the same time, Zehrer remained true to the essential elements of his reform program by insisting that future elections should take place only in the "smallest cells," thereby suggesting that the reconstruction of the state along the lines he had outlined in *Die Tat* was already under way.

The "nationalization of the NSDAP," argued Zehrer, would provide the state with a "firm people's organization" that would be necessary only so long as governmental instruments of socialization such as the school, the labor service, and the militia were still in the process of being built up. At the same

69. The DNVP's role in this developments prompted Ewald von Kleist-Schmenzin to leave the party in protest since in his eyes the new cabinet was "essentially a party government," while he demanded "a leadership of the state that was completely free of all party and interest considerations." See Hiller von Gaertringen, "Deutschnationale Volkspartei," p. 636.

70. Zehrer, "Um die Nachfolge des Reichspräsidenten," *Die Tat*, 24, no. 12 (March 1933): 1028.

71. In this respect, see Zehrer, "Die Revolution von Rechts," *Die Tat* 25, no. 2 (May 1933): 1–16.

72. See Fritzsche, *Politische Romantik*, pp. 301–02.

time, this would impose a certain self-discipline upon the NSDAP and deprive competing parties of their formal right to exist. The implications of Zehrer's short-circuited thinking could not have been more disastrous. The idea that governmental responsibility would somehow hold Hitler and the NSDAP in check would resurface after 30 June 1934 on the occasion of the Röhm purge. In the meantime, Zehrer agreed that the NSDAP had destroyed the liberal state, but he went on to speculate that in Germany – in sharp contrast to the situation in Fascist Italy – "the old pre-liberalist tradition of the state" had swallowed up the party "by imposing itself from above [*indem sie sich aufoktroyiert*]." The celebration held in the Potsdam garrison church in March 1933 had therefore represented "a delayed victory for Frederick, the Great."[73] By this time, Oswald Spengler, upon whose ideas Zehrer based much of his argument, had already broken with such pipe dreams, whereas Carl Schmitt and most of his disciples still agreed with Zehrer.[74]

The proposal to transform the NSDAP into a governmental organization was taken up in December 1933 by the Nazi Minister of the Interior, Wilhelm Frick, and was incorporated into the draft of a "Law for Securing the Unity of Party and State" that was never formally adopted. This represented a feeble expedient to accommodate still persistent hopes that the NSDAP would follow the example of the other Weimar parties and initiate its own self-dissolution. The idea that the NSDAP should be transformed into a political order for the selection and training of future leaders was at that time quite popular, not only in the circle around Hermann Göring, but also in the ministry of the interior, where Helmut Nicolai strongly supported such a solution before being expelled from the NSDAP and dismissed from the civil service as a result of his strong-willed and idiosyncratic ways.[75] As late as June 1933, the neoconservative theorist Jung publicly demanded at a conference of the Catholic Academic Association (Katholischer Akademikerverband) in Maria Laach that as a corollary to the dissolu-

73. Zehrer, "Der Umbau des deutschen Staates," *Die Tat* 25, no. 2 (May 1933): 103ff.

74. Felken, *Oswald Spengler*, pp. 192–93.

75. See P. Diehl-Thiele, *Partei und Staat im Dritten Reich. Untersuchungen zum Verhältnis von NSDAP und allgemeiner Staatsverwaltung 1933–1945* (Munich, 1969), p. 57.

tion of the Weimar party state the NSDAP should dissolve itself as well.[76]

The fact that this sort of thinking surfaced for a relatively brief period of time in the early stages of the Third Reich may help explain why these ideas left such a faint trace in the existing historical record. Such ideas stemmed ultimately from the wishful thinking of those who either staffed the presidential cabinets of the late Weimar Republic or offered ideological defenses on their behalf and contributed in no small measure to the fact that the bourgeois Right so tragically underestimated the full implications of Hitler's appointment as chancellor in January 1933. Instead of being a purely transitional phenomenon that would in time vanish from the historical stage, the NSDAP succeeded in establishing itself as the heir to the destroyed Weimar party system. The widespread anxiety among the NSDAP's prospective allies and sympathizers in the conservative camp that it might slip back into the morass of parliamentarism accelerated the dynamic that led to the formation of the cabinet of national concentration in January 1933. This, in turn, made it easier for Hitler to dispose of the last institutional chains – including the need to heed the various right-wing parties and groups united in the Combat Front Black-White-Red (Kampffront Schwarz-Weiß-Rot) – that had been attached to his appointment as chancellor. While it was Papen who, through the mediation of Kurt von Schröder, set in motion the fateful intrigues that culminated in the installation of the Hitler cabinet, the German public saw nothing but the alternative between parliamentarism and dictatorship. On 3 January 1933, for example, the *Deutsche Führerbriefe* claimed that if efforts to integrate the NSDAP in a "national front" behind the Schleicher government failed, the only way out of the current crisis lay in the choice between "total dictatorship" or a "return to the full-blown parliamentarism of the past [*alter Vollparlamentarismus*]."[77] It was precisely this perception of the political situation that led Robert von der Goltz on the extreme right wing of the DNVP to remark that the dangers of a return to the parliamentary system made the leaders of the Right all the more inclined to reach a reconciliation. According to Goltz,

---

76. See L.E. Jones, "Edgar Julius Jung: The Conservative Revolution in Theory and Practice," *Central European History* 21 (1988): 142–74.

77. *Deutsche Führerbriefe*, 3 January 1933, no. 1.

only Hitler's chancellorship could guarantee that "the parliamentary system provided for in the holy Weimar Constitution [would] belong to the past [*überwundene*] episodes of recent German history."[78]

The almost universal fear on the German Right of a return to the "full-blown parliamentarism of the past" caused whatever political and social reservations Hugenberg and his party associates might have had against a coalition with the NSDAP to fade into the background. In January 1933 Hitler's conservative coalition partners accepted conditions from the Nazi party leader that they had rejected in November and December. The virtual monomaniacal phobia that leaders of Germany's bourgeois Right felt with respect to the existing party system led directly to the establishment of the National Socialist party dictatorship. All of this fed the grandiose self-delusion throughout the conservative camp – in the Ring Movement and German Lords' Club, in the Tat-Circle, in the Reichswehr and DNVP, and among the various agricultural and industrial interest groups that sympathized with the conservative cause – that National Socialism was only a transitory phenomenon that had been temporarily forced to assume the form of a party movement in order to wage its struggle against the parties of the Marxist Left. It was this same delusion that contributed so decisively to the fact that resistance to the National Socialist usurpation of power failed to materialize or – as in the tragic case of Edgar Jung – came too late.

78. W.M., "Bild der Lage," *Deutschlands Erneuerung. Monatsschrift für das deutsche Volk* 6, no. 12 (December 1932): 756.

12

Organized Rural Women and the Conservative Mobilization of the German Countryside in the Weimar Republic*

Renate Bridenthal

Introduction

In 1895 at Cranz, a resort on the Baltic Sea, a group of visiting women of the Junker class often breakfasted together and discussed their shared problems about estate management. One of them, Elisabet Boehm, was inspired to take this exchange of information seriously enough to create a permanent organization, an association of agricultural housewives. Started in 1897 with four of her friends, by 1934 it would claim to have one hundred thousand members when, as the National Federation of Agricultural Housewives' Associations (Reichsverband land-wirtschaftlicher Hausfrauenvereine or RLHV), it assumed nominal leadership of all countrywomen in the Nazi-organized Peasant Estate. How did it arrive at such recognition? By what mechanisms did it mobilize a constituency previously immune to any except religious organization? How did its originally modest goals come to fit into the Nazi agenda? The answers lie in the history of associational life in Germany, about whose relevance to the rise of National Socialism much has been written.[1]

*Research for this article was made possible by grants from the International-al Research and Exchanges Board and by the National Endowment for the Humanities. I have benefited greatly from critical readings by the German Women's History Group, Larry Eugene Jones, Robert G. Moeller, and Lisa DiCaprio.
    1. For example, see *Organizing Interests in Western Europe*, ed. S. Berger (Cambridge, Ma., 1981); D. Blackbourn and G. Eley, *The Peculiarities of German History: Bourgeois Society and Politics in Nineteenth-Century Germany* (Oxford

Another clue is in the widespread German propensity to identify with occupational status, which helped the Nazis to make an ideological counterpoint to class analysis.[2]

What specifically shaped the countrywomen's organization was the prior organization of women and of agrarians. The Federation of German Women's Associations (Bund deutscher Frauenvereine or BDF) was formed in 1894 with the broad goal of improving women's position in society, yet due to legal and political restraints, as well as intellectual and social tradition, the BDF differed from the more radical British and American organized women's movement in that it rarely questioned the notion of separate spheres for women and men.[3] The National Federation of Agricultural Housewives' Associations therefore had to assert its claims within this relatively narrow framework, and this willingness to do so made it a prime candidate for participation in the Nazi attempt to reorganize society along the lines of exaggerated gender distinctions and occupational corporatism.

Another feature that facilitated the conservative mobilization of countrywomen was the somewhat grudging but nevertheless crucial support of the men's agrarian establishment. The Agrarian League (Bund der Landwirte) of Imperial Germany and its successor in the Weimar Republic, the National Rural League (Reichs-Landbund or RLB), have a well-documented history of conservative and ultimately radical rightwing mobilization of the peasantry.[4] Inasmuch as the RLHV

and New York, 1984); G. Eley, *Reshaping the German Right: Radical Nationalism and Political Change after Bismarck* (New Haven, Conn., 1980); R. Koshar, *Social Life, Local Politics, and Nazism: Marburg 1880–1935* (Chapel Hill, N.C., 1986); *Interessenverbände in Deutschland*, ed. H.J. Varain (Gütersloh, 1973); and *Organisierter Kapitalismus. Voraussetzungen und Anfänge*, ed. H.A. Winkler (Göttingen, 1974).

2. T. Childers, "The Social Language of Politics in Germany: The Sociology of Political Discourse in the Weimar Republic," *American Historical Review* 95 (1990): 331–58.

3. In this respect, see A.T. Allen, *Feminism and Motherhood in Germany, 1800–1914* (New Brunswick, N.J., 1991); R.J. Evans, *The Feminist Movement in Germany, 1894–1933* (London, 1976); U. Gerhard, *Unerhört: Die Geschichte der deutschen Frauenbewegung* (Hamburg, 1990); B. Greven-Aschoff, *Die bürgerliche Frauenbewegung in Deutschland 1894–1933* (Göttingen, 1981); and A.K. Hackett, "The Politics of Feminism in Wilehlmine Germany, 1890–1918" (Ph.D. diss., Columbia University, 1976).

4. *The German Peasantry*, ed. R.J. Evans and W.R. Lee (New York, 1986); J. E. Farquharson, *The Plough and the Swastika: The NSDAP and Agriculture in Germany, 1928–1945* (Beverly Hills, Calif., 1976); J. Flemming, *Landwirtschaftliche Interessen und Demokratie. Ländliche Gesellschaft, Agrarverbände und Staat*

worked within RLB-dominated structures, it served those goals at first inadvertently and eventually quite willingly.

Finally, the RLHV freely and consistently used corporatist language. It defined its constituency of countrywomen as an Estate (*Stand*), although it alternated uneasily between identifying with corporate agriculture and with a separate woman's sphere imagined in quasi-corporate terms. In addition, in its effort to try to make a recognized profession of housewifery, it consistently used the language of occupational status. This was not only a creative attempt to raise the value of women's unpaid work, but also reflected the RLHV's intention to minimize class differences by implying social cohesion through occupational status. In this case, however, the occupation could only highlight class differences, as housewives were identified by their place in families. Nevertheless, the RLHV's appeal to corporate notions contributed to the political discourse that helped pave the way for Nazi ideology.

Origins of the Agricultural Housewives' Associations

The idea of organizing women in the countryside belonged to Elisabet Boehm (1859–1943) née Steppuhn, the daughter of an upwardly mobile East Prussian estate manager and later the wife of a bourgeois landowner, Otto Boehm. She received her secondary education at Königsberg, where she first encountered publications from the women's movement. Her marriage brought her still closer to the women's movement, inasmuch as her sister-in-law was Hanna Bieber-Boehm, an activist in the campaign against state-regulated prostitution. Some time in the mid-1890s, Hanna took Elisabet to a women's conference that changed her life. Later she wrote:

> The deliberations profoundly enthralled me and besides that I took some pride in my sex, that stood there so free and spoke so intelli-

1890–1925 (Bonn, 1978); D. Gessner, *Agrarverbände in der Weimarer Republik. Wirtschaftliche und soziale Voraussetzungen agrarkonservativer Politik vor 1933* (Düsseldorf, 1976); H.-J. Puhle, *Agrarische Interessenpolitik und preußischer Konservatismus in wilhelminischen Reich 1893–1914. Ein Beitrag zur Analyse des Nationalismus in Deutschland am Beispiel des Bundes der Landwirte und der Deutsch-Konservativen Partei* (Bonn-Bad Godesberg, 1975); R.G. Moeller, *German Peasants and Agrarian Politics, 1914–1924* (Chapel Hill, N.C., 1986); *Peasants and Lords in Modern Germany*, ed. R.G. Moeller (Boston, Ma., 1986).

gently and led discussions. So women could do that too? In the only women's association I had ever worked with, the Patriotic Women's Association (Vaterländischer Frauenverein), only men actually spoke. Clerics, who took minutes, laid down the rules. The female executive committee was really just a front and hardly said anything other than "Mr. X may speak.". . . They only spoke up in the meetings of the executive committee itself, when it was about who should do the tasks they, and not the men, carried out.[5]

But Boehm's admiration of the women at this meeting was tempered by her agrarian affiliation and her deep social conservatism:

Resolutions were proposed and accepted before I had even understood what they were about. And other countrywomen felt as I did. And afterwards, when we read these resolutions in peace and quiet, we saw that they had a radical and in any case entirely urban character that we could not agree to. . . . I came home resolved to find a way to bring countrywomen into the women's movement in order to take away its purely urban character. The countryside had a right to be heard; it had to assert itself.[6]

At first Boehm tried to work within the Patriotic Women's Association, but this attempt failed. "I was reproached for being a freethinker, a bluestocking, part of the women's movement. That was bitter for me."[7] Her ire rose with her growing consciousness. At a private gathering, someone asserted that women owed their material support to men.

"Every man?" I asked. They said yes. "Do you support me?" I laughingly asked my husband, knowing how he valued my work as that of a colleague's. But to my astonishment, even my husband believed that of course he supported me.[8]

Pursuing the matter, Boehm asked her husband if he also supported the housemaid, household manager, and cook. No, he did not consider that he did. Housewives, it seemed, had no profession: their work had less value than their upkeep. This personal affront shocked her into action. How had she and her husband drifted so far apart? They had come to the estate equally ignorant of agriculture but now, fifteen years later, he had won recognition in his district, evidenced by hon-

5. E. Boehm, *Wie ich dazu kam!* (Berlin, 1941), pp. 23–24.
6. Ibid.
7. Ibid., p. 14.
8. Ibid., p. 17.

orary offices. He had founded two cooperatives, one for steam-powered plows and the other a dairy, and had come to understand the economy in a way that she did not, although they read the same newspapers and books and scientific works together. Wherein lay the difference? And then, she wrote, "the scales fell from my eyes!" Association was the clue. Collective work was the answer. Landowners had had their agricultural associations for a hundred years: specialty groups, cooperatives, credit unions, the agricultural chambers, and most recently in 1893, the Agrarian League. But there were no women in any of them. Her indignation reached a peak: "Didn't we countrywomen belong to agriculture?. . . Was our work worth nothing?. . . Didn't it bring value to the economy as a whole?"[9]

Equally frustrated with women's exclusion from male-run agricultural associations and with the seemingly too radical and too urban tendencies of the bourgeois women's movement, Boehm resolved to organize countrywomen separately. Rebuffed again by her immediate neighbors, who saw her as a bluestocking, she turned to her reading circle which included some townswomen. Shrewdly, she suggested that the key to their cooperation was political – elections, she argued, showed a widening rift between city and country, but women could mend this social division, thus performing a patriotic duty while also looking after their own interests as women. And so, just before Christmas of 1897, five women met in a coffee shop for a planning meeting and the Agricultural Housewives' Association (Landwirtschaftlicher Hausfrauenverein) came into being. By 2 February 1898 ten more women had joined and the group had drafted goals that hardly changed over the next thirty-six years, when the organization was incorporated into the National Socialist "Peasant Estate." The original goals were: 1) to sponsor instruction in home economics for housewives, their daughters, and hired help; 2) to increase production in gardening and poultrying, i.e., the women's sphere of farming; 3) to improve marketing up to the point of exporting; 4) to bridge differences between the rural and urban interests; and 5) to win recognition for housework as a profession.[10]

Boehm recalled that what really motivated this first gather-

9. Ibid., p. 19.
10. Ibid., pp. 23–24.

ing was her suggestion that the group establish its own market. The price of food was, of course, a major source of dispute between town and country. The first market of the newly organized East Prussian Agricultural Women's Association was inaugurated in October 1898. Commissioned to the owner of a small flower shop, it was supervised by a committee consisting of two townswomen and one countrywoman, at least one of whom had to visit the market each day and report at monthly meetings when accounts were settled. The committee was also empowered to set prices.

Their modest little market succeeded beyond their wildest expectations and they were astonished to find that within a year its income had risen twelve-fold, from an estimated 500 marks to 6,000 marks. "Our husbands were particularly surprised," Boehm wrote. "Now we had our own money and therefore courage."[11] The following year they opened a larger and more professional marketplace, staffed by a paid saleswoman, and in its second year the market brought in 10,000 marks.[12] Word of its success spread to neighboring towns. Boehm was called on to help set up other markets and other agricultural women's associations and thus began her long career as an organizer. The proliferation of these markets in East Prussia was remarkable: by 1942 there were fifty-seven of them with a total turnover of 4.5 million marks, the three largest and most successful of them being in Königsberg.[13] The markets' importance stretched beyond sales. They offered an education by not only providing direct lessons in capitalist marketing, but also teaching their participants about the labor market, about new production technologies, and about the value of higher education and of political contacts. They even learned how to market their own association through the self-advertising function of a logo: a bee in flight to represent industriousness. It was stamped on all their marketed eggs to indicate they had been inspected for freshness. Through the markets, organized countrywomen began to perceive themselves as *feminae economicae*.

11. Ibid., p. 26.
12. E. Siebert, "Die ersten Verkaufsstellen," in *Nutzen und Ordnung. Gegenwartsfragen der Forschung, Lehre und Beratung für Wirtschaft, Haushalt und Familie* (Frankfurt am Main, 1955), Heft 3/4, p. 76.
13. E. Siebert, "Elisabet Boehm," *Ostland Lebt: Kulturbrief* 1967/8 (Hanover, 1967), p. 14. The markets outlived the autonomy of their founding organization, after its coordination (*Gleichschaltung*) in 1934.

Encouraged by their success, they took initiatives to improve poultry breeding and gardening, and fought their way onto a few production committees in the agricultural chambers. However, the resistance they encountered there led them to spend less energy on trying to desegregate male power structures than on developing the "women's sphere" of agriculture. This meant the redefinition of women's work as something economically valuable, that is, as skilled work for which one needed training. The vocation (*Beruf*) of housewifery – both in the sense of a "calling" and of a "career" – became the goal of the home economics movement, both rural and urban, of the late-nineteenth century. This goal combined the contradictory notions of traditional women's work with modern professionalism. There was only one glaring problem: housewifery remained unpaid labor.

Formal academic training in accredited institutions was not the arena of organized countrywomen, and yet their activity in home economics must be understood against that background. The best-known, earliest, and most elite initiative for women's education in the countryside came from Ida von Kortzfleisch (1850–1916), who in 1896 founded an association dedicated to establishing economic schools for women in the country (Verein zur Errichtung wirtschaftlicher Frauenschulen auf dem Lande). She set up a private residential school in Hesse in 1898, which was later moved to Reifenstein Eichsfeld, and by 1923 there were fifteen such accredited schools administered by an umbrella organization, the Reifenstein League (Reifenstein Verband). Like cadet academies, the Reifensteiner schools prided themselves on their strictness and the Spartan lifestyle they offered the daughters of the rural elite. A few of these girls might take up a career in teaching.[14]

For the intermediate constituency of peasant girls (*Landmädchen*) who would become neither servants nor managers, there were itinerant teachers offering eight- to ten-week courses sponsored by district administrations or by voluntary women's associations, aided by state funds after 1910. The number of such district schools peaked in 1913 at 282, serving

---

14. By 1928, the schools enrolled 4,901 students, more than their 4,042 alumnae Maiden, and 683 teacher trainees. For further details, see M. Kanzow, *Über den Zusammenschluß der in der Landwirtschaft arbeitenden Frauen* (Berlin and Leipzig, 1931), p. 35.

perhaps 7,000 students.[15] In short, countrywomen were not exactly saturated with formal education – there was room for innovation.

Boehm had founded her first agricultural housewives' association in East Prussia in the same year that Ida von Kortzfleisch founded her first women's agricultural school. In 1912 the association set up its own school. The property of Methgethen (about 10 acres) was donated by a Frau Weller, a German-American woman. The school's first director was the Baroness (*Freiin*) Irene von Gayl (1882–1960), member of a prominent Prussian family and graduate of a Reifenstein school. Gayl was an officer's daughter, enamored of estate life and disdainful of the world of commerce. She had come to the school directorship out of conviction (it paid only fifty marks a month plus room and board), having turned down a job for 1,000 marks a month supervising personnel and inventory in a large Berlin hotel. When she took over, the building still lacked doors and furniture, but using her family connections Gayl succeeded in getting donations of professional equipment.[16] The school had barely gotten under way when World War I broke out.

World War I

The new school at Methgethen, perilously close to the fortress of Königsberg, was evacuated so that soldiers could be quartered in it. Gayl did war service on the eastern front, mainly in field hospitals. By the fall of 1917, however, she returned to reopen the school with two teachers. To make cooking courses possible she evaded the controlled economy through illegal slaughtering and used her social network to get direct deliveries from the local military district. This assertion of privilege did not go unnoticed by the community, which insisted on get-

15. There are no prewar data about students. I arrived at the number by extrapolating backwards from a 1919 survey of the remaining thirty-five schools reporting 867 students. This suggested an average of twenty-five students per school district. See *Land und Frau*, 1 November 1919. This illustrated weekly became the official organ of the RLHV in 1923.

16. I. von Gayl, *Aus meinem Leben* (n.p., n.d.), pp. 53, 55. This unpublished autobiography, dedicated to Margarete von Spies, the author's "life companion" of thirty-five years, was sent to me by her niece, Elisabeth von Gayl, along with additional personal information in two letters she wrote to me from Hildesheim, 29 November 1983 and 25 January 1984.

ting part of her next delivery: extra coal offered by two students, daughters of Silesian mine owners.[17]

On the whole, the war had a contradictory effect on the agricultural women's associations. On the one hand, with male hands now bearing arms and maids enticed into available industrial jobs, rural women were overworked, even with the forced labor provided by prisoners of war. Food production was further hampered by the blockade on fertilizer and fodder, and the historical tension between city and country intensified as food became scarce and peasants were accused of hoarding in order to drive up prices. Ironically, however, it was precisely this conflict that gave the budding organization of countrywomen their chance for greater recognition. Because one of their stated goals was "to bridge the differences between city and country," the agricultural housewives' associations were now mobilized by the government to do exactly that. Although they were predictably unsuccessful in this and hampered in their other activities, the war effort won them recognition and contacts with government officials that proved invaluable after the war.

From the start the War Food Agency (Kriegsernährungsamt) had a Women's Advisory Council (Frauenbeirat) that included leading countrywomen from the regional organizations. The Agency itself was poorly empowered, having only an advisory role for the individual German states. It included representatives of the states and of interest groups such as agrarian associations, cooperatives, administrators, unions, and women.

The Women's Advisory Council included Elisabet Boehm, founder of the East Prussian Association of Agricultural Housewives, the Countess Schwerin-Löwitz, whose husband, a prominent agrarian, was also a member of the War Food Agency and the Price Control Commission (Reichspreisstelle), and the Countess von Keyserlingk, whose husband was another notable agrarian on the price control commission. Non-agrarians on the Women's Council included representatives of the urban housewives' associations and of the Women's Home Economics Schools. A major task of the Council was to facilitate better cooperation between town and country, and some consideration was given to making the Women's Advisory Council more visible to the public than the War

17. Ibid., pp. 57–58, 68–69.

Food Agency itself, on the grounds that women might be more credible in smoothing over social conflict and "enlightening" the public about home front issues. However, by June 1918, the widening social turmoil was mirrored in the Council's increasingly stormy meetings and it was soon dissolved.[18]

Even earlier, in January 1917, countrywomen had met separately to found their own nationwide organization: the National Federation of Agricultural Housewives Associations. It was organized in the Berlin home of the Countess Schwerin-Löwitz, whose husband was at once head of the prestigious German Agricultural Council, an influential member of the Agrarian League in Pomerania, and in 1918 President of the Prussian Diet. A princess, Therese Hohenlohe-Waldenburg, brought to the association a touch of high nobility from the southern state of Württemburg. And of course there was Elisabet Boehm, tireless organizer of local agricultural housewives' associations, who had been rewarded for her recruitment efforts with a Cross of Honor (*Verdienstkreuz*) in April 1917. The goals of the new organization incorporated those of the original Prussian Association, adding new concerns reflecting the growing insecurity of the agricultural sector. These new goals were: 1) to stem the flight from the land; 2) to heighten awareness that agriculture was the basis of the nation's strength; and 3) to represent these goals to the authorities and to other associations.[19]

However, such a relatively narrow economist program failed to meet the broader agenda of mobilizing the countryside behind the war effort. Therefore, in October 1917, the Countess Schwerin-Löwitz again came to the rescue and ended up heading the more encompassing Central Organization of German Countrywomen (Zentrale der deutschen Landfrauen). This was a loose federation of sixteen different conservative associations representing over one million women from such groups as the Patriotic Women's Association, the Evangelical Women's Aid, the Catholic German Women's Federation, several welfare societies, and the newly

18. Protocol of the meeting of the Women's Advisory Council (Frauenbeirat) of the War Food Agency (Kriegsernährungsamt), 8 November 1916, Archiv des Reichsministeriums für Ernährung und Landwirtschaft, Bundesarchiv, Abteilungen Potsdam (hereafter cited as BA Potsdam), 36.01, No. 30, pp. 2–30.

19. *Deutsche Tageszeitung*, 18 January 1917, BA Potsdam, RLB-Pressearchiv, 3106/120.

founded RLHV. The Central's two deputy heads were Boehm and the Countess Keyserlingk, wife of a leading agrarian and provincial president (*Regierungspräsident*) of East Prussia.

The loosely federated Central never challenged the autonomy of its member associations, concentrating instead on coordinating their work for the war effort and mediating jurisdictional quarrels among them. For example, it helped the RLHV and the Patriotic Women's Association to reach an agreement by which the countrywomen would handle marketing for small producers (usually female), while the nationalist group sponsored support services such as care for infants and the sick.[20] The Central was to raise morale by providing welfare services, by helping to vent grievances, and by distributing war propaganda ("Enlightenment") in the countryside.[21] The Central also had two other objectives unrelated to the immediate needs of the war. One was born out of the prewar women's movement, namely, to expand women's representation in the male-dominated agricultural chambers and to develop women's education in the countryside, especially in the area of social work. By this, it hoped to provide careers for educated women and services for the rest, thus stemming the flight from the land among young women of all rural classes. The other goal was to organize countrywomen for the general agrarian cause of demanding more state aid while fighting the "coerced economy" of price controls and house searches for produce.[22]

For all these purposes the Central developed a countrywomen's press with regular news services, published books, and arranged lectures and conferences. The first German Countrywomen's Conference was held in Berlin in February 1918, with the Crown Princess giving it official recognition by greeting its seven hundred delegates representing two million organized women. The conference mirrored the diverse interests of the Central's member groups, but stressed welfare and education. This conference was only the first of many; thou-

20. BA Potsdam, RLB-Pressearchiv, 3106/140.
21. "Welfare" was defined rather broadly. For example, in March 1918, the Central sought inexpensive vacation spots in estate and country homes for impoverished women of the higher orders (*höhere Stände*), but concluded sadly that the demand was much higher than the supply. BA Potsdam, RLB-Pressearchiv, 3106/157.
22. BA Potsdam, RLB-Pressearchiv, 3106/140.

sands of countrywomen reportedly attended conferences held all over Germany in the ensuing year: in Kiel, Württemburg, Bavaria, the Rhineland, Hanover, Saxony, Silesia, Mecklenburg, and Braunschweig.[23]

The Central survived for three years after the war. One of its first postwar actions was to petition the new national economics ministry to include, in its draft law expanding representation in the agricultural chambers to workers, a section enfranchising women as well.[24] They appealed on the grounds that their votes, as members of the propertied class, would counterbalance those of the laborers. This hit the mark; the new law of 16 December 1920 included a paragraph giving women a quota of representatives (*Zuwahl*), and on 20 March 1921 women first gained entry to the Prussian agricultural chamber.[25] The Central claimed credit for winning this bit of headway, but it was a hollow victory. Soon it was rent with internal conflict as the RLHV made a strong bid for sole representation of rural women in their capacity as producers.

At this point the Central had grown to include twenty-six associations and was planning to develop a provincial infrastructure.[26] The most important member associations were the RLHV, the two major Catholic and Protestant women's federations, and the rural welfare association (Deutscher Verein für landwirtschaftliche Wohlfahrts- und Heimatpflege). At its weeklong conference in Berlin from 21 to 28 February 1921 a major issue of conflict emerged: labor relations, specifically child labor. The welfare interest in the Central brought a speaker from the Association for the Protection of Children (Kinderschutzverband) who spoke at length about the misery of children in the countryside, many of them orphans or half-orphans, some illegitimate or in foster care. She noted the lack of day care and consequent neglect of children whose mothers had to work in the fields. Poor nutrition led to rickets and other health hazards. "Unthinking" parents exploited their children's labor, kept them out of school, and even brutally

23. BA Potsdam, RLB-Pressearchiv, 3106/129, 131, 122, 153, 154.

24. *Land und Frau*, 13 December 1919. Later, they petitioned the Prussian legislature similarly. See *Land und Frau*, 6 November 1920.

25. Annual report of the Central, 1920/21, in Geheimes Staatsarchiv, Preußischer Kulturbesitz, Abteilung Merseburg, Ministerium für Landwirtschaft, Domänen und Forsten, Repositorium 87B (hereafter cited as GStA Merseburg, Rep. 87B), 20546/261–63.

26. Ibid., p. 190.

mishandled them at times. Finally, overcrowding led to physical and moral dangers for children. She urged the Central to recruit more voluntary workers to help official social workers in the countryside. The Central's head, the Countess Schwerin-Löwitz, thereupon requested 50,000 marks for this purpose from the Ministry of the Interior. This ameliorative, liberal position of the Central contrasted and conflicted with the position of the RLHV which, in the interests of productivity, maximized the importance of child labor and minimized its risks.[27]

The two groups finally broke apart in the summer of 1921, when elections for the agricultural chambers took place. The Central claimed corporate representation for all rural women, which would have given it the right to nominate candidates, but the ambitious Elisabet Boehm made the same claim for the RLHV. No compromise seemed possible, and in the fall of 1922 the RLHV took its 50,000 members out of the Central, leaving the greatly weakened federation to deal mainly with social issues until its dissolution, the following year, into a women's committee of the rural welfare association.[28] For a short time, until the Central dissolved, competition between it and the RLHV was intense. Writing to the labor ministry about the establishment of a committee for countrywomen's work, the RLHV contested the Central's claim to be on it. It argued that the Central included no purely economic organizations other than the Professional Association of Civil Servants and Vocational Teachers in Home, Garden, and Agriculture (Berufsverband der Beamtinnen und Fachlehrerrinnen in Haus, Garten und Landwirtschaft), and had only two educational organizations, the Reifensteiner agricultural schools and the Bavarian Association for Women's Rural Home Economics Schools (Verein für wirtschaftliche Frauenschulen auf dem Lande). In another letter to the ministry for nutrition and agriculture, the RLHV forcefully argued its greater suitability for representa-

27. Ibid., pp. 172–74.
28. Letter from the National Federation of Agricultural Housewives' Associations to the National Labor Ministry, 12 August 1922, BA Potsdam, 39.01, Bestand Reichsarbeitministerium, 10398/198, announcing its departure from the Central. The Federation requested direct communications from the Ministry henceforth, on the grounds that it was the only purely economic, religiously neutral organization of rural women and therefore entitled to being their professional representative. See also E. Böhm, *Die Berufsorganisation der Landfrauen* (1928), in GStA Merseburg, Rep. 87B, 20547/405–12.

tion on the proposed committee by citing its success in poultry breeding, gardening, and home economics, as well as its contacts and previous work with authorities such as the agricultural chambers and ministries on the national and provincial levels, the German Agricultural Society, the Agrarian League and, through the latter, the National Committee of German Agriculture (Reichsausschuß der deutschen Landwirtschaft). In short, it made an unabashed claim to be the best support of male-organized agriculture.[29] By the fall of 1922, as noted above, the Central had been defeated. The politically astute Countess Schwerin-Löwitz abandoned the Central and returned to being a major figure in the RLHV.

Meanwhile Boehm tirelessly traveled around at her own expense, bringing new local chapters into being in Württemberg, Saxony, Braunschweig, as well as southern Germany, previously dominated by Catholic organizations.[30] The conferences put on by the Central had helped the organizational efforts of the agricultural housewives associations, who thus benefited from the confluence of forces at work in the women's movement and organized agriculture. In sum, while World War I had surely hurt individual female agriculturalists, it had handsomely contributed propaganda and organizational opportunities to RLHV.

RLHV in the Weimar Republic

As is well known, republican Germany was born in civil war and its political structure was shaped in part by the pressure applied by the victorious allies. Democratic suffrage, including women, having been finally achieved, some hoped for a flexible pluralist society. It was not yet foreseeable that the compromise between organized capital and organized labor, which had warded off further revolutionary activity, would demonstrate fateful rigidities. What it did do was introduce a new political discourse on class parity that was layered over an older corporative language that had masked class divisions and that was soon to serve more modern reactionary purposes.[31]

29. Both letters were dated 30 October 1922, GStA Merseburg, Rep. 87B, 20546/342–46.

30. Siebert, "Elisabet Boehm," p. 12.

31. T. Childers, "Social Language of Politics," pp. 331–58, stresses the role of corporatist terminology, specifically that which addresssed occupational status, in Nazi political mobilization.

Germany had long been a highly associational society. Now prewar organizations strove to redefine themselves in order to enhance or at least preserve their status in the new system, while still retaining their identity. Women's organizations faced this struggle with the extra burdens of inexperience in electoral politics and mistrust of long-politicized male organizations. They had to learn strategy quickly. They could do this either at the side of related male organizations or through alliance with other women's organizations or both. The RLHV chose the last course. In 1921 it joined both the National Rural League, an enlarged and reorganized version of the older Agrarian League, and the League of German Women's Associations. Thus it formalized its double agenda of improving women's position in the agrarian sector and countrywomen's position in the organized women's movement.

For a time this dual membership served the countrywomen well. Through the BDF, the RLHV won access to women parliamentarians and it also enjoyed the new respectability of the women's movement and the public acknowledgement of women's needs. At the same time, it stayed on its earlier course to "correct" what it took to be radical tendencies within the women's movement. Thus, while the RLHV shared some concerns of the BDF, notably access to higher education, its huge membership and collaboration with the equally large organization of urban housewives helped to curtail many reforms in family law, in reproductive rights, and in the rights of employed women.[32]

Affiliation with the RLB provided immediate tangible gains. Twenty-six women, nominated mainly by the local agricultural housewives' associations, were elected into the League-dominated agricultural chambers – including Boehm, who had won a seat in the East Prussian chamber.[33] RLB headquarters in Berlin provided the RLHV with office space and a salary for a business manager. Boehm joined the RLB executive committee and three other RLHV leaders represented countrywomen in the RLB assembly.[34] Though the RLHV kept its organizational autonomy, it was often seen as the RLB's

---

32. Greven-Aschoff, *Die bürgerliche Frauenbewegung*, pp. 112–14.

33. *Deutsche Allgemeine Zeitung*, 22 October 1922, BA Potsdam, RLB-Pressearchiv, 3107/91.

34. *Deutsche Frauenarbeit*, 13 August 1921, GStA Merseburg, Rep. 87B, 20546/261–63.

auxiliary. In exchange for its access to RLB resources, the RLHV propagated agrarian political goals to its own constituency. The RLHV was now wedded – and many of its leaders literally were – to powerful anti-republican forces.

The RLHV's growth mushroomed from 568 locals in 1921 to 1,766 locals by 1929. East Prussia, home base of its leadership, had the largest membership (ca. 36,000). Most significant was the organization's nationwide recruitment: most states had some local chapters, although rural women in Bavaria and the Rhineland were more likely to be organized by the Catholic women's organizations. The incompleteness of the data, however, permits only modest conclusions as to the size and significance of the RLHV. Local chapters, where individual membership is available, ranged in size from forty to seventy women. If one assumes an average of fifty-five women per local chapter and multiplies this by the peak number of 1,766 locals reported for 1929, one arrives at an estimated top membership of 97,130 – a figure reasonably close to the round 100,000 that the organization claimed for representative and public relations purposes.[35]

The meaning of these figures is harder to ascertain. One obvious fact is that Prussia dominated the RLHV by providing over one-third of its membership, although East Prussian leadership appears to have depended at least as much on historicity and its personal connections with the Junker base of the Agrarian League. The figures also show a pattern of rapid organization in the first postwar years, followed by a lower increase or stagnation during the stabilization period, and then another steep rise in 1928 with the onset of a renewed crisis in agriculture.[36] From this one might conclude that crises encouraged organizing. Because the RLHV had limited resources for recruitment, it would seem that it gained from the RLB effort to create an agrarian consensus that now included women. Indeed, the RLHV credited its expansion in part to the increase in RLB locals and to the agricultural chambers they influenced.

Material dependence drew the RLHV ever further into the

35. Annual reports of the RLHV for 1921/22, 1926/27, 1927/28, 1928/29 in GStA Merseburg, Rep. 87B, 20546 and 20547. Available figures are incomplete and often appear to have been rounded out.

36. Württemberg is a notable exception, showing major growth during the years of stabilization.

orbit of the RLB. A key mechanism was female participation in the agricultural chambers. Thanks to a 1920 law, women could both vote for candidates and be elected on a quota basis that provided for the election (*Zuwahl*) of one supplementary member for every ten regular members, with one-third of the supplementary members to be women.[37] After the RLHV joined the RLB, its nominations were favored by the RLB-dominated agricultural chambers over those of other women's groups, such as the confessional ones. This presence supported the RLHV's claim to be *the* corporate representative of German countrywomen, which further enhanced recruitment and made the claim ever more plausible.

Organizational advantage was also derived from the chambers' obligation to establish women's departments. These were headed most often by the business managers of the RLHV's local, district, or provincial affiliates. Where none existed, whoever took the departmental post was expected to help establish an RLHV chapter. Thus, through the personal union of these posts, the local chapters gained legitimacy, expansion, and even monopoly. The women's department post in the chambers also ensured rent-free space and office supplies to the RLHV business managers, as well as an ear and possibly a voice in the corridors of power. Other material advantages of the RLHV local affiliates ensued from membership in the agricultural chambers. The chambers supported their requests for financial aid from the states and from the national minister of agriculture. Such subsidies, in addition to private donations, formed the bulk of the chapters' budgets, whose dues were deliberately set low in order to attract a wider membership. But there was a price to be paid for this partnership with the men's agricultural establishment. In a society where property relations favored men, countrywomen lacked an independent power base. To receive RLB financial aid they had to submit detailed budget reports. State subsidies to the RLHV affiliates were funneled through the RLB-dominated agricultural chambers, and the work of the RLB's women's departments sometimes distracted attention from the RLHV locals' own initiatives. Finally, physical proximity put the women under the direct scrutiny of the chambers'

37. Draft law, records of the Königsberg agricultural chamber, GStA Merseburg, Rep. 87B, 13344/300–305.

male officials. Bit by bit, the RLHV fell into the orbit of the RLB and its political trajectory. Corporate membership in the provincial agrarian leagues had placed the RLHV affiliates squarely into the camp of some of the most virulent anti-republican forces on the Weimar political scene. Despite its continued protestations that women could modify social conflict, the RLHV brought additional mass to the radical reactionary camp.

Activities of the RLHV

While organizational growth may have been facilitated by the overtly political goals of the RLB, recruitment proceeded by way of concrete services to rural women in the areas of production, education and labor relations.

PRODUCTION

The RLHV exhorted its members to make their products more competitive and then helped them to do so. For example, eggs were collected at the stations of the local affiliates, candled, sorted by size, stamped with the RLHV logo of a bee in flight, and cartoned. The East Prussian and Saxon (Prussian) affiliates bought central incubators.[38] In fact, poultry farming became a viable profession for women agriculturalists, as testified by the presence and speech of an RLHV representative with the German delegation to the international world poultry farmers' congress in 1930.[39] But as uniform standards began to be imposed by the agricultural chambers, RLHV locals eventually succumbed to larger egg-collection organizations.

Dairy products were in transition from being homemade to being commercially processed in large establishments that excluded women. Nevertheless, RLHV locals in the dairy country of Baden, Bavaria, Saxony, and Württemberg tried to help peasant women to improve their productivity by offering courses in the care of cattle, hygienic milk production, and the conversion of milk into butter and cheese. In 1926, the RLHV joined the governing council (*Verwaltungsrat*) of the newly formed

38. Annual report of RLHV for 1928/29, GStA Merseburg, Rep. 87B, 20548/155.

39. L. Küssner-Gerhard, "Der Reichsverband landwirtschaftlicher Hausfrauenvereine," in *Deutsches Frauenstreben. Die deutsche Frau und das Vaterland*, ed. C. Mende (Berlin., n.d.), pp. 52–53.

National Dairy Committee (Reichsmilchausschuß), a semi-private, semi-public body aiming to raise effective demand.[40]

Some markets similarly tried to standardize the packaging of fruits and vegetables, but here too they were overcome by better capitalized ventures. In 1924 the three big Königsberg LHV markets, which together turned over 100,000 marks per month, transformed themselves into the first women's cooperative in Germany.[41] By 1928 twenty of the remaining fifty-four LHV markets in East Prussia put themselves under co-op law.[42] The attempt to be individual capitalist *feminae economicae* was faltering.

EDUCATION

The modest results of the RLHV's attempts to enhance countrywomen's productivity led it to focus ever more on education. There were two routes: formal schooling and informal structures devised by the RLHV itself. In the area of formal schooling in home economics, the RLHV played an important part. In 1923 the Prussian ministry of agriculture created a new office for agricultural home economics that joined the women's departments of all twelve Prussian agricultural chambers, most of which were headed, as has been noted, by members of the RLHV regional affiliates. In this way, the RLHV's claim to corporate representation of countrywomen gained further legitimacy. In the same year a Prussian vocational school law (*Berufschulpflicht*) provided the framework for rural schools to provide continuing education for women (*ländliche Fortbildungsschulen*). The number of these schools mushroomed from thirty-one in 1924 to 885 in 1927, with an increase in students – mainly women from small holdings and agricultural laborers – from 881 to 21,420.[43] However, the desired and actual future of female education in the countryside was integration into the male agricultural schools, with parallel, though separate, classes for girls. In 1927, 107 such pioneering classes served 2,621 students.[44]

The RLHV, whose members were themselves not formally

40. Verwaltungsratsitzung of the Reichsmilchausschuß, 12 October 1926, GStA Merseburg, Rep. 87B, 15746/44.
41. *Land und Frau*, 5 January 1925.
42. Siebert, "Elisabet Boehm," p. 15.
43. Kanzow, *Über den Zusammenschluß*, pp. 46, 60.
44. Ibid., p. 48.

qualified to teach, limited itself to helping establish these classes. RLHV members became administrators and provided practicums for home economics students. In 1926, the organization succeeded in instituting courses that included the history of "the agricultural women's movement," which led to a flood of requests for RLHV literature.[45] Here again, its image as a corporate representative of agricultural women was fortified.

This claim was also strengthened through the RLHV's own programs of counseling and apprenticeship. Portrayed as self-help within the housewives' estate (*Hausfrauenstand*), the programs deliberately used corporate notions to elide class differences and to encourage social cohesion in the countryside. This part of the RLHV agenda fit comfortably into that of the RLB. From the founding of the first RLHV affiliate in East Prussia, Elisabet Boehm had proposed that members with particular expertise in such areas as poultry breeding, gardening, beekeeping, or weaving, be designated "advisors," who might visit individual farms to offer specific help.[46] After World War I, with the new national organization reaching into far-flung villages, the system of advisors was elaborated and professionalized. Each local chapter elected at least three advisors, who then took special training courses.[47] Exact figures for the total number of advisors active in the RLHV are not available, but in 1929 the Brandenburg affiliate alone reported 119 for poultry breeding, 145 for gardening, and 104 for home economics. Other chapters simply reported lively exchanges of advice.[48]

Another area of advice was helping new agricultural settlers, particularly in the eastern provinces. One of the RLHV's principal duties during the war had been informing veterans' widows of their rights, which included an option to farm land.[49] Another kind of female settler was the unmarried

45. Annual reports of RLHV for 1926–29, GStA Merseburg, Rep. 87B/20547–48.

46. Boehm, *Wie ich dazu kam!*, p. 37.

47. I. von Gayl, "Vom 'Gluckenverein' zum Deutschen Landfrauenverband. Aus der Entwicklungsgeschichte der landwirtschaftlichen Frauenarbeit in Ostpreussen," *Nutzen und Ordnung. Gegenwartsfragen der Forschung, Lehre und Beratung für Wirtschaft, Haushalt und Familie* (Frankfurt am Main, 1955), Heft 3/4, pp. 71–72.

48. Annual report of RLHV for 1928/29, GStA Merseburg, Rep. 87B, 20548/182.

49. *Land und Frau*, 4 August, 1 and 22 September 1917. The law was the same as for abandonment in peacetime.

mother; Brandenburg experimented with such "mother settlements" (*Müttersiedlungen*) as a substitute for welfare.[50] During
the agrarian crisis that began in 1928/29, bankruptcies freed
up more land for settlement. RLHV affiliates then operated
real estate offices for women, mainly widows, who wished to
buy or sell and sent its advisors to inexperienced women on
isolated farmsteads. The national settlement policy was aimed
at occupying the Polish border as a defense against "the
encroaching Slav nation [*das eindringende Slaventum*]."[51]
Boehm even hinted at crossing the border, in intimation of the
quest for *Lebensraum*.[52] And indeed, five months after Hitler
came to power, the RLHV advisory program for settlers grew
to include the labor service of unemployed city girls deployed
to help settler women.[53] In 1936 new full-time teachers were
hired, often equipped with cars for visiting distant villages.
This confirmed the importance of the project, although by then
the RLHV had lost all control over its program.

Another non-academic approach to education in rural home
economics was the notion of apprenticing daughters to other
experienced housewives. While it never became a widespread
practice, ideologically it crystallized the corporate vision. On
the one hand it asserted guild practices – *exclusive* by definition – and on the other hand it *included* all women in the category "housekeeper," defined alternately as an "estate" and as
a "profession." Sometimes Boehm called it a *Berufsgemein-
schaft*.[54] But, in fact, early on she had seen it as a desirable form
of tracking. Through a system of apprenticeship, women of
high social rank whose long-term "breeding" had created
"valuable" children, would get the help of lower-class women,
in exchange for training them in the household arts for their
own future as housewives, when, presumably, they could
"breed" future help.[55] The system would require some schooling for such employer-teachers as well as a final examination
for apprentices. It was hoped that such a guild-like organization could circumvent unionizing and give housewives firm
control over their servants through the notion of teaching

50. *Land und Frau*, 19 April 1919.
51. *Land und Frau*, 24 January 1925.
52. *Land und Frau*, 30 April 1927.
53. *Land und Frau*, 24 June, 1 July, and 26 August 1933.
54. E. Boehm, *Die deutsche Landfrau und ihr Wirken in Haus und Vaterland* (Berlin, 1924), p. 55.
55. *Land und Frau*, 20 September 1919.

them professional standards. Thus, apprenticeship was an idea that straddled the spheres of both labor relations and education.

In 1919, together with organized urban housewives, the Prussian affiliate of the RLHV submitted a model apprentice contract to Germany's new National Assembly for approval.[56] At the time, such a scheme seemed plausible, given the high rate of unemployment among demobilized women war workers. However, by 1922 the government had killed this approach to "professional housewifery" by excluding such training from educational subsidies.[57] Those apprentices who remained were now retrained for higher ranking positions such as household manager.

Employer-teachers debated the issue of wages. Some even thought apprentices should pay a fee "for the effort and expense of training them and for damages sustained in the process."[58] In 1931 the issue of social insurance further inflamed the debate. Organized housewives had resisted paying for the social insurance of their domestic servants throughout the Weimar period, but now apprentices were to be covered for sickness and unemployment even if they had not been paid wages.[59] This, plus the agrarian depression, had an obvious dampening effect on the apprentice program. Nationally, the number of women affected remained minuscule.[60] Its greatest importance was as an idea. It provided a respectable precedent for the Nazi labor service to seize on, into which the apprentice program eventually dissolved, with the RLHV asking to be permitted to contribute its experience.[61]

LABOR RELATIONS

The home economics movement in the countryside veiled the issue of employer-worker relations. At war's end, agricultural women, having lost both men in their families and prisoner-of-war farm help, cast a predatory eye on the postwar unemployment lines of demobilized women war workers. Howev-

56. *Land und Frau*, 29 September 1919.
57. Finance Ministry Decree of 6 October 1922, cited in *Land und Frau*, 21 April 1923.
58. *Land und Frau*, 29 August 1925.
59. *Land und Frau*, 13 June 1931.
60. Kanzow, *Über den Zusammenschluß*, p. 44.
61. *Land und Frau*, 27 May 1933.

er, the revolution had unleashed labor's demands, too, for collective bargaining rights and a revision of the labor code. The Social Democratic Party was trying to organize domestic servants and agricultural laborers, historically the most difficult to unionize. Negotiating issues appeared in the pages of the countrywomen's newspaper, *Land und Frau*, especially pertaining to room, board, and hours for rural maids.[62]

When the 1921 draft legislation for domestic servants had been completed, it caused a furor among organized countrywomen. They argued, as had the men of their class with respect to agricultural labor, that laws appropriate to industry and commerce did not apply to farms, with their uneven seasonal work rhythms. However, in some contradiction to this, they also pointed out that women's work in the household was unending and therefore impossible to regulate. On behalf of the already overburdened peasant woman, they insisted that her maid be exempt from compulsory social insurance payments and protective legislation. After all, they argued, the peasant wife had to be relieved of excess work in order to attend to her family. The same argument was not made for her hired help.[63] In fact, organized urban and rural housewives won the struggle against organized domestics; the domestic labor law never got out of committee.[64] On another front, in the administration of the National Office for Job Placement and Unemployment Insurance, where the agricultural employers' association had surrendered one of its seats to the RLHV, its representative succeeded in exempting maids from unemployment insurance and from paid leave for sickness and maternity.[65]

If the countrywomen's unsentimental attitude toward their

62. *Land und Frau*, 22 March, 19 and 26 April, 3 May, and 5 July 1919.

63. Küssner-Gerhard in *Deutsches Frauenstreben*, ed. Mende, pp. 58–60.

64. Details of the national debate around domestic service are in R. Bridenthal, "Class Struggle Around the Hearth: Women and Domestic Service in the Weimar Republic," in *Towards the Holocaust: The Social and Economic Collapse of the Weimar Republic*, ed. M. Dobkowski and I. Wallimann (Westport, Conn., 1983), pp. 243–64. The local level of Hanover is discussed in R. Bridenthal, "'Professional' Housewives: Stepsisters of the Women's Movement," in *When Biology Became Destiny: Women in Weimar and Nazi Germany*, ed. R. Bridenthal, A. Grossmann, and M. Kaplan (New York, 1984), pp. 153–73.

65. Annual report of the RLHV for 1927/28, GStA Merseburg, Rep. 87B, 20547/670. The husband of the Countess von Keyserlingk, one of the RLHV founders and leaders, was a founder of and leading figure in the Reichsverband land- und forstwirtschaftlicher Arbeitgebervereinigungen in Silesia.

female hired help as not enough to disabuse anyone of the illusion that they were a fainthearted group of mawkish housewives, the RLHV's stance on child labor should have shattered any remaining doubts. In the name of the sanctity of the family it insisted that child labor legislation violated parents' rights over their children and that rural work, which they trivialized as simple gooseherding, was good for their health. Boehm and another RLHV representative joined the Committee for Child Labor in the German Association for the Care of Rural Welfare and Homeland, which, together with the Society for Social Reform, ensured that agrarian needs were "taken into account" in commentaries on the proposed law.[66] In a counter-proposal notably lacking in maternal feeling, the RLHV recommended a maximum of eighteen hours of work a week during a school week for children under the age of fourteen, thirty-six hours when school was not in session, and as much as seventy-eight hours in peak season. In 1927 and 1928 the RLHV celebrated the exemption of rural households from labor legislation and social policy that might injure its interests.[67]

It is hard to evaluate the weight of RLHV influence on legislation, apart from its own claims. Certainly, it exerted influence through its representation in the agricultural chambers and through personal connections. One must also consider the general weakness of organized labor in the countryside, which gave victories over it the appearance of storming through an open door. On the other hand, agricultural workers continued to vote with their feet, steadily draining the countryside of labor. The organization that claimed to represent the peasant woman could do little to prevent her burden from growing ever heavier.

In sum, the RLHV had only moderate success in reaching most of its stated economic goals: the entry of some female agricultural producers into the capitalist economy and the creation of a modestly-sized female professional class in the modernizing agricultural sector. Still, merely trying to achieve these goals meant seeking empowerment, in other words, formal political activity through organized groups.

66. Annual report of the RLHV for 1925/26, GStA Merseburg, Rep. 87B, 20547/204.
67. Annual report of the RLHV for 1926/27, GStA Merseburg, Rep. 87B, 20547/391.

RLHV Politics

As mentioned above, in 1921 the RLHV joined both the Federation of German Women's Associations and the National Rural League. Its dependence on the latter eventually brought it into the RLB's political wake, but until then the organization struggled for some autonomy. It did this in part by playing off the male agrarian organization and the feminist organization against one another. At best, the RLHV could draw on the strengths of both the BDF and the RLB, gaining access to the public arena through the first and to funds and influence through the second. At worst, it suffered attacks from the feminists and slights from the agrarians. Thus, with the BDF, it cooperated with organized urban housewives in an effort to attain a professional profile for unpaid but arguably productive work, a viewpoint that "modern" paid professional women found difficult to share, especially given the anti-labor attitude of these employers of maids. In addition, by defining its members primarily as mediated by their family relations, that is as house*wives*, the RLHV put a further conservative drag on the already feeble pull within the BDF toward feminist individualism.

The contemporary language of corporatism, refurbished in answer to the class-conscious revolution of 1918, allowed the RLHV to assume alternate corporate identities. Sometimes it claimed to be the corporate representative of *women* of the *landowning estate*; at other times, the corporate representative of *agrarian* women within the *"housewives' estate."* The first stressed their identity as producers, the second their gender identity. When the Nazis came to power, they could easily choose the first, designating the RLHV as the representative of *all* women in the countryside, thus vindicating its own long-standing claim. In order to understand how this could happen we need to look more closely at the double agenda of the RLHV, as women and as members of the landowning class, and their relation to the state in both identities.

Elisabet Boehm had to twist some of her sisters' arms to get their agreement to join the "radical" BDF. Though some labeled her a bluestocking, she used her own conservative prejudices to win them over. The BDF was a kind of women's parliament, she explained, that helped prepare legislation and it was therefore imperative for countrywomen to be represented there to counter some leaders of "alien blood [*fremd-blütig*]."[68] A few months later, these were "identified" (wrongly) as Anita Augspurg, Lida Gustava Heymann and other leaders of the German branch of the Women's International League for Peace and Freedom. Anti-pacifism and anti-Semitism merged in Boehm's query: were other national branches also represented by international Jewry (*völkerverbindendes Judentum*) or only the German one?[69]

Nevertheless, during the brief era of international good will from the mid- to the late-1920s, the RLHV took the opportunity to leap into the global currents of the women's movement. Chief representative of this trend was the Countess Margarete von Keyserlingk, a co-founder of the RLHV and its representative in the BDF executive committee from 1921 to 1928. In 1925 Keyserlingk joined the nine-woman BDF delegation to the congress of the International Council of Women in Washington.[70] In London, in 1929, she co-chaired the founding meeting of the International Countrywomen's Association sponsored by the International Council of Women and the Women's Rural Institutes of England, Scotland, and Wales.[71] Twenty-eight national delegations of the ICA next met in Vienna in 1930 simultaneously with the ICW's own eighth quinquennial meeting.[72] At this meeting, Keyserlingk deplored the agricultural labor legislation proposed at the Washington Convention that would regulate hours and health insurance, even for child labor.[73] The German report of the third meeting in Stockholm in June 1933, with its motto "The Will to Peace," was understandably bland. The ICA's fourth publication in 1936 innocuously focused on festivals, costumes, and pageants.[74]

Toward the end of the 1920s the RLHV, perhaps sensing where its greatest advantage lay, loosened its ties with feminists and strengthened its links to the agrarians, which drew it inexorably toward the radical right. From the time of its joining the RLB, Boehm was on its executive committee, three other RLHV leaders were in its representative assembly, and

68. *Land und Frau*, 5 February 1927.
69. *Land und Frau*, 14 May 1927.
70. *Land und Frau*, 5 September 1925.
71. *What the Country Women of the World are Doing* 1 (1929): 35.
72. Ibid., 2 (1930): 114–16.
73. Ibid., 2 (1930): 142.
74. Ibid., 4 (1933).

still others joined various committees.[75] As has been noted, this affiliation gave the RLHV material advantages but also committed it to propagating RLB policies. Thus, in 1924/25, though claiming political neutrality, it worked to elect anti-republican "black-red-white" candidates to national and provincial parliaments.[76]

The RLB connection also brought the RLHV into the international arena, representing women at world agrarian congresses. At the Thirteenth International Agricultural Congress in Rome in 1927, Keyserlingk was elected vice-president of the two-hundred-member women's section (the president came from the host country). Later, she reported to her constituency that Italy under Mussolini looked good to her and that the new Italian countrywomen's organization was growing well on fascist soil.[77] Keyserlingk was not the only RLHV member to have friendly feelings for fascist Italy. Toward the end of 1927, another conference in Rome – on rationalization, including that of the household – brought praise for the "new Italy" from RLHV member Dr. Mathilde Wolff, head of the Brandenburg regional group. Fascism had a place for women's work in its cultural and economic plans; it knew the value of home economics training, she wrote. Still, Wolff seemed a bit uncomfortable with the military presence at the conference, and with the briefcase searches.[78] That same year an RLHV delegation to Austria, invited by the Women's Section of the Austrian Agrarian League, joined its hosts in looking forward to an eventual *Anschluß*.[79]

By 1928 German agriculture was in crisis. The women's sphere of agriculture – milk products, poultry, eggs, fruit and vegetables – was in particular need of protective tariffs. Bankruptcies brought changes in land ownership, and the RLHV helped widows to sell and buy through its work in the RLB's settlement department. The women also developed a youth committee that cooperated with those of the RLB's male youth

75. Speech by Boehm at RLHV conference in Leipzig, 17 June 1921, GStA Merseburg, Rep. 87B, 20546/261–63.
76. Annual report of RLHV for 1924/25, GStA Merseburg, Rep. 87B, 20547/37.
77. *Land und Frau*, 2 July 1927.
78. Report by Dr. Mathilde Wolff on the Home Economics Section of the Labor Science Congress (Arbeitswissenschaftlicher Kongreß) in *Land und Frau*, 3 December 1927.
79. *Land und Frau*, 2 July 1927.

organization.[80] As the depression deepened the RLHV's journal, *Land und Frau*, made more room for politics, such as the announcement of a course on the dangers of cultural Bolshevism given by Guida Diehl's proto-Nazi German Women's Combat League (Deutscher Frauenkampfbund).[81]

In 1930 Elisabeth Boehm retired as head of the RLHV in order to free herself to support the Nazi party outright. In 1931 she wrote an article for the Nazi newspaper *Völkischer Beobachter* that concluded "German Countrywoman! You belong under the swastika."[82] Soon after, she partly retracted, apparently having been challenged by some women in the RLHV. She denied being a Nazi and contended that the swastika pendant she wore merely represented an old Germanic symbol that she had been wearing for forty years.[83] In fact, she had joined the Nazi party that year.[84]

Whatever debates were fought within the RLHV – and no sources record them – its new leadership tended to follow Boehm's course. In 1931 its new head, Gertrud von Bredow, who had headed the women's section of the Brandenburg local chapter of the RLB where her husband was on the executive committee, co-signed a letter with Liselotte Küssner-Gerhard, long-time business manager of the RLHV, to the Nazi Party welcoming its recruitment within the RLHV and asking its support for their organization in return.[85] By mid-1932, *Land und Frau* was echoing Nazi slogans in an article deploring the evils of the capitalist spirit, Marxist atheism, and materialism in general. This was more than ironic, considering the RLHV's long struggle to enable women to participate more fully in capitalist agricultural production.[86] The journal published a review by Boehm of two pamphlets on Nazi economic proposals, one of them by Walter Darré, which she found "statesmanlike." She urged her readers to try to better understand the Nazi Party, as it was now too important to overlook.[87]

80. Annual report of RLHV for 1928/29, GStA Merseburg, Rep. 87B, 20548/153–54.

81. *Land und Frau*, 13 April 1929. For more on the German Women's Combat League, see C. Koonz, *Mothers in the Fatherland: Women, the Family and Nazi Politics* (New York, 1987), p. 80.

82. BA Potsdam, RLB-Pressearchiv, 3109/69.

83. *Land und Frau*, 19 September 1931.

84. Boehm's personnel file, Berlin Documentation Center.

85. BA Potsdam, RLB-Pressearchiv 3109/76.

86. *Land und Frau*, 4 June 1932.

87. *Land und Frau*, 11 June 1932.

Toward the end of 1932 the pages of *Land und Frau* offered militantly patriotic effusions. A travelling slide show was billed: "*Volk* without space – *Volk* without soul?" A Pomeranian local chapter warned that from the east "a wind threatens to blow out the holy flame of the domestic hearth." As early as the fall of 1932, civil defense courses were offered to women, in preparation for war.[88] Finally, when Hitler became chancellor, Boehm emerged from retirement to lead the RLHV into the newly formed Peasant Front. On the occasion, Darré acknowledged her as an "old fighter," that is, an early Nazi.[89] She now freely espoused racism and expansionism and urged others to adopt these "ideals."[90] On the occasion of the RLHV's coordination (*Gleichschaltung*) into the Nazi Peasant Front, she celebrated full corporate victory: "We are recognized for having worked entirely in the spirit of National Socialism and will be entrusted to preside over all countrywomen."[91] And so the RLHV came to an end as an autonomous women's organization, not to be revived until after World War II.

Conclusion

Lacking minutes of meetings or other clear evidence of the politics of RLHV members at the grass roots, it is not possible to conclude that all of them were as willing to follow the Nazi line as was its leadership. However, the history of the RLHV serves as a good example of the conservative mobilization of women from the Empire through the Weimar Republic. This mobilization assisted the ascendance of the NSDAP to power; it provided a network of communications that reached into many towns and villages throughout Germany, particularly in the Protestant north. Through the provision of various services – which was its main goal – the RLHV expanded organizationally. This made it a valuable conduit for the politics of the male-dominated agrarian establishment of which it was a corporate member as both moved ever further toward the radical right. The RLHV's own need to empower countrywomen to achieve their economic goals might or might not have led them along the same path, but its material dependence on the RLB left it no other choice.

88. *Land und Frau*, 24 September, 12 November, and 24 December 1932.
89. BA Potsdam, RLB-Pressearchiv, 3109/124a.
90. *Land und Frau*, 27 May 1933.
91. *Land und Frau*, 10 June 1933.

The momentum of the countrywomen's associational life, like that of many other interest groups, helped the Nazis come to power as much as electoral politics did .[92] Moreover, the corporatist language used by the RLHV to designate a "profession" of housewifery served here, as it did elsewhere, to mask hierarchy with a false egalitarian universalism and to marshal a mass base for class interests. It also prepared rural women to accept the classic fascist fusion of modern technology with nostalgia, in this case rationalized home economics with the traditional role of mistress of the house.

The case of the RLHV demonstrates that its *material* dependence on the Agrarian League hampered its autonomy, which was *ideologically* derived from the women's movement of its day. Thus, while locally active in the provision of certain services and largely self-recruiting, it increasingly propagated the radical right politics of the RLB. The fact that the RLHV's significant leadership was enthusiastic about administering to "the female sphere" of the Nazi Peasant Estate was a harbinger of its complicity in the initial success of National Socialism in Germany. The absorption of the RLHV by the Peasant Estate effectively ended its relative autonomy altogether, though many of its administrators were kept on.[93] Building on the infrastructure established by the countrywomen, the sub-bureau "Household Economy" of the National Food Estate (Reichsnährstand) from 1935 to 1937 set up over 33,000 meetings, very likely combining agricultural advice with political indoctrination.[94]

Was the political price for the loss of relative autonomy worth paying? Did the RLHV at least succeed in its stated goal

92. Koshar, *Social Life, Local Politics, and Nazism*, p. 284, concludes that voluntary associations were "the unauthorized facilitators of German fascism" through their informal exercise of bourgeois hegemony. Because of their claim to represent universal interests, they could mobilize reactionary opinion more effectively than political parties.

93. Interview, 21–22 August 1981, with Regina Frankenfeld, business manager of an Agricultural Housewives Association in Pomerania from 1928 to 1934, head of the women's section of the Pomeranian Peasant Estate (Landbauernschaft) from 1934 to 1937, and head of the schooling and advisory section of the Women's Bureau (Deutsches Frauenwerk) from 1937 to 1945. Letter from Käte Jakobeit, RLHV representative in the Berlin office of the National Agrarian League from 1927 to 1934, and afterwards given a different appointment by the National Peasant Leader (Reichsbauernführer), to the author, 1 September 1983.

94. C.R. Lovin, "Farm Women in the Third Reich," *Agricultural History* 60 (1986): 112–13.

of furthering its members' economic interests? If those are understood to have been the assimilation of women into capitalist relations of production in the countryside through markets, new techniques, and education, the answer must be no. As in other countries where agriculture had become modernized, women were relegated to the margins. Ultimately, the Nazi law on farm inheritance virtually excluded women, and the onset of World War II simply increased their labors. While the RLHV failed to achieve most of its long-range goals, it nevertheless provides a useful microcosm for the historian who can there observe a local agency dealing with forces beyond local control and note early manifestations of women's consciousness in a specific arena. If nothing else, it compels awareness of the complexity of identity in interest group politics.

13

Convergence on the Right

Agrarian Elite Radicalism and Nazi Populism in Pomerania, 1928–33[*]

Shelley Baranowski

In 1932, the staunchly conservative Pomeranian Junker, Ewald von Kleist-Schmenzin, sharply condemned Nazism for its materialism, its irreligion, its contempt for traditional elites and its "Marxism." What particularly vexed Kleist, a prominent figure in rightist circles, was that Hitler had seduced many in the conservative-nationalist camp, notably the National Rural League (Reichs-Landbund or RLB) and Alfred Hugenberg's disintegrating German National People's Party (Deutschnationale Volkspartei or DNVP), into believing that the Nazis would be useful allies in the rightist campaign to destroy the Weimar "system." Certainly no one rivaled Kleist in his loathing of the Republic, which he wanted dismantled in favor of a restored Hohenzollern monarchy. Those very sentiments had earlier led him to support Hugenberg's virulent anti-republicanism. Yet now, he believed, fellow-traveling with National Socialism had only driven "several thousand nationally-minded people" to vote for Hitler: "National Socialism would never have gone on the upswing if nationalist circles had publicly disengaged themselves from it. The view tolerated in the nationalist camp, that National Socialism could be seen as a nationalist party that clings to a few faults, has conjured up a danger for our future that can only be exorcised by extreme and strenuous efforts." Should conservatives not recognize Nazism for what it is, warned Kleist, their goal of an authoritarian and hierarchically ordered Germany

[*]I wish to thank the National Endowment for the Humanities, the American Council of Learned Societies, Kenyon College, and The University of Akron for funding the research upon which this article is based.

would disintegrate, and their political influence rendered negligible.[1]

Kleist counts as one of the few German conservatives who unambiguously opposed the Nazis before Hitler took power, having feared that the Nazi movement would severely challenge the hegemony of existing elites and institutions. Even as an emerging party during the Weimar Republic's last years, National Socialism not only espoused a resentful anti-elitism, it also accomplished a feat beyond the capacities of the "traditional" Right: it unified dissatisfied and remarkably diverse social constituencies into a potent electoral force. As much recent scholarship has suggested, noting Nazism's diffuse plebeian composition and material independence from elites, the Hitler party represented, for the first time in German history, a populist movement with the capacity to wrest power from the dominant business, civil servant, military and landowning classes.[2] In fact, some historians have argued that the Nazis realized their potential. In comparison to fascist Italy, where the agendas of Italian elites restrained Mussolini, the radical imperatives of Nazism and the relative weakness of German elites ultimately provided Hitler with considerable freedom of action.[3]

Yet what should one make of Kleist's assignment of responsibility for Hitler's rise to the "nationalist circles," whose ranks overrepresented Germany's dominant classes? Should one treat his remarks as having reflected an ingrained, not to

1. "Der Nationalsozialismus – Eine Gefahr," in B. Scheurig, *Ewald von Kleist-Schmenzin. Ein Konservativer gegen Hitler* (Oldenburg and Hamburg, 1968), pp. 255–64. Quotation taken from p. 259.

2. For recent suggestions to this effect, see P. Baldwin, "Social Interpretations of Nazism: Renewing a Tradition," *Journal of Contemporary History* 25 (1990): 5–37; G. Corni, *Hitler and the Peasants. Agrarian Policy of the Third Reich 1930–1939*, trans. D. Kerr (New York, Oxford, and Munich, 1990), pp. 18–34; J. Falter, *Hitlers Wähler* (Munich, 1991); Hans Mommsen, *Die verspielte Freiheit 1918–1933. Der Weg der Republik von Weimar in den Untergang 1918–1933* (Berlin, 1989), pp. 321–60; and Thomas Childers, *The Nazi Voter. The Social Foundations of Fascism in Germany* (Chapel Hill, N.C. and London, 1983).

3. G. Corni, "Die Agrarpolitik des Faschismus: Ein Vergleich zwischen Deutschland und Italien," *Tel Aviver Jahrbuch für deutsche Geschichte,*" 17 (1988): 391–423; and W. Schieder, "Das Deutschland Hitlers und das Italien Mussolinis. Zum Problem faschistischer Regimebildung," in *Die Große Krise der dreißiger Jahre. Vom Niedergang der Weltwirtschaft zum Zweiten Weltkrieg,* ed. G. Schulz (Göttingen, 1985), pp. 44–71. Very much against the stream is A.J. Mayer's *Why Did the Heavens Not Darken? The Final Solution in History* (New York, 1988), which suggests that the virulent anti-Bolshevism that cemented the conservative elite-Nazi alliance throughout the Third Reich propelled the "Judeocide."

mention exaggerated, assumption of elite influence? Or might Kleist's comments, upon closer examination, point to a significant, and even crucial, element in the Nazi party's electoral success? These questions are pertinent at this stage of the historical debate given the Hitler movement's influence among voters in rural areas east of the Elbe River where, arguably, the most important component of the German elite, large estate owners, traditionally held sway. For decades, agrarian elites stood out from the German "establishment" as a whole, by having successfully adapted to the demands of mass politics, creating popular constituencies by a blend of concessions and demagogic manipulation.[4] And, until recently, estate owners held center stage in the scholarly literature as the principal actors in Germany's descent into fascism. Yet now they have begun to appear to many historians as being on the defensive, for under the empire they secured their position with increasing difficulty and during the Weimar period they proved unable to retain their rural dominance and political constituencies in the face of the Nazi populist juggernaut.[5] The debate about the effectiveness of elites thus juxtaposes two issues that on the surface appear contradictory – the extent and duration of the landed elite's power, and the Nazi party's independently acquired mass appeal that ultimately forced the German "establishment" to appoint Hitler chancellor.

One might make sense of the conflicting interpretations by looking, appropriately enough, at Kleist's home province of Pomerania, an east-Elbian region where estate owners held disproportionate political influence, and where Nazism proved extraordinarily successful as other Weimar political parties fragmented. Beginning in 1928, a convergence occurred between the elevated radicalism of agrarian elites and the Nazis' accelerated efforts to attract aggrieved rural voters.

4. See Robert G. Moeller's remarks about the failure of German liberals to do likewise, in "The *Kaiserreich* Recast? Continuity and Change in Modern German History," *Journal of Social History* 17 (1984): 655–83.

5. In addition to the references in note 2 above, see R. Bessel, "Why Did the Weimar Republic Collapse?" in *Why Did Weimar Democracy Fail?*, ed. I. Kershaw (London, 1990), p. 140; G. Eley, "Conservatives and Radical Nationalists in Germany: The Production of Fascist Potentials," in *Fascists and Conservatives. The Radical Right and the Establishment in Twentieth Century Europe*, ed. M. Blinkhorn (London, 1990), pp. 50–70; and B. Peterson, "Regional Elites and the Rise of National Socialism, 1920–33," in *Radical Perspectives on the Rise of Fascism in Germany, 1919–1945*, ed. M. Dobkowski and I. Walliman (New York, 1989), pp. 192–93.

That combination, in turn, generated some of the mass support that the Hitler movement exploited to win the chancellorship. The party's relationship to Pomerania's agrarian elites constituted a volatile mixture of accommodation and competition. Yet I will argue that Kleist's suspicions were, in the final reckoning, entirely justified: the behavior of Pomerania's elites, especially estate owners, contributed heavily to the Nazis' electoral advance. Not only did the party benefit directly from the overt backing of some of Pomerania's large holders, Junkers included, it prospered indirectly from the widely disseminated right radicalism of estate owners that transcended the party political divisions among them. In short, Pomerania's elites created a favorable climate for Nazism to develop as the political alternative for numerous rural dwellers when a significant contingent of these elites, through their incessant attacks on the Weimar "system," persuaded country voters that they had little to lose by choosing Nazism. Though Pomerania might seem, at first glance, to provide but a narrow foundation from which to draw larger conclusions about the Nazi party's electoral independence from or dependence on elites, there is enough that is "typical" in the late Weimar experience of that province to suggest that the now prevailing view of a dynamic, populist party undermining the hegemony of elites deserves qualification.

Pomerania, the Estate Owners' Preserve

The eastern Prussian province of Pomerania was the sort of rural, heavily Protestant region that we know in retrospect to have been fertile ground for the electoral advance of National Socialism. Situated on the Baltic Sea, and now unevenly divided between Poland and eastern Germany, Pomerania was sparcely populated and under-urbanized, possessing an economy thoroughly dominated by agriculture. Politically, Pomerania's countryside was profoundly conservative, having favored the right-wing, anti-republican German National People's Party throughout most of the republican years. The only serious challenger to the DNVP, the Social Democratic Party (Sozialdemokratische Partei Deutschlands or SPD), achieved little success recruiting in rural areas, notwithstanding its strength in Pomerania's few cities. Yet in the Reichstag elections of September 1930, the Nazis, following their stunning performance elsewhere in the Reich, served notice that the DNVP's political hegemony had eroded. The Nazi party's percentages among voters increased from 1.5 percent in the Prussian Landtag elections of May 1928, to 24 percent in 1930. Conversely, the DNVP dropped from 41.6 percent in 1928 to 29 percent in 1930.[6] Thereafter, Nazi voters grew even more numerous, polling 48 percent in the July 1932 Reichstag elections, one of the highest totals in Germany.[7]

Because the Prussian government recognized that a major political realignment was taking place, it pressed for explanations from those directly in touch with voter sentiment, its county magistrates, or *Landräte*. The responses from the field recorded the frenetic desperation of peasants, agricultural laborers, civil servants and shopkeepers struggling to keep their heads above water in Pomerania's collapsing agrarian economy. Noted one magistrate, the Nazi party had become a magnet for the economically and politically disenchanted because it had not been responsible for failed government policies, and because it appealed to the unpretentiousness of rural folk, particularly young voters without firm party ties.[8] In fact, the Nazis aggressively marketed themselves as the champions of rural laborers, peasants and the lower middle class, exhorting them to abandon the other middle-class parties for their movement that was sufficiently radical to undermine the Republic, the source of rural society's ills. And, during that campaign, National Socialist propaganda exposed the full dimensions of the party's populism in its ambivalence toward elites, notably agrarian elites. Large estate owners occupied their necessary place, acknowledged one widely circulated reprint of the Nazi agricultural program. Yet they should exist only "in healthy relationship" to middling and small holders. Furthermore, the state had the right to confiscate landed property in cases where the owner either failed to provide for "the maintenance of the Volk" or did not farm the land directly. Finally, the Nazis' pledge to transform the peasantry into a "new nobility," and their advocacy of internal col-

6. B. Drewniak, *Początki Ruchu Hitlerowskiego na Pomorzu Zachodnim 1923–1934* (Pozna´n, 1962), p. 26.

7. *Nazism: A History in Documents and Eyewitness Accounts*, ed. J. Noakes and G. Pridham, 2nd ed., 2 vols. (New York, 1983/84), p. 83.

8. Landrat Anklam to Regierung Präsident Stettin, 11 November 1930, Wojewódskie Archiwum Pa´nstwowe, Szczecin, Regierung Stettin I (hereinafter cited as WAPS-RS I), Nr. 1841.

onization at the expense of estate owners, obviously gave
estate owners cause to fear them.[9]

Indeed, the Nazis' reaggregation of the Right, as well as
their seeming transformation of the politically and economically dependent into political actors, must have appeared dou-
bly surprising in Pomerania. Next to Mecklenburg, Pomerania
had long been considered the special preserve of large estate
owners (*Großgrundbesitzer*). In addition, that province stereo-
typically embodied the tenacious influence of Prussian
"Junkerdom" and its constituent values of patriarchalism, mil-
itarism, monarchism, Protestantism, ruralism and a social
hierarchy ruled by those appropriately anointed.[10] In fact,
there was much there to justify the stereotype. Despite the
presence of numerous bourgeois estate owners, some of
whom, to the disgust of long resident noble families, purchased their holdings as late as during the First World War,
and despite the widespread practice of tenancy, noble families,
including many with centuries-old pedigrees, figured prominently in the leaderships of the province's myriad associations.[11] The obituary of the Rittergutsbesitzer (knight's estate
holder) Konrad Tessen von Heydebreck, who died in 1926
after falling from his horse, conveys beneath the flattering
prose the degree of Junker involvement in all facets of provincial life: the whole community would miss this man, mourned
the article, not merely the administrators and workers on his
holdings, but also the church where he had been patron, the
War Veterans' Association or *Kriegerverein*, the county legislature (*Kreistag*), the various specialized professional organiza-

9. "Nationalsozialismus und Landwirtschaft. Parteiamtliche Kundgebung
über die Stellung der NSDAP zum Landvolk and Landwirtschaft," 7 March
1930, Wojewódskie Archiwum Pa´nstwowe, Koszalin (hereinafter cited as
WAPK), Landratsamt Bütow, Nr. 11. See also A. Czarnik, *Stosunki polityczne
na Pomorzu Zachodnim w okręsie republiki weimarskiej 1919–1933* (Pozna´n,
1983), p. 300.

10. For interesting accounts of Junker life in Pomerania, and coming to
terms with its demise at the end of World War II, see C. v. Krockow, *Die Reise
nach Pommern. Bericht aus einem verschwiegenen Land* (Stuttgart, 1985), and *Die
Stunden der Frauen. Bericht aus Pommern 1944–1947* (Stuttgart, 1988).

11. For a recent description of the composition and practices of Pomeranian
Großgrundbesitzer prior to World War I, see I. Buchsteiner, "Großgrundbesitz
in Pommern zwischen 1871 and 1914. Soziale und ökonomische Veränderun-
gen als Ausdruck der Integration des Adels in die bürgerliche Gesellschaft,"
Zeitschrift für Geschichtswissenschaft 37, no. 4 (1989): 329–336. See also F.L.
Carsten, *Geschichte der preußischen Junker* (Frankfurt am Main, 1988), p. 162.

tions (*Genossenschaften*), not to mention the local offices of the Rural League and the DNVP. All who came into contact with Heydebreck had benefited from his direction.[12]

The basis of Junker dominion – land ownership – proved remarkably durable, even though in those areas of Germany where large estates (100 hectares and more) traditionally held sway, those estates had declined numerically while middling peasant holdings (20–50 ha) proliferated.[13] Though incomplete, available statistics support the continued hold of the Pomeranian nobility: entailed estates (*Fideikomiße*) stubbornly persisted in Pomerania, the vast majority of them in noble hands, despite their legal dissolution in 1920.[14] As late as 1930, even as mounting indebtedness forced numerous farm foreclosures, seventy-seven Junkers bearing such names as Bonin, Bismarck, Flemming, Kleist, Puttkamer and Zitzewitz, possessed estates of 2,500 hectares and larger.[15] Yet such evidence seemingly contradicts the transformed political environment that county officers described to the Prussian government. Or does it really? The resolution lies primarily in an examination of the political behavior of Pomeranian estate owners, the militance of whom grew notably intense in the last five years of the Weimar Republic's existence.

Rural Crisis, Elite Politics and the Birth of Nazism

At no time during the Republic had agrarian elites felt "at home," much less privileged, as they had during the Second Empire. The Revolution of 1918 cost estate owners both the patronage of the emperor and the Prussian three-class franchise, which had assured them a disproportionate political influence, especially at the commanding heights of government. Simultaneously, landed elites confronted striking agri-

12. *Pommersche Tagespost*, 6 July 1926, no. 156.
13. H. Becker, *Handlungsspielräume der Agrarpolitik in der Weimarer Republik zwischen 1923 und 1929* (Stuttgart, 1990), p. 64.
14. "Die Fideikommiße in der Provinz Pommern," *General-Anzeiger Stettin und die Provinz Pommern*, 30 November 1920, vol. 72, no. 271. See also Becker, *Handlungsspielräume der Agrarpolitik*, p. 53. According to Corni, *Hitler and the Peasants*, p. 126, only the Nazis completed the abrogation of the Fideikommiße, but not until mid-1938.
15. T. Häbich, *Deutsche Latifundien. Ein Beitrag zur Berichtung unserer Vorstellung von der bestehenden Verteilung des ländlichen Grundeigentums* (Königsberg, 1930), pp. 135–37.

cultural laborers (*Landarbeiter*), now free of the repressive Servants' Law (*Gesindeordnung*) that had once outlawed farm worker organizations. They faced the continuation of the hated "controlled economy," or *Zwangswirtschaft*, the government's intervention in the agrarian market place to assure the availability and affordability of essential foodstuffs. And finally, they felt threatened by the prospect of socialization, much discussed during the Republic's early months.

In due course, however, the landowners recovered much of their political influence, an accomplishment that illustrates their skill in popular mobilization and underscores the limits of the postwar revolution. Regaining their place in agrarian society demanded not merely that estate owners organize and propagandize the rural population effectively as they had done before World War I, though they continued to do so.[16] Nor could they depend upon outright coercion, though agrarian elites, as has been well-documented, resorted successfully to the army and Free Corps to contain the estate-laborer strike.[17] Rather, to an unprecedented extent, large landowners, reluctantly to be sure, broadened the social bases of conservatism in the newly constituted German National People's Party, while expanding and "democratizing" the prewar Agrarian League (Bund der Landwirte). In Pomerania, the provincial affiliate of the Agrarian League's postwar successor, the National Rural League, insured that its executive committee included an equal number of large holders, small holders and agricultural laborers, as well as a smattering of other

16. The essential studies of prewar and postwar politicization among landowners are, H.-J. Puhle, *Agrarische Interessenpolitik und Preußischer Konservatismus im Wilhelminischen Reich (1893–1914). Ein Beitrag zur Analyse des Nationalismus in Deutschland am Beispiel des Bundes der Landwirte und der Deutsch-Konservativen Partei* (Hannover, 1966); J. Flemming, *Landwirtschaftliche Interessen und Demokratie. Ländliche Gesellschaft, Agrarverbände und Staat 1890–1925* (Bonn, 1978); and M. Schumacher, *Land und Politik. Eine Untersuchung über politische Parteien und agrarische Interessen 1914–1923* (Düsseldorf, 1978).

17. E. Kohler, "Revolutionary Pomerania, 1919–1920: A Study in Majority Socialist Agricultural Policy and Civil-Military Relations," *Central European History* 9, no. 3 (1976): 250–93; J. Flemming, "Die Bewaffung des Landvolks. Ländliche Schutzwehren und agrarischer Konservatismus in der Anfangsphase der Weimarer Republik," *Militärgeschichtliche Mitteilungen* 2 (1979): 7–29. See also the documentation in H. Hübner and H. Kathe, *Lage und Kampf der Landarbeiter im Ostelbischen Preußen (Vom Anfang des 19. Jahrhundert bis zur Novemberrevolution 1918/19)*, 2 vols. (Vaduz/Liechtenstein, 1977), vol. 2, pp. 550–80.

lower middle-class elements, though its chair and most prominent spokespersons were almost always estate owners.[18] The *Pommersche Tagespost*, the most influential journalistic voice of landowner interests in the province, published the criticisms of peasants against the arrogance of estate owners, ever so gently warning elites of the risks involved in failing to accommodate the needs of small producers.[19] Those and similar actions, undertaken in the name of "the unity of agriculture" against the continued pressures of the controlled economy and the militance on the left, certainly paralleled the reconstitution of east-Elbian conservatism nationally. In Pomerania, they succeeded because significant alternatives to the established channels of agrarian interest representation simply failed to materialize.[20]

By their own efforts, therefore, large landowners did their part to repel the revolutionary extremes of the early postwar years. Yet the reluctance of key republican officials, Socialists included, to sacrifice large-scale agricultural production for land reform played an equally important role in preserving the influence of large landowners, especially in the countryside, which had always nurtured the political leverage of agrarian elites. The searing experience of the wartime blockade and its accompanying food scarcity, helped to give estate agriculture a lease on life by persuading the Republic to abandon agrarian experiments. Before long, the controlled economy evaporated, while the left's initial zeal for the socialization of land dissipated into an infinitely milder program for the creation of rural peasant settlements, one that even the Rural League recognized as the lesser evil. Even the Republic's profound economic difficulties, which the inflation of the early 1920s most obviously reflected, benefited many agrarians, both large and small – inflation enabled landowners to retire their heavy debts.[21]

18. *Pommersche Tagespost*, 13 May 1919, no. 126.

19. "An die Großgrundbesitzer," *Pommersche Tagespost*, 21 May 1919, no. 134.

20. See Eley, "Conservatives and Radical Nationalists in Germany"; and J. Flemming, "Konservatismus als national revolutionäre Bewegung. Konservativer Kritik an der Deutschnationalen Volkspartei 1918–1933," in *Deutscher Konservatismus im 19. und 20. Jahrhundert*, ed. D. Stegmann, B.-J. Wendt and P.-C. Witt (Bonn, 1983), pp. 295–331. The lack of independent peasant leadership in Pomerania, particularly in the province's eastern regions, was noted by the president of the Köslin district: Regierung Präsident Köslin to Minister für Landwirtschaft, 8 June 1928, WAPK, Regierung Köslin (hereinafter cited as WAPK-RK), no. 3407.

21. Becker, *Handlungsspielräume der Agrarpolitik*, pp. 95–131.

Nevertheless, those "achievements," hard-fought as they seemed, did little to allay the suspicions of agrarian elites that the Weimar Republic was, at its very core, hostile to agriculture. Those apprehensions stemmed both from the relative decline of agriculture's contribution to the German economy as compared to that of industry, and from the devastating depression that gripped rural Germany after 1925. The stabilization of the mark brought with it increased taxation, higher interest rates, and renewed indebtedness, while falling prices for agricultural commodities and changing consumer demands placed Pomerania's predominantly rye and potatoes cultivation in serious jeopardy.[22] As estate owners saw it, the succession of republican governments only added to their difficulties by importing food, imposing high taxes, failing to reduce interest rates, and kowtowing to the Allies' demands for reparations, thus mortgaging Germany's assets to foreigners instead of restoring profitability in the countryside. The *Pommersche Tagespost* assiduously recorded the litany of complaints arising from the provincial Rural League and the Chamber of Agriculture (Landwirtschaftskammer), especially those that estate owners articulated.[23] Ultimately, the only solution to the problems of agriculture was the obliteration of the "Marxist" system altogether. To indict the Republic, one prominent landowner, Georg Werner von Zitzewitz, drew upon the stubbornly held myth of the central role of agriculture, both to Germany's economy, and to the very identity of Germans. In his view, agriculture had been engaged in a protracted struggle against a "system" that had done nothing but undermine "the indigenous economy." One could affirm the state in principle, according to Zitzewitz, because it was the collective expression of Germans, but the present "system"

22. For discussions of agriculture's long-term decline, see R. Bessel, "Eastern Germany as a Structural Problem in the Weimar Republic," *Social History* 3, (1978): 199–218; and Corni, *Hitler and the Peasants*, pp. 1–17. While no disagreement exists that German agriculture was in a bad way during the republican years, there is doubt that such was the case under the Second Empire. See K. Heß, *Junker and bürgerliche Großgrundbesitzer im Kaiserreich. Landwirtschaftlicher Großbetrieb, Großgrundbesitz und Familienfideikommiße in Preußen (1867/71–1914)* (Stuttgart, 1990), pp. 215–312.

23. G.W. v. Zitzewitz, Groß-Gansen, "Kampf gegen das System! Für die bodenständige Wirtschaft!", *Pommersche Tagespost*, 25 April 1930, no. 96. H.-J. v. Rohr-Demmin, "Landvolk und Nationale Revolution," *Pommersche Tagespost* 17 March 1931, no. 64; von Flemming-Pätzig, "Vorwärts im Kampf für Heimat und Scholle!," *Pommersche Tagespost*, 28 March 1931, no. 74.

was not only "un-German" but even destructive for the German national character (*Volkstum*).[24]

Claiming to represent not just themselves but the *Landvolk* as a whole, Pomeranian estate owners accelerated their efforts to mobilize all rural classes against the Republic's agrarian policies as the rural crisis turned into rural catastrophe. In early 1928, the mass demonstrations of peasants in Schleswig-Holstein, which culminated in a successful tax boycott there, spurred many Pomeranian landowners to lead a similar initiative in their home province. By early March, nervous Prussian government officials reported intermittent, but none the less well-attended, public protests in various parts of the province, invoked usually at the Rural League's behest. Indeed, the president of the Köslin district, which included most of upper Pomerania, noted that the demonstration he witnessed was highly unusual for a population whose conservatism ill-inclined it to challenge the authority of the state.[25] In many instances, those angry, if peaceful, gatherings were made up of peasants and farm workers, urban and rural artisans, as well as shopkeepers affected by the crisis, not to mention estate owners and an array of nationalist associations, such as the Stahlhelm. Peasants and agricultural laborers, in particular, previously unburdened by the debt that afflicted estate owners, had good reason for joining with their social "superiors" now that pork prices had dropped to record lows. Raising swine contributed to the income of both groups. Furthermore, the disastrous harvest of the previous year, which heavy rains and hail yielded, worked its misery at all levels of rural society, whether directly in lost income for the farmers or indirectly in lost business for the lower middle classes who served the farming community.[26]

Official reports voiced their concern that the Rural League's militance, coupled with the persistence of economic hardship, would continue to radicalize a rural population otherwise accustomed to political quiescence. A few county magistrates

---

24. "Politik und Wirtschaft," *Pommersche Tagespost*, 15 April 1930, no. 89.

25. Draft of letter by Regierung Präsident Köslin to Ministerium der Innern, 9 March 1928, WAPK–RK, no. 3407. In addition to the contents of WAPK-RK, no. 3407, additional reports on the effect of the Schleswig-Holstein protest in Pomerania are found in WAPS-RS I, nos. 12134 and 12135.

26. Bericht der Landwirtschaftskammer für das Provinz Pommern über die Lage der Landwirtschaft, 3 August 1927, WAPK-RK, no. 1812.

hinted that the crisis could bring about the divergence of peasant and estate owner interests, an occasion that would obviously weaken the big landowners' near-exclusive hold on agrarian interest representation in the province.[27] Others, however, suggested quite the opposite: the agrarian crisis in the province was driving all rural classes to extremes under the Rural League's leadership. Explained one rural country official, the parlous state of agriculture enabled the League to instill a solidarity of interest between peasants and large landowners based on their common demand for higher pork and potato prices. That would have been difficult in better economic times, given the spacial distances that existed in his district and the general disinclination of rural dwellers to organize, in comparison to urban workers.[28] In any case, large landowners left nothing to chance: to guarantee the attendance of their laborers at the demonstrations, a number of estate owners gave their workers and their spouses the day off with pay.[29]

The following year, however, the anti-republican drift of the mobilization that surfaced in response to the Schleswig-Holstein protests grew still more feverish as the German Right's referendum against the Young Plan occupied the energies of organized agriculture. Again, Pomeranian estate owners led the way. At work in this instance was not just the disastrous economy, but also the long-standing relationship that existed between such prominent Pomeranian Rural League leaders as Hans Joachim von Rohr-Demmin and Alfred Hugenberg. By the late summer of 1928, in fact, a Rohr-led fronde on Hugenberg's behalf resulted in the defeat of those in the DNVP's provincial leadership, like Hans von Schlange-Schöningen, who preferred to defend the interests of agriculture within the Weimar government. Hugenberg's militant anti-republicanism subsequently found few critics.[30]

The campaign against the Young Plan provided a show case

27. An example being Landrat Anklam to Regierung Präsident Stettin, 8 March 1928, WAPS-RS I, no. 12135.

28. Landrat Bütow to Regierung Präsident Köslin, 5 March 1928, WAPK-RK, no. 3407.

29. Landrat Bublitz to Regierung Präsident Köslin, 5 March 1928, WAPK-RK, no. 3407.

30. H. Holzbach, *Das "System Hugenberg." Die Organisation bürgerlicher Sammlungspolitik vor dem Aufstieg der NSDAP* (Stuttgart, 1981), pp. 110–12, 237–39.

for the demagogic skills of Pomeranian estate owners, including the Junkers among them who clustered together at the
numerous rallies staged throughout the province. They not
only served as speakers and distributed flyers that condemned the Plan for subjecting Germany to another twenty-
seven years of "tribute slavery." Many landowners, according
to the reports of provincial government officials, also pres-
sured their labor forces into supporting the referendum, in
many cases threatening to fire workers who failed to cooperate.[31] To secure additional popular support beyond what coercion could accomplish, landowners, such as the knight's estate
owner von Zitzewitz, insisted that the Young Plan meant the
victimatization of all classes: Germany, he argued, was now
threatened with becoming a "helot people," confronted by virtual "enslavement." The consequences of the plan affected not
only the well-being of the German economy as a whole, but
especially "the prospects for the upward mobility of German
workers."[32]

Although the Rural League, the DNVP and the Stahlhelm
occupied the foreground of the anti-Young Plan campaign,
other rightist groups participated as well, including one that
to this point had enjoyed little popular resonance, the National Socialists. The party had committed itself to agitating in
rural regions, both in Pomerania and elsewhere in Germany,
much earlier than is usually believed. Much of the initiative
arose locally rather than at the behest of central party offices.
In Pomerania, the first party cells appeared as early as 1922
and expanded once again after the "refounding" of the Hitler
movement in 1925. Yet the Nazis had neither created their
extensive agrarian network that would arise after 1930, nor
had they yet capitalized on rural dissatisfaction to the extent
they would, largely as a result of the Young Plan referendum.[33]

31. Reports of the anti-Young Plan agitation are found in WAPS-RS I, nos.
1814 and 1821 and folder nos. 82 and 83 in Rep. 65c, Vorpommerscher Lan-
desarchiv Greifswald.

32. *Stargarder Zeitung*, 19 October 1929, no. 246, found in WAPS-RS I, no.
1821.

33. See J.H. Grill, "The Nazi Party's Rural Propaganda before 1928," *Central
European History* 15 (1982): 149–185; as well as Drewniak's discussion of the
Party's beginnings in Pomerania in *Początki Ruchu Hitlerowskiego*, pp. 17–23;
and Corni, *Hitler and the Peasants*, p. 24. Richard Bessel describes the tenuous-
ness of the Nazis' organization in the Prussian east in his *Political Violence and
the Rise of Nazism. The Storm Troopers in Eastern Germany 1925–1934* (New
Haven, Conn., and London, 1984), pp. 13–21.

Even after September 1930, the NSDAP justified its alliances with the DNVP on "tactical grounds," as a way of expanding its possibilities.[34]

After the 1928 Reichstag election, however, the Nazis increased their rallies, propaganda and membership, as the agrarian crisis deepened. In 1929, they founded their first newspaper, *Die Diktatur*, in the provincial town of Pyritz. Another organ, *Die Parole*, published in Stettin, appeared in the spring of the following year.[35] Though aiming to lure the popular classes in the province under their banner, they also adopted a strategy that would be crucial to their success in the heavily German Nationalist Pomeranian countryside: they opted for informal alliances with estate owners in the numerous organizations in which estate owners were active. As other studies have suggested, the Nazis could not have thrived simply because of the quality of their propaganda and organization, however evocative and efficient those might have been. Rather, their participation in the established associational life of the towns and regions that they targeted transformed them from a movement on the fringes of Weimar politics to a serious contender for power.[36]

As the anti-Young Plan crusade progressed, local officials reported on the growing pro-Nazi sympathies of large landowners in the Stahlhelm, as well as the pro-Nazi agitation of younger peasants in the Artaman League (Artamanenbund), a peasant education and settlement program that many estate owners strongly endorsed by allowing their estates to be used as training facilities.[37] As one of those reports testified, the threat of bankruptcy, a common affliction of landowners during the late Weimar period, would prompt affected estate owners to move closer to the Nazis. The consequences, the author feared, would be disastrous, because the standing of estate owners in their communities would encourage others to

34. "Aus dem Rathaus," *Die Parole*, 1 October 1930, no. 6.

35. Drewniak, *Początki Ruchu Hitlerowskiego*, p. 20.

36. See, for example, R. Koshar, *Social Life, Local Politics and Nazism: Marburg 1880–1935* (Chapel Hill, N.C., and London, 1986); and Z. Zofka, *Die Ausbreitung der Nationalsozialismus auf dem Lande. Eine regionale Fallstudie zur politischen Einstellung der Landbevölkerung in der Zeit des Aufstiegs und der Machtergreifung der NSDAP 1928–1936* (Munich, 1979), pp. 73–92.

37. Landrat Anklam to Regierung Präsident Stettin, 14 September 1929 and 25 September 1929, WAPS-RS I, no. 12121; Regierung Präsident Köslin to Oberpräsident Pommern, 31 August 1929, WAPK-RK, no. 3410.

follow their example. The Young Plan initiative, he concluded, was having a significant impact, given the establishment of working committees that joined together all the elements of the Right.[38]

Despite the failure of the Young Plan referendum, the September 1930 Reichstag elections showed just how successful the Nazis had become in luring the rural electorate into their fold. The party outstripped the DNVP in two of Pomerania's three districts. The German Nationals barely prevailed over the Nazis in the Köslin district, which encompassed the eastern (or upper) part of the province, but even that victory would prove temporary in subsequent elections.[39] In part, the Nazis triumphed because they had not "corrupted" themselves by participating in Weimar governments. The opposite tactic cost the DNVP dearly, not only because participation had alienated many rural supporters of the DNVP as successive Weimar cabinets could not alleviate their suffering, but also because it so divided the party's leadership, both national and provincial, that it could not campaign effectively.[40]

Clearly, the NSDAP, as the local evidence suggests, financed itself primarily from the admission fees it charged at its rallies. In addition, it drew the vast majority of its supporters from the Pomeranian lower middle classes and farm laborers. As Kleist himself rued, the Nazi virus infected workers, artisans, small shopkeepers and peasants, especially younger ones.[41] Yet, the conduct of agrarian elites proved anything but irrelevant. Those landowners who transferred their allegiance to the Nazis did indeed, according to reports, influence many in their villages to follow suit.[42] Those many more large holders

38. Regierung Präsident Köslin to Oberpräsident Pommern, 31 August 1929, WAPK-RK, no. 3410.

39. *General Anzeiger*, 15 September 1930, no. 256, 25 April 1932, no. 115.

40. For fuller discussions, see D. Abraham, *The Collapse of the Weimar Republic. Political Economy and Crisis*, 2nd ed. (New York, 1986), pp. 74–89; Childers, *The Nazi Voter*, pp. 145–59; and A. Chanady, "The Disintegration of the German National People's Party, 1924–1930," *Journal of Modern History* 39, (1967): 65–90.

41. Landrat Demmin to Regierung Präsident Stettin, 5 November 1930, WAPS-RS I, no. 1841. Kleist-Schmenzin, "Der Nationalsozialismus – Eine Gefahr," in B. Scheurig, *Ewald von Kleist-Schmenzin*, p. 255.

42. Polizei Präsident Stettin to Oberpräsident Pommern, 6 January, 1931, WAPS-RS I, 11993, remarks that the estate owner and Nazi party member, von Wedel-Parlow, virtually led his entire district from the DNVP to the Hitler movement.

who remained loyal to the DNVP had nonetheless so outspokenly supported Hugenberg's anti-governmentalism that rural voters could see little harm in choosing a new, and more effective, right radical movement from the alternatives presented to them. One local report stressed how much the Young Plan referendum had helped the Nazi cause because it had provided the party with a dry run for the 1930 campaign. The strength of the support for Hugenberg in the provincial DNVP and the DNVP's disintegration nationally had, in essence, confused the voters.[43] Explained one magistrate, deep disappointment with both the DNVP and the Rural League reigned in rural areas,

> which therefore have had to have grown all the more radical when, in recent years, political parties and professional associations have agitated against the "current system" and every republican government in ever sharper and reckless intensification. The elusiveness of concrete successes, and the increasing radicalization of the DNVP, must have driven the denizens of the countryside, who are usually unpolitical and think only of economic issues, inevitably into the arms of the radical fringe party, the NSDAP.[44]

Few Junkers showed the reserve that Ewald von Kleist would shortly acquire although, ironically and tellingly, Kleist himself had contributed to Hugenberg's capture of the Pomeranian German Nationalist leadership two years previous.[45] If most nobles preferred to remain with the DNVP, not a few actively campaigned for the Hitler party.[46] Even those estate owners who sided with the DVNP, be they noble or bourgeois, were anything but hostile to the Hitler movement. In the words of another county report, "An active advocacy by large landowners on behalf of the National Socialists has probably not taken place in local circles. Against that, however, one

43. Landrat Swinemünde to Regierung Präsident Stettin, WAPS-RS I, no. 1841.
44. Landrat Anklam to Regierung Präsident Stettin, 11 November 1930, WAPS-RS I, no. 1841.
45. Holzbach, *Das "System Hugenberg*," p. 238.
46. In addition to von Wedel-Parlow cited in note 42 above, they included a Kalckreuth, a Knesebeck, an Enckevort and a Puttkamer: Abschrift Polizeiverwaltung, Falkenburg, 29 August 1930, WAPK RK, no. 3410, Landrat Ückermünde to Regierung Präsident Stettin, 27 February 1931, WAPS-RS I, no. 11993, *Swinemünder Zeitung*, 25 February 1931, found in WAPS-RS I, no. 12200, and Abschrift Landjägeramt Misdroy, 25 August 1930, WAPS-RS I, no. 12200.

can identify, in many instances, an attitude of benevolent neutrality by large estate owners toward the NSDAP as a system."[47] In either case, whether DNVP or Nazi, estate owners as a group transformed rural conservatism into right extremism.

But what of the Nazis' anti-elitism that ultimately prompted Kleist to criticize Hugenberg? For most estate owners, the Nazis too inconsistently and intermittently expressed their antagonism to deter them from pursuing the principal goal that both the DNVP and National Socialism held in common – eliminating the Republic. The foremost objective of Pomeranian agrarian elites was to destroy the Weimar "system," and the "only" question, though hardly an insignificant one, was whether Hugenberg, Hitler, or both would achieve it. In addition, both sides engaged in a common discourse, which even circumscribed the disputes that arose between them: both claimed to be populist, both insisted on the central meaning of agriculture to the German *Volkstum*, both advocated similar measures to aid farmers, both professed a militant anti-urbanism, and both aspired to speak for the "whole" above the fractiousness of contemporary Weimar political life.

Anti-Semitism, embracing attacks against both "Jewish high finance" and "the Jew Marx," appeared far more frequently in Nazi stump speeches, according to official reports, than at DNVP rallies, though it was most certainly present in landed elite attitudes.[48] In any case, few Nazis, as one county magistrate astutely observed, could best the demagogic rhetoric of the Junker Hans Joachim von Rohr-Demmin, chair of the Pomeranian Rural League, who was given to public statements filled with pathos and irony. Class antagonisms had grown worse than ever, he noted in 1929 while commemorating the tenth anniversary of the provincial Rural League, but agriculture now stood united against the Republic's destructive agrarian policies. He attacked unnamed sources who sought to polarize large and small holders against each other, and launched a blistering attack against the government's settlement program, which during the last years of Weimar

47. Landrat Naugard to Regierung Präsident Stettin, 29 October 1930, WAPS-RS I, no. 1841.
48. An example of Nazi anti-Semitism can be found in the Bericht, Polizeiverwaltung Cammin, 12 September 1930, WAPS-RS I, no. 1840. The view that Jewry was destructive to aristocratic values can be seen in Jürgen von Ramin's article, "Junker" in the Pomeranian Junkers' monthly periodical, *Pommern-Adel*, 1 November 1927, no. 8.

emerged as a means of occupying bankrupt properties with unemployed workers: "Because of it," Rohr concluded with a somewhat surprising twist for one of his heritage, "the incoming settlers will be condemned to a life of hunger, while at the same time, ten thousand peasants are driven from their soil, a revival of serfdom in new form."[49]

The controversies involving the Nazi party and the monarchist, right-wing paramilitary organization, the Stahlhelm, an organization to which numerous estate owners belonged, best illuminate the odd combination of common discourse and conflict that emerged in the relationship between agrarian elites and the Hitler movement. On the one hand many Stahlhelm members joined the NSDAP as well, yet on the other hand tensions arose over issues ranging from the return of the Hohenzollern monarchy to the Nazis' insistence that its members resign from the Stahlhelm and give their total loyalty to the party. The *Pommersche Tagespost* became the forum for debate between the two sides, indicative of the cross fertilization between the two associations. The Nazi Gauleiter, Walter von Corswant, complained of the Stahlhelm's monarchism, an issue the party could not support. Likewise, he argued that the Stahlhelm was "national," but not sufficiently "social," citing its identification with the DNVP and its failure to press sufficiently for "class reconciliation." In response, the Stahlhelm's leader in Pomerania, Berndt von Wedel-Fürstensee, completely denied Corswant's accusations: the Stahlhelm was not a political party, as Corswant implied, nor an association in the service of a political party. Like National Socialism, it was both "national and social," as well as anti-Marxist, anti-capitalist and anti-liberal. Even when von Wedel acknowledged those points in the Stahlhelm's program dividing it from National Socialism – its monarchism and its explicit Christian principles – he quickly returned to the common ground between them, their affirmation of "community" that bound individuals to the whole. Whatever the tensions between the Stahlhelm and the Nazis, von Wedel pressed for continued cooperation.[50]

If discord periodically arose between the Nazi party and the

49. "Zehn Jahre Pommerscher Landbund," *General Anzeiger*, 19 January 1929, no. 19, located in WAPS-RS I, no. 12134. Landrat Ückermünde to Regierung Präsident Stettin, 27 February 1931, WAPS RS I, no. 11993.

50. "Der Stahlhelm, der Nationalsozialismus," *Pommersche Tagespost*, 31 May 1930, no. 126.

Stahlhelm, then it certainly surfaced between estate owners and the party over the Nazis' ambiguous position on large landed property. Yet the Hitler movement was as capable of reassuring agrarian elites as it was of unnerving them. Three weeks before the crucial 1930 elections, for example, Gauleiter Corswant addressed the issue at a rally: National Socialism upholds private property, he explained, so long as "creative work" maintains it, a phrase sufficiently elastic to permit the most generous interpretation. Once it took power, however, the party would expropriate only that property acquired through speculation or usury. Corswant's reference to high interest rates, a frequent landowner complaint, not to mention his own credentials as a knight's estate owner, might well have neutralized landowner opposition.[51] Nor were his remarks idiosyncratic. The party used the province's newspapers, in addition to their own, to dispel the impression that it would dispossess the rural dweller from his land. Only the land of speculators, Jews, and traitors would be confiscated.[52]

After Nazism's great breakthrough in 1930, the party's latent anti-elitism did grow more pronounced, now that it had acquired a significant popular base. The following year, Corswant was forced out as Gauleiter in favor of the Griefswald lawyer, Wilhelm Karpenstein, one notably less solicitous of big landed interests. Given that Corswant had been accustomed to running the party's affairs from his estate, his removal, at the very least, signified the party's growing professionalism.[53] Tensions between the leaderships of the Stahlhelm and the Nazis' anti-elitist paramilitary organization, the SA, flared repeatedly, not only over the issue as to which force would preside over joint military exercises, but also over the SA's refusal to discourage Stahlhelm members from joining its units.[54] Furthermore, as was common in rural areas throughout Germany, the Nazis proposed their own candidates for offices in the Rural League and the Chamber of Agriculture, openly challenging the Junker chairs of both organizations,

51. Polizei Präsident Stettin, 20 August 1930, WAPS-RS I, no. 12199.
52. "Lügen, Lügen und abermals Lügen," *Swinemünde Zeitung*, 11 September 1930, found in WAPS-RS I, no. 1840.
53. Czarnik, *Stosunki polityczne na Pomorzu Zachodnim*, p. 303; Bessel, *Political Violence and the Rise of Nazism*, p. 23.
54. Polizei Präsident Stettin to Oberpräsident Pommern, 8 March 1932, WAPS-RS I, no. 12182.

Rohr-Demmin and Flemming-Pätzig. Complained one peasant who was critical of the Nazis, the Chamber had never before held elections because, for years, the Rural League had simply appointed its members. That method, he suggested, had served all agriculturalists in the province well.[55] To make its case, Nazi propaganda attacked the Chamber for having swindled Pomeranian peasants, and its leader, Flemming, as well as other estate owners, for having obtained credit on more favorable terms than those extended to small holders.[56] Finally, in 1932, Karpenstein founded, as well as edited, the party's first newspaper with a province-wide distribution, the *Pommersche Zeitung*, not least as a means of attacking the DNVP and estate owners for everything from their arrogance toward the NSDAP to their exploitative treatment of workers.[57]

Despite this trend in the Nazis' relationship to provincial elites, however, Pomeranian estate owners persisted in their goal of toppling the Republic. Far from discouraging the agrarian elite, in fact, the Nazis' electoral performance in 1930 persuaded large landowners to escalate their anti-system crusade; first, by supporting the Stahlhelm referendum of 1931 demanding the dissolution of the Prussian Landtag; and second, by refusing to endorse Hindenburg's reelection as President in 1932. Remarkably, even those estate owners who continued to affiliate with the DNVP insisted on the correctness of the Hugenberg course against charges that the party had been ineffective under his leadership. The landowner Jürgen von Ramin sniffed that criticism represented but "a typically parliamentary and supremely short-sighted observation." Hugenberg's popularity, he claimed, would only increase among the *Volk* with each passing crisis.[58] On top of that, the spiraling radicalism of the Rural League's national leadership under Eberhard von Kalckreuth received the approbation of provincial estate owners; at one Landbund rally in Köslin, the

55. Bericht, Bütow, 25 September 1931, WAPK, Landratsamt Bütow, no. 23. See H. Gies, "The NSDAP and Agrarian Organizations in the Final Phase of the Weimar Republic," in *Nazism and the Third Reich*, ed. H.A. Turner, Jr. (New York, 1972), pp. 45–88.

56. "Sünden der Landwirtschaftskammer," *Die Diktatur*, 21 October 1931, found in WAPS-RS-I, no. 12182.

57. "Die Deutschnationalen am Pranger," *Pommersche Zeitung*, 14 July 1932, "Streikbrecher und Stahlhelm," *Pommersche Zeitung*, 17 July 1932.

58. "Entscheidungsjahr mit Hugenberg," *Pommersche Tagespost*, 9 January 1932, no. 9.

large holder, von Gerlach-Parsow, praised Kalckreuth while condemning the Brüning government for having learned nothing from "the great fermentation of 14 September 1930." It had repeatedly failed to combat "Marxism" forcefully.[59]

To be sure, strains continued to develop in the landowner-Nazi "alliance," even in the context of pursuing their common goal of destroying Weimar. According to the evidence, they became prominent during the brief authoritarian chancellorship of Franz von Papen and his "cabinet of barons," as Hitler pursued the office for himself independently of elites. Before the November 1932 elections, Zitzewitz attacked the Nazi party, with evident exasperation, for its demagoguery and its lack of principle. Now we have a government that is "above party," insisted Zitzewitz, one that has not only ended the "black-and-red corruption," but one that is serious about helping agriculture. What has the NSDAP done about it? Rather than supporting Papen, it now fights him.[60] Yet Zitzewitz's remarks are noteworthy, not merely for the tensions and hostility they convey, but also for the speaker's disappointment in the Nazis for failing to recognize that the Right had won.

Certainly, the agrarian crisis, which brought mounting bankruptcies in its wake, fanned the desperate rage of large estate owners against the "system" whose policies they perceived as having eroded their very existence. Even the Eastern Aid (*Osthilfe*) program, which others interpreted as a shameless boondoggle benefiting principally the large estates, was to estate owners little more than a band aid applied to a gaping wound. According to Rohr, Eastern Aid only undermined the healthy enterprises along with the unhealthy ones. Furthermore, the government's subventions served little purpose when the same government took them back again, directly or otherwise, in high taxes, high interest rates and unfavorable trade treaties with other countries. The only reasonable solution, he argued (in addition to dropping interest rates for agriculture), was a tariff policy like England's that blocked foreign imports and forced the population to consume only what the home market produced.[61]

59. "Die Landbund ist zur Stelle," *Pommersche Tagespost*, 2 April 1931, no. 79.
60. Abschrift re: 24 October 1932 DNVP rally, WAPK, Landratsamt Bütow, no. 23.
61. "Machtvolle Landbund-Kundgebung," *Pommersche Tagespost*, 3 February 1932, no. 28.

Although anti-governmentalism often characterized agrarian politicization in Pomerania and elsewhere before World War I, the Republic's peculiar constellation of economic factions along with the gravity of the depression, now promoted the unprecedented expression of agrarian elite radicalism.[62] That radicalism included staging demonstrations against farm foreclosures, affairs in which large and small holders joined together to support the disinherited.[63] On one such occasion, according to the Nazi paper, *Die Diktatur*, 120 "large and small holders" paraded under the black banner first raised during the Peasants' War of 1525, now the symbol of the peasant protest in Schleswig-Holstein.[64] Yet, as such joint maneuvers reveal, enough remained of the hegemony of Pomeranian estate owners to soften the risks of their own militance as they joined with the Nazis against Weimar. In fact, the Nazis' efforts to remove elites from the leaderships of the province's agrarian interest organizations, though serious, were not notably successful. In 1932, Flemming won reelection as president of the Chamber of Agriculture, though ironically despite the opposition of Rohr who considered the former too "moderate," while Rohr returned as chair of the Rural League. Only after the Nazis assumed power in 1933 did a thoroughgoing synchronization of both associations occur.[65]

Indeed, at the risk of speculation, one might conclude that the confidence, even smugness, of estate owners long dominant in the province contributed to their belief that the Nazis could be used. Nazi rallies continued to mute, or even deny outright, tendencies that the party knew would offend the rural population, including large landowners. A notable example of that was the party's position on Christianity. While on occasion, party radicals often worried clergymen with their threats to undermine the influence of both the Protestant and Catholic churches in German society, many of the party's provincial agitators sang a different tune: at a Nazi rally in the eastern Pomeranian border town of Bütow, the

---

62. See Abraham, *Collapse of the Weimar Republic*, pp. 42–105, 171–219.

63. *Grimmen Kreis Zeitung*, 12 November 1930, no. 290.

64. 7 March 1931, no. 10, found in WAPS-RS I, no. 12134.

65. "Landwirtpolitik," *Pommersche Tagespost*, 13 February 1932, no. 37, *Pommersche Zeitung*, 10 July 1933, 16 July 1933. Folder no. 241, Reichs-Landbund, Bundesarchiv Potsdam, contains the correspondence of the Pomeranian Rural League's leadership related to the conflict between Flemming and Rohr.

speaker assured his audience that the party was not "anti-reli-
gion [*religionsfeindlich*]." More positively, he asserted that
National Socialism backed religious instruction in the schools,
an issue of vital importance to the churches. Given the depth
of religious feeling in the province, the prominence of the
Protestant Church in particular, and the significant role of
estate owners in Pomeranian religious affairs, the Nazis had
little choice but to adhere to the centrality of Christianity in
German culture.[66]

Pomerania, East Elbia and the Consequences of Agrarian Politicization

There can be little doubt that National Socialism's rapid electoral growth during the final years of the Weimar Republic
brought something new to German politics: a genuine, if highly unstable, popular coalition that destroyed those parties in
which traditional elites dominated. Elites certainly remained
necessary for naming Hitler chancellor and stabilizing the
Nazi regime after the "seizure" of power, although who
among the elite should assume the most responsibility for
those decisions remains exceedingly controversial.[67] Despite
this, elites have lately appeared less important than previously believed to acquiring the constituency that made the Hilter
party *salonfähig*. One recent survey of the Weimar Republic
suggests that the accession of Hitler resulted less from the preponderance and power of traditional elites, than from their
weakening in the face of massive politicization from below.[68]
In a similar vein, another view now challenges what used to
be accepted as a "given," the beneficial effect of the Young
Plan referendum on the Nazi party and the valuable exposure
that elites offered the Hitler movement, though recent research
on the Nazi electorate underscores the contributions of the

66. Abschrift Bütow, 16 February 1932, WAPK, Landratsamt Bütow, no. 23.
For more on this theme, see S. Baranowski, "The Sanctity of Rural Life: Protes-
tantism, Agrarian Politics, and Nazism in Pomerania during the Weimar
Republic," *German History* 9 (1991): 1–22.

67. The work most determined to exclude German industrialists from the
indictment of aiding and abetting the Nazi takeover is that of H.A. Turner, Jr.,
German Big Business and the Rise of Hitler (New York, 1985).

68. D.J.K. Peukert, *Die Weimarer Republik: Krisenjahre der Klassischen Moderne*
(Frankfurt am Main, 1987), p. 271.

Reich presidential election of 1925 and the anti-Young Plan campaign to later Nazi successes among voters.[69]

The case of Pomerania, however, might give one reason to reconsider. It suggests that the Nazi party's breakthrough in regions that were customarily the preserve of traditional elites may well have come about at least as much from the invitations those preserves granted them, as from the "pre-political and negative mobilization" of the rural community,[70] or the politicization that the Hitler movement conducted independently of elites. The Pomeranian example also implies that an indispensible relationship existed between the Nazis and agrarian conservatives that survived their periodic conflicts, however intense those were. As such, it reminds us to look beyond the confusion that fascist rhetoric, and sometimes fascist practice, deliberately created, to the political and social matrices where fascism operated most effectively – matrices that in Germany brought National Socialism to power.[71] Yet is Pomerania so "typical" that the insights one draws from its experience are thus valid in other regions where elites and Nazis rivaled each other for political dominance? Might the hegemony of its landowning class and the relative docility of its peasants and farm laborers render the province too stereotypical for generalization?

Although recent scholarship underscores the importance of local notables to the Nazi party's growth,[72] a definitive answer to these questions will arise only from a comparative study of the eastern Prussian provinces, a study that does not yet exist. Nonetheless, there is evidence to suggest, above all, that the behavior of landowners in Pomerania accorded with that of their compatriots elsewhere east of the Elbe River. Anti-republican radicalism appeared most intense in the east-Elbian regions, being less in evidence in other rural areas where peasant agriculture numerically counterbalanced larger

69. Otmar Jung, "Plebiczitärer Durchbrunch 1929? Zur Bedeutung von Volksbegehren und Volksentscheid gegen das Youngplan für die NSDAP," *Geschichte und Gesellschaft* 15 (1989): 489–510. See also Falter, *Hitlers Wähler*, pp. 123–25.

70. Corni, *Hitler and the Peasants*, p. 25.

71. Cf. the remarks of R. Soucy, *French Fascism: The First Wave 1924–1933* (New Haven and London, 1986), p. 237.

72. See, for example, R. Hamilton, *Who Voted for Hitler* (Princeton, N.J., 1982), pp. 364–85 and passim.

holdings.[73] Pomerania was not alone in being infertile territory for the Christian National Peasants' and Farmers' Party (Christlich-Nationale Bauern- und Landvolkpartei or CNBLP), that group of renegades from the DNVP who comprised the best hope for a "moderate" conservative alternative to the Hugenberg Right's alliance with Nazism. Although the CNBLP won significant support from Rural League affiliates throughout Germany prior to the 1930 elections, it was not notably successful in the Prussian east, territory that, as a whole, proved indispensible to the Nazi advance among voters. In any event, the CNBLP's failure to unify German agriculture, evident in those same elections, set the stage not only for the Nazis' reaggregation of agriculture nationally, but also the escalating extremism of the Rural League and the DNVP under the influence of estate owners.[74]

To be sure, the radicalism of Prussian estate owners is not the only issue. One must take into account as well the behavior of the Nazi party in the same region. One need only to look at the SA, certainly the personification of the party's militant tendencies, especially in its hostility toward elites. Yet if Nazi radicalism surfaced here, it was a radicalism that dovetailed with elite interests. Both before and after the "seizure" of power, the SA mostly attacked the Left, the Right's enemy par excellence, while shying away from assaults on the existing social order and the structures that upheld it. Caught between its anti-establishment rhetoric on the one hand, and the logic of the party's position on the other, its influence ultimately dissipated, by mid-1934, with the assassination of its national leadership.[75]

In the final analysis, one might fairly speak of the challenges confronting elites, agrarian elites in particular, as the consequence of two mutually reinforcing factors – an agrarian sector that landowners perceived as losing its premier place in the German economy, and the fermentation of popular rural

73. D. Gessner, "'Grüne Front' oder 'Harzburger Front.' Der Reichs-Landbund in der letzten Phase der Weimarer Republik. Zwischen wirtschaftlicher Interessenpolitik und nationalistischem Revisionsanspruch," *Vierteljahrshefte für Zeitgeschichte* 29 (1981): 110–23.

74. L.E. Jones, "Crisis and Realignment: Agrarian Splinter Parties in the Late Weimar Republic, 1928–33," in *Peasants and Lords in Modern Germany*, ed. R.G. Moeller (Boston, London, and Sydney, 1986), pp. 212, 215.

75. Bessel, *Political Violence and the Rise of Nazism*, pp. 75–155.

discontent. The "decline" of agriculture, though not so complete as to strip rural regions of political influence altogether, was nonetheless sufficiently evident to produce economic and political disaster.[76] It not only galvanized anti-republican estate owners, it also gave birth to the sort of popular dissatisfaction that expressed as much impatience with the hegemony of Germany's traditional power holders as it did with the failure of government to remedy popular grievances. After all, given the political influence of elites, were not the sources of that disaffection virtually one and the same?

Yet one should ponder the irony here: if the Pomeranian case is at all "representative" of the experience of other east-Elbian regions, then popular politicization bore the authorship of agrarian elites, even during the "end phase" of the Republic. National Socialism, the strongest challenger yet to elites, attracted little mass support until after 1928, mushrooming thereafter in the conjuncture of economic crisis and popular disaffection that estate owners themselves aided and abetted. If most estate owners had not intended a fascist alternative to Weimar, their politicization nonetheless spawned the Nazi mass base, the crucial ingredient in the Nazi takeover. That mass mobilization was worth the risk to achieve what agrarian elites desired most: the destruction of the Republic.

76. This is Becker's argument in *Handlungsspielräume der Agrarpolitik*.

14

The Conservative Resistance to Hitler and the Fall of the Weimar Republic, 1932–34

Theodore S. Hamerow

The Germans who opposed the Nazi regime were so diverse in their political loyalties, economic circumstances, social origins, and ideological sympathies that any attempt to generalize about them must at first glance seem futile. The only thing they had in common was their rejection of the Third Reich. Some of them stood quite far to the left; they were communists or socialists who insisted that Hitler was simply the tool of German capitalism. Others were dedicated rightists yearning for a vanished imperial glory, convinced that Hitler was undermining the conservative tradition of selfless service to the state. Opponents of the regime included liberals of various shades, men and women who believed in civil rights and representative institutions. There were also devout Christians, both Protestant and Catholic, who saw in the teachings of National Socialism pagan beliefs and heretical doctrines. A few were well-to-do, even wealthy, born into families of successful businessmen or aristocratic landowners, enjoying a privileged status in the established social system. Most earned a modest or meager livelihood as bureaucrats, soldiers, professionals, intellectuals, shopkeepers, clerks, workers, and farmers. How then is it possible to define the collective ethos of a movement so heterogeneous in its composition?

The only solution is to deal separately with each of the various groups and factions among the adversaries of National Socialism. Here the distinction between "opposition" and "resistance," a distinction made by Martin Broszat some fifteen years ago, is particularly useful. To him the "opposition" included those who, though rejecting the teachings of the Third Reich, were incapable because of their subordinate political and social position of going beyond isolated, futile acts of defiance. The much smaller "resistance," on the other hand, consisted of men who occupied important positions in the armed forces and the civil service and were thus able to develop an organized and systematic plan for the overthrow of the regime. In the summer of 1944 they almost succeeded. What distinguished them from the members of the "opposition," however, was not greater boldness or determination or idealism but greater opportunity.[1]

The purpose of this essay is to examine the political attitudes of leading representatives of the anti-Nazi resistance at the end of the Weimar Republic and to determine how they viewed the transition from Weimar to the Third Reich. It will focus primarily upon that segment of the resistance that Klaus-Jürgen Müller, Hans Mommsen, and other prominent historians have described as "national conservative."[2] In this respect, however, the essay will deal not merely with those opponents of the Nazi regime who held positions of influence in the military and civil bureaucracy but will also discuss the attitudes of influential church leaders from the Protestant and Catholic churches. An analysis of the attitudes they held at the time of the Weimar Republic's collapse will make clear that virtually all those who later came to form the nucleus of the conservative resistance to Hitler initially greeted the establishment of the Hitler regime – or, more precisely, welcomed the end of the republican system – with relief, if not enthusiasm. To be sure, few were out-and-out Nazis. Mostly they regarded Hitler's followers as somewhat crude and simple-minded, often intemperate, sometimes rough, but with their hearts in the right place. More important, National Socialism seemed to them a useful ally in the struggle against the hated Weimar government. Not only did Hitler have popular appeal and mass support, but many of his doctrines and beliefs were essentially sound. Those who later turned against the Third

1. M. Broszat, "Vorwort," in *Bayern in der NS-Zeit*, ed. M. Broszat, E. Fröhlich, F. Wiesemann, A. Grossmann, and H. Mehringer, 6 vols. (Munich and Vienna, 1977–83), vol. 1, pp. 11–12.

2. For example, see K.-J. Müller, "The Structure and Nature of the National Conservative Opposition in Germany up to 1940," in *Aspects of the Third Reich*, ed. H.W. Koch (New York, 1985), pp. 133–78.

Reich did so generally because of differences over policy or method, not over principle.

Some of them said as much. In 1944 Count Nikolaus von Üxküll, under arrest for participating in the attempt to assassinate Hitler, testified that he had initially supported the Third Reich. "After the seizure of power [by the Nazis], I was an avowed adherent of the Führer, and I was also convinced that he would lead us to great achievements." Berthold von Stauffenberg, who joined the resistance long before his better-known brother Claus, was somewhat more restrained in describing to the secret police what his original attitude had been. "In the domestic area we had for the most part completely supported the basic ideas of National Socialism." Indeed, those ideas had seemed to him and his friends "healthy and forward-looking."[3]

Such declarations by men threatened with execution might of course be ascribed to a desire to mitigate the severity of the punishment awaiting them. But ten years after the end of the war Alexander von Stauffenberg, the surviving brother of Claus and Berthold and a historian by profession, was still wrestling with the question of whether the Third Reich represented the same pernicious principles at the beginning as at the end. He wondered whether National Socialism "was absolutely evil from the outset, or whether we should advance here a hypothesis of development." Was it not possible that a state based on law, "though under authoritarian auspices," might have emerged out of the Nazi system, and that only with the passage of time did its leadership degenerate, as the last restraints on its power were removed? "The latter is, on the basis of all historical analogies, the more likely [interpretation]." He was reflecting the views of a generation that had tragically misunderstood the nature of National Socialism.[4]

This misunderstanding derived from a similarity in the underlying beliefs and attitudes of those who consistently supported the Third Reich and those who eventually came to

3. SD-Bericht, 16 October 1944, in *"Spiegelbild einer Verschwörung". Die Opposition gegen Hitler und der Staatsstreich vom 20. Juli 1944 in der SD-Berichterstattung. Geheime Dokumente aus dem ehemaligen Reichssicherheitshauptamt*, ed. H.-A. Jacobsen, 2 vols. (Stuttgart, 1984), vol. 1, pp. 447–48.

4. A. von Stauffenberg, "Die deutsche Widerstandsbewegung und ihre geistige Bedeutung in der Gegenwart," in *Bekenntnis und Verpflichtung. Reden und Aufsätze zur zehnjährigen Wiederkehr des 20. Juli 1944* (Stuttgart, 1955), p. 161.

oppose it. Both rejected the republican system, and for essentially the same reasons. To begin with, the members of the resistance remained convinced that the Weimar regime had originated in a historic act of betrayal, in a treasonable subversion of legitimate authority. The revolution of 1918 seemed to them a violation of a sacred national tradition. Especially to the older generation, to those who had grown up in the imperial era, the years before the First World War always remained a vanished golden age. The Weimar regime, on the other hand, had been born of defeat and rebellion. On this point at least they were in essential agreement with the Nazis.

Three weeks after the Kaiser's abdication, for example, Ludwig Beck, who in the 1930s was to become chief of staff of the army and then the leading military figure in the resistance, wrote that the fall of the old order was "so monstrous" that he often thought he was dreaming. He did not doubt, "even for a moment," that the revolution had been planned "long in advance," attacking the armed forces from the rear at a time when the high command was being forced to exert every effort to prevent a military catastrophe. "I know of no revolution in history that was carried out in such a cowardly fashion, a revolution that – and this is actually much worse – has aggravated beyond any doubt the difficult situation in which we have been for a long time now, leading perhaps to complete ruin." Admittedly, by the time Beck joined the resistance twenty years later, his belief in the "stab-in-the-back" legend had weakened considerably. But he never completely overcame the feeling that the Weimar Republic was a child of radicalism, pacifism, and materialism.[5]

The fall of the monarchy and the defeat of Germany came also as a great shock to Ulrich von Hassell, just starting out on what was to become a distinguished diplomatic career. Like Beck he lamented after the Armistice that the outcome of the war had been "a terrible collapse of our hopes." The return of peace was no occasion for celebration in Germany. For the time being "all roads leading upward again" seemed closed. "German influence in the world [has now proved to be] a dream, destroyed once and for all! [Before us stretches the

5. Beck to his sister-in-law, Gertrud Beck, 28 November 1918, in K.-J. Müller, *General Ludwig Beck. Studien und Dokumente zur politisch-militärischen Vorstellungswelt und Tätigkeit des Generalstabschefs des deutschen Heeres 1933–1938* (Boppard am Rhein, 1980), pp. 323–24.

prospect of] wage slavery at home and a decline to the Netherlands' level of power abroad." And yet the nation's political objectives had not been unreasonable; the government had never pursued plans for "world domination." It had simply acted on the "unmistakable feeling that Germany had to achieve influence in the world, if it did not want to decline spiritually and materially among the Great Powers of the world." Was that so terrible?[6]

Though shaken by the fall of the old order, Hassell refused to despair. He urged his countrymen not to accept their bleak situation as "an unalterable fate." Admittedly, to retain hope required "an enormous store of confidence and faith in the mission of our people." And yet there was no choice. The Germans would have to find strength in the spirit that had animated them at the turn of the century under the monarchy. "A difficult task lies before us, a long struggle upward against foreign resistance and domestic folly." Throughout the Weimar years he remained convinced of the importance of that struggle. And when Hitler came to power, Hassell believed at first that the tragic consequences of the revolution of 1918 would now come to an end in a great and exciting national revival.[7]

Carl Goerdeler was another prominent leader of the resistance to whom the establishment of the republic had represented treachery, defeat, and humiliation. In his case, however, the fall of the old order also meant a terrible personal loss. He recognized that the military collapse meant that his native region, Posen and West Prussia, would become part of the new Polish state. The thought was unbearable. An integral part of Germany would fall under alien rule; its language would be suppressed, its culture eradicated, its people Polonized. Something had to be done, however perilous or desperate, to avert this national calamity. In June 1919, on the eve of the signing of the peace treaty in Versailles, Goerdeler declared that "the only possibility of saving the German nationality in the east and [preserving] the eastern frontier region for the Reich is the military overthrow of Poland." But he had little hope that the National Assembly in Weimar would follow this advice. It was therefore necessary for the east "to act independently." Such a policy, he argued, "if prompt and militarily successful," would

6. *Der Tag*, 24 November 1918.
7. Ibid.

win the support of the population, "even though the party leaders are at present hesitant." Under the circumstances, any means would be justified – sabotage, conspiracy, putsch, or military uprising – to prevent the partition of Germany.[8]

Nothing came of his plan to forestall the execution of the Treaty of Versailles. Posen and West Prussia became part of Poland and proved to be a constant source of friction between Berlin and Warsaw. But Goerdeler could never bring himself to accept the consequences of the defeat of 1918. His criticism of the republican regime, however, shifted increasingly from its military weaknesses to its political ineptitude. Long afterward, while in prison awaiting the executioner's axe, he still boasted of how he and others like him had labored tirelessly to bring order out of the chaos created by the fall of the old order. "Who then crushed the revolution?. . . We worked, worked, worked; we neglected our families; we drudged in order to check the disorder, to purge the administration, to regulate, to modernize, to regulate the finances, to restore justice, decency, and duty, to eliminate homelessness, to rehabilitate the means of transportation and supply, to reaccustom to steady employment those who had forgotten how to work, and to render ineffective the Versailles dictate." How unjust then, he complained, that those great accomplishments were now being ignored. Up to the hour of his death Goerdeler remained proud of the struggle he had once waged against the forces of revolution.[9]

The case of Cardinal Michael von Faulhaber of Munich is more puzzling. The other members of the resistance were mostly conservative bureaucrats and officers who had been brought up in the belief that unquestioning obedience to monarchical authority was a solemn civic duty. But Faulhaber's background and experience were quite different. Fifty years earlier his church had engaged in a bitter struggle against the state. Even after the *Kulturkampf* came to an end in the late 1870s, relations between church and state had remained strained. Catholics were generally regarded by the imperial authorities with suspicion and distrust; when seeking advancement in the civil service or the armed forces, they had

8. G. Ritter, *Carl Goerdeler und die deutsche Widerstandsbewegung* (Stuttgart, 1954), p. 23.
9. Ibid., p. 27.

to face pervasive discrimination. Hence the Center Party, which represented their confessional interests, became a supporter of political liberalization, entering during the First World War into an informal coalition with the parties of the middle and moderate Left in order to achieve democratic reform and a compromise peace.

The establishment of the Weimar Republic thus meant liberation for the Catholics of Germany almost as much as for the Socialists or the Jews. They were now free to broaden their political influence and compete on even terms for the highest offices in government. Indeed, because of its pivotal position, the Center Party succeeded in gaining a parliamentary importance far out of proportion to the size of its following. It held the chancellorship in eight of the seventeen cabinets between 1919 and 1932, and was represented by ministers in each of the remaining nine. A prominent churchman like Faulhaber, a man of lower-class background, the son of a baker, might therefore have been expected to welcome a regime committed to the equality of political opportunity. Yet in fact he never became reconciled to the new order; he found it too radical, too secular, too materialistic. Worst of all, it had originated in an act of disobedience that was unpardonable. Nothing it did could expiate the sin of subverting legitimate authority.

This was the unmistakable implication of Faulhaber's famous speech of 27 August 1922 before a large Catholic gathering in Munich. He conceded that compromise was essential for the reconciliation of opposing views and interests. But principles must stand, "like the eternal stars", above compromise; there is a limit beyond which flexibility and accommodation should not go. For Faulhaber that limit had now been reached in the great national debate over the establishment of the republic. "The revolution was perjury and treason; it will remain in history tainted by hereditary fault and branded with the mark of Cain." The new order did achieve some successes, he admitted; it deserved credit, for example, for expanding the opportunities for Catholics to reach high office. Nevertheless, "[someone of] moral character does not base his assessments on successes; a crime cannot be sanctified because of its successes."[10]

10. *Die Reden gehalten in den öffentlichen und geschlossenen Versammlungen der 62. General-Versammlung der Katholiken Deutschlands zu München 27. bis 30. August 1922* (Würzburg, 1923), p. 4.

The loud public outcry provoked by Faulhaber's speech led him to modify what he had said or at least to explain its meaning. He had not intended to condemn the Weimar Constitution or the republican form of government, he assured the Bavarian envoy to the Vatican. "A constitution can be adopted legally without thereby legitimizing the preceding revolution. A child born out of wedlock can become a decent human being without thereby providing justification for motherhood out of wedlock as such." He had simply sought to oppose the efforts of leftists "to bless the revolution of 1918." The speech, he wrote to a member of the papal state secretariat, had been intended as a warning to the Center Party against "opening for Bolshevism the gates to the German people by endless compromises and alliances with the Social Democrats." For Faulhaber the republic remained permanently branded by its revolutionary beginnings.[11]

For most of the other members of the resistance, however, the most serious weakness of Weimar was not its radical origin but factionalism and divisiveness, what they liked to describe as the "party system." Behind the facade of parliamentary government they saw an endless struggle of private ambitions and class interests. The sense of common purpose that once gained for Germany a respected place among the nations of the world had eroded and dissipated under the republic. In its place had come a selfish, undisciplined individualism that in the name of freedom had unleashed a war of all against all. Faith in traditional values had weakened; duty and responsibility had ceased to be considered civic virtues; personal gain had become more important than collective well-being. How was a national revival possible under a regime that tolerated greed, immorality, corruption, and subversion? Only a new form of government based on the principle of authority could revive the spirit of self-sacrifice that republicanism had undermined.

Some participants in the resistance had declared their hostility toward parliamentary democracy from the outset. As early as 1918 Hassell warned against the consequences of a "mechanistic parliamentarianism" that determined public policy by

11. See Faulhaber to Pizzardo, 19 September 1922, and Faulhaber to Ritter, 19 September 1922, in *Akten Kardinal Michael von Faulhabers 1917–1945*, ed. L. Volk, 2 vols. (Mainz, 1975–78), vol. 1, pp. 279, 283.

counting votes instead of considering national needs and interests. The great danger, he insisted, lay in "that disguising of economic demands with political slogans and that adulteration of political lines of thought with economic egoism." Parliamentary systems based on a universal franchise were bound to become corrupted by private interest posing as collective welfare. Unfortunately, "defenders of the so-called rights of the people" failed to recognize "that they are being manipulated like puppets by the wirepullers of international capitalism, and that the mechanistic realization of their doctrines is incompatible with true freedom." A general suffrage was acceptable only "in an organic form," Hassell explained; that is, "first rebuild local administration organically, and then on this basis let the national representation develop, also organically." In the next fifteen years this argument became part of the standard political rhetoric of conservative opponents of Weimar.[12]

Other members of the resistance were generally less outspoken, at least in the early years of the republic. They were prepared to tolerate it, perhaps even support it, as long as there was a chance that the new order might gradually achieve political and economic stability, regaining for Germany a major influence in international affairs. But when the depression beginning in the late 1920s initiated a period of crisis for Weimar from which it never recovered, their criticism of the regime became loud and persistent.

Johannes Popitz is a case in point. A highly respected economic expert, he served successively as German state secretary under Weimar, as Prussian finance minister in the Third Reich, and finally as member of the cabinet that the resistance hoped to install after Hitler's assassination. This last distinction cost him his life. Even during the heyday of the republic, however, he had expressed occasional doubts about the fairness or effectiveness of parliamentary democracy. Could a legislative structure based on universal suffrage provide adequate representation for those taxpayers who must bear the heaviest financial burden? Could a "polycratic" system of authority claiming to express the popular will bring about the financial reforms that the national welfare demanded?

After the coming of the depression, his criticism of the

12. *Der Tag*, 5 January and 7 September 1918.

regime became more pointed, more explicit. "State and economy are in crisis," he wrote early in 1931. Those in charge – Popitz meant Hindenburg and Brüning – were trying to save the country by following "the will of the constituted leaders" of Germany. One part of the state apparatus, however, the part opposing rule by presidential decree, sought "to undo this work of salvation and render the will of the leaders ineffectual." How would this creeping paralysis of the nation's capacity to function end?[13]

The appointment of Hitler as chancellor seemed to Popitz to offer the way out of a terrible dilemma. Here at last was a government that knew what to do and how to do it. No more doubts, no more debates. Speaking in April 1933 before the exclusive Mittwochs-Gesellschaft, he denounced the Weimar Republic as a "powerless state, alienated from the nation, with only a formal, divided, polycratic constitution, with a civil service that no longer constituted a community based on conviction, and with institutions that were either . . . without any general idea or . . . were only a camouflage for forces alien to the state."[14]

According to Popitz, there had been only two ways to put an end to the national crisis: reform or revolution. Reform was tried by Hindenburg in the shape of presidential government by emergency powers, but without success. That left the revolution represented by Hitler. His had been a unique revolution, however, "without bloodshed or at least without struggle, and in legal form." There could be no doubt that a failure of his attempt to rebuild the state on a "national and authoritarian basis" would result in political and economic chaos. The only question now was whether National Socialism would leave room for "personal values and private initiative," that is, whether it would follow the rigid Italian Fascist model or encourage the emergence of a "caste of leaders based on a sense of responsibility and knowledge, united with the people and serving the people." To Popitz the latter seemed the more likely course.[15]

---

13. J. Popitz, "Finanzausgleich," in *Handwörterbuch der Staatswissenschaften*, 4th ed., 9 vols. (Jena, 1923–29), vol. 3, p. 1031; idem, *Der Finanzausgleich und seine Bedeutung für die Finanzlage des Reichs, der Länder und Gemeinden* (Berlin, 1930), p. 8; *Kölnische Zeitung*, 9 February 1931.

14. Popitz's lecture of 26 April 1933, in *Die Mittwochs-Gesellschaft. Protokolle aus dem geistigen Deutschland 1932 bis 1944*, ed. K. Scholder (Berlin, 1982), p. 67.

15. Ibid., pp. 67–69.

The evolution of Goerdeler's attitude toward the republic followed the same pattern: first a grudging acceptance of Weimar, then growing criticism of the regime, and finally a deep sigh of relief at the establishment of the Third Reich. The coming of the depression helped turn the gifted conservative administrator from municipal government to national politics. As early as 1929 he was complaining that "all parties suffer from fear of the voters," which made them incapable of coping with the approaching economic crisis. In memoranda submitted to Hindenburg in 1931 and 1932, he maintained that the parliamentary system was now finished because it had placed "the interest of the parties above the welfare of the state." That was the "curse of parliamentarianism." The only means of avoiding a national catastrophe was the "mobilization of all popular energies," and that meant a "dictatorship lasting for years." As for the Reichstag, "if it creates difficulties for the task of saving the fatherland," it would have to be dissolved.[16]

Goerdeler thus came to favor an authoritarian regime in Germany long before the fall of Weimar. A Hitler dictatorship seemed to him preferable to the fragmented, ineffectual republican system. Though declining an invitation to join the National Socialist Party, he accepted in 1934 a reappointment as the government's price commissioner. In August of that year, moreover, he addressed a lengthy memorandum to the Führer praising the accomplishments of the Third Reich. He spoke favorably about "the elimination of rule by the parties and its fortunate replacement by the amalgamation of party and state." The logical precondition for this vital reform had been the concentration of "the authority of the party and the authority of the state in the hands of one person." Not only that, the regime had, "by transcending the boundaries of the German [states]," created an opportunity "that had almost never before existed in German history" to forge a unitary Reich.[17]

All this praise served as a prelude to Goerdeler's plea that the regime remain willing to share power with conservative well-wishers like himself. "It would be truly deplorable if the most

16. Ritter, *Goerdeler*, pp. 62–63. See also M. Krüger-Charlé, "Carl Goerdelers Versuch der Durchsetzung einer alternativen Politik 1933 bis 1937," in *Der Widerstand gegen den Nationalsozialismus. Die deutsche Gesellschaft und der Widerstand gegen Hitler*, ed. J. Schmädeke and P. Steinbach (Munich and Zurich, 1985), p. 385.

17. Ritter, *Goerdeler*, p. 61; Memorandum by Goerdeler, "An den Reichskanzler Adolf Hitler," August 1934, BA Koblenz, NL Goerdeler, 12.

sober judgments, best experiences, and finest characters to be found in the German people were not enlisted in making use to the greatest national advantage of the conditions that have thus been created." The government, he maintained, needed the support of all patriotic and loyal forces in the new Germany.[18]

Most of the men in the resistance can best be described in the early 1930s as sympathizers and allies of National Socialism, rather than as dedicated followers. At heart they would have preferred Hindenburg or Papen or even Schleicher to Hitler. But a few, especially among the younger members, were true believers. Fritz-Dietlof von der Schulenburg, for example, born after the turn of the century, became convinced early in life that authoritarian government was the only safeguard of social justice for the lower classes. Weimar, on the other hand, seemed to the "red count" to be the tool of a selfish, unscrupulous plutocracy. By the age of the thirty he was inveighing that under the republican regime the state, "formerly a living organism bound to the entire community," had become a "cover organization for special interests and for functionaries." The system of administration had turned into "a battlefield and a source of booty" for the parties, while "anemic" government officials, increasingly submissive to the "party bosses," were becoming "alienated from the people."[19]

There was only one thing to do; in 1932 Schulenburg joined the National Socialist Party. When a year later Hitler came to power, he was as jubilant as the most ardent of the brownshirts. The Third Reich meant defeat for the "powers of Jewry, capital, and the Catholic Church," he exulted. The republic destroyed "the old Prussian civil service, which possessed outstanding qualities of intelligence, character, and accomplishment." But "the unknown soldier of the World War, Adolf Hitler," had created a new core of resistance, so that the Nazi movement became "the incarnation of the faith and will of the German people." The government promptly rewarded his loyalty by appointing him to an important administrative post in East Prussia.[20]

18. Goerdeler, memorandum of August 1934, BA Koblenz, NL Goerdeler, 12.

19. F.D. von der Schulenburg, "Partei und Beamtentum," *Deutschlands Erneuerung. Monatsschrift für das deutsche Volk* 16, no. 6 (March 1932): 347–48, 352.

20. Schulenburg, "Neuaufbau des höheren Beamtentums," April 1933, and "Reichsreform," spring 1934, both in BA Koblenz, NL Schulenburg, 1.

The vocal and outspoken critics of Weimar in the resistance were generally civilians, most of them bureaucrats whose right to express political views was protected by laws safeguarding the independence of the civil service. The soldiers had to be more circumspect. For one thing, they were legally prohibited from becoming directly involved in politics. But more important, the code of conduct in which they had been schooled by General Hans von Seeckt, chief of the army command in the 1920s, taught them that the officer corps stood above parties and ideologies. Because it had to serve the interests of the nation as a whole, an involvement in political affairs would be incompatible with its status and mission. The armed forces must remain aloof from the partisan conflicts of the republic.

In the course of his interrogation by the security police after the failure of the attempt to assassinate Hitler in 1944, General Hans Oster emphasized the political neutrality of the officer corps during the Weimar period. Under the monarchy, he testified, its members had never doubted that the established system was impregnable. "There were no politics for us. We wore the king's uniform, and that was enough for us." Hence the collapse of the empire brought about by the "revolt of 1918" affected most officers like "a hammer blow to the head." The proud monarchical order was now replaced by a "fragmented party state." But after "the most difficult inner struggles," they decided "with a heavy heart" to serve the "socialist republic," thereby helping the nation in the hour of its greatest need. Under Seeckt "we were trained in the decisive years of our military development to become apolitical soldiers." The policy of strict neutrality in public affairs was accepted as the only way to rebuild a disciplined and effective military force that could form the basis for an expanded army. "The words 'party' and 'politics' had an unpleasant sound, as far as we were concerned."[21]

Yet this portrait of a strictly apolitical officer corps serving only the interests of the nation was in fact too cosmetic, too idealized. The armed forces during the republic were never entirely above party and ideology; they were always tacitly predisposed and partisan. It was probably unrealistic to

21. SD-Bericht, 25 August 1944, in *"Spiegelbild einer Verschwörung,"* ed. Jacobsen, vol. 1, p. 302.

expect otherwise. The leaders of the army carefully avoided taking sides in public on questions of government policy, but their private conversations and letters leave little doubt about their political sympathies. To most officers Weimar's great defects were not only the factionalism and divisiveness resulting from the party system, but diplomatic ineptness and military weakness. Their distrust of the republican regime was reinforced by the pacifism and antimilitarism that some of its supporters embraced. How could Germany regain a position of influence in international affairs under a government unable or unwilling to assert a national will? The question always troubled the professional soldiers, including those who subsequently joined the resistance.

In November 1923, for example, during one of the darkest moments in the history of Weimar, Ludwig Beck declared that only an authoritarian form of political rule could now save Germany from disaster. "Conditions at home and abroad are forcing us to follow a different course," he wrote to his wartime commanding officer. "Social Democracy has mismanaged everything; the democratic blessings are no longer effective. We need iron leadership that can reestablish authority, force people to work, and provide bread for the industrious. I hope that such a personality can be found in Berlin. Otherwise, we will soon have famine and civil war everywhere, and France will have her ultimate success." To him the most important thing was "to prevent a disintegration of the troops," and for that the country would have to rely on methods that "only a dictator" can employ.[22]

While Beck despaired because of the government's political ineffectualness, Henning von Tresckow, another prominent member of the resistance, brooded on its military impotence. After leaving the army following the monarchy's collapse, he had found employment in the Potsdam banking house of the Jewish financier Wilhelm Kann. But that experience did little to shake his conviction, expressed, to be sure, before he rejoined the armed forces early in 1926, that the various races and peoples were so different that an enduring peace between them was highly unlikely. A league of nations of "actual, lasting significance" could be established only through the triumph of "the Anglo-American (also known as Jewish) democ-

22. Beck to von Gossler, 11 November 1923, in Müller, *Beck*, pp. 329–31.

ratic-capitalistic idea." But the triumph of such an idea would also mean the "enslavement of the world by commercialism." Worse still, the forces of the left were now allied with those of capital in a futile quest for eternal harmony among nations. "The communist or Marxist idea, even if it is motivated by the best intentions, performs in this connection the role of a servitor [of the capitalists]." A regime espousing half-baked theories of diplomatic reconciliation and international understanding was by its nature incapable of bringing about a revival of Germany.[23]

The coming of the depression revealed even more clearly the partisan inclinations of the members of the officer corps. Their attitudes hardened; their words became less discreet and ambiguous. Hellmuth Stieff, who manufactured the bomb that came close to blowing up Hitler on 20 July 1944, described in the summer of 1932 the political mood of the army leaders, a mood he himself shared. "The parties are the misfortune of Germany," he wrote to his wife. Their irresponsibility had made impossible a stable or fruitful government policy, which was desperately needed "to lead us out of our misery." Therefore, "the government must be freed from the chains of parliamentarianism so that it can work independently, supported by the confidence of the president and the power of the army." After all, the president and the army embodied, in a symbolic way, "the idea of national unity." Because they stood "above the parties," they alone were qualified, "working solely for the welfare of the state" to bring about a reconciliation of the opposing political and social forces. They, and not the Reichstag, provided "the only basis for a government of the sort we need now." The republic was finished; the time had come for a dictatorship.[24]

After the establishment of the Third Reich, an officer in the war ministry who was known to have reservations about the new order told the French military attaché in Berlin that in 1933 "perhaps 60 percent [of the army] was Nazi." The estimate does not seem farfetched. As early as 1930, Beck had argued that Hitler should be appointed chancellor because he represented the only chance Germany had of regaining mili-

23. B. Scheurig, *Henning von Treskow*, 2nd ed. (Oldenburg and Hamburg, 1973), p. 20.
24. Stieff to his wife, 21 August 1932, in Hellmuth Stieff, *Briefe*, ed. Horst Mühleisen (Berlin, 1991), p. 71.

tary power. When the National Socialists won their first great victory in the parliamentary elections of that year, he was overjoyed. In 1931, moreover, according to an old friend, Beck "declared himself in my presence wholeheartedly in favor of National Socialism and would not admit the validity of my profound doubts." Tresckow began even earlier to voice his anti-republican views. In 1929 he announced in the officers' club in Potsdam his support of the Nazi demand for "breaking the chains of usury," and a year later he was seeking to influence members of his regiment "in favor of National Socialism." By the time Weimar fell, little was left of the army's official nonpartisanship in public affairs.[25]

The last pretensions to political neutrality disappeared amid the jubilation with which the officer corps greeted the appointment of Hitler to the chancellorship. The republic with its endless squabbling and bumbling, its vacillating and meandering, was finally over. The work of national reconstruction could begin. Beck rejoiced at the "political revolution" that was taking place in Germany. "I hoped for it for years, and I am delighted that my hope did not deceive me. This is the first real ray of light since 1918."[26] And Wilhelm Canaris, the enigmatic naval officer who a few years later was simultaneously directing the German counterintelligence and obstructing the German war effort, seemed equally enthusiastic. "As an old nationalist," a former colleague of his recalled, "he was at that time convinced that the new regime was better by far than anything that had preceded it, and that for the time being there was simply no other way."[27]

As for the story that on 30 January 1933 Claus von Stauffenberg, dressed in full uniform, led a jubilant procession in Bamberg celebrating Hitler's appointment as chancellor, that has been proven apocryphal. But there is no reason to question the testimony of a fellow officer regarding his attitude toward the advent of the Third Reich. He was delighted "that the people rose up against the chains of the Versailles Treaty, and that through the creation of work the misery of unemployment

25. G. Castellan, *Le réarmament clandestin du Reich, 1930–1935: Vu par la 2e Bureau de l'état-major français* (Paris, 1954), p. 442; N. Reynolds, *Treason Was No Crime: Ludwig Beck, Chief of the German General Staff* (London, 1976), pp. 38, 43; Scheurig, *Henning von Treskow*, p. 44.

26. Beck to Julie S.E. von Gossler, 17 March 1933, in Müller, *Beck*, pp. 338–39.

27. H. Höhne, *Canaris. Patriot im Zwielicht* (Munich, 1987), p. 135.

was eliminated and other measures providing social relief for the working population were initiated."[28] For Oster the victory of National Socialism meant a chance at last for a "return to older traditions." He appears to have regarded the end of the parliamentary system, the suppression of political freedom, and the dissolution of left-wing organizations as unavoidable steps toward a "national revival" that would lead to a "strong national policy" and the rearmament of Germany.[29] Concerning Tresckow, the description by Hans Bernd Gisevius, one of the few members of the resistance to survive the war, is quite apt: "He was for many years able to see only the side of National Socialism attractive to a soldier: the assertion of discipline, the reestablishment of military primacy, and the revision of the Versailles Treaty." The description could in fact have been applied to most army officers in 1933. What mattered to them above all was that Germany would now regain her place in the sun.[30]

While the military and bureaucratic adversaries of the Third Reich were forced to work in secret, they found important allies of similar social background and political outlook in another group within the "resistance," a group whose members could express their views more openly. A number of church leaders from both major denominations displayed considerable courage in publicly attacking some of the practices and doctrines of the government. A few were imprisoned for their insubordination, but most were too popular and influential to be arrested or silenced or intimidated. They insisted as a rule that they did not really want to become involved in political questions, that they were only dealing with moral and theological issues. Yet it was obvious that what they had to say in the name of religion had a direct bearing on the secular policies of the Nazi regime. Thus the effective opponents of the government were not only disaffected soldiers and disenchanted bureaucrats, but also leading clergymen who perceived in the ideology of the Third Reich a threat to the church.

28. P. Hoffmann, *Widerstand, Staatsstreich, Attentat. Der Kampf der Opposition gegen Hitler* (Munich, 1969), p. 373; J. Kramarz, *Claus Graf Stauffenberg, 15. November 1907–20. Juli 1944: Das Leben eines Offiziers* (Frankfurt am Main, 1965), p. 46.

29. H. Graml, "Hans Oster," in *Der zwangzigste Juli. Alternative zu Hitler?*, ed. H.J. Schultz (Stuttgart and Berlin, 1974), pp. 133–34.

30. H.B. Gisevius, *Bis zum bittern Ende*, 2nd. ed., 2 vols. (Zurich, 1946), vol. 2, p. 263.

The churchmen in the resistance approved of the Third Reich almost as much as the soldiers, but to them it represented a moral rather than a material rebirth. Not that they denied the charges of political and military impotence directed against Weimar. They too believed that the republic had been born with the indelible stain of rebellion against legitimate authority, that it placed the interest of parties above the welfare of the nation, and that it acquiesced in the weakness and humiliation of the state. They saw the most serious fault of the parliamentary system, however, in its indifference to Christian values, its attempt to restrict religious influence in public life, its advocacy of secularism and "materialism," its tolerance of the "immorality" of big-city life, and its flirtation with radicalism and "Bolshevism."

The Protestant church in particular displayed a profound nostalgia for the traditions and pieties that the old monarchical order had championed. The great majority of its clergymen, 80 percent by one estimate, supported the parties of the right. The Catholic church was not as one-sided; the Center Party, after all, had played a major role in republican politics. And yet there was deep within German Catholicism an undercurrent of hostility toward the modernism that Weimar appeared to embody. Both major denominations thus regarded the republic with hostility, suspicion, or at best ambivalence.[31]

Theophil Wurm, the Lutheran Church President of Württemberg – in the summer of 1933 he acquired the title of State Bishop – exemplified the attitude of most Protestant clergymen toward the republican regime. Throughout the period of the Third Reich he was to oppose, boldly, vigorously, and publicly, the efforts of National Socialism to gain a decisive influence in ecclesiastical governance. His defiance even led to a brief suspension from office. And yet during the last desperate years of Weimar he openly greeted the decline of parliamentarianism. In November 1932 he spoke approvingly about the concept of a "Christian state" that the Papen ministry had invoked. This did not mean religious coercion, he maintained. And yet a regime "that makes it possible to be a Christian"

31. F.O. Bonkovsky, "The German State and Protestant Elites," in *The German Church Struggle and the Holocaust*, ed. F. H. Littell and H.G. Locke (Detroit, Mi., 1974), p. 129.

should be welcomed, and a system of "politics based on faith" supported. There were signs now of a new public outlook that "until recently was not even considered possible." There was a quest for "values that have been lost," a quest that could not be lightly dismissed with phrases about "reaction or restoration." Were these not hopeful developments? As for National Socialism, the church should at least show "a measure of understanding" for "a powerful popular movement, even though it contains dubious elements and its leadership is by no means unobjectionable."[32]

Four months later, after the Nazi victory, Wurm's reservations about dubious elements and objectionable leadership in the Party disappeared. At the end of March 1933 he praised the new order for overcoming "the danger of a Bolshevization of the German people, a danger that was becoming ever more threatening as a result of our impoverishment." The youth of the country in particular had finally learned that an improvement in material conditions could not be achieved by "the imitation of Russian methods of coercion," but only through "a reorganization of state and economy reflecting the character of its own nation." By early April, Wurm sounded even more positive. After describing the fate of the "organized Protestant Church in Russia," which had reportedly "ceased to exist," he spoke "with joy" about the efforts of the Hitler government to initiate an "urgently needed purge of public life." German Protestantism would regard this purge "with approval" and would "gladly assist it with advice." Weimar had never received similar promises of assistance from him.[33]

The anti-republicanism of most Protestant clergymen, including those who later turned against the Nazi regime, is even more apparent in the case of Otto Dibelius, General Church Superintendent in the eastern region of Prussia. His differences with the Third Reich, to be sure, began sooner than Wurm's. He was forced into retirement as early as June 1933. Four years later the authorities placed him under arrest and

---

32. Wurm to the Council of German Protestant Churches (Deutscher Evangelischer Kirchenausschuß), 24 November 1932, in *Die Evangelische Landeskirche in Württemberg und der Nationalsozialismus. Eine Dokumentation zum Kirchenkampf*, ed. G. Schäfer, 6 vols. (Stuttgart, 1971–86), vol. 1, pp. 226, 228–29.

33. *Allgemeine Evangelisch-Lutherische Kirchenzeitung*, 24 March and 7 April 1933.

deprived him of the right to speak in public. Yet during the Weimar period he inveighed tirelessly against the sins of parliamentarianism, secularism, and materialism. The Nazi ideology seemed to him far preferable to the liberal faith of the impotent republic.

He therefore greeted Hitler's first great electoral success with undisguised approval. The victory of Nazism was a victory for Christianity. "The National Socialists," in his opinion, "have shown by their program as well as their practical conduct . . . that they have a positive attitude toward Christianity without regard for confessional differences." He remained confident that in the newly elected Reichstag they would prove "faithful to this principle of theirs." By early 1931, moreover, he was urging the adoption of a more assertive foreign policy. It might sound very Christian to preach that a nation should not seek power, he wrote, that it should rather beat its swords into plowshares and its spears into pruning hooks. "In the world of today," however, such a view would only serve "as a reinforcement of injustice and hatred on this earth." The peace of justice for which the Christian church stood could only be achieved among nations enjoying equal rights. "To win back this equality of rights will be the task of the German people in the coming decades. The task has been assigned to us by God!"[34]

Hitler's victory in 1933 seemed to Dibelius to be the fulfillment of his hopes for the revival of Germany. The new regime might be dictatorial, he conceded, but that was a cheap price to pay for an end to national humiliation and demoralization. On March 21, in a sermon delivered on the occasion of the opening of the new Reichstag, Dibelius justified the repressive measures introduced by the National Socialist government: "When the state uses its office against those who undermine the foundations of the political order, especially against those who destroy marriage with corrupting and coarse language, make religion contemptible, and slander the sacrifice of life for the fatherland, then it uses its office in the name of God!" The Third Reich had gained in him an eloquent defender of its lofty moral mission.[35]

34. *Berliner Evangelisches Sonntagsblatt*, 28 September 1930 and 25 January 1931.

35. *Das Evangelische Deutschland. Kirchliche Rundschau für das Gesamtgebiet des Deutschen Evangelischen Kirchenbundes*, 26 March 1933.

Martin Niemöller, the most equivocal and contradictory figure among the clerical members of the resistance, became an
apologist for National Socialism even before Dibelius. For him
too a Hitler dictatorship was preferable to the secular, democratic, materialistic republic. Eventually he turned against the
Third Reich, denouncing the government's policy and paying
for his audacity with seven years in a concentration camp. But
during Weimar he had firmly believed that an authoritarian
right-wing regime was the only salvation for Germany.
Always unpredictable, often inconsistent, he combined faith
in the golden rule with conservative, ultra-nationalist zealotry;
he opposed autocratic rule in the church but supported it in
the state; he embraced simultaneously Christian universalism
and German jingoism. What are we then to make of such a
man? No one can accuse Niemöller of not having enough
courage, but his displays of insufficient discernment, tolerance, compassion, or even common sense are puzzling and
distressing. Long after his death, he remains an enigma.

What is clear is that he was at first quite sympathetic to
National Socialism. He himself testified that since 1924 he had
always voted for its candidates in state as well as national elections. He never joined the Party, but was on friendly terms
with many of its supporters and occasionally even used the
Nazi salute. Toward the end of his life he recalled that "it was
a kind of liberation when Hitler came."[36]

Thus the decision of the new government to withdraw from
the League of Nations in October 1933 met with his whole-
hearted approval. Indeed, he boasted that upon hearing about
it, he "immediately sent the Führer a congratulatory telegram,
probably the first the Führer received regarding this action."
And in a sermon delivered at around the same time, he
rejoiced that under the Third Reich the people had regained
their sense of faith and value. "Occupation and status, race
and nation, are once again accepted by us today as realities.
They make demands on us from which we cannot escape."
This new awareness of collective responsibility represented "a
liberation, in reality, indeed, . . . a deliverance." Society had
been going in circles in a narrow "prison courtyard" of selfish-

---

36. H. Buchheim, "Ein NS-Funktionär zum Niemöller-Prozeß," *Viertel-
jahrshefte für Zeitgeschichte* 4 (1956): 312; J. Bentley, *Martin Niemöller, 1892–1984*
(New York, 1984), pp. 41, 43; Bonkovsky, "German State and Protestant
Elites," pp. 136–37.

ness and greed. "Now the gates have been forced open, and we see numerous tasks to which we are summoned." The Third Reich was making possible at last the moral regeneration of Germany.[37]

The Catholic churchmen in the resistance were somewhat more reserved. Indeed, before 1933 National Socialism and Catholicism had regarded each other with distrust and apprehension. To the Nazis internationalism was as dangerous in religion as in politics. A church with close ties to an alien pope and to its coreligionists in other countries seemed almost as sinister as Freemasonry or "world Jewry." The Catholics, on the other hand, were repelled not only by the invocation of Teutonic mythology and paganism in the rites of the Nazi Party, but by its totalitarian claim to control over all collective civic activity, a claim incompatible with confessional trade unions, peasant associations, and youth organizations. Each side believed that the other was, overtly or covertly, a sworn opponent.

Hitler's victory, however, forced the Catholics to seek an accommodation with the new order. Whatever their private convictions, most of them came to feel that only a reconciliation between church and state could safeguard their religious interests. The government in turn was eager to demonstrate its reasonableness, to show that it was ready to cooperate with all the forces of tradition and stability in society. The way was thus open for an *entente cordiale*. Barely two months after Hitler's appointment as chancellor, Cardinal Faulhaber was urging the Bavarian episcopate "to exercise more tolerance toward the new government in spite of everything." Not only was National Socialism in power, he explained, but it had acquired that power legitimately, "as no revolutionary party has yet done." Besides, the pope himself had described Hitler "as the first statesman, after the Holy Father, who raised his voice against Bolshevism."[38]

This cautious endorsement of the Third Reich was transformed into enthusiastic support by the conclusion of a concordat between Germany and the Vatican on 20 July 1933. Four days later Faulhaber sent a handwritten letter to Hitler

---

37. Buchheim, "NS-Funktionär zum Niemöller-Prozeß," p. 313; *Junge Kirche: Halbmonatschrift für reformatorisches Christentum* 1 (1933): 222.

38. *Akten Faulhabers*, ed. Volk, vol. 1, p. 673.

overflowing with praise for the government's great accomplishment. "What the old parliaments and parties did not achieve in 60 years, your statesmanlike farsightedness has made a reality of world history within six months." For Germany's reputation throughout the world this "handclasp" with the papacy would represent a "great deed of immeasurable benefit."[39]

Bishop Clemens August von Galen of Münster, who a decade later displayed so much boldness in openly condemning the Nazi euthanasia program, was at first equally effusive. In a pastoral letter in October 1933, he thanked God that "the top leaders of our fatherland . . . have recognized and are trying with a firm hand to eliminate the terrible danger that threatened our beloved German people as a result of the open propaganda for godlessness and immorality." The conclusion of the concordat had made it possible for the Church to exercise its influence over "the education of our youth and over family and communal life." Catholicism and National Socialism seemed now to be working together to bring about the "spiritual revival" of Germany.[40]

Most members of the resistance were even initially in agreement with that part of the Nazi program that had the cruelest, most tragic consequences, the part dealing with the "Jewish question." After the failure of the attempt to assassinate Hitler, Berthold von Stauffenberg assured his interrogators that in 1933 he and the others had by and large supported the fundamental ideas of National Socialism on domestic policy including "the concept of race."[41] Alas, an examination of what they had to say on the subject supports his contention.

In all fairness, there was an important difference between them and the rabid, fanatical anti-Semites in the Nazi Party. Theirs was the fashionable bigotry of the exclusive drawing room or the elite gentlemen's club. They looked down with condescension on the Jewish climber or parvenu who might have a great deal of money, but who could never attain the

39. Faulhaber to Hitler, 25 July 1933, in *Katholische Kirche und Nationalsozialismus: Dokumente*, ed. H. Müller (Munich, 1963), pp. 170–71.

40. "Programm zur Bischofsweihe," 28 October 1933, in C.A. von Galen, *Akten, Briefe und Predigten 1933–1946*, ed. P. Löffler, 2 vols. (Mainz, 1988), vol. 1, p. 37.

41. SD-Bericht, 16 October 1944, in *"Spiegelbild einer Verschwörung"*, ed. Jacobsen, vol. 1, pp. 447–48.

social status that only family and tradition bestowed. To them the Jews were an alien element incapable of being assimilated into German society. The differences separating the two "races" were too profound to be bridged by toleration or liberalism. Something had to be done, legally and equitably, of course, to reduce the influence of Jewry, to diminish its importance in commerce and finance, to control its growth in learning and the arts, and to counter its promotion of radicalism and subversion. On this point almost all members of the resistance agreed.

Following his arrest in 1944, Popitz declared that "as a quite knowledgeable expert on conditions in the period of the [party] system, I was entirely of the opinion regarding the Jewish question that the Jews must disappear from political and economic life. I did repeatedly recommend a more gradual approach in the *method* employed, especially for reasons of foreign policy." He was perhaps trying to ingratiate himself with the Nazi authorities by emphasizing his early approval of their anti-Semitic doctrines. Yet there is little reason to question the sincerity of his assertion that during Weimar he had believed the Jewish influence in public life to be excessive and unhealthy. It sounds quite plausible.[42]

Some members of the resistance were not content merely to grumble about the "undue importance" that Jews had acquired in public life. They tried to do something about it. Hassell, for example, who after the fall of the monarchy became a member of the executive committee of the German National People's Party (Deutschnationale Volkspartei), proposed a compromise on its stand regarding the "Jewish question" that sought to avoid both too much bigotry and too much toleration. "The development and training of [the nation's] energies in all areas of public life," he suggested, "is the best protection against an excessive growth of harmful alien influence, especially against the domination of Jewry."[43] But this was not enough for most members of the Party. The platform it adopted in 1920 declared that "we oppose every manifestation of a disintegrative, un-German spirit, whether emanating from Jewish or other circles." It was especially

---

42. Ibid., p. 449.
43. G. Schöllgen, *Ulrich von Hassell 1881–1944. Ein Konservativer in der Opposition* (Munich, 1990), p. 32.

important to put a stop to the "ever more dangerous emergence of a domination of government and public life by Jewry." Even this formulation sounds mild compared to some of the slogans circulating in Germany a decade later.[44]

Like Hassell, Goerdeler was prepared at first to support the program of National Socialism, including its racial policy. He too believed that it was important to curb Jewish influence in politics and economics. But the elimination of alien forces in national life should be carried out fairly and equitably. When the Nazis came to power, Goerdeler personally tried to protect Jewish shopkeepers in Leipzig against plundering SA men. Yet he also, by his own admission, "worked together with the National Socialist Party in the first years after 1933 in complete confidence." His hope had been "to influence the course of events in the best interest of our nation, and to strengthen the good forces within the Party (without belonging to it myself!)."[45]

Thus in his memorandum to Hitler in the summer of 1934 he urged that the government's anti-Semitic policy be enforced with strict adherence to legal norms. "What the law has provided will hardly be questioned by reasonable people abroad as a means of self-protection, as long as everything is now carried with iron discipline and the avoidance of excesses and petty persecutions." If this advice were disregarded, on the other hand, "we will only be forced to make ever greater concessions." There was no reason, for example, why the playing of Mendelssohn's music should not be discouraged or even prohibited, provided it was not done officially on "grounds of racial policy." What seemed to concern Goerdeler most was the execution rather than the content of Nazi racial legislation.[46]

A few members of the resistance even went beyond occasional attempts to check "excessive Jewish influence." They became avowed anti-Semites, maintaining that the attitudes and values of Jewry were fundamentally incompatible with the spirit of Germany. The government, therefore, had good reason for adopting protective measures against a small but

44. "Grundsätze der Deutschnationalen Volkspartei," in W. Treue, *Deutsche Parteiprogramme 1861–1956*, 2nd ed. (Berlin and Frankfurt, 1956), p. 112.
45. Ritter, *Goerdeler*, p. 64.
46. Goerdeler, memorandum of August 1934, BA Koblenz, NL Goerdeler, 12.

dangerous racial minority. At his trial in 1938 Niemöller declared that Jews seemed to him "unpleasant and alien." That would hardly be surprising, he explained, in someone who came from "an old Westphalian family of peasants and theologians," and who was "a former imperial naval officer." Still, Jews who converted had to be accepted as equal members of the Christian community. The Bible did not permit the church "to replace baptism with the family tree." God, moreover, should not be conceived "in our image, the Aryan image." He had to be accepted as He actually was, made manifest "in the Jew Jesus of Nazareth." This "truly distressing and great vexation" had to be endured "for the sake of the Gospel."[47]

His view of conversion helps explain Niemöller's defense in 1933 of "non-Aryan" Protestant clergymen – there were twenty-three of them in the entire country, not counting those who had "non-Aryan" wives – clergymen whom the authorities were trying to remove from their positions in the church. To support them, he admitted, required a high degree of "self-denial" on the part of the Germans, who "as a nation have had to endure a great deal under the influence of the Jewish people." It would also be better if "non-Aryan" clergymen did not belong to the governing body of the church or hold other prominent positions. Yet to deprive them of their clerical office altogether would violate the Christian creed and was therefore impermissible. As for the more than half a million "non-Aryans" who had still not converted to Christianity, their fate seemed to Niemöller to be properly the concern of world Jewry, not of the Protestant community in Germany.[48]

For pure, undisguised animosity toward Jews, however, no member of the resistance surpassed Dibelius. As early as 1928, in a circular letter labeled "confidential" that was distributed among the clergymen under his jurisdiction, he described his position bluntly and unequivocally. "I have always considered myself an anti-Semite, despite the bad sound the word has acquired in many circles." Who could deny that in "all the disintegrative manifestations of modern civilization" Jewry had played a leading role? Cultivation of the nationality "to which

47. Buchheim, "NS-Funktionär," p. 313.
48. Bentley, *Niemöller*, p. 65; *Junge Kirche: Halbmonatschrift für reformatorisches Christentum* 1 (1933): 269–70.

God has assigned us," reinforcement of the love of country, a new sense of rootedness in the soil, and a conscious rejection of "modern asphalt culture," those were the goals to which "every Protestant Church will categorically commit itself!"[49]

For Dibelius the establishment of the Third Reich marked the beginning of that spiritual revival for which he had waited so long and so impatiently. The pernicious influence over national life exerted by Jewry under Weimar would now finally come to an end. Hence the unfavorable reaction of the foreign press to the boycott of Jewish stores and businesses that the authorities organized in April 1933 drove him to fury. He launched into an anti-Semitic tirade that must have won the approval of the most rabid Nazi Jew-baiter.

Public opinion abroad, he charged, was not determined by the politicians. It was shaped by "entirely different forces," namely, "economic capital and the press that is dependent on it." These forces had formed connections between one country and another, connections that, "as everyone knows," were to a large extent "in Jewish hands." They accounted for foreign criticism of the Third Reich. "Jewry understandably feels threatened by a national movement with anti-Semitic tendencies." And yet were not Jews closely implicated in the revolution of 1918 and in "the socialist domination"? Every child in Germany knew the large number of Jewish names that had become prominent in politics since the establishment of the republic. "Even though we as Protestant Christians are ever so sensible of the obligation not to do an injustice to anyone, there can be no doubt that the Jewish element has played a leading role in all the sinister events of the last fifteen years." The Third Reich's anti-Semitic policy was really no more than a justifiable means of self-defense.[50]

Most churchmen in the resistance were admittedly more restrained in their attitude toward Nazi racism. A few even expressed private disapproval of the violence and humiliation inflicted on the Jews of Germany. And yet they almost all felt that their proper concern should be their own religious community, their own denominational interest. To challenge the state on an issue that did not directly affect the church would cross the invisible line separating spiritual from secular

49. NL Dibelius, Evangelisches Zentralarchiv, Berlin, 50/R19.
50. *Berliner Evangelisches Sonntagsblatt*, 9 April 1933.

authority. It would be provocative and divisive. As for the Jews, they should rely primarily on the assistance of their co-religionists throughout the world. Only when the government's anti-Semitism had a direct bearing on the teachings of Christianity did some of the church leaders speak out against it.

Bishop Galen, for example, had little to say about the racial policies of the Third Reich until the fall of 1933, when the school superintendent of Münster issued a directive that religious instruction regarding All Souls' Day should be combined with classroom discussion of the destructive role of Jewry in history. To the bishop this was a clear violation of the boundary between religion and politics. He wrote to the superintendent indignantly that the connection between the latter's directive and the significance of All Souls' Day was "very loose, not to say artificial." There was even the danger, he went on, that the less bright pupils might become confused about "Catholic teachings regarding the historical mission of the people of Israel in salvation during the pre-Christian period, and regarding the obligation to act with Christian charity toward all men." His duty as "an appointed guardian of the values of the Catholic faith" was to oppose any infringement on its authority. In fulfilling it Galen displayed great courage. His definition of that duty, however, remained narrowly limited.[51]

The dilemma of a churchman torn between the opposing imperatives of Christian universalism and denominational self-interest, between the conflicting demands of transcendent faith and religious expediency, is much clearer in the case of Cardinal Faulhaber. Though a man of decidedly conservative political views, he was no narrow-minded bigot, no doctrinaire anti-Semite. In private statements during the spring of 1933 he maintained that while "we certainly want no predominance that is disproportionate to the actual number of Jews, . . . we cannot deny them every right in the German fatherland without destroying the foundation in natural law of our own love of the fatherland." More than that, "this action against the Jews is so unchristian that every Christian, not only every priest, would have to stand up against it." He found it especially "unjust and painful," according to a letter to Eugenio Pacelli, the papal secretary of state, later Pius XII, that "also

---

51. Galen to Glowsky, 6 November 1933, in Galen, *Akten, Briefe und Predigten*, ed. Löffler, vol. 1, pp. 46–47.

those [Jews] who have been baptized for ten or twenty years and are good Catholics, even those whose parents were already Catholic, are still legally considered to be Jews." Indeed, toward the end of the year he reasserted in a series of Advent sermons the central role of Judaism in the Christian Scriptures.[52]

Still, in his public statements regarding the situation of the Jews in Germany, the cardinal sounded much more guarded, much more ambivalent. He declared at the outset of his Advent sermons that "aversion to the Jews of today should not be transferred to the books of pre-Christian Jewry," since they were not really written by Jews, but were "inspired by the Spirit of God." In a letter to the Jewish World Conference in Geneva, he emphasized that he had indeed defended "the old Biblical writings of Israel," but had not taken any position "on the Jewish question of today." He even announced from the pulpit that as far as the church was concerned, "there is no objection to honest research on race and cultivation of race," provided it did not lead to "hatred of other peoples."[53]

The contrast between what Faulhaber said in private and what he said in public can only be explained by his resolve to defend Catholic interests at all costs. Late in March 1933, he warned the Bavarian episcopate that "we confront new situations from day to day, and the present Jew-baiting can turn just as quickly into Jesuit-baiting." A week later he wrote to Pacelli that nothing could be done to oppose the racial policies of the regime, because otherwise "the struggle against the Jews would at the same time become a struggle against the Catholics." It was better to remain silent. Faulhaber was simply too cautious, too diplomatic, too prudent to risk some bold but futile gesture of defiance toward National Socialism.[54]

The only public criticism by the resistance of the Third Reich's anti-Semitic policy came from the young Protestant

52. See Faulhaber to Wurm, 8 April 1933, and Faulhaber to the Bavarian Episcopate, 20 May 1933, in *Akten Faulhabers*, ed. Volk, vol. 1, pp. 705, 726; L. Volk, *Der bayerische Episkopat und der Nationalsozialismus 1930–1934* (Mainz, 1965), p. 78.

53. M. von Faulhaber, *Judentum, Christentum, Germanentum. Advents-predigten gehalten in St. Michael zu München 1933* (Munich, 1934), pp. 19, 116; *Beilage zum Amtsblatt Nr. 20 d. Erzdiöze v. München u. Freising vom 15. November 1934.*

54. Faulhaber to the Bavarian Episcopate, 31 March 1933, in *Akten Faulhabers*, ed. Volk, vol. 1, p. 684; Volk, *Der bayerische Episkopat*, p. 78.

theologian Dietrich Bonhoeffer. Not that he was entirely free of common religious biases and stereotypes. He too believed that there was something called the "Jewish question" with which society had to grapple. After the Nazis came to power, he even declared that "the state is without doubt justified in adopting new approaches" to this question. As for the Christian church, it must view the history of the Jews "with a shudder" as "God's own, free, terrible way of dealing with His people." An end to their suffering could come only with "the conversion of Israel." So far Bonhoeffer was only repeating the cultural and theological commonplaces of traditional Christianity.[55]

And yet there gradually emerged out of those familiar phrases about the historical transgression and punishment of the Jews an indirect but unmistakable rejection of anti-Semitism. "From the point of view of Christ's church," Bonhoeffer wrote, "Judaism is never a racial but a religious concept." One may become a Jew through the acceptance of "God's law," but "one cannot become a racial Jew." More than that, "no state in the world" can deal conclusively with "this enigmatic people," because "God has not yet dealt with it." Hence it was now the task of "humanitarian organizations and of individual Christian men who feel the calling" to point out to the state "the moral aspect of its measures at any given time." Indeed, if necessary, they must not hesitate "to accuse the state of violating morality." It took courage to say things like that in Germany in the spring of 1933.[56]

Still, Bonhoeffer was a rare exception. The great majority of the members of the resistance accepted, with varying degrees of approval, the teachings of National Socialism regarding the illegitimate origin of Weimar, the inadequacy of representative government, the military weakness of the republic, the danger of materialism and radicalism, and the destructive influence of Jewry. They welcomed the coming of the Third Reich; they became its supporters and allies. Yet a decade later many of them risked and lost their lives in trying to overthrow a regime whose establishment they had originally welcomed.

---

55. Bonhoeffer, "Die Kirche vor der Judenfrage," n.d. [before April 1933], in D. Bonhoeffer, *Gesammelte Schriften*, ed. E. Bethge, 6 vols. (Munich, 1958–74), vol. 2, pp. 45, 50–51.
56. Ibid.

How are we to account for such a complete about-face? To answer that question in detail requires an examination of their views and attitudes in the middle and late 1930s and during the Second World War. It is clear, however, that what turned them against National Socialism was not its basic principles but their application, execution, and consequence. When the Hitler dictatorship was first established, they accepted it as a vast improvement over an impotent and corrupt parliamentary system.

15

The Limits of Collaboration

Edgar Jung, Herbert von Bose, and the Origins of the Conservative Resistance to Hitler, 1933–34

Larry Eugene Jones

The role that Germany's conservative elites played in the establishment of the Third Reich has long been the subject of considerable controversy and acrimony.[1] By and large, students of Weimar conservatism have focused either on the role that Germany's industrial, agricultural, and military elites played in the establishment and stabilization of the Nazi dictatorship or on the extreme reluctance with which the more prescient of Germany's conservative leaders greeted the Nazi seizure of power. If the first group accepts industrial, agricultural, and military opposition to the legacy of the German revolution of 1918/19 as *prima facie* evidence of conservative sympathy for National Socialism and continues to remind us that Hitler could never have come to power without the collaboration of individual conservatives such as Franz von Papen and Alfred Hugenberg, the second group insists that conservatives too were victims of Nazi persecution and that for all their hostility to the so-called "Weimar system" they remained profoundly alienated from the "New Order" that Hitler estab-

1. This essay represents the revised and expanded version of a paper that was originally read at the 106th annual meeting of the American Historical Association in Chicago, Illinois, on 29 December 1991. The author is particularly grateful to William S. Allen for his perceptive and thought-provoking criticisms of the paper. The essay also complements an article the author published in the June 1988 issue of *Central European History* under the title of "Edgar Julius Jung: The Conservative Revolution in Theory and Practice," and updates it on the basis of subsequent research conducted in the summer of 1990. The author would like to take this opportunity to thank the Deutscher Akademischer Austauschdienst for having provided the funding that made it possible for him to complete the research for this article.

lished in its place. The intense partisanship that has frequently accompanied this debate has made it all the more difficult to arrive at a fully balanced picture of the expectations and anxieties that accompanied the conservative entry into the Third Reich or to appreciate the deep divisions that the collapse of Weimar and the establishment of the Nazi dictatorship produced within the ranks of Germany's conservative elites.[2]

Whereas most studies of the German Right have ended with the Nazi seizure of power in January 1933, the Röhm purge of 30 June 1934 constitutes a far more logical terminus for such an inquiry than either Hitler's appointment as chancellor or the official dissolution of the German National People's Party (Deutschnationale Volkspartei or DNVP) later that summer. Not only does the way in which conservative organizations were either driven out of existence or forcibly coopted into the organizational structure of the Third Reich constitute an extremely important chapter in the history of the German Right, but the Röhm purge represented a genuine watershed in relations between Germany's conservative elites and the new Nazi regime. For just as the suppression of the left wing of the Nazi Party reassured German conservatives that the Nazi revolution had run its course and that the destruction of the Weimar state was not to be followed by a redistribution of wealth and property, so the murder of ex-chancellor Kurt von Schleicher and several of Papen's associates in the vice chancery had a chilling effect upon those conservatives who were critical of the Nazi regime and put a definitive end to their hopes for some sort of a conservative restoration.[3] This,

2. There has been no systematic or comprehensive treatment of the role that Germany's conservative elites played in the destabilization of the Weimar Republic and the establishment of the Third Reich since the publication of Karl Dietrich Bracher's momentous and authoritative work at the end of the 1950s. See K.D. Bracher, *Die Auflösung der Weimarer Republik. Eine Studie zum Problem des Machtverfalls in der Demokratie*, 3rd ed. (Villingen/ Schwarzwald, 1960). For more recent contributions to this debate, see V. Hentschel, *Weimars letzte Monate. Hitler und der Untergang der Weimarer Republik* (Düsseldorf, 1979); and G. Jasper, *Die gescheiterte Zähmung. Wege zur Machtergreifung Hitlers 1930–1934* (Frankfurt am Main, 1986).

3. By far the most incisive analysis of conservative strategy in the first years of the Third Reich is the unpublished dissertation by K.-M. Grass, "Edgar Jung, Papenkreis und Röhmkrise 1933/34" (Ph.D. diss., Universität Heidelberg, 1966). For a more recent treatment of this problem, see the perceptive study by H. Höhne, *Mordsache Röhm. Hitlers Durchbruch zur Alleinherrschaft 1933–1934* (Reinbek bei Hamburg, 1984). The most authoritative analysis of the crisis that led up to the Röhm purge, however, is still W. Sauer, "Die

in turn, effectively defined the terms of conservative collaboration with the Nazi regime from the death of Reich President Paul von Hindenburg in early August 1934 until the Fritsch-Blomberg affair at the beginning of 1938.[4]

The purpose of this essay will be to examine the efforts of a small, yet nonetheless influential, contingent of conservative activists who in 1933/34 tried to regain a measure of control over a situation they had helped create through their involvement in the delegitimization and overthrow of the Weimar Republic. In doing so, it will address the question of whether or not there was a conservative resistance to Hitler in the first years of the Third Reich and, if so, to what extent did it hope to overthrow the Nazi regime or simply seek to reestablish the terms of the original covenant by which representatives of Germany's conservative elites had allowed Hitler to assume the reins of power. This, in turn, will entail not only a careful examination of what those conservatives who opposed Hitler in the first years of the Third Reich actually hoped to achieve but also an inquiry into the means by which they proposed to accomplish their ultimate objectives. Answering these questions will cast additional light on the precise nature of the relationship that existed between Germany's conservative elites and the Nazi state in the year and a half following Hitler's appointment as chancellor. At the same time, it will enable students of the German resistance to establish a clearer relationship between the conservative conspiracy of 1933/34 and the more celebrated attempts to overthrow the Nazi regime at the end of the Second World War.

Mobilmachung der Gewalt," in K.D. Bracher, W. Sauer, and G. Schulz, *Die nationalsozialistische Machtergreifung. Studien zur Errichtung des totalitären Herrschaftssystems in Deutschland 1933/34* (Cologne and Opladen, 1960), esp. pp. 897–966. By comparison, the study by M. Gallo, *The Night of the Long Knives*, trans. L. Emmet (New York, 1972), tends to be sensationalist and should only be used with great caution. Certainly what Gallo has to say about the conservative role in precipitating the purge is badly outdated.

4. In this respect, see K.-J. Müller, "Nationalkonservative Eliten zwischen Kooperation und Widerstand," in *Der Widerstand gegen den Nationalsozialismus. Die deutsche Gesellschaft und der Widerstand gegen Hitler*, ed. J. Schmädeke and P. Steinbach (Munich and Zurich, 1985), pp. 24–49; as well as the longer English version of this article, "The Structure and Nature of the National Conservative Opposition in Germany up to 1940," in *Aspects of the Third Reich*, ed. H.W. Koch (New York, 1985), pp. 133–78.

* * *

Ever since the last years of the Second Empire, the German Right embraced two distinct and ultimately incompatible traditions – one a governmental conservatism associated with the names of men such as Oskar Hergt, Karl Helfferich, and Count Kuno von Westarp, and the other a radical Pan-German nationalism represented by Alfred Hugenberg and Heinrich Claß. In the first years of the Weimar Republic, the differences between these two strands of right-wing political commitment were obscured by the fact that both stood in unconditional opposition to Germany's new republican order. With the political and economic stabilization of the Weimar Republic in the second half of the 1920s, however, the latent antipathy between the two factions of the German Right was transformed into an open split that continued right up until the collapse of the Weimar Republic and into the early years of the Third Reich. The net effect of this split was to immobilize Germany's conservative elite in the face of the challenge it encountered from Hitler and the Nazi movement. Hitler's appointment as chancellor was possible not so much because of the support he received from certain elements of Germany's conservative elite, but because that elite had become so fractured along political as well as structural lines that it was no longer capable of formulating any sort of coherent response to the crisis in which it found itself caught. The Nazi seizure of power in January 1933 thus presupposed the neutralization of Germany's conservative elite as a force that, had it been more united, could have prevented Hitler's bid for power. From this perspective, the disunity of the German Right thus constituted a prerequisite for the Nazi seizure of power that was every bit as essential as the dissolution of the German liberal parties or the schism of the Marxist Left.

Although individual conservatives such as Alfred Hugenberg or Franz von Papen may have been willing to join Hitler in the formation of a new government, their involvement in the formation of the Hitler cabinet took place against a background of extreme apprehension – and in some cases outright opposition – within the ranks of those elements they supposedly represented.[5]

5. This is particularly true in the case of Hugenberg. For further details, see L.E. Jones, "'The Greatest Stupidity of My Life': Alfred Hugenberg and the Formation of the Hitler Cabinet, January 1933," *Journal of Contemporary History* 27 (1992): 63–87.

The formation of the Hitler cabinet in January 1933 was predicated upon the assumption that the conservatives around Papen and the DNVP's Alfred Hugenberg would be able to "tame" Hitler by saddling him and his movement with the burden of governmental responsibility. Conservative hopes of containing Hitler and of restraining the radicalism of the Nazi movement rested in large part with Papen, who, as Hindenburg's personal favorite, had been appointed vice chancellor in the Hitler cabinet and enjoyed immediate access to the presidential palace.[6] With the outcome of the Reichstag elections of 5 March 1933 and the passage of the Enabling Act less than three weeks later, however, conservative hopes of domesticating the Nazi movement and harnessing it to a restorationist political agenda stood exposed as a naive and dangerous illusion. No incident better conveys the sense of powerlessness that suddenly gripped Hitler's conservative allies in the spring of 1933 than the lament of the DNVP's Martin Spahn three days before the passage of the Enabling Act that he and his colleagues were about to be delivered into the hands of Hitler just as the Girondins had allowed themselves to be delivered into the hands of the Jacobins. "What had happened in 1789," Spahn continued, "was about to repeat itself in 1933."[7]

Papen tried to compensate for the impact that the collapse of the traditional German Right had upon his own position within the cabinet by expanding the staff and resources of the vice chancery in hopes that it might establish itself as an effective conservative counterpoise to Hitler and the Nazi movement. Over the course of the next several months, Papen and his advisors were able to attract a cadre of committed conservative activists to work at the vice chancery. Among those who accepted positions in Papen's vice chancery were Herbert von Bose, Baron Wilhelm von Ketteler, Friedrich-Carl von Savigny, Fritz Günther von Tschirsky, and Count Hans von Kageneck.[8] The

6. The most detailed account of Papen's role in Hitler's appointment as chancellor is to be found in H. Müth, "Das 'Kölner Gespräch' am 4. Januar 1933," *Geschichte in Wissenschaft und Unterricht* 37 (1986): 463–80, 529–41. For Papen's largely self-exculpatory account of these events, see F. von Papen, *Der Wahrheit eine Gasse* (Munich, 1952), pp. 253–81.

7. E. Forschbach, "Die Deutschnationalen. Vom Ende einer Partei," *Politische Meinung* 5 (1960): 12.

8. F. G. von Tschirschky, *Erinnerungen eines Hochverräters* (Stuttgart, 1972), pp. 99–105.

Larry Eugene Jones

Papen circle also included a number of individuals who were not officially employed at the vice chancery but who nevertheless worked closely with the vice chancellor on a more or less informal basis. The most important of these was a self-styled conservative revolutionary by the name of Edgar Julius Jung, who had served as Papen's speech writer in the fall of 1932 and who offered his services to Papen once again as the negotiations that culminated in the formation of the Hitler-Papen cabinet were drawing to a close.[9] With the exception of Jung and Bose, the vast majority of those who accepted positions in the vice chancery were conservative Catholics who were not so much opposed to the new Nazi state as they were anxious to find a place within it for themselves and the social and political values they represented.

Of those who began to gather around Papen in the spring and summer of 1933, the most committed anti-Nazis were Jung and Bose. Not yet forty years of age when Hitler assumed power, Jung had already distinguished himself as the author of *Die Herrschaft der Minderwertigen*, a book that has been labeled the bible of German neoconservatism and a work that undoubtedly did much to help crystallize the antidemocratic sentiments of Germany's conservative elite.[10] Deeply influenced by the German romantic tradition, Jung was also attracted to the corporatist theories of Othmar Spann and had attended the lectures of Vilfredo Pareto while spending a year at the University of Lausanne.[11] By far the most important

9. Jung to Papen, 28 January 1933, Nachlaß Fritz Klein, Sr. (hereafter cited as NL Klein). The author would like to take this opportunity to express his gratitude to Fritz Klein for having placed the papers of his father, Fritz Klein, Sr., at his disposal.

10. For an assessment of Jung's ideas and influence, see W. Struve, *Elites against Democracy: Leadership Ideals in Bourgeois Political Thought in Germany, 1890–1933* (Princeton, N.J., 1973), pp. 317–52. See also B. Jenschke, *Zur Kritik der konservativ-revolutionären Ideologie in der Weimarer Republik. Weltanschauung und Politik bei Edgar Julius Jung* (Munich, 1971), esp. pp. 30–74, 106–90. For an analysis of Jung's ideas in the context of German neoconservatism, see the perceptive Marxist study by J. Petzold, *Wegbereiter des deutschen Faschismus. Die Jungkonservativen in der Weimarer Republik* (Cologne, 1978), esp. pp. 205–18, 310–19.

11. On the origins of Jung's political thought, see his letter to Pareto, 16 Jan. 1930, Nachlaß Edgar Jung (hereafter cited as NL Jung), IXa. The author is indebted to Dr. Karl-Martin Grass for having granted him access to the Jung Nachlaß. The Jung Nachlaß consists of approximately forty folders of correspondence, manuscripts, and other documents from the 1920s and early 1930s. It is not complete and contains virtually nothing on Jung's activities in

470

influence on Jung's intellectual development, however, was neither Spann nor Pareto but Leopold Ziegler, a philosopher of religion who, like Nietzsche, decried the effect that the triumph of science and rationalism had had upon man's capacity to appreciate the mythic and religious dimensions of human existence but who, unlike Nietzsche, sought to bring man back to his lost religious heritage.[12] Critical of his own Calvinist heritage for emphasizing the individual at the expense of the community,[13] Jung not only shared Ziegler's longing for the religious renewal of western man but came to regard this as a necessary precondition for Germany's national recovery after the end of the First World War.[14]

But Jung was more than a theorist; he was also a political activist deeply committed to a conservative regeneration (*Erneuerung*) of the German state. A proud and in many respects typical representative of the so-called "front generation,"[15] Jung had returned home in the fall of 1918 only to find the nation for which he had risked his life on the verge of complete collapse. At no point was his emotional commitment to the survival and welfare of the German nation more apparent than in January 1924, when he stood watch outside the Wittelsbacher Hof in Speyer as confederates carried out the assassination of Franz Josef Heinz-Orbis, the self-proclaimed president of the "government of the autonomous Palatinate" who enjoyed dangerously close ties to pro-French separatists in the Rhine.[16] With the collapse of the separatist movement and the stabilization of the Weimar Republic in the second half of the

---

1933/34. Jung's wife apparently destroyed potentially compromising material following his arrest on 25 July 1934. On this matter, see the letter from Jung's son-in-law Bernhard Spangenberg to the historian Bernhard Schwertfeger, 7 June 1948, Bundesarchiv Koblenz, Nachlaß Schwertfeger (hereafter cited as BA Koblenz, NL Schwertfeger), 258/39.

12. For the most elaborate statement of Ziegler's philosophy of religion, see L. Ziegler, *Überlieferung* (Leipzig, 1936). For Ziegler's views on politics, see L. Ziegler, *Fünfundzwanzig Sätze vom deutschen Staat* (Darmstadt, 1931).

13. E.J. Jung, *Die geistige Krise des jungen Deutschland. Rede vor der Studentenschaft der Universität München* (Berlin, n.d. [1927]), pp. 12–13.

14. For Jung's most explicit statement to this effect, see his article, "Die christliche Revolution," *Deutsche Rundschau* 59, no. 17 (September 1933): 142–47. See also E.J. Jung, *Die Herrschaft der Minderwertigen, ihr Zerfall und ihre Ablösung durch ein Neues Reich*, 2nd ed. (Berlin, 1930), pp. 55–66, 83–93.

15. For example, see Jung, "Die Tragik der Kriegsgeneration," *Süddeutsche Monatshefte* 27, no. 8 (May 1930): 511–34.

16. For further details, see F. Grass, "Edgar Julius Jung (1894–1934)," *Pfälzer Lebensbilder* 1 (1964): 326–29.

1920s, Jung turned his attention to the young conservative movement that had been launched with such great fanfare by the late Arthur Moeller van den Bruck.[17] At the same time, he cultivated increasingly close ties with paramilitary organizations in Bavaria and other parts of the country in hopes that they might hold the key to the unity of the German Right.[18] By the end of 1927 Jung had also begun to establish contact with influential representatives of the Ruhr industrial elite such as Paul Reusch, Albert Vögler, and Karl Haniel.[19] Jung's most important foray into the realm of practical politics, however, came with his decision to support the ill-fated Conservative People's Party (Konservative Volkspartei) in the summer of 1930, an experience that proved profoundly distasteful and that only intensified his disdain for the parliamentary system of government.[20]

Throughout all of this, Jung's objective was not to facilitate an accommodation between the German Right and the Weimar Republic, but to make certain that this did not take place under conditions that endangered the prospects for a genuine renewal of German political life.[21] What Jung ulti-

---

17. Jung's most important contribution on behalf of the young conservative movement was his role in the founding of a series of young academic clubs throughout the country. These clubs were part of a concerted effort by Germany's conservative leadership to attract the support of university students and young professionals. For a retrospective of Jung's own activity in this regard, see his letter to Pechel, 29 October 1932, NL Klein. See also Pechel to Humann, 2 November 1932, ibid. For Jung's own eulogy on the young conservative movement in the early Weimar Republic, see Jung, "Neubelebung von Weimar?" *Deutsche Rundschau* 58, no. 9 (June 1932): 158–60. For further information on the young conservative movement in the late Weimar Republic, see the recent study by Y. Ishida, *Jungkonservative in der Weimarer Republik. Der Ring-Kreis 1928–1933* (Frankfurt am Main, 1988).

18. On Jung's contacts with the paramilitary Right, see his letters to Rudolf Pechel, 4 and 8 May 1926, NL Klein. For further information, see Jung to Pechel, 28 May and 4 November 1926, BA Koblenz, Nachlaß Pechel (hereafter cited as BA Koblenz, NL Pechel), 76.

19. In this respect, see Jung to Pechel, 12 November 1927 and 21 February 1928, both in BA Koblenz, NL Pechel, 76.

20. For example, see Jung to Oldag, 28 October 1930, NL Jung, IXa. For a more detailed analysis of Jung's involvement in the people's conservative movement at the beginning of the 1930s, see L.E. Jones, "Edgar Julius Jung: The Conservative Revolution in Theory and Practice," *Central European History* 21 (1988): 149–55.

21. For the most candid statement of Jung's long-term political strategy, see his long letter to Ziegler, 21 August 1930, in the Badische Landesbibliothek, Karlsruhe, Handschriften-Abteilung, Nachlaß Leopold Ziegler (hereafter cited as BLB Karlsruhe, NL Ziegler), H390.

mately sought as a solution to the crisis in which Germany currently found itself, as he explained in September 1929 in a particularly candid letter to Eugen Mündler of the *Rheinisch-West-fälische Zeitung*, was "the establishment of a dictatorship."[22] Thus, it was only natural that Jung should also develop an interest in the newly emergent Nazi movement. Jung's assessment of the Nazi party and its leadership, however, was characteristically cool. For although Jung applauded "the healthy activism and positive energies of National Socialism," he regarded the movement as little more than another manifestation of the materialistic liberalism that he had singled out for such biting criticism in *Die Herrschaft der Minderwertigen*. Writing to a close friend in early February 1930, Jung observed:

> Seen historically we have three great forms of irreligious, secular, materialistic liberalism: Manchesterism, which ends in bourgeois democracy; then Marxism, which is nothing but the reverse image of bourgeois democracy; and finally as the third counter-movement – this time directed against the Left – National Socialism. In its own way it is a mixture of the other two. It can be shown not only historically, but also from the intellectual orientation of National Socialism that it is a form of liberalism carried to extremes. . ..

Jung, however, reserved his most bitter remarks for Hitler: "Whoever like myself has closely observed the movement for years certainly knows the aspirations of Adolf Hitler. Aside from his disappointing intellectual format, it is hard to imagine that the German people will ever entrust itself to a man who failed as dismally as Adolf Hitler failed in the November days of 1923."[23]

His disdain for Hitler notwithstanding, Jung could hardly ignore the increasing popularity of the Nazi movement or the implications this held for his own political strategy. Writing to Mündler shortly after the Nazi Party's smashing victory in the state and regional elections that were held throughout much of Germany on 24 April 1932, Jung argued:

> In my opinion, the sooner the National Socialists come to power [*ans Ruder kommen*], so much the better. Then the debacle will not be so immeasurably great or damaging as it most certainly would

22. Jung to the editor-in-chief of the *Rheinisch-Westfälische Zeitung*, 5 September 1929, NL Jung, IXa.
23. Jung to Wiessner, 3 February 1930, NL Jung, O.

be if the Nazis should take control of the government by themselves. What I am suggesting, therefore, is that one must speak to the Nazis firmly [*den Nazi gut anzureden*] and make certain that the problems inherent in allowing the strongest opposition party in Germany to come to power at a time when we are still diplomatically constrained be made abundantly clear.[24]

Jung, therefore, clearly belonged to that sector of Germany's conservative elite that sought to bring the Nazis to power, albeit under conditions that would ensure their subordination to a conservative political agenda. The immediate task was not only to disabuse the Nazis of their dictatorial aspirations[25] but also to dampen the unbridled enthusiasm that certain elements of Germany's conservative establishment – most notably within Ruhr heavy industry – had developed for the person of Adolf Hitler.[26] Although Jung found it difficult to accept Papen's selection as the new chancellor in early June 1932,[27] he strongly supported the hard line that Papen and his minister of interior, Baron Wilhelm von Gayl, took in their subsequent dealings with the Nazi party leadership.[28] In the meantime, Jung continued to chastise Hitler and his associates for their "pseudo-democratic" rhetoric against the Papen government and for their refusal to provide the new government with the support it needed in order to achieve a truly revolutionary solution to the existing state crisis.[29]

These sentiments continued to inform Jung's attitude toward National Socialism at the time of Hitler's appointment as chancellor in January 1933. Although Jung himself had no hand whatsoever in the formation of the new government, he nevertheless felt a strong sense of responsibility for having helped create a situation where Hitler could come to power

24. Jung to Mündler, 7 May 1932, NL Jung, N.

25. For example, see Jung, "Revolutionäre Staatsführung," *Deutsche Rundschau* 59, no. 1 (October 1932): 1–8.

26. For an indication of Jung's concern about elite sympathy for Hitler and the Nazi movement, see Forschbach to Jung, 27 November 1931, NL Jung, X, and Jung to Pechel, 4 April 1932, NL Klein.

27. For Jung's initial reaction to Papen's appointment and the composition of his cabinet, see E. Forschbach, *Edgar Julius Jung. Ein konservativer Revolutionär 30. Juni 1934* (Pfullingen, 1984), pp. 44–45. For later assessments of the Papen chancellorship, see Jung to Humann, 14 November 1932, and Jung to Pechel, 15 November 1932, both in NL Klein.

28. Jung to Pechel, 20 August 1932, NL Klein.

29. Jung, "Deutsche Unzulänglichkeiten," *Deutsche Rundschau* 59, no. 2 (November 1932): 81–86.

and recognized a moral obligation to work for his removal from office. At the same time, Jung was well aware of Papen's political limitations and had severe doubts as to whether or not the new vice chancellor possessed the moral requisites necessary to resist Hitler's relentless drive for power. The only way in which Papen could prevail against the Nazis, Jung explained in a letter to Rudolf Pechel, was for the vice chancellor to surround himself with a wall of conservatives who were every bit as committed to the realization of their beliefs as the Nazis were to the realization of theirs.[30] It was with this in mind that Jung wrote to Papen shortly before the installation of the new government to offer the use of his services as a speech writer and political advisor.[31] At the urging of his close friend and associate Hans Humann, Papen accepted Jung's offer of help and immediately assigned him the task of consolidating the DNVP, Stahlhelm, and other right-wing groups into a united phalanx for the national elections that had been set for the first week of March 1933.[32] At the same time, Jung wrote virtually all of the speeches that Papen delivered during the campaign, using them as a forum for the propagation of his own brand of revolutionary conservatism.[33]

The outcome of the 5 March 1933 Reichstag elections came as a bitter disappointment for Jung and dealt a severe setback to his hopes of channeling the Nazi revolution in a more conservative direction. An even more devastating blow came less than three weeks later when the Reichstag passed the Enabling Act, thereby giving the Hitler cabinet virtually unlimited authority to do whatever it deemed necessary for Germany's national recovery and nullifying whatever influence Papen had been able to exercise within the cabinet by virtue of his special relationship with Hindenburg.[34] It was at

30. Jung to Pechel, 1 February 1933, NL Klein.
31. Jung to Papen, 28 January 1933, NL Klein.
32. Jung to Pechel, 2 February 1933, NL Klein.
33. In this respect, see Jung to Ziegler, 15 March 1933, BLB Karlsruhe, NL Ziegler, H390.
34. For Jung's reaction to the passage of the Enabling Act, see E. Forschbach, "Vier Tage, die Deutschland zum Verhängnis wurden. Meine Erlebnisse und Beobachtungen in Berlin und Potsdam vom 20. bis 23. März 1933," n.d. [1978], Archiv für Christlich-Demokratische Politik, Sankt-Augustin, Nachlaß Edmund Forschbach (hereafter cited as ACDP Sankt-Augustin, NL Forschbach), I–199/014/1, reprinted in K. Repgen, "Ungedruckte Nachkriegsquellen zum Reichskonkordat. Eine Dokumentation," *Historisches Jahrbuch* 99 (1979): 407–13.

this point that Jung established close contact with Herbert von Bose. Bose had just been recruited as Papen's press secretary in the vice chancery by Carl Werner von Jordans,[35] a prominent member of the German Lords' Club (Deutscher Herrenklub) who shared Jung's skepticism regarding Papen's political instincts and abilities.[36] The two men, however, could not have been more fundamentally different in temperament and character. Jung was the brash, young intellectual who harbored the ambition of someday succeeding Hitler as the leader of the new Germany; Bose was a former army intelligence officer who shunned the political limelight in order to carry on the struggle against Hitler behind the scenes. In terms of his political beliefs, Bose believed that monarchy was the form of government best suited to the German national character but evinced little, if any, enthusiasm for a restoration of the Hohenzollern dynasty. Having come to politics through the young conservative movement of the early Weimar Republic, Bose was skeptical of organized party politics and never aspired to a prominent political role during the Weimar Republic. His disdain for party politics notwithstanding, Bose served as an adjutant to DNVP Reichstag deputy Otto Schmidt-Hannover and played a major role in the organizational preparations for the much celebrated meeting of the Harzburg Front in the fall of 1931.[37]

For all their differences, Jung and Bose were united by their deep contempt for the Hitler regime and by an abiding com-

35. Hans Wedepohl, "Erinnerungen an den 30. Juni 1934," Sammlung Bose. The author would like to express his gratitude to Herbert von Bose's son, Heinz-Jürgen von Bose, for having granted access to the materials that he has collected on his father's political career and death. This collection is referred to here and elsewhere as the Sammlung Bose. After his death Bose's personal papers were entrusted to Josef März, a professor of journalism, but according to Bose's son they were lost in the course of März's flight from Prague after the end of the Second World War.

36. For Jordans's view of Papen, see his letter to Baron Hermann von Lüninck, 14 September 1932, Nachlaß Ferdinand von Lüninck. The author would like to express his appreciation to Baron Gottfried von Lüninck for having granted him access to the papers of his uncle, Baron Ferdinand von Lüninck.

37. Josef März, biographical notes on Herbert von Bose, n.d. [ca. 1953–55], Sammlung Bose. März was Bose's close friend, and the notes he prepared for a biography of Bose remain the most detailed source of information historians have on his political views and activities. Without independent corroboration, it is difficult to determine just how accurate these notes are. Several important points relating to Bose's affiliation with the DNVP have been contested by former Bose associates. For example, see Forschbach to Bauch, 8 October 1970, ACDP Sankt-Augustin, NL Forschbach, I–199/005/5.

mitment to do whatever they could to mitigate its excesses. If Jung was the theoretician of the conservative opposition to Hitler, Bose was one of its chief practitioners. But whereas Jung sought the public spotlight, Bose preferred to work behind the scenes. One of his favorite stratagems was to use his position as Papen's press secretary to leak news of impending action against an individual or organization in hopes that this would prevent that action from taking place. This ploy proved so successful that the German ambassador in London filed an official complaint about the steady stream of unauthorized antigovernment reports that were appearing in *The Week*, a London tabloid edited by the future Irish press magnate, Claud Cockburn.[38] At the same time, Bose helped provide Jews who felt threatened by Nazi racial policies with safe passage abroad.[39] But Bose's most important asset was his access to potential opponents of the regime in the German officer corps. As a former army officer whose father-in-law was a retired artillery general, Bose enjoyed a wide range of contacts within the German officer corps and served as a liaison between the anti-Nazi activists at the vice chancery and potential sympathizers at the upper echelons of the German military establishment. The fact that the commander-in-chief of the German army, Baron Kurt von Hammerstein-Equord, as well as his successor, Baron Werner von Fritsch, were both critics of the Nazi regime only enhanced the significance of these contacts.[40]

As it became increasingly clear during the course of 1933 that Papen and the other conservatives in the Hitler cabinet had failed to prevent the establishment of a one-party Nazi

38. For the details of this arrangement, see Alex Nathan, "Nach 25 Jahren: Unveröffentlichte Erinnerungen an dem 30. Juni 1934," n.d. [1959], Sammlung Bose.

39. The collection of materials that Heinz-Jürgen von Bose has compiled on his father's political activities contains at least two testimonials from Jews whom Herbert von Bose helped escape from Germany in 1933/34.

40. There is no documentary evidence of contacts between Bose and Hammerstein, Fritsch, or any other high-ranking military officer. The fact that both Hammerstein and Fritsch were highly critical of the Nazi regime, however, is beyond dispute. For further information, see H. Foertsch, *Schuld und Verhängnis. Die Fritsch-Krise im Frühjahr 1938 als Wendepunkt in der Geschichte der nationalsozialistischen Zeit* (Stuttgart, 1951), pp. 26–42; as well as the authoritative study of the army's relations to the Nazi state by K.-J. Müller, *Das Heer und Hitler. Armee und nationalsozialistisches Regime 1933–1940* (Stuttgart, 1969), pp. 34–141, esp. 53–60, 77–78, 102–3.

dictatorship, and that Hindenburg himself could no longer be counted upon to hold Hitler in check, Jung and Bose began to lay the foundation for a broadly-based coalition of conservative forces that, they hoped, could ultimately depose the Nazi regime and seize the reins of power for itself. In this respect, Jung and his associates hoped to turn the dissatisfaction with the Nazi regime that had become increasingly pronounced since the summer of 1933 to their own political advantage. From their perspective, three factors gave their efforts to depose the Nazi regime at least a minimal chance of success. In the first place, the agitation of Ernst Röhm and the leaders of the Storm Troopers (Sturmabteilungen or SA) for a "second revolution" and the prospect of a second wave of SA terror had given rise to growing uneasiness within the ranks of Germany's conservative elites. Second, Germany's military leadership was justifiably alarmed over Röhm's plans for the Reichswehr's absorption into a "people's army" with himself at its head. And third, the Catholic clergy and influential lay Catholics had become increasingly disillusioned with the fruits of the concordat that Germany had concluded with the Holy See in the summer of 1933 and were anxious to redefine the terms of their church's relationship with the Nazi state. All these factors combined to create a sense of growing uneasiness not only on the part of the Nazi party leadership but throughout the country as a whole.[41]

Relations between Hitler and the SA leadership had become increasingly strained since the summer of 1933, when the Nazi party leader intervened to put an end to the revolutionary turmoil that had accompanied the Nazi seizure of power and the destruction of the hated "Weimar system." Speaking at a conference of Nazi Reich governors (*Reichsstatthalter*) on 6 July 1933, Hitler took an important step toward reassuring Germany's conservative elites by informing his subordinates that the Nazi revolution had achieved its most important objectives with the dismantling of Germany's republican institutions, and that the revolution had now entered a phase where

41. For an excellent source of information on the growing unrest in Germany in the spring of 1934, see the reports from the spring and early summer of 1934 in *Deutschland-Berichte der SOPADE* 1, no. 1 (17 May 1934): 9–22; and no. 2 (26 June 1934): 99–122, 164–74. See also H. Krausnick, "Der 30. Juni 1934. Bedeutung – Hintergründe – Verlauf," *Aus Politik und Zeitgeschichte. Beilage zur Wochenzeitung "Das Parlament"* 3, no. 25 (30 June 1954): 317–24.

the immediate task was to consolidate its gains legally and peacefully.[42] In the wake of this announcement, schemes for the corporatist reorganization of the national economy were put on hold, while the powers of the special commissars (*Sonderkommissare*) that had been appointed to oversee this process were summarily revoked.[43] Hitler's decision to terminate the Nazi revolution before it touched the economic sphere came as a bitter disappointment to the leaders of the SA and dealt a severe blow to their hopes for a more radical redistribution of wealth and property that would rectify the social inequities of the capitalist economic order. For their own part, Röhm and his associates were quick to reaffirm the revolutionary élan of the SA and to remind Hitler that without their activism the movement could never have come to power.[44] Röhm's own frustration over this turn of events became increasingly apparent when in the spring of 1934 he began to suggest that the Nazi revolution had not yet run its course and that there was still much to be done before the true aims of National Socialism had been achieved.[45]

Precisely what Röhm meant by all this remained unclear. Still, the specter of a "second revolution" with all that implied

42. Hitler's remarks at a conference of Nazi Reich governors, 6 July 1933, in *Die Akten der Reichskanzlei: Die Regierung Hitler. 30. Januar bis 31. August 1933. 12. September 1933 bis 31. August 1934*, ed. K.-H. Minuth, 2 vols. (Boppard am Rhein, 1983), vol. 1, pp. 629–36.

43. In this respect, see the memorandum by Herle of the National Estate of German Industry (Reichsstand der Deutschen Industrie) on a telephone conversation with Feder, 6 July 1933, Historisches Archiv Krupp, Essen, FAH 4 E 193; and the circular from Frick to the Reich governors and state governments, 10 July 1933, Berlin Document Center (hereafter cited as BDC), Abteilung Research, vol. 272 (Sonderkommissare 1933/34). For further information on the fate of Nazi corporatism in the early Third Reich, see R. Rämisch, "Der berufsständische Gedanke als Episode in der nationalsozialistischen Politik," *Zeitschrift für Politik* 4 (1957): 262–72; as well as the more detailed treatments of this problem by G. Schulz, "Die Anfänge des totalitären Maßnahmenstaates," in Bracher, Sauer, and Schulz, *Die nationalsozialistische Machtergreifung*, pp. 627–41; and A. Barkai, *Das Wirtschaftssystem des Nationalsozialismus. Der historische und ideologische Hintergund 1933–1936* (Cologne, 1977), pp. 92–109.

44. E. Röhm, "S.A. und deutsche Revolution," *Nationalsozialistische Monatshefte* 4, no. 39 (June 1933): 251–54.

45. For the most explicit statement of the SA's revolutionary mission, see E. Röhm, *Die nationalsozialistische Revolution und die SA. Rede vor dem Diplomatischen Korps und der Auslandspresse in Berlin am 18. April 1934* (Berlin, n.d. [1934]), esp. pp. 3–11. See also the report of Röhm's speech to a SA contingent from the Rhein and Ruhr in *Der S.A.-Mann*, 7 April 1934, no. 14. For further information, see H. Mau, "Die 'Zweite Revolution' – Der 30. Juni 1934," *Vierteljahrshefte für Zeitgeschichte* 1 (1953): 119–37.

in terms of a second wave of SA terror sent shock waves through the ranks of Germany's conservative elites. At the same time, it posed a clear and immediate threat to Hitler's alliance with the leaders of the Reichswehr, whose lack of enthusiasm for the goals of the Nazi revolution had provoked Röhm's public scorn on more than one occasion.[46] Relations between the Reichswehr and SA were further soured by Röhm's determination to transform the latter into a national militia into which the Reichswehr would presumably be absorbed. Röhm's plans encountered outright rejection from the leaders of the Reichswehr and would no doubt have done irreparable damage to Hitler's domestic political standing had he seen fit to proceed with their implementation. Under heavy pressure from Germany's military leadership, Hitler managed to broker an agreement with Röhm in late February 1934 whereby the SA would henceforth confine its activities to border defense and premilitary education, while the Reichswehr would form the backbone of the new national army that Hitler planned to build up over the course of the next four to eight years.[47] Röhm, however, had no intention of living up to the terms of this agreement and immediately began to subvert it by providing his units with the most sophisticated weaponry he could procure on the international arms market. As Röhm and his associates continued to ignore the terms of the February accord through the spring and early summer of 1934, relations between Hitler and the Reichswehr deteriorated to the point where it was no longer inconceivable that the leaders of Germany's military establishment might join Jung and Bose in their efforts to overthrow the regime if Hitler did not take action to restore his authority over the mutinous SA leadership.[48]

46. For example, see E. Röhm, *Warum SA? Rede vor dem Diplomatischen Korps am 7. Dezember 1933 zu Berlin* (Berlin, n.d. [1933]), esp. pp. 10–12.

47. For the terms of this agreement, see text of a proposal drafted by Beck on 27 February 1934, reprinted in K.-J. Müller, *Armee und Drittes Reich 1933–1939. Darstellung und Dokumentation* (Paderborn, 1987), pp. 192–95. See also the report of Hitler's speech before Germany's military leadership on 28 February 1934 in the unpublished memoirs of Maxmillian von Weichs, Bundesarchiv-Militärarchiv, Freiburg in Breisgau, Nachlaß Weichs (hereafter cited as BA-MA Freiburg, NL Weichs), N19/5/12.

48. On the crisis in Hitler's relations between the military in 1933/34, see Müller, *Heer und Hitler*, pp. 81–100; and H. Krausnick, "Zum militärischen Widerstand gegen Hitler 1933–1938. Möglichkeiten, Ansätze, Grenzen und Kontroversen," in *Aufstand des Gewissens. Der militärische Widerstand gegen Hitler und das NS-Regime 1933–1945*, ed. Militärgeschichtliches Forschungamt (Herford and Bonn, 1984), pp. 311–64.

The dangers that confronted the Nazi regime in the spring of 1934 were compounded by a crisis in its relations with the Catholic church. In July 1933 the Vatican had concluded a concordat with the German state on the assumption that this would insulate the church and its ancillary organizations from the threat of repression at the hands of state and party officials.[49] The conclusion of the concordat was Papen's most important achievement as vice chancellor and represented an important component of his strategy as protector, or *Schirmherr*, of the Association of Catholic Germans (Arbeitsgemeinschaft Katholischer Deutscher or AKD) to reconcile Germany's twenty million Catholics to the new Nazi state.[50] By early 1934, however, it had become clear to Germany's Catholic leaders that the regime had no intention of extending the protection the concordat afforded the church to ancillary organizations such as the Cartel of Catholic German Student Associations (Cartellverband der katholischen deutschen Studentenverbindungen or CV) or the League of Catholic Young Men (Katholischer Jungmännerverband).[51] Church officials protested vigorously against the efforts of state and party officials to undermine the integrity of these organizations and to place them under the control of their Nazi counterparts. As these protests fell upon deaf ears, many of the Catholic conservatives who had felt inclined to support the new government following its installation in office became increasingly disaffected. In the meantime, Catholic activists who were opposed to the regime began to gravitate more and more into the orbit of the Catholic Action (Katholische Aktion).[52]

49. For further details, see K. Scholder, *The Churches and the Third Reich*, vol. 1: *Preliminary History and the Time of Illusion, 1918–1934*, trans. by J. Bowden (Philadelphia, Pa., 1988), pp. 381–413.

50. For Papen's defense of the concordat at the third sociological congress of the German Academics' Association (Deutscher Akademikerverband) at Maria Laach, 23 July 1933, see Papen, "Zum Reichskonkordat," *Der katholische Gedanke. Eine Vierteljahrsschrift* 6 (1933): 331–35. For a fuller statement of Papen's general strategy with respect to Germany's Catholic population, see F. von Papen, *Der 12. November und die deutschen Katholiken. Rede gehalten vor der Arbeitsgemeinschaft katholischer Deutscher in der Messehalle zu Köln am 9. November 1933* (Münster, 1934).

51. On the situation within the Cartel of Catholic Student Associations, see Forschbach's letters to Brand, 17 December 1948, and to Franken, 19 May 1949, both in ACDP Sankt-Augustin, NL Forschbach, I–199/012/3.

52. K. Scholder, *The Churches and the Third Reich*, vol. 2: *The Year of Disillusionment: 1934 Barmen and Rome*, trans. by J. Bowden (Philadelphia, Pa., 1988), pp. 89–121.

The Catholic Action had originated in Italy in the early 1920s. Established on the initiative of Pope Pius XI, the Catholic Action sought to unite Catholic laymen without regard for party affiliation or social background into a cohesive political force dedicated to infusing public life with the apostolic spirit of the Roman Catholic Church. The organization was first established in Germany in late 1928 through the efforts of the Papal Nuncio Eugenio Pacelli and Cardinal Adolf Bertram, archbishop of Breslau and chairman of the Fulda Bishops' Conference (Fuldaer Bischofskonferenz).[53] With Hitler's installation as chancellor and the dissolution of the German Center Party (Deutsche Zentrumspartei) six months later, the Catholic Action became a refuge for Catholics who rejected the totalitarian claims of the Nazi state and were distrustful of Papen's efforts to facilitate a reconciliation between Catholicism and the German state under the auspices of the Association of Catholic Germans.[54] The leading figure in the Catholic Action in 1933/34 was Erich Klausener, a former Centrist who had served at the Prussian ministry of interior before moving over to the Reich transportation ministry in the spring of 1933. Although Klausener had originally greeted the Nazi seizure of power with a sense of relief and a willingness to wait and see what the new government could do in the various areas where vigorous and effective action was required, he became increasingly disenchanted with the regime following the dissolution of the Catholic Workers' Associations (Katholische Arbeitervereine) and other Catholic labor organizations in the summer of 1933.[55] On the other hand, it seems highly unlikely that Klausener had managed to

53. On the establishment of the Catholic Action in Germany, see A. Bertram, *Im Geiste und Dienste der Katholischen Aktion. Aus meinem Sinnen und Sorgen vom Wirken im Reich des Königs Christus* (Munich, 1929), esp. the letter from Pius XI to Bertram, 13 November 1928, pp. 9–14. For further information on the goals of the Catholic Action, see P. Muckermann, *Katholische Aktion* (Munich, n.d. [1928/29]).

54. On the goals of the Catholic Action after the Nazi seizure of power, see E. Bolz, "Katholische Aktion und Politik," n.d., in *Christentum und Politik. Dokumente des Widerstands. Zum 40. JahAestag der Hinrichtung des Zentrumspolitikers und Staatspräsidenten Eugen Bolz am 23. Januar 1945*, ed. J. Köhler (Sigmaringen, 1985), pp. 23–57.

55. On the details of Klausener's life and political career, see W. Adolph, *Erich Klausener* (Berlin, 1955), esp. pp. 20–25, 73–88.

establish contact with Jung, Bose, and the anti-Nazi activists in the vice chancery.[56]

The specter of an impending SA rebellion, the crisis in the regime's relations with the Reichswehr, and the increasing disaffection of Germany's Catholic population combined to create a highly volatile situation that provided Jung, Bose, and the anti-Nazi activists in the vice chancery with the opportunity for which they had been waiting. In December 1933 Jung began to reestablish contacts with his former patrons in the German conservative establishment in anticipation of a conservative renaissance that, he hoped, would bring the German revolution to its natural and necessary culmination.[57] Over the course of the next six months, Jung and his associates proceeded to establish contact with a broad cross section of Germany's conservative elite[58] that included former Stahlhelm leader Theodor Duesterberg,[59] elements of the Catholic aristocracy in Bavaria,[60] influential conservative journalists such as Fritz Klein, Paul Fechtner, and Rudolf Pechel,[61] retired conservative politicians such as Heinrich Brüning and G. R. Treviranus,[62]

56. Ibid., pp. 99–100. See also E. Forschbach, "Ein Erlebnisbericht aus den Jahren 1931–1939," Bundesarchiv Koblenz, Kleine Erwerbung 345 (hereafter cited as BA Koblenz, Kl.Erw. 345), p. 25.

57. In this respect, see the excerpt from an undated letter from Jung to Reusch, appended to a letter from Reusch to Springorum, 12 January 1934, Haniel-Archiv, Duisburg, Nachlaß Paul Reusch (hereafter cited as Haniel-Archiv, NL Reusch), 400101290/36b.

58. It is extremely difficult to reconstruct the full range of contacts that Jung and other members of the vice chancery developed in the second half of 1933 and first half of 1934. For the most detailed analysis of Jung's activities during this period, see Grass, "Jung, Papenkreis und Röhmkrise," pp. 199–212. See also the recollections by two of Jung's closest associates, R. Pechel, *Deutscher Widerstand* (Erlenbach-Zurich, 1947), pp. 75–77, and Forschbach, *Jung*, pp. 83–104; as well as Tschirschky, *Erinnerungen*, pp. 102–05, 154–55.

59. T. Duesterberg, *Der Stahlhelm und Hitler* (Wolfenbüttel and Hanover, 1949), pp. 74–75.

60. On the reaction of the Bavarian aristocracy to the end of the Weimar Republic and the establishment of the Third Reich, see K.O. von Aretin, "Der bayerische Adel. Von der Monarchie zum Dritten Reich," in *Bayern in der NS-Zeit*, ed. M. Broszat, E. Fröhlich, and A. Grossman, 6 vols. (Munich and Vienna, 1977–83), vol. 3, pp. 513–67.

61. In this respect, see P. Fechtner, *Menschen und Zeiten. Begegnungen aus fünf Jahrzehnten* (Gütersloh, 1948), pp. 358–65; and Pechel, *Widerstand*, pp. 75–78, 281–82.

62. Pechel, *Widerstand*, p. 77. See also Brünning's confused and somewhat unreliable account of his relationship to Jung and the anti-Nazi conspiracy in the first years of the Third Reich in his letter to Theodor Draper, November 1947, in H. Brüning, *Briefe und Gespräche 1934–1945*, ed. C. Nix (Stuttgart, 1974), pp. 26–27, n. 10. For Treviranus's equally unreliable account of these events, see G.R. Treviranus, *Für Deutschland in Exil* (Düsseldorf, 1973), pp. 9–29.

and disgruntled senior army officers such as Fritsch, Gerd von Rundstedt, and Erwin von Witzleben.[63] Jung was also able to enlist the support of Paul Reusch, Fritz Springorum, and influential members of the Ruhr industrial establishment, who in January 1934 agreed to underwrite his efforts with a monthly subsidy of 500 marks.[64] Jung even met with ex-chancellor Schleicher on at least one occasion in the spring of 1934 to pass on the contents of a secret memorandum he had drafted for Papen on the foreign policy objectives of the anti-Nazi conspiracy.[65] In return, Schleicher agreed to use his influence within the Reichswehr to undermine the army's support of Hitler and dispatched another of Jung's associates, newspaper correspondent Franz Mariaux, to Paris with a copy of this memorandum in hopes that it might dispel whatever reservations the French might have about a possible military strike against the Nazi regime.[66] By no means, however, did Jung confine his efforts to Germany's conservative elite. To the contrary, Jung realized that his efforts required at least a modicum of popular support if they were to stand any chance of success and thus began to cultivate close ties with former activists in the Christian labor movement as well as with prominent lay Catholics and leaders of the Catholic clergy.[67]

Throughout all this, Papen had little, if any, direct knowledge of what Jung, Bose, and their confederates in the vice chancery were trying to pull off. In fact, Jung and his associates were by no means certain that they could count on Papen's cooperation, particularly in light of the vice chancellor's blindness to Hitler's political and moral deficiencies. In

63. Tschirschky, *Erinnerungen*, p. 155.

64. Springorum to Reusch, 22 February 1934, Haniel-Archiv, NL Reusch, 400101290/36b. A further indication of Reusch's close association with Jung in the summer of 1934 is the letter that he had his representative in Berlin, Martin Blank, deliver to Jung by hand in mid-June 1934. See Reusch to Blank, 15 June 1934, Haniel-Archiv, NL Reusch, 4001012924/12. No copy of Reusch's letter has survived.

65. Schleicher to Moysischewitz, 16 April 1934, quoted in its entirety in Forschbach, *Jung*, p. 105.

66. Forschbach, "Erlebnisbericht," BA Koblenz, Kl.Erw. 345, p. 15. For further information on Schleicher's activities in the spring and early summer of 1934, see Heinrich Schnee, "Die Ereignisse des 30. Juni 1934," Geheimes Staatsarchiv Berlin-Dahlem, Nachlaß Schnee, Mappe 25, Vorgang 86, pp. 36–42.

67. On Jung's contacts with Christian labor leaders, see the memorandum on "Der Düsseldorfer Widerstandskreis" by Walter Hensel, n.d., reprinted in *Verfolgung und Widerstand 1933–1945. Christliche Demokraten gegen Hitler*, ed. G. Buchstab, B. Kaff, and H.-O. Kleinmann (Düsseldorf, 1986), pp. 235–36.

an attempt to rectify this situation, Jung arranged for Papen to meet with Leopold Ziegler, his former teacher and mentor, during the course of a trip the vice chancellor was scheduled to take to southern Italy in early April 1934.[68] Papen was apparently impressed by an article that Ziegler had recently published in Pechel's *Deutsche Rundschau*, thus suggesting to Jung that by bringing the two together it might be possible "to open Papen's eyes about Hitler."[69] But the meeting, which took place in Sorrento on 9 April, seems to have made a much greater impression upon Ziegler than Papen and produced no appreciable change in the vice chancellor's attitude toward Hitler. Not only did Papen remain impervious to Ziegler's criticism of Hitler's character, but he defended his own role in the formation of the Hitler cabinet by blaming everything on the Reichswehr and its plans to force Hindenburg's removal from the presidency if he did not appoint the Nazi leader as chancellor. For Jung, the meeting in Sorrento proved a disappointing failure and definitively dashed whatever hopes he might have had of enlisting Papen in the anti-Hitler resistance.[70]

Shortly after the fateful meeting in Sorrento, Jung provided Papen with a lengthy memorandum on the goals of the anti-Hitler resistance. Here Jung went beyond reciting the by now all too familiar litany of neoconservative complaints against the liberal, democratic, and Marxist legacies of the French Revolution to pose the issue in terms that made it seem as if the very future of white supremacy throughout the world depended upon the outcome of the struggle for a Christian-conservative regeneration of European culture. The survival not merely of Germany but of Europe itself, Jung insisted, depended upon the creation of a new social order based upon the organic bonding of the individual to state and society. Jung, however, was careful to distinguish what he had in mind from fascism in either its Italian or German variant. For while the establishment of a more organic social order necessarily

68. For further details, see Jung to Ziegler, 26 and 28 March 1934, both in BLB Karlsruhe, NL Ziegler, H390.

69. Ziegler to Binswanger, 10 April 1951, in L. Ziegler, *Briefe 1901–1958* (Munich, 1963), pp. 209–10.

70. For a full account of this meeting, see L. Ziegler, "Edgar Jung: Denkmal und Vermächtnis," *Berliner Hefte für Geistiges Leben* 4 (1949): 125–27. See also Forschbach, *Jung*, pp. 104–5.

presupposed the dissolution of the liberal party state, Jung dismissed the dictatorial rule of a single party such as National Socialism as a temporary expedient that had far more in common with the democratic trappings of the liberal era than it did with Germany's future political development. In other words, the Nazi party should follow the example of the other political parties and dissolve itself in order to create a state truly without parties. By far the most interesting feature of Jung's memorandum, however, was his plan for an end to the European nation state and the establishment of a new European order characterized by the dispersal of centralized power more or less along the lines of the medieval German Empire. In this respect, Jung proposed the introduction an elective monarchy (*Wahlmonarchie*) and the appointment of an imperial regent who would serve as a symbol of central European unity, and whose sovereignty would embrace not only Germany but the territories of the former Habsburg Empire as well.[71]

Jung's memorandum from April 1934 was a truly remarkable document that revealed the essentially utopian, though nonetheless reactionary, impulse that lay at the heart of his political vision. In retrospect, its most astonishing – or perhaps most visionary – feature was its reassessment of the nation state and its place in the future world order. For Jung, like few of his compatriots, had come to realize just how volatile a force nationalism was and just how easy it had been for demagogues such as Hitler to manipulate genuine national feeling for the most insidious of purposes. Jung's proposal for the reconstruction of Europe as a decentralized federation of independent states struck directly at the aggressive character of Nazi nationalism and was designed to reassure recipients of the memorandum in France and other European countries that they had nothing to fear from the conservative revolutionaries who sought to remove Hitler from office.[72] All this represented the culmination of a remarkable political transforma-

71. "Denkschrift Edg. Jungs an Papen, verfasst im April 1934," ACDP Sankt Augustin, NL Forschbach, I–199/014/2. A copy of this document has also been deposited by Jung's associate, Franz Mariaux, in the archives of the Institut für Zeitgeschichte, Munich, FA 98, 2375/59.

72. A copy of this memorandum was taken by Franz Mariaux, the Paris correspondent of the Ullstein press, to France, where it was to have been given to French government authorities in the event that the strike against Hitler succeeded. The Vatican also received a copy of this memorandum. See Forschbach, *Jung*, pp. 105–06.

tion for Jung. Jung, after all, had begun his political career as a terrorist whose dedication to the preservation of German national unity had involved him in at least one act of political assassination. Now he had come to distrust the forces he had once served and sought ways of harnessing them before they led Europe to the brink of self-destruction. Moreover, this was accompanied by Jung's conversion to a species of Christian universalism that stressed the primacy of the shared spiritual values lying at the heart of European culture and rejected the racial and *völkisch* exclusivity that found such powerful expression in the ideology of National Socialism.[73]

Jung's memorandum from April 1934 was supposed to serve as a program of action for Jung and his confederates in the vice chancery. Still, the precise mechanism by which Jung and his associates proposed to translate this program into action remained uncertain. Until late May 1934 Jung seems to have believed that the only way in which he and his associates could achieve their objectives was by assassinating Hitler. As a Calvinist who had fully assimilated the classical arguments for tyrannicide into his own political ethos, Jung was not constrained by the same religious scruple that those of a Catholic or Lutheran background might have felt. After all, Jung had already played an instrumental role in the assassination of Heinz-Orbis in January 1924 and was by all accounts fully prepared to do so again. Moreover, Jung's responsibilities as Papen's personal adjutant often brought him into close physical proximity to the Nazi leader and therefore provided him with ample opportunity to carry out the assassination himself. Jung, therefore, seems to have been fairly strongly committed to assassinating Hitler until 21 May 1934, when during the course of a long conversation with Ziegler he was dissuaded from such a course of action by the argument that complicity in Hitler's murder would almost certainly disqualify him from a leading role in the new Germany that was to emerge from

73. This becomes a persistent theme in Jung's later writings and speeches. For example, see E.J. Jung, *Sinndeutung der deutschen Revolution* (Oldenburg, 1933), pp. 78–103; as well as the fragmentary manuscript of an article entitled "Aussonderung oder Einschmelzung" from the fall of 1933, NL Jung, Ib; and the typescript of a lecture on "Die Sinndeutung der konservativen Revolution in Deutschland" that Jung delivered at the University of Zurich on 7 February 1934, NL Jung, VIII. For further information, see K. Breuning, *Die Vision des Reiches. Deutscher Katholizismus zwischen Demokratie und Diktatur (1929–1934)* (Munich, 1969), pp. 107–13.

the shambles of the Nazi dictatorship.[74] At this point, Jung and his confederates fell back upon an alternative plan that had also been under discussion for the past several months. Here the idea was to mobilize the conservative resistance to Hitler by means of a speech that Papen would make at some point in the near future, presumably in Berlin. This speech would provide Germany's military leadership with the pretext it needed for impressing upon Reich President Hindenburg, by now in rapidly failing heath, the need for quick, decisive action if the descent into total anarchy was to be avoided. Thus assured of Hindenburg's support, the Reichswehr would take action not only to suppress the SA mutiny before it had begun to materialize but also to put an end to Nazi rule.[75]

Jung remained deeply skeptical of the military's political reliability and was not at all certain it could be counted on to support him and his associates in the event of a final showdown with Hitler and the leaders of the Nazi state.[76] Nevertheless, he continued to work on the draft of a speech that Papen had been invited to deliver before the faculty and student body of the University of Marburg on 17 June 1934 in hopes that it might serve as the signal for the long-awaited conservative revolution. That Jung was the author of Papen's Marburg speech is now beyond question. For not only did Jung incorporate significant segments of his April memorandum into the text of the speech, but he read drafts of it to other close associates before ever giving it to Papen.[77] Moreover, it is unlikely that the vice chancellor ever saw the text of the speech until after he had boarded the train that was to take him to Marburg. As it was, Papen was alarmed at some of the things the speech contained and tried to make some last-

74. See Leopold Ziegler's account of his conversation with Jung, 21 May 1934, in Ziegler, "Jung: Denkmal und Vermächtnis," pp. 125–35. An entry in Ziegler's appointment calendar for 21 May 1934 confirms that Jung met with Ziegler on that day but provides no indication of what they may have discussed. See BLB Karlsruhe, NL Ziegler, K3046/F23. Jung's plans to assassinate Hitler have been independently confirmed by Forschbach, *Jung*, pp. 110–13; and F. Mariaux, "Herr von Papen und Dr. Edgar Jung," *Rheinische Zeitung* (Westausgabe), 15 February 1947, a typescript of which is to be found along with accompanying correspondence in BA Koblenz, NL Schwertfeger, 256/52–57.

75. The details of Jung's strategy are spelled out most elaborately in Tschirschky, *Erinnerungen*, pp. 172–79. See also Forschbach, *Jung*, pp. 113–15.

76. Ziegler, "Jung: Denkmal und Vermächtnis," pp. 127–30.

77. Tschirschky, *Erinnerungen*, pp. 164–72.

minute changes in the text before being dissuaded from doing so on the grounds that it had already been released to the foreign press.[78] Papen's concern was well-founded, for the speech, its occasional panegyrics to Hitler notwithstanding, represented a frontal assault upon the legitimacy of the Nazi regime and drew attention to the discrepancies between the promise and practice of the German revolution. Among other things, the speech chided the Nazis for not having liquidated their own party as part of the more general liquidation of the Weimar party state.[79] At the same time, the speech played upon the anxieties that rumors of an impending "second revolution" had caused throughout the German populace.

> Whoever plays so irresponsibly with such ideas [of a second revolution] should not forget that a second wave can easily be followed by a third, that whoever threatens to use the guillotine is most likely to come under its blade. . .. No people can tolerate a permanent rebellion from below if it wants to stand before the bar of history. . .. If therefore a second wave of new life is to pass through the German revolution, then [it will come] not as a social revolution, but as the creative consummation of the work already begun.[80]

As Papen's press secretary, Bose had already taken steps to insure that the Marburg speech received the widest possible circulation.[81] Suddenly the blemishes of the Nazi regime were out in the open, and it seemed only a matter of time until either the Reich President or the Reichswehr would have to intervene in order to check Germany's drift into chaos. But Papen, upon whom so much depended, failed to act and allowed the advantage of the moment to slip from his grasp. Summoned to Hitler for two meetings on 18 and 19 June, Papen offered to resign from the government in order to spare it further embarrassment and ordered that circulation of the Marburg speech be immediately halted.[82] Papen's obsequiousness vis-à-vis Hitler was compounded by Hindenburg's inac-

78. Forschbach, *Jung*, pp. 114–15.

79. F. von Papen, *Rede des Vizekanzlers von Papen vor dem Universitätsbund Marburg 17. Juni 1934* (Berlin, n.d. [1934]), p. 9.

80. Ibid., pp. 14–15.

81. Tschirschky, *Erinnerungen*, p. 171.

82. In this respect, see Papen, "Befehl an das Haus!," 18 June 1934, Bundesarchiv Koblenz, records of the vice chancery, Bestand R 53, 49/28; as well as Papen to Hitler, 27 June 1934, Bundesarchiv Koblenz, records of the records of Hitler's personal adjutant, Bestand R 10 (hereafter cited as BA Koblenz, R 10), 50/15–16.

Larry Eugene Jones

cessibility and the indecisiveness of the Reichswehr, whose leaders refused to act without a direct order from the Reich President.[83] The net effect of all this was to deprive Jung, Bose, and their confederates of whatever advantage they had hoped to gain from the initial wave of excitement over Papen's Marburg speech. In the meantime, Hitler found himself under increasingly heavy pressure from elements within his own movement to clean up "the nest of reactionaries" at the vice chancery. Speaking at a party rally in Berlin on 21 June, Reich Propaganda Minister Joseph Goebbels lashed out against the "clique of critics" who were sewing discord throughout the land and who sought to undo the great work of national reconstruction on the eve of its completion.[84] These sentiments were repeated three days later when Rudolf Heß, Hitler's personal secretary and the deputy leader of the Nazi party organization, ridiculed "those from the day before yesterday [*die ewig Vorgestrigen*]" who thought that National Socialism could be replaced by a monarchy or by the leadership of "respectable conservative forces [*bewährte konservative Kräfte*]," and warned party idealists that they were simply playing into the reactionaries' hands with their agitation for a "second revolution."[85] All this represented part of a concerted campaign to counter the effect of Papen's Marburg speech and to set the stage for a strike against the "reactionaries" who had had the temerity to challenge Nazi rule.

The uneasiness the Nazi elite experienced in the early summer of 1934 was fueled by a further deterioration of the regime's relationship with the Catholic church. Direct negotiations between the German foreign office and the Vatican over just how the Catholic youth movement and Catholic student organizations were to be affected by the concordat had broken down in April 1934.[86] This was to be followed by a second round of negotiations later that summer, though this time between the Reich ministry of the interior and a three-man

83. See the memorandum by Fritsch, 1 February 1938, reprinted in its entirety in F. Hoßbach, *Zwischen Wehrmacht und Hitler, 1934–1938*, 2nd ed. (Göttingen, 1965), pp. 59–62.
84. *Deutsche Allgemeine Zeitung*, 22 June 1934, no. 285.
85. R. Heß, *Reden* (Munich, 1938), pp. 27–28.
86. In this respect, see Buttmann's report from Rome, 9–19 April 1934, in *Dokumente zur Kirchenpolitik des Dritten Reiches*, ed. C. Nicolaisen, 2 vols. (Munich, 1971–75), vol. 2, pp. 96–108. For further details, see Scholder, *Churches and the Third Reich*, vol. 2, pp. 89–121.

490

delegation appointed by the German bishops and headed by Wilhelm Berning, Bishop of Osnabrück.[87] In preparation for the resumption of negotiations with the German governments in late June, the German bishops drafted a pastoral letter that was to be published in church newsletters and read from the pulpit throughout the country on 1 July. This letter constituted a direct attack upon Nazi claims of spiritual primacy and accused the regime of fostering a neo-pagan crusade against more than a thousand years of Christian culture in Germany. More importantly, the letter reaffirmed the church's position that all morality was derived from the commandments of God and that no oath of loyalty could require the Christian to perform an act that was contrary to God's law. At the same time, the letter defended the church's right to take a stand in defense of religious principle and categorically denied charges that this constituted a violation of the pledge the church had taken to abstain from all political activity.[88]

This letter, which was drafted in the course of a three-day conference at the beginning of June, represented a courageous departure from the timid course of action the bishops had followed ever since the Nazi seizure of power. The church, it would seem, was about to take a public stand in defense of the principles it held dear and to break openly with the regime in those areas where differences seemed irreconcilable. The government, however, caught wind of this letter before it could be released to the public and entered into direct negotiations with the church hierarchy to prevent it from being read from the pulpit as originally planned. These negotiations ran parallel to those that were already under way on the future of the Catholic youth and student organizations, and church officials were apparently prepared to back down in the matter of the pastoral letter in return for the government's willingness to relent in its demands that these organizations be "coordinated" into their Nazi counterparts.[89] Neither of these issues, however, had been resolved when the Berlin diocese held its 32nd annual Catholic Day at the race track in Hoppegarten on

87. Scholder, *Churches and the Third Reich*, vol. 2, p. 186.
88. *Gemeinsamer Hirtenbrief der am Grabe des hl. Bonafatius versammelten Oberhirten der Diözesen Deutschlands* (n.p., n.d. [1934]), esp. pp. 7–12. A copy of this document is to be found in the Kommission für Zeitgeschichte, Bonn, Nachlaß Emil Ritter, A11.
89. Scholder, *Churches and the Third Reich*, vol. 2, pp. 185–86.

24 July. The Hoppegarten rally, which had been organized by Klausener in his capacity as leader of the Catholic Action and which attracted an estimated 60,000 participants from all parts of the country, took place in the afterglow of Papen's Marburg speech and featured an unannounced appearance by Klausener as the final speaker of the day.[90] Although Klausener had had no contact with the anti-Nazi activists around Jung and was careful to avoid saying anything that might be construed as an attack or criticism of the Nazi regime,[91] the rally's very success constituted a direct challenge to Nazi authority and did much to confirm Nazi fears of a counterrevolution under the spiritual tutelage of the Catholic Action.[92]

It was against the background of these developments that Hitler ordered Jung's arrest on 25 July, thus setting in motion the series of events that culminated in the "Night of the Long Knives." Jung was subsequently taken into custody by the Gestapo at his Berlin apartment later that evening.[93] In the meantime, Bose and his co-conspirators in the vice chancery continued to pin their hopes on Hindenburg and the intervention of the Reichswehr. In this respect, they were hoping that Hindenburg could be persuaded to provide Fritsch and the Reichswehr with the emergency authorization they needed to begin disarmament of the SA and suspend the constitution so that executive power could be transferred from the cabinet to a special directorate consisting of Hitler and the NSDAP's Hermann Göring, Fritsch and Rundstedt from the Reichswehr, and Papen, Brüning, and Carl Goerdeler as representatives of the conservative forces that now hoped to hold the thus chastened Nazis in check. Not only would the suppression of the SA be left in the hands of the Reichswehr, but high-ranking Nazi officials including Goebbels, Heinrich Himmler, and Reinhard Heydrich as well as most of the party's district lead-

---

90. Adolph, *Klausener*, pp. 91–95. See also the report of the Hoppegarten rally in the *Katholisches Kirchenblatt für das Bistum Berlin* 30, no. 28 (15 July 1934): 4–5.

91. The text of Klausener's remarks has not survived. For a brief summary of his speech at Hoppegarten, see Adolph, *Klausener*, p. 94.

92. In this respect, see the detailed "Lagebericht" on the "Katholische Bewegung" from the Reichsführer SS, Chef des Sicherheitsamtes, May–June 1934, in F. Zipfel, *Kirchenkampf in Deutschland 1933–1945. Religionsverfolgung und Selbstbehauptung der Kirchen in der nationalsozialistischen Zeit* (Berlin, 1965), pp. 272–326, esp. pp. 282–91.

93. For the details of Jung's arrest, see Forschbach, *Jung*, p. 122.

ers (*Gauleiter*) and police officials appointed by the Nazis would be taken into protective custody.[94] Unlike Jung, however, neither Bose nor any other of his associates in the vice chancery were prepared to go ahead with Hitler's assassination for fear that this would only transform the Nazi leader into a martyr. The plan that Bose and his associates formulated in the last days of June 1934, therefore, represented a revised version of the "taming strategy" that Papen and Hugenberg had pursued in January 1933, though in this case under conditions that, from their perspective at least, offered much improved prospects for holding the Nazis in line.

In the final analysis, however, the success or failure of the entire undertaking depended upon Papen's ability to persuade the Reich President to act in support of the plan that his subordinates in the vice chancery had devised for the transfer of power from Nazi to conservative hands. After learning of Jung's arrest, Papen returned to Berlin on 26 July but was unsuccessful in his efforts to secure an audience with Hitler.[95] At this point, Papen decided to travel to the president's private estate in Neudeck, where he would meet with Hindenburg and present him with the details of Bose's plan for a conservative putsch against Hitler and the Nazi party leadership. By this time, even the presidential entourage had become impatient with Papen's inactivity and tried to press him into action by going through former Hindenburg associates such as retired field marshal August von Mackensen.[96] But neither Papen nor any other member of the vice chancery was able to get through to the ailing Reich President, who was shielded from outside contact by his son, Oskar, and his personal secretary, Otto Meissner. As a last resort, Papen met with Oskar

94. For fuller details, see Tschirsky, *Erinnerungen*, pp. 176–79.
95. In this respect, see Papen to Hitler, 27 June 1934, BA Koblenz, Bestand R 10/50/15–16; as well as Papen, *Wahrheit*, pp. 352–53.
96. In this respect, see Feldmann to Mackensen, 27 June 1934; and the handwritten text of a letter from Mackensen to Papen, 29 June 1934, Bundesarchiv-Militärarchiv, Freiburg in Breisgau, Nachlaß August von Mackensen, N39/277/1–3. The second of these two letters was apparently never sent. A former military officer who had played a major role in Hindenburg's 1925 election campaign, Otto von Feldmann belonged to the inner circle of the president's advisors and had met with the Reich President as recently as 23 June to discuss the Marburg speech and its political implications. For a further indication of conservative frustration over Papen's failure to capitalize upon the excitement that had been generated by his Marburg speech, see Ritgen to Mackensen, 27 June 1934, ibid., 4–5.

instead and tried to impress upon him the urgency of the moment by revealing some of the details of the plan that had been concocted within the vice chancery for removing the Nazis from power. After agreeing to arrange a meeting between Papen and his father on the morning of 30 June, Oskar then made the fatal mistake of informing not Fritsch but Defense Minister Werner von Blomberg of his conversation with Papen.[97] Through this indiscretion, Hitler and other members of the Nazi elite were able to get wind of what Jung, Bose, and their associates in the vice chancery were up to. Hitler, who up to this point had shown a characteristic lack of resolve throughout the entire crisis, was finally persuaded by Himmler and Göring – the two men who stood the most to gain from Röhm's elimination – to approve plans for a strike against the SA leadership.[98] At the same time, Hitler announced his determination to eliminate the nest of reactionaries at the vice chancery.[99]

By deciding to act against Röhm and the SA leadership, Hitler effectively removed much of the threat that the Reichswehr posed to his control of the state and isolated the anti-Nazi activists within the vice chancery from their most important source of outside support. Jung had been skeptical about the reliability of the military from the outset, and his fears proved fully warranted. From the military's perspective, however, the real threat to its privileged position as one of the "two pillars" upon which the Nazi state was supposedly based came not from Hitler but from Röhm and the SA.[100] Hitler's most enthusiastic supporters within the Reichswehr were Blomberg and his right-hand man at the ministry of defense, Walther von Reichenau. Both were committed to the Reichs-

97. Tschirsky, *Erinnerungen*, pp. 186–88. There is no mention in Papen's memoirs of this meeting with Oskar von Hindenburg.

98. Most biographers of the two men are in essential agreement that Göring and Himmler were the principal catalysts in persuading Hitler to act. On Göring's role in the preparations for the Röhm purge, see A. Kube, *Pour le merité und Hakenkreuz. Hermann Göring im Dritten Reich* (Munich, 1986), pp. 65–73; and D. Irving, *Göring: A Biography* (New York, 1989), pp. 138–50. On the confusion that surrounds Himmler's role in the purge, see G. Browder, *Foundations of the Nazi Police State: The Formation of the Sipo and SD* (Lexington, Ky., 1990), pp. 139–47.

99. See the entry for 28 June 1934 in *Das politische Tagebuch Alfred Rosenbergs aus den Jahren 1934/35 und 1939/40*, ed. H.–G. Seraphim (Göttingen, 1956), p. 31.

100. Müller, *Heer und Hitler*, pp. 53–56.

wehr's alliance with Hitler, and both used their influence with Hitler to pressure him into taking action against the SA so that a rupture in the regime's relations with the military could be avoided.[101] Reichenau was particularly adept at keeping the Reichswehr in the dark about the true nature of the action that was being planned by the Nazi hierarchy, working closely with Himmler in collecting the evidence necessary to convince Hitler and the Reichswehr leadership that an SA putsch was indeed imminent.[102] The net effect of this subterfuge was not only to neutralize the Reichswehr in the conflict between Hitler and the SA and to ensure its acquiescence in whatever the Nazi hierarchy might decide to do but, more importantly, to provide Fritsch and other Reichswehr leaders, most notably Ludwig von Beck in his capacity as chief of the troop office (Truppenamt), with the moral justification they needed to ensure the success of Hitler's prophylactic strike against the SA leadership. Nowhere was the Reichswehr's complicity in the events of 30 June and 1 July 1934 more apparent than in Bavaria, where army leaders were not only informed of the action against the SA, but dutifully followed orders to keep their troops from becoming involved[103] and helped organize the material and logistical support necessary to suppress the supposed putsch before it had had an opportunity to materialize.[104]

Unbeknownst to the Reichswehr leadership, Hitler's accomplices in Berlin had already begun to compile lists of real and imagined political enemies who were to be eliminated in con-

101. For Blomberg's position, see his article, "Die Wehrmacht im Dritten Reich," *Völkischer Beobachter*, 29 June 1934, no. 180.

102. On Reichenau's role in setting the stage for the Röhm purge, see the memoirs of his one-time aide, E. Röhricht, *Pflicht und Gewissen. Erinnerungen eines deutschen Generals 1932 bis 1944* (Stuttgart, 1965), pp. 41–67.

103. On the behavior of the Reichswehr command in Bavaria, see V. Miller, *Ich fand das wahre Vaterland*, ed. K. Mammach (Berlin, 1963), pp. 352–63. See also A. Hoch and H. Weiß, "Die Erinnerungen des Generalobersten Wilhelm Adam," in *Miscellanea: Festschrift für Helmut Krausnick zum 75. Geburtstag*, ed. W. Benz (Stuttgart, 1980), pp. 32–62, esp. pp. 45–46.

104. The strongest argument for a broader pattern of Reichswehr complicity in the Röhm purge has been made by H. Bennecke, *Die Reichswehr und der "Röhm-Putsch"* (Munich and Vienna, 1964). Essential elements of Bennecke's argument have since been confirmed by the discovery of documents in the records of the Bavarian army command in the Bundesarchiv-Militärarchiv, Freiburg im Breisgau. For further details, see K.-J. Müller, "Reichswehr und 'Röhm-Affäre'. Aus den Akten des Wehrkreiskommandos (Bayer.) VII," *Militärgeschichtliche Mitteilungen* 1 (1968): 107–44.

junction with the strike against the SA. Upon receipt of the appropriate code word from Munich indicating that Röhm and other SA leaders had been taken into custody, Göring and Himmler would launch a strike of their own, aimed – among other things – at decapitating the conservative resistance to Hitler and the new Nazi state. At the head of this list stood the name of Herbert von Bose. Shortly after arriving at the vice chancery on the morning of 30 June, Bose learned of the strike against the SA in Bavaria, though most likely without realizing that it had been initiated by Hitler and not, as he assumed, by the Reichswehr. If so, that would account for Bose's apparent good humor and his feeling that everything was going more or less as planned.[105] But just before noon – and after Papen had been removed from harm's way by a summons from Göring[106] – the vice chancery was occupied by an armed S.S. detachment and sealed off from outside access. Approximately a half hour later Bose – unarmed and with no intention of resisting arrest – was shot and killed in his office at the vice chancery.[107] Bose's murder marked the beginning of a wave of killings that continued throughout the capital for the remainder of the day. Only minutes later Schleicher and his wife were shot at their home in the Berlin suburb of Neubabelsberg. Less than half an hour later Klausener met a similar fate in his offices at the ministry of transportation, while Gregor Strasser, Hitler's erstwhile right-hand man who had withdrawn from public life following his break with the Nazi party leader in December 1932 – and who vehemently denied any connection with those who were challenging the regime[108] – was taken from his home to the SS headquarters in the Hotel Prinz Albrechtsstraße, where he was shot in the early evening of 30 June. Jung, who had been in Gestapo hands since 25 June, was taken later that night from his cell in the basement of the Hotel

105. Forschbach, *Jung*, pp. 126–27.
106. Tschirsky, *Erinnerungen*, pp. 189–91.
107. On the events in the vice chancery, see the two-page report by Kurt Josten, n.d.; Hans Wedepohl, "Erinnerungen an den 30. Juni 1934," n.d.; and the declaration by Walter Hummelsheim, 6 September 1949, all in Sammlung Bose, as well as the affidavit by Hermann Sabath, 15 November 1948, BA Koblenz, Nachlaß Sabath, 16.
108. In this respect, see the letter from Strasser to Heß, 18 Juni 1934, BDC, records of the Oberstes Parteigericht der NSDAP, Vorgang Albert Pietzsch. It should be noted that this letter was written the day after Papen's Marburg speech.

Prinz Albrechtsstraße to a small forest on the outskirts of Berlin, where he too was shot.[109] Other prominent conservatives, including five members of Papen's staff at the vice chancery, escaped execution but were forced to spend several anxious days in confinement before being released as a result of Hindenburg's intercession with Hitler.

* * *

Hitler's subsequent defense of his strike against the SA leadership – first at a ministerial conference on the morning of 3 July,[110] and then before the Reichstag ten days later[111] – did much to obscure the real reasons why the action had been necessary in the first place. As a result, the German public was kept very much in the dark about what had actually transpired and remained essentially ignorant of what the conspirators around Jung and Bose had hoped to accomplish. The confusion sown by Hitler's account of these events has persisted to the present and has done much to diminish historical appreciation of that first cadre of conservative opponents of the Nazi regime, who in 1933/34 risked – and, in some cases, lost – their lives in a perhaps ill-conceived, yet nonetheless courageous attempt to overthrow it. Yet as much as one might be tempted to commend the neoconservative activists around Jung and Bose for their courage and determination in opposing Hitler, it would be a mistake to idealize either their motives or their political acumen. One cannot, for example, deny the essentially reactionary character of Jung's political vision or ignore how restrictive his sense of the German polity actually was. After all, had not Jung insisted that the true aim of the national revolution should be "the depoliticization of the masses and their exclusion from the leadership of the state"? And did he not also chastise the Nazis for having made too many concessions to the democratic ethos of the modern age?[112] By the same token, Papen's Marburg speech fell conspicuously short of calling for a restoration of civil liberties, for

109. On the events of 30 June, see Höhne, *Mordsache Röhm*, pp. 247–96. For a list of those who were killed during the course of the purge, see Bennecke, *Reichswehr und "Röhm-Putsch"*, pp. 87–88.

110. Minutes of a ministerial conference, 3 July 1934, in *Die Regierung Hitler 1933/34*, ed. Minuth, vol. 2, pp. 1354–58.

111. A. Hitler, *Rede des Reichskanzlers vor dem Reichstag am 13. Juli 1934* (Berlin, n.d. [1934]), esp. pp. 18–28.

112. Jung, *Sinndeutung der deutschen Revolution*, pp. 70–71, 91–92.

a return to the rule of law, or for an end to racism as an instrument of governmental policy. All of this, in turn, only underscores the limited political vision of those who in 1933/34 attached themselves to Papen's political star in an ill-fated effort to overthrow the Nazi regime.

It is also easy to criticize Jung and his confederates for the naiveté with which they planned Hitler's demise. In retrospect, it is difficult to imagine how they could ever have succeeded. From beginning to end, too much depended upon imponderables such as Papen's civil courage, Hindenburg's ability to act, and the Reichswehr's willingness to oppose Hitler. The plight of the conspirators was further complicated by Jung's own failure to appreciate the brutality of the regime he was trying to overthrow and the almost casual recklessness with which he plotted its downfall.[113] Yet none of this vitiates the importance of the conspiracy as an index of conservative disaffection in the first years of the Third Reich. Not only were Jung and Bose trying to take advantage of the uneasiness that rumors of a second wave of SA terror had produced within the ranks of Germany's conservative elites, but they made a concerted attempt to broaden the base of the resistance by establishing contact with former leaders of the Christian labor movement as well as with influential representatives of Germany's Catholic establishment. Admittedly, one should be careful about exaggerating the extent and significance of these contacts. They were, after all, still in their infancy and had not had sufficient opportunity to develop before Himmler and his associates preempted whatever the conservatives might have had in mind by taking action into their own hands. At the same time, Jung's efforts to recruit support from such quarters suggest that in spite of his unabashed elitism he realized that the conspiracy would not succeed if it remained an affair of the elites and found no backing among the masses.

The net effect of the Röhm crisis was to redefine relations between Germany's conservative elites and the leaders of the new Nazi state on terms essentially dictated by the latter. Germany's propertied classes were both reassured by Hitler's strike against the more radical elements in the SA leadership and chastened by the murder of Schleicher and other promi-

113. This point has been stressed by Jung's close associate Fechtner, *Menschen und Zeiten*, pp. 359–65.

nent conservatives presumably involved in the anti-Hitler conspiracy. At the same time, the resolve that Hitler had supposedly demonstrated in suppressing the SA rebellion did much to cement his position as a popular leader of the German people. At no point since his appointment as chancellor was Hitler more universally acclaimed as a leader worthy of the nation's respect and admiration than in the immediate aftermath of the Röhm purge.[114] In the meantime, Blomberg moved quickly to reaffirm the army's loyalty to Hitler now that he had disposed of Röhm and the threat his plans for a "people's army" had posed to the Reichswehr's privileged position as one of the "two pillars" upon which the Third Reich was presumably based.[115] Whatever uneasiness the Reichwehr's leadership might have felt over the murders of Schleicher and Major General Ferdinand von Bredow, Schleicher's personal adjutant in the ministry of defense, was at least partly offset by the strong sense of relief, if not gratitude, that many military leaders felt toward Hitler for having interceded on the army's behalf in its conflict with Röhm and the SA.[116]

Nor did the significance of the Röhm purge escape the leaders of Germany's Catholic hierarchy. The boldness the German bishops had shown in drafting the pastoral letter that was to be read from the pulpit on 1 July quickly evaporated in the wake of the murders of Klausener and another prominent lay Catholic, Adalbert Probst of the German Youth Force (Deutsche Jugendkraft). Timidity, not confrontation, was once again the order of the day.[117] A further symptom of conservative timidity in the wake of the Röhm purge was the way in which Goerdeler and other governmental conservatives who

114. M. Jamin, "Das Ende der 'Machtergreifung': Der 30. Juni 1934 und seine Wahrnehmung in der Bevölkerung," in *Die nationalsozialistische Machtergreifung*, ed. W. Michalka (Paderborn, 1984), pp. 207–19. See also I. Kershaw, *The Hitler Myth: Image and Reality in the Third Reich* (Oxford, 1987), pp. 83–95.

115. In particular, see Blomberg's remarks at a conference of the German High Command, 5 July 1934, BA-MA Freiburg, Militärgeschichtliche Sammlung 1/1667/112–20.

116. For further details, see Müller, *Heer und Hitler*, pp. 122–41. For a somewhat more sanguine assessment of the military's response to the events of 30 June 1934, see L.E. Hill, "The National-Conservatives and Opposition to the Third Reich before the Second World War," in *Germans against Nazism: Nonconformity, Opposition and Resistance in the Third Reich. Essays in Honour of Peter Hoffmann*, ed. F.R. Nicosia and L.D. Stokes (New York and Oxford, 1990), pp. 221–51.

117. Scholder, *The Churches and the Third Reich*, vol. 2, pp. 202–7.

had been on the outer fringes of the anti-Hitler conspiracy began to look for ways of ingratiating themselves with the Nazi regime in the illusory hope that the elimination of the radicals around Röhm presaged a return to the principles of law and order.[118] All this, in turn, represented part of a more general pattern of conservative accommodation to the situation that had been created by the Röhm purge, a pattern that was to define the terms of conservative collaboration with the Third Reich until the next major crisis in the Fritsch-Blomberg affair at the beginning of 1938.

To what extent, then, may the anti-Nazi conspiracy in the spring and summer of 1934 be regarded as a precursor to the more celebrated attempts to overthrow the Nazi regime toward the end of the Second World War? To be sure, the personal ties between the conservative resistance of 1933/34 and that of a decade later were extremely weak. By the same token, those who plotted Hitler's assassination in the summer of 1944 have generally failed to acknowledge either an intellectual or moral debt to the conservative victims of the Röhm purge. None of this, however, can obscure a marked affinity between the ideas that Jung expressed in his April 1934 memorandum for Papen and those that later surfaced in the programmatic formulations of the Kreisau Circle (Kreisauer Kreis) under Count Helmuth von Moltke. For while few of Moltke's associates would have been willing to endorse Jung's proposal for the creation of an elective monarchy for all of central Europe or could have accepted the more blatantly reactionary aspects of his political program, they nevertheless shared his disdain for the pluralistic party democracy of the Weimar Republic, his antipathy toward capitalism and his longing for a more organic economic order, and his deep-seated suspicion of nationalism and an international order based upon the modern nation state. Nor would they have had a difficult time accepting Jung's proposition that Germany's national regeneration could take place only on the basis of a revitalized Christianity.[199] Such ideas, after all, were

118. In this respect, see the memorandum by Goerdeler, "An den Reichs-kanzler Adolf Hitler," August 1934, BA Koblenz, NL Goerdeler, 12. See also M. Krüger-Charlé, "Carl Goerdelers Versuche zur Durchsetzung einer alternativen Politik 1933 bis 1937," in *Der Widerstand gegen den Nationalsozialismus*, ed. Schmädeke and Steinbach, pp. 383–404.

119. On the ideas of the Kreisau Circle, see H. Mommsen, "Social Views and Constitutional Plans of the Resistance," in H. Graml, H. Mommsen, H.-J. Reichhardt, and E. Wolf, *The German Resistance to Hitler* (Berkeley, Ca., and

part of a common conservative heritage that situates Jung, Bose, and their co-conspirators within a continuum of young conservative activism that stretched from the early years of the Weimar Republic to the ill-fated attempt on Hitler's life in the summer of 1944.

Los Angeles, 1970), pp. 55–147; and G. van Roon, *German Resistance to Hitler: Count von Moltke and the Kreisau Circle*, trans. by P. Ludlow (London, 1971), pp. 219–68; as well as the recently discovered collection of documents published in *Dossier: Kreisauer Kreis. Dokumente aus dem Widerstand gegen den National-sozialismus. Aus dem Nachlaß von Lothar König S. J.*, ed. R. Blaustein (Frankfurt am Main, 1987), esp. pp. 127–78, 200–38, 278–95.

Select Bibliography on the History of German Conservatism, 1789–1945

The following bibliography provides a brief survey of the most important secondary literature in English and German on the history of German conservatism. No attempt has been made to include all of the specialized monographs, essays, and dissertations that have been written on the subject; only works of major significance have been listed. Many important contributions are included in the editions of collected essays listed below. Unfortunately, limitations of space prohibit listing these essays individually. Scholars who would like a more comprehensive and detailed bibliography on the history of German conservatism before 1918 should consult the monographs by R. Chickering, J. Retallack, and W. Schwenkter listed below. No comparable bibliographies are available for the Weimar and Nazi periods.

Abraham, D. *The Collapse of the Weimar Republic: Political Economy and Crisis*, 2nd rev. ed. New York, 1986.
_____. "Conflicts within German Industry and the Collapse of the Weimar Republic." *Past and Present*, no. 88 (August 1980): 88–128.
_____. "Constituting Hegemony: The Bourgeois Crisis of Weimar Germany." *Journal of Modern History* 51 (1979): 417–33.
_____. "State and Classes in Weimar Germany." *Politics and Society* 9 (1978): 229–66.
Allen, D.Y. "From Romanticism to Realpolitik: Studies in Nineteenth-Century German Conservatism." Ph.D. diss., Columbia University, 1971.
Anderson, E.N. *The Social and Political Conflict in Prussia, 1858–1864*. New York, 1968.
Applegate, C.A. *Nation of Provincials: The German Idea of Heimat*. Berkeley, Calif., 1990.
Aretin, K.O. "Der bayerische Adel. Von der Monarchie zum Dritten Reich." In *Bayern in der NS-Zeit*, edited by M. Broszat, E. Fröhlich, and A. Grossmann, 6 vols., vol. 3, pp. 513–67. Munich and Vienna, 1981.
_____. "Die bayerische Regierung und die Politik der bayerischen Monarchisten in der Krise der Weimarer Republik 1930–1933." In

Festschrift für Hermann Heimpel zum 70. Geburtstag am 19. September 1971, edited by Max-Planck-Institut für die Geschichte, pp. 205–37. Göttingen, 1971.

Bach, J. *Franz von Papen in der Weimarer Republik. Aktivitäten in Politik und Presse 1918–1932*. Düsseldorf, 1977.

Bacheller, C.R. "Class and Conservatism: The Changing Social Structure of the German Right, 1900–1928." Ph.D. diss., University of Wisconsin-Madison, 1976.

Baranowski, S. *The Confessing Church, Conservative Elites, and the Nazi State*. Lewiston, N.Y., 1986.

————. "Continuity and Contingency: Agrarian Elites, Conservative Institutions and East Elbia in Modern German History." *Social History* 12 (1987): 285–308.

————. "The Sanctity of Rural Life: Protestantism, Agrarian Politics, and Nazism in Pomerania during the Weimar Republic." *German History* 9 (1991): 1–22.

Barkin, K. *The Controversy over German Industrialization*. Chicago, 1970.

Beck, H. "Conservatives, Bureaucracy, and the Social Question in Prussia (1815–1848)." Ph.D. diss., University of California-Los Angeles, 1988.

————. "The Social Policies of Prussian Officials: The Bureaucracy in a New Light." *Journal of Modern History* 64 (1992): 263–98.

Behnen, M. *Das Preußische Wochenblatt (1851–1861). Nationalkonservative Publizistik gegen Ständestaat und Polizeistaat*. Göttingen, 1971.

Behrens, R. "Die Deutschnationalen in Hamburg." Ph.D. diss., University of Hamburg, 1973.

Bendersky, J.W. *Carl Schmitt: Theorist for the Third Reich*. Princeton, N.J., 1983.

Berdahl, R.M. "Conservative Politics and Aristocratic Landowners in Bismarckian Germany." *Journal of Modern History* 44 (1972): 1–20.

————. *The Politics of the Prussian Nobility: The Development of a Conservative Ideology, 1770–1848*. Princeton, N.J., 1988.

————. "Prussian aristocracy and conservative ideology: A methodological examination." *Social Science Information* 15 (1976): 583–599.

————. "The Stände and the Origins of Conservatism in Prussia." *Eighteenth-Century Studies* 6 (1973): 298–321.

————. "The Transformation of the Prussian Conservative Party, 1866–1876." Ph.D. diss., University of Minnesota, 1965.

Berding, H. *Moderner Antisemitismus in Deutschland*. Frankfurt am Main, 1988.

Berghahn, V.R. *Der Stahlhelm – Bund der Frontsoldaten 1918–1935*. Düsseldorf, 1966.

————. *Der Tirpitz-Plan. Genesis und Verfall einer innenpolitischen Strategie unter Wilhelm II*. Düsseldorf, 1971.

Bessel, R. "1933: A Counter-Revolution that Failed." In *Revolution and*

Counter-Revolution, edited by E.E. Rice, pp. 109–27. Oxford, 1991.

Bessel, R., and E.J. Feuchtwanger, eds. *Social Change and Political Development in Weimar Germany.* London, 1981.

Bieber, H. Paul *Rohrbach. Ein konservativer Publizist und Kritiker der Weimarer Republik.* Munich-Pullach, 1972.

Blackbourn, D. *Class, Religion, and Local Politics in Wilhelmine Germany: The Centre Party in Württemberg before 1914.* New Haven, Conn., and London, 1980.

————. *Populists and Patricians: Essays in Modern German History.* London, 1987.

Blinkhorn, M., ed. *Fascists and Conservatives: The Radical Right and the Establishment in Twentieth-Century Europe.* London, 1990.

Bonham, G. *Ideology and Interests in the German State.* New York and London, 1991.

Booms, H. *Die Deutschkonservative Partei. Preußischer Charakter, Reichsauffassung, Nationalbegriff.* Düsseldorf, 1954.

Borg, D.R. *The Old-Prussian Church and the Weimar Republic: A Study in Political Adjustment, 1917–1927.* Hanover, N.H., and London, 1984.

Bowen, R.H. *German Theories of the Corporative State.* New York, 1947.

Braatz, W. "Die agrarisch-industrielle Front in der Weimarer Republik 1930–1932. Die Rolle der Interessentengruppen als Triebkräfte des sozio-ökonomischen Wandels während der Weltwirtschaftskrise." *Schmollers Jahrbuch für Wirtschafts- und Sozialwissenschaften* 91 (1971): 541–65.

————. "Franz von Papen and the Preußenschlag, 20 July 1932: a move by the 'New State' toward Reichsreform." *European Studies Review* 3 (1973): 157–80.

Bracher, K.D. *Die Auflösung der Weimarer Republik. Eine Studie zum Problem des Machtverfalls in der Demokratie,* 4th ed. Villingen Schwarzwald, 1960.

Brakelmann, G., M. Greschat, and W. Jochmann. *Protestantismus und Politik. Werk und Wirkung Adolf Stöckers.* Hamburg, 1982.

Bramsted, E.K. *Aristocracy and the Middle Classes in Germany: Social Types in German Literature, 1830–1900.* London, 1937.

Braun, W. *Evangelische Parteien in historischer Darstellung und sozialwissenschaftlicher Beleuchtung.* Mannheim, 1939.

Braune, F. *Edmund Burke in Deutschland. Ein Beitrag zur Geschichte des historisch-politischen Denkens.* Heidelberg, 1917.

Breuning, K. *Die Vision des Reiches. Deutscher Katholizismus zwischen Demokratie und Diktatur (1929–1934).* Munich, 1969.

Broszat, M., and K. Schwabe, eds. *Die deutschen Eliten und der Weg in den Zweiten Weltkrieg.* Munich, 1989.

Bullivant, K. "The Conservative Revolution." In *The Weimar Dilemma: Intellectuals in the Weimar Republic,* edited by A. Phelan, pp. 47–70. Manchester, 1985.

Buttlar, M. v. *Die politische Vorstellungen des Friedrich August Ludwig von der Marwitz. Ein Beitrag zur Genesis und Gestalt konservativen Denkens in Preußen*. Frankfurt am Main, 1980.

Caplan, J. *Government with Administration: State and Civil Service in Weimar and Nazi Germany*. Oxford, 1988.

Carsten, F.L. *A History of the Prussian Junkers*. Aldershot, 1989.

_____. *The Reichswehr and Politics 1918 to 1933*. Oxford, 1966.

Cecil, L. "The Creation of Nobles in Prussia, 1871–1918." *American Historical Review* 75 (1970): 757–95.

_____. *Wilhelm II: Prince and Emperor, 1859–1900*. Chapel Hill, N.C., 1989.

Chamberlin, B. "The Enemy on the Right: The 'Alldeutscher Verband' in the Weimar Republic, 1918–1926." Ph.D. diss., University of Maryland, 1972.

Chanady, A.A. "The Disintegration of the German National People's Party, 1924–1930." *Journal of Modern History* 39 (1967): 65–91.

Chickering, R. *We Men Who Feel Most German: A Cultural Study of the Pan-German League, 1886–1914*. Boston, Mass., 1984.

Childers, T. *The Nazi Voter: The Social Foundations of Fascism in Germany, 1919–1933*. Chapel Hill, N.C., 1983.

_____. "The Social Language of Politics in Germany: The Sociology of Political Discourse in the Weimar Republic." *American Historical Review* 95 (1990): 331–58.

Christensen, M.K. "Ernst Wilhelm Hengstenberg and the Kirchenzeitung Faction: Throne and Altar in Nineteenth-Century Prussia." Ph.D. diss., University of Oregon, 1972.

Clark, C.M. "Jewish Mission in the Christian State: Protestant Missions to the Jews in Eighteenth and Nineteenth-Century Prussia." Ph.D. diss., Cambridge University, 1991.

Clemens, G. *Martin Spahn und der Rechtskatholizismus in der Weimarer Republik*. Mainz, 1983.

Coetzee, M.S. *The German Army League: Popular Nationalism in Wilhelmine Germany*. New York and Oxford, 1990.

Conze, W. "Brüning als Reichskanzler: Eine Zwischenbilanz." *Historische Zeitschrift* 224 (1972): 310–34.

Corni, G. "Alfred Hugenberg as Minister of Agriculture: Interlude or Continuity." *German History* 7 (1989): 204–25.

Craig, G.A. *The Politics of the Prussian Army, 1640–1945*. Oxford, 1955.

Demand, E. *Von Schleicher zu Springer. Hans Zehrer als politischer Publizist*. Mainz, 1971.

Diehl, J.M. *Paramilitary Politics in the Weimar Republic*. Bloomington, Ind., 1977.

_____. "Von der 'Vaterlandspartei' zur 'nationalen Revolution'. Die 'Vereinigten Vaterländischen Verbände Deutschlands (VVVD)' 1922–1932." *Vierteljahrshefte für Zeitgeschichte* 33 (1985): 617–39.

Dierks (née Nax), M. *Die preußischen Altkonservativen und die Juden-frage* 1810/1847. Rostock, 1939.

Dobkowski, M.N., and I. Wallimann, eds. *Radical Perspectives on the Rise of Fascism in Germany, 1919–1945.* New York, 1989.

Donohoe, J. *Hitler's Conservative Opponents in Bavaria, 1930–1945: A Consideration of Catholic, Monarchist, and Separatist Anti-Nazi Activities.* Leiden, 1961.

Dorpalen, A. *Hindenburg and the Weimar Republic.* Princeton, N.J., 1964.

Dörr, Manfred. "Die Deutschnationale Volkspartei 1925 bis 1928." Ph.D. diss., University of Marburg, 1964.

Droz, J. "Préoccupations sociales et préoccupations réligieuses aux origines du parti conservateur prussien." *Revue d'Histoire Moderne et Contemporaine* 2 (1955): 280–300.

Edmundson, N. "The Fichte Society: A Chapter in Germany's Conservative Revolution." *Journal of Modern History* 38 (1966): 161–80.

Eley, G. *From Unification to Nazism: Reinterpreting the German Past.* Winchester, Mass., 1986.

————. *Reshaping the German Right: Radical Nationalism and Political Change after Bismarck.* New Haven, Conn., 1980.

Elm, L., ed. *Falsche Propheten. Studien zum konservativ-anti demokratischen Denken im 19. und 20. Jahrhundert.* Berlin, 1984.

Elm, L., C. Remer, and H. Sonntag. *Konservatismus-Forschung.* Jena, 1985.

Ender, W. *Konservative und rechtsliberale Deuter des Nationalsozialismus 1930–1945. Eine historisch-politische Kritik.* Frankfurt am Main, 1984.

Engelberg, E. *Bismarck: Das Reich in der Mitte Europas.* Berlin, 1990.

————. *Bismarck: Upreuße und Reichsgründer,* 6th ed. Berlin, 1986.

Epstein, K. *The Genesis of German Conservatism.* Princeton, N.J., 1966.

Erger, J. *Der Kapp-Lüttwitz Putsch. Ein Beitrag zur deutschen Innenpolitik 1919/20.* Düsseldorf, 1967.

Etue, G.E., Jr. "The German Fatherland Party, 1917–1918." Ph.D. diss., University of California-Berkeley, 1959.

Evans, R.J., ed. *Society and Politics in Wilhelmine Germany.* London, 1978.

Evans, R.J., and W.R. Lee, eds. *The German Peasantry: Conflict and Community in Rural Society from the Eighteenth to the Twentieth Centuries.* New York, 1986.

Fairbairn, B. "Authority vs. Democracy: Prussian Officials in the German Elections of 1898 and 1903." *Historical Journal* 34 (1990): 811–38.

————. "The Limits of Nationalist Politics: Electoral Culture and Mobilization in Germany, 1890–1903." *Journal of the Canadian Historical Association* (New Series) 1 (1990): 145–69.

Felken, D. *Oswald Spengler. Konservativer Denker zwischen Kaiserreich und Diktatur.* Munich, 1988.

Feldman, G.D. "Big Business and the Kapp Putsch." *Central European History* 4 (1971): 99–130.

Fenske, H. *Konservatismus und Rechtsradikalismus in Bayern nach 1918.* Bad Homburg, 1969.

Fischer, F. *From Kaiserreich to Third Reich: Elements of Continuity in German History, 1871–1945*, trans. R. Fletcher. London and Boston, Mass., 1986.

————. *Moritz August von Bethmann Hollweg und der Protestantismus.* Berlin, 1938; reprint, Vaduz, 1965.

————. *War of Illusions: German Politics from 1911 to 1914.* London, 1975.

Fischer, H. "Der 'Treubund mit Gott für König und Vaterland'. Ein Beitrag zur Reaktion in Preußen." *Jahrbücher für die Geschichte Ost- und Mitteldeutschlands* 24 (1975): 60–127.

Flemming, J. "Die Bewaffnung des 'Landvolks'. Ländliche Schutzwehren und agrarischer Konservatismus in der Anfangsphase der Weimarer Republik." *Militärgeschichtliche Mitteilungen* 31 (1979): 7–36.

————. *Landwirtschaftliche Interessen und Demokratie. Ländliche Gesellschaft, Agrarverbände und Staat 1890–1925.* Bonn, 1978.

Fricke, D. "Zur Erforschung konservativer Politik und Ideologie in der Geschichte bürgerlicher Parteien." *Zeitschrift für Geschichtswissenschaft* 27 (1979): 1139–55.

Fricke, D., et al., eds. *Die bürgerlichen Parteien in Deutschland. Handbuch der Geschichte der bürgerlichen Parteien und anderer bürgerlicher Interessenorganisationen vom Vormärz bis zum Jahre 1945.* 2 vols. Leipzig, 1968, and Berlin, 1970.

————, eds. *Lexikon zur Parteiengeschichte. Die bürgerlichen und kleinbürgerlichen Parteien und Verbände in Deutschland (1789–1945).* 4 vols. Leipzig, 1983–86.

Friedenthal, E. "Volksbegehren und Volksentscheid über den Young-Plan und die deutschnationale Sezession." Ph.D. diss., University of Tübingen, 1957.

Fritzsche, K. *Politische Romantik und Gegenrevolution: Fluchtwege in der Krise der bürgerlichen Gesellschaft. Das Beispiel des "Tat"-Kreises.* Frankfurt am Main, 1976.

————. "Konservatismus." In *Handbuch Politischer Theorien und Ideologien*, edited by F. Neumann, pp. 65–105. Hamburg, 1977.

————. "Konservatismus im gesellschaftlich-geschichtlichen Prozeß." *Neue Politische Literatur* 24 (1979): 1–23, 295–317; 25 (1980): 150–69.

Fritzsche, P. *Rehearsals for Fascism: Populism and Political Mobilization in Weimar Germany.* New York and Oxford, 1990.

Führer, K. "Der Deutsche Reichskriegerbund Kyffhäuser 1930–1934. Politik, Ideologie und Funktion eines 'unpolitischen' Verbandes."

Militärgeschichtliche Mitteilungen 36 (1984): 57–76.

Füßl, W. *Professor in der Politik: Friedrich Julius Stahl (1801–1861). Das monarchische Prinzip und seine Umsetzung in die parlamentarische Praxis.* Göttingen, 1988.

Gall, L. *Bismarck: The White Revolutionary,* trans. J.A. Underwood. 2 vols. London, 1986.

Garber, J. "Drei Theoriemodelle frühkonservativer Revolutionsabwehr. Altständischer Funktionalismus, spätabsolutistisches Vernunftrecht, evolutionärer 'Historismus.'" *Jahrbuch des Instituts für Deutsche Geschichte* 8 (1979): 65–101.

————. "Politische Spätaufklärung und vorromantische Frühkonservativismus. Aspekte der Forschung." Afterword to F. Valjavec, *Die Entstehung der politischen Strömungen in Deutschland 1770–1815.* 2nd ed. Kronberg/Ts., 1978.

Garber, J., ed. *Kritik der Revolution. Theorien des deutschen Frühkonservativismus 1790–1810,* vol. 1: *Dokumentation.* Kronberg/ Ts., 1976.

Gellately, R. *The Politics of Economic Despair: Shopkeepers and German Politics, 1890–1914.* London, 1974.

Gemein, G. "Die DNVP in Düsseldorf 1918–1933." Ph.D. diss., University of Cologne, 1969.

Gerlach, E.L. von *Von der Revolution zum Norddeutschen Bund. Politik und Ideengut der preußischen Hochkonservativen 1848–1866. Aus dem Nachlaß von Ernst Ludwig von Gerlach,* ed. H. Diwald. 2 vols. Göttingen, 1970.

Gerschenkron, A. *Bread and Democracy in Germany.* New York, 1943.

Gerstenberger, H. *Der revolutionäre Konservatismus. Ein Beitrag zur Analyse des Liberalismus.* Berlin, 1969.

Gessner, D. *Agrardepression und Präsidialregierungen in Deutschland 1930–1933. Probleme des Agrarkonservatismus am Ende der Weimarer Republik.* Düsseldorf, 1977.

————. "Agrarian Protectionism in the Weimar Republic." *Journal of Contemporary History* 12 (1977): 759–78.

————. *Agrarverbände in der Weimarer Republik. Wirtschaftliche und soziale Voraussetzungen agrarkonservativer Politik vor 1933.* Düsseldorf, 1976.

Glum, F. *Konservatismus im 19. Jahrhundert. Eine Auswahl Europäischer Porträts.* Bonn, 1969.

Götting, H. "Die sozialpolitische Idee in den konservativen Kreisen der vormärzlichen Zeit." Ph.D. diss., University of Berlin, 1920.

Gottwald, H., ed. "Konservative Politik und Ideolgie." Special issue of the *Jenaer Beiträge zur Parteiengeschichte* 44 (July 1980).

Grass, K.M. "Edgar Jung, Papenkreis und Röhmkrise 1933/34." Ph.D. diss., University of Heidelberg, 1966.

Grathwohl, R.P. *Stresemann and the DNVP: Reconciliation or Revenge in German Foreign Policy.* Lawrence, Kans., 1980.

Grebing, H. *Aktuelle Theorien über Faschismus und Konservatismus. Eine Kritik.* Stuttgart, 1974.

Grebing, H., et al., eds. *Konservatismus – eine deutsche Bilanz.* Munich, 1971.

Greiffenhagen, M. *Das Dilemma des Konservatismus in Deutschland.* 2nd ed. Munich, 1977.

Gründer, H. "Rechtskatholizismus im Kaiserreich und in der Weimarer Republik unter besonderer Berücksichtigung der Rheinlande und Westfalens." *Westfälische Zeitschrift* 134 (1984): 107–55.

Guratzsch, D. *Macht durch Organisation. Die Grundlegung des Hugenbergschen Presseimperiums.* Düsseldorf, 1974.

Hahn, A. *Die Berliner Revue. Ein Beitrag zur Geschichte der konservativen Partei zwischen 1855 und 1875.* Berlin, 1934.

Hamel, I. *Völkischer Verband und nationale Gesellschaft. Der Deutschnationale Handlungsgehilfen-Verband 1893–1933.* Hamburg, 1967.

Hamerow, T.S. *Restoration, Revolution, Reaction: Economics and Politics in Germany, 1815–1871.* Princeton, N.J., 1958.

————. *The Social Foundations of German Unification, 1858–1871.* 2 vols. Princeton, N.J., 1969–72.

Hartwig, E. "Die 'Mittelstandspolitik' des Bundes der Landwirte 1893 bis 1914." 2 vols. Ph.D. diss., University of Jena, 1980.

Hayes, P. *Interest and Ideology: I.G. Farben in the Nazi Era.* Cambridge, 1987.

————. "A 'Question Mark with Epaulettes'? Kurt von Schleicher and Weimar Politics." *Journal of Modern History* 52 (1980): 35–65.

Heffter, H. *Die Kreuzzeitungspartei und die Kartellpolitik Bismarcks.* Leipzig, 1927.

Heinemann, U. *Ein konservativer Rebell. Fritz-Dietlof Graf von der Schulenburg und der 20. Juli.* Berlin, 1990.

Henderson, C.R. "Heinrich Leo: A Study in German Conservatism." Ph.D. diss., University of Wisconsin-Madison, 1977.

Hennig, E. and R. Sarge, eds. *Konservatismus – eine Gefahr für die Freiheit?* Munich and Zurich, 1983.

Hentschel, V. *Weimars letzte Monate. Hitler und der Untergang der Weimarer Republik.* Düsseldorf, 1979.

Herberger, K.V. *Die Stellung der preußischen Konservativen zur sozialen Frage, 1848–62.* Meißen, 1914.

Herf, J. *Reactionary Modernism: Technology, Culture, and Politics in Weimar and the Third Reich.* Cambridge, 1984.

Hertzman, L. *DNVP: Right-Wing Opposition in the Weimar Republic, 1918–1924.* Lincoln, Nebr., 1963.

Heß, K. *Junker und bürgerliche Großgrundbesitzer im Kaiserreich. Landwirtschaftlicher Großbetrieb, Großgrundbesitz und Familienfideikommiß in Preußen (1867/71–1914).* Stuttgart, 1990.

Hietala, M. *Der neue Nationalismus. In der Publizistik Ernst Jüngers und des Kreises um ihn 1920–1933*. Helsinki, 1975.

Hill. L.E. "The National-Conservatives and Opposition to the Third Reich before the Second World War." In *Germans against Nazism: Nazism, Opposition, and Resistance in the Third Reich. Essays in Honour of Peter Hoffmann*, edited by F.R. Nicosia and L.D. Stokes, pp. 221–51. New York and Oxford, 1990.

Hiller von Gaertringen, F. "Die Deutschnationale Volkspartei." In *Das Ende der Parteien 1933*, edited by E. Matthias and R. Morsey, pp. 543–652. Düsseldorf, 1960.

_____. "Zur Beurteilung des Monarchismus in der Weimarer Republik." In *Tradition und Reform in der deutschen Politik. Gedenkschrift für Waldemar Besson*, edited by G. Jasper, pp. 138–86. Frankfurt am Main, 1976.

Hindelang, S. *Konservatismus und soziale Frage. Victor Aimé Hubers Beitrag zum sozialkonservativen Denken im 19. Jahrhundert*. Frankfurt am Main, 1983.

Hoepke, K.-P. *Die deutsche Rechte und der italienische Faschismus. Ein Beitrag zum Selbstverständnis und zur Politik von Gruppen und Verbänden der deutschen Rechten*. Düsseldorf, 1968.

Hörster-Philipps, U. *Konservative Politik in der Endphase der Weimarer Republik. Die Regierung Franz von Papen*. Cologne, 1982.

Hoffmann, P. *The History of the German Resistance, 1933–1945*, trans. R. Barry. Cambridge, Ma., 1977.

Holmes, K.A. *The NSDAP and the Crisis of Agrarian Conservatism in Lower Bavaria: National Socialism and the Peasants' Road to Modernity*. New York and London, 1991.

Holzbach, H. *Das "System Hugenberg." Die Organisation bürgerlicher Sammlungspolitik vor dem Aufstieg der NSDAP*. Stuttgart, 1981.

Hubatsch, W. *Hindenburg und der Staat. Aus den Papieren des Generalfeldmarschalls und Reichspräsidenten von 1878 bis 1934*. Göttingen, 1966.

Hughes, H.S. *Oswald Spengler: A Critical Estimate*. New York and London, 1952.

Hunt, J.C. "The 'Egalitarianism' of the Right: The Agrarian League in Southwest Germany, 1893–1914," *Journal of Contemporary History* 10 (1974): 513–530.

Ishida, Y. *Jungkonservative in der Weimarer Republik. Der Ring-Kreis, 1928–1933*. Frankfurt am Main, 1988.

Jarausch, K.H. *The Enigmatic Chancellor: Bethmann Hollweg and the Hubris of Imperial Germany*. New Haven, Conn., and London, 1973.

_____. "Illiberalism and Beyond: German History in Search of a Paradigm." *Journal of Modern History* 55 (1983): 268–84.

Jasper, G. *Die gescheiterte Zähmung. Wege zur Machtergreifung Hitlers, 1930–1934*. Frankfurt am Main, 1986.

Jenschke, B. *Zur Kritik der konservativ-revolutionären Ideologie in der*

511

Weimarer Republik. Weltanschauung und Politik bei Edgar Julius Jung. Munich, 1971.

Jonas, E. *Die Volkskonservativen. Entwicklung, Struktur, Standort und staatspolitische Zielsetzung.* Düsseldorf, 1965.

Jones, L.E. "Between the Fronts: The German National Union of Commercial Employees from 1928 to 1933." *Journal of Modern History* 48 (1976): 462–82.

————. "Crisis and Realignment: Agrarian Splinter Parties in the Late Weimar Republic, 1928–33." In *Peasants and Lords in Modern Germany: Recent Essays in Agricultural History,* edited by R.G. Moeller, pp. 198–232. Boston, Mass., 1986.

————. "Edgar Julius Jung: The Conservative Revolution in Theory and Practice." *Central European History* 21 (1988): 142–74.

————. "'The Greatest Stupidity of My Life': Alfred Hugenberg and the Formation of the Hitler Cabinet, January 1933." *Journal of Contemporary History* 27 (1992): 63–87.

Jones, L.E., and J. Retallack, eds. *Elections, Mass Politics, and Social Change in Modern Germany: New Perspectives.* Cambridge, 1992.

Jordan, E. *Die Entstehung der konservativen Partei und die preußische Agrarverhältnisse von 1848.* Munich and Leipzig, 1914.

Kaltenbrunner, G.-K., ed. *Die Herausforderung der Konservativen.* Freiburg, 1974.

————. ed. *Rekonstruktion des Konservatismus.* Freiburg, 1972.

Kann, R.A. "Friedrich Julius Stahl: A Re-examination of his Conservatism." *Leo Baeck Institute Year Book* 12 (1967): 55–74.

Kardorff, S. von *Wilhelm von Kardorff. Ein nationaler Parlamentarier im Zeitalter Bismarcks und Wilhelms II. 1828–1907.* Berlin, 1936.

Kaufmann, W.H. *Monarchism in the Weimar Republic.* New York, 1953.

Kehr, E. *Der Primat der Innenpolitik. Gesammelte Aufsätze zur preußisch-deutschen Sozialgeschichte im 19. und 20. Jahrhundert,* edited by H.-U. Wehler. Frankfurt am Main, 1965.

————. *Schlachtflottenbau und Parteipolitik 1894–1901. Versuch eines Querschnitts durch die innenpolitischen, sozialen und ideologischen Voraussetzungen des deutschen Imperialismus.* Berlin, 1930.

Keinemann, F. *Soziale und politische Geschichte des westfälischen Adels.* Hamm, 1976.

Kennedy, P., and A.J. Nicholls, eds. *Nationalist and Racialist Movements in Britain and Germany Before 1914.* London and Oxford, 1981.

Kessler, H. *Wilhelm Stapel als politischer Publizist. Ein Beitrag zur Geschichte des konservativen Nationalismus zwischen den beiden Weltkriegen.* Nuremberg, 1967.

Klatte, K. "Die Anfänge des Agrarkapitalismus und der preußische Konservatismus." Ph.D. diss., University of Hamburg, 1974.

Kleine, G.H. "Adelsgenossenschaft und Nationalsozialismus." *Vierteljahrshefte für Zeitgeschichte* 26 (1978): 100–43.

Klotzbücher, A. "Der politische Weg des Stahlhelm, Bund der Frontsoldaten, in der Weimarer Republik. Ein Beitrag zur Geschichte der 'Nationalen Opposition' 1918–1933." Ph.D. diss., University of Erlangen, 1964.

Knobel, E. *Die Hessische Rechtspartei. Konservative Opposition gegen das Bismarckreich.* Marburg, 1975.

Knoll, J.H. "Der autoritäre Staat: Konservative Ideologie und Staatstheorie am Ende der Weimarer Republik." *Lebendiger Geist. Hans-Joachim Schoeps zum 50. Geburtstag von Schülern dargestellt*, edited by H. Diwald, pp. 200–24. Leiden and Cologne, 1959.

Kondylis, P. *Konservativismus. Geschichtlicher Gehalt und Untergang.* Stuttgart, 1986.

Koselleck, R. *Preußen zwischen Reform und Revolution*, 2nd ed. Stuttgart, 1975.

Kovan, A.S. "The Reichs-Landbund and the Resurgence of Germany's Agrarian Conservatives, 1919–1923." Ph.D. diss., University of California-Berkeley, 1972.

Kraehe, E. *Metternich's German Policy.* 2 vols. Princeton, N.J., 1963 and 1983.

Krausnick, H. "Zum militärischen Widerstand gegen Hitler 1933–1938: Möglichkeiten, Ansätze, Grenzen und Kontroversen." In *Aufstand des Gewissens. Der militärische Widerstand gegen Hitler und das NS-Regime 1933–45*, edited by Militärgeschichtliches Forschungsamt, pp. 311–64. Herford and Bonn, n.d. [1984].

Krauss, E. *Ernst von Bülow-Cummerow, ein konservativer Landwirt und Politiker des 19. Jahrhunderts.* Berlin, 1937; reprint, Vaduz, 1965.

Kreuder, T., and H. Loewy, eds. *Konservatismus in der Strukturkrise.* Frankfurt am Main, 1987.

Kruck, A. *Geschichte des Alldeutschen Verbandes 1890–1939.* Wiesbaden, 1954.

Lamberti, M.E. "The Rise of the Prussian Conservative Party, 1840–1858." Ph.D. diss., Yale University, 1966.

Large, D.C., ed. *Contending with Hitler: Varieties of German Resistance in the Third Reich.* Cambridge, 1991.

Lebovics, H. *Social Conservatism and the Middle Classes in Germany, 1914–1933.* Princeton, N.J., 1969.

Lees, A. "Critics of Urban Society in Germany, 1854–1914." *Journal of the History of Ideas* 40 (1979): 61–83.

Lenk, K. *Deutscher Konservatismus.* Frankfurt am Main, 1989.

Leopold, J.A. *Alfred Hugenberg: The Radical Nationalist Campaign against the Weimar Republic.* New Haven, Conn., 1977.

Lettner, G. *Das Rückzugsgefecht der Aufklärung in Wien 1790–1792.* Frankfurt am Main and New York, 1988.

Leuß, H. *Wilhelm Freiherr von Hammerstein 1881–1895. Chefredakteur der Kreuzzeitung.* Berlin, 1905.

Levy, R.S. *The Downfall of the Anti-Semitic Political Parties in Imperial Germany.* New Haven, Conn., 1975.

Liebe, W. *Deutschnationale Volkspartei 1918–1924.* Düsseldorf, 1956.

Lohalm, U. *Völkischer Radikalismus. Die Geschichte des Deutschvölkischen Schutz- und Trutz-Bundes 1919–1923.* Hamburg, 1970.

Lokatis, S. "Hanseatische Verlagsanstalt. Politisches Buch-Marketing im 'Dritten Reich'." Ph.D. diss., University of Bochum, 1991.

Lougee, R.W. *Paul de Lagarde, 1827–1891: A Study of Radical Conservatism in Germany.* Cambridge, Mass., 1962.

Maltzahn, C. von *Heinrich Leo (1799–1878). Ein Politisches Gelehrtenleben zwischen Romantischem Konservatismus und Realpolitik.* Göttingen, 1979.

Mannheim, K. *Conservatism: A Contribution to the Sociology of Knowledge,* edited by D. Kettler, V. Meja, and N. Stehr. London and New York, 1986.

Martin, A. von "Weltanschauliche Motive im altkonservativen Denken." In *Deutsche Parteien vor 1918,* edited by G.A. Ritter, pp. 142–64. Cologne, 1973.

Maurensberger, V. *Rudolf Pechel und die "Deutsche Rundschau." Eine Studie zur konservativ-revolutionären Publizistik in der Weimarer Republik (1918–1933).* Bremen, 1971.

Mehnert, G., ed. *Programme Evangelischer Kirchenzeitungen im 19. Jahrhundert.* Witten, 1972.

Mende, D. "Kulturkonservatismus und konservative Erneuerungsbestrebungen." In *Adolf Grabowsky. Leben und Werk,* edited by H. Thierbach, pp. 87–129. Cologne, 1963.

Moeller, R.G. "Peasants and Tariffs in the Kaiserreich: How Backward were the Bauern?" *Agricultural History* 55 (1981): 370–84.

_____. *German Peasants and Agrarian Politics, 1914–1924: The Rhineland and Westphalia.* Chapel Hill, N.C., and London, 1986.

Moeller, R.G., ed. *Peasants and Lords in Modern Germany: Recent Studies in Agricultural History.* Boston, 1986.

Mohler, A. *Die konservative Revolution in Deutschland 1918–1932. Ein Handbuch,* 2nd ed. Darmstadt, 1972.

Mommsen, H. *Beamtentum im Dritten Reich.* Stuttgart, 1966.

_____. "Fritz-Dietlof Graf von der Schulenburg und die preußische Tradition." *Vierteljahrshefte für Zeitgeschichte* 32 (1984): 213–39.

_____. *From Weimar to Auschwitz,* trans. P. O'Connor. Princeton, N.J., 1991.

_____. "Social Views and Constitutional Plans of the Resistance." In H. Graml, H. Mommsen, H.J. Reichhardt, and E. Wolf, *The German Resistance to Hitler,* with an introduction by F.L. Carsten, pp. 55–147. Berkeley, Calif., 1970.

_____. *Die verspielte Freiheit. Der Weg der Republik von Weimar in den Untergang.* Berlin, 1989.

_____. "Zur Verschränkung traditioneller und faschistischer Führungsgruppen in Deutschland bei dem Übergang von der Bewegung- zur Systemphase." In *Faschismus als soziale Bewegung*, edited by W. Schieder, pp. 157–81. Hamburg, 1976.

Mosse, G.L. *The Crisis of German Ideology: Intellectual Origins of the Third Reich*. New York, 1964.

_____. "Die deutsche Rechte und die Juden." In *Entscheidungsjahr 1932. Zur Judenfrage in der Endphase der Weimarer Republik*, edited by W.E. Mosse, 2nd ed., pp. 183–246. Tübingen, 1966.

_____. *The Nationalization of the Masses: Political Symbolism and Mass Movements in Germany from the Napoleonic Wars through the Third Reich*. New York, 1975.

Müller, H. *Der Preußische Volks-Verein*. Berlin, 1914.

Müller, J. *Die Jugendbewegung als deutsche Hauptrichtung neukonservativer Reform*. Zurich, 1971.

Muller, J.Z. "Justus Möser and the Conservative Critique of Early Modern Capitalism." *Central European History* 23 (1990): 153–78.

_____. *The Other God that Failed: Hans Freyer and the Deradicalization of German Conservatism*. Princeton, N. J., 1987.

Müller, K.-J. *The Army, Politics, and Society in Germany, 1933–45: Studies in the Army's Relation to Nazism*. New York, 1987.

_____. *Das Heer und Hitler. Armee und nationalsozialistisches Regime 1933–1940*. Stuttgart, 1969.

_____. "The Structure and Nature of the National Conservative Opposition in Germany up to 1940." In *Aspects of the Third Reich*, edited by H.W. Koch, pp. 133–78. New York, 1985.

Muncy, L.W. *The Junker in the Prussian Administration under William II, 1888–1914*. Providence, R.I., 1944.

Muth, Heinrich. "Das 'Kölner Gespräch' am 4. Januar 1933." *Geschichte in Wissenschaft und Unterricht* 37 (1986): 463–80, 529–41.

Neebe, R. *Großindustrie, Staat und NSDAP 1930–1933. Paul Silverberg und der Reichsverband der Deutschen Industrie in der Krise der Weimarer Republik*. Göttingen, 1981.

Neumann, S. *Die Stufen des preußischen Konservatismus. Ein Beitrag zum Staats- und Gesellschaftsbild Deutschlands im 19. Jahrhundert*. Berlin, 1930, reprint Vaduz, 1965.

Nipperdey, T. *Die Organisation der deutschen Parteien vor 1918*. Düsseldorf, 1961.

Nolte, E. "Konservativismus und Nationalsozialismus." *Zeitschrift für Politik* 11 (1964): 3–20.

Nowak, K. *Evangelische Kirche und Weimarer Republik. Zum politischen Weg des deutschen Protestantismus zwischen 1918–1933*. Göttingen, 1981.

Nußer, H.G.W. *Konservative Wehrverbände in Bayern, Preußen und Österreich 1918–1933*. 2 vols. Munich, 1972.

O'Donnell, A.J. "National Liberalism and the Mass Politics of the German Right, 1890–1907." Ph.D. diss., Princeton University, 1973.

Oertel, G. *Der Konservatismus als Weltanschauung.* Leipzig, 1893.

Oertzen, D. von *Adolf Stöcker,* 2nd ed. 2 vols. Berlin, 1911.

Opitz, G. *Der Christlich-soziale Volksdienst. Versuch einer protestantischen Partei in der Weimarer Republik.* Düsseldorf, 1969.

Orr, W.J., Jr. "The Foundation of the Kreuzzeitung Party in Prussia, 1848–1850." Ph.D. diss., University of Wisconsin, Madison, 1971.

_____. "The Prussian Ultra Right and the Advent of Constitutionalism in Prussia." *Canadian Journal of History* 11 (1976): 295–310.

Panzer, A. "Parteipolitische Ansätze der deutschen Bauernbewegung bis 1933." In *Europäische Bauernparteien im 20. Jahrhundert,* edited by H. Gollwitzer, pp. 524–42. Stuttgart and New York, 1977.

Patch, W., Jr. *Christian Trade Unions in the Weimar Republic, 1918–1933: The Failure of "Corporate Pluralism."* New Haven, Conn., 1985.

Peck, A.J. *Radicals and Reactionaries: The Crisis of Conservatism in Wilhelmine Germany.* Washington, D.C., 1978.

Pedlow, G.W. *The Survival of the Hessian Nobility, 1770–1870.* Princeton, N.J., 1988.

Petersdorff, H. von *Kleist-Retzow. Ein Lebensbild.* Berlin, 1907.

Petzold, J. "Alternative zur faschistischen Diktatur? Die Regierungskonzeption des Generals Kurt von Schleicher." *Militärgeschichte* 22 (1983): 16–31.

_____. *Wegbereiter des deutschen Faschismus. Die Jungkonservativen in der Weimarer Republik.* Cologne, 1978.

Pflanze, O. *Bismarck and the Development of Germany.* 3 vols. Princeton, N.J., 1990.

Plehve, F.-K. von *Reichskanzler Kurt von Schleicher. Weimars letzte Chance gegen Hitler.* Eßlingen, 1983.

Puhle, H.-J. *Agrarische Interessenpolitik und preußischer Konservatismus im wilhelminischen Reich 1893–1914. Ein Beitrag zur Analyse des Nationalismus in Deutschland am Beispiel des Bundes der Landwirte und der Deutsch-Konservativen Partei,* 2nd ed. Bonn Bad-Godesberg, 1975.

_____. "Conservatism in Modern German History." *Journal of Contemporary History* 13 (1978): 689–720.

_____. "Radikalisierung und Wandel des deutschen Konservatismus vor dem Ersten Weltkrieg." In *Die deutschen Parteien vor 1918,* edited by G.A. Ritter, pp. 165–86. Cologne, 1973.

_____. *Von der Agrarkrise zum Präfaschismus. Thesen zum Stellenwert der agrarischen Interessenverbände in der deutschen Politik am Ende des 19. Jahrhunderts.* Wiesbaden, 1972.

Puhle, H.-J., and H.-U. Wehler, eds. *Preußen im Rückblick.* Göttingen, 1980.

Pulzer, P. *The Rise of Political Anti-Semitism in Germany and Austria*, rev. ed. Cambridge, Mass., 1988.

Pyclik, H.P. "Friedrich Julius Stahl: A Study of the Development of German Conservative Thought 1802–1861." Ph.D. diss., University of Minnesota, 1972.

Ramlow, G. *Ludwig von der Marwitz und die Anfänge konservativer Politik und Staatsanschauung in Preußen*. Berlin, 1930.

Retallack, J. "Anti-Semitism, Conservative Propaganda, and Regional Politics in Late Nineteenth-Century Germany." *German Studies Review* 11 (1988): 377–403.

_____. "Conservatives *contra* Chancellor: Official Responses to the Spectre of Conservative Demagoguery from Bismarck to Bülow." *Canadian Journal of History* 20 (1985): 203–36.

_____. "'Ideology without Vision'? Recent Literature on Nineteenth-Century German Conservatism." *Bulletin of the German Historical Institute* London 13 (1991): 3–22.

_____. *Notables of the Right: The Conservative Party and Political Mobilization in Germany, 1876–1918*. London and Boston, Ma., 1988.

_____. "'What Is to Be Done?' The Red Specter, Franchise Questions, and the Crisis of Conservative Hegemony in Saxony, 1896–1909." *Central European History* 23 (1990): 271–312.

Ribhegge, W. *Konservative Politik in Deutschland. Von der Französischen Revolution bis zur Gegenwart*. Darmstadt, 1989.

Ritter, G. "Die preußischen Konservativen in der Krise von 1866." Ph.D. diss., University of Heidelberg, 1913; reprint, Nendeln, 1976.

_____. *Carl Goerdeler und die deutsche Widerstandsbewegung*. Stuttgart, 1954.

Ritter, G.A. "Kontinuität und Umformung des deutschen Parteiensystems 1918–1920." In *Entstehung und Wandel der modernen Gesellschaft. Festschrift für Hans Rosenberg zum 65. Geburtstag*, edited by G.A. Ritter, pp. 342–76. Berlin, 1970.

Ritthaler, A. *Karl Ludwig Freiherr von und zu Guttenberg. Ein politisches Lebensbild*. Würzburg, 1970.

Roder, H. *Der christlich-nationale Deutsche Gewerkschaftsbund (DGB) im politisch-ökonomischen Kräftefeld der Weimarer Republik. Ein Beitrag zur Funktion und Praxis der bürgerlichen Arbeiterbewegung vom Kaiserreich bis zur faschistischen Diktatur*. Frankfurt am Main, Bern, and New York, 1986.

Roeske, U. "Brüning und die Volkskonservativen (1930)." *Zeitschrift für Geschichtswissenschaft* 19 (1971): 904–15.

Rogge, H., and E. Weber, eds. *The European Right: A Historical Profile*. Berkeley, Calif., and Los Angeles, 1966.

Rosenberg, H. *Bureaucracy, Aristocracy and Autocracy: The Prussian Experience, 1660–1815*. Boston, 1958.

_____. *Machteliten und Wirtschaftskonjunktur. Zur neueren deutschen Sozial- und Wirtschaftsgeschichte.* Göttingen, 1978.

Rothfels, H. *The German Opposition to Hitler.* Hinsdale, Ill., 1948.

Rudolph, H. *Kulturkritik und konservative Revolution. Zum kulturell-politischen Denken Hofmannstahls und seinem problemgeschichtlichen Kontext.* Tübingen, 1971.

Ruge, W. *Hindenburg. Porträt eines Militaristen.* Cologne, 1981.

Rürup, R. *Emanzipation und Antisemitismus. Studien zur "Judenfrage" der bürgerlichen Gesellschaft,* 2nd ed. Frankfurt am Main, 1987.

Saage, R. *Rückkehr zum starken Staat? Studien über Konservatismus, Faschismus und Demokratie.* Frankfurt am Main, 1983.

Saile, W. *Hermann Wagener und sein Verhältnis zu Bismarck. Ein Beitrag zur Geschichte des konservativen Sozialismus.* Tübingen, 1958.

Saul, K. "Der 'Deutsche Kriegerbund.' Zur innenpolitischen Funktion eines 'nationalen' Verbandes im kaiserlichen Deutschland." *Militärgeschichtliche Mitteilungen* 2 (1969): 95–159.

_____. "Der Staat und die 'Mächte des Umsturzes.' Ein Beitrag zu den Methoden antisozialistischer Repression und Agitation vom Scheitern des Sozialistengesetzes bis zur Jahrhundertwende." *Archiv für Sozialgeschichte* 12 (1972): 293–350.

Scheel, W. *Das "Berliner Politische Wochenblatt" und die politische und soziale Revolution in Frankreich und England. Ein Beitrag zur konservativen Zeitkritik in Deutschland.* Göttingen, 1964.

Scheurig, B. *Ewald von Kleist-Schmenzin. Ein Konservativer gegen Hitler.* Oldenburg and Hamburg, 1968.

Schildt, A. *Militärdiktatur mit Massenbasis? Die Querfrontkonzeption der Reichswehrführung um General von Schleicher am Ende der Weimarer Republik.* Frankfurt am Main, 1981.

Schilling, K. "Beiträge zu einer Geschichte des radikalen Nationalismus 1890–1909." Ph.D. diss., University of Cologne, 1968.

Schissler, H. *Preußischer Agrargesellschaft im Wandel. Wirtschaftliche, gesellschaftliche und politische Transformationsprozesse von 1763 bis 1847.* Göttingen, 1978.

Schmädeke, J. and P. Steinbach, eds. *Der Widerstand gegen den Nationalsozialismus. Die deutsche Gesellschaft und der Widerstand gegen Hitler.* Munich, 1985.

Schmidt, G. "Parlamentarisierung oder 'Präventive Konterrevolution'? Die deutsche Innenpolitik im Spannungsfeld zwischen konservativer Sammlungspolitik und latenten Reformbestrebungen 1907–1914." In *Gesellschaft, Parlament und Regierung. Zur Geschichte des Parlamentarismus in Deutschland,* edited by G.A. Ritter, pp. 249–74. Düsseldorf, 1974.

Schmidt, S. "Junkertum und Genesis des deutschen Konservatismus im 19. Jahrhundert." *Zeitschrift für Geschichtswissenschaft* 27 (1979): 1058–72.

Schneller, M. *Zwischen Romantik und Faschismus. Der Beitrag Othmar Spanns zum Konservatismus der Weimarer Republik.* Stuttgart, 1970.

Schoeps, H.-J. *Das andere Preußen. Konservative Gestalten und Probleme im Zeitalter Friedrich Wilhelms IV.*, 5th ed. Honnef am Rhein, 1981.

_____. *Studien zur unbekannten Religions- und Geistesgeschichte.* Göttingen, 1963.

Schoeps, M. "Der deutsche Herrenklub. Ein Beitrag zur Geschichte des Konservativismus in der Weimarer Republik." Ph.D. diss., University of Erlangen-Nürnberg, 1968.

Schöllgen, G.A. *Conservative Against Hitler – Ulrich von Hassell: Diplomat in Imperial Germany, the Weimar Republic and the Third Reich, 1881–1944.* New York, 1990.

Schönhoven, K. *Die Bayerische Volkspartei 1924–1932.* Düsseldorf, 1972.

_____. "Zwischen Anpassung und Ausschaltung. Die bayerische Volkspartei in der Endphase der Weimarer Republik 1932/33." *Historische Zeitschrift* 224 (1977): 340–78.

Schrettenseger, U. "Der Einfluß Karl Ludwig von Hallers auf die preußische konservative Staatstheorie und -praxis." Ph.D. diss., University of Munich, 1949.

Schreyer, H. "Monarchismus und monarchistische Restaurationsbestrebungen in der Weimarer Republik." *Jahrbuch für Geschichte* 29 (1984): 291–320.

Schroeder, W. "Junkertum und preußisch-deutsches Reich. Zur politischen Konzeption des Junkertums und zu ihrer Widerspiegelung in der Kreuz-Zeitung 1871–1873," in *Die großpreußisch-militaristische Reichsgründung 1871. Voraussetzungen und Folgen*, edited by H. Bartel and E. Engelberg, vol. 2, pp. 170–234. 2 vols. East Berlin, 1971.

Schüddekopf, O.-E. *Die deutsche Innenpolitik im letzten Jahrhundert und der konservative Gedanke. Die Zusammenhänge zwischen Aussenpolitik, innere Staatsführung und Parteiengeschichte, dargestellt an der Geschichte der Konservativen Partei von 1807 bis 1918.* Braunschweig, 1951.

Schulz, G. "Der 'Nationale Klub von 1919' zu Berlin. Zum politischen Verfall einer Gesellschaft." *Jahrbuch für die Geschichte Mittel- und Ostdeutschlands* 11 (1962): 207–37.

_____. "Über Johann Popitz (1884–1945)." *Der Staat* 24 (1985): 485–509.

Schumacher, M. *Land und Politik. Eine Untersuchung über politische Parteien und agrarische Interessen 1914–1923.* Düsseldorf, 1979.

_____. *Mittelstandsfront und Republik. Die Wirtschaftspartei – Reichspartei des deutschen Mittelstandes 1919–1933.* Düsseldorf, 1972.

Schumann, H.G., ed. *Konservatismus.* Cologne, 1974.

Schwarz, H.-P. *Der konservative Anarchist. Politik und Zeitkritik Ernst Jüngers.* Freiburg in Breisgau, 1962.

Schwentker, W. "Conservatism in Nineteenth and Twentieth Century German History." *Bulletin of the German Historical Institute London* 23 (1986): 3–15.

_____. *Konservative Vereine und Revolution in Preußen 1848/49. Die Konstituierung des Konservativismus als Partei.* Düsseldorf, 1988.

Schwerin, G. "Wilhelm Frhr. v. Gayl, der Innenminister im Kabinett Papen 1932." Ph.D. diss., University of Erlangen, 1972.

Schwierskott, H.-J. *Arthur Moeller van den Bruck und der revolutionäre Nationalismus in der Weimarer Republik.* Göttingen, 1962.

Shanahan, W.O. *German Protestants Face the Social Question, vol. 1: The Conservative Phase, 1815–1871.* Notre Dame, Ind., 1954.

Seeber, G., and K.-H. Noack, eds. *Preußen in der deutschen Geschichte nach 1789.* Berlin, 1983.

Sieh, H. "Der Hamburger Nationalistenklub. Ein Beitrag zur Geschichte der christlich-konservativen Strömungen in der Weimarer Republik." Ph.D. diss., University of Mainz, 1963.

Silverman, D.P. "Nazification of the German Bureaucracy Reconsidered: A Case Study." *Journal of Modern History* 60 (1988): 496–539.

Sommer, F. *Die Wiener Zeitschrift (1792–93). Die Geschichte eines antirevolutionären Journals.* Zeulenroda-Leipzig, 1932.

Sontheimer, K. *Antidemokratisches Denken in der Weimarer Republik. Die politischen Ideen des deutschen Nationalismus zwischen 1918 und 1933.* Munich, 1962.

Sperber, J. *Popular Catholicism in Nineteenth-Century Germany.* Princeton, N.J., 1984.

Stark, G. *Entrepreneurs of Ideology: Neoconservative Publishers in Germany, 1890–1933.* Chapel Hill, N.C., 1981.

Stegmann, D. *Die Erben Bismarcks. Parteien und Verbände in der Spätphase des Wilhelminischen Deutschlands. Sammlungspolitik 1897–1918.* Cologne, 1970.

_____. "Hugenberg contra Stresemann. Die Politik der Interessenverbände am Ende des Kaiserreiches." *Vierteljahrshefte für Zeitgeschichte* 24 (1976): 329–78.

_____. "Kapitalismus und Faschismus in Deutschland 1929–1934. Thesen und Materialien zur Restituierung des Primats der Großindustrie zwischen Weltwirtschaftskrise und beginnender Rüstungskonjunktur." *Gesellschaft. Beiträge zur Marxschen Theorie,* no. 6 (1976), pp. 19–91.

_____. "Konservativismus und nationale Verbände im Kaiserreich. Bemerkungen zu einigen neueren Veröffentlichungen." *Geschichte und Gesellschaft* 10 (1984): 409–20.

_____. "Zum Verhältnis von Großindustrie und Nationalsozialismus 1930–1933. Ein Beitrag zur Geschichte der sog. Machtergreifung." *Archiv für Sozialgeschichte* 13 (1973): 399–482.

————. "Zwischen Repression und Manipulation. Konservative Machteliten und Arbeiter- und Angestelltenbewegung 1910–1918. Ein Beitrag zur Vorgeschichte der DAP/NSDAP." *Archiv für Sozialgeschichte* 12 (1972): 351–432.

Stegmann, D., B.-J. Wendt, and P.-C. Witt, eds. *Deutscher Konservatismus im 19. und 20. Jahrhundert. Festschrift für Fritz Fischer.* Bonn, 1983.

————, ed. *Industrielle Gesellschaft und politisches System. Beiträge zur politischen Sozialgeschichte: Festschrift für Fritz Fischer zum siebzigsten Geburtstag.* Bonn, 1978.

Steinbach, P. *Die Zähmung des politischen Massenmarktes. Wahlen und Wahlkämpfe im Bismarckreich im Spiegel der Hauptstadt- und Gesinnungspresse.* 3 vols. Passau, 1990.

Stern, F. *The Failure of Illiberalism: Essays on the Political Culture of Modern Germany.* New York, 1972.

————. *The Politics of Cultural Despair: A Study in the Rise of the Germanic Ideology.* Berkeley, Calif., 1961.

Stillich, O. *Die politischen Parteien in Deutschland, vol. 1: Die Konservativen.* Leipzig, 1911.

Streisow, J. *Die Deutschnationale Volkspartei und die Völkisch-Radikalen 1918–1922.* 2 vols. Frankfurt am Main, 1981.

Struve, W. *Elites against Democracy: Leadership Ideals in Bourgeois Political Thought in Germany, 1890–1933.* Princeton, N.J., 1973.

Stupperich, A. *Volksgemeinschaft oder Arbeitersolidarität. Studien zur Arbeitnehmerpolitik in der Deutschnationalen Volkspartei (1918–1933).* Göttingen, 1982.

Suval, S. *Electoral Politics in Wilhelmine Germany.* Chapel Hill, N.C., 1985.

Sweet, P.R. *Friedrich von Gentz: Defender of the Old Order.* Madison, Wis., 1941.

Thimme, A. *Flucht in den Mythos. Die Deutschnationale Volkspartei und die Niederlage von 1918.* Göttingen, 1969.

Tims, R.W. *Germanizing Prussian Poland: The H-K-T Society and the Struggle for the Eastern Marches in the German Empire, 1894–1919.* New York, 1941.

Tirrell, S.R. *German Agrarian Politics after Bismarck's Fall: The Formation of the Farmers' League.* New York, 1951.

Trumpp, T. "Franz von Papen, der preußisch-deutsche Dualismus und die NSDAP in Preußen. Ein Beitrag zur Vorgeschichte des 20. Juli 1932." Ph.D. diss., University of Tübingen, 1963.

Turner, H.A., Jr. *German Big Business and the Rise of Hitler.* Oxford, 1985.

————. "The Ruhrlade: Secret Cabinet of Heavy Industry in the Weimar Republic." *Central European History* 3 (1970): 195–228.

Valjavec, F. "Die Anfänge des österreichischen Konservativismus: L.A. Hoffmann." In *Festschrift Karl Eder*, pp. 155–68. Innsbruck, 1959.

_____. *Die Entstehung der politischen Strömungen in Deutschland 1770–1815*. 2nd unrev. ed. Kronberg/Ts., 1978.

Van Roon, G. *German Resistance to Hitler: Conrad von Moltke and the Kreisau Circle*, trans. P. Ludlow. London, 1971.

Vascik, G. "Rural Politics and Sugar: A Comparative Study of National Liberal Politics in Hannover and Prussian Saxony, 1871–1914." Ph.D. diss., University of Michigan, 1988.

Vierhaus, R. "Konservativ, Konservatismus." In *Geschichtliche Grundbegriffe. Historisches Lexikon zur politisch-sozialen Sprache in Deutschland*, edited by O. Brunner, W. Conze, and R. Kosselleck, vol. 3, pp. 531–65. Stuttgart, 1982.

Vogel, U. *Konservative Kritik an der bürgerlicher Revolution: August Wilhelm Rehberg*. Darmstadt and Neuwied, 1972.

Vogel, W. *Katholische Kirche und nationale Kampfverbände in der Weimarer Republik*. Mainz, 1989.

Vogelsang, T. *Kurt von Schleicher. Ein General als Politiker*. Göttingen, 1965.

_____. *Reichswehr, Staat und NSDAP. Beiträge zur deutschen Geschichte 1930–1932*. Stuttgart, 1962.

Volkov, S. *The Rise of Popular Antimodernism in Germany: The Urban Master Artisans, 1873–1896*. Princeton, N.J., 1978.

Von Klemperer, K. *German Resistance against Hitler: The Search for Allies Abroad, 1938–1945*. Oxford, 1992.

_____. *Germany's New Conservatism: Its History and Dilemma in the Twentieth Century*. Princeton, N.J., 1957.

_____. "Glaube, Religion, Kirche und der deutsche Widerstand gegen den Nationalsozialismus." *Vierteljahrshefte für Zeitgeschichte* 28 (1980): 293–309.

Walker, D.P. "Alfred Hugenberg and the 'Deutschnationale Volkspartei,' 1918–1930." Ph.D. diss., Cambridge University, 1976.

_____. "The German National People's Party: The Conservative Dilemma in the Weimar Republic." *Journal of Contemporary History* 14 (1979): 627–47.

Wallraf, L. "Zur Politik der Deutschkonservativen Partei in den letzten Jahrzehnten ihres Bestehens (1898–1918) unter den Bedingungen der imperialistischen Epoche." Ph.D. diss, University of Jena, 1970.

Wawrzinek, K. *Die Entstehung der deutschen Antisemitenparteien (1873–1890)*. Berlin, 1927.

Wehler, H.-U. *The German Empire, 1871–1918*, trans. K. Traynor. Leamington Spa, 1985.

Weisbrod, B. "Economic power and political stability reconsidered: heavy industry in Weimar Germany." *Social History* 4 (1979): 241–63.

_____. *Schwerindustrie in der Weimarer Republik. Interessenpolitik zwischen Stabilisierung und Krise.* Wuppertal, 1978.

Weißbecker, M. "Konservative Politik und Ideologie in der Konterrevolution 1918/19." *Zeitschrift für Geschichtswissenschaft* 27 (1979): 707–20.

Westarp, K. von *Konservative Politik im letzten Jahrzehnt des Kaiserreichs.* 2 vols. Berlin, 1935.

Wiegand, H.-J. *Das Vermächtnis Friedrich Julius Stahls. Ein Beitrag zur Geschichte konservativen Rechts- und Ordnungsdenkens.* Königstein/Ts., 1980.

Williamson, J.G. *Karl Helfferich, 1872–1924: Economist, Financier, Politician.* Princeton, N.J., 1971.

Wolf, S.P. *Konservatismus im liberalen Baden. Studien zur badischen Innen-, Kirchen- und Agrarpolitik sowie zur süddeutschen Parteiengeschichte 1860–1893.* Karlsruhe, 1990.

Woods, R. *Ernst Jünger and the Nature of Political Commitment.* Stuttgart, 1982.

Wortmann, K. *Geschichte der Deutschen Vaterlandspartei 1917–1918.* Halle, 1926.

Wright, J.R.C. *"Above Parties": The Political Attitudes of the German Protestant Church Leadership, 1918–1933.* Oxford, 1974.

Notes on Contributors

SHELLEY BARANOWSKI is associate professor of history at the University of Akron in Akron, Ohio. She is the author of *The Confessing Church, Conservative Elites, and the Nazi State* (Toronto, Queensland, 1986) and is currently working on a book-length monograph entitled *The Sanctity of Rural Life: Agrarian Conservatism in Pomerania, 1918–1933* that is to be published by Oxford University Press.

DAVID E. BARCLAY is professor of history at Kalamazoo College in Kalamazoo, Michigan. He is the author of *Rudolf Wissel als Sozialpolitiker 1890–1933* (Berlin, 1984) and has published extensively on the monarchy, court, and Prussian society in the age of Frederick William IV. His most recent book, *Frederick William IV and the Prussian Monarchy, 1840–61*, is scheduled to be published in 1995 by Oxford University Press and in German translation by the Siedler Verlag of Berlin.

HERMANN BECK is assistant professor of history at the University of Miami in Coral Gables, Florida. He is the author of "The Social Policies of Prussian Officials: The Bureaucracy in a New Light," *Journal of Modern History* 64 (1992): 263–98, and is currently preparing a monograph on "The Origins of the Authoritarian Welfare State in Prussia, 1815–1871" that will be published by the University of Michigan Press in its series on Social History, Popular Culture, and Politics in Germany.

RENATE BRIDENTHAL is professor of history at Brooklyn College, the City University of New York. She has written extensively on German women's history in the late nineteenth and twentieth centuries. She has also co-edited two collections of essays on European women's history, the first with Claudia Koonz and Susan Mosher-Stuard, *Becoming Visible: Women in European History*, 2nd ed. (Boston, 1987), and the second with Atina Grossmann and Marion Kaplan, *When Biology Became Destiny: Women in Weimar and Nazi Germany* (New York, 1984).

CHRISTOPHER M. CLARK is college lecturer in modern European history at St. Catharine's College at the University of Cambridge. He recently completed his dissertation entitled "Jewish Mission in the Christian State: Protestant Missions to the Jews in Eighteenth- and Nineteenth-Century Prussia" (Ph.D. diss., University of Cambridge,

1991).

GEOFF ELEY is professor of history at the University of Michigan in Ann Arbor, Michigan. He is the author of *Reshaping the German Right: Radical Nationalism and Political Change after Bismarck* (New Haven, Conn., and London, 1980) and *From Unification to Nazism: Reinterpreting the German Past* (Boston, 1986). He also collaborated with David Blackbourn in writing *The Peculiarities of German History: Bourgeois Society and Politics in Nineteenth-Century Germany* (Oxford and New York, 1984). His current field of research is the history of German liberalism from 1860 to 1930.

PETER FRITZSCHE is associate professor of history at the University of Illinois in Champaign-Urbana, Illinois. He is the author of *Rehearsals for Fascism: Populism and Political Mobilization in Weimar Germany* (New York, 1990) and *A Nation of Fliers: German Aviation and the Popular Imagination* (Cambridge, Ma., 1992). He is currently working on a study of boulevard newspapers and the metropolitan experience in Berlin at the turn of the century.

THEODORE S. HAMEROW is professor emeritus of history at the University of Wisconsin-Madison. He is the author of *Restoration, Revolution, Reaction: Economics and Politics in Germany, 1815–1871* (Princeton, N.J., 1958) and *The Social Foundations of German Unification, 1858–1871*, 2 vols. (Princeton, N.J., 1969–72). He is currently writing a book on the German resistance to Hitler.

LARRY EUGENE JONES is professor of history at Canisius College in Buffalo, New York, and is the author of *German Liberalism and the Dissolution of the Weimar Party System, 1918–1933* (Chapel Hill, N.C., and London, 1988). He also collaborated with Konrad Jarausch in editing *In Search of a Liberal Germany: Studies in the History of German Liberalism from 1789 to the Present* (New York, Oxford, and Munich, 1990), and with James Retallack in editing *Elections, Mass Politics, and Social Change in Modern Germany: New Perspectives* (New York and Cambridge, 1992).

HANS MOMMSEN is professor of history at the University of the Ruhr in Bochum, Germany. He has published extensively on the social and political history of the Weimar Republic and the Third Reich and was co-editor with Dietmar Petzina and Bernd Weisbrod of *Industielle Entwicklung und politisches System in der Weimarer Republik* (Düsseldorf, 1974). His most recent publications include *Die verspielte Freiheit: Der Weg der Republik von Weimar in den Untergang 1918 bis 1933* (Berlin, 1989), and *From Weimar to Auschwitz*, translated by Philip O'Connor (Princeton, N.J., 1991).

JAMES RETALLACK is associate professor of history at the University of Toronto in Toronto, Ontario. He is the author of *Notables of the Right: The Conservative Party and Political Mobilization in Germany, 1876–1918* (London and Boston, 1988) and collaborated with Larry Eugene Jones in editing *Elections, Mass Politics, and Social Change in Modern Germany: New Perspectives* (New York and Cambridge, 1992). He is currently working on the history of political journalism in Germany from 1770 to 1920 and electoral politics in the Kingdom of Saxony from 1866 to 1918.

WOLFGANG SCHWENTKER is lecturer in modern European history at the University of Düsseldorf. He is the author of *Konservative Vereine und Revolution in Preußen 1848/49: Die Konstituierung des Konservatismus als Partei* (Düsseldorf, 1988) and co-editor of *Max Weber und seine Zeitgenossen* (Göttingen, 1988). He is currently writing a book on the impact of Max Weber on Japanese social and political thought.

DIRK STEGMANN is professor of history at the University of Lüneburg and is the author of *Die Erben Bismarcks: Parteien und Verbände in der Spätphase des Wilhelminischen Deutschlands – Sammlungspolitik 1897–1918* (Cologne and Berlin, 1970). He is also the co-author of *Die Republik von Weimar*, 2 vols. (Düsseldorf, 1979) and has co-edited two *Festschriften* in honor of Fritz Fischer, *Industrielle Gesellschaft und politisches System. Beiträge zur politischen Sozialgeschichte* (Bonn, 1978), and *Deutscher Konservatismus im 19. und 20. Jahrhundert* (Bonn, 1983). He is currently working on the history of the German Fatherland Party from 1917 to 1920.

ALAN STEINWEIS is assistant professor of history at the University of Nebraska in Lincoln, Nebraska, and holds the Hymen Rosenberg Professorship of Modern European History and Judaic Studies. He is also author of a forthcoming book entitled *Art, Ideology, and Economics in Nazi Germany: The Reich Chambers of Music, Theater, and the Visual Arts* (Chapel Hill, N.C. and London: University of North Carolina Press, 1993).

GEORGE VASCIK is associate professor of history at the Hamilton Campus of Miami University in Hamilton, Ohio, and the author of various articles on peasant politics and the rural economy in late Wilhelmine Germany. He is currently revising his dissertation "Rural Politics and Sugar: A Comparative Study of National Liberal Politics in Hannover and Prussian Saxony, 1871–1914" (Ph.D. diss., University of Michigan, 1988) for publication as a book.

Index

528

Index

Index

Index

Index

Index

23, 301–2, 304–15, 319, 322–28, 347, 472
Mohl, Robert von, 98, 109
Möllendorff, Wichard von, 324
Moltke, Count Helmuth von, 500
Mommsen, Hans, 27, 434
monarchism, 101, 104, 123, 131–33, 135, 137, 148, 151, 155, 407, 424, 438, 450
monarchy, 15, 66, 68, 79, 78, 91–93, 150, 155, 172
  conservative relationship to, 68
  ties to the lower classes, 79
  collapse, 436
Montesquieu, Charles de Secondat, 69
Moser, Hans Joachim, 343–44, 346
Möser, Justus, 5
Mosse, George, 6, 7
mother settlements (*Müttersiedlungen*), 395
Mühsam, Erich, 306
Müllensiefen, Hermann, 164
Müller, Adam, 15, 42, 101, 103
Müller, Klaus-Jürgen, 27, 434
Müller, Oskar, 304
Mündler, Eugen, 473
music, 331, 334, 338, 340, 343–44
Mussolini, Benito, 401, 408

Napoleon Bonaparte, 112, 133
Nassau, 43
National Assembly, (1919), 316, 318, 396, 437–38
National Association (Nationalverein), 169
National Committee of German Agriculture (Reichsausschuß der deutschen Landwirtschaft, 388
National Dairy Committee (Reichsmilchausschuß), 393
National Federation of Agricultural Housewives' Associations (Reichsverband landwirtschaftlicher Hausfrauenvereine or RLHV), 375–77, 384–95, 397–405
  affiliation with RLB, 399–403
  concept of housewives' estate (Hausfrauenstand), 394
  in Prussia, 396

Land und Frau, 397, 403
  affinity with Nazism, 402
  youth committee, 401–2
National Food Estate (Reichsnährstand), 404
National Liberal Party (Nationalliberale Partei or NLP), 29, 157, 161–68, 174–76, 178, 183, 198–99, 201, 203–4, 206, 208, 210, 214, 218–26, 238–39, 243–46 248, 253, 257, 262–63, 266, 270–72, 274, 276–79, 287, 290–92
  alliance with BdL, 220
  in Hanover, 244–47
  in Hesse, 203–4
National Liberals. *See* National Liberal Party
National Office for Job Placement and Unemployment Insurance, 397
National Party, proposal for and discussion of, 171–79, 181
national renewal, 1914, 301
National Rural League (Reichs-Landbund or RLB), 376–77, 389–92, 394, 399–404, 407, 413–19, 422, 425–26, 431
National Socialism, 22, 25, 190, 301, 305–6, 330–31, 333–34, 336, 338–39, 343–46, 353–55, 357, 359–60, 363, 366, 373, 375, 403–4, 407–8, 410, 422–23, 425, 429–30, 432, 433–35, 442, 444, 448–55, 461–63, 465, 473–74, 486–87, 490
  and conservatism, 340
  and cultural conservatism, 345
  anti-elitism, 407, 411, 423–27
  Diktatur, Die, 420, 428
  ideology, 377, 452
  anti-Marxism, 407
  anti-modernism, 340
  critique of modernist culture, 331, 336
  racism, 459
  Kampfbund für deutsche Kultur, 339–40, 345
National Socialist Factory Cell Organization (Nationalsozialistische Betriebszellenorganisation or NSBO), 354

542

Index